Prof. MARK Hall
hallma@wfu.edu

THE LAW OF HEALTH CARE FINANCE AND REGULATION

ASPEN SELECT SERIES

THE LAW OF HEALTH CARE FINANCE AND REGULATION

Fourth Edition

Mark A. Hall
Fred D. and Elizabeth L. Turnage Professor of Law and Public Health
Wake Forest University

Nicholas Bagley
Professor of Law
University of Michigan

David Orentlicher
Cobeaga Law Firm Professor of Law
UNLV William S. Boyd School of Law

Mary Anne Bobinski
Professor
Allard School of Law University of British Columbia

Wolters Kluwer

Published by Wolters Kluwer in New York.

Wolters Kluwer Legal & Regulatory U.S. serves customers worldwide with CCH, Aspen Publishers, and Kluwer Law International products. (www.WKLegaledu.com)

To contact Customer Service, e-mail customer.service@wolterskluwer.com, call 1-800-234-1660, fax 1-800-901-9075, or mail correspondence to:

Wolters Kluwer
Attn: Order Department
PO Box 990
Frederick, MD 21705

Printed in the United States of America.

1 2 3 4 5 6 7 8 9 0

ISBN 978-1-4548-9038-6

About Wolters Kluwer Legal & Regulatory U.S.

Wolters Kluwer Legal & Regulatory U.S. delivers expert content and solutions in the areas of law, corporate compliance, health compliance, reimbursement, and legal education. Its practical solutions help customers successfully navigate the demands of a changing environment to drive their daily activities, enhance decision quality and inspire confident outcomes.

Serving customers worldwide, its legal and regulatory portfolio includes products under the Aspen Publishers, CCH Incorporated, Kluwer Law International, ftwilliam.com, and MediRegs names. They are regarded as exceptional and trusted resources for general legal and practice-specific knowledge, compliance and risk management, dynamic workflow solutions, and expert commentary.

About Wolters Kluwer Legal & Regulatory U.S.

To Larry C. Hall, Ph.D., for showing me the joys of an academic life.
— *M.A.H.*

To Celia and Sebastian, who have brought so
much joy and meaning to my life.
— *N.B.*

To the memory of Prof. Herman I. Orentlicher, for his commitment to
"neutral skepticism," rigorous standards, and, above all, decency.
— *D.O.*

To my partner Holly and our daughter Anna, and to my parents, for their
encouragement.
— *M.A.B.*

To Bill Curran, for his guiding light.

Summary of Contents

Contents

3 ■ *Health Care Financing and Reform* *113*

Preface

The Content and Organization of This Book

This book contains the materials from *Health Care Law and Ethics* (9th ed. 2018) that are focused on health care finance and regulation. As the larger book passes its half-century anniversary, we pause to reflect on the remarkable metamorphosis of health care law from a subspecialty of tort law, to a mushrooming academic and practice field whose tentacles reach into myriad scholarly disciplines and areas of substantive law. This book's eight prior editions reflect important stages in this evolutionary growth. Health care law originated as a separate field of professional practice and academic inquiry during the 1960s, when this book was first published. Under the somewhat grandiose label of "medical jurisprudence," the primary focus at first was on medical proof in all kinds of criminal and civil litigation, on medical malpractice actions against physicians, and on public health regulation. The principal concern was how traditional bodies of legal doctrine and practice—such as criminal, tort, and evidence law—should apply in medical settings.

During the 1970s, bioethics became a major additional area of concern as a consequence of the right to die movement spawned by the *Quinlan* case, and the focus on individual autonomy contained in the informed consent doctrine and the landmark decision on reproductive decisionmaking in Roe v. Wade. Law courses during this and earlier periods were taught under the heading of "law and medicine."

In the 1980s, economic and regulatory topics formed the third component of health care law, as exemplified by the increasing application of antitrust laws to the health care industry and the growing body of legal disputes under Medicare and Medicaid. This newer dimension accelerated its growth into the 1990s with the theoretical perspectives. Behavioral disciplines such as psychology, sociology, and anthropology help to illuminate the nature of medical knowledge and the lived experience of illness, dependency, and trust as they occur in real-life medical encounters. Findings from health services research published in the health policy literature create a stronger empirical and theoretical base for exploring health care law, one that better exposes its broad social impact. Analytical disciplines, such as economics and moral and political theory, create the foundation for understanding developments in financing, regulation, and bioethics. And, the perspectives of feminist, communitarian, and critical race theory demonstrate the limitations of conventional analytical models and help us understand how health care law must evolve to accommodate viewpoints and concerns that have been excluded in the past.

The 1992 death of Bill Curran, the original author of this casebook, left us with a considerable burden to shoulder. Although Prof. Curran was involved in the conceptual reorganization of these materials, he was unable to contribute to their selection and editing. Still, his presence is felt in every part of these materials through the inspiration of his mentoring, his friendship, and his vast body of work.

We intend that this book will continue to serve as both a teaching tool and an ongoing resource for conducting research in health care law. To that end, we provide substantial bibliographic notes in each section. Also, we have created a dedicated Web site to serve this book: www.health-law.org. It extends the book's content with interesting background materials, updates of important events since publication, additional relevant topics that were excluded due to space constraints, and links to other resources on the internet.

The following is a bibliography of resources and readings that relate to research in health care law generally. Additional bibliographic references can be found at pages 39 and 339, and on the casebook Web site.

Treatises and Texts: Barry Furrow et al., Health Law (2d ed. 2001); Mark A. Hall, David Orentlicher, and Ira Mark Ellman, Health Care Law and Ethics in a Nutshell (3d ed. 2011); Eleanor Kinney, Administrative Law of Health care in a Nutshell (2016); Hooper, Lundy & Bookman, Treatise on Health Care Law; John H. Robinson, Roberta M. Berry & Kevin McDonnell, eds., A Health Law Reader: An Interdisciplinary Approach (1999); World Health Organization, International Digest of Health Legislation.

Health Care Law Journals: American Journal of Law and Medicine (Boston Univ.); Annals of Health Law (Loyola-Chicago); DePaul Journal of Health Care Law; Food, Drug and Cosmetic Law Journal; Health Law & Policy Abstracts and Public Health Law Abstracts (SSRN online journals); Health Matrix (Case Western Univ.); Houston Journal of Health Law & Policy; Indiana Health Law Review (Indiana Univ.-Indianapolis); Journal of Contemporary Health Law and Policy (Catholic Univ.); Journal of Health & Biomedical Law (Suffolk), Journal of Health and Life Sciences Law (St. Louis Univ., AHLA); Journal of Health Care Law & Policy (Univ. of Maryland); Journal of Law and Health (Cleveland-Marshall); Journal of Law, Medicine and Ethics (ASLME); Journal of Legal Medicine (So. Illinois Univ.); Medical Trial Technique Quarterly; Journal of Medicine and Law; St. Louis Univ. Law Journal (recurring symposia); Seton Hall Law Review (same); Quinnipiac Health Law Journal; Whittier Law Review; Yale Journal of Health Policy, Law and Ethics.

Leading Medical, Industry, and Health Policy Journals: American Journal of Public Health; American Medical News (AMA); Health Affairs (published by Project Hope); Health Care Financing and Delivery (SSRN online journal), Medicare &

Medicaid Research Review (DHHS/CMS); Health Economics, Policy and Law (Cambridge Press); Health Services Research; Inquiry (published by Excellus, a Blue Cross plan in Rochester, NY); Hospitals and Health Networks (AHA); Journal of the American Medical Association; Journal of Health Politics, Policy and Law; Medical Care; Milbank Quarterly; Modern Healthcare; New England Journal of Medicine.

Health Law Societies, Digests, and Newsletters: ABA Section on Health Law (newsletter and journal); American College of Legal Medicine (journal); American Society of Law, Medicine, and Ethics (two journals); BNA Health Law Reporter (weekly); American Health Lawyers Association (monthly digest and newsletter, bimonthly journal).

Acknowledgments

This manuscript could not have been prepared without the diligent help of those students and staff who assisted us over the past few years (Hailey Cleek, Travis Edwards, Victoria Hall-Palerm, Dorothy Hector, Colin Herd, Amy Lai, John Minkley, Robert Petito, Lena Rieke, Michael Shapiro, and Jacob Steiner), and without the superhuman patience of our families (who, curiously, wish to remain anonymous). We also thank the authors and publishers who granted permission to use each of the excerpts of copyrighted material in these readings.

American Health Lawyers Association Public Interest Committee, "A Public Policy Discussion: Taking the Measure of the Stark Law" (2009). Copyright © 2009 by the American Health Lawyers Association. Reprinted by permission. All rights reserved.

Bagley, Nicholas, "Bedside Bureaucrats: Why Medicare Reform Hasn't Worked," Georgetown Law Journal 101, no. 3 (2013): 519-80. Copyright © 2013 by Georgetown Law Journal. Reprinted by permission. All rights reserved.

Bennett, Amanda, "End-of-life Warning at $618,616 Makes Me Wonder Was It Worth It." Bloomberg News (March 4, 2010). Copyright © 2010 by Bloomberg BNA. Reprinted by permission. All rights reserved.

Blumenthal, David, "Making Medical Errors into 'Medical Treasures.'" JAMA 272, no. 23 (1994): 1867-68. Copyright © 1994 by the American Medical Association. Reprinted by permission. All rights reserved.

Bodenheimer, Thomas, and Kevin Grumbach, "Reimbursing Physicians and Hospitals." JAMA 272, no. 12 (1994): 971-77. Copyright © 1994 by the American Medical Association. Reprinted by permission. All rights reserved.

Buckman, Robert, and Karl Sabbagh, Magic or Medicine? An Investigation of Healing and Healers (1995). Copyright © 1995 by Prometheus Books. Reprinted by permission. All rights reserved.

Cohodes, Donald R., "Where You Stand Depends on Where You Sit: Musings on the Regulation/Competition Dialogue." Journal of Health Politics, Policy and Law 7, no. 1 (1982): 54-79. Copyright © 1982 by Duke University Press. Reprinted by permission. All rights reserved.

Crosson, Francis J., and Laura A. Tollen, Partners in Health: How Physicians and Hospitals Can Be Accountable Together (2010). Copyright © 2010 by John Wiley & Sons. Reprinted by permission. All rights reserved.

Dworkin, Ronald, "Will Clinton's Plan Be Fair?" The New York Review of Books 41, no. 1/2 (1994). Copyright © 1994 by the New York Review of Books. Reprinted by permission. All rights reserved.

Eddy, David M., Clinical Decision Making: From Theory to Practice (1996). Copyright © 1996 by Jones & Bartlett. Reprinted by permission. All rights reserved.

Greely, Henry T., "Direct Financial Incentives in Managed Care: Unanswered Questions." Health Matrix 6 (1996): 53-88. Copyright © 1996 by Case Western Reserve University School of Law. Reprinted by permission. All rights reserved.

Goodman, John C., and Gerald L. Musgrave, Patient Power: Solving America's Health Care Crisis (1992). Copyright © 1992 by the Cato Institute. Reprinted by permission. All rights reserved.

Hall, Mark A., Making Medical Spending Decisions: The Law, Ethics, and Economics of Rationing Mechanisms (1997). Copyright © 1997 by Oxford University Press. Reprinted by permission. All rights reserved.

Havighurst, Clark C., "Health Care Choices: Private Contracts as Instruments of Health Reform" (1995). Copyright © 1995 by American Enterprise Institute. Reprinted by permission. All rights reserved.

Havighurst, Clark C., "The Professional Paradigm of Medical Care: Obstacle to Decentralization." Jurimetrics 30, no. 4 (1990): 415-429. Copyright © 1990 by the American Bar Association. Reprinted by permission. All rights reserved.

Jost, Timothy Stoltzfus, "The Necessary and Proper Role of Regulation to Assure the Quality of Health Care." Houston Law Review 25 (1988): 525-98. Copyright © 1988 by Houston Law Review. Reprinted by permission. All rights reserved.

Kaplan, Richard L., "Reflections on Medicare at 50: Breaking the Chains of Path Dependency for a New Era." Elder Law Journal 23 (2015): 1-38. Copyright © by 2015 by the University of Illinois Board of Trustees. Reprinted by permission. All rights reserved.

Kauper, Thomas E., "The Role of Quality of Health Care Considerations in Antitrust Analysis." Law and Contemporary Problems 51, no. 2 (1988): 273-340. Copyright © 1988 by Duke University Press.

Krugman, Paul, and Robin Wells, "The Health Care Crisis and What to Do About It." The New York Review of Books 53, no. 5 (2006). Copyright © 2006 by the New York Review of Books. Reprinted by permission. All rights reserved.

Kuttner, Robert, "Columbia/HCA and the Resurgence of the For-Profit Hospital Business." New England Journal of Medicine 335, no. 5 (1996): 362-68. Copyright © 1996 by the Massachusetts Medical Society. Reprinted by permission. All rights reserved.

Marmor, Theodore R., and Jonathan Oberlander, "The Health Bill Explained at Last." The New York Review of Books 57, no. 13 (2010). Copyright © 2010 by the New York Review of Books. Reprinted by permission. All rights reserved.

Nelson III, Leonard J., "Rationing Health Care in Britain and the United States." Journal of Health and Biomedical Law 7, no. 2 (2011): 175-232. Copyright © 2011 by Suffolk University School of Law. Reprinted by permission. All rights reserved.

Note, "Right of Corporation to Practice Medicine," Yale Law Journal 48, no. 2 (1938): 346-351. Copyright © 1938 by the Yale Law Journal Company. Reprinted by permission. All rights reserved.

Peters Jr., Philip G., "Health Care Rationing and Disability Rights." Indiana Law Journal 70, no. 2 (1995): 491-547. Copyright © 1995 by Indiana Law Journal. Reprinted by permission. All rights reserved.

Peterson, Mark A., "Health Care Into the Next Century." Journal of Health Politics, Policy and Law 22 (1997): 291-313. Copyright © 1997 by Duke University Press. Reprinted by permission. All rights reserved.

Reid, Tom R., The Healing of America: A Global Quest for Better, Cheaper, and Fairer Health Care (2009). Copyright © 2009 by Tom R. Reid. Reprinted by permission. All rights reserved.

Reinhardt, Uwe, "Uncompensated Hospital Care," in Uncompensated Hospital Care: Rights and Responsibilities (Frank A. Sloan, James F. Blumstein, and James M. Perrin eds., 1986). Copyright © 1986 by Johns Hopkins University Press. Reprinted by permission. All rights reserved.

Rosenblatt, Rand E., "Health Care, Markets, and Democratic Values." Vanderbilt Law Review 34 (1981): 1067-1115. Copyright © 1981 by Vanderbilt Law Review. Reprinted by permission. All rights reserved.

Sawicki, Nadia N., "Character, Competence, and the Principles of Medical Discipline." Journal of Health Care Law and Policy 13 (2010): 285-323. Copyright © 2010 by the University of Maryland School of Law. Reprinted by permission. All rights reserved.

Somers, Herman Miles, and Anne Ramsay Somers, Doctors, Patients, and Health Insurance: The Organization and Financing of Medical Care (1961). Copyright © 1961 by the Brookings Institution. Reprinted by permission. All rights reserved.

Tanner, Michael D., "Bad Medicine: A Guide to the Real Costs and Consequences of the New Health Care Law" (2010). Copyright © 2010 by the Cato Institute. Reprinted by permission. All rights reserved.

Tanner, Michael D., "The Grass Is Not Always Greener: A Look at National Health Care Systems Around the World" (2008). Copyright © 2008 by the Cato Institute. Reprinted by permission. All rights reserved.

White, Joseph, "Competing Solutions: American Health Care Proposals and International Experience" (1995). Copyright © 1995 by the Brookings Institution. Reprinted by permission. All rights reserved.

Mark Hall
Nick Bagley
David Orentlicher
Mary Anne Bobinski

April 2018

1

Introduction

All of us have had some exposure to the world of medicine, but few law students have reason to understand the intricacies of this financing and delivery system and how it has developed. This understanding is essential in a course that focuses on the full range of legal and public policy issues pertaining to the delivery and payment for medical care. Those issues have naturally taken shape according to the structural components and historical growth of the health care sector and its various institutions.

As you read through what sometimes seems to be an alphabet soup of actors, institutions, and acronyms, rather than memorizing all the details, try to construct a coherent story line of how the health care sector took shape over time and how its various pieces interconnect at present. You don't need to master all the details now, as they will reemerge throughout the course, but it will be easier to remember them at the end if you have an initial framework to which you can attach them.

A. THE NATURE OF MEDICAL PRACTICE

We begin with a description of the human condition of illness and the professional practice of medicine, since these are what distinguish health care law from other fields of legal study. It is essential throughout this book to have some appreciation of the impact that illness has on how people function, the intricacies of medical decisionmaking, and how doctors and patients interact. To focus your thoughts on these issues, reflect on your own experiences with medical care, and consider the following list of popular "misconceptions" (developed by Alain Enthoven). What observations and evidence emerge from these readings to rebut or qualify each of these commonly held notions?

1. The doctor should be able to know what conditions the patient has, to answer the patient's questions precisely, and to prescribe the right treatment. If the doctor doesn't, that is incompetence or even malpractice.
2. For each medical condition, there is a "best" treatment. It is up to the doctor to know about that treatment and to use it. Anything else is unnecessary surgery, waste, fraud, or underservice.
3. Medicine is an exact science. Unlike 50 or 100 years ago, there is now a firm scientific base for what the doctor does. Standard treatments are supported by scientific proof of efficiency.
4. Medical care consists of standard products that can be described precisely and measured meaningfully in standard units such as "inpatient days," "outpatient visits," or "doctor office visits."
5. Much of medical care is a matter of life and death or serious pain or disability.
6. More medical care is better than less care.
7. People have no control over the timing of their need for medical care. Whatever care is needed is needed right away.

1. Patients, Doctors, and Hospitals

■ HEALTH CARE PAST AND PRESENT
Robert Rhodes
Health Care Politics, Policy, and Distributive Justice: The Ironic Triumph*

Death before the nineteenth century was an ever-looming presence in our ancestors' thoughts and a frequent visitor to their families. They feared it and had little control over it. Sudden death was as central to attitudes prior to the twentieth century as the cemetery was to every village and town. . . .

Resignation and fatalism toward natural occurrences characterize preindustrial societies, just as a sense of self-direction and control characterize modern society. . . . Modern societies have faith that they can control the future. A futurist orientation allows for savings, capital formation, long periods of education, and lifestyles that deny instant gratification for future health. Preindustrial conditions do not reward such faith. . . . Uncontrollable natural or supernatural forces took away life, and one needed to reconcile one's fate to the four horsemen of the apocalypse: disease, famine, pestilence, and drought.

The twentieth century represents perhaps the clearest triumph of science over fatalism. . . . The modern hospital, the professionalism of physicians and nurses, and effective pharmaceuticals have dramatically altered mortality rates and improved the quality of life in postindustrial states.

For those entering a hospital prior to 1900, the probability of treatment helping, rather than harming, would be less than fifty-fifty, and the odds would be considerably poorer prior to 1870. Today, we identify hospitals as technologic citadels of sophisticated medical practice. But their preindustrial origins were as religious and charitable institutions for the hopelessly sick and poor. They were places to comfort the indigent dying.

For the first three quarters of the nineteenth century, medical personnel were not in charge of hospitals. . . . In the main, hospitals at that time were places for the homeless poor and insane to die. The affluent classes were treated at home. For a variety of reasons, however, hospitals became central to medical practice and education between 1870 and 1910.[1] . . .

[T]he development of the medical profession parallels particular developments of the hospital. This is especially true of surgery, which enjoyed a dramatic increase of prestige and precision during this time. Technological advances played a major role in changing surgery. Before painkilling drugs, surgical methods in the first half of the nineteenth century depended upon powerful and swift physicians whose craft and tools were closer to the corner butcher. Mortality rates of about 40 percent followed amputation.

Three developments altered the brutality and mortality rates and allowed abdominal surgery, which was rarely performed prior to 1890. Dentist William Morton's demonstration of ether at Massachusetts General Hospital in 1846 ushered in a means of eliminating pain and allowed more careful and delicate surgery. Joseph Lister's discovery of antisepsis in 1867 gradually led to new procedures during surgery to prevent infection. However, antisepsis was poorly understood. Lister's technique was based on the use of carbolic acid spray, but his methods were adopted only over a long period of time. Fatal infections continued even after using the spray because antiseptic procedures were not followed carefully until after 1880. Soon, sterile procedures were properly followed and surgery rapidly expanded. Finally, the development of the X-ray in 1895, along with other diagnostic tools, opened the way for abdominal surgery for appendicitis, gallbladder, and stomach ulcers. Thoracic surgery and surgery of the nervous and cardiovascular systems developed in the early 1900s.

Triumph and Tragedy

By 1950, the cliché a "medical miracle" had rich meaning. Infant mortality rates in the United States were fewer than 15 per 100,000 births, down from 300 or so per 100,000 at the turn of the century. Pneumonia, once whispered by medical staff who witnessed the suffering of the dying to be the "old man's relief," now was easily controlled with penicillin. Infectious diseases in particular dramatically declined in the first half of the twentieth century. Improvement in health was a triumph of modernity, and part of that triumph was a consequence of modern

1. Paul Starr, The Social Transformation of American Medicine 151 (1982).

medicine. There is, however, much debate about the weight of medicine's contribution, compared to other modern factors. . . .

Our dramatic advances in health are also related to improved nutrition, life-style, and education, as well as to medical advancements. The literature of health care points, in particular, to . . . proper diet, minimal tension, absence of smoking or heavy drinking, daily exercise, and a life-style that provides low-risk factors for accidents. Advances in health and longevity are more closely tied to higher income, better diets, and especially greater education than to advances in medicine. . . .

Yet, American perception of well-being is closely identified with medicine. Paradoxically, much of the public's present disenchantment with medicine is the consequence of this identification. Modern medicine has advanced to the frontiers of preserving life, but only by increasingly more expensive therapies and diagnoses to preserve life "on its margins." That is, additional expenditures and efforts to treat disease produce diminishing results in proportion to the effort. We are just beginning to learn that our scientific capacity to triumph over illness, physical anomalies, and death, on many occasions with medical miracles, brings with it a special brand of tragedy.

We have become totally modern. No more can we explain death and suffering as a consequence of fate. It is our medicine, or lack of it, that denies death and suffering. We know we must choose who receives scarce resources and who does not. No longer can we attribute to fate or to God the responsibility for making life-and-death decisions. Yet, these life-and-death decisions involve very expensive procedures and technologies and often contribute only marginally to extending life. Examples are well known and regularly make front-page newspaper drama: organ transplants, aggressive treatment of terminal patients, neonates under 750 grams, or long-term comatose patients.

These new choices challenge our basic values and frequently produce conflict. . . . Conflict is father to politics and law, and politics determines who gets what, when, and how. Conflict also forces moral reassessment of traditional attitudes and postures, including the justice question: "Who *should* get what, when and how."

How do we distribute health care? How should we? How does political power within the present economic system determine the distribution of health care? These questions obviously spill over the boundaries of economics, politics, sociology, law, medicine, history, and philosophy. In particular, looming over the politics of health care is a sense of the tragic, as well as the majestic. Tragedy points to human endeavors that are virtuous and honorable, yet carry the seeds of their own downfall. Our efforts to lessen the suffering and lengthen the lives of Americans through accessible, affordable, quality health care represent the best of our traditions and have been, on balance, an American success story. Sometimes we fall short in that effort because some group is unreasonably left behind in the political shuffle. The [45] million Americans who [have] no health coverage represent[] such a group. At other times, our very success leads to exasperating dilemmas of bioethics and distributive justice that would cross the eyes of a Solomon. Our dilemma over public financing for costly organ transplants at the expense of other badly needed programs or continued aggressive treatment of comatose or terminally ill loved ones are poignant, modern examples. It is here where triumph merges with tragedy.

END-OF-LIFE WARNING AT $618,616 MAKES ME WONDER WAS IT WORTH IT

Amanda Bennett

Bloomberg News, Mar. 4, 2010*

It was some time after midnight on Dec. 8, 2007, when [the doctor] told me my husband might not live till morning. The kidney cancer that had metastasized almost six years earlier was growing in his lungs. He was in intensive care at the Hospital of the University of Pennsylvania in Philadelphia, and had begun to spit blood.

Terence Bryan Foley, 67 years old, my husband of 20 years, father of our two teenagers, a Chinese historian who earned his Ph.D. in his 60s, a man who played more than 15 musical instruments and spoke six languages, a San Francisco cable car conductor and sports photographer, an expert on dairy cattle and swine nutrition, film noir and Dixieland jazz, was confused. He knew his name, but not the year. He wanted a Coke.

Should Terence begin to hemorrhage, the doctor asked, what should he do? This was our third end-of-life warning in seven years. We fought off the others. Perhaps we could dodge this one too. [Terence's oncologist] and I both believed that a new medicine he had just begun to take would buy him more time. Keep him alive if you can, I said. Let's see what the drug, Pfizer Inc.'s Sutent, can do.

Terence died six days later, on Friday, Dec. 14, 2007. What I couldn't know then was that the thinking behind my request—along with hundreds of decisions we made over seven years—was a window on the impossible calculus at the core of the U.S. health-care debate.

Expensive Last Chances

Terence and I didn't have to think about money, allocation of medical resources, the struggles of [millions of] uninsured Americans, or the impact on corporate bottom lines. Backed by medical insurance provided by my employers, we were able to fight his cancer with a series of expensive last chances like the one I asked for that night.

How expensive? The bills totaled $618,616, almost two-thirds of it for the final 24 months, much of it for treatments that no one can say for sure helped extend his life. In just the last four days of trying to keep him alive—two in intensive care, two in a cancer ward—our insurance was charged $43,711 for doctors, medicines, monitors, X-rays and scans. Two years later, the only thing I know for certain that money bought was confirmation that he was dying.

Some of the drugs probably did Terence no good at all. At least one helped fewer than 10 percent of all those who took it. Pharmaceutical companies and insurers will have to sort out the economics of treatments that end up working for only a small subset. Should everyone have the right to try them? Terence and I

*Excerpted with permission. For a fuller account, see Amanda Bennett, The Cost of Hope (2012).

answered yes. Each drug potentially added life. Yet that too led me to a question I can't answer. When is it time to quit?

Science, Emotion, Costs

Congress didn't touch the issue in [the Patient Protection and Affordable Care Act of 2010]. The mere hint of somehow limiting the ability to choose care as aggressively as Terence and I did, created a whirlwind of accusations that the ill, aged and infirm would be forced before government "death panels."

As the debate heated up, I remembered the fat sheaf of insurance statements that arrived after Terence's death . . . [from] six hospitals, four insurers, Medicare, three oncologists, and a surgeon. Those papers tell the story of a system filled with people doing their best. And they raise complex questions about a health-care system that consumes 17 percent of the economy. As I leafed through the stack of documents, it was easy to see why 31 percent of the money spent on health care goes to paperwork and administration. . . .

The documents revealed an economic system in which the sellers don't set and the buyers don't know the prices. The University of Pennsylvania hospital charged more than 12 times what Medicare at the time reimbursed for a chest scan. One insurer paid a hospital for 80 percent of the $3,232 price of a scan, while another covered 24 percent. Insurance companies negotiated their own rates, and neither my employers nor I paid the difference between the sticker and discounted prices.

'It's Completely Insane'

In this economic system, prices of goods and services bear little relation to the demand for them or their cost to make—or, as it turns out, the good or harm they do. "No other nation would allow a health system to be run the way we do it. It's completely insane," said Uwe E. Reinhardt, a political economy professor at Princeton University. . . . Taking it all into account, the data showed we had made a bargain that hardly any economist looking solely at the numbers would say made sense. Why did we do it?

I was one big reason. Not me alone, of course. The medical system has a strong bias toward action. My husband, too, was unusual . . . in his passionate willingness to endure discomfort for a chance to see his daughter grow from a child to a young woman, and his son graduate from high school.

After Terence died, [his doctor] drew me a picture of a bell curve, showing the range of survival times for kidney cancer sufferers. Terence was way off in the tail on the right-hand side, an indication he had indeed beaten the odds. An explosion of research had made it possible to extend lives for years—enough to keep our quest from having been total madness.

Terence used to tell a story, almost certainly apocryphal, about his Uncle Bob. Climbing aboard a landing craft before the invasion of Normandy, so the story went, Bob's sergeant told the men that by the end of the day, nine out of 10 would be dead. Said Bob, on hearing that news: "Each one of us looked around and felt so sorry for those other nine poor sonsabitches."

For me, it was about pushing the bell curve. Knowing that if there was something to be done, we couldn't not do it. Believing beyond logic that we were going to escape the fate of those other poor sonsabitches. It is very hard to put a price on that kind of hope.

Pricing Hope

We found the cancer by accident [a decade ago]. . . . Within a month, Terence was in surgery, and [another doctor] had taken out the diseased kidney. . . . "We got it all," he said. Terence was visibly moved. "Thank you for saving my life," he said. . . . The statistics looked good. By the traditional method of staging—a 7-centimeter tumor with no sign of having spread—Terence had an 85 percent chance of surviving five years.

The bills from Regence Blue Cross & Blue Shield of Oregon show the operation was relatively inexpensive, too, just over $25,000, or only about 4 percent of the total [eventually] charged to keep Terence alive. Insurance paid a discounted $14,084. Terence and I paid $209.87. The lab soon cast a chill on our optimism.

Terence had "collecting duct" cancer, the rarest and most aggressive form. . . . If that was correct, Terence had almost no chance of making it to the end of the year. . . . "Watchful waiting" was the recommended path. Waiting for him to die was what we feared. He didn't die. He got better. We didn't know why. We tried not to think about it. . . .

Then, on May 6, 2002, I was at work when [our son] Terry called, panic in his voice. "Mom, come home. Dad is very sick." . . . His father was in bed, his face flaming with fever, shaking with chills under a pile of blankets. He could barely speak. "The cancer is in my lungs," he said. "I've got six to nine months left."

A scan had spotted the cancer's spread. Not wanting to worry us, Terence had secretly begun taking Interleukin-2. If he recovered, he figured, we would never know how close he came; if he died, he would have spared us months of anguish. . . . What he didn't reckon on was that the drug would make him violently ill. But it was the only possible therapy at that time. Injections of the protein—at $735 a dose—were intended to stimulate the immune response to help fight off the cancer's invasion. The overall response rate was about 10 percent. For most, it did nothing.

That evening, for the one and only time, I felt pure terror. I spent the night awake in our dark living room. . . . Knowing the long odds, [the oncologist later] told me he had prescribed Interleukin-2 simply because it was all there was. Terence stopped taking it after just a few weeks, unable to stand the side effects.

I shook off my fear and plunged into the Internet. If there was something out there that could save him, I was going to find it. One colleague had been snatched from dying of AIDS by a chance introduction to a doctor who prescribed an experimental antiviral cocktail. Another had beaten leukemia with a cutting-edge bone marrow transplant. We could defeat this, too. . . .

The entire medical bill for seven years . . . was steeply discounted. The $618,616 became $254,176 when the insurers paid their share and imposed their discounts. Of that, Terence and I were responsible for $9,468—less than 4 percent. . . .

[A]s summer in Philadelphia turned to autumn. Terence resumed [another treatment which he had ceased earlier due to side effects]. Because he wasn't in a clinical trial, our insurance company was billed: $27,360 a dose, for four treatments. [But that also failed to stop the cancer's spread.] . . .

Reading Their Goodbyes

[A few months later] I signed the papers transferring Terence to hospice. The next day, Tuesday, the hospital staff took away the machines and the monitors. The oncologists and radiologists and lab technicians disappeared. Another group of people—hospice nurses, social workers, chaplains and counselors for me and the children—began to arrive one by one, as the focus shifted from treating Terence to easing our transition.

For the next three days, with Terence in the same hospital bed, we spent $14,022 on [pain and anxiety medications], and on monitoring for him and counseling for a different kind of pain management for the children and me. The cost was less than a third of the previous four days' $43,711.

Terence drifted into a coma on Tuesday. I e-mailed his friends and read their goodbyes aloud, hoping he could hear and understand. I slept in a chair. At about 2:30 A.M. Friday, a noise in the hall startled me. I awoke just in time to hold his hand as he died. They gave me back his wedding ring the next day.

Looking back, memories of my zeal to treat are tinged with sadness. Since I didn't believe my husband was going to die, I never let us have the chance to say goodbye. . . .

Would I do it all again? Absolutely. I couldn't not do it again. But I think had he known the costs, Terence would have fought the insurers spending enough, at roughly $200,000, to vaccinate almost a quarter-million children in developing countries. That's how he would have thought about it. . . .

Did we help Terence? Or harm him? . . . [His doctor] and I looked at the numbers. The average patient in his [clinical] trial got 14 months of extra life. Without any treatment, [his doctor] estimates that for someone at Terence's stage of the disease it was three months. Terence got 17 months—still within the realm of chance, but way, way up on the bell curve.

There's another bell curve that starts about where Terence's left off. It charts the survival times for patients treated not just with [the dugs Terence received] but also Novartis's Afinitor and GlaxoSmithKline's Votrient, made available within the past three years. Doctors and patients now are doing what we dreamed of, staggering one drug after another and buying years more of life. . . .

[Terence's] 17 months included an afternoon looking down at the Mediterranean with Georgia from a sunny balcony in Southern Spain. Moving Terry into his college dorm. Celebrating our 20th anniversary with a carriage ride through Philadelphia's cobbled streets. A final Thanksgiving game of charades with cousins Margo and Glenn.

And one last chance for Terence to pave the way for all those other poor sonsabitches.

■ DOCTORS, PATIENTS, AND HEALTH INSURANCE: THE ORGANIZATION AND FINANCING OF MEDICAL CARE

Herman Miles Somers & Anne Ramsay Somers

1961

. . . The popular conception of the doctor-patient relationship is a mixture of fact and fancy. Until World War II the general practitioner family doctor was still in the majority. The one-to-one relationship of a personally chosen physician—where economic and other factors permitted any choice—with his patient was the most common form of medical practice. In big cities, the doctor had an office, usually mahogany and leather, sparsely equipped with simple diagnostic aids, a few surgical tools, and some antiseptic drugs. But, especially in rural areas and suburbs, he was more often found in the homes of his patients doing his rounds, working at the bedside of the sick and injured. His black bag held almost all his equipment. His records were kept partly in a small notebook, mostly in his mind and heart. He appeared indefatigable, compassionate, and available wherever and whenever needed. . . .

This doctor of the past has been idealized in story, picture, and legend. . . . Despite its apparent anachronisms, the picture still appeals to people's sentiments—even to those fully aware of its use as a public relations device. It has the warmth and intimate concern that no hypodermic needle—no complex of steel and tubing—can replace, however effective they may be. Although medical miracles are now performed successfully between strangers, doctors and patients both believe that the absence of continuity, personal concern, and individual attention are detrimental to the best medical care. This is not without foundation.

The origin of the "traditional" doctor-patient relationship reaches deep into the past. From the beginning of medical history, the practicing physician has been part priest, part technician, part personal or family counselor. In early days, when medicine had very little in the way of scientific knowledge to rely on, it was inevitable that the subjective priestly element should be dominant. . . .

In modern times medicine has become more scientific. But the traditional reliance on mystical forces and a highly authoritarian doctor-patient relationship persists to a degree unknown in other contemporary human relations. . . . The relationship of citizen and state, of employer and employee, of teacher and pupil, parent and child, even of husband and wife, have undergone profound and acknowledged changes as a result of the technological and socio-economic trends of the past few centuries. But there is no general acknowledgment or acceptance of the significant change that has, in fact, been taking place in the doctor-patient relationship. Of the manifold and complex reasons, only a few of the more important can be noted here.

First and basic is the persistence—in spite of scientific progress—of large elements of uncertainty and fear regarding illness and medical care which are conducive to continued reliance on hope, faith, confidence and other subjective factors on the part of both doctor and patient. "Honor thy physician because of the need thou hast of him," so said apocryphal Ecclesiastes to the Hebrews thousands of years ago. And still, today, patients yearn to have confidence in their doctors, to idealize them, to endow them with superhuman powers. Talcott Parsons, the Harvard sociologist, reconciles the use of such subjective factors—the use of "modern magic"—with the scientific basis of modern medicine by calling it a "functional bias."

> The basic function of magic is to bolster the self-confidence of actors in situations where energy and skill *do* make a difference but where, because of uncertainty factors, outcomes cannot be guaranteed. This fits the situation of the doctor, but in addition on the side of the patient it may be argued the *belief* in the possibility of recovery is an important factor in it. If from purely a technical point of view both the individual doctor and the general tradition are optimistically biased it ought to help. . . . Of course, this argument must not be pressed too far.

As the boundaries of medical ignorance and uncertainty are pushed back, one would expect this resort to supra-scientific factors to decline, and, indeed, it has in the case of bacterial and other diseases where the cause and cure are clearly established. But the reduced role of subjective factors in the treatment of specific cases has been more than offset by an increasing interest in the role of the emotions in illness. A widespread increase in psychotherapy and psychosomatic medicine has renewed the emphasis on a personal doctor and a personal doctor-patient relationship of a type that permits knowledge of the "whole [person]." . . .

Moreover, it is now widely believed that illness, *per se,* tends to create—even in the most intellectual of patients—an attitude of dependence, of "regression" to helplessness, and perhaps to childlike behavior. . . . In this state, confidence in the authority and benevolence of the doctor, as well as in his scientific knowledge and technical skill—the now-familiar "father-image"—is generally desired and often desirable.

Finally, there is the impenetrable mystery of death. The physician's relation to this event—however helpless he in fact may be—has endowed him, in the eyes of centuries of patients, with an aura of the mystery. To the extent that the physician identifies himself with this priestly role and takes on himself the burden associated therewith, or at least appears to do so through the gravity of his personal demeanor and behavior, his supra-scientific role continues to be respected and perpetuated, reinforcing in the eyes of individual patients and society at large his status as a dispenser of increasingly scientific medicine.

■ COMPETING SOLUTIONS: AMERICAN HEALTH CARE PROPOSALS AND INTERNATIONAL EXPERIENCE

Joseph White

1995

America's systems for delivering and paying for medical care are notably more complex than those of most other countries. Many doctors work in more than one hospital, making governance of medical staffs difficult; specialists are harder to coordinate because there are more of them; and the proliferation of forms of managed care means rapid change in patterns of gatekeeping and referral.

Physicians

American doctors go through extensive training to work long hours for high pay. The typical medical school program requires, after four years of college, four more years of "undergraduate" medical education. During the final two years, students receive some clinical training. Virtually all graduates then must complete some graduate medical education in order to be licensed to practice medicine. This education is obtained in residency programs, mainly in hospitals affiliated with medical schools. Normally only one year of residency (as an intern) is needed for licensure, but up to eight years (for neurosurgeons) may be required for certification as a specialist.

. . . Given the length of their training and the size of their debts, it is understandable that most physicians feel entitled to incomes that are much higher than those of most other Americans. . . . [The median physician salary is about $200,000, roughly five times that of the average American worker. The range across specialties is broad. Pediatricians and general practitioners typically earn around $175,000, common medical specialists (cardiology, dermatology, anesthesiology) are in the $250,000-$350,000 range, while heart surgeons and brain surgeons can earn well over $500,000. Some doctors earn substantially more from entrepreneurial activities such as medical patents and investments in various health care organizations.]

An unusually high proportion of American doctors are trained to specialize. Fewer than 10 percent of American doctors [call] themselves general practitioners (GPs), the standard term for primary care physicians. But because a specialist such as a family practitioner, internist, pediatrician, or obstetrician-gynecologist may be a person's regular physician, between 33 and 40 percent of physicians (depending on who is counting) are mainly primary care providers. [Specialists who receive several years of extra training and pass additional exams are designated as "Board Certified," meaning that they comply with voluntary, private standards set by the American Specialty Boards, which operate under the auspices of the AMA. At one time, board certification was relatively rare, but now the vast majority of new doctors obtain certification. About two dozen boards now exist, covering not only standard specialties but also areas of general practice such as family medicine and internal medicine.] . . .

Two-thirds of physicians practice in offices, the vast majority with admitting privileges to a hospital. Many practice in more [than one hospital] (for example, a nice suburban hospital for simple cases, and a high-tech academic medical center for difficult ones). Hospitals therefore must compete for admissions by making those physicians happy, such as by having the fanciest equipment. . . .

Institutional Care

Long-term or chronic care, especially for the aged, is a complicated system on its own, and the potential expenses of long-term care are so great that it is highly unlikely that any reform will do much about it. [Therefore, the focus here is] on the costs of the current American health care system, of which one major component is hospital services for acute care.

The American supply of hospitals is dominated by private nonprofit hospitals—many owned by religious organizations. [About two-thirds] of hospital beds [are] provided by the nonprofits, 10 percent by the for-profit sector. The rest, just over a quarter of the beds, [are] in federal, state, or local facilities. It is hard to identify much difference between the behavior and efficiency of the for-profit and private nonprofits. If private institutions are more efficient, the savings go largely or entirely to investors.

Americans spend a great deal of money on hospitals: [about 40 percent] of all spending on patient care. But . . . the hospital is not as dominant a provider as it once was or still is in other countries. Hospitals and doctors tried to avoid regulation by moving care to ostensibly freestanding ambulatory care facilities. Examples include kidney dialysis units, and radiology group practices with close relations with hospitals. Some payers encouraged the shift, believing those facilities would be cheaper. . . .

Back in the traditional hospitals, the nature of care depends greatly on hospitals' relationships with doctors and medical schools, and on hospitals' catchment areas—the areas from which they get most of their patients. . . .

A suburban hospital can generally provide sophisticated care, such as cardiac bypass surgery, but it is not as likely to have clinical professors who are able to provide extremely specialized care for "interesting" cases. All hospitals want the most advanced equipment, but the academic medical centers must have it for research and training. These centers rely heavily on residents and interns for delivery of care and, most important, are likely to have a much lower-class population of patients.

Many of the [academic medical centers] are in inner cities. They are likely to have large outpatient departments to train the students (residents) and serve the local population, which feeds into the inpatient wards; the emergency room not only gets emergencies but also serves as an outpatient clinic for some of the population. All of this is the good news: If a major teaching hospital is in the inner city, then either a large and endowed institution or a state government pays for some care for the inner-city poor.

When local hospitals receive little funding for education, poor populations must frequently rely on a hospital financed by a strapped city or county budget. Such hospitals—for example, Cook County in Chicago, Boston City, and Charity in New Orleans—have interns and residents to do the work because of their relationship with a training program, but nowhere near the resources of a freestanding university hospital. All hospitals in the inner city try to convince Medicare that they deserve an extra subsidy for treating a poorer, less-insured, and often sicker population. The federal government calls these disproportionate share payments. One of the huge issues for American health care reform is what will happen to the academic medical centers and the remaining urban public hospitals if payment systems allow competing insurers to favor hospitals that are less expensive because they have lesser teaching and subsidy burdens.

Another major issue is how a bias toward specialized, high-technology medicine, created in part by how medical education is financed and how physicians are paid, is reinforced by arrangements for capital investment in American medicine. There are hardly any measures in place to prevent a "medical arms race" among hospitals that seek the most advanced technology in order to attract physicians and generate revenue. . . .

Because for years insurers would pay whatever physicians and hospitals billed, and hospitals relied on physicians to provide patients, hospitals competed for patients by having the best equipment, and insurers ended up paying for excess treatments and higher charges per treatment. Also, at one time, physicians could refer patients to any specialist they wished, and patients could go directly to a specialist without referral.

The rise of managed care and of more aggressive bargaining by insurers has change[d] this basic pattern. Insurers have become more likely to refuse to approve a given service or to insist on a lower price. Hospitals still need to attract physicians by offering the best equipment, however, so they are caught between the demands of doctors and payers. Meanwhile insurers are limiting choice of and access to specialists by building closed panels, in which a person covered by a plan either cannot use or must pay a surcharge to use any provider who is not on special contract to the plan. A patient might find that her doctor of 20 years' standing is no longer part of her insurance plan; a physician might find that many of his patients can afford referral only to three nephrologists whom he does not know. One of the key issues in reform is whether these . . . restrictions on choice of physician are necessary.

DOCTORS, PATIENTS, AND HEALTH INSURANCE: THE ORGANIZATION AND FINANCING OF MEDICAL CARE

Herman Miles Somers & Anne Ramsay Somers

1961

[T]he conflict between [hospital] medical staff and [hospital] management has become both sharper and more open in recent years. The roots of this conflict—the basic dichotomy in hospital organization—go back to eighteenth century Britain and the establishment of the Anglo-American tradition of voluntary hospitals. There was no such dichotomy in medieval days when hospitals were operated, with little medical assistance, by monastic orders for the sick poor. There is generally no such duality in the major Continental hospitals which are usually run, with unquestioned authority, by full-time chiefs of medical services. The distinguishing feature of the Anglo-American voluntary hospital, however, has been its use by private physicians for private patients with little or no accompanying administrative or financial responsibility. . . .

Recent developments—the hospital's changing role, its increase in size, complexity, utilization, cost, and its greatly altered financial base—have intensified the inherent instability of this administrative structure. . . . Lay influences on hospital administration and policy are clearly increasing. Ultimate policy responsibility has always rested with lay trustees. Traditionally, they limited their oversight to balancing the books. With the tremendous increase in hospital costs, however, this single concern has led to increasing surveillance over the hospital's total functioning, including the organization of the medical staff. The hospital administrator, traditionally an untrained individual content to play a fairly subservient role and socially outranked by doctor and trustee alike, is being transformed into a professional with increasing self-confidence and authority. . . .

At the same time the hospital has become an indispensable workshop for the modern physician, who finds it virtually impossible to practice good medicine without hospital affiliation. The hospital is the center of his professional world, and he is acknowledged to be its key figure. Fully 40 percent of private physician income is now earned in the hospital. Naturally he wants "his" institution equipped with the latest scientific and technological facilities. But the doctor's relationship to the hospital is peculiarly ambiguous. As a rule he assumes neither administrative nor financial responsibility. Yet, in practice, his is the most powerful voice in the organization. He alone admits and discharges patients; he alone can diagnose, prescribe, and treat patients—still the chief purpose for which the hospital exists. With his high professional status, he may, in most hospitals, countermand administrative orders and defy lay authority with relative impunity. The result is the confusing duality that prevails today throughout the hospital system, public and private. . . .

It is sometimes proposed that hiring the medical staff on a salary or contract basis would increase the doctors' sense of responsibility for hospital administration and help clarify lines of accountability. It could integrate the administrative structure without restricting professional integrity. This is the general pattern in a few of the nation's best hospitals, such as the Henry Ford in Detroit and the Cleveland Clinic Hospital. Most of the profession is, however, vigorously opposed to such practice, alleging "hospital domination," "lay control," or the "corporate practice of medicine." Some hospitals have taken a middle road—employing full-time medical directors (this is frequently the practice in government hospitals) and in a few instances, full-time chiefs of medical services. This too is generally frowned on by physicians in private practice. . . .

Many hospital spokesmen, however, content themselves with pleading for physician cooperation in assuring some responsibility for hospital operations and costs. . . . But such recommendations are usually set in a purely hortatory context. It is not clear how such preachments are to influence the individual doctor. The "medical staff" of which he is a member is in most instances simply a term for the collectivity of physicians authorized to practice in a particular hospital. The staff can be as disciplinary an instrument as it chooses to be, but in most places it has chosen minimal responsibility. . . . By and large the staff still prefers not to interfere with the practices of the individual physician.

■ CLINICAL DECISION MAKING: FROM THEORY TO PRACTICE

David M. Eddy

1996

Medical practice is in the middle of a profound transition. Most physicians can remember the day when, armed with a degree, a mission, and confidence, they could set forth to heal the sick. Like Solomon, physicians could receive patients, hear their complaints, and determine the best course of action. While not every patient could be cured, everyone could be confident that whatever was done was the best possible. Most important, each physician was free, trusted, and left alone to determine what was in the best interest of each patient.

All of that is changing. . . . Now physicians must deal with second opinions, precertification, skeptical medical directors, variable coverage, outright denials, utilization review, threats of cookbook medicine, and letters out of the blue chiding that Mrs. Smith is on two incompatible drugs. Solomon did not have to call anyone to get permission for his decisions. What is going on?

What is going on is that one of the basic assumptions underlying the practice of medicine is being challenged. This assumption is not just a theory about cholesterol, antiarrhythmia, or estrogens. This assumption concerns the intellectual foundation of medical care. Simply put, the assumption is that whatever a physician decides is, by definition, correct. The challenge says that while many decisions no doubt *are* correct, many are not, and elaborate mechanisms are needed to determine which are which. Physicians are slowly being stripped of their decisionmaking power.

Notes: Doctors and Hospitals

1. *The Two-Headed Monster.* The unique structure of American hospitals, in which doctors are independent but essential to their financial well-being, has been described as "attractive as a two-headed monster" and as "stable as a three-legged stool." See H. L. Smith, Two Lines of Authority Are One Too Many, 84 Modern Hosp. 59 (Mar. 1955). This division of authority is mirrored throughout the organizational structure of the health care system. For instance, hospitals, unlike any other business organization, are required by state licensure laws and private accreditation standards to have *two* sets of corporate bylaws; one for the hospital administration

and a second for the medical staff. Similarly, health insurance traditionally pays hospitals separately from doctors, as reflected in the distinctions between Blue Cross (hospital insurance) vs. Blue Shield (physician insurance) and between Medicare Part A vs. Part B.

2. *Power Relationships in Medicine.* Medical sociologists and organizational theorists have produced a rich literature discussing the role of physicians within medical institutions. Leading examples are Eliot Freidson, Doctoring Together (1975); Eliot Freidson, Profession of Medicine (1970); Paul Starr, The Social Transformation of American Medicine (1982); Jeffrey Harris, The Internal Organization of Hospitals: Some Economic Implications, 8 Bell J. Econ. 467 (1977). For an exploration of how these insights illuminate a variety of legal doctrines and public policy debates, see Mark A. Hall, Institutional Control of Physician Behavior: Legal Barriers to Health Care Cost Containment, 137 U. Pa. L. Rev. 431 (1988) ("Because the law absorbs and reflects the values and relationships of traditional medicine, it has codified the ethic of professional dominance, effectively shielding physicians from the institutional influence contemplated by revolutionary changes in health care policy."); Sara Rosenbaum, The Impact of United States Law on Medicine as a Profession, 289 JAMA 1546 (2003); Symposium, 29 J. Health Pol. Pol'y & L. 557 (2004); Symposium, 4 Ind. Health L. Rev. 205-286 (2007).

3. *History and Description.* For **general histories and descriptions** of the health care delivery system, see David Smith & Arnold Kaluzny, The White Labyrinth: A Guide to the Health Care System (2d ed. 2000); Kristina M. Young & Philip J. Kroth, Health Care USA: Understanding Its Organization and Delivery (9th ed. 2018); David Johnson & Nancy Kane, The U.S. Health Care System: A Product of American History and Values, *in* E. Elhauge ed., The Fragmentation of U.S. Health Care (2010); Hamilton Moses et al., The Anatomy of US Health Care, 310 JAMA 1947 (2013). For more extensive historical accounts of the transformation of hospitals and their role in modern medicine, see Guenter B. Risse, Mending Bodies, Saving Souls: A History of Hospitals (1999); Charles Rosenberg, The Care of Strangers (1987); David Rosner, A Once Charitable Enterprise (1982); Rosemary Stevens, In Sickness and in Wealth: American Hospitals in the Twentieth Century (1989).

2. *The Nature of Medical Judgment*

CLINICAL DECISION MAKING: FROM THEORY TO PRACTICE
David M. Eddy*
1996

. . . Why do physicians vary so much in the way they practice medicine? At first view, there should be no problem. There are diseases—neatly named and categorized by textbooks, journal articles, and medical specialty societies. There are various procedures physicians can use to diagnose and treat these diseases. It should be

*Reprinted with permission. Dr. Eddy is a physician researcher, formerly on the faculty of Duke University, and now a consultant in Jackson Hole, Wyoming.

possible to determine the value of any particular procedure by applying it to patients who have a disease and observing the outcome. And the rest should be easy—if the outcome is good, the procedure should be used for patients with that disease; if the outcome is bad, it should not. Some variation in practice patterns can be expected due to differences in the incidence of various diseases, patients' preferences, and the available resources, but these variations should be small and explainable.

The problem of course is that nothing is this simple. Uncertainty, biases, errors, and differences of opinions, motives, and values weaken every link in the chain that connects a patient's actual condition to the selection of a diagnostic test or treatment. . . . Uncertainty creeps into medical practice through every pore. Whether a physician is defining a disease, making a diagnosis, selecting a procedure, observing outcomes, assessing probabilities, assigning preference, or putting it all together, he is walking on very slippery terrain. It is difficult for nonphysicians, and for many physicians, to appreciate how complex these tasks are, how poorly we understand them, and how easy it is for honest people to come to different conclusions.

Defining a Disease

If one looks at patients who are obviously ill, it is fairly easy to identify the physical and chemical disorders that characterize that illness. On the other hand, a large part of medicine is practiced on people who do not have obvious illnesses, but rather have signs, symptoms, or findings that may or may not represent an illness that should be treated. Three closely related problems make it difficult to determine whether or not a patient actually has a disease that needs to be diagnosed or treated.

One problem is that the dividing line between "normal" and "abnormal" is not nearly as sharp as a cursory reading of a textbook would suggest. . . . A second problem is that many "diseases," at least at the time they are diagnosed, do not by themselves cause pain, suffering, disability, or threat to life. They are considered diseases only because they increase the probability that something else that is truly bad will happen in the future. . . .

The difficulty of defining a disease is compounded by the fact that many of the signs, symptoms, findings, and conditions that might suggest a disease are extremely common. If a breast biopsy were performed on a random sample of senior citizens, fully 90 percent of them could have fibrocystic disease. If obesity is a disease, the average American is diseased. . . . Morbid obesity is defined as 100 percent above the ideal weight. But what is "ideal," and why 100 percent? The lesson is that for many conditions a clinician faces, there is no clear definition of disease that provides an unequivocal guide to action, and there is wide room for differences of opinion and variations in practice. . . .

[E]ven when sharp criteria are created, physicians vary widely in their application of these criteria—in their ability to ask about symptoms, observe signs, interpret test results, and record the answers. The literature on "observer variation" has been growing for a long time. . . . Thirteen pathologists were asked to read 1,001 specimens obtained from biopsies of the cervix, and then to repeat the readings at a later time. On average, each pathologist agreed with himself only 89 percent of the time (intraobserver agreement), and with a panel of "senior" pathologists only

87 percent of the time (interobserver agreement). Looking only at the patients who actually had cervical pathology, the intraobserver agreement was only 68 percent and the interobserver agreement was only 51 percent. The pathologists were best at reading more advanced disease and normal tissue, but were labeled "unsatisfactory" in their ability to read the precancerous and preinvasive stages.

Similar studies have been reported for . . . many other signs, symptoms, and procedures. Even if there were no uncertainty about what constitutes a disease and how to define it, there would still be considerable uncertainty about whether or not a patient has the signs, symptoms, and findings needed to fit the definition.

Selecting a Procedure

The task of selecting a procedure is no less difficult. There are two main issues. First, for any patient condition there are dozens of procedures that can be ordered, in any combination, at any time. The list of procedures that might be included in a workup of chest pain or hypertension would take more than a page, spanning the spectrum from simply asking questions, to blood studies, to X-rays. Even for highly specific diagnostic problems, there can be a large choice of procedures. For example, if a woman presents with a breast mass and her physician wants to know its approximate size and architecture, the physician might contemplate an imaging procedure. The choice could include mammography, ultra-sonography, thermography, diaphanography, computed tomography, lymphography, Mammoscan, and magnetic resonance imaging. . . . And why should a diagnostic workup be limited to one test? Why not follow a negative mammogram with a computed tomogram (or vice versa)? For the detection of colorectal cancer, a physician can choose any combination of fecal occult blood tests (and there are more than a dozen brands), digital examination, rigid sigmoidoscopy, flexible 30 cm sigmoidoscopy, flexible 60 cm sigmoidoscopy, barium enema (either plain or air contrast), and colonoscopy. These choices are not trivial. Most procedures have different mechanisms of action and a long list of pros and cons. . . . These procedures are for relatively well-defined diseases; imagine the problems of selecting procedures to evaluate symptoms like fatigue, headache, or fever that can have about a dozen causes. . . .

In theory, much of the uncertainty just described could be managed if it were possible to conduct enough experiments under enough conditions, and observe the outcomes. Unfortunately, measuring the outcomes of medical procedures is one of the most difficult problems we face. The goal is to predict how the use of a procedure in a particular case will affect that patient's health and welfare. Standing in the way are at least a half dozen major obstacles. The central problem is that there is a natural variation in the way people respond to a medical procedure. Take two people who, to the best of our ability to define such things, are identical in all important respects, submit them to the same operative procedure, and one will die on the operating table while the other will not. Because of this natural variation, we can only talk about the probabilities of various outcomes—the probability that a diagnostic test will be positive if the disease is present (sensitivity), the probability that a test will be negative if the disease is absent (specificity), the probability that a treatment will yield a certain result, and so forth.

One consequence of this natural variation is that to study the outcomes of any procedure it is necessary to conduct the procedure on many different people, who are thought to represent the particular patients we want to know about, and then average the results. . . . Some diseases are so rare that, in order to conduct the ideal clinical trials, it would be necessary to collect tens of thousands, if not hundreds of thousands, of participants. A good example concerns the frequency of the Pap smear. One might wonder why the merits of a three-year versus one-year frequency cannot be settled by a randomized controlled trial. Because of the low frequency of cervical cancer, and the small difference in outcomes expected for the two frequencies, almost one million women would be required for such a study. . . .

Finally, even when the best trials are conducted, we still might not get an answer. Consider the value of mammography in women under fifty, and consider just one outcome—the effect on breast cancer mortality. Ignore for the time being the radiation hazard, false-positive test results, inconvenience, financial costs, and other issues. This is one of the best-studied problems in cancer prevention, benefiting from the largest (60,000 women) and longest (more than 15 years) completed randomized controlled trial, and an even larger uncontrolled study involving 270,000 women screened for five years in 29 centers around the country. Yet we still do not know the value of mammography in women under 50. . . .

Unable to turn to a definitive body of clinical and epidemiological research, a clinician or research scientist who wants to know the value of a procedure is left with a mixture of randomized controlled trials, nonrandomized trials, uncontrolled trials, and clinical observations. The evidence from different sources can easily go in different directions, and it is virtually impossible for anyone to sort things out in his or her head. Unfortunately, the individual physician may be most impressed by observations made in his or her individual practice. This source of evidence is notoriously vulnerable to bias and error. What a physician sees and remembers is biased by the types of patients who come in; by the decisions of the patients to accept a treatment and return for follow-up; by a natural desire to see good things; and by a whole series of emotions that charge one's memory. On top of these biases, the observations are vulnerable to large statistical errors because of the small number of patients a physician sees in a personal practice. . . .

Now assume that a physician can know the outcomes of recommending a particular procedure for a particular patient. Is it possible to declare whether those outcomes are good or bad? Unfortunately, no. The basic problem is that any procedure has multiple outcomes, some good and some bad. The expected reduction in chest pain that some people will get from coronary artery bypass surgery is accompanied by a splitting of the chest, a chance of an operative mortality, days in the hospital, pain, anxiety, and financial expense. Because the outcomes are multiple and move in different directions, tradeoffs have to be made. And making tradeoffs involves values. . . . Imagine the variation in how different people value pain, disability, operative mortality, life expectancy, a day in a hospital, and who is going to feed the dogs. . . .

Putting It All Together

The final decision about how to manage a patient requires synthesizing all the information about a disease, the patient, signs and symptoms, the effectiveness of dozens of tests and treatments, outcomes and values. All of this must be done without knowing precisely what the patient has, with uncertainty about signs and symptoms, with imperfect knowledge of the sensitivity and specificity of tests, with no training in manipulating probabilities, with incomplete and biased information about outcomes, and with no language for communicating or assessing values. If each piece of this puzzle is difficult, it is even more difficult for anyone to synthesize all the information and be certain of the answer. It would be an extremely hard task for a research team; there is no hope that it could occur with any precision in the head of a busy clinician. Hence the wide variability in the estimates physicians place on the values of procedures.

[A] final example document[s] how difficult it is to combine information from many sources to estimate the value of a particular procedure. . . . A survey of 1,000 11-year-old schoolchildren in New York City found that 65 percent had undergone tonsillectomy. The remaining children were sent for examinations to a group of physicians and 45 percent were selected for tonsillectomy. Those rejected were examined by another group of physicians and 46 percent were selected for surgery. When the remaining children were examined again by another group of physicians, a similar percent were recommended for tonsillectomy, leaving only 65 students. At that point, the study was halted for lack of physicians.

Consequences

The view of anyone who wants a close look at the consequences of different medical procedures is, at best, smoky. Some procedures may present a clear picture, and their value, or lack of it, may be obvious; putting a finger on a bleeding carotid artery is an extreme example. But for many, if not most medical procedures, we can only see shadows and gross movements. . . . We certainly do not know how a particular individual will respond. Words like "rare," "common," and "a lot" must be used instead of "one out of 1,000," or "seven on a scale of one to ten." . . .

In the end, given all the uncertainties, incentives, and heuristics, a physician will have to do what is comfortable. If it is admitted that the uncertainty surrounding the use of a procedure is great, and that there is no way to identify for certain what is best, or to prove that any particular action is right or wrong, the safest and most comfortable position is to do what others are doing. The applicable maxim is "safety in numbers." A physician who follows the practices of his or her colleagues is safe from criticism, free from having to explain his or her actions, and defended by the concurrence of colleagues.

COMPLICATIONS: A SURGEON'S NOTES ON AN IMPERFECT SCIENCE

Atul Gawande*

2002

The Case of the Red Leg

Seeing patients with one of the surgery professors in his clinic one afternoon, I was struck by how often he had to answer his patients' questions, "I do not know."

*Excerpted with permission, Henry Holt and Company. The author is a physician on the faculty of Harvard's Schools of Medicine and of Public Health. This true story uses fictionalized names.

These are four little words a doctor tends to be reluctant to utter. We're supposed to have the answers. We want to have the answers. But there was not a single person he did not have to say those four little words to that day. . . . The core predicament of medicine—the thing that makes being a patient so wrenching, being a doctor so difficult, and being a part of a society that pays the bills they run up so vexing—is uncertainty. With all that we know nowadays about people and diseases and how to diagnose and treat them, it can be hard to see this, hard to grasp how deeply the uncertainty runs. As a doctor, you come to find, however, that the struggle in caring for people is more often with what you do not know than what you do. Medicine's ground state is uncertainty. And wisdom—for both patients and doctors—is defined by how one copes with it.

This is the story of one decision under uncertainty.

It was two o'clock on a Tuesday afternoon in June. . . . I had just finished admitting someone with a gallbladder infection and was attempting to sneak out for a bite to eat when one of the emergency room physicians stopped me with yet another patient to see: a twenty-three-year-old, Eleanor Bratton, with a red and swollen leg. . . . "It's probably only a cellulitis" [he said]—a simple skin infection. . . . But he wanted me to make sure there wasn't anything "surgical" going on—an abscess that needed draining or some such. "Would you mind taking a quick look?" Groan. No. Of course not. . . .

She looked fit, athletic, and almost teenage, with blond hair tight in a ponytail, nails painted gold, and her eyes fixed on a television. There did not seem anything seriously ill about her. . . . That weekend she had gone back home to Hartford, Connecticut, to attend a wedding . . . and she had kicked off her shoes and danced the whole night. The morning after, however, she woke up with her left foot feeling sore. She had a week-old blister on the top of her foot from some cruddy sandals she had worn, and now the skin surrounding the blister was red and puffy. . . . The redness spread, and during the night she got chills and sweats and a fever of one hundred and three degrees. . . . I asked Eleanor if she had had any pus or drainage from her leg.

No. Any ulcers open up in her skin? No. A foul smell or blackening of her skin? No. Any more fevers? Not in the last two days. I let the data roll around in my head. . . . Objectively, the rash had the exact appearance of a cellulitis, something antibiotics would take care of. But another possibility lodged in my mind now, one that scared the hell out of me. . . .

Decisions in medicine are supposed to rest on concrete observations and hard evidence. But just a few weeks before, I had taken care of a patient I could not erase from my mind. . . . He was found to have a small and very ordinary skin rash on his chest and was sent home with antibiotic pills for cellulitis. That night the rash spread eight inches. The following morning he spiked a fever of one hundred and two degrees. By the time he returned to the emergency room, the skin involved had become numb and widely blistered. Shortly after, he went into shock. He was transferred to my hospital and we quickly took him to the OR.

He didn't have a cellulitis but instead an extremely rare and horrendously lethal type of infection known as necrotizing fasciitis (fah-shee-EYE-tiss). The tabloids have called it a disease of "flesh-eating bacteria" and the term is not an exaggeration. Opening the skin, we found a massive infection, far worse than what appeared from the outside. All the muscles of the left side of his chest, going around to his back, up to his shoulder, and down to his abdomen, had turned gray and soft and foul with invading bacteria and had to be removed. . . . The next day we had to remove his arm. For a while, we actually thought we had saved him. . . . One by one, however, his kidneys, lungs, liver, and heart went into failure, and then he died. It was among the most awful cases I have ever been involved in.

What we know about necrotizing fasciitis is this: it is highly aggressive and rapidly invasive. It kills up to 70 percent of the people who get it. No known antibiotic will stop it. . . . It is an organism that usually causes little more than a strep throat, but in certain strains it has evolved the ability to do far worse. No one knows where these strains come from. As with a cellulitis, they are understood to enter through breaks in the skin. The break can be as large as a surgical incision or as slight as an abrasion. . . . Survival is possible only with early and radical excisional surgery, often requiring amputation. To succeed, however, it must be done early. By the time signs of deep invasion are obvious—such as shock, loss of sensation, widespread blistering of the skin—the person is usually unsalvageable.

Standing at Eleanor's bedside, bent over examining her leg, I felt a little foolish considering the diagnosis. . . . True, in the early stages, a necrotizing fasciitis can look just like a cellulitis, presenting with the same redness, swelling, fever, and high white blood cell count. But . . . [o]nly about a thousand cases of necrotizing fasciitis occur in the entire United States each year, mainly in the elderly and chronically ill—and well over *three million* cases of cellulitis.

What's more, Eleanor's fever had gone away; she didn't look unusually ill; and I knew I was letting myself be swayed by a single, recent, anecdotal case. If there were a simple test to tell the two diagnoses apart, that would have been one thing. But there is none. The only way is to go to the operating room, open the skin, and look—not something you want to propose arbitrarily. . . .

Eleanor and her father looked on with new dread when [the general surgeon, Dr.] Studdert arrived in his scrubs and operating hat to see her. He had her tell her story again and then uncovered her leg to examine it. He didn't seem too impressed. Talking by ourselves, he told me that the rash looked to him only "like a bad cellulitis." But could he say for sure that it was not necrotizing fasciitis? He could not. It is a reality of medicine that choosing to *not* do something—to not order a test, to not give an antibiotic, to not take a patient to the operating room—is far harder than choosing to do it. . . .

Studdert sat down on the edge of her bed . . . and, in a quiet and gentle voice, he went on to explain the unquiet and ungentle effects of necrotizing fasciitis. . . . "I think it is unlikely you have it," he told Eleanor. "I'd put the chances"—he was guessing here—"at well under five percent." But, he went on, "without a biopsy, we cannot rule it out." He paused for a moment to let her and her father absorb this. Then he started to explain what the procedure involved. . . .

Eleanor went rigid. "This is crazy," she said. "This doesn't make any sense." She looked frantic, like someone drowning. "Why don't we just wait and see how the antibiotics go?" Studdert explained that this was a disease that you cannot sit on, that you had to catch it early to have any chance of treating it. Eleanor just shook her head and looked down at her covers.

Studdert and I both turned to her father to see what he might have to say. He . . . asked what would happen if the biopsy were positive for the disease. Studdert . . . hesitated before going on. "This can mean an amputation," he said. Eleanor began to cry. "I don't want to do this, Dad." Mr. Bratton swallowed hard, his gaze fixed somewhere miles beyond us.

In recent years, we in medicine have discovered how discouragingly often . . . medicine still lacks the basic organization and commitment to make sure we do what we know to do. But spend almost any amount of time with doctors and patients, and you will find that the larger, starker, and more painful difficulty is the still abundant uncertainty that exists over what should be done in many situations. The gray zones in medicine are considerable, and every day we confront situations like Eleanor's—ones in which clear scientific evidence of what to do is missing and yet choices must be made.

Exactly which patients with pneumonia, for example, should be hospitalized and which ones sent home? Which back pains treated by surgery and which by conservative measures alone? Which patients with a rash taken to surgery and which just observed on antibiotics? For many cases, the answers can be obvious. But for many others, we simply do not know. . . . In the absence of algorithms and evidence about what to do, you learn in medicine to make decisions by feel. You count on experience and judgment. And it is hard not to be troubled by this. . . . But in the face of uncertainty, what other than judgment does a physician have—or a patient have, for that matter? . . .

Eleanor and her dad now agreed to go ahead. "Let's get it over with," she said. But then I brought her the surgical consent form to sign. On it, I had written not only that the procedure was a "biopsy of the left lower extremity" but also that the risks included a "possible need for amputation." She cried out when she saw the words. It took her several minutes alone with her father before she could sign. . . .

There is, in fact, another approach to decision making, one advocated by a small and struggling coterie in medicine. The strategy, long used in business and the military, is called decision analysis, and the principles are straightforward. On a piece of paper (or a computer), you lay out all your options, and all the possible outcomes of those options, in a decision tree. You make a numeric estimate of the probability of each outcome, using hard data when you have it and a rough prediction when you don't. You weigh each outcome according to its relative desirability (or "utility") to the patient. Then you multiply out the numbers for each option and choose the one with the highest calculated "expected utility." The goal is to use explicit, logical, statistical thinking instead of just your gut. The decision to recommend annual mammograms for all women over age fifty was made this way and so was the U.S. decision to bail out Mexico when its economy tanked. Why not, the advocates ask, individual patient decisions?

Recently, I tried "treeing out" (as the decision buffs put it) the choice Eleanor faced. The options were simple: to biopsy or not biopsy. The outcomes quickly got complicated, however. There was: not being biopsied and doing fine; not being biopsied, getting diagnosed late, going through surgery, and surviving anyway; not being biopsied and dying; being biopsied and getting only a scar; being biopsied and getting a scar plus bleeding from it; being biopsied, having the disease and an amputation, but dying anyway; and so on. When all the possibilities and consequences were penciled out, my decision tree looked more like a bush. Assigning the probabilities for each potential twist of fate seemed iffy. I found what data I could from the medical literature and then had to extrapolate a good deal. And determining the relative desirability of the outcomes seemed impossible after talking to

Eleanor about them. Is dying a hundred times worse than doing fine, a thousand times worse, a million? Where does a scar with bleeding fit in? Nonetheless, these are the crucial considerations, the decision experts argue, and when we decide by instinct, they say, we are only papering this reality over.

Producing a formal analysis in any practical time frame proved to be out of the question, though. It took a couple of days—not the minutes that we had actually had—and a lot of back and forths with two decision experts. But it did provide an answer. According to the final decision tree, we should *not* have gone to the OR for a biopsy. The likelihood of my initial hunch being right was too low, and the likelihood that catching the disease early would make no difference anyway was too high. Biopsy could not be justified, the logic said. I don't know what we would have made of this information at the time. We didn't have the decision tree, however. And we went to the OR. . . .

At first glance beneath her skin, there was nothing apparent to alarm us. . . . When we probed with the tip of a clamp inside the calf incision, however, it slid unnaturally easily along the muscle, as if bacteria had paved a path. This is not a definitive finding, but enough of one that Studdert let out a sudden, disbelieving, "Oh shit." . . . The features he saw were "consistent with necrotizing fasciitis[.]" . . . "She's got it," he finally announced grimly. . . .

Decisions compound themselves, in medicine like in anything else. No sooner have you taken one fork in the road than another and another come upon you. The critical question now was what to do. . . . "I thought about a BKA," a below-knee amputation, Studdert says, "even an AKA," an above-knee amputation. No one would have faulted him for doing either. But he found himself balking. "She was such a young girl," he explains. "It may seem harsh to say, but if it was a sixty-year-old man I would've taken the leg without question." This was partly, I think, a purely emotional unwillingness to cut off the limb of a pretty twenty-three-year-old—the kind of sentimentalism that can get you in trouble. But it was also partly instinct again, an instinct that her youth and fundamentally good health might allow him to get by with just removing the most infested tissue (a "debridement") and washing out her foot and leg. Was this a good risk to take, with one of the deadliest bacteria known to man loose in her leg? Who knows? But take it he did. . . . We ended up operating on her leg four times in four days. . . . Only then was Studdert confident that not only had Eleanor survived, but her foot and leg had, too. . . .

For close to thirty years, Dartmouth physician Jack Wennberg has studied decision making in medicine, . . . [a]nd what he has found is a stubborn, overwhelming, and embarrassing degree of inconsistency in what we do. His research has shown, for example, that the likelihood of a doctor sending you for a gallbladder-removal operation varies 270 percent depending on what city you live in; for a hip replacement, 450 percent; for care in an intensive care unit during the last six months of your life, 880 percent. A patient in Santa Barbara, California, is five times more likely to be recommended back surgery for a back pain than one in Bronx, New York. This is, in the main, uncertainty at work, with the varying experience, habits, and intuitions of individual doctors leading to massively different care for people.

How can this be justified? The people who pay for the care certainly do not see how. (That is why insurers bug doctors so constantly to explain our decisions.) Nor might the people who receive it. Eleanor Bratton, without question, would have been treated completely differently depending on where she went, who she saw, or even just when she saw me (before or after that previous necrotizing fasciitis case I'd seen; at 2 A.M. or 2 P.M.; on a quiet or a busy shift). She'd have gotten merely antibiotics at one place, an amputation at another, a debridement at a third. This result seems unconscionable.

People have proposed two strategies for change. One is to shrink the amount of uncertainty in medicine—with research, not on new drugs or operations (which already attracts massive amounts of funding) but on the small but critical everyday decisions that patients and doctors make (which gets shockingly little funding). Everyone understands, though, that a great deal of uncertainty about what to do for people will always remain. (Human disease and lives are too complicated for reality to be otherwise.) So it has also been argued, not unreasonably, that doctors must agree in advance on what should be done in the uncertain situations that arise—spell out our actions ahead of time to take the guesswork out and get some advantage of group decision. This last goes almost nowhere, though. For it runs counter to everything we doctors believe about ourselves as individuals, about our personal ability to reason out with patients what the best course of action for them is. . . .

The possibilities and probabilities are all we have to work with in medicine, though. What we are drawn to in this imperfect science, what we in fact covet in our way, is the alterable moment—the fragile but crystalline opportunity for one's know-how, ability, or just gut instinct to change the course of another's life for the better. In the actual situations that present themselves, however—a despondent woman arrives to see you about a newly diagnosed cancer, a victim bleeding from a terrible injury is brought pale and short of breath from the scene, a fellow physician asks for your opinion about a twenty-three-year-old with a red leg—we can never be sure whether we have such a moment or not. Even less clear is whether the actions we choose will prove either wise or helpful. That our efforts succeed at all is still sometimes a shock to me. But they do. . . .

Notes: Medical Decisionmaking

1. *The Nature of Medical Judgment.* Medical decisionmaking is best appreciated by examining a range of particular medical cases. One example of a full-length case discussion, which illustrates many of the dimensions of uncertainty of judgment described by Doctors Gawande and Eddy is linked on the Web site for this book, www.health-law.org. For additional readings on the nature of medical judgment, see Kathryn Montgomery, How Doctors Think (2006); Jerome Groopman, How Doctors Think (2007); Kathryn Hunter, Doctors' Stories: The Narrative Structure of Medical Knowledge (1991).

Dr. Gawande mentions the work of Dartmouth researchers documenting dramatic variations in physicians' practice styles in different communities. Dr. Gawande brought this research to widespread attention in The Cost Conundrum: What a Texas Town Can Teach Us About Health Care, The New Yorker, June 1, 2009. Efforts to standardize medical practice and reduce variations in practice are discussed in Chapters 3.D. For additional discussion of treatment variation, see Institute of Medicine, Variation in Health Care Spending (2013).

2. *Medical Terminology.* Early editions of this book contained information about medical terminology, medical science, and anatomy. Lawyers who practice in this

field must eventually acquire a fair amount of medical knowledge, and many law students enjoy learning something about a different profession's specialized vocabulary. Others see medical terminology as an obstacle to understanding what's really happening in these cases. We have chosen to cater to the latter group; our feeling is that if you end up working in this field, you will have plenty of opportunity to learn the terminology later. Here, when cases contain uncommon medical terms, we will define them for you. If we fail to do so, most terms used in this book are contained in better-quality general dictionaries. For those who want more specialized information, here is a sampling of various medical texts and treatises, some written especially for lawyers and others for medical professionals or for the lay public. **Medical Dictionaries:** Dorland's Illustrated Medical Dictionary; Stedman's Medical Dictionary; Taber's Cyclopedic Medical Dictionary. Links to the online versions of these can be found on this casebook's Web site, www.health-law.org. A comprehensive guide to medical research for legal purposes is Caroline Young, Medico-Legal Research Using Evidence-Based Medicine, 102 Law Libr. J. 449 (2010).

B. THE "CRISIS" IN ACCESS, COST, AND QUALITY

HEALTH AND MEDICAL CARE REFORM IN THE UNITED STATES: ETHICAL QUESTIONS AND CONCERNS

Thomas W. Merrill, David G. Miller, Joseph A. Raho & Ginger Gruters
President's Council on Bioethics, Staff Background Paper
2008

The reform of health and medical care in the United States has been a topic on our national agenda for decades now. . . . [A]t present, we seem to be witnessing a remarkable coalescence—of the public, health professionals and organizations, and policymakers—around the conclusion that the American "system" of health and medical care is ailing. Three problems—of access and coverage, of quality, and of cost—are usually cited as the signs and symptoms of this increasingly worrisome state. . . . [W]e offer a purely descriptive account of the problems of access, quality, and cost, in order to illustrate their complexity and to draw out their implications for ethical questioning. . . .

I. The Problem of Access to Health and Medical Care

In [2010], according to the Current Population Survey of the U.S. Census Bureau, [50] million Americans were uninsured. This statistic is often cited in ways that suggest that it—and it alone—constitutes the whole of the problem of access to health and medical care in the United States. . . . There are other dimensions to the problem of access. The underinsured, who have some coverage but are inadequately protected against high out-of-pocket costs, are the subjects of a growing literature. Difficulties with the supply and geographical distribution of health care professionals, along with some types of health care facilities (for example, emergency rooms), are also constituents of the problem of access. Our focus here, however, is on the uninsured. . . .

According to one estimate, some 18,000 premature deaths per year in the United States (as well as a number of other serious health conditions) could have been prevented by better access to health care.[3] To be sure, the uninsured do have access to emergency room care . . . , but care through this source tends to be less than optimal. Conditions are often treated only when they have become very serious. Moreover, the use of emergency care by the uninsured exacerbates the burdens placed on often strained emergency rooms and centers. . . . Those hospitals and professionals incur costs that eventually lead to higher charges for the insured or to increasing outlays of federal and state funds for uncompensated care. . . .

The preceding review of statistical data underscore[s] one conclusion: the situation of the uninsured in the United States is a complicated one, far more so than the oft-cited figure of [50] million reveals. As this review has shown, that number does not capture how long the uninsured lack this essential component of access to care, nor does it provide important information on who the uninsured are. The number of individuals who lack insurance for a year or more is lower than [50] million—probably somewhere between 30 and 40 million. Nor is it the case that the uninsured are all poor and thus unable to purchase insurance. More than one-third have household incomes above the median national income. Moreover, about a fifth are not citizens. . . . It is also noteworthy that the rates of uninsurance are higher among the poor and among African-American and Hispanic communities. . . .

II. The Problem of Health Care Costs and Financing

Just as few, if any, would dispute the fact that there are many millions of uninsured Americans, so too would few take issue with the claims that health care costs in the United States are high compared to other industrialized nations and that these costs are increasing in seemingly unconstrained ways. These facts are cause for concern on a number of fronts. Such broad measures of population health as infant mortality and life expectancy, for example, indicate that the U.S. does no better, and in some cases does far worse, than similar countries that spend less on health care: we may not be getting good value for our money. . . . [T]he current situation is made more worrying still by the historical trends in the growth of health care spending. . . . According to some estimates made by the Congressional Budget Office, if current trends continue, health care spending could rise to almost 50 percent of total Gross Domestic Product (GDP) by 2082. . . .

There is much controversy, of course, over the causes of those increases and the ways we might address those causes. Here, we simply lay out some well-known facts about health care spending in the United States: as a portion of GDP and per capita; as it affects employees and employers; and as it affects federal and state budgets.

Today [as of 2016], the United States spends about [$3.3] trillion per year on health care, which amounts to [18] percent of GDP and about [$10,000] per person. Of course, compared with the poorer nations of the world, all of the wealthier

3. See the Institute of Medicine report *Hidden Costs, Value Lost: Uninsurance in America* (2003). Other scholars point out, however, that it is difficult to establish clear evidence of causation (as opposed to correlation) between insurance status and health status. . . .

nations spend a greater proportion of their income on health care. The United States, however, spends more on health care—both on a per capita basis and as a percentage of its GDP—than *any* other nation in the world. . . . National spending on health care as a share of GDP increased from about 5 percent in 1960 to our current level of [18] percent today and is projected to continue to grow. . . . The cumulative effect of those growth rates is this: The United States has experienced a *twenty-fold increase* in health care expenditures—a four-fold increase over the consumer price index over the same period. . . .

Of course, the rising share of health care as a portion of GDP may not necessarily be cause for concern. As mentioned above, as countries become wealthier, their citizens tend to spend more money on health care, and there is no way to determine *a priori* what the "appropriate" level of spending on health care may be. Moreover, the percentage of GDP representing health care also depends on the size and character of what happens in other sectors of the economy. Above all, the costs by themselves do not tell us anything about the quality or value of the care being provided. . . . Nevertheless, as the cost of health care rises so quickly relative to growth in GDP, it cannot fail to strain private and public budgets and to make it ever more difficult to solve or ameliorate other problems. . . .

For individuals, rising health care costs lead to increased premiums and to insurance plans that attempt to restrain *their* costs by using higher deductibles, co-pays, and the like. Because individuals and families in the United States tend to get their insurance through their employers, who choose and purchase coverage from an insurer, those employers are often in the middle between the insurance companies and their employees who actually use the insurance. For this reason, employers are often the parties that complain most loudly about rising costs. They also tend to look to devices for holding down costs through cost sharing and the like. In [2017] the average cost of [group] insurance (including both the part of the premium paid by the employer and the employee) was [over $6,000] per year for an individual and [over $18,000] per year for a family. . . .

Most economists argue that, despite appearances, employers are not really paying the insurance premiums of their employees. Rather, the insurance premium is simply part of the total compensation package for the employee. Because of the tax exemption for health insurance, it makes sense for an employee to take part of their compensation as (untaxed) health benefits. For most Americans, our employer picks the insurance company, chooses the plan, and sends in the check, but the employer does not bear the final cost of the insurance premiums. That comes out of whatever the total amount of compensation the employer is willing to pay to the employee. In times of rising health care costs, that means that more of the total compensation has to go to insurance and less can go to increased wages. . . . Rather than coming out of corporate profits, the increasing cost of health care has resulted in relatively flat real wages for 30 years. That is the real health care cost-wage trade-off. . . .

Increased health care costs also put a burden on federal and state governments, primarily through Medicare and Medicaid. . . . [P]ublic funds, including Medicare, Medicaid, Veterans health care, and other programs account for about 45 percent of total health spending in any given year. For the governments that pay for these programs, rising health care costs mean some hard choices: reducing benefits, restricting eligibility, cutting other public programs, raising taxes.

For the states, health care costs are already the single largest part of state budgets. . . . Not surprisingly, states have tended to respond by cutting other programs, most commonly funding for public higher education. . . . For the federal government, rising health care costs . . . could threaten to swamp the budget. . . .

III. The Problem of Health Care Quality

In light of the fact that the United States spends much more on health care than other countries, it is reasonable to ask: Are we getting good value for the money? But with respect to the question of the quality of our health care, we find significant division between, on the one hand, those who cite the technological marvels produced in America and the outcomes in the treatment of complex diseases and, on the other hand, those who look to various aggregate measures of population health and find significant defects. . . . Of course, these seemingly opposed arguments are not mutually incompatible: America could produce the world's best technologies while also failing to provide the right care in many routine instances, not to mention the problems of the uninsured. And so we ask: What do we know about the quality of American health care?

On the one hand, it is true that by many measures of population health, the United States does quite poorly: infant mortality rates are higher in the United States than in many other comparable nations, and life expectancy rates are also low compared to other industrialized nations. A study by the World Health Organization (WHO) found that the United States ranked 37th . . . behind many other industrialized nations, all of which, as we have seen, spend far less per capita on health care than the U.S. does. . . .

Yet there is controversy over these facts. Some scholars argue, for example, that the cross-national comparisons fail to take into account differences in the underlying populations in different countries. They suggest that if we control for factors like homicide rates and car accidents—both of which are higher in the United States than in other countries—the measures of population health begin to look more similar to other nations. They also point out that rates of survival after the diagnosis of various serious ailments like cancer tend to be higher in the U.S. than elsewhere. Moreover, defenders of health care in United States point to the medical technologies and innovations developed here: The United States has produced more winners of the Nobel Prize in medicine than any other country. . . . Additionally, the U.S. spends far more of its public and private monies on biomedical research and development than does the European Union. Thus, defenders of U.S. health care argue that we cannot evaluate the level of quality of health care in the United States without keeping in mind the increased quality of the technologies used in health care.

As is often noted, Americans tend to be strongly attached to medical innovation and new medical technologies, more so than citizens of other countries. And there is a respectable body of literature which argues that the benefits of new technologies far outweigh their costs (as heavy as the latter may be). The [Harvard] economist David Cutler . . . and colleagues find that the cost of treating a heart attack has increased by some $10,000 in the 1990s, but that life expectancy after heart attack also rose by about one year. The treatment for low-birth weight infants presents a similarly positive picture. Cutler and colleagues conclude that "technological changes have proved to be worth far more than their costs."[35] . . .

Of course, . . . even the best technology cannot help very much if a particular patient does not have access to it—or does not have *timely* access. [Moreover], with respect to three different indicators—patient safety, receipt of recommended care, and variations in the intensity and outcomes of treatment—evidence suggests troublesome inadequacies in the quality of health care in America.

Patient Safety: Marked and seemingly widespread deficiencies in patient safety were the focus of the Institute of Medicine's *To Err Is Human,* a report published in 2000. According to the IOM, as many as 98,000 deaths are the result of medical error each year in the United States. That is more deaths from medical error than from motor vehicle accidents (around 45,000 deaths annually), from breast cancer (also around 45,000 deaths annually), or from AIDS (around 16,000 deaths annually). . . .

Receipt of Recommended Care: In the last few decades, professional societies along with such government agencies as the Agency for Healthcare Research and Quality have sought to develop and promulgate clinical practice guidelines and clinical pathways that stipulate the evidence-based recommendations for the most effective diagnosis and treatment of a wide range of diseases and disorders, from childhood asthma to adult hypertension. Nonetheless, [the] first national, comprehensive study on quality of care for adults in the U.S. . . . found that patients received the recommended care only 54.9 percent of the time.[41] . . . As [the author] testified before the U.S. Senate, "We spend nearly $2 trillion annually on health care and we get it right about half the time. That may be the best in the world, but I think you would agree that we can and should do better."

Variations in Intensity and Outcomes of Treatment: A substantial body of evidence also supports the finding of wide variations of the amount of money spent and of treatments performed between different areas of the country, but without any corresponding variations in health outcomes. In fact, the evidence seems to suggest that geographical areas that spend more actually have lower levels of quality of care. Researchers at Dartmouth led by Jack Wennberg and Elliott Fisher have shown, for example, that the amount of money spent per capita on Medicare recipients varies widely between different areas of the country, by almost as much as a threefold difference, even after controlling for differences in age, race, and sex. But, . . . the correlation with quality is low.

Many researchers have concluded that increased spending does not translate into better outcomes—in fact it may translate into worse outcomes. Wennberg and Fisher contend that much of the health care spending in Medicare, perhaps as much as 20 percent to 30 percent, does not bring added health benefits and that there may well be a similar proportion of private spending on health care that does not bring better outcomes. Economists suggest that in many cases Americans

35. David Cutler, *Your Money or Your Life: Strong Medicine for America's Healthcare System* (New York: Oxford University Press, 2004).

41. McGlynn, Asch, Adams, et al., "The Quality of Health Care Delivered to Adults in the United States," *New England J. Med.*, vol. 328: 2635-2645, June 26, 2003.

may be at the "flat of the curve," that is, at that place in a cost-benefit analysis when further resources may not only bring added benefit but may, in fact, bring less benefit. . . . Peter Orszag, director of the Congressional Budget Office, has recently written: "With health care spending currently representing 16 percent of gross domestic product (GDP), [Wennberg and Fisher's results] would suggest that nearly 5 percent of GDP—or roughly $700 billion each year—goes to health care spending that can't be shown to improve health outcomes." Of course, as Orszag observes, trying to figure out how to reduce inappropriate or unnecessary care is no easy task. . . .

Leaving aside the difficult problems of designing the right policies to make American health care more efficient, however, there is a more fundamental question about what we—as patients and as citizens—expect from modern medical technology. Do we have extravagant expectations from medical science? Are we so accustomed to having someone else pay the bill that we no longer question whether a particular intervention is worth its cost? While evaluating the cost-effectiveness of various interventions or organizing the health care system to be more cost effective will not solve all of our health care problems, it may be a necessary condition of a more sustainable system that we come to see that more is not always better.

A variety of problems—access, cost, and quality—make health care in the United States an unavoidably complicated affair, and this is not the place to elaborate specific policy proposals. But we should remember that the health care system is one in which each of us will find ourselves in various capacities at various points in our lives, and the decisions we make about the various aspects of health care reflect our identity as a nation and the type of social union we wish to create and advance. . . .

International Comparison of Spending on Health, 1980–2010

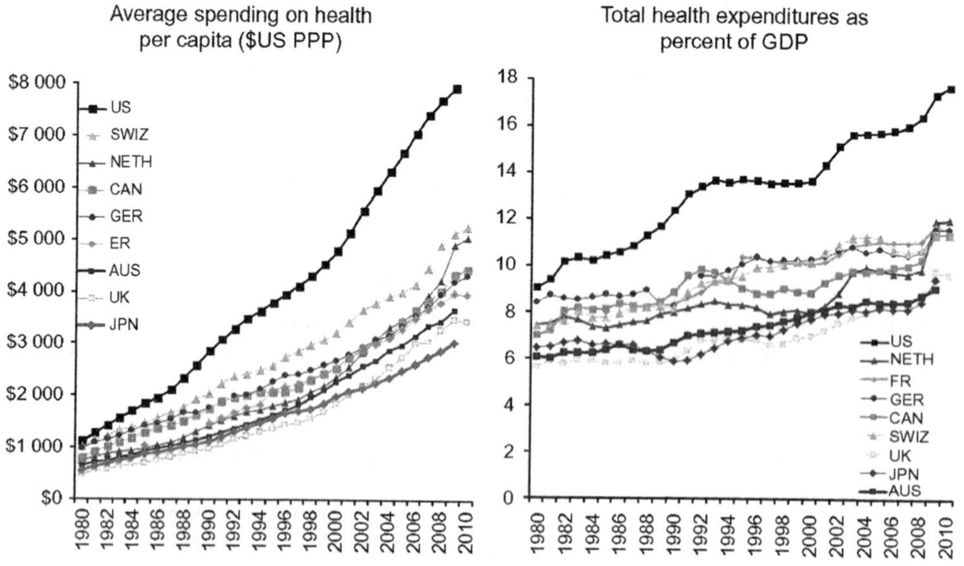

Notes: PPP = purchasing power parity; GDP = gross domestic product.
Source: Commonweath Fund, based on OECD Health Data 2012.

Notes: The Crisis in American Medicine

1. *The Perpetual Crisis.* American medicine has been declared to be in a "crisis" since at least the early 1960s. See Marion Sanders, The Crisis in American Medicine (1961). Can things really be all that bad if they've been like this so long? Note the competing viewpoint of Harvard economist David Cutler, cited above, that major increases in medical spending can be traced to substantial gains in health that, at least in certain areas, are clearly worth their costs.

Even if there is not a "crisis," there is still clearly a serious problem in American medicine. In case you're still not convinced, consider the following additional facts, opinions, and anecdotes.

> Medicine, like many other American institutions, suffered a stunning loss of confidence in the 1970s. Previously, two premises had guided government health policy: first, that Americans needed more medical care—more than the market alone would provide; and second, that medical professionals and private voluntary institutions were best equipped to decide how to organize those services. . . . In the 1970s this mandate ran out. The economic and moral problems of medicine displaced scientific progress at the center of public attention. Enormous increases in cost seemed ever more certain; corresponding improvements in health ever more doubtful. The prevailing assumptions about the need to expand medical care were reversed: The need now was to curb its apparently insatiable appetite for resources. In a short time, American medicine seemed to pass from stubborn shortages to irrepressible excess, without ever having passed through happy sufficiency. [Paul Starr, The Social Transformation of American Medicine 379 (1982).]
>
> How much does an overnight stay at a Virginia hospital cost? . . . A year ago, Mr. Shipman, a 43-year-old former furniture salesman from Herndon, Va., experienced severe chest pains during the night. . . . Suspecting a heart attack, doctors first performed a cardiac catheterization to examine and unblock the coronary arteries. Then, they inserted a stent, a small metal device that props open a blocked artery so the blood flows better to the heart. Lacking health insurance, Mr. Shipman . . . checked himself out of the hospital against medical advice. Since then, Mr. Shipman and his wife, Alina, have received hospital bills totaling $29,500. . . . In addition, there were other bills: some $1,000 for the ambulance trip, $6,800 from the cardiologist who performed the stent procedure, and several thousand dollars for the local emergency-room visit. In all, the two-day health crisis left the Shipmans saddled with medical bills totaling nearly $40,000. Once solidly middle class, the couple says the debt triggered a gradual unraveling of their lives. "Middle class or not, when you have a bill of $37,000 hanging over your head, that's all you think about," says Ms. Shipman. . . . "You eat, sleep and breathe that bill." [Lucette Lagnado, Anatomy of a Hospital Bill, Wall St. J., Sept. 21, 2004, at B1.]
>
> In its technical brilliance, American health care is unsurpassed. Its best care would have seemed miraculous just a few years ago. But the bad side of American health care is very bad, and there is reason to think that it will get worse before it gets better. For one thing, the coming years will see a further increase in both the number of the elderly in the population and their percentage of the population. The growth will be particularly great among those over 85, the people most likely to make heavy use of the medical system. New technology, for which one can almost always read "expensive" new technology, continues to invade medicine. [Henry T. Greely, The Future of the American Health Care System, 3 Stan. L. & Pol'y Rev. 16 (1991).]
>
> There are few other areas of the U.S. economy where waste is so apparent and the possibility of savings is so tangible. . . . Perhaps the most troubling . . . [fact] is

> the amount spent on administration. For every office-based physician in the United States, there are 2.2 administrative workers. That exceeds the number of nurses, clinical assistants, and technical staff put together. One large physician group in the United States estimates that it spends 12 percent of revenue just collecting revenue. . . . The situation is no better in hospitals. . . . Duke University Hospital, for example, has 900 hospital beds and 1,300 billing clerks. On top of this are the administrative workers in health insurance. [David Cutler & Dan P. Ly, The (Paper) Work of Medicine, 25 J. Econ. Perspect. 3 (2011).]
>
> There is no U.S. health care system. What we call our health care system is, in daily practice, a hodgepodge of historic legacies, philosophical conflicts, and competing economic schemes. Health care in America combines the tortured, politicized complexity of the U.S. tax code with a cacophony of intractable political, cultural, and religious debates about personal rights and responsibilities. Every time policymakers, corporate health benefits purchasers, or entrepreneurs try to fix something in our health care system, they run smack into its central reality: the primary producers and consumers of medical care are uniquely, stubbornly self-serving as they chew through vast sums of other people's money. Doctors and hospitals stumble their way through irresolvable conflicts between personal gain and ethical responsibilities; patients struggle with the acrimony and anguish that accompany life-and-death medical decisions; consumers, paying for the most part with everybody's money but their own, demand that the system serve them with the immediacy and flexibility of other industries; and health insurers are trapped in the middle, trying to keep everybody happy. A group of highly imaginative, energetic people armed with the world's largest Mark-n-Wipe board could not purposefully design a more complex, dysfunctional system if they tried. It is a $1.3 trillion per year fiasco narrated with moral shrillness and played out one competing anecdote after another. [J. D. Kleinke, Oxymorons: The Myth of a U.S. Health Care System 1 (2001).]

2. *International Comparisons and Medical Tourism.* According to one analysis, the poor U.S. performance on aggregate health statistics noted above (life expectancy, infant death rate) is not due to major differences in health habits or lifestyles, since the United States is similar in many ways to the comparison European countries. Instead, this author argues that the lower U.S. rankings are due in large part to the relatively inadequate system of primary care physicians and the overuse of high-risk procedures. Barbara Starfield, Is U.S. Health Really the Best in the World?, 284 JAMA 483 (2000). Another prominent study found that the British are much healthier than Americans in all major disease areas, such as diabetes, heart disease, stroke, lung disease, and cancer, even after controlling for all relevant sociodemographic factors. J. Banks, M. Marmot et al., Disease and Disadvantage in the United States and England, 295 JAMA 2037 (2006). Consider also, the following, from a health policy expert at Harvard:

> Finally, if you take a big step back and look at the data, Americans do better than average in timely access [to care], especially to specialty services and "elective" surgery (which is often not that elective). They tend to be among the [world] leaders in acute care quality, when healthcare means the difference between life and death, although the quality of primary care could surely be better. And America is the innovation engine of the world, pumping out new drugs and treatments that benefit the whole world. . . . [O]verall, while the U.S. healthcare system has a lot of work ahead, we should not overlook its strengths – and they are sizeable.

Ashish Jha, Judging Health Systems: Focusing on What Matters (Sept. 2017). See Chapter 3.F for additional international discussion.

One sign of better medical value elsewhere is the extent to which Americans who are footing the bill are willing to receive care in other countries, even lesser-developed ones such as India, Mexico, or the Caribbean. See note 3 for readings on this growing phenomenon of "medical tourism" and its host of legal issues.

3. *More Facts, Figures, and Opinions.* There is seemingly an endless appetite for **facts and figures** about the U.S. health care delivery system. Those who wish for more, or more recent numbers, can find them in the annual reports of the Medicare Payment Advisory Commission (MedPac), in periodic issues of Health Affairs, and on the Web pages for the U.S. Census Bureau and the Centers for Medicare and Medicaid Services (CMS), which are linked to the Web page for this book, www.health-law.org.

For more discussion of **what's right or wrong with the U.S. health care system (note 1)**, see Elisabeth Rosenthal, An American Sickness (2017); Jonathan Cohn, Sick: The Untold Story of America's Health Care Crisis (2007); Shannon Brownlee, Overtreated: Why Too Much Medicine Is Making Us Sicker and Poorer (2007); David Goldhill, How American Health Care Killed My Father, The Atlantic, Sept. 2009; Tom Daschle, Critical: What We Can Do About the Health-Care Crisis (2008); Einer Elhauge ed., The Fragmentation of U.S. Health Care (2010); Julius B. Richmond & Rashi Fein, The Health Care Mess: How We Got into It and What It Will Take to Get Out (2005); Paul Krugman & Robin Wells, The Health Care Crisis and What to Do About It, 53 N.Y. Review of Books No. 5 (Mar. 23, 2006); Jonathan Gruber & Helen Levy, The Evolution of Medical Spending Risk, 23 J. Econ. Perspec. 25 (2009); Robert E. Hall & Charles I. Jones, The Value of Life and the Rise in Health Spending, 122 Q. J. Econ. 39 (2007); Kevin Murphy & Robert Topel eds., Measuring the Gains from Medical Research (2003); Elliott S. Fisher, Medical Care: Is More Always Better?, 349 New Eng. J. Med. 1665 (2003); Nortin M. Hadler, The Last Well Person (2004); Henry Aaron & Paul Ginsburg, Is Health Spending Excessive? If So, What Can We Do About It?, 28(5) Health Aff. 1260 (Oct. 2009); Symposium, 39 J.L. Med. & Ethics 111 (2011); President's Council of Economic Advisors, The Economic Case for Health Care Reform (2009); Thomas Bodenheimer, High and Rising Health Care Costs, 142 Annals Intern. Med. 847, 932 (2005); Symposium, 28 Health Aff. 1250 (Oct. 2009); Symposium, 362 New Eng. J. Med. 1 (2010); Symposium, 22(1) Health Aff. 1 (Jan. 2003).

On **international comparisons (note 2)**, see Cathy Schoen et al., U.S. Health System Performance: A National Scorecard, 25 Health Aff. w457 (Sept. 2006); David Squires, Explaining High Health Care Spending in the United States: An International Comparison (Commonwealth Fund 2012); S.H. Woolf, U.S. Health in International Perspective: Shorter Lives, Poorer Health (Institute of Medicine, 2013).

On **medical tourism (note 2)**, see Glenn Cohen & Holly Lynch, Patients with Passports: Medical Tourism, Law and Ethics (2013); Glenn Cohen, Protecting Patients with Passports: Medical Tourism and the Patient Protective Argument, 95 Iowa L. Rev. 1467 (2010); Nathan Cortez, Cross-Border Health Care and the Hydraulics of Health Reform (2012); Nathan Cortez, Recalibrating the Legal Risks of Cross-Border Health Care, 10 Yale J. Health Pol'y L. & Ethics 1 (Winter 2010); Nicolas P. Terry, Under-Regulated Health Care Phenomena in a Flat World: Medical Tourism and Outsourcing, 29 W. New Eng. L. Rev. 421 (2007); Kerrie S. Howze, Medical Tourism: Symptom or Cure?, 41 Ga. L. Rev. 1013 (2007); Thomas R. McLean, The Offshoring of American Medicine, 14 Annals Health L. 205 (2005); Note, 18 Kennedy Inst. Ethics J. 193 (2008) (bibliography); Symposium, 26 Wis. Int'l L.J. 591-964 (2008).

C. COMPETING PARADIGMS IN HEALTH LAW

This section briefly introduces various analytical perspectives that give greater depth to our understanding of health care law, ethics, and public policy. Most of these analytical frameworks spring from some branch of moral and political theory that addresses fundamental questions of individual and social justice, such as how best to distribute scarce medical resources, and whose decision over medical treatment should govern when there is conflict. Necessarily, this must be a grab bag of somewhat disconnected lines of thought drawn from many different intellectual disciplines—primarily philosophy, economics, and political science. This is due to what Einer Elhauge below calls the "paradigm pathology" of health care law: See also the sources cited in note 2 of the Preface.

Although health law may have a core set of concerns, it lacks a dominant analytical mode. In classic fields of law such as contracts or torts, most people seem at least to be asking the same sorts of questions, even if they don't arrive at the same answers. Health care law has so many interdisciplinary, intellectual currents that courts and scholars sound at times like the mythical builders of the Tower of Babel. Some order can be brought to this mélange of ideologies by categorizing and critiquing different "paradigms" of thought. As the second and third readings in this section explain, the dominant paradigms in past decades have been professionalism and patient autonomy, and the contending analytical paradigms respond to these. Rather than attempt any neat packaging of the contenders, for they are still very untidy, try to identify throughout the course which currents of thought are consistent with or opposed to the professionalism or patient autonomy paradigms and in what ways.

■ ALLOCATING HEALTH CARE MORALLY*
Einer Elhauge
82 Cal. L. Rev. 1449 (1994)

Health law policy suffers from an identifiable pathology. . . . [I]t employs four different paradigms for how decisions to allocate resources should be made: the market paradigm, the professional paradigm, the moral paradigm, and the political paradigm. . . . [R]ather than coordinate these decisionmaking paradigms, health law policy employs them inconsistently, such that the combination operates at cross-purposes.

This inconsistency results in part because, intellectually, health care law borrows haphazardly from other fields of law, each of which has its own internally coherent conceptual logic, but which in combination results in an incoherent legal framework and perverse incentive structures. In other words, health care law has not—at least not yet—established itself to be a field of law with its own coherent conceptual logic, as opposed to a collection of issues and cases from other legal fields connected only by the happenstance that they all involve patients and health care providers.

 (The author's name is pronounced "EL-hague.")

In other part, the pathology results because the various scholarly disciplines focus excessively on their favorite paradigms. Scholars operating in the disciplines of economics, medicine, political science, and philosophy each tend to assume that their discipline offers a privileged perspective. This leads them either to press their favored paradigm too far or to conceptualize policy issues solely in terms of what their paradigm can and cannot solve.

Instead, health law policy issues should be conceived in terms of comparative paradigm analysis. Such analysis focuses on the strengths and weaknesses of the various decisionmaking paradigms, determining which is *relatively* better suited to resolving various decisions, and then assigning each paradigm to the roles for which it is best suited. . . .

Luckily, this is a mode of analysis in which legal scholars, as cross-disciplinary generalists, have some plausible claim to comparative scholarly advantage. Unluckily, it is hard and arduous. Nevertheless, it offers the promise that health law scholars will provide insights into health policy that so far have been missed. In a field as intellectually new as modern health law, it should hardly be surprising that this task has only begun.

THE PROFESSIONAL PARADIGM OF MEDICAL CARE: OBSTACLE TO DECENTRALIZATION*

Clark C. Havighurst

30 Jurimetrics J. 415 (1990)

The thesis of this article is that, despite all the organizational and financial changes that occurred in the health care sector in the 1980s, we still cannot fight the battle for efficiency effectively because we are saddled as a society with a particular paradigmatic conception of the medical care enterprise. The source of this paradigm is a deep-seated belief, long fostered by the medical profession, that medical care is not a commodity, that its characteristics are scientifically determined, and that decisions concerning it must be entrusted exclusively to professionals. That this paradigm is ideologically attractive and contains some significant kernels of truth simply complicates the problem of adapting it to accord with current economic realities.

The professional paradigm of the medical enterprise is a venerable one, stemming from the days early in this century when the medical profession rose to what sociologist Paul Starr has called a position of "cultural authority, economic power, and political influence."[5] Although its tenets are nowhere officially set down, some of them can be deduced from the profession's performance during the era when it exercised rather complete hegemony over health care and its financing. Judging from that experience, the profession's ideology has included the following themes:

5. P. Starr, The Social Transformation of American Medicine 5 (1982).

- medical care should be evaluated only on the basis of safety and efficacy;
- cost considerations should not enter into medical decisionmaking because counting costs implies both a willingness to trade off a patient's welfare against other societal needs and a tolerance for differences based on ability to pay;
- decisions on the appropriate utilization of medical services should be based exclusively on scientific evidence and expert opinion;
- although patient preferences should be honored under the principle of informed consent, there is no similar urgency about giving people opportunities to express their preferences qua consumers, with cost differences in view; and
- professional norms alone should set the limits of a physician's judgment.

Under these general principles, the role of payers was long limited to ensuring that professional norms were followed, so that only care that was virtually useless or positively harmful was excluded. . . .

The professional paradigm derives much of its force from the egalitarian ideal in medicine—the belief that every citizen is entitled to medical care of the same quality and that "two-tier" medicine is unthinkable. Even though society has not seen fit to adopt an egalitarian policy by accepting either the heavy tax burden or the stringent rationing necessary to achieve it, the egalitarian ideal colors much thinking about medical care. Indeed, even in the absence of any actual legal or contractual entitlement, a powerful entitlement mentality must be confronted by anyone seeking to economize in the provision of health services. The professional paradigm generally supports this view of things, while the profession as a whole resists most of the measures that would be necessary to create an affordable, truly egalitarian system. There is here a marriage of convenience—between physicians' desires to resist infringements on their clinical freedom and a particularly extreme view of the requirements of social justice.

The scientific character of medicine has also provided vital support for the professional paradigm. Indeed, the success of the medical profession in establishing its scientific character in the early part of the century—in the Flexner Report,[6] for example—laid the groundwork for its claim of exemption from market forces and for its autonomy as a profession. Once medical care was viewed as the application of science to human problems rather than as a commercial service to be bought and sold in market transactions, the profession was able to resist most of the pressures that naturally arose and to head off, by effective lobbying or collective action, market developments that might have threatened its hegemony. . . .

Residues of the professional paradigm can be found in many places but are particularly significant in the legal system. Not only does the law tend to defer to the medical profession's presumed scientific authority on many points, but it is often administered with an egalitarian mentality that tends to define issues in terms of abstract rights. Indeed, the law frequently goes to great lengths to avoid appearing to concede that some persons might ever have a legal or even a contractual right to better medical care than someone else. This refusal to recognize the reality that some consumers might choose, or wish to choose, to purchase more or better health

6. A. Flexner, *Medical Education in the United States and Canada* (Carnegie Foundation for the Advancement of Technology, Bull. No. 4, 1910).

care than others—or have a lesser entitlement because of inability or unwillingness to pay—greatly complicates efforts to economize in the private sector. It also raises, perhaps inappropriately, the cost to government of providing for those who cannot support themselves. As long as the legal system does not acknowledge inequality or recognize efforts to escape the costly standards implicit in the professional/scientific/egalitarian paradigm, neither self-supporting consumers nor taxpayers are in a good position to economize on health care by refusing to buy too much of a good thing.

THE PRACTICE OF AUTONOMY: PATIENTS, DOCTORS, AND MEDICAL DECISIONS
Carl E. Schneider
1998

Bioethicists, like lawyers, live in danger of what I once called "hyper-rationalism." Hyper-rationalism has both a methodological and a substantive aspect. As a method, [h]yper-rationalism is essentially the substitution of reason for information and analysis. It has two components: First, the belief that reason can reliably be used to infer facts where evidence is unavailable or incomplete, and second, the practice of interpreting facts through a narrow set of artificial analytic categories. Hyper-rationalism, in other words, tempts us to believe that we can understand how people think and act merely by reasoning, and not by investigating. . . .

For one thing, the assumptions of hyper-rationalism can lead us into a tendency to see human nature and conduct as verging on the uniform. . . . As empiricists in fields ranging from sociology to psychology to anthropology have been at pains to show, this view exaggerates human rationality and understates the role of social and cultural factors in patient's lives. . . .

Hyper-rationalists' . . . picture of human nature is too simple, too disembodied, to be convincing. They present a bloodless, flat, distant, abstract, depersonalized, impoverished view of the way people think, feel, and act, of the social circumstances in which people live, of the ethical lives they lead. And hyper-rationalism's simplifications are particularly injurious in [health law and ethics], a field that treats people in their least rational moments, in their most emotional travails, in their most contextual complexity.

Hyper-rationalism, of course, has its uses. It promotes the kind of generalization that frees courts and commentators to reason logically about the normative problems that are, after all, one of their central concerns. And some simplification of life's complexity is necessary if human problems are to be dealt with practically and promptly, if comprehensible rules are to be devised, if useful precedent is to be developed, if institutions are to function smoothly. But we should want to insinuate as much of that complexity as possible into normative discourse. A failure to do so perilously distances norms from the people and circumstances they seek to govern.

This is a peril with which law is all too familiar.[7] . . . One of the great truths about law is that, with unnerving frequency, it fails to achieve the effects intended

7. The remainder of this excerpt interpolates parts of another publication by the same author, Bioethics in the Language of the Law, 24(4) Hastings Center Rep. (July 1994).

for it, and sometimes quite fails to have any effect at all. Some of the most fascinating modern legal scholarship reminds lawyers how removed their talk is from the world's ken. That literature reveals that, to the lawyer's chagrin, businesses resist using contracts, ranchers do not know what rules of liability govern damage done by wandering cattle, suburbanites do not summon the law to resolve neighborhood disputes, engaged couples do not know the law governing how they will own property when they marry, citizens repeatedly reject the due process protections proffered them, and, what is worse, all these people simply don't care what the law says. . . .

What is going on here? Well, of course, lots of things. But central among them is society's enormous complexity and the narrow relevance of the law to it. People are enticed by many pressures beyond those the law creates. They have their own agendas and, more important, their own normative systems. The law writes rules, but the governed—when they know the rules—often have the incentives, time, and energy to avoid them.

Consider advance directives [for end-of-life care]. They offer an apparently irresistible way of speaking in one of life's greatest crises. Yet people spurn them. They do so because they have their own lives to lead. Momentous as the crisis may be, it will generally not seem urgent until it arrives. People resist contemplating their own mortality. They heartily dislike and don't easily understand legal forms; they find them obscure and darkly imagine how they might be misused. For that matter, people may doubt that they will be used at all. Further, many people have trouble envisioning their circumstances years into the future or how they would respond to those hypothetical circumstances. And I suspect that people expect that decisions about their welfare would in any case fall to people they trust—to their families. In short, advance directives were formulated and promoted by people—bioethicists, lawyers, and doctors, for instance—who know what they want to do through them and keenly want to do it. But many of us are not clear about what we want and about whether getting it is worth the costs.

In short, while the language of the law may have penetrated into the bosom of society, it must still, in quotidian life, compete with the many other languages that people speak more comfortably, more fluently, and with much more conviction. These are languages of religion and morality, of love and friendship, of pragmatism and social accommodation, of custom and compromise. The danger for [health law and ethics], then, is believing too deeply that law can pierce the Babel, can speak with precision, can be heard. . . .

But what is the antidote to hyper-rationalism? There are several. For instance, [Howard] Brody writes that philosophy of medicine "can indeed advance by . . . abstract discussions; but it can advance only so far. At some point we will require a richer context for the discussion to proceed fruitfully. This context can be provided by stories of sickness." . . .

We need, then, to inhabit all the mansions available in the house of bioethics. And among the least inhabited of those mansions is that of empirical research. Such research offers a breadth, rigor, and precision of understanding that is available in no other way. It provides a disciplined way of reviewing our assumptions and a systematic means of identifying neglected issues. In sum, empirical research provides a fruitful means of obtaining a more detailed, complex, and acute understanding of what patients want, think, and do which can deepen—and darken—our understanding of bioethical problems.

Notes: Professionalism, Empiricism, and Other Paradigms

1. *Defending Professionalism.* Contrasting with Prof. Havighurst's views, a number of scholars have defended the important role that professionalism plays in medicine and analyzed how law should promote or accommodate desirable features of professionalism. See, e.g., Andrew Fitcher, The Law of Doctoring: A Study of the Codification of Medical Professionalism, 19 Health Matrix 317 (2009); Gail Agrawal, Resuscitating Professionalism: Self-Regulation in the Medical Marketplace, 66 Mo. L. Rev. 341 (2001). On professionalism generally, see Eliot Freidson, Professionalism: The Third Logic (2001).

2. *Outsider Jurisprudence.* Feminist critique, critical race theory, and critical legal studies are flourishing in health care law, as they are elsewhere in legal analysis. See, e.g., Symposium, Deconstructing Traditional Paradigms in Bioethics: Race, Gender, Class, and Culture, 15 St. Louis U. Pub. L. Rev. 183 (1996). Leading critical legal scholars are David Frankford and Gregg Bloche. Examples of their work include Privatizing Health Care: Economic Magic to Cure Legal Medicine, 66 S. Cal. L. Rev. 1 (1992) (Frankford); The Invention of Health Law, 91 Cal. L. Rev. 247 (2003) (Bloche). Professors Dorothy Roberts and Lisa Ikemoto have been especially prominent scholars on critical race theory. Examples of their work include Killing the Black Body: Race, Reproduction, and the Meaning of Liberty (1997) (Roberts); The Genetic Tie, 62 U. Chi. L. Rev. 209 (1995) (Roberts); In the Shadow of Race: Women of Color in Health Disparities Policy, 39 U.C. Davis L. Rev. 1023 (2006) (Ikemoto). See also Michele Goodwin, Black Markets: The Supply and Demand of Body Parts (2006); David B. Smith, Health Care Divided: Race and Healing a Nation (1999); Vernellia R. Randall, Slavery, Segregation and Racism: An African American Perspective on Bioethics, 15 St. Louis U. Pub. L. Rev. 191 (1996). Feminist critique is multidisciplinary, but is especially rich with respect to reproductive issues. For a broad introduction, see articles published in Symposium, Feminist Bioethics, 26 J. Med. & Phil. 339 (2001). See also Susan M. Wolf, Feminism & Bioethics: Beyond Reproduction (1996); Symposium, 44 U. Balt. L. Rev. 163 (2015); Symposium, 9 Duke J. Gender L. & Pol'y 1 (2002).

3. *Empiricism and Narratives.* Whichever philosophical or analytical camp one hails from, all agree that legal and public policy analysis is greatly enhanced with good empirical information. That is why we try to provide a good amount of empirical data throughout the notes in this book. For other general overviews of empirical work relevant to health care law and ethics, see Michelle M. Mello & Kathryn Zeiler, Empirical Health Law Scholarship: The State of the Field, 96 Geo. L.J. 649-702 (2008); Jeremy Sugarman et al., A Quarter Century of Empirical Research in Biomedical Ethics, *in* Methods in Medical Ethics (2d ed. 2010); Scott Burris, From Health Care Law to the Social Determinants of Health: A Public Health Law Research Perspective, 159 U. Pa. L. Rev. 1649 (2011).

Empiricism can also take a more anecdotal form, by deepening understanding of legal and public policy problems through the rhetorical device of narrative. Telling personal stories can be a powerful way to demonstrate how law actually affects people in real lives. Several compelling examples are contained in these materials, see pages 5 and 30, and others are cited in the bibliography at page 24 and are discussed in Carl Schneider's book. For additional narratives, see Elizabeth A. Pendo, Images of Health Insurance in Popular Film: The Dissolving Critique, 37

J. Health L. 267 (2004); Stacey A. Tovino, Incorporating Literature into a Health Law Curriculum, 9 J. Med. & L. 213 (2005); Dena Davis, Tell Me a Story: Using Short Fiction in Teaching Law, 47 J. Leg. Educ. 240 (1997); and a recurring column in Health Affairs. Narrative approaches have also been criticized as excessively anecdotal and tending to be misrepresentative. See David A. Hyman, Patient Dumping: Lies, Damned Lies, and Narrative, 73 Ind. L.J. 797 (1998).

2

Institutional Liability

Ordinarily, the patient-provider relationship is a consensual one to which both parties must agree. Therefore, an individual physician may, generally speaking, refuse to accept patients for any reason or for no reason. The same is true to a lesser extent for hospitals and other institutions. But this general freedom of contract is limited in several important ways. Hospitals may not turn patients away in emergencies until they have at least stabilized the patient's condition. Neither may doctors or hospitals refuse patients for certain discriminatory reasons, such as the patient's race, sex, or HIV status. Once treatment has begun, it may not be ceased without proper arrangements being made. And providers may not impose unreasonable conditions on their agreement to treat. While historically a physician's freedom to turn away patients found its limitations primarily in the law, the growth of formal arrangements between managed care health plans and physicians means that a provider's obligation to treat is being increasingly defined by the private agreements among the patient, insurance plan, and provider. The following materials explore the origins of, and limits on, this freedom of contract between providers and patients.

A. THE DUTY TO TREAT

■ HURLEY v. EDDINGFIELD

59 N.E. 1058 (Ind. 1901)

BAKER, Justice.

The appellant sued appellee for $10,000 damages for wrongfully causing the death of his intestate. The court sustained appellee's demurrer to the complaint, and this ruling is assigned as error.

The material facts may be summarized thus: At and for years before decedent's death appellee was a practicing physician at Mace, in Montgomery county, duly licensed under the laws of the state. He held himself out to the public as a general practitioner of medicine. He had been decedent's family physician. Decedent became dangerously ill, and sent for appellee. The messenger informed appellee of decedent's violent sickness, tendered him his fee for his services, and stated to him that no other physician was procurable in time, and that decedent relied on him for attention. No other physician was procurable in time to be of any use, and decedent did rely on appellee for medical assistance. Without any reasons whatever, appellee refused to render aid to decedent. No other patients were requiring appellee's immediate service, and he could have gone to the relief of decedent if he had been willing to do so. Death ensued, without decedent's fault, and wholly from appellee's wrongful act. The alleged wrongful act was appellee's refusal to enter into a contract of employment. Counsel do not contend that, before the enactment of the law regulating the practice of medicine, physicians were bound to render professional service to everyone who applied. The act regulating the practice of medicine provides for a board of examiners, standards of qualification, examinations, licenses to those found qualified, and penalties for practicing without license. The act is a preventive, not a compulsive, measure. In obtaining the state's license (permission) to practice medicine, the state does not require, and the licensee does not engage, that he will practice at all or on other terms than he may choose to accept. Counsel's analogies, drawn from the obligations to the public on the part of innkeepers, common carriers, and the like, are beside the mark. Judgment affirmed.

■ WILMINGTON GENERAL HOSPITAL v. MANLOVE

174 A.2d 135 (Del. 1961)

SOUTHERLAND, Chief Justice.

This case concerns the liability of a private hospital for the death of an infant who was refused treatment at the emergency ward of the hospital. The facts are these:

On January 4, 1959, Darien E. Manlove, the deceased infant, then four months old, developed diarrhea. The next morning his parents consulted Dr. Hershon. They asked whether the medicine they had for him was all right and the doctor said that it was. In the evening of the same day Mrs. Manlove took the baby's temperature.

It was higher than normal. They called Dr. Hershon, and he prescribed additional medication (streptomycin), which he ordered delivered by a pharmacy.

Mrs. Manlove stayed up with the child that night. He did not sleep. On the morning of January 6th, the parents took the infant to Dr. Hershon's office. Dr. Thomas examined the child and treated him for sore throat and diarrhea. He prescribed a liquid diet and some medicine. . . .

On the morning of January 7th (a Wednesday) [the infant's] temperature was still above normal—102. Mr. and Mrs. Manlove determined to seek additional medical assistance. They knew that Dr. Hershon and Dr. Thomas were not in their offices on Wednesdays, and they took their infant to the emergency ward of the Wilmington General Hospital.

There is no real conflict of fact as to what occurred at the hospital. The parents took the infant into the reception room of the Emergency Ward. A nurse was on duty. They explained to the nurse what was wrong with the child, that is, that he had not slept for two nights, had a continuously high temperature, and that he had diarrhea. Mr. Manlove told the nurse that the child was under the care of Dr. Hershon and Dr. Thomas, and showed the nurse the medicines prescribed. The nurse explained to the parents that the hospital could not give treatment because the child was under the care of a physician and there would be danger that the medication of the hospital might conflict with that of the attending physician. The nurse did not examine the child, take his temperature, feel his forehead, or look down his throat. The child was not in convulsions, and was not coughing or crying. There was no particular area of body tenderness.

The nurse tried to get in touch with Dr. Hershon or Dr. Thomas in the hospital and at their offices, but was unable to do so. She suggested that the parents bring the baby Thursday morning to the pediatric clinic.

Mr. and Mrs. Manlove returned home. Mrs. Manlove made an appointment by telephone to see Dr. Hershon or Dr. Thomas that night at eight o'clock. At eight minutes past three o'clock in the afternoon the baby died of bronchial pneumonia. . . .

It was assumed by both parties below that the hospital was a private hospital and not a public one—that is, an institution founded and controlled by private persons and not by public authority. The trial court disagreed, finding a quasi-public status in the receipt of grants of public money and tax exemptions. . . . Hence, the court concluded, liability may be imposed on the defendant in an emergency case.

We are compelled to disagree with the view that the defendant has become a public (or quasi-public) hospital. It is admitted (although the record does not show it) that it is privately owned and operated. We find no dissent from the rule that such a hospital is a private hospital, and may, at least in the absence of control by the legislature, conduct its business largely as it sees fit. . . .

Moreover, the holding that the receipt of grants of public money requires the hospital to care for emergency cases, as distinguished from others, is not logical. Why emergency cases? If the holding is sound it must apply to all the hospital services, and that conclusion, as we shall see, is clearly unsound. . . .

We are of opinion that the defendant is a private and not a public hospital, in so far as concerns the right of a member of the public to demand admission or treatment. What, then, is the liability of a private hospital in this respect?

Since such an institution as the defendant is privately owned and operated, it would follow logically that its trustees or governing board alone have the right to determine who shall be admitted to it as patients. No other rule would be sensible or workable. Such authority as we have found supports this rule. "A private hospital owes the public no duty to accept any patient not desired by it, and it is not necessary to assign any reason for its refusal to accept a patient for hospital service." 41 C. J. S. Hospitals §8, p.345. . . .

. . . Does that rule apply to the fullest extent to patients applying for treatment at an emergency ward? . . .

It may be conceded that a private hospital is under no legal obligation to the public to maintain an emergency ward, or, for that matter, a public clinic. But the maintenance of such a ward to render first-aid to injured persons has become a well-established adjunct to the main business of a hospital. If a person, seriously hurt, applies for such aid at an emergency ward, relying on the established custom to render it, is it still the right of the hospital to turn him away without any reason? In such a case, it seems to us, such a refusal might well result in worsening the condition of the injured person, because of the time lost in a useless attempt to obtain medical aid. Such a set of circumstances is analogous to the case of the negligent termination of gratuitous services, which creates a tort liability. Restatement, Law of Torts, "Negligence," §323. . . .

As above indicated, we are of opinion that liability on the part of a hospital may be predicated on the refusal of service to a patient in case of an unmistakable emergency, if the patient has relied upon a well-established custom of the hospital to render aid in such a case. . . .

Applying this rule here, we inquire, was there an unmistakable emergency? Certainly, the record does not support the view that the infant's condition was so desperate that a layman could reasonably say that he was in immediate danger. The learned judge indicated that the fact that death followed in a few hours showed an emergency; but with this we cannot agree. It is hindsight. And it is to be noted that the attending physician, after prescribing for the child one morning before, did not think another examination that night or the next morning was required. If this case had gone to the jury on the record here made, we would have been required to hold that it was insufficient to establish liability. We cannot agree that the mere recitation of the infant's symptoms was, in itself, evidence of an emergency sufficient to present a question for the jury. Before such an issue could arise there would have to be evidence that an experienced nurse should have known that such symptoms constituted unmistakable evidence of an emergency. . . .

The possibility that the case might turn on additional evidence respecting the matters we have touched upon was not considered either by the court or counsel. In these circumstances, we think the case should go back for further proceedings. We should add, however, that if plaintiff cannot adduce evidence showing some incompetency of the nurse, or some breach of duty or some negligence, his case must fail. Like the learned judge below, we sympathize with the parents in their loss of a child; but this natural feeling does not permit us to find liability in the absence of satisfactory evidence.

For the reasons above set forth the order denying summary judgment is affirmed, without approving the reasons therefor set forth in the court's opinion.

WIDEMAN v. SHALLOWFORD COMMUNITY HOSPITAL

826 F.2d 1030 (11th Cir. 1987)

HILL, Circuit Judge.

This case presents the novel question of whether a county government's alleged practice of using its emergency medical vehicles only to transport patients to certain county hospitals which guarantee the payment of the county's medical bills violates a right protected by the federal constitution. We hold that such a practice, even if proved, would not violate any established constitutional right. . . .

I. BACKGROUND

The facts underlying this case are undeniably tragic. On April 12, 1984, Toni Wideman, who at the time was four months pregnant, began experiencing abdominal pain. She called her obstetrician, Dr. John Ramsey, who instructed her to come immediately to Piedmont Hospital. Ms. Wideman called the 911 emergency telephone number in DeKalb County and requested an ambulance to take her to Piedmont. Three employees of the DeKalb County Emergency Medical Service (EMS) responded to this call. Ms. Wideman claims that she again informed the EMS employees to take her to Piedmont where her doctor was waiting, but they refused and, instead, took her against her wishes to Shallowford Community Hospital. After a substantial delay, during which the attending physician at Shallowford spoke by phone with Dr. Ramsey, Ms. Wideman was transferred to Piedmont. At that point, however, Dr. Ramsey was unable to stop her labor, and Ms. Wideman gave birth to a premature baby, named Ebony Laslun Wideman, who survived for only four hours. . . .

. . . It seems that both parties, as well as the district court, have assumed that the alleged policy violates a cognizable constitutional right, which the plaintiffs characterize as their right to the provision of essential medical treatment and services by the county.[1] However, . . . the proper resolution of this case requires us first to determine whether the Constitution grants a right to medical care and treatment in these circumstances. . . .

III. A. EXISTENCE OF A CONSTITUTIONAL RIGHT TO ESSENTIAL MEDICAL CARE

Beginning from the broadest prospective, we can discern no general right, based upon either the Constitution or federal statutes, to the provision of medical treatment and services by a state or municipality. If such a right exists at all, it must derive from the Fourteenth Amendment's due process clause, which forbids a state to deprive anyone of life, liberty or property without due process of law. The due process clause, however, has traditionally been interpreted as protecting certain

1. The constitutional right alleged by the plaintiffs arguably may be characterized as the much more specific right to the medical care and services of their choice. Ms. Wideman was provided with medical care in this case; indeed, she was rushed to a hospital in an ambulance provided by the county. Her claim appears to be that she should have been able to direct the ambulance wherever she wanted to go. For purposes of our analysis, however, we shall consider the plaintiffs' alleged constitutional right as they have characterized it.

"negative liberties," i.e., an individual's right to be free from arbitrary or discriminatory action taken by a state or municipality. This circuit has recognized the "well established notion that the Constitution limits the actions the states can take rather than mandating specific obligations." Bradberry v. Pinellas County, 789 F.2d 1513, 1517 (11th Cir. 1986). . . .

Two Supreme Court decisions dealing with access to abortions also support our conclusion that there is no general right to medical care or treatment provided by the state. In Maher v. Roe, 432 U.S. 464 (1977), two indigent women brought suit challenging a Connecticut regulation prohibiting the funding of abortions that were not medically necessary. The plaintiffs argued under the Fourteenth Amendment that the state regulation impinged on their constitutional right to an abortion, as recognized in Roe v. Wade, 410 U.S. 113 (1973). The Court upheld the state regulation, concluding that *Roe* did not declare an unqualified constitutional right to an abortion; rather, that case declared a woman's right to be protected from unduly burdensome interference with her freedom to decide whether to terminate her pregnancy. Significantly, in reaching this result, the Court noted that "the Constitution imposes no obligation on the states to pay the pregnancy-related medical expenses of indigent women, or indeed to pay any of the medical expenses of indigents." *Maher*, 432 U.S. at 469 (footnote omitted).

The Court's subsequent decision in Harris v. McRae, 448 U.S. 297 (1980), reinforced the constitutional distinction between requiring the state to provide medical services and prohibiting the state from impeding access to such services. The plaintiffs in *Harris* challenged the constitutionality of the Hyde amendment, which denied public funding for certain medically necessary abortions, as violating their due process liberty interest in deciding whether to terminate a pregnancy. The Supreme Court held that although the liberty protected by the due process clause prohibits unwarranted government interference with freedom of choice in the context of certain personal decisions, "it does not confer an entitlement to such funds as may be necessary to realize all the advantages of that freedom." . . . More recently, the Court has interpreted *Maher* and *Harris* as standing for the proposition that, "as a general matter, the state is under no constitutional duty to provide substantive services for those within its border." Youngberg v. Romeo, 457 U.S. 307, 317 (1982).

Several courts of appeals decisions have addressed the issue of whether a state or municipality has a duty under the Fourteenth Amendment to provide various protective services to its citizens. Almost without exception, these courts have concluded that governments are under no constitutional duty to provide police, fire, or other public safety services. . . .

B

That there exists no such general right to the provision of medical care and services by the state, however, does not end our inquiry. Both the Supreme Court and various circuit courts have indicated that the existence of a "special custodial or other relationship" between an individual and the state may trigger a constitutional duty on the part of the state to provide certain medical or other services. In these special circumstances, the state's failure to provide such services might implicate constitutionally protected rights.

For example, the Supreme Court has held that the Eighth Amendment prohibition against cruel and unusual punishments, applicable to the states via the Fourteenth Amendment, requires states to provide medical care for those whom it is punishing by incarceration. . . . Similarly, the Court has held that an involuntarily committed mental patient retains . . . a clear Fourteenth Amendment right "to adequate food, shelter, clothing, and medical care." *Youngberg*, 457 U.S. at 315. . . .

Following this rationale, a constitutional duty can arise only when a state or municipality, by exercising a significant degree of custody or control over an individual, places that person in a worse situation than he would have been had the government not acted at all. Such a situation could arise by virtue of the state affirmatively placing an individual in a position of danger, effectively stripping a person of her ability to defend herself, or cutting off potential sources of private aid. The key concept is the exercise of coercion, dominion, or restraint by the state. . . .

In the present case, we conclude that DeKalb County did not exercise a degree of coercion, dominion, or restraint over Ms. Wideman sufficient to create a "special relationship." . . . The county did not force or otherwise coerce her into its ambulance; it merely made the ambulance available to her, and she entered it voluntarily. Ms. Wideman's physical condition at the time might have required her to seek immediate medical help, and that need might have induced her to make use of the service provided by the county, hoping that she could convince the EMS employees to take her where she wanted to go. Her physical condition, however, cannot be attributed to the county. . . . Therefore, the county was under no affirmative constitutional duty to provide any particular type of emergency medical service for her. . . .

. . . Because the Constitution does not require municipalities to provide any emergency medical services at all, it would be anomalous indeed to hold them liable for providing limited services which happen to be less extensive than a particular citizen may desire. . . .

Notes: The Differing Obligations of Physicians and Hospitals; Hospitals as Quasi-Public Facilities

1. *The "No Duty" Rule.* The complaint and brief in Hurley v. Eddingfield reveal that the deceased patient was in distress during childbirth, yet, as the *Hurley* court suggests, physicians are not obligated to provide care to a particular patient unless they have agreed to do so. A standard characterization of this principle appears in Oliver v. Brock, 342 So. 2d 1, 3 (Ala. 1976):

> A physician is under no obligation to engage in practice or to accept professional employment, but when the professional services of a physician are accepted by another person for the purposes of medical or surgical treatment, the relation of physician and patient is created. The relation is a consensual one wherein the patient knowingly seeks the assistance of a physician and the physician knowingly accepts him as patient. The relationship between a physician and patient may result from an express or implied contract, either general or special, and the rights and liabilities of the parties thereto are governed by the general law of contract. . . . 61 Am. Jur. 2d, Physicians, Surgeons, and Other Healers, §96.

This "no duty" rule is consistent with tort law's normal "Good Samaritan" doctrine, which does not require individuals, even professionals, to come to the aid of strangers in distress. A physician's *ethical*, as opposed to legal, duty is somewhat more demanding, however. The American Medical Association's Principles of Medical Ethics state that a "physician shall, in the provision of appropriate patient care, except in emergencies, be free to choose whom to serve. . . ." (Principle VI). Why couldn't this ethical pledge to provide emergency care be converted into an implied promise that physicians make to the public at large? See William E. May, Medical Ethics: Code and Covenant or Philanthropy and Contract? 5(6) Hastings Ctr. Rep. 29 (1975). Doesn't the public rely on physicians as much as they do on hospital emergency departments? Consider especially Dr. Eddingfield's status as the plaintiff's family physician. Despite these qualms, *Hurley* is still thought to state the prevailing law for physicians.

2. *Triggering a Treatment Relationship.* A physician's complete freedom to refuse treatment exists only if a treatment relationship has not been initiated. Here, the fact that Dr. Eddingfield may have treated the *Hurley* patient in the past did not suffice, because the law considers treatment relationships to coincide with "spells of illness." Thus, once a patient recovers from an illness or stops seeking treatment, a new treatment relationship must be formed in order to invoke a duty of continuing treatment. See, e.g., Grubbs v. Rawls, 369 S.E.2d 683, 685-686 (Va. 1988).

Consider how this issue might come out differently when the patient receives medical care from a health maintenance organization (HMO). In this regard, see Hand v. Tavera, 864 S.W.2d 678 (Tex. Ct. App. 1993) (holding that "when the health-care plan's insured shows up at a participating hospital emergency department, and the plan's doctor on call is consulted about treatment or admission, there is a physician-patient relationship between the doctor and the insured").

3. *The Hospital's Duty.* Despite the reluctance of the *Manlove* court to find a duty to treat, it is considered a groundbreaking case in that it paved the way for other courts to make more definitive findings of hospital liability for the refusal of emergency care. See, e.g., Stanturf v. Sipes, 447 S.W.2d 558 (Mo. 1969) (hospital may be liable for refusing to treat frostbite victim who could not post $25 deposit); Mercy Medical Center v. Winnebago County, 206 N.W.2d 198 (Wis. 1973) ("It would shock the public conscience if a person in need of medical emergency aid would be turned down at the door of a hospital."); but see Campbell v. Mincey, 413 F. Supp. 16 (N.D. Miss. 1975) (no obligation of hospital emergency department to care for pregnant woman in labor). Many states impose a requirement of open emergency departments by statute or regulation. See generally Karen Rothenberg, Who Cares? The Evolution of the Legal Duty to Provide Emergency Care, 26 Hous. L. Rev. 21 (1989).

How do you explain the fact that hospitals have a duty to provide emergency care to all who seek it while physicians are under no such obligation? Arguably, it does not make sense to expect physicians to be available at all times, while hospitals can reasonably be expected to always have someone staffing their emergency departments. But what about just expecting physicians to be available during their regular office hours for emergencies? Can't doctors factor into their scheduling the possibility of emergencies? Don't they in fact already do that? Is part of the issue that physicians may not necessarily have the expertise for any emergency patient that comes through the door? Suppose the physician is a dermatologist and is confronted with a cardiac emergency. Is there anything the doctor reasonably could do besides call 911? How might it actually not serve patients' interests in less populated areas if physicians have a duty to provide care to those in need?

Hospitals, too, may be able to limit their obligation according to their capacity or expertise. Suppose a hospital has no emergency department because it specializes in elective surgeries. Or suppose the emergency department is full. When this happens, hospital emergency departments often place themselves on "drive-by" status, which means they alert ambulances not to stop there. One court held this was permissible in the case of a child who consequently suffered brain damage, even though the hospital had treated the child many times in the past and had encouraged his parents to pass up other closer hospitals and come there if he had serious problems. Davis v. Johns Hopkins Hospital, 622 A.2d 128 (Md. 1993). Regulations under the Emergency Medical Treatment and Active Labor Act (EMTALA) come to the same conclusion. 42 C.F.R. §489.24(b)(4).

4. *The Meaning of Reliance.* Why is the *Manlove* reliance theory limited to just emergency care? Observe the court's reasoning that "such a refusal [of treatment] might well result in worsening the condition of the injured person, because of the time lost in a useless attempt to obtain medical aid." Presumably, this is true only in a very serious or "unmistakable" emergency. It might be possible, however, to argue for other types of reliance. Suppose, for instance, that a prospective patient chose to live in the community because of the presence of a hospital, and it would thereby frustrate his or her reliance if the hospital could deny care in nonemergencies as well as emergencies. On the other hand, while such patients may have a psychological reliance, they would not suffer a *detrimental* reliance in the sense of a material change in one's position for the worse.

Where reliance is detrimental, should the patient have to demonstrate actual reliance in the particular case, rather than reliance being assumed? The *Manlove* court appeared to treat only the detriment part as requiring proof, not the psychological expectation. Should we presume that patients always legitimately expect emergency departments to be open to them? Consider, for instance, Guerrero v. Copper Queen Hospital, 537 P.2d 1329 (Ariz. 1975), which found that a hospital in a border town owned by a local mining company had a duty to render emergency aid to two severely burned Mexican children who were injured in their home across the border.

5. *Physicians "On Call." Hurley* and *Manlove* appear consistent because one is about doctors and the other is about hospitals. But does it make sense for hospitals to have a duty to accept emergency patients if the doctors who work there are free to refuse treatment? Courts generally have resolved this problem by holding that a doctor who is "on call" for a hospital emergency department voluntarily undertakes the hospital's greater duty of care. The leading decision is Hiser v. Randolph, 617 P.2d 774 (Ariz. 1980). At 11:45 P.M. one night, Bonita Hiser came to the emergency department at Mojave County General Hospital in a semi-comatose condition arising out of an exacerbation of her juvenile onset diabetes. Along with the seven other doctors in the area, Dr. Randolph took turns as the on-call physician for the emergency department, a duty for which he was paid $100 per 12-hour shift, and he was on call when Mrs. Hiser came to the hospital. When the emergency department nurse called Dr. Randolph, he refused to come in. He claimed this was because he lacked the expertise to treat diabetes, but there was also evidence that his refusal was based on personal animosity toward Mrs. Hiser or the fact that Mrs. Hiser's husband was a lawyer. Mrs. Hiser died because of the delay in treatment. The court

found that Dr. Randolph breached his duty of care arising from his status as an on-call physician. According to the court,

> the obviously intended effect of the [hospital's] bylaws and rules and regulations was to obligate the emergency room doctor "on call" to provide emergency treatment to the best of the doctor's ability to any emergency patient of the hospital. Under these circumstances, the lack of a consensual physician-patient relationship before a duty to treat can arise has been waived by the signatory doctors.

But see Childs v. Weis, 440 S.W.2d 104 (Tex. Ct. App. 1969) (physicians on emergency call were under no specific duty to see all patients who presented themselves to the emergency department).

A similar analysis is possible for HMO physicians. See St. Charles v. Kender, 646 N.E.2d 411 (Mass. Ct. App. 1995) (HMO subscriber is a third-party beneficiary of an HMO's contracts with its physicians; contract was breached when physician failed to return patient's calls for an appointment). In Hand v. Tavera, 864 S.W.2d 678 (Tex. Ct. App. 1993), Lewis Hand went to the Humana Hospital (Village Oaks) emergency department because of a three-day headache. He also had high blood pressure, and his medical history revealed that his father had died of an aneurysm. The emergency department physician was able to control Mr. Hand's blood pressure and headache temporarily with medication but ultimately concluded that Mr. Hand should be admitted to the hospital. Hospital admissions required the approval of another physician under the Humana Health Care Plan, so the emergency department physician called Dr. Robert Tavera, the physician responsible that evening for authorizing admissions of Humana patients. Dr. Tavera decided that Mr. Hand should be treated as an outpatient. A few hours after returning home, Mr. Hand suffered a stroke. The trial court granted Dr. Tavera summary judgment on the ground that no patient-physician relationship had been formed, but the appellate court held that a patient-physician relationship existed by virtue of Mr. Hand's membership in the Humana Health Care Plan and Dr. Tavera's designation "as the doctor acting for the Humana plan that night." As the court observed, "Hand paid premiums to Humana to purchase medical care in advance of need . . . and Tavera's medical group agreed to treat Humana enrollees in exchange for the fees received from Humana. In effect, Hand had paid in advance for the services of the Humana plan doctor on duty that night, who happened to be Tavera, and the physician-patient relationship existed."

6. *The Quasi-Public Status of Hospitals.* Another basis for imposing a duty to treat, distinct from the reliance theory, is the assertion that physicians or hospitals owe duties to the public at large simply by virtue of their having chosen to become licensed health care providers. It is a version of this argument that the *Hurley* court rejects with the cryptic comment that "analogies, drawn from the obligations to the public on the part of innkeepers, common carriers, and the like, are beside the mark."

In ancient common law, certain occupations and businesses were considered to be "common callings," meaning that they could not turn away customers without a good reason. Innkeepers and public transport ("common carriers") were the classic examples. The reasons for these heightened public service duties were the importance of the service, the monopoly status of the business, and the support it received from the government. See Charles Burdick, The Origin of the Peculiar

Duties of Public Service Companies, 11 Colum. L. Rev. 514, 616, 742 (1911); O.W. Holmes, Jr., Common Carriers and the Common Law, 13 Am. L. Rev. 40 (1879).

In modern times, these "businesses affected with a public interest" are the public utilities (electric, phone, trains, etc.), and common-law duties of public service have been supplanted by overt government regulation. This body of common law has therefore become somewhat archaic, but it is still sometimes invoked against trade associations or labor unions that refuse membership. See generally Comment, 49 U. Chi. L. Rev. 840 (1982); Note, 102 Harv. L. Rev. 1993 (1989).

In Chapter 4, we will see that this body of law has been used to characterize hospitals as "quasi-public" facilities for purposes of giving *physicians* rights of access to their medical staffs. Considering that patients are the ultimate customers for whom public benefit is intended, shouldn't this analogy have even more application to them? It would be ironic indeed to insist on physician access but deny patient access. Nevertheless, the *Manlove* court rejected this view. In other states, later decisions have been more receptive to the quasi-public characterization. For instance, in Thompson v. Sun City Community Hospital, 688 P.2d 605 (Ariz. 1984), the court found that a cause of action exists against a hospital that stabilized a patient with a severed artery and then transferred him for financial reasons. The court based the duty to treat on the general public policy embodied in hospital licensing regulations and private accreditation standards. Also, in Payton v. Weaver, 182 Cal. Rptr. 225 (Cal.App. 1982), the court suggested in dictum that this public service theory could be used to impose a community-wide obligation on kidney dialysis centers to share the burden of treating an unwanted disruptive patient. Cf. A.J.G. Priest, Possible Adaptation of Public Utility Concepts in the Health Care Field, 35 Law & Contemp. Probs. 839 (1970).

7. *The Private Status of Physicians.* Reconsider the situation of physicians. Why shouldn't medical practice by physicians be considered a "common calling" or a quasi-public service? Indeed, it turns out that, in fifteenth-century English law, physicians were included on the list of common callings along with blacksmiths and other important professions. Perhaps today, the missing ingredient is that a physician rarely has a local monopoly; usually there are several in town. But not always. One court found a common-law duty to treat where the sole physician practice group in town refused to accept a patient who had filed a complaint against one of the doctors in the group. Leach v. Drummond Medical Group, 192 Cal. Rptr. 650 (Cal. Ct. App. 1983).

There is an alternative explanation for the law no longer treating physicians as being engaged in a common calling. Consider this perspective:

> Although the law was ambiguous, there is a substantial argument that the duty to serve the public extended to all businesses that held themselves out as open to the public. Only around the time of the Civil War did this rule begin formally to narrow, and only after the Civil War, when civil rights were extended to African-Americans for the first time, did the courts clearly state for the first time that most businesses had no common-law duties to serve the public. The rule achieved its present form only when the issue became enmeshed in the problem of race relations. This change in the law had the effect – and without doubt the purpose – of enabling businesses to continue to serve white customers while choosing to exclude black customers. [Joseph W. Singer, No Right to Exclude: Public Accommodations and Private Property, 90 Nw. U. L. Rev. 1283, 1294-1295 (1996).]

In a few state statutes, regulatory law imposes some limited duties on physicians to provide care for patients. In Massachusetts, for instance, physicians, as a condition of being licensed, must agree to charge Medicare patients no more than Medicare's "reasonable charge." This has been held not to violate the constitutional rights of physicians. Dukakis v. Massachusetts Medical Society, 815 F.2d 790 (1st Cir. 1987).

8. *Paying vs. Indigent Patients.* Perhaps this body of law is not more developed because doctors and hospitals rarely turn away patients who can pay. For patients who cannot pay, the public service theory is usually no help, since the common law never required common callings to serve people for free. Only the reliance theory reaches this result, but it is restricted to serious emergencies, those in which the patient is worse off for having made a futile attempt to secure service. Only in Arizona have courts used a public service theory to impose a duty to treat patients who cannot pay, and there too the duty is limited to emergency care. (Should it be?) For the view that physicians, hospitals, and other providers should be regulated as a public utility, both to promote access and contain costs, see Nicholas Bagley, Medicine as a Public Calling, 114 Mich. L. Rev. 57 (2015).

9. *Enforcement of Public Rights.* For patients who cannot pay, regulatory law may place hospitals under somewhat greater duties than the common law to treat both emergency and nonemergency patients, but these public law duties have been limited and are not enforceable by individual patients.

Consider, for example, tax law. Nonprofit hospitals are considered to be "charities" that are exempt from property and income tax. Part of this charitable status includes an obligation to treat some patients for free. As discussed in Chapter 4.B.2, federal law restricts this free-care obligation to emergency patients, as do most states, but a few states are beginning to require hospitals to devote a certain percentage of their overall services to patients who cannot pay. Once again, however, this is a community service obligation owed to the public at large, not to individual patients, and so it cannot be enforced very easily by private action. Finally, the Joint Commission on Accreditation of Healthcare Organizations (JCAHO) private accreditation standards require hospitals to accept patients without regard to "source of payment," but this is interpreted to mean accepting all patients with some source of payment (e.g., not turning away Medicaid patients) rather than a duty to accept patients who cannot pay.

This leaves us with the following patchwork of laws: for physicians, no common-law duty to treat, even in emergencies. For hospitals: (1) a common-law duty to treat emergency patients regardless of payment, but only in serious emergencies; (2) common law and regulatory duties to treat all patients who can pay; but (3) no enforceable duty to treat nonemergency or mild emergency patients who cannot pay. This set the stage for enactment of a new federal statute, the Emergency Medical Treatment and Active Labor Act (EMTALA).

Notes: Moral and Constitutional Rights to Health Care

1. *Moral Rights to Treatment.* The discussion of legal rights to treatment surely must be informed by how our society views moral rights to health care. What message does society send when the law limits the right to treatment so narrowly as to encompass only serious emergencies? Does the emergency care limitation suggest that we

are trying to limit care to the most compelling needs and to avoid people demanding too much care (emergencies being thought of as unpredictable)? This might be seen as a partial embodiment of the "rescue principle" discussed in Chapter 3.D.1, which declares that the strongest ethical demand in medicine is to help those in greatest need. In this regard, the moral dimension of medicine is stronger than in any other commercial arena, because there is no equivalent requirement that grocers, restaurants, or hotels provide their services for free to people in dire straits. What justifies this distinction? Is it that if food and housing were available on demand, it would be too easy to abuse the privilege? But what kinds of incentives for patients does a right only to emergency care generate? Is the reluctance of the courts to find even broader rights to health care a reflection of the difficulty in deciding who to hold responsible for vindicating these rights? Or perhaps it reflects the difficulty in defining what a right to health care would include. Consider in this regard the difference between defining a right to food or housing and a right to health care.

The moral issue can also be debated from a broader, social perspective. So far, we have thought only about whether patients have a right to demand treatment from particular doctors and hospitals. Even where they do not have these private rights, perhaps they have a claim to a more public right, one that society as a whole owes to provide minimally decent health care to all. Arguments to this effect are explored in Chapter 3. For some time, we have recognized this claim to basic social support for education and to a more limited extent for food and housing. But for health care, there was no national safety net until the enactment of the Patient Protection and Affordable Care Act in 2010. Importantly, the Act expands Medicaid coverage to all persons whose family income is no more than 138 percent of the federal poverty level. Still, even with the Act's implementation, more than 25 million Americans (many of them undocumented immigrants) lack health insurance of any kind. Perhaps it was politically and morally sustainable to deny coverage to so many people before enactment of the Affordable Care Act—and to continue denying coverage to millions of Americans—only because private hospital emergency departments exist as a last resort for those without insurance. Could it be, then, that the heightened private law duties of hospitals weakened our nation's public law commitment to health care access? See Mark A. Hall, The Unlikely Case in Favor of Patient Dumping, 28 Jurimetrics 389 (1988). For an argument that private law duties tend to undermine voluntary charity, see Richard Epstein, Mortal Peril: Our Inalienable Right to Health Care? (1997). For responses to Epstein, see Symposium: Is America's Health Care System in Mortal Peril?, 1998 U. Ill. L. Rev. 683.

2. *Positive vs. Negative Liberty.* If there is a moral right to health care generally, it is clearly not vindicated as a substantive due process right by the U.S. Constitution. *Wideman* is a classic statement of the principle that the Bill of Rights embodies primarily negative, not positive, liberties, that is, it is concerned mainly with freedoms from government imposition, not rights to government assistance. Thus, the Constitution becomes relevant to health care when the government bans treatment choices or forces treatment, but not when it simply declines to assist in obtaining treatment. In this regard, the U.S. Constitution differs markedly from constitutional models in Europe. B. Jessie Hill, What Is the Meaning of Health? Constitutional Implications of Defining "Medical Necessity" and "Essential Health Benefits" Under the Affordable Care Act, 38 Am. J.L. & Med. 445 (2012); John A.

Robertson, Controversial Medical Treatment and the Right to Health Care, 36(6) Hastings Center Rep. 15 (2006).

Wideman was followed by an important Supreme Court opinion confirming its general analysis in this regard. In DeShaney v. Winnebago County Department of Social Services, 489 U.S. 189 (1989), the Court held that no constitutional violation occurred in a case where a child was left with permanent brain damage when a state social services agency failed to intervene aggressively enough to prevent child abuse. The state had received several reports of severe beatings by the father. The Court reaffirmed "that the due process clauses generally confer no affirmative right to governmental aid," and it reasoned that the state agency had not assumed a "special relationship" with the child by virtue of having made some ineffectual efforts to protect him since the agency did nothing to make him more vulnerable to the danger. See also Archie v. Racine, 847 F.2d 1211 (7th Cir. 1988) (en banc) (§1983 action not maintainable for city rescue service's negligent failure to dispatch ambulance; no constitutional right to treatment exists).

As *Wideman* indicates, government will assume duties to provide health care when it confines individuals in psychiatric hospitals, prisons, or other facilities. Before the enactment of the Affordable Care Act, occasional press reports described cases of uninsured people committing crimes so they would have access to health care while incarcerated. Katie Moisse & James Verone, The Medical Motive for His $1 Bank Robbery, ABC News, June 23, 2011.

3. *Equal Protection.* In Maher v. Roe, 432 U.S. 464, 469-470 (1977), discussed in *Wideman*, the Court identified another possible source of a constitutional duty to treat: "The Constitution imposes no obligation on the states to pay . . . any of the medical expenses of indigents. But when a state decides to alleviate some of the hardships of poverty by providing medical care, the manner in which it dispenses benefits is subject to constitutional limitations." For example, in Memorial Hospital v. Maricopa County, 415 U.S. 250 (1974), the Court struck down Arizona's requirement of a year's residence in a county as a condition of receiving nonemergency medical care at county expense as infringing on the right to travel. Might a state be subject to an equal protection attack for funding some procedures but not others? See Doe v. Colautti, 592 F.2d 704 (3d Cir. 1978) (finding no violation of the equal protection clause when Pennsylvania's medical assistance program provided less generous benefits for psychiatric care than for general medical care). See Chapter 3.D.1 for discussion of statutory protections against discrimination in access to health care.

4. *Legislative Mandates.* In Harris v. McRae, 448 U.S. 297 (1980), another abortion funding case discussed in *Wideman*, the Court addressed a nonconstitutional theory for compelling government funding of health care. States that participate in Medicaid are, generally speaking, required to fund most medically necessary forms of treatment. Beal v. Doe, 432 U.S. 438, 444 (1977). Although *McRae* found this statutory requirement to be inapplicable to abortions, in other cases the medical necessity mandate has proved to be an effective tool for obtaining Medicaid coverage. Pittman v. Secretary, Florida Dept. Health & Rehab. Services; 998 F.2d 887 (11th Cir. 1993) (requiring coverage of a liver-intestine transplant for a child); Rush v. Parham, 625 F.2d 1150 (5th Cir. 1980) (requiring funding for sex change operations in certain circumstances). However, there is no statutory requirement that Medicaid

be funded at a level sufficient to cover all people who need it. See Chapter 3.D for additional discussion.

BURDITT v. U.S. DEPARTMENT OF HEALTH AND HUMAN SERVICES

934 F.2d 1362 (5th Cir. 1991)

REAVLEY, Circuit Judge.

Hospitals that execute Medicare provider agreements with the federal government pursuant to 42 U.S.C. §1395cc must treat all human beings who enter their emergency departments in accordance with the Emergency Medical Treatment and Active Labor Act (EMTALA), 42 U.S.C. §1395dd. Hospitals and responsible physicians found to have violated EMTALA's requirements are subject to civil money penalties. [This case is an appeal by Dr. Burditt of a $20,000 fine assessed against him by the Department of Health and Human Services. EMTALA also provides for a private cause of action, with prevailing plaintiffs entitled to monetary damages from the offending hospital and appropriate equitable relief. Damages may not be recovered from physicians in a private cause of action, however.]

I.A. FACTS

Mrs. Rosa Rivera arrived in the emergency room of DeTar Hospital in Victoria, Texas at approximately 4:00 P.M. on December 5, 1986. At or near term with her sixth child, she was experiencing one-minute, moderate contractions every three minutes and her membranes had ruptured. Two obstetrical nurses, Tammy Kotsur and Donna Keining, examined her and found indicia of labor and dangerously high blood pressure. Because Rivera had received no prenatal care, and had neither a regular doctor nor means of payment, Kotsur telephoned Burditt, who was next on DeTar's rotating call-list of physicians responsible for such "unaligned" obstetrics patients. Upon hearing Rivera's history and condition, Burditt told Kotsur that he "didn't want to take care of this lady" and asked her to prepare Rivera for transfer to John Sealy Hospital in Galveston, Texas, 170 miles away. Burditt agreed to call back in five to ten minutes.

Kotsur and Keining told the nursing supervisor, Jean Herman, and DeTar's administrator, Charles Sexton, of their belief that it would be unsafe to transfer Rivera. When Burditt called back, Keining told him that, according to Sexton's understanding of hospital regulations and federal law, Burditt would have to examine Rivera and personally arrange for John Sealy to receive her before he could legally transfer her. Keining asked Burditt for permission to start an intravenous push of magnesium sulfate as a precaution against convulsive seizures. Burditt told Keining to begin administering this medication only if Rivera could be transported by ambulance. . . .

Burditt arrived at approximately 4:50 to examine Rivera. He confirmed her blood pressure to be the highest he had ever seen, 210/130, and he assumed that she had been hypertensive throughout her pregnancy. As the experienced head of DeTar's obstetrics and gynecology department, Burditt knew that there was a strong possibility that Rivera's hypertension would precipitate complications which might kill both Rivera and her baby. He also knew that the infants of hypertensive mothers are at higher-than-normal risk of intrauterine growth retardation. He estimated that Rivera's baby was six pounds—less than normal weight—and arranged her transfer to John Sealy, a perinatal facility better equipped than DeTar to care for underweight infants. . . .

At approximately 5:00, Herman showed Burditt DeTar's guidelines regarding EMTALA, but he refused to read them. Burditt told Herman that Rivera represented more risk than he was willing to accept from a malpractice standpoint. Herman explained that Rivera could not be transferred unless Burditt signed a DeTar form entitled "Physician's Certificate Authorizing Transfer." Burditt asked for "that dang piece of paper" and signed his name under the following:

> I have examined the patient, ________, and have determined that, based upon the information available to me at this time, the medical benefits reasonably expected from the provision of appropriate medical treatment at another medical facility outweigh the increased risks to the patient's medical condition from effecting [the] transfer. The basis for my conclusion is as follows: ________

Burditt listed no basis for his conclusion and remarked to Herman that "until DeTar Hospital pays my malpractice insurance, I will pick and choose those patients that I want to treat."

Burditt then went to care for another unaligned patient, Sylvia Ramirez, while the nurses arranged Rivera's transfer. They found another obstetrical nurse, Anita Nichols, to accompany Rivera to John Sealy. Burditt returned to the nurses' station and stayed there from 5:30 to 6:18. He never again examined Rivera or asked about her medical condition, though he inquired several times about the status of her transfer. Burditt delivered the Ramirez baby at 6:22. Afterward, Nichols told him the results of her examination of Rivera and informed him that the ambulance had arrived. Based exclusively on Nichols' statements, Burditt concluded that Rivera's condition had not changed since his examination two hours before. Burditt did not reexamine Rivera though he saw her being wheeled to the ambulance. He did not order any medication or life support equipment for Rivera during her transfer.

Nichols delivered Rivera's healthy baby in the ambulance approximately 40 miles into the 170-mile trip to John Sealy. She directed the driver to nearby Ganado Hospital to get a drug called pitocin to staunch Rivera's bleeding. While there, Nichols telephoned Burditt, who ordered her to continue to John Sealy despite the birth. Instead, per Rivera's wishes, Nichols returned Rivera to DeTar, where Burditt refused to see her because she failed to proceed to John Sealy in accordance with his instructions. Burditt directed that Rivera be discharged if she was stable and not bleeding excessively. A DeTar official pressed Burditt to allow Dr. Shirley Pigott to examine Rivera. Rivera stayed at DeTar under Pigott's care for three days and left in good health. . . .

II.A.1. SCREENING

Because Rivera presented herself to DeTar's emergency department and a request was made on her behalf for care, EMTALA required DeTar to

> provide for an *appropriate* medical screening examination *within the capability of the hospital's emergency department* to determine whether or not an emergency medical condition . . . exists or to determine if the individual is in active labor. . . .

42 U.S.C. §1395dd(a) (emphasis added). The parties agree that DeTar appropriately screened Rivera and discovered that she had an "emergency medical condition"—severe hypertension—within the meaning of 42 U.S.C. §1395dd(e)(1).[2]

II.A.2. EMERGENCY MEDICAL CONDITION AND ACTIVE LABOR

Patients diagnosed with an "emergency medical condition" or "active labor" must either be treated or be transferred in accordance with EMTALA. Burditt claims that Rivera received all of the care that she was due under EMTALA because he stabilized her hypertension sufficiently for transfer and she was not in active labor when she left DeTar for John Sealy.

II.A.2.a. Unstable Emergency Medical Condition

Rivera's blood pressure was 210/130 at 4:00 and 5:00. This was the last reading known to Burditt before he facilitated her transfer. Nurses also measured her blood pressure as 173/105 at 5:30, 178/103 at 5:45, 186/107 at 6:00, and 190/110 at 6:50. Experts testified that Rivera's hypertension put her at high risk of suffering serious complications, including seizures, heart failure, kidney dysfunction, tubular necrosis, stroke, intracranial bleeding, placental abruption, and fetal hypoxia. This is substantial, if not conclusive evidence that Rivera entered and exited DeTar with an emergency medical condition.

Burditt argues that he fulfilled EMTALA's requirements with respect to Rivera's hypertension by "stabilizing" it, or

> provid[ing] such medical treatment of the condition as may be necessary to assure, within reasonable medical probability, that no material deterioration of the condition is likely to result from [a] transfer. . . .

42 U.S.C. §1395dd(e)(4)(A). He claims that the magnesium sulfate that he ordered for Rivera has an antihypertensive effect that complements its primary anticonvulsive purpose.

Development of any of the possible complications could have killed or seriously injured Rivera, her baby, or both, and thus would constitute a "material deterioration"

2. EMTALA defines "emergency medical condition" as

> a medical condition manifesting itself by acute symptoms of sufficient severity (including severe pain) such that the absence of immediate medical attention could reasonably be expected to result in—
> (A) placing the patient's health in serious jeopardy,
> (B) serious impairment to bodily functions, or
> (C) serious dysfunction of any bodily organ or part.

42 U.S.C. §1395dd(e)(1) (Supp. IV 1987).

under 42 U.S.C. §1395dd(e)(4)(A). Any deterioration would "result" from transfer in that Rivera would have received better care for any complication at DeTar than in the ambulance. Thus, Burditt could not have stabilized Rivera unless he provided treatment that medical experts agree would prevent the threatening and severe consequences of Rivera's hypertension while she was in transit. [The HHS appeals board] could properly disregard Burditt's testimony and accept that of all other testifying experts in holding that Burditt provided no such treatment, and thus did not stabilize Rivera's emergency medical condition. . . .

II.A.2.b. Active Labor

EMTALA defines "active labor" as labor at a time when

> (B) there is inadequate time to effect safe transfer to another hospital prior to delivery, or
> (C) a transfer may pose a threat [to] the health and safety of the patient or the unborn child.

42 U.S.C. §1395dd(e)(2)(B)-(C). This statutory definition renders irrelevant any medical definition of active labor. . . .

Burditt challenges the ALJ's finding that, at approximately 5:00, there was inadequate time to safely transfer Rivera to John Sealy before she delivered her baby. Dr. Warren Crosby testified that, based on Burditt's own examination results, Rivera would, more likely than not, deliver within three hours after Burditt [made the decision to transfer her to] John Sealy. . . . Burditt does not challenge [the] conclusion that the ambulance trip from DeTar to John Sealy takes approximately three hours. We therefore hold that [the HHS appeals board] properly concluded that Rivera was in active labor under 42 U.S.C. §1395dd(e)(2)(B).

The ALJ also found that Rivera was in active labor under clause C at the time Burditt examined her. There is always some risk of a vehicular accident in transit, so transfer always "may" pose a threat to the health and safety of the patient or fetus. . . . We believe that Congress intended clause C to extend EMTALA's . . . protection to women in labor who have any complication with their pregnancies regardless of delivery imminency. Because better medical care is available in a hospital than in an ambulance, whether a transfer "may pose a threat" under 42 U.S.C. §1395dd(e)(2)(C) depends on whether the woman in labor has any medical condition that could interfere with the normal, natural delivery of her healthy child. Under the statutory language, a woman in labor is entitled to EMTALA's . . . protections upon a showing of possible threat; it does not require proof of a reasonable medical probability that any threat will come to fruition. . . .

The record overwhelmingly confirms that Rivera's hypertension could have interfered with a normal delivery, and she was thus in active labor under 42 U.S.C. §1395dd(e)(2)(C). . . .

II.A.3. TREAT OR TRANSFER

Upon discovery of active labor or an emergency medical condition, EMTALA usually requires hospitals to treat the discovered condition. Under certain circumstances, however, EMTALA allows hospitals to transfer patients instead of treating them. 42 U.S.C. §1395dd(b)(1)(B). . . . [The court went on to find that Burditt had not satisfied the requirements under EMTALA for a transfer before stabilization. Under EMTALA, transfer is permitted if the patient requests transfer *or* the physician has certified in writing that the medical benefits of transfer outweigh the increased risks to the patient. In addition, the receiving hospital must be capable of providing the needed treatment and must have agreed to accept the transfer. Finally, the transfer must occur with appropriate personnel and transportation, including appropriate life support measures. While Burditt had obtained consent from John Sealy before the transfer, he had not reasonably concluded that the benefits of transfer outweighed the risks nor had he arranged for the transfer with appropriate personnel and transportation.]

II.C. EMTALA's Constitutionality

As his final attempt to escape [liability], Burditt claims that EMTALA effects a public taking of his services without just compensation in contravention of the Constitution's Fifth Amendment.

Assuming *arguendo* that professional services constitute property protected by the takings clause, Burditt has not shown that EMTALA effects a taking. EMTALA imposes no responsibilities directly on physicians; it unambiguously requires hospitals to examine and stabilize, treat, or appropriately transfer all who arrive requesting treatment. Its provision for sanctions against physicians who knowingly violate its requirements is merely an enforcement mechanism that does not alter its explicit assignment of duties.

Governmental regulation that affects a group's property interests "does not constitute a taking of property where the regulated group is not required to participate in the regulated industry." Whitney v. Heckler, 780 F.2d 963, 972 (11th Cir.), *cert. denied*, 479 U.S. 813 (1986).

Two levels of voluntariness undermine Burditt's taking assertion. Only hospitals that voluntarily participate in the federal government's Medicare program must comply with EMTALA. Hospitals must consider the cost of complying with EMTALA's requirements in deciding whether to continue to participate in the Medicare program.

Second, Burditt is free to negotiate with DeTar or another hospital regarding his responsibility to facilitate a hospital's compliance with EMTALA. Thus, physicians only voluntarily accept responsibilities under EMTALA if they consider it in their best interest to do so. Accordingly, Burditt's claim under the takings clause is without merit. . . .

Notes: The Federal Patient Dumping Statute

1. *Historical Background.* Congress passed the Emergency Medical Treatment and Active Labor Act (EMTALA) as part of the Consolidated Omnibus Reconciliation Act of 1986 (COBRA), in response to the perception that state law was too weak to prevent widespread patient dumping. While EMTALA, or COBRA, has worked better than previous legal efforts, in part because of the private right of action, there are still concerns that patient dumping persists at unacceptable levels. One scholar argues, however, that

> EMTALA is a virtual catalogue of how to get a statute wrong. First, generalize from unrepresentative anecdotal evidence in identifying the problem. Draft the statute sloppily, and leave the most important words undefined or defined too broadly. Finance the resulting open-ended entitlement with an unfunded mandate imposed on private parties. . . . [Design the enforcement system] to reward the wrong people. Finally, apply the statute even after the world on which it depended has vanished. Any one of these problems would be bad enough in isolation, but their combined effect is devastating to the interests EMTALA was intended to protect.

David A. Hyman, Dumping EMTALA: When Bad Laws Happen to Good People (1998) (unpublished). As you read the following notes, see if you can determine why someone might reach such a conclusion. Nevertheless, Prof. Hyman acknowledges that

> the statute is wildly popular across the entirety of the political spectrum and among such disparate interest groups as physicians, advocates for the poor, [academics,] and consumer groups. Unlike many reforms, EMTALA does not create a new administrative bureaucracy; it does not favor the interests of the well-connected against the less fortunate; its on-budget costs are modest; and it seems to be no more intrusive than is absolutely necessary to accomplish its objectives.

David A. Hyman, Patient Dumping and EMTALA: Past Imperfect/Future Shock, 8 Health Matrix 29, 29 (1998).

As the *Burditt* court indicated, courts have not thought EMTALA poses constitutional problems. But not everyone agrees. E. Haavi Morreim, EMTALA: Medicare's Unconstitutional Condition on Hospitals, 43 Hastings Const. L.Q. 61 (2015).

Dr. Michael Burditt was the first physician fined for an EMTALA violation, and his actions were vigorously defended by the Texas Medical Association. For a critical view of the Fifth Circuit's decision in the *Burditt* case, see David Hyman, Lies, Damned Lies, and Narrative, 73 Ind. L.J. 797, 824-832 (1998). As a general matter, the government rarely penalizes individual physicians under EMTALA, levying most of its fines on hospitals. Sophie Terp et al., Individual Physician Penalties Resulting from Violation of Emergency Medical Treatment and Labor Act, 24 Academic Emergency Med. 442 (2017).

2. *Screening and Stabilizing.* EMTALA creates two distinct duties. First, the duty to screen patients is triggered by their arrival at the hospital, and it ceases if it is determined they are not in what the statute defines as an "emergency" condition. Second, if patients are in an emergency condition, then the hospital must stabilize them. (The statutory requirements are similar for patients in active labor.) Most litigation has arisen at the first stage, in cases where patients claim the hospital failed entirely to evaluate or recognize their emergency condition.

But that is not our main concern in this note. Our concern is, if there clearly is an emergency, how far does the duty to treat extend? Do hospitals have to perform bypass surgery after they halt a heart attack? Although *Burditt* found that "stabilizing" care was not rendered in that case, what about other typical situations? Consider whether the outcome would be any different under EMTALA than it was under this state law decision: Joyner v. Alton Ochsner Medical Foundation, 230 So. 2d 913 (La. Ct. App. 1970) (auto accident victim did not "require immediate admission" after stabilizing care was rendered, despite "multiple deep facial lacerations, a possible head injury, traumatic damage to the teeth and multiple bruises and contusions of the body, resulting in considerable loss of blood"). Consider whether the duty to treat under EMTALA is as strong as it is under this state law decision: Thompson v. Sun City Community Hospital, 688 P.2d 605 (Ariz. 1984) (a cause of action exists against a hospital that stabilized a patient with a severed artery and then transferred him for financial reasons). Is the federal statute any more demanding than the *Manlove* reliance theory?

Moreover, courts have applied the stabilization requirement of EMTALA only when a hospital discharges a patient or transfers the patient to another hospital, and not when the hospital provides care. Harry v. Marchant, 291 F.3d 767, 770-772 (11th Cir. 2002) (en banc) (observing that the stabilization requirement of EMTALA is defined in terms of transfer or discharge). See also Alvarez-Torres v. Ryder Memorial Hospital, Inc., 582 F.3d 47, 51-52 (1st Cir. 2009); Bryan v. Rectors and Visitors of the University of Virginia, 95 F.3d 349, 352 (4th Cir. 1996).

For a view that EMTALA has blocked blatantly discriminatory practices without actually improving the quality of health care received by disadvantaged populations, see Karin V. Rhodes & Kristofer L. Smith, Short-term Care with Long-term Costs, 69 Annals Emergency Med. 163 (2017). For proposals to make EMTALA work more effectively, see Katharine Van Tassel, Modernizing the Emergency Medical Treatment & Labor Act to Harmonize with the Affordable Care Act to Improve Equality, Quality and Cost of Emergency Care, 15 Hous. J. Health L. & Pol'y 131 (2015).

There are other consequences of an obligation only to stabilize. For example, hospitals may send undocumented immigrants back to their home countries, and many of these patients die because of their inability to access follow-up care upon their return.

Although EMTALA only requires stabilization, other federal rules may extend the duty to provide care. Medicare's conditions for participation require safe discharge planning for hospitalized patients, and it may not be safe to discharge a patient who has only been stabilized. Jennifer L. Herbst, Permanent Patients, 47(1) Hastings Center Rep. 6 (2017).

In its requirement to stabilize emergency patients, EMTALA does not require the impossible. If a hospital does not have the facilities or personnel necessary to fully stabilize a patient, and the patient must be transferred to a more sophisticated hospital to receive needed care, the first hospital can transfer the patient to the more sophisticated hospital without violating EMTALA. The transferring hospital must do all it can to stabilize the patient's condition, but it need not do what it cannot do. Cherukuri v. Shalala, 175 F.3d 446 (6th Cir. 1999) (absolving physician at small rural hospital after the physician transferred two patients who needed surgery to stop internal bleeding from an automobile accident).

And to ensure that potential receiving hospitals do not undermine patient protections, EMTALA imposes on those hospitals a duty to accept appropriate transfers (no "reverse dumping"). St. Anthony Hospital v. U.S. Dept. HHS, 309 F.3d 680 (10th Cir. 2002).

3. *The Patient's Indigency.* While the passage of EMTALA was motivated by concerns about private hospitals "dumping" indigent or uninsured patients on public hospitals, the statutory language imposes no requirement that patients show that they were denied emergency services because of indigency or lack of insurance. See 42 U.S.C. §1395dd(a) ("if any individual . . . comes to the emergency department . . . ,

the hospital must provide for an appropriate medical screening examination within the capability of the hospital's emergency department").

Accordingly, courts have generally held that it is irrelevant why a person did not receive an appropriate screening exam or, if an emergency was identified, why a person did not receive stabilizing care before discharge or transfer. As one court observed, "[EMTALA] applies to any and all patients, not just to patients with insufficient resources." Brooker v. Desert Hospital Corp., 947 F.2d 412, 415 (9th Cir. 1991). Accord Summers v. Baptist Medical Center, 91 F.3d 1132 (8th Cir. 1996); Gatewood v. Washington Healthcare Corp., 933 F.2d 1037, 1040 (D.C. Cir. 1991).

The Supreme Court addressed the motive question in the context of EMTALA's stabilization requirement and rejected any need to show an improper motive. Roberts v. Galen of Virginia, Inc., 525 U.S. 249 (1999). The Court "express[ed] no opinion" on the need to show an improper motive for a claim of inappropriate medical screening.

Perhaps the most controversial extension of EMTALA beyond economic discrimination occurred in the *Baby K* case, which involved a baby with anencephaly—a baby missing the major part of the brain that is necessary for conscious thought. In In re Baby K, 16 F.3d 590 (4th Cir. 1994), parents of an anencephalic child sought ventilatory treatment of their child during periodic bouts of respiratory distress. After the second of three such episodes, the hospital sought judicial permission to withhold the ventilator when the child next came to the emergency department. In the view of the hospital, it was medically and ethically inappropriate to ventilate the child given her limited life expectancy, her total absence of consciousness, and the futility of treatment at improving her condition. According to the hospital, the only appropriate treatment for the child was the treatment "it would provide other anencephalic infants—supportive care in the form of warmth, nutrition, and hydration." The court rejected the hospital's argument. It observed that EMTALA requires stabilizing treatment in the event of a medical emergency, and the child's respiratory distress met EMTALA's definition of a medical emergency. If there was to be an exception for "futile" care under EMTALA, Congress would have to write that exception into the statute. The *Baby K* decision raises serious questions about the ability of society to contain health care costs. If the hospital in the case could not deny a ventilator to an anencephalic child, how could any emergency medical care be withheld on the ground that its high costs were not justified by its minimal benefit? Is there a distinction between the economic or other discrimination prohibited by EMTALA and the denial of care that results when a hospital is concerned about the limits of society's resources?

Perhaps in recognition of these concerns, the Fourth Circuit limited the impact of *Baby K* two years later. In Bryan v. Rectors and Visitors of the University of Virginia, 95 F.3d 349 (4th Cir. 1996), an EMTALA claim was brought on behalf of a patient who died of a heart attack after her physicians decided that "no further efforts to prevent her death should be made." Twenty days before the heart attack, the patient had been admitted to the hospital in respiratory distress. Eight days before the heart attack, apparently because of the hopelessness of the patient's condition, her physicians decided to withhold further life-sustaining treatment, including cardiopulmonary resuscitation, in the event of a cardiac arrest. When she suffered her heart attack, no efforts were made to prevent her death. According to the court, there was no EMTALA violation because EMTALA "was intended to regulate the hospital's care of the patient only in the immediate aftermath of the act of admitting her for emergency treatment and while it considered whether it would undertake longer-term full treatment or instead transfer the patient to a hospital that could and would undertake that treatment." Id. at 352.

4. *Preventive Dumping.* There has been concern that hospitals would try to evade their EMTALA obligations by dumping patients before they reach the emergency department. For example, when called by a paramedic or emergency medical technician who is transporting a patient by ambulance, the emergency department staff might direct the ambulance to another hospital. Early cases suggested that hospitals would have considerable freedom to prevent patients from reaching the emergency department. See Miller v. Medical Center of Southwest Louisiana, 22 F.3d 626 (5th Cir. 1994) (hospital not liable under EMTALA for refusing to accept the transfer of a patient who needed specialized emergency care beyond the capabilities of the transferring hospital); Johnson v. University of Chicago Hospitals, 982 F.2d 230 (7th Cir. 1992) (hospital not liable for diverting an ambulance to another hospital).

Subsequent amendment of the EMTALA regulations and case law interpreting the amendment have limited the ability of hospitals to engage in preventive dumping. Under one regulation, patients have come to the hospital's emergency department for purposes of EMTALA once they have reached any part of the hospital's property, including a hospital-owned ambulance service. 42 C.F.R. §489.24(b) (2011) (applied in Hernandez v. Starr County Hospital District, 30 F. Supp. 2d 970 (S.D. Tex. 1999); Preston v. Meriter Hospital, Inc., 700 N.W.2d 158 (Wis. 2005)). The same regulation permits hospitals to divert non-hospital-owned ambulance services if the emergency department "does not have the staff or facilities to accept any additional emergency patients." 42 C.F.R. §489.24(b)(4). The Ninth Circuit has interpreted this provision to mean that a hospital violates EMTALA when it diverts a non-hospital-owned ambulance in the absence of an inability to provide treatment for the patient. Arrington v. Wong, 237 F.3d 1066 (9th Cir. 2001); see also Morales v. Sociedad Espanola de Auxilo Mutuo y Beneficencia, 524 F.3d 54 (1st Cir. 2008). See Caroline J. Stalker, Comment, How Far Is Too Far?: EMTALA Moves from the Emergency Room to Off-Campus Entities, 36 Wake Forest L. Rev. 823 (2001).

Note that there is some ambiguity to §489.24(b). Although the regulation seems to limit the ability of hospitals to divert non-hospital-owned ambulances, it also states that "[a]n individual in a non-hospital-owned ambulance off hospital property is not considered to have come to the hospital's emergency department even if a member of the ambulance staff contacts the hospital by telephone or telemetry communications and informs the hospital that they want to transport the individual to the hospital for examination and treatment."

As indicated, under 42 C.F.R. §489.24(b), EMTALA is triggered when an individual comes to areas of the hospital other than the emergency department. Thus, a First Circuit decision emphasizes the point that a hospital's duty to stabilize before transfer applies to any patient in the hospital, "regardless of how that person enters the institution or where within the walls he may be when the hospital identifies the problem." Lopez-Soto v. Hawayek, 175 F.3d 170, 173 (1st Cir. 1999) (observing that the stabilization requirement of EMTALA applies to an individual who "comes to a hospital" and holding that EMTALA applies when a pregnant woman is admitted to the maternity ward and taken to the operating room for a cesarean section, and her infant is born with respiratory distress and needs emergency care).

5. *Dumping After Admission to the Hospital.* Courts disagree as to whether EMTALA's stabilization requirement continues to apply once the patient has been admitted to the hospital. Cases have arisen in which patients were admitted to the hospital for treatment and, after a few or more days of treatment, been transferred to another hospital or discharged before their illness was fully treated. Or as in *Lopez-Soto, supra* note 4, the emergency condition may develop after the individual has become an inpatient or outpatient at the hospital.

Some courts have concluded that the obligation to stabilize exists throughout the patient's visit to the hospital. In addition to *Lopez-Soto,* see Thornton v. Southwest Detroit Hospital, 895 F.2d 1131 (6th Cir. 1990).

Other courts have concluded that the stabilization requirement ceases upon the patient's admission to the regular hospital. Bryan v. Rectors and Visitors of the University of Virginia, 95 F.3d 349, 352 (4th Cir. 1996); James v. Sunrise Hospital, 86 F.3d 885 (9th Cir. 1996); Bryant v. Adventist Health Systems/West, 289 F.3d 1162 (9th Cir. 2002). Note that in *Bryan* and *Bryant,* the courts were deciding about the stabilization requirement for care rendered during the patient's hospital stay and not in the context of a transfer or discharge. Hence, it is not surprising that the courts were especially concerned about converting state malpractice claims into federal EMTALA claims. In *Bryant,* the Court observed that the stabilization requirement would not cease upon the patient's admission to the hospital "if a patient demonstrates in a particular case that inpatient admission was a ruse to avoid EMTALA's requirements." 289 F.3d at 1169. A federal district court invoked that point in a case in which a patient was sent home after admission but before his injuries had been stabilized. Morgan v. North Mississippi Medical Center, Inc., 403 F. Supp. 2d 1115, 1130 (S.D. Ala. 2005). Although the court denied the hospital's motion to dismiss the EMTALA claim, it ultimately concluded on summary judgment that the hospital had not engaged in a ruse to avoid EMTALA's requirements when it admitted the patient. Morgan v. North Mississippi Medical Center, Inc., 458 F. Supp. 2d 1341 (S.D. Ala. 2006).

In a final rule that took effect in 2003, the Centers for Medicare & Medicaid Services took the position that EMTALA does not apply to individuals who are inpatients or outpatients at a hospital. 42 C.F.R. §489.24(b), (d)(2). The Sixth Circuit, which concluded in the *Thornton* case, supra, that the obligation to stabilize persists through the patient's hospitalization, has rejected the regulation. Moses v. Providence Hospital & Medical Centers, Inc., 561 F.3d 573, 583 (6th Cir. 2009). The Third Circuit, on the other hand, has upheld the regulation. Torretti v. Main Line Hospitals, Inc., 580 F.3d 168, 174-176 (3d Cir. 2009) (interpreting 42 C.F.R. §489.24(b) when an EMTALA claim was brought by an outpatient). So too have many district courts. Thornhill v. Jackson Parish Hospital, 184 F. Supp. 3d 392, 399-400 (W.D. La. 2016) (citing cases).

6. *Appropriate Medical Screening.* In interpreting EMTALA's requirement of an "appropriate medical screening examination," courts have recognized an important tension between ensuring access to emergency care for all persons and creating a federal cause of action for charges of malpractice in the emergency department. If a person is sent home from the emergency department after a physician wrongly concludes that there is no serious health problem, the mistaken diagnosis may reflect either the negligent provision of care or the purposeful denial of care. A hospital trying to evade its EMTALA obligations might do so by giving undesired patients short

shrift when screening them. At the same time, patients who have been injured by malpractice may try to bring their claim under both state tort law and federal EMTALA law, thereby increasing their potential recovery, gaining access to a federal forum and its quicker judgments, and increasing their bargaining power with the hospitals by virtue of the latter's possible loss of its participation in Medicare. EMTALA claims are often appended to state tort claims when people sue for injuries allegedly caused by inadequate emergency care. Singer, supra note 1, 33 Hous. L. Rev. at 118 & n.22.

Courts have consistently stated that EMTALA cannot be used to bring claims for medical malpractice, and they have tried to distinguish between a denial of care and the negligent provision of care by looking at whether the hospital screened the patient in the same way it screens similarly situated patients. As the D.C. Circuit explained, the issue is whether the hospital "conform[ed] its treatment of a particular patient to its standard screening procedures. . . . [A]ny departure from standard screening procedures constitutes inappropriate screening." Gatewood v. Washington Healthcare Corp., 933 F.2d 1037, 1041 (D.C. Cir. 1991). Similarly, the Fourth Circuit has stated that EMTALA's screening requirement is designed to prevent "disparate treatment." Vickers v. Nash General Hospital, Inc., 78 F.3d 139, 143 (4th Cir. 1996). Hospitals are obligated only to "apply uniform screening procedures to all individuals coming to the emergency room." In re Baby K, 16 F.3d 590, 595 (4th Cir. 1994). Accord Correa v. Hospital San Francisco, 69 F.3d 1184 (1st Cir. 1995); Summers v. Baptist Medical Center, 91 F.3d 1132, 1138 (8th Cir. 1996); Repp v. Anadarko Municipal Hospital, 43 F.3d 519, 522 (10th Cir. 1994); Holcomb v. Monahan, 30 F.3d 116, 117 (11th Cir. 1994).

The Sixth Circuit has adopted a similar standard, although it has indicated that the departure from the hospital's standard screening procedures must have resulted from some invidious motive like bias against the patient on the basis of "race, sex, politics, occupation, education, personal prejudice, drunkenness, spite . . . distaste for the patient's condition (e.g., AIDS patients). . . ." Cleland v. Bronson Health Care Group, Inc., 917 F.2d 266, 271-272 (6th Cir. 1990); Roberts v. Galen of Virginia, 111 F.3d 405, 408-409 (6th Cir. 1997), rev'd in part, 525 U.S. 249 (1999). Even if the Sixth Circuit requires some invidious motive, would it ever be difficult to find a bias lurking that would be unacceptable under the *Cleland* standard? Perhaps not often, but see Garrett v. Detroit Medical Center, 2007 U.S. Dist. LEXIS 17584 (E.D. Mich. Mar. 14, 2007) (dismissing patient's EMTALA claim on grounds that the defendant hospital transferred the patient to a hospital so he could be treated at a hospital that was "in-network" for his insurance).

Since EMTALA requires hospitals to apply their standard screening procedures, cases can turn on whether the defendant hospital had established standard screening guidelines and whether the defendant physician had followed those guidelines. See, e.g., Delibertis v. Pottstown General Hospital, 152 F. Supp. 3d 394, 399-400 (E.D. Pa. 2016) (rejecting summary judgment since hospital presented evidence that treating physician followed his own standard practices rather than the hospital's standard practices).

For an argument that trial courts are too quick to grant summary judgment for hospitals on the question of whether patients received an appropriate screening, see Note, 87 N.Y.U. L. Rev. 591 (2012).

Despite the courts' admonition that EMTALA does not create a federal malpractice cause of action, there inevitably will be some overlap between EMTALA claims and malpractice claims. Do you see how a requirement that hospitals provide all patients with their standard screening procedures amounts to requiring that the hospitals provide nonnegligent care? See Demetrios G. Metropoulos, Note, Son of COBRA: The Evolution of a Federal Malpractice Law, 45 Stan. L. Rev. 263 (1992).

As the preceding discussion indicates, courts have interpreted the requirement of an appropriate screening examination as an equal treatment right rather than an entitlement right. But isn't EMTALA a statute that grants an entitlement rather than a right of equal treatment? Is there a way to define appropriate screening examination as an entitlement without turning it even more clearly into the equivalent of nonnegligent care?

7. *Further Reading.* On EMTALA and its **role in the health care system** (note 1), see Russell Korobkin, Determining Health Care Rights from Behind a Veil of Ignorance, 1998 U. Ill. L. Rev. 801; Paul T. Menzel, Justice and Fairness, 40 J.L. Med. & Ethics 582 (2012); Sara Rosenbaum, The Enduring Role of the Emergency Medical Treatment and Active Labor Act, 32 Health Aff. 2075 (2013); Sara Rosenbaum et al., EMTALA and Hospital "Community Engagement," 53 Buff. L. Rev. 499 (2005); Karen Rothenberg, Who Cares? The Evolution of the Legal Duty to Provide Emergency Care, 26 Hous. L. Rev. 21 (1989); Dana E. Schaffner, Note, EMTALA: All Bark and No Bite, 2005 U. Ill. L. Rev. 1021; Lawrence E. Singer, Look What They've Done to My Law, Ma: COBRA's Implosion, 33 Hous. L. Rev. 113 (1996); Annot., 104 A.L.R. Fed. 166.

On the **duty to stabilize** (note 2), see Mark A. Hall, The Unlikely Case in Favor of Patient Dumping, 28 Jurimetrics J. 389 (1990) ("In the great majority of cases, the federal standard will do nothing to prevent patient dumping. . . . Even for those patients who do require stabilization prior to transfer, the federal law will result only in a delay in the transfer."); Kenneth R. Wing & John R. Campbell, The Emergency Room Admission: How Far Does the "Open Door" Go?, 63 U. Det. L. Rev. 119 (1985); Will Jay Pirkey, Shameful Practice, 39 L.A. Law. 20 (July/Aug. 2016).

On the ethical and financial concerns with **undocumented immigrants** (note 2), see Maya Babu & Joseph Wolpin, Undocumented Immigrants, Healthcare Access and Medical Repatriation Following Serious Medical Illness, 3 J. Health & Life Sci. L. 83 (2009); Janet L. Dolgin & Katherine R. Dieterich, When Others Get Too Close, 19 Cornell J.L. & Pub. Pol'y 283 (2010); Svetlana Lebedinski, EMTALA: Treatment of Undocumented Aliens and the Financial Burden It Places on Hospitals, 7 J.L. Soc'y 146 (2005-2006); Jennifer M. Smith, Screen, Stabilize, and Ship: EMTALA, U.S. Hospitals, and Undocumented Immigrants, 10 Hous. J. Health L. & Pol'y 309 (2010); Michael J. Young & Lisa Soleymani Lehmann, Undocumented Injustice, 370 New Eng. J. Med. 669 (2014).

B. HOSPITAL LIABILITY

While most doctors are well insured, some are not; and even those who are do not always make the most attractive targets for suit. Moreover, many medical errors do not result from physicians' mistakes. Therefore, plaintiffs are sometimes eager to hold the institutions in which physicians practice responsible for bad medical outcomes. There are two prominent institutions: hospitals and insurers, especially

HMOs. These institutional targets of suit entail both unique theories of liability and unique defenses against liability, which the following material explores.

You will learn shortly that two distinct theories of liability have emerged: vicarious and direct. In the former, the institution is held strictly liable for acts of negligence by member physicians, based on the physician's relationship with the institution. Observe how this branch of liability takes shape according to differences in how types of physicians are connected with hospitals. Direct liability, the second branch, depends on showing some wrongdoing by the institution's management with respect to physician competence and patient care. Here, the issue is what responsibility is it realistic to assign to lay managers with respect to clinical matters? Overarching this development of legal doctrine is an evolution in judicial and public attitudes about the role that institutions play in the delivery of health care. This change has occurred both with respect to hospital liability and in the migration of liability from hospitals to HMOs. To set these materials in their historical context, then, we begin with a now outmoded but still seminal decision.

SCHLOENDORFF v. SOCIETY OF NEW YORK HOSPITAL

105 N.E. 92 (N.Y. 1914)

Cardozo, J.

In the year 1771, by royal charter of George III, the Society of the New York Hospital was organized for the care and healing of the sick. During the century and more which has since passed, it has devoted itself to that high task. It has no capital stock; it does not distribute profits; and its physicians and surgeons, both the visiting and the resident staff, serve it without pay. Those who seek it in search of health are charged nothing if they are needy, either for board or for treatment. The well-to-do are required by its by-laws to pay $7 a week for board, an amount insufficient to cover the per capita cost of maintenance. Whatever income is thus received is added to the income derived from the hospital's foundation, and helps to make it possible for the work to go on. The purpose is not profit, but charity. . . .

To this hospital, the plaintiff came in January, 1908. She was suffering from some disorder of the stomach. She asked the superintendent or one of his assistants what the charge would be, and was told that it would be $7 a week. She became an inmate of the hospital, and after some weeks of treatment, the house physician, Dr. Bartlett, discovered a lump, which proved to be a fibroid tumor. He consulted the visiting physician, Dr. Stimson, who advised an operation. The plaintiff's testimony is that the character of the lump could not, so the physicians informed her, be determined without an ether examination. She consented to such an examination, but notified Dr. Bartlett, as she says, that there must be no [surgical removal]. She was taken at night from the medical to the surgical ward and prepared for an operation by a nurse. On the following day ether was administered, and, while she was unconscious, a tumor was removed. Her testimony is that this was done without her consent or knowledge. She is contradicted both by Dr. Stimson and by Dr. Bartlett, as well as by many of the attendant nurses. For the purpose of this appeal, however, since a verdict was directed in favor of the defendant, her narrative, even if improbable, must be taken as true. Following the operation, and, according to the testimony of her witnesses, because of it, gangrene developed in her left arm, some of her fingers had to be amputated, and her sufferings were intense. She now seeks to charge the hospital with liability for the wrong.

Certain principles of law governing the rights and duties of hospitals, when maintained as charitable institutions have, after much discussion, become no longer doubtful. It is the settled rule that such a hospital is not liable for the negligence of its physicians and nurses in the treatment of patients. Hillyer v. St. Bartholomew's Hospital, [1909] 2 K.B. 820. This exemption has been placed upon two grounds. The first is that of implied waiver. It is said that one who accepts the benefit of a charity enters into a relation which exempts one's benefactor from liability for the negligence of his servants in administering the charity. The hospital remains exempt, though the patient makes some payment to help defray the cost of board. Such a payment is regarded as a contribution to the income of the hospital, to be devoted, like its other funds to the maintenance of the charity. The second ground of the exemption is the relation subsisting between a hospital and the physicians who serve it. It is said that this relation is not one of master and servant, but that the physician occupies the position, so to speak, of an independent contractor, following a separate calling, liable, of course, for his own wrongs to the patient whom he undertakes to serve, but involving the hospital in no liability, if due care has been taken in his selection. On one or the other, and often on both of these grounds, a hospital has been held immune from liability to patients for the malpractice of its physicians. The reasons that have led to the adoption of this rule are, of course, inapplicable where the wrong is committed by a servant of the hospital and the sufferer is not a patient. It is therefore also a settled rule that a hospital is liable to strangers—i.e., to persons other than patients—for the torts of its employees committed within the line of their employment.

In the case at hand, the wrong complained of is not merely negligence. It is trespass. Every human being of adult years and sound mind has a right to determine what shall be done with his own body; and a surgeon who performs an operation without his patient's consent commits an assault, for which he is liable in damages. This is true, except in cases of emergency where the patient is unconscious, and where it is necessary to operate before consent can be obtained. The fact that the wrong complained of here is trespass, rather than negligence, distinguishes this case from most of the cases that have preceded it. . . . [The plaintiff] had never waived the right to recover damages for any wrong resulting from this operation, for she had forbidden the operation. In this situation, the true ground for the defendant's exemption from liability is that the relation between a hospital and its physicians is not that of master and servant. The hospital does not undertake to act through them, but merely to procure them to act upon their own responsibility. . . .

The wrong was not that of the hospital; it was that of physicians, who were not the defendant's servants, but were pursuing an independent calling, a profession sanctioned by a solemn oath, and safeguarded by stringent penalties. If, in serving their patient, they violated her commands, the responsibility is not the defendant's; it is theirs. There is no distinction in that respect between the visiting and the resident physicians. Whether the hospital undertakes to procure a physician from afar, or to have one on the spot, its liability remains the same. . . .

It is true, I think, of nurses, as of physicians, that, in treating a patient, they are not acting as the servants of the hospital. The superintendent is a servant of the hospital; the assistant superintendents, the orderlies, and the other members of the administrative staff are servants of the hospital. But nurses are employed to carry out the orders of the physicians, to whose authority they are subject. The hospital undertakes to procure for the patient the services of a nurse. It does not undertake, through the agency of nurses, to render those services itself. The reported cases make no distinction in that respect between the position of a nurse and that of a physician and none is justified in principle. If there are duties performed by nurses foreign to their duties in carrying out the physician's orders, and having relation to the administrative conduct of the hospital, the fact is not established by this record, nor was it in the discharge of such duties that the defendant's nurses were then serving. The acts of preparation immediately preceding the operation are necessary to its successful performance, and are really part of the operation itself. They are not different in that respect from the administration of the ether. Whatever the nurse does in those preliminary stages is done, not as the servant of the hospital, but in the course of the treatment of the patient, as the delegate of the surgeon to whose orders she is subject. The hospital is not chargeable with her knowledge that the operation is improper any more than with the surgeon's.

If, however, it could be assumed that a nurse is a servant of the hospital, . . . [w]as she to infer from the plaintiff's words that a distinguished surgeon intended to mutilate the plaintiff's body in defiance of the plaintiff's orders? Was it her duty, as a result of this talk, to report to the superintendent of the hospital that the ward was about to be utilized for the commission of an assault? I think that no such interpretation of the facts would have suggested itself to any reasonable mind. The preparation for an ether examination is to some extent the same as for an operation. The hour was midnight, and the plaintiff was nervous and excited. . . . There may be cases where a patient ought not to be advised of a contemplated operation until shortly before the appointed hour. To discuss such a subject at midnight might cause needless and even harmful agitation. About such matters a nurse is not qualified to judge. She is drilled to habits of strict obedience. She is accustomed to rely unquestioningly upon the judgment of her superiors. No woman occupying such a position would reasonably infer from the plaintiff's words that it was the purpose of the surgeons to operate whether the plaintiff forbade it or not. I conclude, therefore, that the plaintiff's statements to the nurse on the night before the operation are insufficient to charge the hospital with notice of a contemplated wrong. . . .

The conclusion, therefore, follows that the trial judge did not err in his direction of a verdict. A ruling would, indeed, be an unfortunate one that might constrain charitable institutions, as a measure of self-protection, to limit their activities. A hospital opens its doors without discrimination to all who seek its aid. It gathers in its wards a company of skilled physicians and trained nurses, and places their services at the call of the afflicted, without scrutiny of the character or the worth of those who appeal to it, looking at nothing and caring for nothing beyond the fact of their affliction. In this beneficent work, it does not subject itself to liability for damages, though the ministers of healing whom it has selected have proved unfaithful to their trust.

Notes: Hospital Liability; Charitable and Governmental Immunity

1. Schloendorff. For a fascinating account of the history of this famous case, see Paul Lombardo, Phantom Tumors and Hysterical Women: Revising Our View of the Schloendorff Case, 33 J.L. Med. Ethics 791 (2005). He reveals that the unconsented operation was a hysterectomy.

Is Justice Cardozo's rejection of hospital liability as absolute as it first appears? What about the qualification, "if due care has been taken in [the doctor's] selection"? What if the court were more demanding about the nurse's duty to speak up?

2. *Charitable Immunity.* The rule of charitable immunity was subjected to an increasing number of exceptions—distinguishing between paying and nonpaying patients, patients and strangers, and administrative vs. professional acts—until it eventually crumbled in most states. The leading decision is President of Georgetown College v. Hughes, 130 F.2d 810 (D.C. Cir. 1942), which observed that charitable hospitals could simply purchase insurance to protect themselves from economic catastrophe. The gist of this changed attitude is best captured in a colorful dissent by the renowned Pennsylvania Justice Musmanno in Michael v. Hahnemann Medical College and Hospital of Philadelphia, 172 A.2d 769 (Pa. 1961):

> Hospitals then were little better than hovels in which the indigent were gathered for the primitive cures available. The wealthy and the well-to-do were cared for in their homes. The hospital or infirmary was more often than not part of the village parish. Charity in the biblical sense prevailed. And if it happened that some poor mortal was scalded by a sister of mercy, who exhausted from long hours of vigil and toil, accidentally spilled a ladle of hot soup on a hand extended for nourishment, there was no thought of lawsuits against the philanthropists who made the meager refuge possible. But if, following such a mishap, litigation should have been initiated in the courts, it is not difficult to understand why judges would be reluctant to honor such a complaint, convinced on the basis of humanity, that an enterprise utterly devoid of worldly gain should be exempt from liability. A successful lawsuit against such a feeble structure might well have demolished it and have thus paralyzed the only helping hand in the world of unconcern for the rag-clothed sick and the crutchless disabled.
>
> The situation today is quite different. Charitable enterprises are not housed in ramshackle wooden structures. They are not mere storm shelters to succor the traveler and temporarily refuge those stricken in a common disaster. Hospitals today, to a large extent, are mighty edifices, in stone, glass and marble. They maintain large staffs, they use the best equipment that science can devise, they utilize the most modern methods of helping themselves to the noblest purpose of man, that of helping one's stricken brother. But they do all this on a business basis, and properly so. . . . And if the hospital is a business for the purpose of collecting money, it must be a business for the purpose of meeting its obligations. . . .

So be it for hospitals, but what about physician groups? In an unusual but important decision, the Virginia Supreme Court considered whether faculty at the state's premier medical school qualified for charitable immunity. The Court held no, despite the organization's charitable tax exemption, because it operated much more as a normal for-profit business than as a charity. University of Virginia Health Services Foundation v. Morris, Va., 657 S.E.2d 512 (Va. 2008). Despite this shift in attitude, a number of states retain a version of charitable immunity in statutes that limit the amount of damages that can be recovered against nonprofit hospitals or charities generally. See Conners v. Northeast Hospital Corp., 439 Mass. 469 (2003) ($20,000 cap on damages against any charitable corporation protects a hospital in a suit by someone who slipped in its icy parking lot); Annot., 25 A.L.R.4th 517 (1983).

3. *Governmental Immunity.* Public hospitals might also claim governmental immunity under the common-law concept that "the king can do no wrong." See,

e.g., Withers v. University of Kentucky, 939 S.W.2d 340 (Ky. 1997) (university hospital is a "state agency" immune from suit). Most states, however, have abrogated governmental immunity to some degree by statute, as has the federal government. This abrogation is often limited, though, to "ministerial" or "proprietary" functions, thus preserving many of the same arcane distinctions that arose under charitable immunity and the *Schloendorff* rule. See, e.g., Moser v. Heistand, 681 A.2d 1322 (Pa. 1996) (immunity exists only for suits based simply on physician error, not for suits based on failures in administration that result in physician error). See generally John Akula, Sovereign Immunity and Health Care: Can Government Be Trusted?, 19(6) Health Aff. 152 (Dec. 2000). Substantial immunity is still common in many states for psychiatric hospitals, and full immunity is still preserved for injuries suffered during the course of active military duty. See Feres v. United States, 340 U.S. 135 (1950). In sharp contrast, Veterans Administration (VA) hospitals are subject by statute to a form of strict liability, without regard to negligence. See Brown v. Gardner, 513 U.S. 113 (1994).

4. *Subsequent Developments in Vicarious Liability.* The refusal to apply ordinary principles of respondeat superior even to employed nurses gave way in later decades to a rule that held the hospital responsible for "administrative" errors, in contrast with errors in medical judgment. What resulted was a string of arcane distinctions and inconsistent decisions concerning such routine medical acts as administering medication, giving injections, and applying casts. For instance, giving a blood transfusion to the wrong patient was considered "administrative," whereas giving the wrong blood to the right patient was labeled an error of medical judgment. See generally Bing v. Thunig, 143 N.E.2d 3 (N.Y. 1957). As will be seen in the next case, these cracks in hospitals' liability armor eventually led to the outright reversal of *Schloendorff* by *Bing*. The modern issue, then, becomes how does standard respondeat superior apply to physicians who are not, strictly speaking, employees.

On the modern status of hospital liability generally, see James Smith, Hospital Liability; Mary Bertolet & Lee Goldsmith, Hospital Liability: Law and Practice; Aspen Hospital Law Manual. Documenting a sharp rise in suits against nursing homes, see David G. Stevenson & David M. Studdert, The Rise of Nursing Home Litigation: Findings from a National Survey of Attorneys, 22(2) Health Aff. 219 (Mar. 2003).

DIGGS v. NOVANT HEALTH, INC.
628 S.E.2d 851 (N.C. App. 2006)

GEER, Judge.

In September 1999, plaintiff, who was in her early eighties, was diagnosed [with gall stone disease]. . . . Plaintiff chose to have [a surgeon] perform the gall bladder surgery [who] had hospital privileges at Forsyth Medical Center ("FMC") . . . [which] in turn is owned by Novant Health Inc. Plaintiff's gall bladder surgery required general anesthesia. Piedmont Anesthesia & Pain Consultants, P.A. ("Piedmont") had a contract . . . that granted Piedmont the exclusive right to provide anesthesia services at FMC. Piedmont employees Dr. Joseph McConville and nurse Sheila Crumb were responsible for administering anesthesia to plaintiff through an induction and intubation process. Ms. Crumb performed the intubation, which involved inserting a tube into plaintiff's trachea, under the supervision of Dr. McConville. Ms. Crumb made three attempts before successfully completing the intubation. At some point during the attempts, Ms. Crumb perforated plaintiff's esophagus, a fact that was not discovered until many hours after the gall bladder surgery was over. Plaintiff contends that as a result of that perforation, she has suffered severe and permanent injuries.

On 11 October 2002, plaintiff filed suit against not only the hospital defendants, but also Ms. Crumb, Dr. McConville, and Piedmont, . . . [alleging] that the hospital defendants were vicariously liable for the anesthesiology defendants' negligence, as well as the negligence of the hospital floor nurses who, following plaintiff's surgery, failed to immediately notice the perforation. . . . [The trial court granted summary judgment for the hospital defendants.]

A. Liability Based on Actual Agency

As this Court has held, "[u]nder the doctrine of *respondeat superior,* a hospital is liable for the negligence of a physician or surgeon acting as its agent. There will generally be no vicarious liability on an employer for the negligent acts of an independent contractor." This Court has established that "[t]he vital test in determining whether an agency relationship exists is to be found in the fact that the employer has or has not retained the right of control or superintendence over the contractor or employee as to details." Specifically, the principal must have the right to control *both the means and the details of the process* by which the agent is to accomplish his task in order for an agency relationship to exist.

In arguing that an agency relationship existed, plaintiff relies exclusively on two contracts entered into between Piedmont and FMC: the Anesthesia Agreement and the Anesthesia Services Agreement. The Anesthesia Services Agreement specifically provided, however, that FMC "shall neither have nor exercise any control or direction over the methods by which [Piedmont] or any Physician shall perform it or his work and functions." . . . Further, under the agreements, (1) the physicians associated with Piedmont are not prohibited from practicing outside of the Hospital; (2) Piedmont and the hospital bill patients separately for their respective services; (3) Piedmont is responsible for meeting its own hiring needs; and (4) Piedmont is responsible for managing its own scheduling. . . .

We hold that the provisions in the agreements between Piedmont and FMC are materially indistinguishable from those in . . . Hoffman v. Moore Reg'l Hosp., Inc., 114 N.C. App. 248, 251, 441 S.E.2d 567, 569 (1994) (upholding grant of summary judgment when the physician was a member of a private group, the physician's schedule was determined by the group rather than the hospital, and the patient was billed for the physician's services by the group and not the hospital). . . . Plaintiff has, therefore, failed to present sufficient evidence to establish a *prima facie* case of actual agency.

B. Liability Based on Apparent Agency

It is well-established that even in the absence of an agency relationship, "'[w]here a person, by words or conduct, represents or permits it to be represented that another is his agent, he will be estopped to deny the agency as against third persons, who have dealt, on the faith of such representation, with the person so held out as agent, even if no agency exists in fact.' " This doctrine of apparent agency was first considered by our Supreme Court as a basis for hospital liability for malpractice in Smith v. Duke Univ., 14 S.E.2d 643 (NC 1941): . . . [Citing *Schloendorff*, the court rejected both actual and apparent agency on the part of Duke University, even though it employed the doctor in question as a member of its medical school faculty, because he was employed to teach and treat indigent patients, and this patient was seen as part of his private practice, for which the patient paid the doctor separately.] . . .

Our Supreme Court has since recognized that, in the years following *Smith*, the nature of hospitals has substantially changed. After observing that the *Smith* assumptions regarding hospitals were "no longer appropriate in this era," the Court explained: "First of all, hospitals are now in the business of treatment. As stated in [Bing v. Thunig, 143 N.E.2d 3 (NY 1957), which overturned *Schloendorff*]:

> The conception that the hospital does not undertake to treat the patient, does not undertake to act through its doctors and nurses, but undertakes instead simply to procure them to act upon their own responsibility, no longer reflects the fact. Present day hospitals, as their manner of operation plainly demonstrates, do far more than furnish facilities for treatment. They regularly employ on a salary basis a large staff of physicians, nurses and internes [sic], as well as administrative and manual workers, and they charge patients for medical care and treatment, collecting for such services, if necessary, by legal action. Certainly, the person who avails himself of hospital facilities' expects that the hospital will attempt to cure him, not that its nurses or other employees will act on their own responsibility.

In applying the doctrine of apparent agency, courts throughout the country have struggled with this change in the nature of hospitals from institutions providing only facilities to institutions actually providing medical services, such as emergency room care or, as in this case, anesthesia. In Sword v. NKC Hosps., Inc., 714 N.E.2d 142 (Ind. 1999), the Indiana Supreme Court . . . noted that courts have employed apparent agency to hold hospitals liable for the negligence of independent contractors in both emergency room and anesthesia contexts. The court . . . pointed out that some jurisdictions ask whether the plaintiff reasonably believed that the hospital was providing the pertinent medical care, while other jurisdictions presume reliance. Over all, the court concluded that "[c]entral to both of these factors—that is, the hospital's manifestations and the patient's reliance—is the question of whether the hospital provided notice to the patient that the treating physician was an independent contractor and not an employee of the hospital." . . . According to *Sword*, . . . "a hospital generally will be able to avoid liability by providing meaningful written notice to the patient, acknowledged at the time of admission." The court noted, however, that written notice might not suffice if the patient did not have an adequate opportunity to make an informed choice, such as in the case of a medical emergency.

After conducting a similar survey of the development of the law nationwide, the South Carolina Supreme Court also chose to adopt [an apparent agency] approach. Simmons v. Tuomey Reg'l Med. Ctr., 533 S.E.2d 312, 322 (SC 2000). . . . The court limited application of this test "to those situations in which a patient seeks services at the hospital as an institution, and is treated by a physician who reasonably appears to be a hospital employee." It stressed that its holding did "not extend to situations in which the patient is treated in an emergency room by the patient's own physician after arranging to meet the physician there. Nor does our holding encompass situations in which a patient is admitted to a hospital by a private, independent physician whose only connection to a particular hospital is that he or she has staff privileges to admit patients to the hospital. Such patients could not reasonably believe his or her physician is a hospital employee." Comparable tests have been adopted in numerous other jurisdictions, particularly with respect to the rendering of anesthesia or emergency services. . . .

Defendants point to [our prior decision in] *Hoffman* as establishing a different test. . . . Although the plaintiff in *Hoffman*, who was admitted to a hospital at the request of her private physician for a particular procedure, did not choose the doctor who would perform that procedure, the consent form specifically listed five possible doctors and the patient was looking to one of those doctors to provide her care. The case fell squarely within the traditional *Smith* analysis regarding treating physicians. There was no indication in the opinion that the hospital was holding itself out as providing the services involved as opposed to simply providing facilities for the performance of the procedure by private practitioners. Under those circumstances, this Court required evidence "that Mrs. Hoffman would have sought treatment elsewhere or done anything differently had she known for a fact that [the doctor] was not an employee of the hospital."

When, however, a hospital does hold itself out as providing services, we . . . are . . . persuaded by the weight of authority from other jurisdictions. Under this approach, a plaintiff must prove that (1) the hospital has held itself out as providing medical services, (2) the plaintiff looked to the hospital rather than the individual medical provider to perform those services, and (3) the patient accepted those services in the reasonable belief that the services were being rendered by the hospital or by its employees. A hospital may avoid liability by providing meaningful notice to a patient that care is being provided by an independent contractor. See, e.g., Cantrell v. Northeast Ga. Med. Ctr., 235 Ga. App. 365, 368, 508 S.E.2d 716, 719-720 (1998) (concluding that trial court did not err in granting a directed verdict to hospital when "conspicuous signage was posted and forms signed by the patient or representative revealed the independent contractor status of the doctor").

Plaintiff has submitted sufficient evidence to meet this test. The hospital had a Department of Anesthesiology with a Chief of Anesthesiology and a Medical Director, a fact that a jury could reasonably find indicated to the public that FMC was providing anesthesia services to its patients. Further, defendants chose to provide those services by contracting with Piedmont to provide anesthesia services to the hospital on an exclusive basis. Piedmont doctors served as the hospital's Chief of Anesthesiology and anesthesia Medical Director. As Dr. McConville put it, his group "provide[d] the anesthesia services for the operating room at Forsyth." . . . Plaintiff and other surgical patients had no choice as to who would provide anesthesia services for their operations.

Plaintiff's affidavit states that she was unaware that Dr. McConville and Ms. Crumb were not employees of the hospital. . . . In addition, plaintiff pointed to the form on FMC letterhead that she signed entitled "Consent to Operation and/or Other Procedures." The form specified: "I therefore authorize *my physician*, his or her associates or assistants to perform such surgical procedures as they, in the exercise of their professional judgment, deem necessary and advisable." (Emphasis added.) By contrast, with respect to anesthesia services, the form stated: "I authorize the administration of such anesthetics as may be necessary or advisable *by the anesthetist/anesthesiologist responsible for this service and I request the administration of such anesthetics.*" . . . A jury could decide based on this form that plaintiff was, through this form, requesting anesthesia services from FMC and that—given the distinction made between plaintiff's personal physician and the unnamed anesthesiologist—plaintiff was accepting those services in the reasonable belief that the services would be provided by the hospital and its employees. . . .

Given the current record, we hold that the trial court erred in granting summary judgment with respect to plaintiff's claims based on apparent agency. . . . Plaintiff has also argued (1) that the hospital defendants owed plaintiff a non-delegable duty and (2) that the hospital defendants are liable, even apart from agency principles, for the failure to obtain informed consent from plaintiff regarding anesthesia services. . . . [B]ecause of our resolution of this appeal, we need not address these alternative arguments. . . .

Notes: Hospital Vicarious Liability

1. *Employed Physicians.* Under modern law, there is universal agreement that hospitals are vicariously liable for their employed physicians and nurses. Principles of actual agency determine when doctors are hospital agents even when they are not official employees. Notice how the hospital in *Diggs* had carefully arranged its anesthesiology contract to avoid actual agency, following factors specified in an earlier N.C. appellate court decision. But, what about different contracts at other hospitals? In Adamski v. Tacoma General Hospital, 579 P.2d 970 (Wash. App. 1978), the court allowed a jury trial on actual agency for emergency room physicians when the hospital billed patients for their services, among other factors.

2. *Hospital Control.* Is it consistent with the corporate practice of medicine doctrine, discussed in Chapter 4.B.3, to hold a hospital responsible for the professional mistakes of its agent-physicians? The corporate practice of medicine doctrine holds that it is illegal for corporations to subject physicians to the control of lay management because this would constitute the unlicensed practice of medicine. If respondeat superior liability is premised on the principal's control of an agent's actions, how can it coexist with this prohibition of corporate control of physicians? One court, agreeing with this logic, surprisingly held that a health center cannot, as a matter of law, be held responsible for a physician's negligence. Daly v. Aspen Center for Women's Health, 134 P.3d 450 (Colo. App. 2005). Another decision, issued with respect to an HMO, found it necessary to declare the corporate practice of medicine doctrine "totally abolished" in order to hold the HMO vicariously liable for an employed physician's mistake. Sloan v. Metropolitan Health Council of Indianapolis, 516 N.E.2d 1104 (Ind. Ct. App. 1987). The court also reasoned, consistent with other decisions, that respondeat superior does not require actual control but merely a finding that the negligent acts occurred within the course and scope of employment. Otherwise, hospitals could not be held responsible for employed nurses, or airlines for employed pilots. Perhaps based on this thinking, other courts have not found it necessary to abolish the corporate practice of medicine doctrine in order to hold hospitals liable for physicians' errors. See, e.g., McDonald v. Hampton Training School for Nurses, 486 S.E.2d 299 (Va. 1997) (vicarious liability attaches

even though hospital does not control actual medical judgment); Dias v. Brigham Medical Associates, Inc., 438 Mass. 317 (2002) (same, for a medical group).

3. *"Captain of the Ship."* One hospital defense against vicarious liability that still remains is the "captain of the ship" or borrowed servant doctrine. The effect of this doctrine is not only to hold physicians (usually surgeons) responsible for subordinate doctors and nurses, but sometimes also to relieve the hospital from vicarious responsibility. This occurs when a hospital employee's negligent acts are directed or supervised by a physician who is not an agent of the hospital; then, the independent physician can be found to have temporarily "borrowed" the hospital's employee. Courts usually find that the hospital and the physician in charge share the employee and therefore share liability. See, e.g., Tonsic v. Wagner, 329 A.2d 497 (Pa. 1974). However, courts sometimes hold the doctor solely liable if he instructs the nurse to perform an act that contravenes hospital policy. See, e.g., Hoffman v. Wells, 397 S.E.2d 696 (Ga. 1990). See also Restatement (Second) of Agency §227.

4. *Indemnification Agreements.* The principles of vicarious liability introduced here apply to other medical institutions than just hospitals. Materials below explore for instance how vicarious liability applies to HMOs. Earlier, it was observed that physician practice groups or clinics can be held liable as an entity for the negligence of one of their members. It is possible in all of these circumstances, however, to reallocate liability among the parties through the use of indemnification agreements. These agreements do not alter the rights of the injured patient, but they do affect which of several joint tortfeasors can seek contribution or indemnification from the others. Negotiating these indemnification agreements is a major aspect of contract drafting, especially in managed care settings.

5. *Ostensible Agency.* Even though the *Diggs* court claims that facts and circumstances matter, how different would the next case be if the surgical consent form refers to "*my* anesthesiologist" rather than "*the* anesthesiologists"? Or, what if the hospital were to have patients sign a separate disclaimer form acknowledging that all doctors are independent contractors and not hospital agents? In the emergency room context, most modern courts hold that hospitals are subject to a jury finding of ostensible agency for emergency room physicians regardless of the specifics of the arrangement. The courts' reasoning is reflected in the following cases: Gilbert v. Sycamore Municipal Hospital, 622 N.E.2d 788 (Ill. 1993) (hospital advertising itself as offering quality care contributes to the impression that doctors work for the hospital); Simmons v. Tuomey Regional Medical Center, 533 S.E.2d 312 (S.C. 2000) (patient did not specifically choose any of the emergency room physicians that treated her); Whitlow v. Rideout Memorial Hospital, 237 Cal. App. 4th 631 (2015) (disclaimer of agency in admission form and on wall signs may not have been adequate notice for patient in excruciating pain). To the contrary, see Frezados v. Ingalls Memorial Hosp., 991 N.E.2d 817 IIll. App. 2013) ("Nearly everyone who seeks emergency treatment is in some physical or emotional distress, and were we to hold that such distress could operate to nullify provisions in an otherwise duly signed treatment consent form, hospitals would always be required to proceed to trial on claims of vicarious liability.").

In non-emergency contexts like that in *Diggs*, where ostensible agency is applied to hospital-based specialists such as radiologists and anesthesiologists, some courts are more open to argument both ways, depending on the facts and circumstances. See, e.g., Milliron v. Francke, 793 P.2d 824 (Mont. 1990) (providing radiologist with office, equipment, personnel, and billing is not sufficient to establish agency relationship; in a rural setting, it is understood this is necessary to maintain adequate staffing). However, most courts find their way to allowing the case to go to trial. E.g., Burless v. West Virginia University Hospitals, Inc., 601 S.E.2d 85 (W. Va. 2004) (disclaimer in a consent form was not sufficient to inform patient giving birth that university physicians were not hospital employees); Sword v. NKC Hospitals, 714 N.E.2d 142 (Ind. 1999) (anesthesiologist could be found to be an apparent agent of a hospital that "aggressively marketed its services to the public . . . [as] 'the most technically sophisticated birthplace in the region' and touted the 'full availability of a special anesthesiology team, experienced and dedicated exclusively to OB patients' "); York v. Rush-Presbyterian-St. Luke's Medical Center, 854 N.E.2d 635 (Ill. 2006) (similar, based on 28-page analysis of detailed testimony, even for a patient who himself was a surgeon and who picked most of his own doctors).

6. *Office-Based Physicians.* Do you think the ostensible agency doctrine could apply to specialists who are not entirely hospital based, such as surgeons or consultants referred by a patient's primary care physician? After all, hospitals also have departments of cardiology and surgery, and patients often do not pick their own surgeons or cardiologists (for instance, if their heart or surgical problem develops while they're in the hospital for a different problem, or if they enter the hospital through the emergency room before being transferred to a regular hospital room). So far, only Puerto Rico courts have not gone this far, holding hospitals vicariously liable whenever a patient "goes directly to the hospital seeking medical aid and the hospital 'provides' the physicians who treat him [or her], . . . because [then] the patient has entrusted his or her health to the hospital." Casillas-Sanchez v. Ryder Memorial Hosp., 960 F.Supp.2d 362 (D.P.R. 2013). In contrast, this court held that the hospital cannot be held vicariously liable "when the patient has first gone directly to the physician's private office and then is treated at the hospital on the physician's recommendation merely because said institution is one of several which the physician has the privilege of using." At present, this is a distinctly minority position, but a few other courts appear willing to expand vicarious liability to any situation where "a patient seeks treatment from a hospital and not from a particular physician of the patient's choosing." Syracuse v. Diao, 707 N.Y.S.2d 570 (App. Div. 2000) (allowing case to go to trial where a patient simply called a specialized surgery center to request an appointment but did not ask for a particular physician).

7. *Enterprise Liability.* Notice the *Diggs* court's brief mention at the end of an argument based on "non-delegable duty," also known as "enterprise liability." This concept would hold hospitals automatically liable for all acts of negligence, either within particular departments or for all physicians within their walls, regardless of the specifics of actual or apparent agency—even if the doctor is conceded to be an obvious independent contractor. The rationale for a nondelegable duty is that the public policy supporting hospital responsibility is so strong that, as a matter of law, the hospital may not avoid responsibility by delegating the function to an independent contractor. The classic example is an airline that attempts to shield itself from liability by retaining pilots as independent contractors.

So far, this nondelegable duty concept has been applied in only a few cases and only to emergency room care. The leading case is Jackson v. Power, 743 P.2d 1376 (Alaska 1987). Based on hospital licensing statutes and Joint Commission accreditation standards, the court observed that the hospital had assumed a duty to ensure adequate emergency room services. The court then concluded that a hospital "may not shield itself from liability by claiming that it is not responsible for the results of negligently performed health care when the law imposes a duty on the hospital to provide that health care. . . . We simply cannot fathom why liability should depend upon the technical employment status of the emergency room physician who treats the patient." Is this reasoning necessarily limited to emergency room care? So far, this is as far as courts have taken it. See Fletcher v. South Peninsula Hospital, 71 P.3d 833 (Alaska 2003) (refusing to extend the doctrine to surgeons).

8. *The Next Stage.* Falling between vicarious liability for some physicians and enterprise liability for all physicians is a position known as "direct institutional liability," in which hospitals are held liable even for acts of independent physicians, but only if the hospital management breached a duty of care owed directly to patients with respect to selecting or supervising the physician. That theory of liability is thought to have been introduced by the next case. See if you can discern in this case a major shift in liability, or instead whether its holding rests on a more conventional application of vicarious liability. To the extent it presages a new duty of hospitals, precisely what is the content of that duty?

■ DARLING v. CHARLESTON COMMUNITY MEMORIAL HOSPITAL

211 N.E.2d 253 (Ill. 1965), cert. denied, 383 U.S. 946 (1966)

SCHAEFER, Justice.

. . . On November 5, 1960, the plaintiff, who was 18 years old, broke his leg while playing in a college football game. He was taken to the emergency room at the defendant hospital where Dr. Alexander, who was on emergency call that day, treated him. Dr. Alexander, with the assistance of hospital personnel, applied traction and placed the leg in a plaster cast. A heat cradle was applied to dry the cast. Not long after the application of the cast plaintiff was in great pain and his toes, which protruded from the cast, became swollen and dark in color. They eventually became cold and insensitive. On the evening of November 6, Dr. Alexander "notched" the cast around the toes, and on the afternoon of the next day he cut the cast approximately three inches up from the foot. On November 8, he split the sides of the cast with a Stryker saw; in the course of cutting the cast the plaintiff's leg was cut on both sides. Blood was observed by the nurses and others, and there was a stench in the room, which one witness said was the worst he had smelled since World War II. The plaintiff remained in Charleston Hospital until November 19, when he was transferred to Barnes Hospital in St. Louis and placed under the care of Dr. Fred Reynolds, head of orthopedic surgery at Washington University School of Medicine and Barnes Hospital. Dr. Reynolds found that the fractured leg contained a considerable amount of dead tissue which in his opinion resulted from interference with the circulation of blood in the limb caused by swelling or hemorrhaging of the leg against the construction of the cast. Dr. Reynolds performed several operations in a futile attempt to save the leg but ultimately it had to be amputated eight inches below the knee.

The evidence before the jury is set forth at length in the opinion of the Appellate Court and need not be stated in detail here. The plaintiff contends that it established that the defendant was negligent in permitting Dr. Alexander to do orthopedic work of the kind required in this case, and not requiring him to review his operative procedures to bring them up to date; in failing, through its medical staff, to exercise adequate supervision over the case, especially since Dr. Alexander had been placed on emergency duty by the hospital, and in not requiring consultation, particularly after complications had developed. Plaintiff contends also that in a case which developed as this one did, it was the duty of the nurses to watch the protruding toes constantly for changes of color, temperature and movement, and to check circulation every ten to twenty minutes, whereas the proof showed that these things were done only a few times a day. Plaintiff argues that it was the duty of the hospital staff to see that these procedures were followed, and that either the nurses were derelict in failing to report developments in the case to the hospital administrator, he was derelict in bringing them to the attention of the medical staff, or the staff was negligent in failing to take action. Defendant is a licensed and accredited hospital, and the plaintiff contends that the licensing regulations, accreditation standards, and its own bylaws define the hospital's duty, and that an infraction of them imposes liability for the resulting injury.

The defendant's position is stated in the following excerpts from its brief:

> It is a fundamental rule of law that only an individual properly educated and licensed, and not a corporation, may practice medicine. . . . Accordingly, a hospital is powerless under the law to forbid or command any act by a physician or surgeon in the practice of his profession. . . . A hospital is not an insurer of the patient's recovery, but only owes the patient the duty to exercise such reasonable care as his known condition requires and that degree of care, skill and diligence used by hospitals generally in that community. . . . Where the evidence shows that the hospital care was in accordance with standard practice obtaining in similar hospitals, and Plaintiff produces no evidence to the contrary, the jury cannot conclude that the opposite is true even if they disbelieve the hospital witnesses. . . . A hospital is not liable for the torts of its nurse committed while the nurse was but executing the orders of the patient's physician, unless such order is so obviously negligent as to lead any reasonable person to anticipate that substantial injury would result to the patient from the execution of such order. . . . The extent of the duty of a hospital with respect to actual medical care of a professional nature such as is furnished by a physician is to use reasonable care in selecting medical doctors. When such care in the selection of the staff is accomplished, and nothing indicates that a physician so selected is incompetent or that such incompetence should have been discovered, more cannot be expected from the hospital administration.

The basic dispute, as posed by the parties, centers upon the duty that rested upon the defendant hospital. That dispute involves the effect to be given to . . . hospital regulations adopted by the State Department of Public Health under the Hospital Licensing Act, to the Standards for Hospital Accreditation of the American Hospital Association, and to the bylaws of the defendant. . . .

> The conception that the hospital does not undertake to treat the patient, does not undertake to act through its doctors and nurses, but undertakes instead simply to procure them to act upon their own responsibility, no longer reflects the fact. Present-day hospitals, as their manner of operation plainly demonstrates, do far more than furnish facilities for treatment. They regularly employ on a salary basis a large staff of physicians, nurses and internes, as well as administrative and manual workers, and they charge patients for medical care and treatment, collecting for such services, if necessary, by legal action. Certainly, the person who avails himself

> of "hospital facilities" expects that the hospital will attempt to cure him, not that its nurses or other employees will act on their own responsibility. (Fuld, J., in Bing v. Thunig (1957), 2 N.Y.2d 656, 163 N.Y.S.2d 3, 11, 143 N.E.2d 3, 8.)

The Standards for Hospital Accreditation, the state licensing regulations and the defendant's bylaws demonstrate that the medical profession and other responsible authorities regard it as both desirable and feasible that a hospital assume certain responsibilities for the care of the patient.

We now turn to an application of these considerations to this case. . . . [W]e need not analyze all of the issues submitted to the jury. Two of them were that the defendant had negligently:

> 5. Failed to have a sufficient number of trained nurses for bedside care of all patients at all times capable of recognizing the progressive gangrenous condition of the plaintiff's right leg, and of bringing the same to the attention of the hospital administration and to the medical staff so that adequate consultation could have been secured and such conditions rectified; . . .
>
> 7. Failed to require consultation with or examination by members of the hospital surgical staff skilled in such treatment; or to review the treatment rendered to the plaintiff and to require consultants to be called in as needed.

We believe that the jury verdict [against the hospital] is supportable on either of these grounds. On the basis of the evidence before it the jury could reasonably have concluded that the nurses did not test for circulation in the leg as frequently as necessary, that skilled nurses would have promptly recognized the conditions that signalled a dangerous impairment of circulation in the plaintiff's leg, and would have known that the condition would become irreversible in a matter of hours. At that point, it became the nurses' duty to inform the attending physician, and if he failed to act, to advise the hospital authorities so that appropriate action might be taken. As to consultation, there is no dispute that the hospital failed to review Dr. Alexander's work or require a consultation; the only issue is whether its failure to do so was negligence. On the evidence before it the jury could reasonably have found that it was. . . .

Judgment affirmed.

■ JOHNSON v. MISERICORDIA COMMUNITY HOSPITAL

301 N.W.2d 156 (Wis. 1981)

COFFEY, Justice.

. . . This action arose out of a surgical procedure performed at Misericordia by Dr. Salinsky on July 11, 1975, in which he unsuccessfully attempted to remove a pin fragment from Johnson's right hip. During the course of this surgery, the plaintiff's common femoral nerve and artery were damaged causing a permanent paralytic condition of his right thigh muscles with resultant atrophy and weakness and loss of function. . . .

[T]he jury found that Salinsky was negligent with respect to the medical care and treatment he afforded the plaintiff and attributed 20 percent of the causal negligence to him and 80 percent to the hospital. . . . [T]he only facts material to this review are those connected with Misericordia Hospital in appointing Dr. Salinsky to the medical staff with orthopedic privileges.

The record establishes that Misericordia was formerly . . . a nursing home known as Downtown Nursing Home, Inc. Subsequently, . . . all of the nursing home services were discontinued and the name "Misericordia Community Hospital" was adopted. The hospital known as Misericordia Community Hospital was not and has not been accredited by the Joint Commission on Accreditation of Hospitals. . . .

Dr. Salinsky applied for orthopedic privileges on the medical staff. In his application, Salinsky stated that . . . his privileges at other hospitals had never "been suspended, diminished, revoked, or not renewed." In another part of the application form, he failed to answer any of the questions pertaining to his malpractice insurance. . . .

Mrs. Jane Bekos, Misericordia's medical staff coordinator (appointed April of 1973), testifying from the hospital records, noted that Salinsky's appointment to the medical staff was recommended by the then hospital administrator, David A. Scott, Sr., on June 22, 1973. Salinsky's appointment and requested orthopedic privileges, according to the hospital records, were not marked approved until August 8, 1973. This approval of his appointment was endorsed by Salinsky himself. Such approval would, according to accepted medical administrative procedure, not be signed by the applicant but by the chief of the respective medical section. Additionally, the record establishes that Salinsky was elevated to the position of Chief of Staff shortly after he joined the medical staff. However, the court record and the hospital records are devoid of any information concerning the procedure utilized by the Misericordia authorities in approving either Salinsky's appointment to the staff with orthopedic privileges, or his elevation to the position of Chief of Staff.

Mrs. Bekos, testified that . . . she failed to contact any of the references in Salinsky's case. . . . Further, Mrs. Bekos stated that an examination of the Misericordia records reflected that at no time was an investigation made by anyone of any of the statements recited in his application. . . .

Dr. A. Howell, the hospital's medical director, stated that the hospital did not have a functioning credentials committee at this time, and therefore the executive committee . . . assume[d] the responsibility of evaluating and approving applications for medical staff privileges. . . . [T]he minutes of [the June 21st] meeting list Salinsky as an attending member of the defendant's medical staff at the meeting despite the fact that Salinsky's application for staff privileges had neither been recommended for approval, nor approved by the committee as of this date. . . .

At trial, the representatives of two Milwaukee hospitals, . . . gave testimony concerning the accepted procedure for evaluating applicants for medical staff privileges. Briefly, they stated that the hospital's governing body, i.e., the board of directors or board of trustees, has the ultimate responsibility in granting or denying staff privileges. However, the governing board delegates the responsibility of evaluating the professional qualifications of an applicant for clinical privileges to the medical staff. The credentials committee (or committee of the whole) conducts an investigation of the applying physician's or surgeon's education, training, health, ethics and experience through contacts with his peers in the specialty in which he is seeking privileges, as well as the references listed in his application to determine the veracity of his statements and to solicit comments dealing with the applicant's credentials.

Once the credentials committee (or committee of the whole) has conducted their investigation and reviewed all of the information bearing on the applicant's qualifications, it relays its judgment to the governing body, which, as noted, has the final appointing authority.

The record demonstrates that had the executive committee of Misericordia, in the absence of a current credentials committee, adhered to the standard and accepted practice of investigating a medical staff applicant's qualifications and thus examined Salinsky's degree, postgraduate training, and contacted the hospitals referred to in his application, it would have found, contrary to his representations, that he had in fact experienced denial and restriction of his privileges, as well as never having been granted privileges at the very same hospitals he listed in his application. This information was readily available to Misericordia, and a review of Salinsky's associations with various Milwaukee orthopedic surgeons and hospital personnel would have revealed that they considered Salinsky's competence as an orthopedic surgeon suspect, and viewed it with a great deal of concern. . . .

[W]e hold that a hospital has a duty to exercise due care in the selection of its medical staff. . . . [O]ur holding is supported by the decisions of a number of courts from other jurisdictions. See . . . Annot., 51 A.L.R.3d 981 (1973). These cases hold that a hospital has a direct and independent responsibility to its patients, over and above that of the physicians and surgeons practicing therein, to take reasonable steps to (1) insure that its medical staff is qualified for the privileges granted and/or (2) to evaluate the care provided. . . .

The resolution of the issue of whether the hospital was negligent in granting Salinsky orthopedic surgical privileges and appointing him to its medical staff depends on whether Misericordia exercised that degree of care and skill as the average hospital exercises in selecting its medical staff. Applying this standard to the facts of this case, Johnson was only required to show that the defendant did not exercise reasonable care (that degree of care ordinarily exercised by the average hospital) to determine whether Salinsky was competent. . . . Therefore, the trial court's instruction that the hospital was required to exercise reasonable care in the granting of medical staff privileges and that reasonable care "meant that degree of care, skill and judgment usually exercised under like or similar circumstances by the average hospital," was proper.

Turning to the plaintiff's proof requirements, since the procedures ordinarily employed by hospitals in evaluating applications for staff privileges are not within the realm of the ordinary experience of mankind, we agree with the ruling of the appellate court that expert testimony was required to prove the same. . . .

There was credible evidence to the effect that a hospital, exercising ordinary care, would not have appointed Salinsky to its medical staff. Mr. Harden, administrator for Family Hospital, testified a hospital governing board with knowledge that an applicant for medical staff privileges had his orthopedic surgical privileges revoked at one hospital, on the recommendation of a panel of three orthopedic surgeons, and that his orthopedic privileges at another hospital were confined to simple operative procedures, would not, on the basis of this information, have granted him surgical privileges in that specialty. Dr. Sam Neeseman stated that a hospital's credentials committee, with knowledge of such events would not, in the exercise of ordinary care, have approved the applicant's request for orthopedic privileges. . . . Thus, the jury's finding of negligence on the part of Misericordia must be upheld as the testimony of Mr. Harden and Dr. Neeseman constituted credible evidence which reasonably supports this finding. . . .

[A]lthough [a hospital] must rely on the medical staff and in particular the credentials committee (or committee of the whole) to investigate and evaluate an applicant's qualifications for the requested privileges, . . . this delegation of the responsibility to investigate and evaluate the professional competence of applicants for clinical privileges does not relieve the governing body of its duty to appoint only qualified physicians and surgeons to its medical staff and periodically monitor and review their competency. . . . The facts of this case demonstrate that a hospital should, at a minimum, require completion of the application and verify the accuracy of the applicant's statements, especially in regard to his medical education, training and experience. Additionally, it should: (1) solicit information from the applicant's peers, including those not referenced in his application, who are knowledgeable about his education, training, experience, health, competence and ethical character; (2) determine if the applicant is currently licensed to practice in this state and if his licensure or registration has been or is currently being challenged; and (3) inquire whether the applicant has been involved in any adverse malpractice action and whether he has experienced a loss of medical organization membership or medical privileges or membership at any other hospital. The investigating committee must also evaluate the information gained through its inquiries and make a reasonable judgment as to the approval or denial of each application for staff privileges. The hospital will be charged with gaining and evaluating the knowledge that would have been acquired had it exercised ordinary care in investigating its medical staff applicants. . . . This is not to say that hospitals are insurers of the competence of their medical staff, for a hospital will not be negligent if it exercises the noted standard of care in selecting its staff.

Notes: Hospitals' Direct Liability; Risk Management Programs

1. *Direct vs. Vicarious Liability. Darling* is undoubtedly the most significant hospital liability case in the past 50 years. It is frequently referred to as a landmark decision in the field of hospital liability because it placed at least some degree of direct responsibility on the hospital for the maintenance of an acceptable standard of care of patients. Direct or "corporate" liability contrasts with vicarious liability in that it imposes on hospitals a duty of care owed directly to patients with respect to medical judgment. Conventional forms of direct liability entail primarily administrative, not medical, functions such as maintaining safe premises, sterile equipment, and adequate rules and regulations. *Darling* is recognized as extending direct corporate liability to substandard medical care rendered by independent doctors. Hospitals thus can be found liable for some act of negligence on their part with respect to patient care decisions made by independent doctors; vicarious liability, on the other hand, attaches regardless of the degree of hospital care but only when doctors are actual or apparent agents.

2. Darling*'s Progeny.* Consider whether the *Darling* court actually intended to announce a new theory of liability. How else could the case have been reasoned, using principles from the previous case and notes? Commentators have observed that *Darling* achieved its status largely by virtue of the importance that academic

commentators and subsequent decisions attached to it, and the vocal reaction of hospitals and physicians. The leading commentator was health law professor Arthur Southwick, in The Hospital's New Responsibility, 17 Clev.-Marshall L. Rev. 146 (1968); and The Hospital as an Institution—Expanding Responsibilities Change Its Relationship with the Staff Physician, 9 Cal. W.L. Rev. 429 (1973). See generally Annot., 62 A.L.R.4th 692 (1988).

3. *Enterprise Liability and the Balance of Power.* What reaction to *Darling* would you expect from the medical profession and the hospital industry? Surprisingly, *Darling* was openly embraced by hospitals but vehemently attacked by physicians. It greatly influenced the standards of the Joint Commission and virtually became the official philosophy of the American Hospital Association. The AMA's reaction to the *Darling* decision was immediate and negative. In considering why this would be so, consider what *Darling* signals about the power relationship between hospitals and physicians. Would it be fair to impose hospital responsibility for patient care without allowing hospital authority? In its comment on the case in 12 Citation 82 (1965), the AMA said, "The effect of this decision is unfortunate since it appears to place a hospital in a position where it must exercise control over the practice of medicine by physicians on its attending staff in order to avoid liability. This is apt to encourage control of the practice of medicine by persons who are not licensed physicians."

A similar reaction occurred in 1993 when President Clinton's health care reform task force aired an idea for medical malpractice reform known as exclusive enterprise liability. As discussed at page 104, exclusive enterprise liability would change existing law in two ways: (1) it would hold hospitals and HMOs vicariously liable for all negligent injuries caused by any member physician, regardless of status or contractual relationship with the institution; and (2) the institution would be solely liable, letting doctors entirely off the hook. Surprisingly, the hospital industry was interested in this idea but the AMA vehemently opposed it, causing the Clinton administration to quickly back away. Even though the AMA was clamoring for relief from medical malpractice, it viewed this proposal for abolishing physician liability as a Trojan Horse because of its implications for the relative power balance between doctors and medical institutions. See Frances Miller, Malpractice Liability and Physician Autonomy, 342 Lancet 973 (1993); Robert A. Berenson, Do Physicians Recognize Their Own Best Interests?, 13(2) Health Aff. 185 (1994).

Despite this hostility, some HMOs, most teaching hospitals, and virtually all government hospitals implement a de facto form of exclusive enterprise liability in which the institution pays for the physicians' malpractice insurance (usually as part of its own self-insured retention fund), defends all suits, and pays all judgments for claims arising from treatment at the institution. Reinforcing the policy argument in favor of a more general form of hospital enterprise liability, research documents that many medical errors in hospitals are due to flaws in the system of care rather than purely individual physician mistakes, but that hospitals lack a sufficient "business case" to improve patient safety because they internalize only a small percentage of the costs of medical error. See Michelle M. Mello et al., Who Pays for Medical Errors? An Analysis of Adverse Event Costs, the Medical Liability System, and Incentives for Patient Safety Improvement, 4 J. Empirical Leg. Stud. 835 (2007).

For these reasons, most legal scholars strongly favor broader hospital enterprise liability. See, e.g., Kenneth Abraham & Paul Weiler, Enterprise Liability and the Evolution of the American Health Care System, 108 Harv. L. Rev. 381 (1994); Barry Furrow,

Patient Safety and the Fiduciary Hospital, 1 Drexel L. Rev. 439 (2009); Philip G. Peters, Resuscitating Hospital Enterprise Liability, 73 Mo. L. Rev. 369-397 (2008).

4. *Duty to Supervise and Nursing Negligence. Darling* and its progeny identify two forms of hospital negligence with respect to physicians: negligent selection and retention, and negligent supervision. The first of these, which is developed in Johnson v. Misericordia Community Hospital, is much less controversial. Observe that it was recognized in passing even in *Schloendorff*, supra. It entails reviewing physicians' competency and performance history before admission to the medical staff and periodically (typically every two years) thereafter. Surprisingly, however, one modern court has refused to recognize a tort for negligent credentialing, reasoning that regulatory oversight of hospitals suffices. Paulino v. QHG of Springdale, Inc., 386 S.W.3d 462 (Ark. 2012).

The duty to supervise, in contrast, assumes *contemporaneous* supervision of daily treatment decisions *as they are made*. Several subsequent decisions have alluded to this duty of contemporaneous supervision, but few have squarely imposed it, distinct from the duty of care in selection and retention. Indeed, subsequent decisions in Illinois have expressly disavowed any such duty arising from *Darling*. See Essig v. Advocate BroMenn Medical Center, 33 N.E.3d 288 (Ill. App. Ct. 2015) ("the only logical inference from [plaintiffs'] argument is that [the hospital] should have appointed . . . a fully trained and licensed urologist to oversee [the surgeon] . . . and to veto the allegedly negligent course of treatment . . . . Of course, the law does not impose such a duty on hospitals").

Other courts, however, have rather explicitly imposed such a duty of active supervision, at least in dictum. See, e.g., Thompson v. Nason Hospital, 591 A.2d 703 (Pa. 1991). Usually, these are cases of gross negligence in which the departure from medical standards is so blatant that it is possible to attribute to hospital administrators' constructive knowledge of the error in progress. One route for attributing this knowledge is through nurses, under the logic that, at some point, nurses should object to or call to a supervisor's attention treatment that is going extremely badly. Because nurses are hospital employees, this theory essentially holds hospitals vicariously liable for nurses' failure to speak up or intervene. See Strubhart v. Perry Memorial Hospital, 903 P.2d 263 (Okla. 1995); T. Hardy, 61 Tul. L. Rev. 86 (1986) (the test under *Darling* should be "whether in a given situation a reasonable, prudent nurse would have spoken up about a physician's negligence"). Is this explanation consistent with the facts in *Darling*? Is it consistent with the practical realities of the doctor-nurse relationship? Recall Justice Cardozo's treatment of this very same theory of liability in *Schloendorff*, supra. See also Essig v. Advocate, supra ("it would be entirely inconsistent with both the scope of nursing practice and the applicable standard of care for an attending nurse to attempt to interfere with a surgeon, *in the midst of an ongoing surgery*").

5. *Risk Management.*

> The newly created role in hospitals of "risk manager" marks the official recognition of a role that has become central to the way hospitals are run. Their role is clearly defined . . . "to avoid or minimize potential legal, and hence, financial loss for the health care provider." Although they may fulfill several different administrative functions, . . . I contend that current risk management practices in hospitals have risen to a pitch of near hysteria. They embody actions that are unprecedented in

their intrusiveness into the doctor-patient relationship and are unethical in violating the rights of patients. . . . The typical responses of risk managers are wildly overactive. If people in ordinary life were to act in accordance with the minuscule probabilities on which risk management bases its decisions, we would all be in a constant state of paralysis. . . . Hospital administrators have refused to permit competent adult patients to reject burdensome treatment even when physicians concur with the patient's wish. It is not uncommon for administrators to request that a court order be obtained whenever there is a shred of doubt (which almost always exists) about what the law says. Where it was once physicians who overtreated patients because they believed it was their moral obligation to continue therapy, it is now hospital administrators and risk managers who more often insist on overtreatment out of fear of medical-legal liability. It is not a great exaggeration to view risk managers as enemies of patients. . . .

Who are these risk managers, and what is the origin of their role in the hospital? Some risk managers have law degrees, but most do not. Some are nurses who rose to the rank of supervisor and then moved into hospital administration, often after obtaining a master's degree. Others come from the ranks of hospital administrators, some with a degree in hospital or business administration. More rare are individuals with an advanced degree in a field such as sociology, and still others made their career in health planning or administration and were around long before the occupation of risk manager was invented. Large medical centers typically have an office of risk management in addition to in-house counsel. The staff of lawyers works together with risk management both in devising hospital policies that affect patients and in dealing with individual cases in which anyone suspects that there may be a risk of some sort.

The overall movement can be traced back to the late 1960s and early 1970s, when efforts were begun in industrial and other workplaces to reduce the costs of liability payments by underwriters and insurance companies. The trend widened, and in the 1980s risk management offices began to be established in hospitals . . . to deal with concerns about possible liability arising out of incident reports in the hospital: a patient falling out of bed, a visitor slipping in a puddle of water in the corridor, an inadvertent injury to a patient in the course of treatment. . . . The original worries about legal liability have now expanded to encompass everything that might place the hospital in a bad light. Risk managers are now charged with the task of minimizing risks other than those of liability. They look out for the projected risks of bad publicity, the actions of a disgruntled employee, or the possible political ramifications of a medical decision or hospital policy. . . . Even when the patient has no family, and there is no one around who would sue the hospital, risk management is brought into the case. One of the peculiar features of this situation is the nearly automatic response by many physicians to call risk management whenever the slightest uncertainty is voiced about an ethical matter or vaguely perceived to have legal implications. . . .

Ruth Macklin, Enemies of Patients (1993). Does this account confirm the fears of the AMA about the consequences for physicians of exposing hospitals to liability?

Hospitals are now required to have risk management programs by Joint Commission accreditation standards, and, in a few states, by hospital licensing laws. Risk management programs are now common also in nursing homes and HMOs. On their structure and content generally, see American Society for Healthcare Risk Management, Risk Management Handbook for Health Care Facilities (1990); B. Youngberg, Essentials of Hospital Risk Management (1990).

6. *Informed Consent Liability*. One form of physician supervision for which courts have been especially reluctant to impose hospital liability is the duty to obtain informed consent. One might suppose that it easily falls within the hospital's administrative functions to ensure that patients have signed the proper paperwork before major operations are conducted, especially since nurses usually have a central role in obtaining informed consent. Most courts, however, hold that informed consent is solely the responsibility of the physician because the delicate considerations of what exactly to tell the patient and when are matters "particularly calling for the exercise of medical judgment." Valles v. Albert Einstein Medical Center, 805 A.2d 1232 (Pa. 2002) (no liability even for employed physician because "a medical facility cannot maintain control over this aspect of the physician-patient relationship"). For a critique, see Robert Gatter, The Mysterious Survival of the Policy Against Informed Consent Liability for Hospitals, 81 Notre Dame L. Rev. 1203 (2006); Note, 1 Ind. Health L. Rev. 253 (2004).

7. *Self-Imposed Standards*. The hospital licensing regulations, accreditation standards, and hospital bylaws referred to in the *Darling* opinion contained statements such as the following:

[REGULATIONS]

The [hospital] board [of directors] shall be responsible for the maintenance of proper standards of professional work in the hospital and shall require that the medical staff function in conformity with reasonable standards of competency. . . .

[ACCREDITATION STANDARDS]

Maintaining high standards of medical care will depend upon the character of the [medical] staff and the effectiveness of its organization to carry out the following duties: 1. Selection of those recommended for staff appointments and hospital privileges. 2. Constant analysis and review of the clinical work done in the hospital. . . . It is the duty of the hospital [medical] staff through its chiefs of service and Executive Committee to see that members of the staff do not fail in the matter of calling consultants as needed.

[MEDICAL STAFF BYLAWS]

The purpose of this organization shall be to insure that all patients admitted to the hospital or treated in the outpatient department receive the best possible care.

Another important aspect of the court's holding is that standards such as these, to which the hospital subscribed or was bound, can be introduced as evidence, but not conclusive proof, of the customary standard of administrative care that prevails in the hospital industry. Is the effect of these standards to make a hospital strictly liable for any mistakes that doctors make? How would you revise these standards in order to perform their intended function in these various legal documents while at the same time moderating their liability effect?

8. *Hospital Custom*. Most courts hold hospitals to a national standard of care in selecting medical staff members. Would a similar locality standard be more appropriate? Consider the history and accreditation status of Misericordia Community

Hospital, which was a very small hospital with relatively few medical staff. Under the national standard, are these factors relevant to the "like or similar circumstances" qualifier? See Note, 1983 Wis. L. Rev. 453 (arguing that the *Misericordia* standards are too demanding for some hospitals). Observe, though, that the duty to fully investigate physicians' credentials is greatly eased now that hospitals can obtain records of past malpractice lawsuits and disciplinary actions by other hospitals from the National Practitioner Data Bank.

Hospital negligence cases are not as dependent on expert witnesses as are physician negligence cases, despite the *Johnson* court's holding on this point. Once the issue of physician negligence is established, issues of administrative care and proper oversight are subject to the "reasonable person" standard. Other courts sometimes hold that these issues are subject to commonsense understanding. If you were on a jury, would you consider a hospital negligent if it approved a physician who had been sued for malpractice three times in the past five years? If he had lost or settled two of the three suits for substantial amounts?

9. *Medical Staff Committees.* Observe the brief discussion at the end of *Johnson* concerning the legal effect of the hospital's delegating the task of medical staff credentialing to members and committees of the medical staff. Recall that medical staff members are, generally speaking, not agents of the hospital. Therefore, could a hospital not claim in a typical case, where it merely follows the medical staff's recommendation, that it is not responsible for their sloppiness or poor judgment? Assume the hospital board has no way to know that the medical staff did a poor job or made a bad decision. This defense does not work for two reasons: (1) Although medical staff members are independent contractors in their medical status as practicing doctors, they are agents of the hospital in their administrative status while sitting on medical staff committees. Therefore, ordinary respondeat superior applies to their committee mistakes. (2) The duty to screen medical staff members is considered nondelegable.

Distributing liability in the opposite direction, would it be possible to hold medical staff members individually liable for doing a poor job in evaluating an applicant? Alternatively, could the medical staff be held liable as an entity? In practice, physicians are not individually exposed since hospitals usually assume responsibility for liability arising from medical staff review activities. See generally J. Horty & D. Mulholland, The Legal Status of the Hospital Medical Staff, 22 St. Louis U.L.J. 485 (1978).

10. *Puzzles to Ponder.* In *Johnson,* the jury found Dr. Salinsky negligent. Is this necessary to hold the hospital liable for its own negligence? If a hospital negligently admits a bad doctor to the medical staff, shouldn't it be liable for any injury the doctor causes, under the notion that the hospital's negligence is distinct from the doctor's? This question seems to never have been addressed directly by the courts. Uniformly, they find hospital negligence only where the doctor is also negligent. The best explanation for this limitation is one of proximate cause. A hospital's negligent screening of a physician is not sufficiently proximate to a patient's injury, even if it literally causes the injury, unless the injury results from the physician's own negligence as well.

Another doctrinal puzzle is whether hospitals who negligently credential a physician are liable to patients who are injured off premises in the doctor's private office. Although standard foreseeability and but-for causation tests would appear to be met, most courts hold that hospitals are liable only for injuries to hospital patients, even where the plaintiff can prove she relied on the hospital credentials in selecting the doctor. Again, the notion appears to be one of proximate cause, influenced by older notions of privity of contract. See Insinga v. LaBella, 543 So. 2d 209 (Fla. 1989) (no hospital liability for giving admitting privileges to a person masquerading as a physician, where injury occurred outside hospital). But see Copithorne v. Framingham Union Hospital, 520 N.E.2d 139 (Mass. 1988) (hospital duty extends to medical staff member who drugged and raped patient in her home). Should it make any difference if the doctor practices in a hospital-owned and -leased medical office building right next door? What if the hospital owns an HMO that the doctor and patient belong to?

C. MANAGED CARE LIABILITY

We turn now to a new form of institution, one that combines medical delivery with medical financing. When confronted with HMOs' institutional liability, courts quickly applied the same structure of analysis that had developed for hospitals. Because HMOs differ in important respects from hospitals, however, the result of this analysis may not be the same. In the following materials, consider how different types of managed care entities and arrangements should be treated under the various theories and branches of no liability, vicarious liability, and direct liability.

■ BOYD v. ALBERT EINSTEIN MEDICAL CENTER

547 A.2d 1229 (Pa. Super. Ct. 1988)

OLSZEWSKI, Judge:

This is an appeal from the trial court's order granting summary judgment in favor of defendant/appellee, Health Maintenance Organization of Pennsylvania (hereinafter HMO). Appellant asserts that the trial court erred in granting the motion for summary judgment when there existed a question of material fact as to whether participating physicians are the ostensible agents of HMO. For the reasons stated below, we reverse the grant of summary judgment.

The facts, as averred by the parties in their pleadings and elicited through deposition testimony, reveal that at the time of her death, decedent and her husband were participants in the HMO. HMO is a medical insurance provider that offers an alternative to the traditional Blue Cross/Blue Shield insurance plan.[1] Decedent's husband became eligible for participation in a group plan provided by HMO through his employer. Upon electing to participate in this plan, decedent and her husband were provided with a directory and benefits brochure which listed

1. A Health Maintenance Organization is an organized system of health care which provides or arranges for a comprehensive array of basic and supplemental health care services. These services are provided on a prepaid basis to voluntarily enrolled members living within a prescribed geographic area. Responsibility for the delivery, quality and payment of health care falls to the managing organization—the HMO.

the participating physicians. Restricted to selecting a physician from this list, decedent chose Doctor David Rosenthal and Doctor Perry Dornstein as her primary care physicians.

In June of 1982, decedent contacted Doctor David Rosenthal regarding a lump in her breast. Doctor Rosenthal ordered a mammogram to be performed which revealed a suspicious area in the breast. Doctor Rosenthal recommended that decedent undergo a biopsy and referred decedent to Doctor Erwin Cohen for that purpose. Doctor Cohen, a surgeon, is also a participating HMO physician. The referral to a specialist in this case was made in accordance with the terms and conditions of HMO's subscription agreement.[2]

On July 6, 1982, Doctor Cohen performed a biopsy of decedent's breast tissue at Albert Einstein Medical Center. During the procedure, Doctor Cohen perforated decedent's chest wall with the biopsy needle, causing decedent to sustain a left hemothorax. Decedent was hospitalized for treatment of the hemothorax at Albert Einstein Hospital for two days.

In the weeks following this incident decedent complained to her primary care physicians, Doctor David Rosenthal and Doctor Perry Dornstein, of pain in her chest wall, belching, hiccoughs, and fatigue. On August 19, 1982, decedent awoke with pain in the middle of her chest. Decedent's husband contacted her primary care physicians, Doctors Rosenthal and Dornstein, and was advised to take decedent to Albert Einstein Hospital where she would be examined by Doctor Rosenthal. Upon arrival at Albert Einstein emergency room, decedent related symptoms of chest wall pain, vomiting, stomach and back discomfort to Doctor Rosenthal. Doctor Rosenthal commenced an examination of decedent, diagnosed Tietz's syndrome,[3] and arranged for tests to be performed at his office where decedent underwent X-rays, EKG, and cardiac isoenzyme tests.[4] Decedent was then sent home and told to rest.[5]

During the course of that afternoon, decedent continued to experience chest pain, vomiting and belching. Decedent related the persistence and worsening of these symptoms by telephone to Doctors Rosenthal and Dornstein, who prescribed, without further examination, Talwin, a pain medication. At 5:30 that afternoon decedent was discovered dead in her bathroom by her husband, having expired as a result of a myocardial infarction.

2. Doctor Rosenthal admitted in his deposition that HMO limited specifically the doctors to whom decedent could have been referred.

3. Tietze's Syndrome is an inflammatory condition affecting the costochondral cartilage. It occurs more commonly in females, generally in the 30 to 50 age range.

4. HMO avers that decedent was returned to the doctor's office for testing because it was more comfortable and convenient for her. Appellant, however, asserts that the tests were performed in the doctor's office, rather than the hospital, in accordance with the requirements of HMO whose primary interest was in keeping the medical fees within the corporation.

5. Appellant contends that Doctor Rosenthal acted negligently in ordering the tests to be performed in his office when decedent exhibited symptoms of cardiac distress. The safer practice, avers appellant, would have been to perform the tests at the hospital where the results would have been more quickly available. Appellant further contends that, despite Doctor Rosenthal's diagnosis of Tietze's Syndrome, the nature of the tests he ordered indicates that he was concerned about the possibility of a heart attack.

Appellant's complaint and new matter aver that HMO advertised that its physicians and medical care providers were competent, and that they had been evaluated for periods of up to six months prior to being selected to participate in the HMO program as a medical provider. The complaint further avers that decedent and appellant relied on these representations in choosing their primary care physicians. The complaint then avers that HMO was negligent in failing to

> qualify or oversee its physicians and hospital who acted as its agents, servants, or employees in providing medical care to the decedent nor did HMO of Pa. require its physicians, surgeons and hospitals to provide adequate evidence of skill, training and competence in medicine and it thereby failed to furnish the decedent with competent, qualified medical care as warranted.

Finally, appellant's new matter avers that HMO furnished to its subscribers documents which identify HMO as the care provider and state that HMO guarantees the quality of care.

Appellant's theory of recovery before the trial court was primarily one of vicarious liability under the ostensible agency theory. In granting defendant HMO's motion for summary judgment, the trial court found that plaintiff/appellant had failed to establish either of the two factors on which the theory of ostensible agency, as applied to hospitals in *Capan,* is based. On appeal, appellant contends that the evidence indicates that there exists a question of fact regarding whether HMO may be held liable under this theory. . . .

The group master contract provides that HMO "operates a comprehensive prepaid program of health care which provides health care services and benefits to Members in order to protect and promote their health, and preserve and enhance patient dignity." HMO was incorporated in 1975 under the laws of Pennsylvania and converted from a nonprofit to a for-profit corporation in 1981. HMO is based on the individual practice association model (hereinafter IPA), which means that HMO is comprised of participating primary physicians who are engaged in part in private practice in the HMO service area. Under the plan, IPA contracts with HMO to provide medical services to HMO members. IPA selects its primary and specialist physicians and enters into an agreement with them obligating the physician to perform health services for the subscribers of HMO.

The primary physician's role is defined as the "gatekeeper into the health care delivery system." "An HMO member must consult with his primary physician before going to a specialist and/or the hospital." If the primary physician deems it necessary, he arranges a consultation with an HMO participating specialist, which constitutes a second opinion. "Basically, with the primary physicians 'screening' the members' illnesses, excessive hospitalization and improper use of specialists can be reduced."

Member-patients use a physician directory and choose a conveniently located office of a participating primary physician. HMO members will only receive reimbursement from nonparticipating providers when the condition requiring treatment was of an immediate nature. Determinations of immediacy are made by the HMO quality assurance committee. In any event, persons desiring emergency nonprovider benefits must notify HMO or their primary physician of the emergency within 48 hours and must give written proof of the occurrence within ninety days after service is rendered. . . .

Primary physicians are paid through a mechanism termed "capitation." Capitation is an actuarially determined amount prepaid by HMO to the primary physician for each patient who has chosen his office. The dollar amount is based upon a predetermined rate per age group. The primary physicians are paid 80 percent of the capitation amount and the remaining 20 percent is pooled by IPA and goes back into a pooled risk-sharing fund as a reserve against specialty referral costs and hospital stays. Each primary care office has its own specialist fund and hospital fund established by allocating a predetermined amount each month for each member who has chosen that primary care office. The surplus from the specialist fund is returned to the primary care office. The hospital fund, however, is governed by a hospital risk/incentive-sharing scheme which anticipates a number of inpatient days per members per year. If the actual hospital utilization is less than anticipated, the HMO and IPA each receive 50 percent of the savings. IPA must place the savings in the Special IPA risk-sharing account and must use the funds to offset losses resulting from unanticipated physician costs. If utilization is greater than anticipated, IPA is responsible for 50 percent of the loss up to the amount of uncommitted funds in the Special IPA risk sharing account. . . .

HMO asserts that because the theory of ostensible agency has been applied in Pennsylvania only to the relationship between hospitals and independent contractor physicians, the theory is not appropriate in the instant situation. We emphasize, however, that when this court introduced the concept of ostensible agency to this Commonwealth in *Capan*, supra, we based that decision in large part upon "the changing role of the hospital in society [which] creates a likelihood that patients will look to the institution" for care. Because the role of health care providers has changed in recent years, the *Capan* rationale for applying the theory of ostensible agency to hospitals is certainly applicable in the instant situation. . . .

We find that the facts indicate an issue of material fact as to whether the participating physicians were the ostensible agents of HMO. HMO covenanted that it would "[provide] health care services and benefits to Members in order to protect and promote their health. . . . " "HMOPA operates on a direct service rather than an indemnity basis." Appellant paid his doctor's fee to HMO, not to the physician of his choice. Then, appellant selected his primary care physicians from the list provided by HMO. Regardless of who recommended appellant's decedent to choose her primary care physician, the fact remains that HMO provides a limited list from which a member must choose a primary physician. Moreover, those primary physicians are screened by HMO and must comply with a list of regulations in order to honor their contract with HMO.

Further, as mandated by HMO, appellant's decedent could not see a specialist without the primary physician's referral. As HMO declares, the primary physician is the "gatekeeper into the health care delivery system." "An HMO member must consult with his primary physician before going to a specialist and/or the hospital." Moreover, appellant's decedent had no choice as to which specialist to see. In our opinion, because appellant's decedent was required to follow the mandates of HMO and did not directly seek the attention of the specialist, there is an inference that appellant looked to the institution for care and not solely to the physicians; conversely, that appellant's decedent submitted herself to the care of the participating physicians in response to an invitation from HMO. See comment (a), Restatement (Second) Agency §267. . . .

We conclude, therefore, that the trial court erred when it granted HMO's motion for summary judgment on the ground that the participating physicians were not the ostensible agents of HMO. . . .

McEwen, Judge, concurring.

I concur in the result reached by the majority since the author, after a very careful analysis of the issues presented in this appeal, reaches the quite basic principle that issues of material fact may not be resolved by summary judgment.

I write only because it appears to me that the learned trial court improperly resolved by summary judgment the basic factual issue of whether the literature, in which HMO "guaranteed" and "assured" the quality of care provided to its subscribers, had been distributed to appellant or to other subscribers of HMO.

It might also be mentioned that while the court was understandably uncertain as to the theories upon which plaintiff was proceeding,[1] it appears that the amended complaint of plaintiff does contain factual averments supporting a breach of warranty claim.

WICKLINE v. STATE

239 Cal. Rptr. 810 (Cal. Ct. App. 1986)

Rowen, Associate Justice.

[Lois Wickline, who was treated under California's Medicaid program (known as "Medi-Cal"), sued the State, but not her physician, for negligently causing her premature discharge from the hospital, resulting in complications that eventually necessitated amputation of her right leg. Wickline alleged that her premature discharge was the fault of Medi-Cal's erroneous withholding of its authorization for her continued hospitalization.] This is an appeal from a judgment for plaintiff entered after a trial by jury. For the reasons discussed below, we reverse the judgment.

Principally, this matter concerns itself with the legal responsibility that a third party payor, in this case, the State of California, has for harm caused to a patient when a cost containment program is applied in a manner which is alleged to have affected the implementation of the treating physician's medical judgment. . . .

I

Responding to concerns about the escalating cost of health care, public and private payors have in recent years experimented with a variety of cost containment mechanisms. We deal here with one of those programs: The prospective utilization review process.

1. The trial court noted in its opinion that

> the gravamen of plaintiff's complaint is that HMO of PA guaranteed or warranted the quality of care provided. . . . Plaintiff's theory of recovery . . . is not entirely clear. A reading of the complaint suggests Plaintiff is proceeding upon grounds of corporate liability. However, in his answer to the motion of HMO of PA for summary judgment, plaintiff contends HMO of PA is vicariously liable through ostensible agency.

At the outset, this court recognizes that this case appears to be the first attempt to tie a health care payor into the medical malpractice causation chain and that it, therefore, deals with issues of profound importance to the health care community and to the general public. For those reasons we have permitted the filing of amicus curiae briefs in support of each of the respective parties in the matter to assure that due consideration is given to the broader issues raised before this court by this case. . . .

Early cost containment programs utilized the retrospective utilization review process. In that system the third party payor reviewed the patient's chart after the fact to determine whether the treatment provided was medically necessary. If, in the judgment of the utilization reviewer, it was not, the health care provider's claim for payment was denied.

In the cost containment program in issue in this case, prospective utilization review, authority for the rendering of health care services must be obtained before medical care is rendered. Its purpose is to promote the well-recognized public interest in controlling health care costs by reducing unnecessary services while still intending to assure that appropriate medical and hospital services are provided to the patient in need. However, such a cost containment strategy creates new and added pressures on the quality assurance portion of the utilization review mechanism. The stakes, the risks at issue, are much higher when a prospective cost containment review process is utilized than when a retrospective review process is used.

A mistaken conclusion about medical necessity following retrospective review will result in the wrongful withholding of payment. An erroneous decision in a prospective review process, on the other hand, in practical consequences, results in the withholding of necessary care, potentially leading to a patient's permanent disability or death.

II

Though somewhat in dispute, the facts in this case are not particularly complicated. In 1976, Wickline a married woman in her mid-40's, with a limited education, was being treated by Dr. Stanley Z. Daniels (Dr. Daniels), a physician engaged in a general family practice, for problems associated with her back and legs. Failing to respond to the physical therapy type of treatment he prescribed, Dr. Daniels had Wickline admitted to Van Nuys Community Hospital (Van Nuys or Hospital) in October 1976 and brought in another physician, Dr. Gerald E. Polonsky (Dr. Polonsky), a specialist in peripheral vascular surgery, to do a consultation examination. Peripheral vascular surgery concerns itself with surgery on any vessel of the body, exclusive of the heart.

Dr. Polonsky examined plaintiff and diagnosed her condition as arteriosclerosis obliterans with occlusion of the abdominal aorta, more generally referred to as Leriche's Syndrome. . . .

According to Dr. Polonsky, the only treatment for Leriche's Syndrome is surgical. In Wickline's case her disease was so far advanced that Dr. Polonsky concluded that it was necessary to remove a part of the plaintiff's artery and insert a synthetic (Teflon) graft in its place.

After agreeing to the operation, Wickline was discharged home to await approval of her doctor's diagnosis and authorization from Medi-Cal for the recommended surgical procedure and attendant acute care hospitalization. It is conceded that at all times in issue in this case, the plaintiff was eligible for medical benefits under California's medical assistance program, the "Medi-Cal Act," which is more commonly referred to as Medi-Cal. (Welf. & Inst. Code, §§14000 et seq., 14000.4.)

As required, Dr. Daniels submitted a treatment authorization request to Medi-Cal, sometimes referred to as form "161," "MC-161" or "TAR." In response to Dr. Daniels' request, Medi-Cal authorized the surgical procedure and 10 days of hospitalization for that treatment.

On January 6, 1977, plaintiff was admitted to Van Nuys by Dr. Daniels. On January 7, 1977, Dr. Polonsky performed a surgical procedure in which a part of plaintiff's artery was removed and a synthetic artery was inserted to replace it. Dr. Polonsky characterized that procedure as "a very major surgery."

Later that same day Dr. Polonsky was notified that Wickline was experiencing circulatory problems in her right leg. He concluded that a clot had formed in the graft. As a result, Wickline was taken back into surgery, the incision in her right groin was reopened, the clot removed and the graft was resewn. Wickline's recovery subsequent to the two January 7th operations [was] characterized as "stormy." She had a lot of pain, some spasm in the vessels in the lower leg and she experienced hallucinating episodes. On January 12, 1977, Wickline was returned to the operating room where Dr. Polonsky performed a lumbar sympathectomy.

A lumbar sympathectomy is a major operation in which a section of the chain of nerves that lie on each side of the spinal column is removed. The procedure causes the blood vessels in the patient's lower extremity to become paralyzed in a wide open position and was done in an attempt to relieve the spasms which Wickline was experiencing in those vessels. Spasms stop the outflow of blood from the vessels causing the blood to back up into the graft. Failure to relieve such spasms can cause clotting.

Dr. Polonsky was assisted in all three surgeries by Dr. Leonard Kovner (Dr. Kovner), a board-certified specialist in the field of general surgery and the chief of surgery at Van Nuys. Dr. Daniels was present for the initial graft surgery on January 7, 1977, and for the right lumbar sympathectomy operation on January 12, 1977.

Wickline was scheduled to be discharged on January 16, 1977, which would mean that she would actually leave the hospital sometime before 1 P.M. on January 17, 1977. On or about January 16, 1977, Dr. Polonsky concluded that "it was medically necessary" that plaintiff remain in the hospital for an additional eight days beyond her then scheduled discharge date. Drs. Kovner and Daniels concurred in Dr. Polonsky's opinion.

Dr. Polonsky cited many reasons for his feeling that it was medically necessary for plaintiff to remain in an acute care hospital for an additional eight days, such as the danger of infection and/or clotting. His principal reason, however, was that he felt that he was going to be able to save both of Wickline's legs and wanted her to remain in the hospital where he could observe her and be immediately available, along with the hospital staff, to treat her if an emergency should occur.

In order to secure an extension of Wickline's hospital stay, it was necessary to complete and present to Medi-Cal a form called "Request for Extension of Stay in Hospital," commonly referred to as an "MC-180" or "180." . . .

At Van Nuys, Patricia N. Spears (Spears), an employee of the hospital and a registered nurse, had the responsibility for completing 180 forms. In this case, as requested by Dr. Polonsky, Spears filled out Wickline's 180 form and then presented it to Dr. Daniels, as plaintiff's attending physician, to sign, which he did, in compliance with Dr. Polonsky's recommendation. All of the physicians who testified agreed that the 180 form prepared by Spears was complete, accurate and adequate for all purposes in issue in this matter.

Doris A. Futerman (Futerman), a registered nurse, was, at that time, employed by Medi-Cal as a Health Care Service Nurse, commonly referred to as an "on-site nurse." . . .

Futerman, after reviewing Wickline's 180 form, felt that she could not approve the requested eight-day extension of acute care hospitalization. While conceding that the information provided might justify some additional time beyond the scheduled discharge date, nothing in Wickline's case, in Futerman's opinion, would have warranted the entire eight additional days requested and, for those reasons, she telephoned the Medi-Cal Consultant. She reached Dr. William S. Glassman (Dr. Glassman), one of the Medi-Cal Consultants on duty at the time in Medi-Cal's Los Angeles office. The Medi-Cal Consultant selection occurred randomly. As was the practice, whichever Medi-Cal Consultant was available at the moment took the next call that came into the office. . . .

After speaking with Futerman on the telephone, Dr. Glassman rejected Wickline's treating physician's request for an eight-day hospital extension and, instead, authorized an additional four days of hospital stay beyond the originally scheduled discharge date. . . .

After review of Wickline's 180 form, Dr. Glassman testified that the factors that led him to authorize four days, rather than the requested eight days, was that there was no information about the patient's temperature which he, thereupon, assumed was normal; nothing was mentioned about the patient's diet, which he then presumed was not a problem; nor was there any information about Wickline's bowel function, which Dr. Glassman then presumed was functioning satisfactorily. Further, the fact that the 180 form noted that Wickline was able to ambulate with help and that whirlpool treatments were to begin that day caused Dr. Glassman to presume that the patient was progressing satisfactorily and was not seriously or critically ill. . . .

In essence, respondent argues, Dr. Glassman based his decision on signs and symptoms such as temperature, diet and bowel movements, which were basically irrelevant to the plaintiff's circulatory condition for which she was being treated and did not concern himself with those symptoms and signs which an ordinary prudent physician would consider to be pertinent with regard to the type of medical condition presented by Wickline.

Complying with the limited extension of time authorized by Medi-Cal, Wickline was discharged from Van Nuys on January 21, 1977. Drs. Polonsky and Daniels each wrote discharge orders. At the time of her discharge, each of plaintiff's three treating physicians were aware that the Medi-Cal Consultant had approved only four of the requested eight-day hospital stay extension. While all three doctors were aware that they could attempt to obtain a further extension of Wickline's hospital stay by telephoning the Medi-Cal Consultant to request such an extension, none of them did so. . . .

At trial, Dr. Polonsky testified that in the time that had passed since the first extension request had been communicated to Medi-Cal, on January 16th or 17th, and the time of her scheduled discharge on January 21, 1977, Wickline's condition had neither deteriorated nor become critical. In Dr. Polonsky's opinion no new symptom had presented itself and no additional factors had occurred since the original request was made to have formed the basis for a change in the Medi-Cal Consultant's attitude regarding Wickline's situation. In addition, he stated that at the time of Wickline's discharge it did not appear that her leg was in any danger.

Dr. Polonsky testified that at the time in issue he felt that Medi-Cal Consultants had the state's interest more in mind than the patient's welfare and that that belief influenced his decision not to request a second extension of Wickline's hospital stay. In addition, he felt that Medi-Cal had the power to tell him, as a treating doctor, when a patient must be discharged from the hospital. Therefore, while still of the subjective, noncommunicated, opinion that Wickline was seriously ill and that the danger to her was not over, Dr. Polonsky discharged her from the hospital on January 21, 1977. He testified that had Wickline's condition, in his medical judgment, been critical or in a deteriorating condition on January 21, he would have made some effort to keep her in the hospital beyond that day even if denied authority by Medi-Cal and even if he had to pay her hospital bill himself. . . .

All of the medical witnesses who testified at trial agreed that Dr. Polonsky was acting within the standards of practice of the medical community in discharging Wickline on January 21, 1977. . . .

Wickline testified that in the first few days after she arrived home she started feeling pain in her right leg and the leg started to lose color. In the next few days the pain got worse and the right leg took on a whitish, statue-like marble appearance. Wickline assumed she was experiencing normal recovery symptoms and did not communicate with any of her physicians. Finally, when "the pain got so great and the color started changing from looking like a statue to getting a grayish color," her husband called Dr. Kovner. It was Wickline's memory that this occurred about the third day after her discharge from the hospital and that Dr. Kovner advised Mr. Wickline to give extra pain medicine to the plaintiff.

Thereafter, gradually over the next few days, the plaintiff's leg "kept getting grayer and then it got bluish." The extra medication allegedly prescribed by Dr. Kovner over the telephone did not relieve the pain Wickline was experiencing. She testified that "by then the pain was just excruciating, where no pain medicine helped whatsoever." Finally, Wickline instructed her husband to call Dr. Kovner again and this time Dr. Kovner ordered plaintiff back into the hospital. Wickline returned to Van Nuys that same evening, January 30, 1977, nine days after her last discharge therefrom. . . .

Attempts to save Wickline's leg through the utilization of anticoagulants, antibiotics, strict bed rest, pain medication and warm water whirlpool baths to the lower extremity proved unsuccessful. On February 8, 1977, Dr. Polonsky amputated Wickline's leg below the knee because had he not done so "she would have died." The condition did not, however, heal after the first operation and on February 17, 1977, the doctors went back and amputated Wickline's leg above the knee. . . .

In Dr. Polonsky's opinion, to a reasonable medical certainty, had Wickline remained in the hospital for the eight additional days, as originally requested by him and her other treating doctors, she would not have suffered the loss of her leg. . . .

Dr. Polonsky testified that in his medical opinion, the Medi-Cal Consultant's rejection of the requested eight-day extension of acute care hospitalization and his authorization of a four-day extension in its place did not conform to the usual medical standards as they existed in 1977. He stated that, in accordance with those standards, a physician would not be permitted to make decisions regarding the care of a patient without either first seeing the patient, reviewing the patient's chart or discussing the patient's condition with her treating physician or physicians.

III

From the facts thus presented, appellant takes the position that it was not negligent as a matter of law. Appellant contends that the decision to discharge was made by each of the plaintiff's three doctors, was based upon the prevailing standards of practice, and was justified by her condition at the time of her discharge. It argues that Medi-Cal had no part in the plaintiff's hospital discharge and therefore was not liable even if the decision to do so was erroneously made by her doctors. . . .

As to the principal issue before this court, i.e., who bears responsibility for allowing a patient to be discharged from the hospital, her treating physicians or the health care payor, each side's medical expert witnesses agreed that, in accordance with the standards of medical practice as it existed in January 1977, it was for the patient's treating physician to decide the course of treatment that was medically necessary to treat the ailment. It was also that physician's responsibility to determine whether or not acute care hospitalization was required and for how long. Finally, it was agreed that the patient's physician is in a better position than the Medi-Cal Consultant to determine the number of days medically necessary for any required hospital care. The decision to discharge is, therefore, the responsibility of the patient's own treating doctor.

Dr. Kaufman testified that if, on January 21, the date of the plaintiff's discharge from Van Nuys, any one of her three treating doctors had decided that in his medical judgment it was necessary to keep Wickline in the hospital for a longer period of time, they, or any of them, should have filed another request for extension of stay in the hospital, that Medi-Cal would expect those physicians to make such a request if they felt it was indicated, and upon receipt of such a request further consideration of an additional extension of hospital time would have been given.

Title 22 of the California Administrative Code §51110, provided, in pertinent part, at the relevant time in issue here, that: "The determination of need for acute care shall be made in accordance with the usual standards of medical practice in the community."

The patient who requires treatment and who is harmed when care which should have been provided is not provided should recover for the injuries suffered from all those responsible for the deprivation of such care, including, when appropriate, health care payors. Third party payors of health care services can be held legally accountable when medically inappropriate decisions result from defects in the design or implementation of cost containment mechanisms as, for example, when appeals made on a patient's behalf for medical or hospital care are arbitrarily ignored or unreasonably disregarded or overridden. However, the physician who complies without protest with the limitations imposed by a third-party payor, when his medical judgment dictates otherwise, cannot avoid his ultimate responsibility for his patient's care. He cannot point to the health care payor as the liability scapegoat when the consequences of his own determinative medical decisions go sour.

There is little doubt that Dr. Polonsky was intimidated by the Medi-Cal program but he was not paralyzed by Dr. Glassman's response nor rendered powerless to act appropriately if other action was required under the circumstances. If, in his medical judgment, it was in his patient's best interest that she remain in the acute care hospital setting for an additional four days beyond the extended time period originally authorized by Medi-Cal, Dr. Polonsky should have made some effort to keep Wickline there. He himself acknowledged that responsibility to his patient. It was his medical judgment, however, that Wickline could be discharged when she was. All the plaintiff's treating physicians concurred and all the doctors who testified at trial, for either plaintiff or defendant, agreed that Dr. Polonsky's medical decision to discharge Wickline met the standard of care applicable at the time. Medi-Cal was not a party to that medical decision and therefore cannot be held to share in the harm resulting if such decision was negligently made.

In addition, thereto, while Medi-Cal played a part in the scenario before us in that it was the resource for the funds to pay for the treatment sought, and its input regarding the nature and length of hospital care to be provided was of paramount importance, Medi-Cal did not override the medical judgment of Wickline's treating physicians at the time of her discharge. It was given no opportunity to do so. Therefore, there can be no viable cause of action against it for the consequences of that discharge decision. . . .

V

This court appreciates that what is at issue here is the effect of cost containment programs upon the professional judgment of physicians to prescribe hospital treatment for patients requiring the same. While we recognize, realistically, that cost consciousness has become a permanent feature of the health care system, it is essential that cost limitation programs not be permitted to corrupt medical judgment. We have concluded, from the facts in issue here, that in this case it did not.

For the reasons expressed herein, this court finds that appellant is not liable for respondent's injuries as a matter of law. That makes unnecessary any discussion of the other contentions of the parties.

Notes: Managed Care Liability

1. *The Components of Managed Care.* Managed care is a term that applies broadly to a wide variety of arrangements that restrict the generosity of traditional health insurance. Managed care (1) restricts choice of physicians through networks and gatekeepers, (2) alters discrete treatment decisions through utilization review and prior authorization requirements, and (3) creates cost-constrained financial incentives through capitation payments and risk-sharing pools. Each of these components has distinct liability implications and can exist separately from the others. For instance, "managed indemnity" insurance does (2) but not (1) or (3), simply by adding utilization review to traditional insurance. Preferred provider organizations (PPOs) do (1) but not (3), and may do (2) but not necessarily. HMOs are the fullest embodiment of managed care because they incorporate all three components. In analyzing these cases and others that are likely to arise in the future, however, be

sure to think individually about each of these components and observe how they might arise in a variety of different institutional forms.

2. *HMO Immunity*. In a few jurisdictions, HMOs are immune from suit for negligent treatment, in some states by statute and in one state formerly by court decision. Williams v. Good Health Plus, Inc., 743 S.W.2d 373 (Tex. Ct. App. 1987), resonates with hospital decisions early in the century by holding that an HMO logically cannot be held liable because the corporate practice of medicine doctrine prevents it from controlling physicians' treatment decisions. That decision has since been overturned by statute, however. Comment, 30 Tex. Tech. L. Rev. 1227 (1999). But California, by statute, declares that health insurers may not be held vicariously liable for medical decisions by independent physicians. Martin v. PacifiCare of California, 198 Cal. App. 4th 1390 (2011). Economist Patricia Danzon is one who argues for HMO immunity under the theory that holding physicians individually liable is sufficient, unless the HMO agrees by contract to assume liability. Patricia M. Danzon, Tort Liability: A Minefield for Managed Care, 24 J. Leg. Stud. 491 (1997). Do you agree?

3. *Vicarious Liability*. There are two basic types of HMOs, with several permutations. The HMO type in *Boyd* was an Independent Practice Association (IPA), which is composed of a large contractual network of physicians who maintain practices in their own offices and see patients with many different types of insurance. For a decision similar to *Boyd*, see Villazon v. Prudential Health Care Plan, 843 So. 2d 842 (Fla. 2003). An agency relationship is much easier to establish with the other type of HMO, a staff or group model, in which a smaller number of physicians work exclusively for a single HMO in a centralized clinic. What about a PPO (preferred provider organization) or POS (point of service) plan with an open network in which patients are encouraged to stay with the designated physicians but are free to go outside the network and select any doctor they want by paying a higher deductible or copayment? What about a closed network that is very large but has no gatekeeping restrictions, that is, patients can see anyone they want when they want, but only within the network? See generally Comment, Managed Health Care: HMO Corporate Liability, Independent Contractors, and the Ostensible Agency Doctrine, 15 J. Corp. L. 535 (1990).

How might an IPA HMO alter its structure or operations to avoid the attribution of agency and vicarious liability? See Chase v. Independent Practice Ass'n, 583 N.E.2d 251 (Mass. App. Ct. 1991) (vicarious liability rejected where HMO contract stated the IPA only "arranged for" services but did not provide services directly); Jones v. U.S. Healthcare, 723 N.Y.S.2d 478 (App. Div. 2001) (an HMO "cannot be held vicariously liable for defendant doctors' and hospital's alleged malpractice in discharging plaintiff and her baby prematurely, where the . . . Group Master Contract, membership card and Member Handbook clearly state that doctors and hospitals participating in defendant's health care program are independent contractors"). But see Petrovich v. Share Health Plan, 719 N.E.2d 756 (Ill. 1999) (exculpatory language in insurance documents does not control if the patient didn't actually read or understand the documents). Because IPAs are now the dominant form of HMOs, and because HMO lawyers have widely adopted these techniques, the working assumption among both plaintiff's and defense lawyers is that HMOs generally cannot be held vicariously liable simply by virtue of forming a network and requiring gatekeeping. This is also confirmed in several of the state managed care liability statutes discussed in the next note. See Agrawal & Hall, infra.

4. *HMO Direct Liability.* The focus of *Boyd* is vicarious liability, but HMOs have also been held to the same type of direct corporate liability ushered in by Darling v. Charleston Community Memorial Hospital. Recall that for hospitals, direct corporate liability takes two basic forms: a duty of care in the selection of physicians, and a duty of care in the contemporaneous supervision of physicians. The former is readily applicable to HMOs as well. Several courts have held that they have the same obligation hospitals do to review the credentials and competency of physicians that they select for their network. See, e.g., McClellan v. Health Maintenance Organization, 604 A.2d 1053 (Pa. Super. Ct. 1992); Pagarigan v. Aetna, 2005 WL 2742807 (Cal. Ct. App. 2005). HMOs are required under their own accreditation standards to engage in a hospital-like credentialing process, and increasingly they are required to do so by state regulation as well. Nevertheless, many managed care networks accept virtually "any willing provider," that is, anyone with a license who agrees to the network's payment terms. A "Dear Doctor" letter sent by one PPO to California physicians stated, "Welcome to the PPO network. You are now part of a carefully selected panel of more than 300 hospitals and 21,000 physicians." Robert A. Berenson, Beyond Competition, 16(2) Health Aff. 171, 175 (1997). Some states require by statute that HMOs accept any qualified provider. Does either voluntary or mandatory nonselectivity undermine the basis for a duty of care in selection?

Recall that the second branch of *Darling*—the duty of contemporaneous supervision—is highly controversial with respect to hospitals and is accepted in only a very limited fashion in most jurisdictions because it doesn't make sense to require hospital administrators to actively intervene in medical treatment decisions. Is the case for an HMO's duty to supervise any stronger? Even if there is no such mandatory duty, however, consider whether HMOs have voluntarily assumed such a duty through their utilization review function. Is this not the essential point of *Wickline,* that when insurance companies choose to intervene in treatment decisions, they assume a duty of care in doing so? Accord Shannon v. McNulty, 718 A.2d 828 (Pa. Super. Ct. 1998) ("When . . . an insurer interjects itself into the rendering of medical decisions affecting a subscriber's care it must do so in a medically reasonable manner.").

To remove any doubt about this issue, about a dozen states have adopted statutes that hold insurers liable for personal injuries caused by negligent or inappropriate administration of health insurance benefits. See Agrawal & Hall, infra; Note, 74 Temp. L. Rev. 507 (2001). It is unlikely, however, that these statutes can be applied to employer-provided health insurance, due to the federal preemption doctrine discussed in the following case.

5. *Medical Tourism.* Complex medical care can be quite good in some less developed countries such as India and Malaysia, but considerably less expensive, even factoring in travel costs—with net savings of tens of thousands of dollars per procedure for many common surgeries. Thus, it may be just a matter of time before insurers, or self-insured employers, begin offering strong incentives (in the form of discounts or rebates) to people who opt to use "preferred providers" overseas. Would doing only that give rise to insurer liability for any medical injuries? If so, under what theory(ies) of institutional liability? And, what standard of care (domestic or foreign) should determine the provider's underlying negligence? For discussion, but no resolution, of these fascinating questions, see Glenn Cohen, Protecting Patients with Passports, 95 Iowa L. Rev. 1467 (2010).

6. Wickline's *Holding.* The precise holding or nonholding of *Wickline* has been a source of considerable confusion, both in the courts and among lawyers and commentators. This confusion is due in part to the unusual tactical decision by the plaintiff's lawyer not to sue the treating physicians. As a result, the plaintiff was able to use the treating physicians as experts for her side, but the physicians were unwilling to indict themselves by testifying that the four-day stay fell below a minimally acceptable standard of care. Without such testimony, the court was forced to find no liability. Without any basis in the clinical evidence for finding anyone liable, much of what the court said about the competing responsibilities of physicians and insurers was rendered dictum.

Nevertheless, *Wickline* is still the seminal case on the issues it addresses. In trying to make sense of what the opinion means for future disputes, distinguish these two issues: (1) whether insurers are potentially on the liability hook for making bad coverage decisions, and (2) whether physicians are off the liability hook when insurers are at fault. Realize it is possible to answer "yes" to (1) and "no" to (2); in other words, both can be held liable at the same time. Others sometimes interpret *Wickline* to mean, however, that the doctor's ultimate responsibility absolves the insurance company from blame. The most prominent instance of this reading of *Wickline* is a subsequent California decision, Wilson v. Blue Cross of Southern California, 271 Cal. Rptr. 876 (Cal. Ct. App. 1990). There, a psychiatric patient committed suicide after being released from the hospital when his private insurer stopped paying for his hospitalization benefits due to lack of medical necessity. The court found it necessary to distinguish and disapprove *Wickline* in order to allow the case to be tried against the insurer under a negligence theory. Is anything in *Wickline* opposed to such a holding? For a sampling of the extensive commentary on these two cases, see John Blum, An Analysis of Legal Liability in Health Care Utilization Review and Case Management, 26 Hous. L. Rev. 191 (1989); Comment, 52 Ohio St. L.J. 1289 (1991).

Under *Wickline,* could insurer liability be imposed not only based on the substance of the utilization review decision, but also based on the process? What flaws were present in Medi-Cal's UR process? How feasible would it be to improve on that process?

If insurers can be found liable for negligent failures to approve necessary care, can they also be held accountable for negligent approvals of harmful care?

7. *Bringing Liability and Payment into Sync.* Does the potential liability under *Wickline* make sense from the physician's perspective? Physicians complain that it is unfair to hold them responsible for failing to provide treatment that insurance will not pay for. See Note, 59 Duke L. Rev. 955 (2010). What realistic options did Mrs. Wickline's physicians have? How might the tort standard of medical appropriateness be brought more into sync with the insurance standard? One possibility is by referring to the law of abandonment, which holds that physicians are able to terminate care in certain circumstances if they give proper notice and an opportunity to locate another physician. Whether lack of payment is a permissible reason to give this notice has not yet clearly been decided.

Consider also whether physicians practicing under managed care constraints should be held to a lower standard of care than under fee-for-service insurance.

8. *Few Cases but Big Verdicts.* One reason for the lack of clarity about the respective responsibilities of physicians and insurers is that there have been surprisingly few cases like *Wickline* and *Wilson* with decisions on the merits. This suggests that

perhaps in practice insurers rarely deny coverage for care that is required by the minimal standard of medical practice. The paucity of suits may also be due to the preemption of state law by the federal ERISA statute, discussed in the next case. Others attribute the favorable malpractice record of staff model HMOs like Kaiser to their detailed programs of malpractice prevention and physician monitoring and to the availability of a grievance process for dissatisfied patients. These characteristics typically do not exist, however, in the broad network model HMOs that currently prevail in the market. Further explanation for the small number of suits comes from the fact that plaintiffs' lawyers are reluctant to name health insurers in medical malpractice suits since this greatly complicates the litigation and is usually unnecessary given the fact that the treating physician is "on the hook" in any event (for reasons explained in *Wickline*). Also, plaintiffs' lawyers report seeing few or no cases where harm results from health insurers' refusing to pay for treatment that physicians request. Agrawal & Hall, infra.

Although there have been few successful cases against health insurers, when plaintiffs have succeeded, they sometimes win very large punitive damages awards, in the range of $50 million to $100 million or more. For instance, in Fox v. Health Net (1993), a California jury awarded $77 million in punitive damages (plus $12 million compensatory) against an HMO that had refused to pay for an innovative cancer treatment, which the surviving family claimed resulted in the patient's death. This was eclipsed by the $120 million verdict in Goodrich v. Aetna U.S. Healthcare (1999), $116 million of which were punitive damages. Like *Fox*, the *Goodrich* verdict was based on an HMO's reluctance to authorize expensive, state-of-the-art treatment for terminal cancer that it considered to be experimental. Then, in 2013, a Nevada jury returned a whopping $524 million verdict against an HMO for contracting with a physician whose sloppy procedures resulted in infecting the patient with Hepatitis C, Meyer v. Health Plan of Nevada.

Does this track record of very few successful verdicts, but some that are extremely large, create appropriate incentives for plaintiffs to sue? Is it likely to send appropriate deterrence signals to health insurers? Does the small number of suits suggest a need to remove barriers to suing health plans? Would a "floodgate" of litigation threaten the viability of the managed care industry or of its core cost-containment practices? For discussion from various perspectives, see the literature cited in note 14.

9. *Financial Incentives*. Another potential basis for direct liability against HMOs and managed care arrangements is the use of financial incentives to encourage physicians to economize. An insurer might avoid the entire issue of liability for second-guessing medical judgment by paying doctors in a way that encourages them to economize in their own clinical decisionmaking. Using *Wickline*'s notion of "defects in the design or implementation of cost containment mechanisms," is it possible nevertheless to argue that some financial incentives are too strong per se, or that in practice they caused a physician to err? Answering "yes," see Pagarigan v. Aetna, 2005 WL 2742807 (Cal. Ct. App. 2005). Consider by analogy the suits in the 1990s against Domino's Pizza for pressuring its deliverers to drive too fast. Financial incentives might also lead to claims for punitive damages in medical malpractice cases against physicians, or might give rise to a claim for breach of fiduciary duty.

10. *Breach of Contract*. The *Boyd* concurrence suggests that HMO liability might also be based on a contractual or quasi-promissory theory, such as warranty or fraud.

Is there a difference between the nature of the promises an HMO makes and those made by typical hospitals or doctors? Professor Brewbaker argues that, because HMOs, unlike hospitals, sell medical services, they undertake an implied warranty of quality which, as with doctors, promises nonnegligent care. Therefore, he argues that HMOs should be automatically liable for any negligent care delivered under their auspices, regardless of whether they fall under the theories of liability devised for hospitals. William Brewbaker, Medical Malpractice and Managed Care Organizations: The Implied Warranty of Quality, 60 Contemp. Probs. 117 (Spring 1997).

11. *Employer Liability.* If insurers can be held liable for lack of care in selecting physicians and supervising treatment decisions, how about employers who construct their own managed care plans? Many large employers eliminate the "middle man" by contracting directly with hospitals and physicians on a self-insured basis. In doing so, an employer may either "rent a network," that is, contract with an existing network of providers, or it might form its own network. In either event, is it plausible to impose the same type of managed care liability on employers as on the insurers they have ousted? If such liability existed under state law, it would likely be preempted for reasons addressed in the following case. For discussion, see Dana M. Muir, Fiduciary Status as an Employer's Shield: The Perversity of ERISA Fiduciary Law, 2 U. Pa. J. Lab. & Emp. L. 391 (2000).

12. *Exclusive Enterprise Liability.* The furthest extension of the concepts of enterprise liability developed for hospitals, HMOs, and other forms of managed care would be to hold a network of hospitals, doctors, and insurers exclusively liable at the highest institutional level for any medical mistake that occurs within any component part. If the health care delivery system were to move toward the "integrated delivery system" structure described in Chapter 4, commentators have speculated whether these networks should or will be the final point of liability focus. So far, most networks are only loosely formed contractual affiliations in which the parties (hospitals, doctors, and insurers) agree on a nonexclusive basis to market their services collectively to employers or other insurers. Does this entail sufficient integration, coordination, selection, and supervision to justify imposition of enterprise liability? Consider whether it is feasible for integrated delivery systems to influence the quality of care if these affiliations are nonexclusive, that is, if doctors and hospitals belong to several such networks. See Michelle M. Mello & Allen Kachalia, Evaluation of Options for Medical Malpractice System Reform, Report to MedPAC, 2010.

> [T]he plan's liability could be limited to injuries caused by physicians who receive the greatest share of their reimbursement from that payer, or could extend to any injury incurred by the plan's insured patients. The former would better peg liability to the plan's ability to influence the physician's practice, since the plan's threat not to contract with physicians in the future if they did not improve would have greater financial consequence for the physician. However, it could allow plans that did not have a large market share to evade liability altogether.

13. *Consumer-Driven Health Care.* As insurers recede from aggressive managed care, will these liability threats likewise recede, or will they be replaced with new theories of liability? According to one professor, consumer-driven health care opens up an entirely new arena of potential health plan liability in the form of failure to provide full or accurate information about health care options. Kristin Madison, ERISA and Liability for Provision of Medical Information, 84 N.C. L. Rev. 471-546

(2006). See also E. Haavi Morreim, High-Deductible Health Plans: Litigation Hazards for Health Insurers, 18 Health Matrix 1 (2008).

14. *Further Reading.* For commentary and analysis on **managed care liability** generally, see Haavi Morreim, Holding Health Care Accountable (2001); Jennifer Arlen & William MacLeod, Malpractice Liability for Physicians and Managed Care Organizations, 78 N.Y.U. L. Rev. 1929 (2003); Gail Agrawal & Mark Hall, What If You *Could* Sue Your HMO? Managed Care Liability Beyond the ERISA Shield, 47 St. Louis U. L. J. 235 (2003); Clark Havighurst, Vicarious Liability: Relocating Responsibility for the Quality of Medical Care, 26 Am. J.L. & Med. 7 (2000); Peter Jacobson & Neena Patil, Managed Care Litigation: Legal Doctrine at the Boundary of Tort and Contract, 57 Med. Care Res. & Rev. 440 (2000); David Studdert et al., Expanded Managed Care Liability: What Impact on Employer Coverage?, 18(6) Health Aff. 7 (Dec. 1999); Richard A. Epstein & Alan O. Sykes, The Assault on Managed Care: Vicarious Liability, Class Actions, and the Patient's Bill of Rights, 30 J. Leg. Stud. 625 (2002).

On **enterprise liability** (note 12), see K. Abraham & P. Weiler, Enterprise Medical Liability and the Choice of the Responsible Enterprise, 20 Am. J.L. & Med. 29 (1994); Clark C. Havighurst, Making Health Plans Accountable for the Quality of Care, 31 Ga. L. Rev. 587 (1997); William Sage, Enterprise Liability and the Emerging Managed Care Health Care System, 60 Law & Contemp. Probs. 159 (Spring 1997); Randall R. Bovbjerg & Robert Berenson, Enterprise Liability in the Twenty-First Century, *in* Medical Malpractice and the U.S. Health Care System (W. Sage & R. Kersh eds., 2006); Note, 121 Harv. L. Rev. 1192 (2008).

Problem: Enterprise Liability

Mike Mulligan is administrator of Florence Nightingale Hospital, a large facility in a metropolitan area. Mary Anne is the local lawyer. Mike has a plan to protect the hospital from the erosion of business that has resulted from managed care contracts taking more and more patients into the larger facilities nearby. Mulligan's plan is for the hospital to form its own managed care network. Mulligan would like to include as many of the local physicians as possible in the network. (Assume this is legal under antitrust law.) The network will then sell HMO-type insurance to local residents. The premium revenues will be split 50/50 between the hospital and the doctors, with the physician half going mostly to the primary care physicians. These primary care physicians will act as gatekeepers for hospitalization decisions, referrals to specialists in town, and referrals to larger hospitals for more complex care.

Mulligan consults Mary Anne about advice on the liability implications of this plan. The hospital has been named in a number of suits recently, and he is concerned at the formation stage about what new liability exposure the network will create and what steps are possible to manage or reduce that exposure. Taking the position of Mike Mulligan, how desirable would each of the following alternative ideas be from a business or practical perspective? Taking the position of Mary Anne, how desirable would each be from a legal perspective?

1. Automatically accept into the network any doctor with medical staff privileges at the hospital.
2. In contracting with doctors, insist on an indemnification clause that requires them to compensate the hospital system for any paid claims that arise from the doctor's own fault.

3. Agree to purchase malpractice insurance for network physicians, defend any claims brought by patients, and pay for any resulting liability. Consider this option both for hospital-based care only and for all medical care.
4. Increase the size and authority of the risk management department, school them in the techniques of quality assurance and "total quality management," and impose a passel of practice guidelines that cover liability-sensitive areas of medicine.
5. Write insurance contracts so as to notify subscribers that network physicians are independent contractors. Post similar statements in doctors' waiting rooms, at hospital entrances, on hospital admission forms, and on informed consent forms. Review stationery, billing forms, and uniform dress to avoid creating the unintended impression of an agency relationship between the hospital system and network physicians.
6. Have the risk management department and Mary Anne review all advertising and marketing materials to eliminate any statements that might create an expectation or image of receiving quality care.
7. Write insurance contracts so as to specifically promise an "adequate level of care, consistent with the coverage provided by this insurance and within the standards of care that prevail in other, similar locations in this state."

■ AETNA HEALTH INC. v. DAVILA

542 U.S. 200 (2004)

Justice THOMAS delivered the opinion of the Court.

In these consolidated cases, two individuals sued their respective HMOs for alleged failures to exercise ordinary care in the handling of coverage decisions, in violation of a duty imposed by the Texas Health Care Liability Act (Texas Act). We granted certiorari to decide whether the individuals' causes of action are completely preempted by the . . . Employee Retirement Income Security Act of 1974 (ERISA) . . .

[Davila was covered by Aetna through his employer, and Calad was covered by CIGNA through her husband's employer.] Respondents both suffered injuries allegedly arising from Aetna's and CIGNA's decisions not to provide coverage for certain treatment and services recommended by respondents' treating physicians. Davila's treating physician prescribed Vioxx to remedy Davila's arthritis pain, but Aetna refused to pay for it. Davila did not appeal or contest this decision, nor did he purchase Vioxx with his own resources and seek reimbursement. Instead, Davila began taking Naprosyn, from which he allegedly suffered a severe reaction that required extensive treatment and hospitalization. [Editors' note: The Court fails to mention that Davila nearly died from bleeding ulcers and that, although Vioxx is much more expensive than Naprosyn, it has fewer side effects relating to bleeding ulcers.]

Calad underwent surgery, and although her treating physician recommended an extended hospital stay, a CIGNA discharge nurse determined that Calad did not meet the plan's criteria for a continued hospital stay. CIGNA consequently denied coverage for the extended hospital stay. Calad experienced postsurgery complications forcing her to return to the hospital. She alleges that these complications would not have occurred had CIGNA approved coverage for a longer hospital stay.

[In separate state-court suits,] respondents . . . argued that petitioners' refusal to cover the requested services violated their "duty to exercise ordinary care when making health care treatment decisions," and that these refusals "proximately caused" their injuries. Petitioners removed the cases to Federal District Courts, arguing that respondents' causes of action fit within the scope of, and were therefore completely preempted by, ERISA . . . The United States Court of Appeals for the Fifth Circuit consolidated their cases with several others raising similar issues . . . After examining the causes of action available under [ERISA], the Court of Appeals determined that respondents' claims could possibly fall under . . . §502(a)(1)(B), which provides a cause of action for the recovery of wrongfully denied benefits. . . . [However, the court ruled that this case does not fall under ERISA because] respondents "are not seeking reimbursement for benefits denied them," but rather request "tort damages" arising from "an external, statutorily imposed duty of 'ordinary care.' " . . .

II

Congress enacted ERISA to "protect . . . the interests of participants in employee benefit plans and their beneficiaries" by setting out substantive regulatory requirements for employee benefit plans and to "provid[e] for appropriate remedies, sanctions, and ready access to the Federal courts." 29 U.S.C. §1001(b). The purpose of ERISA is to provide a uniform regulatory regime over employee benefit plans. To this end, ERISA includes expansive preemption provisions, see ERISA §514, which are intended to ensure that employee benefit plan regulation would be "exclusively a federal concern." ERISA's "comprehensive legislative scheme" includes "an integrated system of procedures for enforcement." . . . As the Court said in *Pilot Life Ins. Co. v. Dedeaux,* 481 U.S. 41 (1987):

> [T]he detailed provisions of §502(a) set forth a comprehensive civil enforcement scheme that represents a careful balancing of the need for prompt and fair claims settlement procedures against the public interest in encouraging the formation of employee benefit plans. The policy choices reflected in the inclusion of certain remedies and the exclusion of others under the federal scheme would be completely undermined if ERISA-plan participants and beneficiaries were free to obtain remedies under state law that Congress rejected in ERISA. The six carefully integrated civil enforcement provisions found in §502(a) of the statute as finally enacted . . . provide strong evidence that Congress did *not* intend to authorize other remedies that it simply forgot to incorporate expressly.

Therefore, any state-law cause of action that duplicates, supplements, or supplants the ERISA civil enforcement remedy conflicts with the clear congressional intent to make the ERISA remedy exclusive and is therefore pre-empted. . . . It follows that if an individual brings suit complaining of a denial of coverage for medical care, where the individual is entitled to such coverage only because of the terms of an ERISA-regulated employee benefit plan, and . . . if an individual, at some point in time, could have brought his claim under ERISA §502(a) . . . then the individual's cause of action is completely preempted by ERISA. . . .

III

The only action [Davila] complained of was Aetna's refusal to approve payment for Davila's Vioxx prescription. Further, the only relationship Aetna had with Davila was its partial administration of Davila's employer's benefit plan. Similarly . . . Calad contests only CIGNA's decision to refuse coverage for her hospital stay . . . It is clear, then, that respondents complain only about denials of coverage promised under the terms of ERISA-regulated employee benefit plans. Upon the denial of benefits, respondents could have paid for the treatment themselves and then sought reimbursement through a §502(a)(1)(B) action, or sought a preliminary injunction. . . .[1]

Respondents contend, however, that the complained-of actions violate legal duties that arise independently of ERISA or the terms of the employee benefit plans at issue in these cases. Both respondents brought suit specifically under the Texas Act, alleging that petitioners "controlled, influenced, participated in and made decisions which affected the quality of the diagnosis, care, and treatment provided" in a manner that violated "the duty of ordinary care." . . . The Texas Act does impose a duty on managed care entities to "exercise ordinary care when making health care treatment decisions," and makes them liable for damages proximately caused by failures to abide by that duty. However, if a managed care entity correctly concluded that, under the terms of the relevant plan, a particular treatment was not covered, the managed care entity's denial of coverage would not be a proximate cause of any injuries arising from the denial. Rather, the failure of the plan itself to cover the requested treatment would be the proximate cause.[2] More significantly, the Texas Act clearly states that "[it] . . . create[s] no obligation on the part of the health insurance . . . entity to provide to an insured or enrollee treatment which is not covered by the health care plan of the entity." Hence, . . . interpretation of the terms of respondents' benefit plans forms an essential part of their [state law] claim, and [state law] liability would exist here only because of petitioners' administration of ERISA-regulated benefit plans. Petitioners' potential liability under the Texas Act in these cases, then, derives entirely from the particular rights and obligations established by the benefit plans. . . . [R]espondents bring suit only to rectify a wrongful denial of benefits promised under ERISA-regulated plans, and do not attempt to remedy any violation of a legal duty independent of ERISA. . . .

[T]he Court of Appeals found significant that respondents "assert a tort claim for tort damages" rather than "a contract claim for contract damages," and that respondents "are not seeking reimbursement for benefits denied them." But, distinguishing between preempted and non-preempted claims based on the particular label affixed to them would "elevate form over substance and allow parties to evade" the preemptive scope of ERISA simply "by relabeling their contract claims as claims for tortious breach of contract." . . . In [previous Supreme Court cases

1. Respondents also argue that the benefit due under their ERISA-regulated employee benefit plans is simply the membership in the respective HMOs, not coverage for the particular medical treatments that are delineated in the plan documents. Respondents did not identify this possible argument in their brief in opposition to the petitions for certiorari, and we deem it waived.

2. To take a clear example, if the terms of the health care plan specifically exclude from coverage the cost of an appendectomy, then any injuries caused by the refusal to cover the appendectomy are properly attributed to the terms of the plan itself, not the managed care entity that applied those terms.

finding preemption], the plaintiffs all brought state claims that were labeled either tort or tort-like. . . .

Respondents also argue—for the first time in their brief to this Court—that the Texas Act is a law that regulates insurance, and hence that ERISA §514(b)(2)(A) saves their causes of action from preemption.[3] This argument is unavailing. . . . ERISA §514(b)(2)(A) must be interpreted in light of the congressional intent to create an exclusive federal remedy in ERISA §502(a). Under ordinary principles of conflict preemption, then, even a state law that can arguably be characterized as "regulating insurance" will be preempted if it provides a separate vehicle to assert a claim for benefits outside of, or in addition to, ERISA's remedial scheme.

IV

Respondents, their *amici,* and some Courts of Appeals have relied heavily upon Pegram v. Herdrich, 530 U.S. 211 (2000), in arguing that ERISA does not preempt or completely preempt state suits such as respondents'. . . . *Pegram* cannot be read so broadly. In *Pegram,* the plaintiff sued her physician-owned-and-operated HMO (which provided medical coverage through plaintiff's employer pursuant to an ERISA-regulated benefit plan) and her treating physician, both for medical malpractice and for a breach of an ERISA fiduciary duty. The plaintiff's treating physician was also the person charged with administering plaintiff's benefits; it was she who decided whether certain treatments were covered. We reasoned that the physician's "eligibility decision and the treatment decision were inextricably mixed." We concluded that "Congress did not intend [the defendant HMO] or any other HMO to be treated as a fiduciary to the extent that it makes mixed eligibility decisions acting through its physicians." . . .

[I]it was essential to *Pegram*'s conclusion that the decisions challenged there were truly "mixed eligibility and treatment decisions," *i.e.,* medical necessity decisions made by the plaintiff's treating physician *qua* treating physician and *qua* benefits administrator. Put another way, the reasoning of *Pegram* "only make[s] sense where the underlying negligence also plausibly constitutes medical maltreatment by a party who can be deemed to be a treating physician or such a physician's employer." Cicio v. Does, 321 F.3d 83, 109 (C.A.2 2003) (Calabresi, J., dissenting in part). Here, however, petitioners are neither respondents' treating physicians nor the employers of respondents' treating physicians. Petitioners' coverage decisions, then, are pure eligibility decisions, and *Pegram* is not implicated. . . .

Justice GINSBURG, with whom Justice BREYER joins, concurring.

. . . [This] decision is consistent with our governing case law on ERISA's preemptive scope. I therefore join the Court's opinion. But, with greater enthusiasm . . . I also join "the rising judicial chorus urging that Congress and [this] Court revisit what is an unjust and increasingly tangled ERISA regime." DiFelice v. AETNA U.S. Healthcare, 346 F.3d 442, 453 (C.A.3 2003) (Becker, J., concurring). Because the Court has coupled an encompassing interpretation of ERISA's preemptive force with a cramped construction of the "equitable relief" allowable under §502(a)(3), a "regulatory vacuum" exists: "[V]irtually all state law remedies are preempted but very few federal substitutes are provided."

A series of the Court's decisions has yielded a host of situations in which persons adversely affected by ERISA-proscribed wrongdoing cannot gain make-whole relief [because] "there is a stark absence in [ERISA] itself and in its legislative history of any reference to an intention to authorize the recovery of extracontractual damages" for consequential injuries. . . . [F]resh consideration of the availability of consequential damages under §502(a)(3) is plainly in order. See 321 F.3d, at 106, 107 (Calabresi, J., dissenting in part) ("gaping wound" caused by the breadth of preemption and limited remedies under ERISA, as interpreted by this Court, will not be healed until the Court "start[s] over" or Congress "wipe[s] the slate clean"); DiFelice, 346 F.3d, at 467 ("The vital thing . . . is that either Congress or the Court act quickly, because the current situation is plainly untenable."); Langbein, What ERISA Means by "Equitable": The Supreme Court's Trail of Error in *Russell, Mertens,* and *Great-West,* 103 Colum. L. Rev. 1317, 1365 (2003). . . . The Government notes a potential amelioration. . . . [It] suggests that the Act, as currently written and interpreted, may "allo[w] at least some forms of 'make-whole' relief." . . . As the Court points out, respondents here declined the opportunity to amend their complaints to state claims for relief under §502(a). . . . But the Government's suggestion may indicate an effective remedy others similarly circumstanced might fruitfully pursue.

"Congress . . . intended ERISA to replicate the core principles of trust remedy law, including the make-whole standard of relief." *Langbein* 1319. I anticipate that Congress, or this Court, will one day so confirm.

Notes: ERISA Preemption

1. *Damages Under ERISA.* Under ERISA, patients who are wrongly denied health insurance benefits can recover compensation only for the costs of treatment, but not for consequential damages, pain and suffering, wrongful death, or punitive damages. Corcoran v. United Healthcare, Inc., 965 F.2d 1321 (5th Cir. 1992), dramatically illustrates the hardship caused by this restriction in available remedies. There, a woman miscarried late in her pregnancy due, she alleged, to the HMO's refusal to authorize hospitalization for pregnancy complications. The court limited her potential remedies under ERISA to an order for treatment or compensation for treatment costs. But, because the fetus had died, these remedies were meaningless. This restriction of damages is much more severe even than that imposed by ordinary contract law. See Sullivan v. O'Connor, 296 N.E.2d 183 (Mass. 1973). Therefore, it is important to note the concurring Justices' argument in *Davila* that this limitation can and should be revisited. See Sarah Spisich, The Aftermath of *Davila*: Are Healthcare Enrollees Now in a Sinking Ship Without a Paddle?, 17(4) The Health Lawyer 22 (Aug. 2005); Comment, 2006 B.Y.U. L. Rev. 1589 (2007).

The majority in *Davila* appears to think the outcome makes perfect sense according to congressional intent. Legislative history, however, reveals that Congress wrote ERISA primarily with pension benefits in mind, and long before managed care health insurance existed. Do you see why limiting damages to the costs of treatment might have made a lot more sense under traditional insurance? Assuming, as the concurrence argues, that ERISA's remedies no longer make sense for managed care insurance, whose responsibility is it to fix the problem: Congress's or the courts'? See Andrews-Clarke v. Travelers Insurance Co., 948 F. Supp. 49 (D. Mass. 1997) ("Although the [failure of the utilization reviewer to approve hospitalization for a deeply troubled alcoholic who later committed suicide] is extraordinarily troubling, even more disturbing to this Court is the failure of Congress to amend a statute that, due to the changing realities of the modern health care system, has gone conspicuously awry from its original intent. Does anyone care? Do you?").

2. *ERISA Terminology Is Obscure and Confusing.* Essentially, an ERISA "plan" exists any time an employer pays for health insurance. If the employer simply purchases health insurance, then technically there may be a distinction between the "plan," which is the decision to purchase, and the insurance, which is the contracted-for benefit. Would it be possible, using this distinction, to argue that ERISA preempts only suits against employers for failing to provide insurance, but not suits against insurers for failing to provide the benefits covered by the insurance? Observe how *Davila* avoids this issue in footnote 2 of the opinion, but a few lower courts have adopted this position. See, e.g., Washington Physicians Service Ass'n v. Gregoire, 147 F.3d 1039 (9th Cir. 1998) ("The mere fact that many [employers] choose to buy health insurance for their [employees] does not cause a regulation of health insurance automatically to 'relate to' any employee benefit plan—just as a decision to buy an apple a day for every employee, or to offer employees a gym membership, does not cause all state regulation of apples and gyms to 'relate to' employee benefit plans."). But see Hotz v. Blue Cross & Blue Shield of Massachusetts, 292 F.3d 57, 59-60 (1st Cir. 2002) ("Although the [employer plan/insurance plan] distinction is linguistically possible, it would mean that numerous past ERISA suits brought to secure payment for medical services from third-party providers under ERISA plans lacked a legal basis."). See generally Russell Korobkin, The Failed Jurisprudence of Managed Care, and How to Fix It: Reinterpreting ERISA Preemption, 51 UCLA L. Rev. 457 (2003).

Regardless, ERISA preemption would still apply to situations where the employer self-insures, that is, pays for health care directly out of its own funds. In that case, ERISA clearly preempts state law liability against the employer. So far, courts have applied ERISA preemption equally to both purchased and self-funded health insurance, where tort and contract claims are concerned. This distinction is relevant, however, for purposes of preemption of state insurance regulation, as discussed in Chapter 3.C.

3. *Which Claims Are Preempted?* The end of the *Davila* opinion briefly alludes to ERISA's effect on more conventional medical malpractice claims that arise under managed care insurance. Lower court decisions clarify the following: ERISA clearly does not apply to a malpractice claim against only the treating physician for a medical mistake that is unaffected by health insurance. . . . Likewise, courts usually find no preemption if a plaintiff attempts to hold a health insurer vicariously liable for a treating physician's mistake. Pacificare of Oklahoma v. Burrage, 59 F.3d 151 (10th Cir. 1995); Rice v. Panchal, 65 F.3d 637 (7th Cir. 1995). This helps to explain *Davila*'s reference to the fact that the plaintiffs' physicians in that case were not employees of the health plans.

The law is unsettled, however, when there is a medical treatment mistake and the plaintiff attempts to hold the insurer *directly* responsible because it selected bad physicians or influenced their treatment decisions. This is similar to the situation in Pegram v. Herdrich, 530 U.S. 211 (2000), which is discussed in *Davila.* There, the patient claimed that her doctor was influenced by profit distributions from the HMO and that this financial tie violates ERISA fiduciary standards. In the course of rejecting that claim under ERISA, the Court noted that the patient was free to pursue her claim in state court in the form of a medical malpractice suit. This strongly suggests that direct liability actions against HMOs for care provided by treating physicians are not preempted by ERISA, even after *Davila.*

In short, courts must distinguish between tort claims based on insurance coverage decisions, which are preempted, and medical malpractice liability, which is not preempted. In drawing this line, many lower courts have followed a rule of thumb that distinguishes between claims based on the *quantity* of care and those based on its *quality.* See, e.g., Dukes v. U.S. Healthcare, 57 F.3d 350 (3d Cir. 1995); Bauman v. U.S. Healthcare, Inc., 193 F.3d 151 (3d Cir. 1999). The *Davila* case makes no reference to this concept, however. Instead, it focuses on whether the insurer or the treating physician made the critical decision. Is that distinction likely to be sufficiently clear in most cases? What about situations where the treating physician is employed full time by an HMO, and the HMO instructs the physician that a particular treatment option is not approved, for instance, that women should not remain in the hospital longer than 48 hours following normal childbirth? That might be regarded as a quantity decision based on the insurance policy's medical appropriateness criteria, or it might be regarded as a form of direct HMO liability for interfering with physicians' ability to make good treatment decisions. Does *Davila* resolve which is the correct characterization?

One further complication: If it is possible to find an agency relationship between the HMO and the treating physician, should it matter that the HMO is not the physician's employer? Isn't the critical factor whether or not the physician agreed with, or acquiesced in, the HMO's decision? In *Davila,* the HMO refused to pay for treatments the physicians ordered, but, in many other cases, physicians may not order treatment they know the HMO won't pay for or that will cost the physician money under the HMO's payment incentives. Shouldn't patients be able to blame the HMO, at least in part, when this happens? In such cases, should *Davila* apply?

There is a large amount of academic literature discussing these issues, but most of it predates *Davila.* For subsequent analysis, see Aaron S. Kesselheim & Troyen A. Brennan, The Swinging Pendulum: The Supreme Court Reverses Course on ERISA and Managed Care, 5 Yale J. Health Pol'y L. & Ethics 451 (2005); Leonard A. Nelson, Aetna v. Davila: A Missed Opportunity, 31 Wm. Mitchell L. Rev. 843-896 (2005); Comment, 88 U. Colo. L. Rev. 1169 (2017); Note, 84 Tex. L. Rev. 1347-1383 (2006).

4. *Medicare Preemption.* Preemption issues might also arise under Medicare, which has a restrictive set of remedies for beneficiaries (discussed in Chapter 3.D.2). One court has held that Medicare's administrative review process does not preempt a state tort action against a private HMO that contracted to deliver Medicare services. McCall v. Pacificare of California, Inc., 21 P.3d 1189 (Cal. 2001). But, a later court has disagreed, finding that Medicare's 2006 amendments preempt liability suits against private Medicare insurers. Morrison v. Health Plan of Nevada, 328 P.3d 1165 (Nev. 2014).

3

Health Care Financing and Reform

The organization of health care law can be thought of in terms of concentric rings. At the center is the core treatment relationship between physician and patient. Outside this core are various external interests that might affect individual medical decisions. This book looks at the financial and intuitional arrangements that surround the treatment relationship; this chapter explores who pays for medical care, and under what terms. The next chapter explains the structure of medical facilities and how they relate to member physicians and to each other. It also examines the most complex layer in this set of rings: the emerging interconnections among insurers, facilities, and physicians as the marketplace for health care delivery undergoes rapid and fundamental transformation.

The dominant themes are political and economic: as our society struggles to solve the problems that confront the health care financing and delivery system, should we rely primarily on a market model that treats medicine as a consumer good, or on a social model that looks to regulatory governmental intervention to correct the perceived failures of the marketplace? This theme is introduced in Chapter 1.C, and is developed in more depth below, especially in Chapter 3.F.

Our fragmented system of paying for health care makes it difficult to cover comprehensively all of the complex legal regimes created by the many different sources of insurance. Rather than dividing the world of insurance into public vs. private, and conventional vs. managed care, we have chosen to organize this chapter around the generic issues that affect all sources of insurance: who is eligible, what services are covered, how is insurance regulated, how are disputes resolved, and how are doctors and hospitals paid? Along the way, it will be necessary, however, to learn whether answers to these questions differ according to the particular source of insurance. Therefore, we begin with a description of the entire, complex financing system.

A. SOURCES OF HEALTH INSURANCE

1. *The Right to Health Care*

■ UNCOMPENSATED HOSPITAL CARE: RIGHTS AND RESPONSIBILITIES*
Uwe Reinhardt

While honest economists long ago despaired of developing an overarching theory of distributive justice, political philosophers continue to hammer away at the problem. The several distinct theories of distributive justice emerging from these efforts are elegant in their internal logic, and eminently stimulating even to a skeptic. In the end, however, that literature fails as a guide towards a universally acceptable principle of justice. On the contrary, it persuades one that there cannot possibly be such a principle. For however tight the internal logic of any particular philosopher's theory of justice may be, that logic is ultimately anchored on some overarching value for which that author claims primacy on purely subjective grounds. Collectively, the political philosophers writing on the subject teach us that justice, like beauty, rests in the eye of the beholder.

Libertarian philosophers, for example, elevate individual liberty to the status of the single, overriding social value to which all other values are subordinate, and which can never justly be traded off against any subordinate value. Implicit in the libertarian's concept of "liberty" is the tenet that the individual is entitled to dispose of his or her possessions as he or she sees fit. Extreme versions of the theory—articulated, for example, in Robert Nozick's Anarchy, State, and Utopia (1974)—hold that any governmental infringement on this presumed property right is ipso facto unjust. Thus, to tax one person's wealth in order to finance another person's health care is unjust, as is a policy that compels physicians or privately owned facilities to render health care to designated individuals. In the libertarian's credo, it is the health care provider's right to determine whom to serve and whom not to serve, and also what price to exact for health services rendered. Health care providers must find this a comforting credo.

Diametrically opposed to the libertarian credo are the various theories of distributive justice espoused by egalitarian philosophers. Egalitarian philosophers elevate "equal respect for all individuals" or "equality of opportunity" to the overriding value of a just society to which all other values—among them individual liberty—are deemed subordinate. Equality of opportunity, argue these philosophers, requires as a minimum that all members of society have equal access to certain basic commodities, access to which determines an individual's range of opportunities and measure of self-respect. Health care, along with food, shelter, and education, is among these basic commodities.

* This reading is excerpted from the first chapter of a book by this title edited by F. Sloan, J. Blumstein & J. Perrin (1986). Reprinted with permission of Johns Hopkins University Press. The author was a well-known health economist at Princeton (and his first name is pronounced "OO-vay").

The entitlements implicit in the egalitarian tenet seem rather open-ended, and as recent history in this country has shown, they certainly are. Egalitarians, however, do not glibly ignore resource constraints. They merely argue that, in the face of such constraints, need, rather than ability to pay, should be the basis for rationing. Clearly, this theory of justice implies redistribution of the sort libertarians consider coercive and hence unjust.

One's own predilections aside, it is certainly no more logically compelling to let equal opportunity triumph completely over individual liberty than it is to do the reverse. Indeed, outside the ivory tower, any prevailing sense of justice is apt to be an amalgam in which each of the pure theories is somewhat compromised. While purist philosophers may deplore such compromises, policymakers must not only countenance them but actively lead in forging the amalgam.

A remarkable and unique feature of American health policy has been its attempt to accommodate simultaneously both the egalitarian and the libertarian theories of justice in their extreme purity. No other nation in the industrialized West has been quite so bold, or quite so naive, as to attempt that feat. Ironically, no other nation finds itself, in the mid-1980s, with the unsolved problem of uncompensated indigent care at the center stage of its health policy debate. There appears to be a causal link between schizoid thinking on the ethical plane and impotence at the level of policy.

Throughout the postwar period, and possibly even earlier, our policies on the distribution of health care have been firmly rooted in the egalitarian credo: It has been a widely shared notion that health care in the United States should be distributed on the basis of medical need rather than ability to pay. Furthermore, with appeal to the overarching principle of "equal respect for all individuals," it has generally been held (at least in public debate) that the nation should aim for equality in the process of—that there should be equity in the so-called amenities accompanying the delivery of health care, including the travel and wait time during access and the degree of free choice among providers. Politicians of all ideological stripes have supported these tenets (at least none has openly questioned them), and providers have endorsed them as well.

Cynics may argue that no one seriously entertained these lofty maxims and that they were recited by politicians mainly for public consumption. Some glaring remaining inequalities in access to health care may be cited to buttress that case. But a fair reading of health legislation during the 1960s and 1970s should persuade even a skeptic that public policy in those years was motivated by a genuine desire to move the country closer to an egalitarian distribution of health care. By the end of the 1970s, few policy analysts and even fewer public officials still questioned the proposition that access to all medically necessary and technically feasible health care on equal (process) terms is one of an American citizen's basic rights.

The pursuit of an egalitarian health care system is, of course, not a uniquely American phenomenon. Most other industrialized nations have shared that goal, and some of them seem to have been rather more successful than have we in approaching it. A uniquely American phenomenon, however, has been the endeavor to extract an egalitarian distribution of health care from a delivery system still firmly grounded in libertarian principles.

To be sure, our health care delivery system does not measure up in all respects to a libertarian's dream. Some individual liberties are being compromised by government for the sake of quality control, and even the staunchest defenders of the libertarian credo, America's physicians, have from time to time enlisted the government's coercive power to protect their economic turf through occupational licensing. We share such infringements with other modern societies. But in no other modern society espousing egalitarian principles for the distribution of health care have physicians and hospitals been quite so free as they have in the United States to organize their facilities as they see fit, to practice medicine as they see fit, and to price their services as they see fit. In these realms, libertarian principles have prevailed, and every legislative attempt to compromise them for the sake of cost control or greater equity in distribution has, until very recently, been beaten back successfully, with overt appeals to the libertarian credo. "If you want an egalitarian distribution of health care," providers have said, "we endorse it heartily, and we shall do our best to bring it about—but for a fee, and we want that fee to be reasonable as we define that term."

Libertarian and egalitarian purists wrestle with one another in any democratic society. The politician's task, as noted earlier, is to fashion from this struggle a sustainable social compromise. It is on that count that American health policy has performed poorly relative to other democracies. For, in seeking to cater to both extremes among notions of distributive justice, American policymakers have bestowed upon the nation a maze of public health programs that make a Rube Goldberg contraption appear streamlined by comparison.

There has been extraordinarily generous public health insurance coverage for some services and for some individuals—replete with completely free choice of providers by patients and with virtually open-ended reimbursement formulas for providers, . . . entitlements that have, on occasion, bordered on handing providers the key to the public treasury. . . . Yet, attempts to curb that flow of public funds into private treasuries have always been decried and, until very recently, rejected as an intolerable, regulatory infringement on private liberties.

Congressional respect for this peculiar conception of "liberty" naturally carried the danger of turning any federal health program into a fiscal hemorrhage. Too timid to prevent that outcome through controls on providers, our politicians have pursued the next logical policy to contain public health budgets: They simply have left glaring gaps in health insurance coverage, particularly for the near poor and the unemployed (whose health insurance coverage typically ceases with employment). . . . [O]ne would be hard put to identify any other industrialized society today that would still visit upon an unemployed worker's family, already down on its luck in so many material and emotional ways, the added anxiety and potential real hardship of going without health insurance coverage. It happens only in America.

It has become fashionable to attribute our long-standing failures in this area to a streak of meanness in the American character. Having lived both outside and inside this nation, I do not accept that interpretation. The special genius of nations who have long settled these problems lies not in their citizens' superior character, but lies, as noted, in a political process capable of forging a more stable ethical foundation for their health care systems. In all of these nations, the providers of health care enjoy fewer liberties than do their American counterparts. But, in addition, a good many of these countries—for example, the United Kingdom, West Germany, France, Switzerland, and Holland—have been rather more tolerant of some degree of tiering in their health systems than have the champions of egalitarianism in the United States. Perhaps the time has come for Americans, too, to debate more openly—and without the customary rancor and slander—just what are the essential ingredients of a just health care system.

THE RIGHT TO A DECENT MINIMUM OF HEALTH CARE*
Tom L. Beauchamp & James F. Childress

The history of the right to health care has been characterized more by political rhetoric than by careful analysis. The primary question has been whether the government should be involved in health care allocation and distribution, rather than leaving these matters to the marketplace. Libertarians insist that all rights to social goods based on enforced beneficence violate the principle of respect for autonomy. Society has often allowed this libertarian-supported rule of ability to pay to determine the distribution of health goods and services, but we will argue that this rule should not be allowed to serve as our only principle of distributive justice.

Two main arguments support a right to health care: (1) an argument from collective social protection and (2) an argument from fair opportunity. The first argument focuses on the similarities between health needs and other needs that have conventionally been protected by government. Threats to health are relevantly similar to threats presented by crime, fire, and polluted environments. The latter threats are conventionally resisted by collective actions and resources. . . . If government has an obligation to provide one type of essential service, then it must have an obligation to provide another. . . . However, . . . these public programs pertain to social goods, such as public health, whereas health care is largely a matter of the individual's private good. . . .

A second argument buttresses this first argument by appealing to the fair-opportunity rule. From this perspective, the justice of social institutions is gauged by their tendency to counteract lack of opportunity caused by unpredictable bad luck and misfortune over which the person has no meaningful control. Insofar as injury, disability, or disease creates profoundly significant disadvantages and reduces agents' capacity to function properly, justice is done if societal health care resources are used to counter these morally arbitrary, disadvantaging effects and to restore to persons a fair chance to use their capacities. . . .

This general guideline of fair opportunity suggests a path for giving content to the idea of a decent minimum of health care and for setting priorities in the allocation of resources. . . . The rule of fair opportunity asserts that collective moral obligations exist to provide health care at the level needed for persons to receive as fair a chance in life as possible.

Even if the arguments we have presented for a moral right to health care are rejected on grounds that justice does not support this right, a legal right or entitlement to health care can be supported on a different moral basis such as compassion and beneficence. . . . According to the "enforced beneficence argument," as Allen Buchanan terms it, beneficent citizens who do not believe that the needy have a

* This excerpt is from Principles of Biomedical Ethics (4th ed. 1994).

right to health care would still establish certain health programs for the needy while coercively requiring those with the resources to sustain the programs. . . . If the goals are sufficiently fundamental and important, coercion can be morally justified to fulfil the goals independent of the existence of rights.

A directly related argument from societal beneficence focuses on the expression of social virtue and excellence in public policies, with an emphasis on creating a morally worthy society with which citizens can identify. This communitarian approach concentrates on compassion for victims of the various lotteries of life. Themes from this approach echo in the influential report of the President's Commission for the Study of Ethical Problems in Medicine and Biomedical Research on Securing Access to Health Care (1983): "The depth of a society's concern about health care can be seen as a measure of its sense of solidarity in the face of suffering and death. . . . A society's commitment to health care reflects some of its most basic attitudes about what it means to be a member of the human community."

The Scope of the Right to Health Care

Apart from the contest between libertarian and nonlibertarian views of justice, an intractable, and ultimately the most important, problem is how to specify the entitlements and limits established by a right to health care. Two broad views have attracted wide contemporary support: a right to equal access to health care and a right to a decent minimum of health care. Both rely on egalitarian premises. The former represents a strong egalitarian perspective of equal access to all bona fide health care resources. The latter incorporates only a weak egalitarian point of view, viz., equal access to fundamental health care resources. . . . The societal obligation can be discharged at various levels, but the decent-minimum approach entails acceptance of [a] two-tiered system of health care: enforced social coverage for basic and catastrophic health needs (tier 1), together with voluntary private coverage for other health needs and desires (tier 2). . . .

Although some parties will be distressed to learn that the standard is "decent" care rather than "optimum" care, only the former can be justified in a socially funded policy. When we later . . . discuss explicit health policies such as the pioneering Oregon health plan, we will see that it is unrealistic to expect a higher level than adequate care. Rationing will also be an essential part of the process. Otherwise priorities cannot be set and maintained.

This proposal has the advantage of holding out the potential for compromise among libertarians, utilitarians, communitarians, and egalitarians, because it incorporates some moral concerns stressed by each of these theories. It guarantees basic health care for all on a premise of equal access, while allowing unequal additional purchase by individual initiative and contract. It mixes private and public forms of distribution, and it affirms collective as well as free-market methods of delivering health care. . . .

Despite these attractions, the decent-minimum proposal has proved difficult to explicate and implement. . . . Those who promote access to a decent minimum or adequate level of care usually do not specify where to set limits on expenditures for health care that confer precise entitlements. . . . [This] raises problems of whether society can fairly, consistently, and unambiguously devise a public policy that recognizes a right to care for primary needs without creating a right to exotic and expensive forms of treatment, such as liver transplants costing over $200,000 for what many deem to be marginal benefits in quality-adjusted life-years. More importantly, the model is purely programmatic until society defines what decent minimum means in operational terms. This task is, we believe, the major problem confronting health policy in the United States today.

Notes: The Right to Health Care

1. *The Right to Health Care.* Consider these additional perspectives on whether there is a moral or social right to health care, and what that right might be:

> There is a moral right to health care, but not of the sort often claimed. It is a right grounded not in purchasing power, merit, or social worth, but in human need. The right to health care finds its rationale in a social concept of the self, in a sense of common humanity, and in a knowledge of common vulnerability to disease and death. The right begins in a recognition that we all fall ill and are susceptible to disability and death. That is our nature and, whatever cultural variations there may be . . . , the root awareness we have of this is not an invention but a discovery. Second, while some illnesses are self-induced diseases generally are not the sort of things which are distributed by merit. We are all very likely to incur needs for health care for which we are not responsible and which are, in many instances, unforeseeable. Third, health care . . . is effective. Ill health is, in sum, the sort of thing which is universally experienced, but unevenly distributed, over which we have little control or predictive powers and for which there is frequently effective help. A just society is one in which the right to health care is based on the elemental fact of human need. . . . A more complete statement of a right to health care is as follows: *A right to health care based on need means a right to equitable access based on need alone to all effective care society can reasonably afford.* [The author defines "need alone" to mean that a person's entitlement to health care depends on the person's need for care, not the person's race, wealth, status, or other social attributes. Larry R. Churchill, Rationing Health Care in America 90-94 (1987) (emphasis in original).]
>
> [P]ermitting a noticeably lower tier of services for the poor can be based on respect for poor persons' own preferences. If poor, I will rationally and knowledgeably prefer to spend less on preserving health and saving life than if I am well off. Especially in choosing whether to cover and pay for statistically expensive, marginally beneficial procedures, lower income people will properly choose differently. To flatten out these differences through uniform health services *without* changing the basic distribution of income rides roughshod over poor people's preferences for the only lives they have to live. If wider injustice is the problem, it should be attacked by redistributing economic resources generally, not by restricting the choices of the poor when those choices are plausibly rational within their real-life context. [Paul T. Menzel, Some Ethical Costs of Rationing, 20 L. Med. & Health Care 57, 62-63 (1992).]
>
> [T]he United States [has] never really come close to forging the chain of public policies necessary to empower consumers to purchase health care according to their respective needs and circumstances. . . . [W]here other nations have more or less arranged their health care systems so that those who want more or better care than is suitable for the median citizen must pay more for it, the United States has structured things so that lower- and middle-income premium payers bear heavy burdens so that the elite classes can continue to enjoy the style of health care to

which they are accustomed. [Clark Havighurst, How the Health Care Revolution Fell Short, 65 Law & Contemp. Probs. 55, 77-78, 89 (Autumn 2002).]

2. *"Safety Net" Care for Uninsured Patients.* In the United States, health insurance is the main vehicle for providing access to affordable medical care, but insurance is not the only way. Lower-income uninsured patients have direct access to care through a number of "safety net" providers—those who, as a last resort, will take all patients regardless of their ability to pay.

Most prominently, hospitals may not refuse at least "stabilizing" treatment to emergency patients (see Chapter 2.A.1). But, beyond that, many hospitals will accept indigent uninsured patients for free or at very steep discounts. These safety net facilities include public hospitals owned by large municipalities or state medical schools, as well as (to varying degrees) nonprofit private hospitals that are tax-exempt. The United States also has a large number of "community health centers" and free clinics that provide primary care services on the safety net basis. These are supported by federal and state funds, or by charity and volunteer workers. Public hospitals and clinics are also operated by the federal government for Native Americans (the Indian Health Service), military personnel, and veterans (VA hospitals).

What are the inadequacies of such safety net systems? First, safety net providers are absent in many locations, and where they do exist, funding is usually deficient. Several prominent suits attempting to force municipalities to better fund their public hospitals have achieved only moral victories due to procedural obstacles. See, e.g., Evelyn V. v. Kings County Hospital Center, 819 F. Supp. 183 (E.D.N.Y. 1993) (public hospital's level of service may violate state and federal statutes, but federal courts lack authority to order compliance); Tailfeather v. Board of Supervisors, 48 Cal. App. 4th 1223 (Cal. 1996) (county not obligated to adopt formal standards specifying maximum waiting times for indigents' receipt of medical care); Franklin Memorial Hospital v. Harvey, 575 F.3d 121 (1st Cir. 2009) (finding no constitutional infirmity in requiring private hospitals to provide free indigent care). But see Saint Alphonsus Regional Medical Center, Inc. v. Board of County Commissioners of Ada County, 190 P.3d 870 (Idaho 2008) (requiring county to pay some of the $187,000 medical bill incurred by an illegal immigrant). See generally Gary Jones, Regulatory Takings and Emergency Medical Treatment, 47 San Diego L. Rev. 145 (2010).

Second, most of the safety net is focused on primary care and on hospital care for acute or emergency conditions. Often lacking is any well-organized system to provide specialist outpatient services and diagnostic testing. But, where these and other deficiencies do not exist, well-coordinated, comprehensive safety net systems have been shown to provide levels of care similar to that provided by private or public insurance. See Mark A. Hall, Access to Care Provided by Better Safety Net Systems for the Uninsured, 68 Med. Care Res. Rev. 441 (2011). The Veterans Health Administration is sometimes held out as a prime example, although not without some controversy. See Adam Oliver, The Veterans Health Administration: An American Success Story?, 85 Milbank Q. 5 (2007); Phillip Longman, Best Care Anywhere: Why VA Healthcare Is Better Than Yours (2007).

3. *Further Reading.* For discussions of the **moral foundation and meaning of the right to health care**, see Norman Daniels, Just Health Care 27-29 (1985); Richard Epstein, Mortal Peril: Regulating Health Care in America (1997), which contains an

extensive argument against entitlements and positive rights to health care; Timothy Jost, Disentitlement: Health Care Entitlements and the Threats That They Face (2003); Christina Ho, Are We Suffering From an Undiagnosed Health Right?, 42 Am. J. L. & Med. 743 (2016); Lindsay Wiley, From Patient Rights to Health Justice: Securing the Public's Interest in Affordable, High-Quality Health Care, 37 Cardozo Law Review 833 (2016); Sidney Watson, Metaphors, Meaning, and Health Reform, 54 St. Louis U. L.J. 1313 (2010); Einer Elhauge, Allocating Health Care Morally, 82 Cal. L. Rev. 1449 (1995); Andre Hampton, Markets, Myths, and a Man on the Moon: Aiding and Abetting America's Flight from Health Insurance, 52 Rutgers L. Rev. 987 (2000); Kevin P. Quinn, Viewing Health Care as a Common Good: Looking Beyond Political Liberalism, 73 S. Cal. L. Rev. 277 (2000); Jennifer P. Ruger, Toward a Theory of a Right to Health, 18 Yale J.L. & Human. 273 (2006); Note, Universal Access to Health Care, 108 Harv. L. Rev. 1323 (1995); and Symposium, 36 J. Med. & Phil. 529 (2011).

For discussions of a **legal right to health care**, generally, see Mila Versteeg & Emily Zackin, American Constitutional Exceptionalism Revisited, 81 U. Chi. L. Rev. 1641 (2014) (observing that "a whopping 72% [of the world's written constitutions] include a right to health care"); Erin C. Fuse Brown. Developing a Durable Right to Health Care, 14 Minn. J.L. Sci. & Tech. 439 (2013); Abigail Moncrieff, The Freedom of Health, 159 Penn. L. Rev. 2209 (2011); Puneet K. Sandhu, A Legal Right to Health Care: What Can the United States Learn from Foreign Models of Health Rights Jurisprudence?, 95 Cal. L. Rev. 1151 (2007) (arguing, based on experience in other countries, that a legal right to health care is justiciable); Elizabeth Weeks Leonard, State Constitutionalism and Health Care, 12 U. Pa. J. Const. L. 1327 (2010) (noting lack of enforcement of relevant state constitutional provisions); Alan Jenkins & Sabrineh Ardalan, Positive Health: The Human Right to Health Care Under the New York State Constitution, 35 Fordham Urb. L.J. 479 (2008).

For discussions of the **safety net**, see Mark Hall & Sara Rosenbaum eds., The Health Care Safety Net in a Post-Reform World (2012); Mark A. Hall, Approaching Universal Coverage with Better Safety-Net Programs for the Uninsured, 11 Yale J. Health Pol'y, L. & Ethics 9 (2011); Symposium, 31(8) Health Aff. (2012); Symposium, 26(5) Health Aff. (2007); Symposium, 25(3) Health Aff. (2006).

2. *Private Health Insurance*

THE MARKET STRUCTURE OF THE HEALTH INSURANCE INDUSTRY

D. Andrew Austin & Thomas L. Hungerford

Congressional Research Service, 2009

The market structure of the modern U.S. health insurance industry not only reflects the complexities and uncertainties of health care, but also its origins in the 1930s and its evolution in succeeding decades. . . . As population shifted from rural agricultural regions to industrialized urban centers, . . . [m]any workers obtained accident or sickness policies through fraternal organizations, labor unions, or private insurers. These policies were usually indemnity plans, that would pay a set cash amount in the event of a serious accident or health emergency. . . .

HOW THE "BLUES" BEGAN

The modern health insurance industry in the United States was spurred by the onset of the Great Depression. In 1929, the Baylor University Hospital in Dallas created a pre-paid hospitalization benefit plan for school teachers after a hospital executive discovered that unpaid bills accumulated by local educators were a large burden on hospital finances as well as on the teachers themselves. Unlike earlier health insurance policies, subscribers were entitled to hospital care and services rather than a cash indemnity. . . . Other hospitals in Dallas quickly followed suit with their own group hospitalization plans as a means of ensuring a steady revenue source in difficult economic times.[11] . . . Community-based plans in St. Paul, Minnesota, Washington, D.C., and Cleveland were created soon afterwards. The Blue Cross emblem, first used by the St. Paul plan, was widely adopted by other prepaid hospital benefit plans adhering to American Hospital Association (AHA) guidelines. . . .

The health insurance market in the United States, according to many historians, was originally structured to avoid competition among providers.[15] . . . Hospital and professional groups . . . soon pushed for joint plans that required "free choice of physicians and hospital," rather than plans offered by individual hospitals. Joint plans dampened incentives for local hospitals to compete on the basis of price or generosity of plan benefits. The American Hospital Association strongly favored joint plans that allowed a subscriber to obtain care from any licensed local hospital and viewed single-hospital plans as a threat to the economic stability of community hospitals. . . .

Insurance coverage of physician services lagged behind the growth of Blue Cross hospital plans due to opposition from the American Medical Association (AMA) and restrictive state laws.[19] In several states, however, medical societies set up prepaid service plans to preempt proposed state or federal plans, which evolved into Blue Shield plans. . . . Blue Cross plans accelerated their growth during World War II and extended to almost all states by 1946. Wartime wage and price controls authorized in October 1942 excluded "reasonable" insurance and pension benefits. As industries struggled to expand war production, many employers used health insurance and other fringe benefits to attract new workers. In the late 1940s, the National Labor Relations Board (NLRB) successfully sued employers that refused to bargain collectively over fringe benefits, opening the way for unions to negotiate with employers over health insurance, which further helped boost enrollments in health insurance plans. . . .

[Today, most] private health insurance is offered through employers. With employer-sponsored plans, employers may simply offer health benefit plans through

11. Robert Cunningham III and Robert M. Cunningham Jr., *The Blues: A History of the Blue Cross and Blue Shield System* (Dekalb, IL: Northern Illinois University Press, 1997).

15. Rosemary Stevens, *In Sickness and In Wealth: American Hospitals in the 20th Century* (New York: Basic Books, 1989), p. 156.

19. Paul Starr, *The Social Transformation of American Medicine* (New York: Basic Books, 1983), pp. 296-297.

an insurance company for a negotiated price and bear no insurance risk. At the other extreme, the employer may self-insure and handle the plan itself, thus bearing all of the insurance risk and the administrative burden of the plan. Often, the extent of employer involvement depends on the number of employees. Research has found that 80% of large employers (500 or more employees) choose to self-insure rather than purchase coverage from a health insurer. . . .

Tax Advantages for Employer-Provided Health Insurance Benefits

. . . Health insurance is subsidized through the tax system in several ways. First, . . . [the] Internal Revenue Code of 1954 included section 106, which explicitly allowed the exclusion of employer contributions for health insurance. . . . The Joint Committee on Taxation (JCT) estimates that the federal government forgoes [over $250 billion] annually in tax revenue because of this exclusion. . . . The tax exemption for employer-provided health care made health insurance cheaper than non-exempt forms of consumption for individuals. One study found that health insurance coverage following the 1954 tax changes expanded more rapidly among employees with higher incomes, who generally had marginal tax rates, which could indicate that the tax exclusion led workers to demand more extensive or generous plans. Other factors, such as rising income levels, competition for workers, and rising medical costs, also spurred growth in employer-provided health benefits. . . .

Commercial Insurers Enter

Before World War II, many commercial insurers doubted that hospital or medical costs were an insurable risk. Insurers traditionally considered a risk insurable only if the potential losses were definite, measurable and not subject to control by the insured. The financial risks linked to illness or injury, however, could vary depending on the judgment of medical personnel, and behavior of the insured could affect the probability of ill health in many ways. After the rapid spread of Blue Cross plans in the mid-1930s, however, several commercial insurers began to offer similar health coverage. By the 1950s, commercial health insurers had become potent competitors and began to cut into Blue Cross's market share in many parts of the country. The large-scale entry of commercial insurers into the health insurance market changed the competitive environment. . . .

[T]he commercial health insurers were not bound to set premiums using the Blue Cross community rating principle, which linked premiums to average claims costs across a geographic area rather than to the claims experience of particular groups or individuals. Therefore, commercial insurers using an "experience rating" approach were able to underbid Blue Cross for firms that employed healthier-than-average individuals, which on average were cheaper to insure.

The loss of healthier groups then raised average costs among remaining groups, which . . . compelled Blue Cross to adopt experience rating. . . . The shift toward experience rating changed the nature of competition in the health insurance market. Insurers could cut costs by shifting risks to others, by recruiting firms whose employees and their families were healthier than average, rather than finding more efficient ways of managing risks for a given pool of subscribers. . . .

By the 1980s, health researchers and policymakers had begun to view the differences between Blue Cross/Blue Shield insurers, which were organized as non-profit organizations, and for-profit commercial health insurers as having narrowed. . . . In 1994, Blue Cross/Blue Shield guidelines were amended to let affiliates reorganize as for-profit insurers, leading the way for more than a dozen Blue Cross/Blue Shield affiliates to convert to for-profit status. Other Blue Cross/Blue Shield insurers bought other insurers, merged, or restructured in other ways. At the same time, private insurers acquired HMOs and other managed care organizations. Consolidations reduced both the number of commercial and Blue Cross/Blue Shield organizations, leading to the emergence of a small number of very large insurers with strong market positions across the country. . . .

Introduction of Medicare and Medicaid

. . . While Blue Cross/Blue Shield and commercial insurance plans covered a large portion of employees and their dependents at the end of the 1950s, many low-income and elderly people had trouble obtaining affordable health insurance or paying for health care. . . . Social Security was extended to pay providers to cover certain medical costs incurred by aged, blind, and disabled beneficiaries starting in 1950. . . . State governments, subject to certain federal requirements, retained substantial discretion over benefit levels and income limits, which were typically linked to welfare assistance programs. . . .

In 1965, the Johnson Administration worked with Ways and Means Committee Chairman Wilbur Mills to create the Medicare program, which provided health insurance for nearly all Americans over age 65. Medicare combined a compulsory hospital insurance program (Part A) with a voluntary physician services plan (Part B). While some had worried that Medicare would displace private insurers, Blue Cross organizations became fiscal intermediaries for Medicare, responsible for issuing payments to providers and other back office operations. Medicaid, created in the same 1965 act, is a means-tested program financed by federal and state funds. Each state designs and administers its own program under federal rules. Over time, Medicaid eligibility standards and federal requirements have become more complex. . . .

The Rise of Managed Care [and "Consumer-Directed" Care]

In some parts of the country, plans combining insurance with the direct provision of health care evolved into important players in local markets despite the strong opposition of the AHA and AMA. A health plan designed for southern California construction workers in the mid-1930s eventually became the Kaiser Health Plan. . . . While some of these plans prospered locally or regionally, they did not achieve national reach until the 1970s.

In 1971, President Nixon announced a program to encourage prepaid group plans that joined insurance and care functions as a way to constrain the growth of medical care costs, which had risen sharply in the years following the startup of the Medicare and Medicaid programs, and to enhance competition in the health insurance market. Advocates claimed that health maintenance organizations (HMOs), which integrate health care and health insurance functions, would have a financial motive to promote wellness and would lack incentives to overprovide care. . . .

While this ambitious goal was not reached in the 1970s, by the late 1980s policymakers and businesses began to view greater use of managed care organizations such as HMOs and similar organizations as a key strategy for controlling health care costs. In the mid-1990s, the broader use of more restrictive forms of managed care (such as stringent gatekeeper, second medical opinion, and pre-approval requirements) sparked strong consumer resistance, which forced an industry retreat from some of those strategies. Networks of providers, known as preferred provider organizations (PPOs), grew rapidly in the late 1980s and early 1990s. PPOs, often owned by hospital systems and other providers, typically contract with insurers or self-insured firms and offer discounted fee-for-service (FFS) rates. PPO enrollees who receive care outside of the network typically must obtain plan approval or pay more. Thus, PPO plans provided patients with more flexibility than staff-model HMOs, which generally did not cover care provided outside of the HMO. As various types of managed care plans such as HMOs and PPOs became widespread, more employers offered choices among competing health plans to let workers willing to pay higher premiums avoid restrictive plans. . . .

The predominant type of health insurance plan has changed dramatically over the past 25 years. Over 90% of the privately insured were covered by an indemnity or traditional "unmanaged" health insurance plan in 1980; now the share is less than 10%. Today, most people covered by private insurance are covered by some kind of managed care plan ranging from a managed indemnity plan (e.g., PPOs, where the insurers negotiate fees with providers) to a staff HMO (the insurer and the provider are the same, and patients see physicians who are on salary). . . .

In the 1990s, proponents of "consumer-directed" health care proposed measures intended to make consumers more sensitive to medical care costs. In . . . 2003 . . . Congress passed legislation to allow consumers with high-deductible health insurance plans to set up Health Savings Accounts (HSAs) that allow people to pay for out-of-pocket expenses through a tax-advantaged medical savings account. . . .

Description of the Health Insurance Market

Individuals and families typically buy insurance to avoid risks by paying a known premium in order to receive benefits if an adverse event were to occur during the insurance policy's term. Most individuals are willing to pay an insurer to assume the bulk of financial risks associated with unpredictable health outcomes of uncertain severity. . . . Some insured people will become sick or injured and incur significant medical expenses. Most people, however, will remain relatively healthy, thus incurring little or no medical expenses.[54] . . . In essence, money is shifted from those who remain healthy to those who become sick or injured.

The health insurance market is tightly interrelated with other parts of the health care system. . . . Health insurers not only reimburse providers, but also

54. A analysis of 2002 Medical Expenditure Panel Survey data found that "[h]alf of the population spends little or nothing on health care, while 5 percent of the population spends almost half of the total amount." . . . [See also National Institute for Health Care Management, The Concentration of Health Care Spending (2012).]

typically have some control over the number and types of services covered and negotiate contracts with providers on the payments for health services. . . .

The health insurance market has many features that push it far from the economic benchmark of perfect competition. . . . How insurers design health care networks influences how consumers use health care. Consumers typically choose a primary physician who selects tests and treatments and makes referrals to medical specialists. Employers negotiate with insurers on behalf of their workers, and labor unions negotiate with employers over health benefits on behalf of their members. Health insurers, in turn, negotiate contracts with providers and handle payments for individual services. A primary physician's admitting privileges typically determine where his patient goes for non-emergency hospital care. Patients must go through a physician to obtain most medical tests and pharmaceuticals. Health care consumers typically rely on these intermediaries instead of interacting directly with other parts of the health care system. This heavy reliance on intermediaries is a key characteristic of the current health care market. . . .

Using intermediaries such as health insurers protects consumers from financial risks linked to serious medical problems, but it also insulates consumers from information about costs and prices for specific health care goods and services. When a third-party, such as a private insurer or a government, pays for the bulk of health care costs, consumers may demand more care and providers may wish to supply more care. Links among intermediaries and providers can also limit consumers' choices. For example, a person's job may limit her health insurance choices, and another person's choice of physician may limit choices among hospitals. Some families and individuals lacking these intermediaries must navigate the health insurance and health care system themselves, which may be a serious challenge. . . .

Finally, how intermediaries interact has important consequences in the health care market. For instance, employers and health insurers, which both intermediate on behalf of individuals, interact through negotiations over insurance benefits packages. Politicians can also act as intermediaries for their constituents by helping to determine reimbursement rates for public insurance programs and by changing the regulatory environment facing health insurers. . . .

Moral Hazard

Moral hazard, which occurs when insurance status changes behavior, is another problem in the health insurance market. Moral hazard occurs if an insured individual consumes more medical services than she would have had she been uninsured. For example, having health insurance could induce someone to seek medical care for minor conditions (e.g., a sore throat), choose a high-amenity health care setting (e.g., a more hotel-like hospital), or neglect his health (e.g., by eating fatty foods). Consequently, moral hazard leads the insurer to pay providers more for an insured person's medical services than that person would have paid out of his own pocket had he not been insured. Of course, non-monetary costs, such as the pain and inconvenience of obtaining unnecessary medical care, may help limit moral hazard among patients.

Insurers typically react to moral hazard by raising premiums to cover the costs of additional services and by limiting care, either directly (e.g., through prior approval requirements) or through cost-sharing measures such as copayments and deductibles. . . . The lack of transparency in the pricing of medical services contributes to this problem—most people do not know the cost of medical services (both what the provider normally charges and what the insurance company reimburses the provider).

The Principal-Agent Problem

A patient (here, a *principal*), as noted above, typically relies on a physician (an *agent*) for care and advice. The physician, or other intermediary, might face incentives to act to further their own interests, rather than those of the patient, by providing a higher quantity or lower quality of care than would be appropriate for a patient. . . . [P]ayment and incentive systems may mitigate conflicts of interests. Professional standards and professional organizations may also help mitigate those conflicts. . . .

While that arrangement may avoid some problems, it may not solve others. In fee-for-service (FFS) arrangements, physicians and other providers may face financial incentives to provide more care than would best suit the patient's interests. When insurance pays most of the costs associated with health care, providers have little financial incentive to control costs and may overprovide health care services. One study randomly selected doctors into a salary group and a fee-for-service group during a nine-month study. The results showed that doctors in the fee-for-service group scheduled more office visits than salaried doctors, and almost all of the difference was due to the fee-for-service doctors seeing well patients rather than sick patients. Defensive medicine, in which physicians or other providers order tests that may reduce the probability of medical malpractice litigation, but which provide limited therapeutic benefits to the patient, presents a similar problem. . . .

Responses to . . . moral hazard and principal-agent problems affect the structure of the health financing system. Health insurers, as noted above, use coinsurance and pre-approval requirements to limit potential moral hazard among patients. Health insurers concerned about moral hazard and principal-agent problems among providers design incentive systems to limit overprovision of care. For example, the rapid transition to managed care in the 1990s might be seen as an attempt to control costs due to moral hazard. In addition, research and development (R&D) decisions made by medical technology and pharmaceutical firms may be indirectly guided by how health insurance coverage affects choices of providers and patients. Reforms that change the health financing system without taking into account potential moral hazards that previous structures and practices were designed to mitigate could encounter unanticipated problems. . . .

47 MILLION AND COUNTING: WHY THE HEALTH CARE MARKETPLACE IS BROKEN

Testimony of Mark A. Hall

U.S. Senate Committee on Finance Hearing (2008)

The high concentration of most medical costs in a relative few people is the single most important fact for understanding the private insurance market. It is hard to find the right words to describe this foundational statistical phenomenon in terms that are sufficiently compelling, so I will start with a graphic depiction. Arraying the population by health care spending in [2014, Figure 3.1 below] shows that

- the top 1% [who averaged more than $100,000] accounted for [over one-fifth] of total spending
- the top 5% [who averaged more than $50,000] accounted for [almost] half of all spending
- and the top 20% . . . accounted for [over] 80% of spending.

The bottom half of the population distribution [who averaged $264 that year] incurred [3%] of total costs.

FIGURE 3.1 The Concentration of Health Care Spending

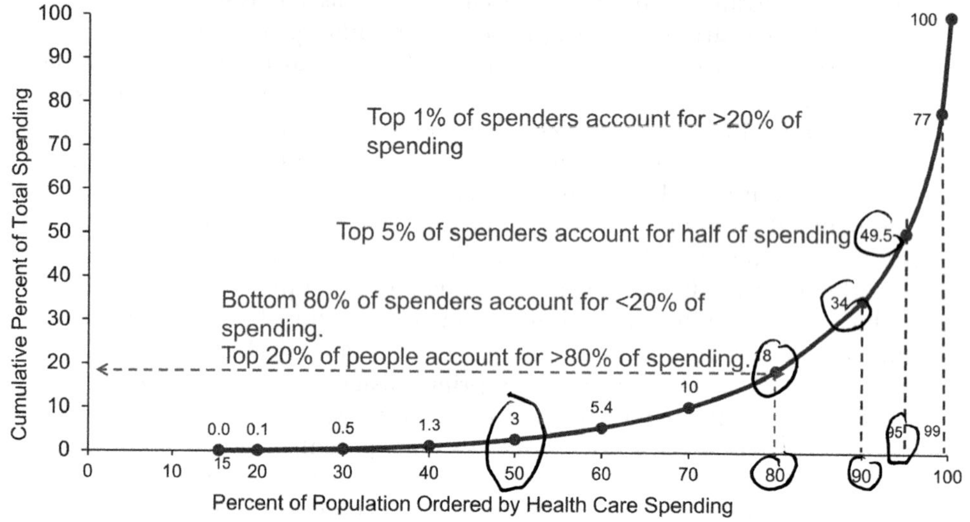

Source: NIHCM Foundation analysis from the 2009 Medical Expenditure Panel Survey.

For convenience, I refer to this as "the 80/20 rule." I call it a rule because the pattern is remarkably universal. This pattern has a fractal geometry that appears wherever one looks. It holds true both for the population at large and for just about any subpopulation of any size one might choose to examine. . . . The extreme concentration of health care costs is an economic law of nature that has been observed as early as the 1930s and that will be with us for as long as anyone can foresee—regardless of how we deliver and pay for health care.

I stress the 80/20 rule because it is the most elemental fact of health insurance. It is as fundamental as gravity, and as pervasive as the weather. It is the endemic First Cause that reaches everywhere and explains just about everything of importance in the market for insurance. The high concentration of medical costs is why we need and have insurance in the first place. Pooling expenses across a population keeps them affordable for everyone, but the extreme costs at the high end also explain why insurance is so expensive, especially for those who anticipate no real need.

The extreme magnitude of differences in health risks also explains the private insurance market's most perplexing dynamics. I will describe several troubling phenomena, each of which derives from the basic fact that insurers stand to gain a great deal by avoiding or appropriately pricing people with higher risks. They also stand to lose a great deal if they do not attract a good number of lower risks. Therefore, competitive forces in health insurance markets inevitably focus on risk selection (or risk segmentation). Other points of competitive focus—such as product design, benefit coverage, sales vehicles, and care management—either have much less impact on profitability or are themselves surrogates for risk selection or segmentation. . . .

The natural dynamics of risk segmentation are so strong that risk selection occurs even without overt [screening by insurers]. Subscribers naturally sort themselves by risk to some extent, according to the covered benefits and plan features they find most attractive. Insurers and employers have learned that features such as deductibles, managed care, and particular benefits that are covered or excluded appeal differently to people with lesser versus greater health care needs. This is one reason many health policy analysts favor uniform benefits and why most employers limit their workers' choice of health plans. . . .

Risk selection practices flow directly from the very nature of how competitive markets should and must respond to highly concentrated health risks. Therefore, these effects will never be eliminated unless the market is fundamentally restructured. . . .

BAD MEDICINE: A GUIDE TO THE REAL COSTS AND CONSEQUENCES OF THE NEW HEALTH CARE LAW

Michael D. Tanner

*Cato Institute, July 2010**

On March 21, 2010, in an extraordinary Sunday night session, the House of Representatives gave final approval to President Obama's long-sought health insurance plan in a partisan 219-212 vote. The bill had earlier passed the Senate on Christmas Eve, 2009. Not a single Republican in either chamber voted for the bill. . . . More than 2,500 pages and 500,000 words long, the Patient Protection and Affordable Care Act (PPACA) [also known as the Affordable Care Act or ACA] represents the most significant transformation of the American health care system since Medicare and Medicaid. It will fundamentally change nearly every aspect of health care from insurance to the final delivery of care.

The final legislation is, in some ways, an improvement over earlier versions. It is not the single-payer system sought by many liberals. Nor did it include the interim step of a so called "public option" that would likely have led to a single-payer system in the long run. . . . But that does not mean that this is, as the president has claimed, a "moderate" bill. It mandates that every American purchase a government-designed insurance package, while fundamentally reordering the insurance market and turning insurers into something resembling public utilities. . . .

Insurance coverage will be extended to millions more Americans as government subsidies are expanded deep into the middle class. Costs will be shifted between groups, though ultimately not reduced. And a new entitlement will be created, with the threat of higher taxes and new debt for future generations. In many ways, it has rewritten the relationship between the government and the people, moving this country closer to European-style social democracy. . . .

Individual and Employer Mandates

Perhaps the single most important piece of this legislation is its individual mandate, a legal requirement that every American obtain health insurance coverage that meets the government's definition of "minimum essential coverage." Those who don't receive such coverage through government programs, their employer, or some other group would be required to purchase individual coverage on their own. This individual mandate is unprecedented in U.S. governance. . . .

Under the new law, beginning in 2014, those who fail to obtain insurance would be subject to a tax penalty. That penalty would be quite mild at first, either $95 or one percent of annual income in 2014, whichever is greater. But it ramps up quickly after that, . . . [to] the greater of $695 or 2.5 percent of annual income. . . . Individuals will be exempt from the penalties if they . . . are unable to obtain insurance that costs less than 8 percent of their gross incomes. . . . While the law imposes penalties for failure to comply, . . . it does not contain any criminal penalties for failing to comply, and it forbids the use of liens or levies to collect the penalties. However, the IRS . . . may withhold tax refunds to individuals who fail to comply with the mandate. . . .

The new law also contains an employer mandate, although it is watered down from the proposal that passed the House last year. . . . [B]eginning in 2014, if a company with 50 or more full-time employees (or the equivalent) does not provide health insurance to its workers, . . . the company must pay a tax penalty of $2,000 for every person they employ full time (minus 30 workers). . . . [A]s with the individual mandate, the penalty may be low enough that many businesses may find it less costly to "pay" than to "play" . . .

Insurance Regulations

The Patient Protection and Affordable Care Act imposes a host of new federal insurance regulations that will significantly change the way the health insurance industry does business. Some of these regulatory changes are likely to be among the law's most initially popular provisions. But many are likely to have unintended consequences. Perhaps the most frequently discussed regulatory measure is the ban on insurers denying coverage because of preexisting conditions. . . . Specifically, . . . insurers would be prohibited from making any underwriting decisions based on health status, mental or physical medical conditions, claims experience, medical history, genetic information, disability, [or] other evidence of insurability. . . .

Finally, there will be limits on the ability of insurers to vary premiums on the basis of an individual's health. That is, insurers must charge the same premium for someone who is sick as for someone who is in perfect health. Insurers may consider age in setting premiums, but those premiums cannot be more than three times higher for their oldest than their youngest customers. Smokers may also be charged up to 50 percent more than nonsmokers. . . . While the ban on medical underwriting may make health insurance more available and affordable for those with preexisting conditions and reduce premiums for older and sicker individuals, it will also increase premiums for younger and healthier individuals. . . .

Perhaps the most fundamental reordering of the current insurance market is the creation of "exchanges" in each state. . . . The exchanges would function as a clearinghouse, a sort of wholesaler or middleman, matching customers with providers and products. Exchanges would also allow individuals and workers in small companies to take advantage of the economies of scale, both in terms of administration and risk pooling, which are currently enjoyed by large employers. . . . Exactly how significant the exchanges will prove to be remains to be seen. . . . However, one should be skeptical of claims that the exchange will reduce premiums. . . .

Insurance plans offered for sale within the exchanges [are] grouped into four categories based on actuarial value: bronze, the lowest cost plans, providing 60 percent of the actuarial value of a standard plan as defined by the secretary of HHS; silver, providing 70 percent of the actuarial value; gold, providing 80 percent of the actuarial value; and platinum, providing 90 percent of the actuarial value. In addition, exchanges may offer a special catastrophic plan to individuals who are under age 30 or who have incomes low enough to exempt them from the individual mandate. . . . CBO estimates that premiums for bronze plans would probably average between $4,500 and $5,000 for an individual and between $12,000 and $12,500 for family policies. The more inclusive policies would have correspondingly higher premiums. . . .

SUBSIDIES

The number one reason that people give for not purchasing insurance is that they cannot afford it. Therefore, the legislation's principal mechanism for expanding coverage (aside from the individual and employer mandates) is to pay for it, either through government-run programs such as Medicaid . . . or through subsidizing the purchase of private health insurance.

Starting in 2011, states are required to expand their Medicaid programs to cover all U.S. citizens with incomes below 133 percent of the poverty level [which is roughly $15,000 for an individual or $30,000 for a family of four]. . . . [T]he primary result of the law's Medicaid expansion would be to extend coverage to the parents in low-income families and to childless adults. In particular, single, childless men will now be eligible for Medicaid. . . .

Individuals with incomes too high to qualify for Medicaid but below 400 percent of the poverty level ($88,000 per year, for family of four) will be eligible for subsidies . . . in the form of refundable tax credits. . . . The credit is calculated on a sliding scale according to income in such a way as to limit the total proportion of income that an individual would have to pay for insurance. Thus, individuals with incomes between 133 and 200 percent of the poverty level will receive a credit covering the cost of premiums up to four percent of their income, while those earning 300-400 percent of the poverty level will receive a credit for costs in excess of 9.5 percent of their income. . . . As with many tax credits, the phase-out of these benefits creates a high marginal tax penalty as wages increase. In some cases, workers who increase their wages could actually see their after-tax income decline as the subsidies are reduced. . . .

All together, this law represents a massive increase in the welfare state, adding millions of Americans to the roll of those dependent, at least to some extent, on government largess. Yet for all the new spending, the Patient Protection and Affordable Care Act falls short of its goal of achieving universal coverage. . . . According to the Congressional Budget Office, the legislation would reduce the number of uninsured Americans by about [25] million people by 2019. . . . Supporters of the legislation point out that that would decrease the number of uninsured Americans to roughly [8] percent of non-elderly Americans, a far cry from universal coverage, but undoubtedly better than today's 15 percent. . . .

Increased Spending, Increased Debt

Health-care costs are rising faster than GDP growth and now total more than $[2.5] trillion—more than Americans spend on housing, food, national defense, or automobiles. However, the Patient Protection and Affordable Care Act fails to do anything to reduce or even restrain the growth in those costs. . . . This should not come as a big surprise. The primary focus of the legislation was to expand insurance coverage. Giving more people access to more insurance, not to mention mandating that current insurance cover more services, will undoubtedly result in more spending. . . .

It is also worth noting that cost estimates for government programs have been wildly optimistic over the years, especially for health care programs. . . . There is certainly reason to believe that the costs of this law will exceed projections. For example, as discussed above, increased insurance coverage could lead to increased utilization and higher subsidy costs. At the same time, if companies choose to drop their current insurance and dump employees into subsidized coverage or Medicaid, it could substantially increase the program's costs. . . .

This is all taking place at a time when the government is facing an unprecedented budgetary crisis. The U.S. budget deficit hit $1.4 trillion in 2009, and we are expected to add as much as $9 trillion to the national debt over the next 10 years, a debt that is already in excess of $12 trillion and rising at a rate of nearly $4 billion per day. Under current projections, government spending will rise from its traditional 20-21 percent of our gross domestic product to 40 percent by 2050. That would require a doubling of the tax burden just to keep up. . . .

Conclusion

Health care reform was designed to accomplish three goals: (1) provide health insurance coverage for all Americans, (2) reduce insurance costs for individuals, businesses, and government, and (3) increase the quality of health care and the value received for each dollar of health care spending. . . . The legislation comes closest to success on the issue of expanding the number of Americans with insurance. . . . The law also makes some modest insurance reforms that will prohibit some of the industry's more unpopular practices. However, those changes will come at the price of increased insurance costs, especially for younger and healthier individuals, and reduced consumer choice.

At the same time, the legislation is a major failure when it comes to controlling costs. While we were once promised that health care reform would "bend the cost curve down," this law will actually *increase* U.S. health care spending. . . . Clearly the trajectory of U.S. health care spending under this law is unsustainable. Therefore, it raises the inevitable question of whether it will lead to rationing down the road.

We should be clear, however. With a few minor exceptions governing Medicare reimbursements, the law would not directly ration care or allow the government to dictate how doctors practice medicine. There is no "death board" as Sarah Palin once wrote about in her Facebook posting. Even so, . . . this law represents a fundamental shift in the debate over how to reform health care. It rejects consumer-oriented reforms in favor of a top-down, "command and control," government-imposed solution. As such, it sets the stage for potentially increased government involvement. . . . One thing is certain—the debate over health care reform is far from over. . . .

THE HEALTH BILL EXPLAINED AT LAST

Theodore R. Marmor & Jonathan Oberlander*

New York Review of Books, August 2010

. . . Republicans have sought to make health care reform Barack Obama's "Waterloo" . . . by scaring the public. Ominous and utterly false warnings about "death panels," a government "takeover" of American medicine, and "pulling the plug on grandma" followed. . . . The irony is that for all the apocalyptic rhetoric, the new health reform law is anything but radical. In fact, it closely resembles the 2006 reform in Massachusetts supported by then-governor Republican Mitt Romney. And most strikingly, it does not replace the current mix of US health insurance schemes with a single public health insurance program like Medicare. Instead, the 2010 reform legislation introduces a complex system of subsidies, mandates, regulations, and programs that build on our present patchwork arrangements. . . .

Despite such deep flaws in the US health care system, the central assumption of both the Obama administration and the Democratic leadership in Congress was that only legislation that did not seek to radically change it had a chance of success. That political calculation, in turn, was based on the view that the Clinton administration's health reform effort failed during 1993-1994 because it tried to change too much and provoked too much opposition from insurance companies and other powerful interests.

This time around, reformers hoped to reassure the large number of insured Americans who say they are satisfied with their current coverage that they had nothing to fear from change. Democrats also wanted to work with rather than fight against the health care industry. They hoped to gain support from the insurance, hospital, and pharmaceutical industries, which stood to gain financially from expanded insurance coverage and had the financial resources and political influence to undercut reforms they opposed. As a consequence, the creation of a Canadian-style health program, in which universal insurance—Medicare for all—is provided by the government, was never seriously considered. Such a reform

* The authors are (or were) political science professors in the public health departments of Yale University and the University of North Carolina, respectively.

would have caused, in the administration's view, too much disruption of prevailing arrangements and led to an inflammatory and unwinnable debate over "socialized medicine." . . .

How Will the New Law Work?

First, all Americans who earn less than 133 percent of the federal poverty level [which amounts to roughly $15,000 for an individual or $30,000 for a family of four] will become eligible for Medicaid [in states that opt to expand Medicaid]. For the first time, Medicaid will offer coverage solely on the basis of income and regardless of family circumstance—including the single adults without children who are now excluded. . . .

Most Americans under age sixty-five will continue to receive employer-sponsored coverage. As a new feature, children can stay on their parents' insurance plans until age twenty-six. New regulations banning insurers from imposing caps on both annual and lifetime payments will also benefit policyholders. Larger employers will have to offer health coverage to their workers or pay a penalty ($2,000 per worker) to the federal government. Smaller employers with fewer than fifty workers will be exempt from this requirement, and, depending on their average wage, businesses with twenty-five or fewer workers are eligible for tax credits to help them buy health insurance for their workers.

The law also expands coverage by offering subsidies to uninsured Americans to purchase insurance in newly formed health benefit exchanges. Each state is expected to set up and administer these exchanges as a regulated market for health insurance. If a state chooses not to do so, its residents can join a federally sponsored exchange. In either case, people will choose from a variety of private insurance plans within each exchange, with federal subsidies available on a sliding scale to help them pay their premiums. Those with incomes up to 400 percent of the federal poverty level (i.e., now up to about [$50,000 for singles or twice that for a family of four]) will be eligible for subsidies. In all, 29 million Americans are expected to obtain insurance through the exchanges by 2019. . . .

The insurance exchanges will be regulated extensively. Starting in 2014, insurers will not be able to deny coverage to would-be policyholders or charge them higher premiums because of their health status (though insurers can vary premiums by age). Insurers will also be prohibited from retroactively canceling coverage for sick policyholders. Most Americans will be required to obtain health insurance or pay a federal tax penalty—starting in 2014 at $95 per person or 1 percent of taxable income, whichever is greater, and then increasing to $695 or 2.5 percent of taxable income by 2016.

The CBO estimates that [about 25] million Americans will gain coverage through the expansion of Medicaid, subsidies, and insurance exchanges. This will make an enormous difference to the financial circumstances of many Americans with modest means and large medical expenses. Contrary to what conservative critics have claimed, the reform will undoubtedly mean less, not more, rationing of medical care as tens of millions of uninsured persons gain access to health insurance.

By broadening health insurance coverage, the law moves the United States closer to the principle that no one should go without access to medical care. In regulating the health insurance industry, with provisions to end discrimination on the basis of preexisting conditions, it brings about a long-overdue expansion of federal authority. In these ways and more, the Affordable Care Act is a substantial achievement.

At the same time, large gaps remain between the problems of American medicine and the remedies that Congress has adopted. Even if the Affordable Care Act were fully implemented, an estimated [30] million people would still lack insurance [by 2020]. We cannot know precisely who will be without coverage a decade from now. But analysts expect that the uninsured will be made up of three groups: undocumented immigrants who are ineligible for federal subsidies or Medicaid; Americans who still find coverage, even with subsidies, too expensive to purchase on their own but aren't poor enough to qualify for Medicaid; and healthy people who can afford to buy coverage but will instead choose the cheaper option of paying the penalty for not having insurance. In any case, the United States, alone among industrialized democracies, will likely continue to have a large uninsured population for years to come. . . .

In fact, the expansion of insurance coverage and regulation described in the law is hardly straightforward. . . . [I]nsurers whose profits are at stake can be expected to seek loopholes to evade the new regulations. According to the law, the secretary of health and human services must write the thousands of pages of regulations necessary to implement it, and these will be subject to congressional scrutiny and intense lobbying by the health care industry. . . . One consequence, then, of building on the existing system is that the new law will require coordination of a great many disparate policies if coverage goals are to be met and if the health insurance marketplace is to be transformed.

Perhaps the largest shortcoming of the reform, though, is the absence of reliable, system-wide controls on medical costs. The law takes steps to slow down the rate of increase in Medicare spending, such as cutting projected payments to hospitals. . . . Outside of Medicare, the measures to slow health care spending are far less impressive. . . . The law's strategy to contain costs additionally rests on a series of reforms aimed at improving medical care delivery and health outcomes: paying hospitals on the basis of quality; bundling payments together for inpatient and outpatient care; funding research that compares the clinical effectiveness of medical treatment options; and providing greater coverage of preventive services. It also encourages the formation of so-called accountable care organizations that create networks of primary care doctors, specialists, and hospitals to care (and receive payments) for a defined set of patients. Many of these reforms will be implemented initially in Medicare—a newly established Medicare innovations center is charged with testing payment reform—with the hope that successful policies will then spread through the private sector.

Health and Human Services Secretary Kathleen Sebelius says that "every cost-cutting idea that every health economist has brought to the table is in this bill." That is probably true—but it also shows that American health policy researchers pay scant attention to international experience. . . . The new law seems based on the hope that if a large variety of reforms are tested, at least some will succeed; but nobody knows how many will work in practice or whether they will save money at all.

We do know that other rich democracies that spend much less than the US on medical care do so largely by adopting budgetary targets for health expenditures and by tightly regulating what the governments and insurers pay hospitals, doctors, and other medical care providers. Outside of Medicare, the current reform contains no such measures.

The Obama administration, confronting enormous opposition over proposals to expand coverage, chose mostly to defer addressing the political problems of cost control. But the . . . issue cannot be avoided for long. . . . The expansion of coverage and the requirement that individuals purchase insurance, alongside rising premium costs, . . . will increase [pressure] on the federal government to moderate the growth in health care costs—especially in view of sizable budget deficits. . . . As a result, there is enormous uncertainty about how well and how long the patchwork of health reforms adopted in 2010 will hold together.

Notes: Health Care Reform—A Work in Progress

1. *"The More Things Change, . . ."* The ACA fundamentally changed how the individual health insurance market works and expanded who among those in poverty can qualify for Medicaid. However, the ACA's changes to employer-based insurance and Medicare (elderly and disabled) were modest to minor; those sources of coverage remain fundamentally the same. Also, employers have not dropped coverage nearly to the extent that many analysts predicted. Accordingly, despite all the *sturm und drang*, most people have not actually been affected very much by the ACA, at least directly. The following pie charts nicely illustrate how coverage has, and has not, changed following implementation of the ACA.

FIGURE 3.2

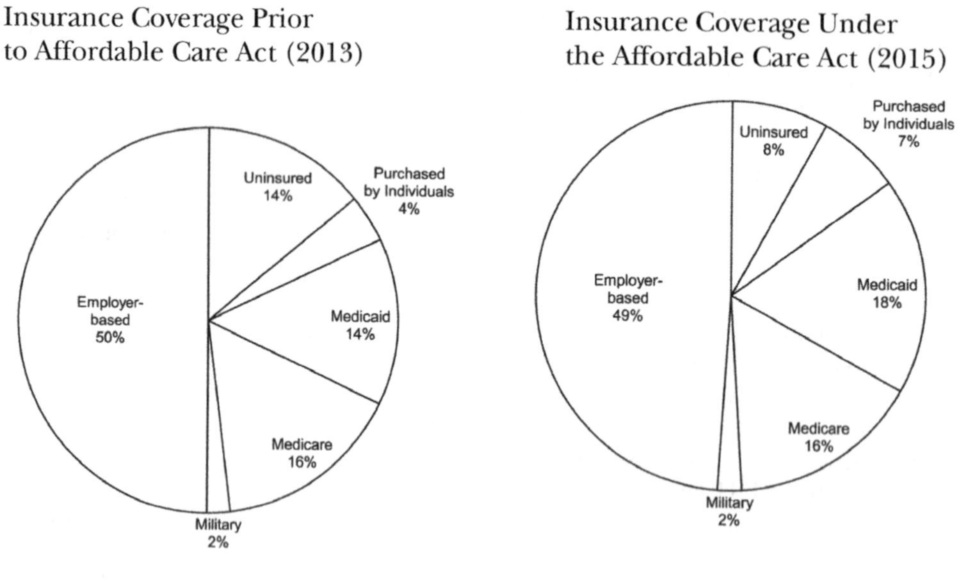

2. *Agreeing to Disagree.* Public and political views on the ACA have been highly polarized from the beginning, both due to differences in ideology, but also due to raw partisan politics—much of which focused on President Obama. In contrast, notice the degree of commonality between the two selections presented above, which come from thoughtful policy analysts at distinctly different positions in the

political spectrum. On which points do they agree? On which do they fundamentally disagree—more than simply a choice of emphasis (glass half full vs. half empty)?

Among the full range of views, consider also those of liberal physicians who favor a "single-payer" national health insurance system:

> As much as we would like to join the celebration . . . , in good conscience we cannot. We take no comfort in seeing aspirin dispensed for the treatment of cancer. Instead of eliminating the root of the problem—the profit-driven, private health insurance industry—this costly new legislation will enrich and further entrench these firms. . . .
>
> Millions of middle-income people will be pressured to buy commercial health insurance policies costing up to 9.5 percent of their income but covering an average of only 70 percent of their medical expenses, potentially leaving them vulnerable to financial ruin if they become seriously ill. Many will find such policies too expensive to afford or, if they do buy them, too expensive to use because of the high co-pays and deductibles.
>
> Insurance firms will be handed at least $447 billion in taxpayer money to subsidize the purchase of their shoddy products. This money will enhance their financial and political power, and with it their ability to block future reform. . . .
>
> The much-vaunted insurance regulations—e.g., ending denials on the basis of pre-existing conditions—are riddled with loopholes, thanks to the central role that insurers played in crafting the legislation. Older people can be charged up to three times more than their younger counterparts. . . .
>
> Congress and the Obama administration have saddled Americans with an expensive package of onerous individual mandates, new taxes on workers' health plans, countless sweetheart deals with the insurers and Big Pharma, and a perpetuation of the fragmented, dysfunctional, and unsustainable system that is taking such a heavy toll on our health and economy today. This bill's passage reflects political considerations, not sound health policy. . . . We pledge to continue our work for the only equitable, financially responsible and humane remedy for our health care mess: single-payer national health insurance, an expanded and improved Medicare for All.

Physicians for a National Health Program, Health Bill Leaves 23 Million Uninsured: A False Promise of Reform (Mar. 22, 2010).

3. *What Does the Public Think?* Democrats predicted that the Affordable Care Act would become popular with the American public once it took full effect. Instead, opinion has remained bitterly divided, substantially along political lines, with almost half the country viewing it unfavorably. Republican repeal-and-replace efforts, however, have apparently made the ACA more popular: by June 2017, and for the first time, more than half of the public reported favorable views on the law.

People who have gained private coverage through the ACA's exchanges are generally happy with their insurance, with 80 percent reporting that they are "very" or "somewhat" satisfied, according to surveys by the Commonwealth Fund. Many of those who have enrolled in private plans, however, are frustrated with the price of coverage, and in particular with the high deductibles that are common in exchange plans. (The average deductible in 2017 for a typical Obamacare plan was $3,572 for individuals and $7,474 for families.) Also, some people (such as younger, healthier males) are upset that they can no longer purchase more bare bones coverage (that excludes, for instance, mental health and maternity care), at rates that are adjusted for their gender and age. Thus, unless they qualify for a substantial subsidy, some people have to pay several times more for insurance than before the ACA, when they purchase individually.

Major industry interest groups (hospitals, doctors, insurers, pharmaceuticals) continue to support the ACA or at least to oppose its repeal. Their stocks have generally performed better than overall market indices since reform.

4. *What Has Health Reform Accomplished?* The ACA's most singular achievement is not universal insurance, but universal insur*ability*. Not everyone is covered, but everyone may now obtain coverage. Put another way, no one need worry about becoming uninsurable. Consider what life choices this basic guarantee enhances, from jobs to career paths to family relationships. Some analysts have detected an uptick in start-up companies, career changes, and early retirements following the ACA. Despite accusation that the ACA hurts employment, there is no evidence that it has increased job terminations or slowed job growth, nor have employers dropped health coverage in substantial numbers.

Measured against its core goal of actually expanding coverage, the ACA has been a partial success. In the glass half-full column, the National Center for Health Statistics estimates that "[i]n 2016, 28.6 million (9.0%) persons of all ages were uninsured at the time of interview—20.0 million fewer persons than in 2010." The portion of the population without insurance is lower than it has ever been in the United States.

In the half-empty column, nearly 30 million people remain uninsured. Who are they? Many are people who choose to (or feel they have to) pay the "individual mandate" tax penalty for remaining uninsured rather than purchase insurance, even when insurance is partially subsidized. In the 19 states that have chosen not to accept federal money to expand their Medicaid programs, stringent eligibility rules continue to disqualify many nonelderly adults near poverty. Even in states that have expanded, many people are unaware of their options or struggle with the enrollment process. Undocumented immigrants make up another substantial fraction of the uninsured population.

The ACA's exchanges work well in many states, especially those that chose to run their own exchanges. But the exchanges in some states (rural states in particular) have struggled to attract sufficient insurers, and insurer participation is diminishing on account of the political uncertainty over the ACA. Also, premiums in the individual market have increased sharply. Initially, these premiums were considerably lower than expected, due to intense competition among insurers for a large bolus of new enrollment. Since then, however, premiums have increased at double-digit rates in order to keep up with the level of medical costs that new enrollees are incurring. Despite these increases, average premiums on the exchanges are generally in line with, or not a great deal more than, what employers pay for similar group coverage, and premium increases have been much more moderate in states (mostly blue) that have openly embraced the ACA. Nevertheless, premiums are especially high in some parts of the country, and are expected to rise still higher as uncertainty over the ACA's fate makes healthier people more reluctant to enroll.

5. *Who Pays for All of This?* When it was enacted in 2010, the ACA was projected to cost the federal government almost $1 trillion over the first ten years. Over half of this was financed from a variety of taxes, such as taxes on medical devices

and prescription drugs, increased Medicare payroll taxes for high-wage earners, and, oddly, a tax on tanning beds. Most of the remainder of the ACA's price tag was financed by reductions in Medicare payments to providers and insurers. On balance, the Congressional Budget Office projected that these tax increases and spending cuts would exceed the ACA's costs by roughly $100 billion over ten years, and would slightly reduce the federal deficit. However, the cuts to Medicare and the increase in Medicare payroll taxes used to finance the ACA make it more difficult to enact reforms needed to keep Medicare solvent for the next generation.

Partly because of the Great Recession, and partly because not all states took advantage of the Medicaid expansion, actual spending on the law's coverage provisions has been about one-third lower than anticipated. As a result, according to CBO, "repealing the ACA would increase federal budget deficits by $137 billion over the 2016-2025 period."

6. *Repeal, Replace, or Repair?* The election of Donald Trump gave Republicans unified control of the White House and Congress for the first time since the ACA's adoption. Yet Republicans were unable to muscle a repeal-and-replace bill through Congress. The political scientist Jonathan Oberlander explained where matters stood in the fall of 2017:

> The repeal-and-replace debate revealed Republicans' failure to meet another challenge: developing a decent, let alone better, alternative to Obamacare. The House-passed AHCA would have repealed the ACA's mandates, reduced insurance subsidies for low-income persons, cut taxes for wealthier persons, loosened insurance regulations, and rolled back funding for Medicaid expansion while capping federal Medicaid spending. That combination of reforms . . . would result in tens of millions of Americans losing coverage and paying more for health insurance.
>
> [The replacement proposals] also underscored the success of ACA policies in making insurance more accessible for persons with preexisting conditions and more affordable for lower-income Americans. . . . The fact that GOP repeal proposals would have left much of the ACA in place confirmed that reality. . . . Although Republican politicians highlighted the soaring premiums in ACA insurance exchanges in many states, in a legislative "bait and switch," their repeal plans retained the exchanges and instead targeted Medicaid, which has nothing to do with the rising premiums in the individual insurance market. . . .
>
> Since 2010, Republicans have campaigned against a mythical Obamacare that they demonized as a disaster. The real Obamacare has serious shortcomings, but it also provides essential, popular benefits to tens of millions of Americans. . . . By comparison with the GOP's dystopian health care vision, Obamacare has never looked better. Republicans could not mobilize public support for their plan, which was the least popular major legislation of the past three decades. Instead, the Republican threats to Obamacare inspired widespread protests and a movement to protect the law. . . .
>
> Still, Obamacare's fortunes remain uncertain. . . . [T]he president could create a self-fulfilling prophecy of ACA failure [by refusing to fund key payments to insurers as discussed below, and by declining to enforce the individual mandate]. . . . Alternatively, Democrats and Republicans could cooperate to stabilize the ACA's insurance marketplaces and adopt other reforms . . . .
>
> Since 2010, the ACA has been an existential issue for Republicans who made its elimination a political cause. Abandoning that commitment to repeal Obama

> care, and instead working with Democrats on incremental measures to improve the law, will not be easy. The demise, for now, of Senate repeal legislation will not end the Obamacare debate. But could it mark a turning point?

Jonathan Oberlander, Repeal, Replace, Repair, Retreat: Republicans' Health Care Quagmire, 377 New Eng. J. Med. 1001 (2017).

With repeal-and-replace on life support, congressional Republicans took a different approach. In the closing days of 2017, they passed a tax reform bill that (among many other things) zeroed out the individual mandate. Premiums on the exchanges are expected to surge as a result, and an estimated 13 million people could lose coverage in the coming decade. See Congressional Budget Office, Repealing the Individual Health Insurance Mandate: An Updated Estimate (Nov. 2017). The repeal is due to take effect in 2019.

7. *Further Reading.* For accounts of the law's **enactment and general descriptions of its contents**, see Washington Post, Landmark: The Inside Story of America's New Health Care Law (2010); Jonathan Gruber, Health Care Reform: What It Is, Why It's Necessary, How It Works (2011); Paul Starr, Remedy and Reaction: The Peculiar American Struggle over Health Care Reform (2011); Stuart Altman, Power, Politics and Universal Health Care (2011); John McDonough, Inside National Health Reform (2011); Lawrence Jacobs & Theda Skocpol, Health Care Reform and American Politics (2010).

For more about the Massachusetts precursor to the ACA, see Edward Zelinsky, The New Massachusetts Health Law: Preemption and Experimentation, 49 Wm. & Mary L. Rev. 229 (2008); Michael Tanner, No Miracle in Massachusetts: Why Governor Romney's Health Care Reform Won't Work (Cato Institute, 2006); Symposium, 55 U. Kan. L. Rev. 1091 (2007); Symposium, 28(4) Health Aff. w578 (July-Aug. 2009); Symposium, 36(5) Hastings Center Rep. 14 (Oct. 2006); Symposium, 354 New Eng. J. Med. 2093 (2006).

■ NATIONAL FEDERATION OF INDEPENDENT BUSINESS v. SEBELIUS

567 U.S. 1 (2012)

Chief Justice ROBERTS.

Today we resolve constitutional challenges to two provisions of the Patient Protection and Affordable Care Act of 2010: the individual mandate, which requires individuals to purchase a health insurance policy providing a minimum level of coverage; and the Medicaid expansion, which gives funds to the States on the condition that they provide specified health care to all citizens whose income falls below a certain threshold. . . .

I

The individual mandate requires most Americans to maintain "minimum essential" health insurance coverage. 26 U.S.C. §5000A. . . . Many individuals will receive the required coverage through their employer, or from a government program such as Medicaid or Medicare. But for individuals who are not exempt and do not receive health insurance through a third party, the means of satisfying the requirement is to purchase insurance from a private company.

Beginning in 2014, those who do not comply with the mandate must make a "[s]hared responsibility payment" to the Federal Government, . . . calculated as a percentage of household income, subject to a floor based on a specified dollar amount and a ceiling based on the average annual premium the individual would have to pay for qualifying private health insurance. In 2016, for example, the penalty will be 2.5 percent of an individual's household income, but no less than $695 and no more than the average yearly premium for ["bronze level"] insurance. The Act . . . bars the IRS from using several of its normal enforcement tools, such as criminal prosecutions and levies. And some individuals who are subject to the mandate are nonetheless exempt from the penalty—for example, those with income below a certain threshold and members of Indian tribes.

On the day the President signed the Act into law, Florida and 12 other States filed a complaint . . . subsequently joined by 13 more States, several individuals, and the National Federation of Independent Business. The plaintiffs alleged, among other things, that the individual mandate provisions of the Act exceeded Congress's powers under Article I of the Constitution. The District Court agreed, holding that . . . the individual mandate could not be severed from the remainder of the Act, and therefore struck down the Act in its entirety. . . . The Court of Appeals for the Eleventh Circuit . . . struck down only the individual mandate, leaving the Act's other provisions intact. . . .

III. A

The Government's first argument is that the individual mandate is a valid exercise of Congress's power under the Commerce Clause and the Necessary and Proper Clause. According to the Government, the health care market is characterized by a significant cost-shifting problem. Everyone will eventually need health care at a time and to an extent they cannot predict, but if they do not have insurance, they often will not be able to pay for it. Because state and federal laws nonetheless require hospitals to provide a certain degree of care to individuals without regard to their ability to pay, hospitals end up receiving compensation for only a portion of the services they provide. To recoup the losses, hospitals pass on the cost to insurers through higher rates, and insurers, in turn, pass on the cost to policy holders in the form of higher premiums. Congress estimated that the cost of uncompensated care raises family health insurance premiums, on average, by over $1,000 per year.

In the Affordable Care Act, Congress addressed the problem of those who cannot obtain insurance coverage because of preexisting conditions or other health issues. It did so through the Act's "guaranteed-issue" and "community-rating" provisions. These provisions together prohibit insurance companies from denying coverage to those with such conditions or charging unhealthy individuals higher premiums than healthy individuals.

The guaranteed-issue and community-rating reforms do not, however, address the issue of healthy individuals who choose not to purchase insurance to cover potential health care needs. In fact, the reforms sharply exacerbate that problem, by providing an incentive for individuals to delay purchasing health insurance until they become sick, relying on the promise of guaranteed and affordable coverage.

The reforms also threaten to impose massive new costs on insurers, who are required to accept unhealthy individuals but prohibited from charging them rates necessary to pay for their coverage. This will lead insurers to significantly increase premiums on everyone.

The individual mandate was Congress's solution to these problems. By requiring that individuals purchase health insurance, the mandate prevents cost-shifting by those who would otherwise go without it. In addition, the mandate forces into the insurance risk pool more healthy individuals, whose premiums on average will be higher than their health care expenses. This allows insurers to subsidize the costs of covering the unhealthy individuals the reforms require them to accept. The Government claims that Congress has power under the Commerce and Necessary and Proper Clauses to enact this solution.

1

. . . Given its expansive scope, it is no surprise that Congress has employed the commerce power in a wide variety of ways to address the pressing needs of the time. But Congress has never attempted to rely on that power to compel individuals not engaged in commerce to purchase an unwanted product. . . . The power to regulate commerce presupposes the existence of commercial activity to be regulated. . . . As expansive as our cases construing the scope of the commerce power have been, they all have one thing in common: They uniformly describe the power as reaching "activity." . . .

The individual mandate, however, does not regulate existing commercial activity. It instead compels individuals to become active in commerce by purchasing a product, on the ground that their failure to do so affects interstate commerce. Construing the Commerce Clause to permit Congress to regulate individuals precisely because they are doing nothing would open a new and potentially vast domain to congressional authority. Every day individuals do not do an infinite number of things. . . .

To consider [an] example in the health care market, many Americans do not eat a balanced diet, . . . [which] increases health care costs to a greater extent than the failure of the uninsured to purchase insurance. . . . Under the Government's theory, Congress could address the diet problem by ordering everyone to buy vegetables. . . . That is not the country the Framers of our Constitution envisioned. . . . Congress already enjoys vast power to regulate much of what we do. Accepting the Government's theory would give Congress the same license to regulate what we do not do, fundamentally changing the relation between the citizen and the Federal government. . . .

The individual mandate's regulation of the uninsured as a class is, in fact, particularly divorced from any link to existing commercial activity. The mandate primarily affects healthy, often young adults who are less likely to need significant health care and have other priorities for spending their money. . . . The Government, however, . . . regards it as sufficient to trigger Congress's authority that almost all those who are uninsured will, at some unknown point in the future, engage in a health care transaction. . . . The Commerce Clause is not a general license to regulate an individual from cradle to grave, simply because he will predictably engage in particular transactions. Any police power to regulate individuals as such, as opposed to their activities, remains vested in the States.

The Government argues that the individual mandate can be sustained as a sort of exception to this rule, because health insurance is a unique product. According to the Government, upholding the individual mandate would not justify mandatory purchases of items such as cars or broccoli because, as the Government puts it, "[h]ealth insurance is not purchased for its own sake like a car or broccoli; it is a means of financing health-care consumption and covering universal risks." But cars and broccoli are no more purchased for their "own sake" than health insurance. They are purchased to cover the need for transportation and food. . . . And for most of those targeted by the mandate, significant health care needs will be years, or even decades, away. The proximity and degree of connection between the mandate and the subsequent commercial activity is too lacking to justify an exception of the sort urged by the Government. . . .

2

The Government next contends that Congress has the power under the Necessary and Proper Clause to enact the individual mandate because the mandate is an "integral part of a comprehensive scheme of economic regulation"—the guaranteed-issue and community-rating insurance reforms. . . . [Interpreting the] power to "make all Laws which shall be necessary and proper for carrying into Execution" the powers enumerated in the Constitution, Art. I, §8, cl. 18, we have been very deferential to Congress's determination that a regulation is "necessary." We have thus upheld laws that are " 'convenient, or useful' or 'conducive' to the authority's 'beneficial exercise.' " But we have also carried out our responsibility to declare unconstitutional those laws that undermine the structure of government established by the Constitution. . . .

Applying these principles, the individual mandate cannot be sustained under the Necessary and Proper Clause as an essential component of the insurance reforms. Each of our prior cases upholding laws under that Clause involved exercises of authority derivative of, and in service to, a granted power. . . . The individual mandate, by contrast, vests Congress with the extraordinary ability to create the necessary predicate to the exercise of an enumerated power, . . . reach[ing] beyond the natural limit of its authority and draw[ing] within its regulatory scope those who otherwise would be outside of it. Even if the individual mandate is "necessary" to the Act's insurance reforms, such an expansion of federal power is not a "proper" means for making those reforms effective. . . . The commerce power thus does not authorize the mandate.

[Justices Scalia, Kennedy, Thomas, and Alito concurred with, but did not join, the Commerce Clause portion (III.A) of this opinion. The other four justices dissented from this portion.]

B

That is not the end of the matter. . . . [T]he Government asks us to read the mandate not as ordering individuals to buy insurance, but rather as imposing a tax on those who do not buy that product. . . . The most straightforward reading of the mandate is that it commands individuals to purchase insurance. . . . [But] if an individual does not maintain health insurance, the only consequence is that he must make an additional payment to the IRS when he pays his taxes. . . . Under that theory, the mandate is not a legal command to buy insurance. Rather, it makes going without insurance just another thing the Government taxes, like buying gasoline or earning income. . . .

The question is not whether that is the most natural interpretation of the mandate, but only whether it is a "fairly possible" one. . . . Granting the Act the full measure of deference owed to federal statutes, it can be so read, for the reasons set forth below. . . . First, for most Americans the amount due will be far less than the price of insurance, and, by statute, it can never be more.[4] . . . While the individual mandate clearly aims to induce the purchase of health insurance, it need not be read to declare that failing to do so is unlawful. . . . Indeed, it is estimated that four million people each year will choose to pay the IRS rather than buy insurance. . . .

Neither the Act nor any other law attaches negative legal consequences to not buying health insurance, beyond requiring a payment to the IRS. . . . [Instead], the shared responsibility payment merely imposes a tax citizens may lawfully choose to pay in lieu of buying health insurance. . . .

[Justices GINSBURG, Breyer, Sotomayor, and Kagan joined this tax power portion of the opinion (III.B). The portion of the decision addressing Medicaid expansion is excerpted at page 159.]

Justice GINSBURG, concurring in part and dissenting in part.

. . . Although every [person] will incur significant medical expenses during his or her lifetime, the time when care will be needed is often unpredictable. An accident, a heart attack, or a cancer diagnosis commonly occurs without warning. Inescapably, we are all at peril of needing medical care without a moment's notice. To manage the risks associated with medical care—its high cost, its unpredictability, and its inevitability—most people in the United States obtain health insurance. Many (approximately 170 million in 2009) are insured by private insurance companies. Others, including those over 65 and certain poor and disabled persons, rely on government-funded insurance programs, notably Medicare and Medicaid. Combined, private health insurers and State and Federal Governments finance almost 85% of the medical care administered to U. S. residents.

Not all U.S. residents, however, have health insurance. In 2009, approximately 50 million people were uninsured, either by choice or, more likely, because they could not afford private insurance and did not qualify for government aid. . . . Unlike markets for most products, however, the inability to pay for care does not mean that an uninsured individual will receive no care. Federal and state law, as well as professional obligations and embedded social norms, require hospitals and physicians to provide care when it is most needed, regardless of the patient's ability to pay. As a consequence, medical-care providers deliver significant amounts of care to the uninsured for which the providers receive no payment. . . .

Health-care providers do not absorb these bad debts. Instead, they raise their prices, passing along the cost of uncompensated care to those who do pay reliably:

4. In 2016, for example, individuals making $35,000 a year are expected to owe the IRS about $60 for any month in which they do not have health insurance. Someone with an annual income of $100,000 a year would likely owe about $200. The price of a qualifying insurance policy is projected to be around $400 per month.

the government and private insurance companies. In response, private insurers increase their premiums, shifting the cost of the elevated bills from providers onto those who carry insurance. . . . And it is hardly just the currently sick or injured among the uninsured who prompt elevation of the price of health care and health insurance. . . . [B]ecause any uninsured person may need medical care at any moment and because health-care companies must account for that risk, every uninsured person impacts the market price of medical care and medical insurance. . . .

Aware that a national solution was required, Congress could have taken over the health-insurance market by establishing a tax-and-spend federal program like Social Security. Such a program, commonly referred to as a single-payer system (where the sole payer is the Federal Government), would have left little, if any, room for private enterprise or the States. Instead of going this route, Congress enacted the ACA, a solution that retains a robust role for private insurers and state governments. To make its chosen approach work, however, Congress had to use some new tools, including a requirement that most individuals obtain private health insurance coverage. As explained below, by employing these tools, Congress was able to achieve a practical, altogether reasonable, solution. . . .

Congress knew that encouraging individuals to purchase insurance would not suffice to solve the problem, because most of the uninsured are not uninsured by choice. Of particular concern to Congress were people who, though desperately in need of insurance, often cannot acquire it: persons who suffer from preexisting medical conditions. Before the ACA's enactment, private insurance companies took an applicant's medical history into account when setting insurance rates or deciding whether to insure an individual. Because individuals with preexisting medical conditions cost insurance companies significantly more than those without such conditions, insurers routinely refused to insure these individuals, charged them substantially higher premiums, or offered only limited coverage that did not include the preexisting illness.

To ensure that individuals with medical histories have access to affordable insurance, Congress devised a three-part solution. First, Congress imposed a "guaranteed issue" requirement, which bars insurers from denying coverage to any person on account of that person's medical condition or history. Second, Congress required insurers to use "community rating" to price their insurance policies. Community rating, in effect, bars insurance companies from charging higher premiums to those with preexisting conditions.

But these two provisions, Congress comprehended, could not work effectively unless individuals were given a powerful incentive to obtain insurance. In the 1990's, several States—including New York, New Jersey, Washington, Kentucky, Maine, New Hampshire, and Vermont—enacted guaranteed-issue and community-rating laws without requiring universal acquisition of insurance coverage. The results were disastrous. All seven states suffered from skyrocketing insurance premium costs, reductions in individuals with coverage, and reductions in insurance products and providers.

Congress comprehended that guaranteed-issue and community-rating laws alone will not work. When insurance companies are required to insure the sick at affordable prices, individuals can wait until they become ill to buy insurance. Pretty soon, those in need of immediate medical care—i.e., those who cost insurers the most—become the insurance companies' main customers. This "adverse selection" problem leaves insurers with two choices: They can either raise premiums dramatically to cover their ever-increasing costs or they can exit the market. In the seven States that tried guaranteed-issue and community-rating requirements without a minimum coverage provision, that is precisely what insurance companies did. See, e.g., Hall, An Evaluation of New York's Reform Law, 25 J. Health Pol. Pol'y & L. 71, 91-92 (2000).

Massachusetts, Congress was told, cracked the adverse selection problem. By requiring most residents to obtain insurance, the Commonwealth ensured that insurers would not be left with only the sick as customers. As a result, federal lawmakers observed, Massachusetts succeeded where other States had failed. In coupling the minimum coverage provision with guaranteed-issue and community-ssssrating prescriptions, Congress followed Massachusetts' lead.

In sum, Congress passed the minimum coverage provision as a key component of the ACA to address an economic and social problem that has plagued the Nation for decades: the large number of U. S. residents who are unable or unwilling to obtain health insurance. Whatever one thinks of the policy decision Congress made, it was Congress' prerogative to make it. Reviewed with appropriate deference, the minimum coverage provision, allied to the guaranteed-issue and community-rating prescriptions, should survive measurement under the Commerce and Necessary and Proper Clauses. . . .

II

. . . The inevitable yet unpredictable need for medical care and the guarantee that emergency care will be provided when required are conditions nonexistent in other markets. That is so of the market for cars, and of the market for broccoli as well. Although an individual might buy a car or a crown of broccoli one day, there is no certainty she will ever do so. And if she eventually wants a car or has a craving for broccoli, she will be obliged to pay at the counter before receiving the vehicle or nourishment. She will get no free ride or food, at the expense of another consumer forced to pay an inflated price. Upholding the minimum coverage provision on the ground that all are participants or will be participants in the health-care market would therefore carry no implication that Congress may justify under the Commerce Clause a mandate to buy other products and services.

. . . The Chief Justice also calls the minimum coverage provision an illegitimate effort to make young, healthy individuals subsidize insurance premiums paid by the less hale and hardy. This complaint, too, is spurious. . . . In the fullness of time, moreover, today's young and healthy will become society's old and infirm. Viewed over a lifespan, the costs and benefits even out: The young who pay more than their fair share currently will pay less than their fair share when they become senior citizens. And even if, as undoubtedly will be the case, some individuals, over their lifespans, will pay more for health insurance than they receive in health services, they have little to complain about, for that is how insurance works. Every insured person receives protection against a catastrophic loss, even though only a subset of the covered class will ultimately need that protection. . . .

Recall that one of Congress' goals in enacting the Affordable Care Act was to eliminate the insurance industry's practice of charging higher prices or denying coverage to individuals with preexisting medical conditions. The commerce power allows Congress to ban this practice, a point no one disputes. Congress knew, however, that simply barring insurance companies from relying on an applicant's medical history would not work in practice. Without the individual mandate, Congress learned, guaranteed-issue and community-rating requirements would trigger an adverse-selection death-spiral in the health-insurance market: Insurance premiums would skyrocket, the number of uninsured would increase, and insurance companies would exit the market. When complemented by an insurance mandate, on the other hand, guaranteed issue and community rating would work as intended. . . .

Asserting that the Necessary and Proper Clause does not authorize the minimum coverage provision, The Chief Justice focuses on the word "proper," . . . declar[ing] the minimum coverage provision not "proper" because it is less "narrow in scope" than other laws this Court has upheld under the Necessary and Proper Clause. . . . The Chief Justice [fails] to explain why the [individual mandate] is more far-reaching than other implied powers this Court has found meet under the Necessary and Proper Clause. These powers include the power to enact criminal laws; the power to imprison, including civil imprisonment; and the power to create a national bank. . . . How is a judge to decide, when ruling on the constitutionality of a federal statute, whether Congress employed an "independent power," or merely a "derivative" one. Whether the power used is "substantive," or just "incidental"? The instruction The Chief Justice, in effect, provides lower courts: You will know it when you see it. . . .

Justices Scalia, Kennedy, Thomas, and Alito, dissenting.

. . . In our view, both these central provisions of the [ACA]—the Individual Mandate and Medicaid Expansion—are invalid. It follows, as some of the parties urge, that all other provisions of the Act must fall as well. . . . The whole design of the Act is to balance the costs and benefits affecting each set of regulated parties. Thus, individuals are required to obtain health insurance. Insurance companies are required to sell them insurance regardless of patients' pre-existing conditions and to comply with a host of other regulations. And the companies must pay new taxes. States are expected to expand Medicaid eligibility and to create regulated marketplaces called exchanges where individuals can purchase insurance. Some persons who cannot afford insurance are provided it through the Medicaid Expansion, and others are aided in their purchase of insurance through federal subsidies available on health-insurance exchanges. The Federal Government's increased spending is offset by new taxes and cuts in other federal expenditures, including reductions in Medicare and in federal payments to hospitals. Employers with at least 50 employees must either provide employees with adequate health benefits or pay a financial exaction if an employee who qualifies for federal subsidies purchases insurance through an exchange.

In short, the Act attempts to achieve near-universal health insurance coverage by spreading its costs to individuals, insurers, governments, hospitals, and employers—while, at the same time, offsetting significant portions of those costs with new benefits to each group. . . . [The dissenters therefore conclude that a defect in any major provision should bring down the entire Act.]

Notes: Access to Private Health Insurance

1. *Who Would Have Guessed?* No one was surprised that the Supreme Court split 5-4 on the ACA's constitutionality. What was surprising, though, were the two

particular bases for the ruling. In all the litigation leading up to the Supreme Court, not a single lower court (out of the dozen or so) had ruled either that the mandate is merely a tax, or that the Medicaid expansion coerces the states unless they are allowed to opt out.

Also surprising was that the four conservative dissenters declined to join Justice Roberts's opinion on the Commerce Clause issues. They dissented based on the tax issue and on severability, but elsewhere in their dissent, they expressed the same reasoning as Roberts on the Commerce Clause issues. According to several journalists, Roberts initially sided with the other conservatives, but he switched during the opinion-drafting process. Jeffrey Toobin, The Oath: The Obama White House and the Supreme Court (2012).

2. *The Way It Was*. As noted above, Congress repealed the individual mandate in late 2017 (effective 2019). Many congressional Republicans remain committed to undoing the rest of the ACA. As the debate over the future of health reform plays out, however, it is important not to lose sight of the way things were before. People not covered by group insurance could be turned down, or charged more, for the slightest reasons, including common conditions such as hay fever or ear infections. According to the Senate testimony excerpted above, "about 70 percent of people who appl[ied] for health insurance receive[d] an offer of coverage at standard rates or better. The rest [were] either declined (12%), offered higher rates (6%), or offered coverage that exclude[d] one or more particular pre-existing conditions (13%). In field studies, market testers found that conditions as common as asthma, ear infections, and high blood pressure [created] problems obtaining coverage." Even in groups, covered people could have "pre-existing conditions" excluded for up to a year.

A dense thicket of federal and state laws tried to ameliorate the worst effects of this "medical underwriting," but only in a patchwork fashion. The federal Health Insurance Portability and Accountability Act (HIPAA) prevented group insurers (those who cover employers) from turning anyone down, but did not regulate insurance rates. That was left to the states, most of which allowed insurers to charge older or sicker people substantially more. HIPAA protected people from undergoing new waiting periods for preexisting conditions when they changed jobs, but it did not help them if they went without insurance for more than two months. Another federal law, called COBRA, allows people to stay on their employer's plan for up to three years after they leave a job, but only if they are able to pay the entire premium themselves.

3. *The Fairness of Community Rating*. Notice how the Justices differed in their characterizations of the ACA's community rating rule. Chief Justice Roberts emphasizes that the ACA requires younger, healthy people to pay more than they actually expect to incur in medical expense, on average, in order to subsidize other people. Is this a form of redistribution? If so, is it fair? Justice Ginsburg reminds us that no one knows when he or she might suffer medical misfortune, so we all face a similar set of risks from basic human frailty and brute luck. Although the magnitude of risk differs over time, Justice Ginsburg is willing to take more of a lifetime perspective.

Another principle of justice, however, might say that people who deliberately engage in risky behavior should not be allowed to force those who do not to pay their extra costs of insurance. Note that, despite community rating, the ACA allows insurers to charge smokers up to 50 percent more, and it also allows employers to pay substantial rebates to workers who participate in health-improving "wellness" programs. How much of medical costs do you speculate are caused by other voluntary behaviors? Which of these behaviors should be "punished" with higher insurance premiums or tolerated as legitimate lifestyle choices? Consider each of the following: eating meat, obesity, having children, drinking while pregnant, failing to exercise regularly, hang gliding.

Related to this debate is whether health insurance is more of a social financing mechanism for expected costs, rather than simply a private contingency fund for unexpected events. Economists observe that medical expense does not fit the classic model for insurable costs that applies to conventional insurance lines such as life, fire, and liability. These types of "casualty insurance" are designed for unpredictable, high-cost events, but most people's medical expenses are predictable to a significant extent. Nevertheless, we insure these expenses in order to make them more affordable, by spreading them more broadly across society. This is most obvious for the "social insurance" government programs of Medicare and Medicaid. But private health insurance also serves important social functions. Thus, whether to conceive of medical benefits coverage as a fundamental social good or a purely private good lies at the heart of many of the controversies explored in these notes, such as how comprehensive health insurance should be, whether insurers should be allowed to pick and choose among subscribers, and whether health insurance should be community rated.

4. *What About Employer Sponsored Coverage?* Even as the ACA transformed the individual market for health insurance, it made relatively few changes to the employer-sponsored market. The reason is simple: Employer-sponsored insurance already represents a naturally occurring form of community rating, in the sense that the premium cost is viewed as being equal for each member of the group. Even though each member contributes a different amount to the overall group cost, when the group is of sufficient size, insurers feel no need, even in unregulated markets, to assess each person's risk status in order to predict the group's overall expected medical cost (because groups' historical averages predict future expenses well enough). These and other natural economies of scale help explain why employer-based health insurance has been so successful. In a sense, the ACA's reforms are meant to help the individual and small-group market work as well as the large-group employer market already works on its own.

Tax law also strongly encourages employer-based insurance. Insurance premiums paid by employers are not taxed as income, and employees' premium contributions are paid on a pre-tax basis through payroll deduction. In contrast, individual (non-group) insurance is usually paid entirely through after-tax earnings. Is it fair that people who buy their own insurance do not receive the same tax breaks as employer-sponsored insurance? Note that the employment-based tax advantage is highly regressive, since it gives the most support to people with the greatest income. Covering people through the workplace also restricts their choices to plans that employers want to offer.

From time to time, proposals surface to decouple health insurance from employment. This could occur in several ways, to a greater or lesser degree. One idea, known as "defined contribution," is for employers to give employees a fixed budget that employees can use to shop for insurance anywhere they want, rather than the employer's paying for a benefit plan the employer selects. A second approach is to provide a tax credit (rather than deduction) to anyone who purchases health insurance, whether or not insurance comes as a job benefit.

When the ACA was adopted, many commentators predicted that employers would stop offering insurance and send their employees to the exchanges. So far, however, the ACA has had little effect on employer-based coverage. See Jean Abraham & Anne Beeson Royalty, How Has the Affordable Care Act Affected Work and Wages? (Jan. 2017). Many employees prefer employer-sponsored coverage on account of its favorable tax treatment. In addition, the exchanges in some states have struggled to attract a sufficient number of insurers, contributing to market instability. For those reasons, as well as uncertainty over the ACA's future, employers and employees have proven reluctant to disturb existing arrangements.

5. *Workplace Wellness Programs.* Although employers are generally prohibited from discriminating against their employee on the basis of health status, the ACA relaxes the community rating rules in connection with employer-sponsored "wellness programs." There are two types of wellness programs. *Participatory wellness programs* offer employees a financial incentive based on their participation alone. An employee might get a reduction in her monthly premium, for example, for filling out a detailed assessment designed to gauge her overall health. *Health-contingent wellness programs* require employees to achieve health-related targets in order to receive the financial incentive. Employees might have to go to the gym a certain number of times each month or keep their blood pressure under control. Supporters of wellness programs have argued that a healthier workforce will reduce employer health care costs, perhaps substantially. Prior to the ACA, however, federal rules prohibiting discrimination on the basis of health status discouraged employers from adopting health-contingent wellness programs. The ACA has spurred their broader adoption by authorizing employers to offer financial incentives of up to 30 percent of the cost of the employee's premiums. Partly in response, most large employers have adopted wellness programs of one kind or another, although programs that offer extremely large incentives to promote adherence remain rare. Soeren Mattke et al., RAND Health, Workplace Wellness Programs Study (2013). Wellness is now a $6 billion industry.

Rigorous studies indicate, however, that workplace wellness programs rarely reduce spending or improve employee health. Indeed, many wellness programs actually increase expenses because employees receive unnecessary care arising as a result of their wellness screenings. Although some specialized wellness programs that target employees with chronic diseases may result in savings, such programs are not the norm. See Adrianna McIntyre et al., The Dubious Empirical and Legal Foundations of Workplace Wellness Programs, 27 Health Matrix 59 (2017).

Wellness programs have also come under fire for violating the Americans with Disabilities Act. To forestall disability discrimination, the ADA prohibits employers from asking employees about their medical histories unless their responses are "voluntary." In early 2016, the EEOC finalized a rule clarifying that a health assessment would be considered "voluntary" within the meaning of the ADA if the incentives of the wellness program stayed within the limits marked out in the ACA. 81 Fed. Reg. 31126 (2016). Critics have argued that the rule is too permissive: Because the average premium for a family plan in 2015 was $17,545, employers can offer incentives of up to $5,263 in connection with adherence to a wellness program. With potential incentives that large, it is not clear how a health assessment can be considered "voluntary." See AARP v. EEOC, 2017 WL 3614430 (D.D.C. Aug. 22, 2017) (holding that the EEOC rule is arbitrary and capricious).

In addition, wellness programs raise concerns about patient privacy. In 2013, for example, employees at Penn State were outraged when they were asked to take a health assessment that asked whether they "have recently had problems with a supervisor, a separation or a divorce, their finances or a fear of job loss; another question asks female employees whether they plan to become pregnant over the next year." Natasha Singer, On Campus, a Faculty Uprising Over Personal Data, N.Y. Times (Sept. 14, 2013).

6. *Additional Reading.* For **commentary on the Supreme Court's decision**, see The Health Care Case: The Supreme Court's Decision and Its Implications (Nathaniel Persily et al. eds. 2013); David A. Hyman, Why Did Law Professors Misunderestimate the Lawsuits Against PPACA?, 2014 U. Ill. L. Rev. 805; Josh Blackman, Unprecedented: The Constitutional Challenge to Obamacare (2013); Symposium, Health Care and the Constitution: A Forum on the Supreme Court's Affordable Care Act Decision, 81 Fordham L. Rev. 1697 (2013); Einer Elhauge, Obamacare on Trial (2012); Andrew Koppleman, The Tough Luck Constitution and the Fight over Health Care Reform (2013); Symposium, 38 J. Health Pol. Pol'y & L. 215 (2013); Martha Minow, Affordable Convergence: "Reasonable Interpretation" and the Affordable Care Act, 126 Harv. L. Rev. 117 (2012) ("Reading the two opinions . . . is a bit like traveling between two countries speaking different languages.").

On the **fairness of community rating** (note 3), see Jessica L. Roberts, "Healthism": A Critique of the Antidiscrimination Approach to Health Insurance and Health-Care Reform, 2012 U. Ill. L. Rev. 1159; Allison K. Hoffman, Three Models of Health Insurance: The Conceptual Pluralism of the Patient Protection and Affordable Care Act, 159 U. Pa. L. Rev. 1873 (2011); Deborah Stone, The Struggle for the Soul of Insurance, 18 J. Health Pol. Pol'y & L. 287 (1993); Lisa Klautzer et al., Can We Legally Pay People for Being Good?, 49 Inquiry 268 (2012).

On **insurance markets and regulation under the ACA**, see Tom Baker, Health Insurance, Risk, and Responsibility After the Patient Protection and Affordable Care Act, 159 U. Pa. L. Rev. 1577 (2011); Amy Monahan, On Subsidies and Mandates: A Regulatory Critique of the ACA, 36 J. Corp. L. 781 (2011); Allison K. Hoffman, Oil and Water: Mixing Individual Mandates, Fragmented Markets, and Health Reform, 36 Am. J. Law Med. & Ethics 7 (2010); Timothy Jost, Loopholes in the Affordable Care Act, 5 St. Louis U. J. Health L. & Pol'y 27 (2011).

On the **merits of decoupling insurance from employment** (note 4), see Edward A. Zelinsky, The Defined Contribution Paradigm, 114 Yale L.J. 451 (2004); Symposium, 38 Inquiry 175 (2001); Symposium, 25(6) Health Aff. 1474 (Dec. 2006). On the possible demerits, see David A. Hyman & Mark A. Hall, Two Cheers for Employment-Based Health Insurance, 2 Yale J. Health Pol'y L. & Ethics 23 (2002). See generally Mark V. Pauly, Health Benefits at Work (1998).

For discussions of **wellness programs** (note 5), see Symposium, 27 Health Matrix 1 (2017); Special Issue, 39 Journal of Health, Politics, Policy and Law 955 (2014); Jill R. Horwitz et al., Wellness Incentives in the Workplace: Cost Savings Through Cost Shifting to Unhealthy Workers, 32 Health Aff. 468 (2013).

An excellent textbook on **health insurance economics and regulation** generally is Michael A. Morrisey, Health Insurance (2013).

7. *Insurance Exchanges and States' Options.* Health insurance exchanges are quasi-public entities that facilitate the online sale and purchase of insurance and that determine people's eligibility for the ACA's subsidies. Under the ACA, states had the option of establishing their own insurance exchange or falling back on a federally operated exchange. The ACA's drafters anticipated that most states, even those hostile to health reform, would rather run their own exchanges than cede that authority to the

federal government. But the choice of whether to establish an exchange became, in many states, a referendum on the state's support for the broader project of health reform. In the end, 34 states declined to establish exchanges. Rather unexpectedly, those choices became the subject of a second Supreme Court case over the future of the ACA.

■ KING v. BURWELL

576 U.S. ___ (2015)

Chief Justice ROBERTS delivered the opinion of the Court [in which Justices KENNEDY, GINSBURG, BREYER, SOTOMAYOR, and KAGAN joined].

The Patient Protection and Affordable Care Act adopts a series of interlocking reforms designed to expand coverage in the individual health insurance market. First, the Act bars insurers from taking a person's health into account when deciding whether to sell health insurance or how much to charge. Second, the Act generally requires each person to maintain insurance coverage or make a payment to the Internal Revenue Service. And third, the Act gives tax credits to certain people to make insurance more affordable.

In addition to those reforms, the Act requires the creation of an "Exchange" in each State—basically, a marketplace that allows people to compare and purchase insurance plans. The Act gives each State the opportunity to establish its own Exchange, but provides that the Federal Government will establish the Exchange if the State does not.

This case is about whether the Act's interlocking reforms apply equally in each State no matter who establishes the State's Exchange. Specifically, the question presented is whether the Act's tax credits are available in States that have a Federal Exchange.

I. A

The Patient Protection and Affordable Care Act grew out of a long history of failed health insurance reform. In the 1990s, several States began experimenting with ways to expand people's access to coverage. One common approach was to impose a pair of insurance market regulations—a "guaranteed issue" requirement, which barred insurers from denying coverage to any person because of his health, and a "community rating" requirement, which barred insurers from charging a person higher premiums for the same reason. Together, those requirements were designed to ensure that anyone who wanted to buy health insurance could do so.

The guaranteed issue and community rating requirements achieved that goal, but they had an unintended consequence: They encouraged people to wait until they got sick to buy insurance. Why buy insurance coverage when you are healthy, if you can buy the same coverage for the same price when you become ill? This consequence—known as "adverse selection"—led to a second: Insurers were forced to increase premiums to account for the fact that, more and more, it was the sick rather than the healthy who were buying insurance. And that consequence fed back into the first: As the cost of insurance rose, even more people waited until they became ill to buy it.

This led to an economic "death spiral." As premiums rose higher and higher, and the number of people buying insurance sank lower and lower, insurers began to leave the market entirely. As a result, the number of people without insurance increased dramatically. . . .

In 1996, Massachusetts adopted the guaranteed issue and community rating requirements and experienced similar results. But in 2006, Massachusetts added two more reforms: The Commonwealth required individuals to buy insurance or pay a penalty, and it gave tax credits to certain individuals to ensure that they could afford the insurance they were required to buy. The combination of these three reforms—insurance market regulations, a coverage mandate, and tax credits—reduced the uninsured rate in Massachusetts to 2.6 percent, by far the lowest in the Nation.

B

The Affordable Care Act adopts a version of the three key reforms that made the Massachusetts system successful. First, the Act adopts the guaranteed issue and community rating requirements. . . . Second, the Act generally requires individuals to maintain health insurance coverage or make a payment to the IRS. . . . In Congress's view, that coverage requirement was "essential to creating effective health insurance markets." Congress also provided an exemption from the coverage requirement for anyone who has to spend more than eight percent of his income on health insurance. Third, the Act seeks to make insurance more affordable by giving refundable tax credits to individuals with household incomes between 100 percent and 400 percent of the federal poverty line. . . .

These three reforms are closely intertwined. As noted, Congress found that the guaranteed issue and community rating requirements would not work without the coverage requirement. And the coverage requirement would not work without the tax credits. The reason is that, without the tax credits, the cost of buying insurance would exceed eight percent of income for a large number of individuals, which would exempt them from the coverage requirement. . . .

C

In addition to those three reforms, the Act requires the creation of an "Exchange" in each State where people can shop for insurance, usually online. An Exchange may be created in one of two ways. First, the Act provides that "[e]ach State shall . . . establish an American Health Benefit Exchange . . . for the State." Second, if a State nonetheless chooses not to establish its own Exchange, the Act provides that the Secretary of Health and Human Services "shall . . . establish and operate such Exchange within the State."

The issue in this case is whether the Act's tax credits are available in States that have a Federal Exchange rather than a State Exchange. The Act . . . provides that the amount of the tax credit depends in part on whether the taxpayer has enrolled in an insurance plan through "an Exchange established by the State under section 1311 of the Patient Protection and Affordable Care Act." The IRS addressed the availability of tax credits by promulgating a rule that made them available on both State and Federal Exchanges. . . . At this point, 16 States and the District of Columbia have established their own Exchanges; the other 34 States have elected to have HHS do so. 1/3 2/3

Petitioners are four individuals who live in Virginia, which has a Federal Exchange. They do not wish to purchase health insurance. In their view, Virginia's Exchange does not qualify as "an Exchange established by the State," so they should not receive any tax credits. That would make the cost of buying insurance more than eight percent of their income, which would exempt them from the Act's coverage requirement. . . .

II

. . . When analyzing an agency's interpretation of a statute, we often apply the two-step framework announced in Chevron U. S. A. Inc. v. Natural Resources Defense Council, Inc., 467 U. S. 837 (1984). Under that framework, we ask whether the statute is ambiguous and, if so, whether the agency's interpretation is reasonable. This approach "is premised on the theory that a statute's ambiguity constitutes an implicit delegation from Congress to the agency to fill in the statutory gaps." FDA v. Brown & Williamson Tobacco Corp., 529 U. S. 120, 159 (2000). "In extraordinary cases, however, there may be reason to hesitate before concluding that Congress has intended such an implicit delegation."

This is one of those cases. The tax credits are among the Act's key reforms, involving billions of dollars in spending each year and affecting the price of health insurance for millions of people. Whether those credits are available on Federal Exchanges is thus a question of deep "economic and political significance" that is central to this statutory scheme; had Congress wished to assign that question to an agency, it surely would have done so expressly. It is especially unlikely that Congress would have delegated this decision to the IRS, which has no expertise in crafting health insurance policy of this sort. This is not a case for the IRS.

It is instead our task to determine the correct reading of [this provision]. If the statutory language is plain, we must enforce it according to its terms. But oftentimes the "meaning—or ambiguity—of certain words or phrases may only become evident when placed in context." Brown & Williamson, 529 U. S., at 132. So when deciding whether the language is plain, we must read the words "in their context and with a view to their place in the overall statutory scheme." Our duty, after all, is "to construe statutes, not isolated provisions."

A

We begin with the text of Section 36B. As relevant here, Section 36B allows an individual to receive tax credits only if the individual enrolls in an insurance plan through "an Exchange established by the State under [42 U.S.C. §18031]." . . . Section 18031 provides that "[e]ach State shall . . . establish an American Health Benefit Exchange . . . for the State." Although phrased as a requirement, the Act gives the States "flexibility" by allowing them to "elect" whether they want to establish an Exchange. If the State chooses not to do so, Section 18041 provides that the Secretary "shall . . . establish and operate such Exchange within the State." By using the phrase "such Exchange," Section 18041 instructs the Secretary to establish and operate the same Exchange that the State was directed to establish under Section 18031. In other words, State Exchanges and Federal Exchanges are equivalent . . . .

Second, we must determine whether a Federal Exchange is "established by the State" for purposes of Section 36B. At the outset, it might seem that a Federal

Exchange cannot fulfill this requirement. . . . But when read in context, "with a view to [its] place in the overall statutory scheme," the meaning of the phrase "established by the State" is not so clear. . . . [Various technical] provisions suggest that the Act may not always use the phrase "established by the State" in its most natural sense. Thus, the meaning of that phrase may not be as clear as it appears when read out of context. . . .

The upshot of all this is that the phrase "an Exchange established by the State under [§18031]" is properly viewed as ambiguous. The phrase may be limited in its reach to State Exchanges. But it is also possible that the phrase refers to all Exchanges—both State and Federal—at least for purposes of the tax credits. . . . The Affordable Care Act contains more than a few examples of inartful drafting. . . . Several features of the Act's passage contributed to that unfortunate reality. . . . Congress passed much of the Act using a complicated budgetary procedure known as "reconciliation," which limited opportunities for debate and amendment, and bypassed the Senate's normal 60-vote filibuster requirement. As a result, the Act does not reflect the type of care and deliberation that one might expect of such significant legislation. Cf. Frankfurter, Some Reflections on the Reading of Statutes, 47 Colum. L. Rev. 527, 545 (1947) (describing a cartoon "in which a senator tells his colleagues 'I admit this new bill is too complicated to understand. We'll just have to pass it to find out what it means.' ").

Rushed enactment

Anyway, we "must do our best, bearing in mind the fundamental canon of statutory construction that the words of a statute must be read in their context and with a view to their place in the overall statutory scheme." Utility Air Regulatory Group, 573 U. S., at ___. . . .

B

Given that the text is ambiguous, we must turn to the broader structure of the Act to determine the meaning of Section 36B. . . . Here, the statutory scheme compels us to reject petitioners' interpretation because it would destabilize the individual insurance market in any State with a Federal Exchange, and likely create the very "death spirals" that Congress designed the Act to avoid. . . . It is implausible that Congress meant the Act to operate in this manner. . . . Congress made the guaranteed issue and community rating requirements applicable in every State in the Nation. But those requirements only work when combined with the coverage requirement and the tax credits. So it stands to reason that Congress meant for those provisions to apply in every State as well. . . .

Finally, the structure of Section 36B itself suggests that tax credits are not limited to State Exchanges. Section 36B(a) initially provides that tax credits "shall be allowed" for any "applicable taxpayer." [It] then defines an "applicable taxpayer" as someone who (among other things) has a household income between 100 percent and 400 percent of the federal poverty line. Together, these two provisions appear to make anyone in the specified income range eligible to receive a tax credit. . . .

In a democracy, the power to make the law rests with those chosen by the people. Our role is more confined—"to say what the law is." Marbury v. Madison, 1 Cranch 137, 177 (1803). That is easier in some cases than in others. But in every case we must respect the role of the Legislature, and take care not to undo what it has done. A fair reading of legislation demands a fair understanding of the legislative plan.

Congress passed the Affordable Care Act to improve health insurance markets, not to destroy them. If at all possible, we must interpret the Act in a way that is consistent with the former, and avoids the latter. . . .

Justice SCALIA, with whom Justice THOMAS and Justice ALITO join, dissenting.

. . . This case requires us to decide whether someone who buys insurance on an Exchange established by the Secretary gets tax credits. You would think the answer would be obvious—so obvious there would hardly be a need for the Supreme Court to hear a case about it. . . . Words no longer have meaning if an Exchange that is not established by a State is "established by the State." It is hard to come up with a clearer way to limit tax credits to state Exchanges. . . .

The Court persists that these provisions "would make little sense" if no tax credits were available on federal Exchanges. Even if that observation were true, it would show only oddity, not ambiguity. Laws often include unusual or mismatched provisions. The Affordable Care Act spans 900 pages; it would be amazing if its provisions all lined up perfectly with each other. This Court "does not revise legislation . . . just because the text as written creates an apparent anomaly." Michigan v. Bay Mills Indian Community, 572 U. S. ___, ___ (2014). . . .

[In various places, the dissent describes the majority's analysis as "feeble," "interpretive jiggery-pokery," "outlandish[]," "indefensible," a "dismal failure," and "[p]ure applesauce."]

Even less defensible, if possible, is the Court's claim that its interpretive approach is justified because this Act "does not reflect the type of care and deliberation that one might expect of such significant legislation." . . . It is not our place to . . . make everything come out right when Congress does not do its job properly. It is up to Congress to design its laws with care, and it is up to the people to hold them to account if they fail to carry out that responsibility. Rather than rewriting the law under the pretense of interpreting it, the Court should have left it to Congress to decide what to do about the Act's limitation of tax credits to state Exchanges. If Congress values above everything else the Act's applicability across the country, it could make tax credits available in every Exchange. . . . And if Congress thinks that the present design of the Act works well enough, it could do nothing. Congress could also do something else altogether, entirely abandoning the structure of the Affordable Care Act. The Court's insistence on making a choice that should be made by Congress both aggrandizes judicial power and encourages congressional lassitude. . . .

The Act that Congress passed makes tax credits available only on an "Exchange established by the State." This Court, however, concludes that this limitation would prevent the rest of the Act from working as well as hoped. So it rewrites the law to make tax credits available everywhere. We should start calling this law SCOTUScare.

Perhaps the Patient Protection and Affordable Care Act will attain the enduring status of the Social Security Act or the Taft-Hartley Act; perhaps not. But this Court's two decisions on the Act will surely be remembered through the years. The somersaults of statutory interpretation they have performed ("penalty" means tax, . . .) will be cited by litigants endlessly, to the confusion of honest jurisprudence. And the cases will publish forever the discouraging truth that the Supreme Court of the United States favors some laws over others, and is prepared to do whatever it takes to uphold and assist its favorites.

Notes: The Exchanges

1. *Hurricane Season.* King v. Burwell was preceded by almost as much fevered anticipation as NFIB v. Sibelius. And for good reason: Had the case come out the other way, the exchanges would likely have collapsed in the 34 states that had chosen the federal default exchange. See Nicholas Bagley et al., Predicting the Fallout from King v. Burwell, 372 New Eng. J. Med. 101 (2015). Republican congressional leaders would have come under intense pressure to propose a statutory fix that President Obama would have been willing to sign into law. No one knows, though, whether such an imagined bipartisan compromise could have been achieved.

2. *Tea Leaves.* Does the Court's decision signal a desire to bring an end to judicial challenges to the ACA's fundamentals? Another flashpoint of legal controversy arose in *House of Representatives v. Price* (formerly *House v. Burwell*), where House Republicans argued that the Obama administration was spending money to support the ACA without the required appropriation from Congress. The ACA provision in question requires insurers to give their lowest-income enrollees a discount on their out-of-pocket spending (in the forms of deductibles and copayments); in exchange, the federal government is supposed to reimburse the insurers. The Obama administration asked Congress to appropriate the needed funds, but Congress declined. To prevent the ACA's collapse, the administration then interpreted the statute to allow it to make the payments out of an existing appropriation.

The lawsuit was initially seen as a political stunt. Fights over the appropriations power are worked out between the political branches; historically, they have never been the subject of litigation. Observers on both sides of the aisle believed that the House of Representatives lacked standing to bring the case. But a federal district court disagreed, reasoning that a violation of the appropriations power would infringe on the House's constitutionally assigned powers and would thus cause it a concrete injury. House v. Burwell, 130 F. Supp. 3d 53 (D.D.C. 2015). On the merits, the court also sided with the House: In its view, the ACA included no appropriation for the cost-sharing subsidies. House v. Burwell, 185 F. Supp. 3d 165 (D.D.C. 2016). The court enjoined the government from making cost-sharing payments, but stayed its injunction pending appeal to the D.C. Circuit.

In October 2017, while the appeal was still pending, President Trump reversed the Obama administration's legal determination and ordered the payments to cease. Although many observers feared that the exchanges would unravel with the loss of the cost-sharing payments, the real-world consequences have been surprisingly muted. The vast majority of insurers had already raised their premiums to account for the risk that President Trump might cut off their payments, and state insurance commissioners took creative steps to shield their insurance markets from the worst effects. Higher premiums will harm those people who do not quality for premium subsidies, but the ACA protects those making less than four times the poverty level by capping their premiums at a fixed percentage of income. Although a bipartisan group of senators has proposed legislation to temporarily fund the cost-sharing payments, it is unclear as of late 2017 whether the legislation has any chance of passing.

3. *Correcting Congress's Mistakes.* The drafting anomaly in King v. Burwell was initially seen as an obvious mistake arising from the somewhat rushed manner in which its final language was hammered together. Senate committees had drafted two earlier versions, one that relied entirely on state exchanges and the other that

had only a single federal exchange. Although the enacted bill merged the two ideas—states would take the lead, but with a federal fallback—drafters failed to clean up all of the exchange-related phrasing. Do you find it curious that neither the challengers nor the government openly characterized the legislative language as a mistake? Or that the Court's opinion only vaguely hints at this possibility?

Instead of claiming a drafting error, the challengers argued—implausibly and with essentially no evidentiary support—that Congress deliberately withheld subsidies from the federal fallback exchange in order to compel states to establish their own exchanges. If Congress did use subsidies in this manner, would it have amounted to unconstitutional coercion? Consider the question in light of the portion of NFIB v. Sebelius that we turn to below.

4. *The Health of the Exchanges.* The rollout of the exchanges was initially rocky. HealthCare.gov, the federally operated exchange, did not function for the first months of its operation, and a number of newly established "cooperative health plans" failed. These growing pains notwithstanding, however, the exchanges have proven successful at enrolling people in coverage. More than 12.2 million people selected coverage for 2017 through the state and federal exchanges, and about 84 percent of them qualified for premium subsidies. See CMS, Health Insurance Marketplaces 2017 Open Enrollment Period Final Enrollment Report (Mar. 2017).

But the top-level numbers mask wide variability. In 2016, the prices for a typical silver-level exchange plan ran from a high of $719 per month in Anchorage, Alaska to a low of $186 per month in Albuquerque, New Mexico. Many rural counties have struggled to attract enough insurers to assure a competitive marketplace. Today, more than one in five exchange enrollees had a choice of only one insurer. See Cynthia Cox et al., 2017 Premium Changes and Insurer Participation in the Affordable Care Act's Health Insurance Marketplaces, Kaiser Family Foundation, Oct. 24, 2016. On the other hand, by the end of 2016, premiums and range of choice were not dramatically different for ACA individual coverage than what most employers typically pay and what most employees have to choose from.

Large premium increases for 2017, together with the withdrawal of several large insurers who were leaving the exchanges, raised questions about the long-term stability of the exchanges. Although most independent observers believed that prices in 2018 would stabilize and that the exchanges would remain viable, the election of Donald Trump has changed the calculus. The president's decision to cut off cost-sharing payments, together with concerns that the administration may not vigorously enforce the individual mandate, has sent jitters through the insurance industry.

5. *Rate Regulation.* Although the ACA imposes a host of new requirements for the individual and small-group insurance markets, it does relatively little to regulate the price of insurance. The important exception is the ACA's "medical loss ratio," which requires insurers to spend at least 80 percent of what they earn in premiums on their enrollees' medical expenses. (To an insurer, any payment for health care is a "medical loss.") If an insurer spends less than the required amount, it must remit the difference to its customers. The medical loss ratio aims to discourage insurers from denying good claims, to stop them from spending too much on sales and administration, and to prevent them from pocketing excessive profits. But the requirement is controversial. Smaller insurers, for example, may spend more on administration relative to their larger competitors, making it more difficult for them to hit the medical loss ratio.

The ACA also requires insurers to inform the federal government if they plan on increasing their premiums by more than 10 percent and to explain the reasons for the rate increase. See 76 Fed. Reg. 29964 (2011). The ACA, however, does not empower the federal government to reject unreasonable rate increases; that authority remains with the states, which vary greatly in the rigor of their rate review processes. See Department of Health and Human Services, Rate Review Annual Report (Dec. 2015).

6. *Further Reading.* For some of the voluminous commentary on King v. Burwell, see Josh Blackman, Unraveled: Obamacare, Religious Liberty, and Executive Power (2016); Abbe R. Gluck, Imperfect Statutes, Imperfect Courts: Understanding Congress's Plan in an Era of Unorthodox Lawmaking, 129 Harv. L. Rev. 62 (2015); Nicholas Bagley, Three Words and the Future of the Affordable Care Act, 40 J. Health Pol. Pol'y & L. 589 (2015); Jonathan H. Adler & Michael F. Cannon, Taxation Without Representation: The Illegal IRS Rule to Expand Tax Credits under the PPACA 23 Health Matrix 119 (2013).

For background on House v. Price (note 2), see Nicholas Bagley, Legal Limits and the Implementation of the Affordable Care Act, 164 Penn. L. Rev. 1715, 1729-1735 (2016).

For discussion of the **medical loss ratio** (note 4), see Michael McCue et al., Impact of Medical Loss Regulation on the Financial Performance of Health Insurers, 32 Health Aff. 1546 (2013); Michael McCue & Mark A. Hall, The Federal Medical Loss Ratio Rule: Implications for Consumers in Year 3 (2013); Benjamin Day et al., The Affordable Care Act and Medical Loss Ratios: No Impact in First Three Years, 45 Int'l J. Health Servs. 127 (2015).

3. Medicaid

NATIONAL FEDERATION OF INDEPENDENT BUSINESS v. SEBELIUS

567 U.S. 1 (2012)

Chief Justice ROBERTS.

. . . On the day the President signed the [Patient Protection and Affordable Care] Act into law, Florida and 12 other States filed a complaint . . . subsequently joined by 13 more States . . . and the National Federation of Independent Business. The plaintiffs alleged, among other things, that . . . the Medicaid expansion, which gives funds to the States on the condition that they provide specified health care to all citizens whose income falls below a certain threshold, . . . exceeds Congress's authority under the Spending Clause . . . [because it coerces them] by threatening to withhold all of a State's Medicaid grants, unless the State accepts the new expanded funding and complies with the conditions that come with it. This, they argue, violates the basic principle that the Federal Government may not compel the States to enact or administer a federal regulatory program. . . .

Enacted in 1965, Medicaid offers federal funding to States to assist [low-income] pregnant women, children, needy families, the blind, the elderly, and the disabled in obtaining medical care. See 42 U.S.C. §1396a(a)(10). In order to receive that funding, States must comply with federal criteria governing matters such as who receives care and what services are provided at what cost. By 1982 every State had chosen to participate in Medicaid. . . .

There is no doubt that the Act dramatically increases state obligations under Medicaid. The current Medicaid program requires States to cover only certain discrete categories of needy individuals—pregnant women, children, needy families, the blind, the elderly, and the disabled. There is no mandatory coverage for most childless adults, and the States typically do not offer any such coverage.[6] The States also enjoy considerable flexibility with respect to the coverage levels for parents of needy families. On average States cover only those unemployed parents who make less than 37 percent of the federal poverty level, and only those employed parents who make less than 63 percent of the poverty line.[7]

The Medicaid provisions of the Affordable Care Act, in contrast, require States to expand their Medicaid programs by 2014 to cover all individuals under the age of 65 with incomes below 133 percent of the federal poverty line. . . . The Affordable Care Act provides that the Federal Government will pay 100 percent of the costs of covering these newly eligible individuals through 2016. In the following years, the federal payment level gradually decreases, to a minimum of 90 percent. In light of the expansion in coverage mandated by the Act, the Federal Government estimates that its Medicaid spending will increase by approximately $100 billion per year, nearly 40 percent above current levels. . . .

In this case, the financial "inducement" Congress has chosen is much more than "relatively mild encouragement"—it is a gun to the head. . . . [T]he Medicaid Act provides that if a State's Medicaid plan does not comply with the Act's requirements, the Secretary of Health and Human Services may declare that "further payments will not be made to the State." A State that opts out of the Affordable Care Act's expansion in health care coverage thus stands to lose not merely "a relatively small percentage" of its existing Medicaid funding, but all of it. Medicaid spending accounts for over 20 percent of the average State's total budget, with federal funds covering 50 to 83 percent of those costs. . . . The threatened loss of over 10 percent of a State's overall budget . . . is economic dragooning that leaves the States with no real option but to acquiesce in the Medicaid expansion. . . .

[T]he Government claims that the Medicaid expansion is properly viewed merely as a modification of the existing program because the States agreed that Congress could change the terms of Medicaid when they signed on in the first place. . . . Congress has in fact done so, sometimes conditioning only the new funding, other times both old and new. The Medicaid expansion, however, accomplishes a shift in kind, not merely degree.

The original program was designed to cover medical services for four particular categories of the needy: the disabled, the blind, the elderly, and needy families with dependent children. Previous amendments to Medicaid eligibility merely

6. [Actually, about half the states provide at least some coverage for low-income childless adults, but the coverage usually is more limited than Medicaid's full benefits and federal funding is provided only through special "waivers" of normal Medicaid funding rules.—Eds.]

7. [The federal poverty level is about $12,000 for a single person and about twice that for a family of four, with other levels similarly scaled to household size.—Eds.]

altered and expanded the boundaries of these [mandatory] categories. Under the Affordable Care Act, Medicaid is transformed into a program to meet the health care needs of the entire nonelderly population with income below 133 percent of the poverty level. It is no longer a program to care for the neediest among us, but rather an element of a comprehensive national plan to provide universal health insurance coverage. . . . A State could hardly anticipate that Congress's reservation of the right to "alter" or "amend" the Medicaid program included the power to transform it so dramatically. . . .

[Justices Breyer and Kagan joined this portion of the opinion (IV.A). Justices Scalia, Kennedy, Thomas, and Alito concurred with, but did not join, this portion. Thus, seven justices agreed that the Medicaid expansion is unconstitutional.]

B

Nothing in our opinion precludes Congress from offering funds under the Affordable Care Act to expand the availability of health care, and requiring that States accepting such funds comply with the conditions on their use. What Congress is not free to do is to penalize States that choose not to participate in that new program by taking away their existing Medicaid funding. . . . As a practical matter, that means States may now choose to reject the expansion; that is the whole point. But that does not mean all or even any will. Some States may indeed decline to participate, either because they are unsure they will be able to afford their share of the new funding obligations, or because they are unwilling to commit the administrative resources necessary to support the expansion. Other States, however, may voluntarily sign up, finding the idea of expanding Medicaid coverage attractive, particularly given the level of federal funding the Act offers at the outset. . . .

[Justices Ginsburg, Breyer, Sotomayor, and Kagan joined this subsection B, regarding the consequence of finding the Medicaid expansion coercive. The other four justices (Scalia, Kennedy, Thomas, and Alito) dissented on the remedy, arguing instead that the consequence should be to strike down the entire Affordable Care Act. See page 156.]

Justice GINSBURG [with whom Justice SOTOMAYOR joined], dissenting in part.

. . . Medicaid is a prototypical example of federal-state cooperation in serving the Nation's general welfare. Rather than authorizing a federal agency to administer a uniform national health-care system for the poor, Congress offered States the opportunity to tailor Medicaid grants to their particular needs, so long as they remain within bounds set by federal law. In shaping Medicaid, Congress did not endeavor to fix permanently the terms participating states must meet; instead, Congress reserved the "right to alter, amend, or repeal" any provision of the Medicaid Act. . . . And from 1965 to the present, States have regularly conformed to Congress' alterations of the Medicaid Act.

The Chief Justice's . . . conclusion rests on [the premise that] . . . the Medicaid expansion is . . . a new grant program, not an addition to the Medicaid program existing before the ACA's enactment. Congress, The Chief Justice maintains, has threatened States with the loss of funds from an old program in an effort to get them to adopt a new one. . . . The Chief Justice therefore—for the first time ever—finds an exercise of Congress' spending power unconstitutionally coercive.

Medicaid, as amended by the ACA, however, is not two spending programs; it is a single program with a constant aim—to enable poor persons to receive basic health care when they need it. . . . States have no entitlement to receive any Medicaid funds; they enjoy only the opportunity to accept funds on Congress' terms. . . . The Federal Government, therefore, is not, as The Chief Justice charges, threatening States with the loss of "existing" funds from one spending program in order to induce them to opt into another program. Congress is simply requiring States to do what States have long been required to do to receive Medicaid funding: comply with the conditions Congress prescribes for participation. . . .

Expansion has been characteristic of the Medicaid program. Akin to the ACA in 2010, the Medicaid Act as passed in 1965 augmented existing federal grant programs jointly administered with the States. Huberfeld, Federalizing Medicaid, 14 U. Pa. J. Const. L. 431, 444-445 (2011). States were not required to participate in Medicaid. But if they did, the Federal Government paid at least half the costs. To qualify for these grants, States had to offer a minimum level of health coverage to beneficiaries of four federally funded, state-administered welfare programs: Aid to Families with Dependent Children; Old Age Assistance; Aid to the Blind; and Aid to the Permanently and Totally Disabled. At their option, States could enroll additional "medically needy" individuals; these costs, too, were partially borne by the Federal Government at the same, at least 50%, rate.

Since 1965, Congress has amended the Medicaid program on more than 50 occasions, sometimes quite sizably. Most relevant here, between 1988 and 1990, Congress required participating States to include among their beneficiaries pregnant women with family incomes up to 133% of the federal poverty level, children up to age 6 at the same income levels, and children ages 6 to 18 with family incomes up to 100% of the poverty level. These amendments added millions to the Medicaid-eligible population. . . .

Compared to past alterations, the ACA is notable for the extent to which the Federal Government will pick up the tab. Medicaid's 2010 expansion is financed largely by federal outlays. In 2014, federal funds will cover 100% of the costs for newly eligible beneficiaries; that rate will gradually decrease before settling at 90% in 2020. By comparison, federal contributions toward the care of beneficiaries eligible pre-ACA range from 50% to 83%, and averaged 57% between 2005 and 2008. . . .

Finally, any fair appraisal of Medicaid would require acknowledgment of the considerable autonomy States enjoy under the Act. . . . Subject to its basic requirements, the Medicaid Act empowers States to "select dramatically different levels of funding and coverage, alter and experiment with different financing and delivery modes, and opt to cover (or not to cover) a range of particular procedures and therapies. States have leveraged this policy discretion to generate a myriad of dramatically different Medicaid programs over the past several decades." Ruger, Of Icebergs and Glaciers, 75 Law & Contemp. Probs. 215, 233 (2012). . . .

The alternative to conditional federal spending, it bears emphasis, is not state autonomy but state marginalization. In 1965, Congress elected to nationalize health coverage for seniors through Medicare. It could similarly have established Medicaid as an exclusively federal program. Instead, Congress gave the States the opportunity to partner in the program's administration and development. . . . Congress must of course have authority to impose limitations on the States' use of the federal dollars. This Court, time and again, has respected Congress' prescription of spending conditions, and has required States to abide by them. . . . That is what makes this such a simple case, and the Court's decision so unsettling. . . .

■ MEDICAID EVOLUTION FOR THE 21ST CENTURY

John V. Jacobi
102 Ky. L.J. 357 (2014)

Medicaid was created in 1965 as a companion to Medicare. Unlike Medicare, which was intended as a contributory social insurance system for the elderly, Medicaid was intended to shore up the existing patchwork of state systems, and, funded in part by the federal government, to provide health care services to the poor. From the beginning, Medicaid recognized the historical primacy of the states as providers for the poor, but also initiated an increased regulatory role for the federal government to enforce some basic coverage principles as conditions of states' receipt of the federal funds available under the program. Like its sister program, Medicare, Medicaid did not interfere with the financial freedom of health care providers; like private health insurance coverage, it set about creating payment mechanisms that would lead providers to participate voluntarily in Medicaid as they did in private insurance programs. Medicaid, then, deviated from precursor systems: "[I]n its essential structure, Medicaid resembled not a grant program to clinics and hospitals, but instead a 'third party payment' system structured to operate like insurance, paying 'participating' health care professionals and institutions for covered services furnished to enrolled persons."

Medicaid was set up as something akin to a public insurance system, but became increasingly cabined over time by statutory and regulatory provisions that bar the states' Medicaid programs from running, as private insurance does, on a market-oriented, risk-sensitive basis. As Medicaid has developed, it has deviated more and more from the private insurance model on which it was loosely based, in three essential ways: first, those covered are mostly uninsurable in private markets; second, the services covered extend beyond those covered in commercial insurance; and third, the structure, adjusted by many amendments over the years, is much more complex than any private insurance product.

A. Who is Covered?

Prior to the expansions permitted by the ACA, Medicaid enrollees have been limited to the most medically precarious: the poor and vulnerable. In short, they are exactly the people private insurers do not wish to cover. They are poor, and also "categorically eligible." That is, in addition to meeting income and assets requirements, enrollees are required to be blind, disabled, elderly, pregnant women, children, or in families with children. These groups represent predictably high-cost insureds. A child with disabilities, for example, requires about four times the health expenditures of a child without disabilities, and people over the age of sixty-five are similarly expensive to cover. In Medicaid, the elderly and people with disabilities comprise only about 25% of enrollees, but account for about 65% of the program's cost. The distribution of health care usage generally, and predictably, is very skewed toward the elderly and people with disabilities and chronic illnesses, with

1/4 2/3

the most-ill 5% utilizing about half of the health care resources, and the least-ill 50% accounting for only about 3% of annual health expenditures. On the basis of their age and health history, then, Medicaid enrollees are likely to need a great deal of care and will be essentially uninsurable under the circumstances.

In addition, people in the Medicaid program raise identity issues beyond disability and age. The non-elderly enrollment in Medicaid is over 53% Black or Hispanic, although those two groups comprise only about 30% of the American population. The long history of race- and ethnicity- based health disparities in American health care strongly suggests that the overrepresentation of people of color in Medicaid will reflect poorer health outcomes—regardless of any faults of the Medicaid program itself. "For example, relative to whites, African Americans and Hispanics are less likely to receive appropriate cardiac medication . . . or to undergo coronary artery bypass surgery, even when the variations in such factors as insurance status, income, age, co-morbid conditions, and symptom expression are taken into account." In addition to the effects of race and ethnicity, socioeconomic status has a demonstrable effect on health status, independent of insurance status. Regardless of the causes of these effects, they establish that people covered by Medicaid are more medically fragile, have more complex health conditions, and are affected by determinants of poor health, independent of their access to health coverage or care.

B. What is Covered?

Medicaid also differs from other health finance programs in the breadth of services covered. The program covers services included in commercial insurance, including preventive, curative, and restorative physician, pharmacy, and hospital services. In addition, however, Medicaid mandates that states cover long-term care services, home care services, transportation services to and from service providers, Federally Qualified Health Center services, and rural health clinic services. In addition, many states have added "optional" services that are not mandated, but for which the federal government will provide funding if added by a state plan. The most common of these services include dental, eyeglass, prostheses, and personal care services, as well as intermediate care facility services for individuals with intellectual disabilities.

This broad coverage fits Medicaid's programmatic mission to assist the states in fulfilling their traditional mission of serving the health needs of the poor and vulnerable. Some of the additional services included in many Medicaid programs, such as coverage of eyeglasses and dental services, simply reflect a recognition that the poor do not have the disposable income to pay for services and devices that have a relatively low expected cost. Other benefits, like intermediate care facilities for people with intellectual disabilities and home care services, reflect the need to provide services for the very conditions that give rise to the vulnerability entitling individuals to Medicaid services. The slate of covered services, then, reflects the poor, elderly, or disabled condition of Medicaid enrollees.

C. Complex Structure

The structure of Medicaid is famously complex. Unlike Medicare, which is wholly federally funded and governed, Medicaid requires that the federal and state governments work in partnership—a relationship that has been notably strained recently. Its basic structure, as leading historians of Medicaid have observed, lacked coherence and clarity as a social insurance system for three reasons: first, it failed to cover all of the poor, but extended only to the categorically eligible; second, the definition and scope of medical services covered were variable from state to state; and third, the income eligibility standards varied, in some cases dramatically, from state to state. In sum, the program remained a balkanized system funded by the federal government but largely run by the states. Perhaps most critically, states retained substantial power to determine how much to pay providers for their services, and states have taken advantage of that power.

Medicaid was criticized as rather "ill-designed" and "vague" from the beginning. It paid providers on a fee-for-service basis, as did insurers. But federal payments, forming the majority of Medicaid financing, were structured as a grant-in-aid program for the states, which were largely in charge of maintaining a network of willing providers. Unlike private insurance, the Medicaid program has grown, adding components over the years ranging beyond traditional medical care to address the needs of the target population. In addition, millions of low-income elderly persons and persons with long-term disabilities qualify for both Medicaid and Medicare, and use Medicare as the primary payer for services. They rely on Medicaid, however, to pay for Medicare's coinsurance and deductibles, and for those health care services covered by Medicaid but not Medicare. One major source of Medicaid's complexity has been states' gradual movement away from the role of public insurer to the role of public payor, devolving many insurer functions to commercial HMOs.

The movement toward then-novel HMOs as fiscal and programmatic intermediaries began within five years of Medicaid's creation. California was a pioneer in the use of Medicaid HMOs. Widespread claims of fraudulent sales practices and inadequate provider networks frustrated these efforts and led federal regulators to impose relatively stringent requirements for the use of Medicaid managed care. By 1980, only about 1% of Medicaid enrollees were in HMOs. During the 1980s, however, Medicaid officials in the Reagan and George H.W. Bush administrations relaxed many of the restrictions on the use of Medicaid HMOs, although these efforts only raised the percentage of enrollees to about 12%. During the 1990s, mostly through the use of [administrative] waivers, the number of Medicaid enrollees in HMOs grew dramatically "from 9.5 percent of total Medicaid enrollment in 1991 to 40.1 percent in 1996." These waivers from usual Medicaid regulatory requirements were necessary because state managed care programs limited the range of enrollees' choice of providers and varied, by location within states, enrollees' access to services. Then, as part of the Balanced Budget Act of 1997, states obtained the authority to mandate HMO enrollment for most Medicaid beneficiaries.

In an effort to contain Medicaid costs, states have continued to move toward managed care. By 2010, most states had moved the majority of their enrollees to HMOs, and almost two-thirds of Medicaid enrollees were in managed care. For most states, the movement to HMOs for Medicaid enrollees has not resulted in the hoped-for cost savings, and the shift seems not to have improved the quality of care or access to providers. Medicaid programs have, then, largely moved from directly administering provider payments to purchasing insurance coverage for enrollees from private vendors. In other words, most states have largely privatized what had been among their most important programmatic functions: selecting, maintaining, monitoring, and compensating health care providers for many of their Medicaid enrollees. This "decentralization" of government function not only saved states the administrative and staffing costs of network formation and maintenance, but also, to some extent, relieved them of the always-delicate task of intermediating between providers and enrollees.

Notes: Medicaid

1. *Medicaid Quandaries.* The Supreme Court's decision in NFIB v. Sebelius allowed states to refuse the ACA's Medicaid expansion while retaining funding for traditional Medicaid. As of this writing, 19 states, concentrated in the South and the Great Plains, have refused the Medicaid expansion. Does it make financial sense for those states to refuse the expansion considering that federal funds will pay for at least 90 percent of the costs? What other reasons might states have for refusing to expand? What effect does a refusal to expand have on physicians and hospitals? Even though Medicaid pays them substantially less than private insurance, many of them are already treating the people who would be added to Medicaid, but are

FIGURE 3.3 Medicaid's Role for Selected Populations

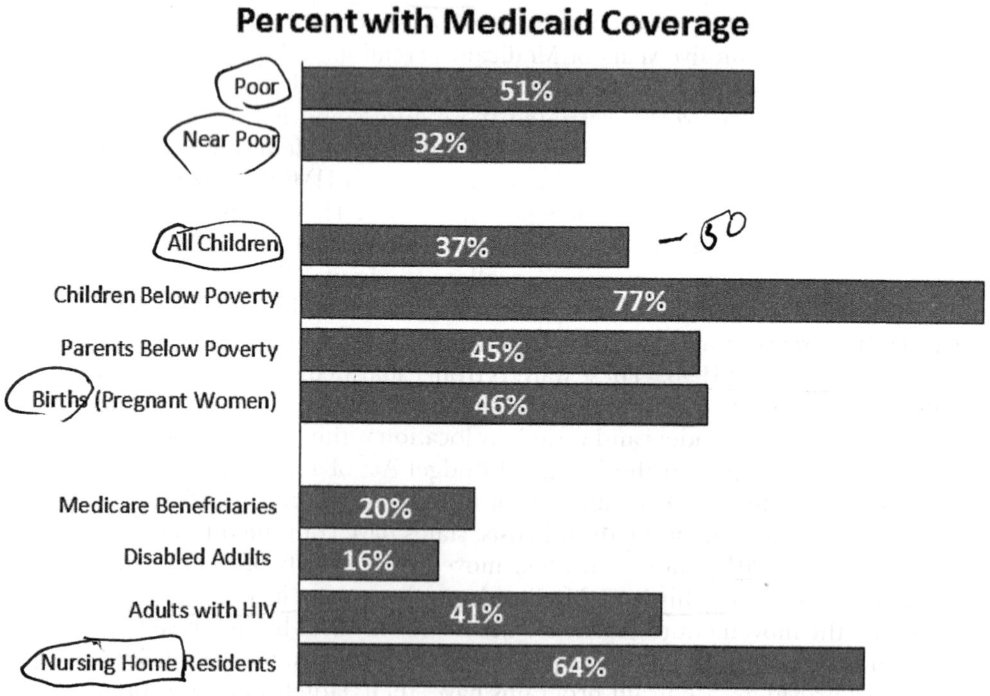

SOURCE: Kaiser Commission on Medicaid and the Uninsured (KCMU) and Urban Institute analysis of various federal data sources for 2013 or earlier, prior to Medicaid expansion under the ACA.

doing so for almost no money, as indigent uninsured patients. See Mark Hall, States' Decisions Not to Expand Medicaid, 92 N.C. L. Rev. 1459 (2014).*

2. *Block Grants.* With Donald Trump's election, the debate over repealing and replacing the ACA has raised questions about the future of the Medicaid expansion and even about Medicaid's basic structure:

> Congressional Republicans hope to transform Medicaid from an individual entitlement to a block grant—a fixed sum of money that places few restrictions on the purposes that states can use it for. In some respects, block grant proposals promote federalism: they afford states more discretion about how to put Medicaid dollars to work. A state, for example, could place limits on eligibility or benefits; more creatively, it could use some of its Medicaid money for lead abatement in urban cores, as Michigan has recently been allowed to do on a small scale. But the devil is in the details. A fixed block grant that increases with economy-wide inflation and is insensitive to the business cycle would not give states the fiscal flexibility necessary to cope with a recession. Over time, as well, the galloping pace of medical inflation would erode the value of the block grants, requiring states to ration access to medical care, either through cuts to benefits or to eligibility. Proposals to transform Medicaid into a block-grant program may trade on the rhetoric of states' rights, but they have the perverse effect of inhibiting state power.
>
> Alternative approaches could mitigate the concern. Per capita grants anchored to a formula that accounted for the number of people within a state under a particular income threshold, for example, would avoid the countercyclical trap: federal outlays would then increase as more people lost their jobs and became dependent on government assistance. But because the data necessary to calculate funding levels may lag the economy by several years, a state could find itself in a financial pinch just as a recession takes hold. Nor would a per capita grant account for unanticipated cost spikes associated with the release of costly new therapies (like the new Hepatitis C drugs) or epidemics (like the Zika outbreak). Of greater concern, the size of per capita grants would have to increase with medical inflation. Yet Republicans anticipate achieving large cost reductions through Medicaid reform—suggesting that the goal is not to provide sufficient funds to cover those who are currently eligible, but instead to force states to shrink their programs through eligibility restrictions and benefit cuts.

Nicholas Bagley, Federalism and the End of Obamacare, 127 Yale L.J.F. 1 (2017). For an in-depth discussion of block grants and changing Medicaid's status as an entitlement program, see David A. Super, The Political Economy of Entitlement, 104 Colum. L. Rev. 633 (2004).

* See also, Jonathan Oberlander, Repeal, Replace, Repair, Retreat: Republicans' Health Care Quagmire, ___ New Eng. J. Med. ___ (2017): "Medicaid's remarkable scope (it covers more than 70 million Americans), array of sympathetic constituencies (it covers 49 percent of all children, 39 percent of births, 35 percent of persons with disabilities, and 64 percent of nursing home residents), role in financing vital medical services (including mental-health, HIV, and opioid-addiction treatments and long-term care), and importance to health system stakeholders (including hospitals, physicians, and states) means that it is not an easy mark" for funding cuts.

3. *Federalism on Steroids.* The intricate structure of federal and state roles in the ACA—not just under Medicaid, but also regarding the regulation of private health insurance—raises a host of federalism issues that scholars will debate for years to come. For a start, see Abbe Gluck, Intrastatutory Federalism and Statutory Interpretation: State Implementation of Federal Law in Health Reform and Beyond, 121 Yale L.J. 534, 582 (2011); I. Glenn Cohen, Conscientious Objection, Coercion, the Affordable Care Act, and U.S. States, 20 Ethical Perspectives 163 (2013); David K. Jones, Lavatories of Democracy? Health Reform and Federalism in the Trump Era, 95 Milbank Q. 470 (2017); Elizabeth McCuskey, Agency Imprimatur & Health Reform Preemption, 89 Ohio St. L.J. (2017); Nicole Huberfeld et al., Plunging into Endless Difficulties: Medicaid and Coercion in National Federation of Independent Business v. Sebelius, 93 B.U. L. Rev. 1 (2013); Elizabeth Weeks Leonard, Rhetorical Federalism: The Value of State-Based Dissent to Federal Health Reform, 39 Hofstra L. Rev. 111 (2010); Abigail Moncrieff, Cost-Benefit Federalism: Reconciling Collective Action Federalism and Libertarian Federalism in the Obamacare Litigation and Beyond, 37 Am. J.L. & Med. 288 (2012).

4. *Enforcing the Medicaid Entitlement.* For eligible beneficiaries, Medicaid creates an entitlement to medically necessary care. Paying for that care, however, puts an enormous strain on state budgets. Especially in hard times, states may try to save money by reducing their Medicaid payments to hospitals, physicians, and other providers. On average, Medicaid pays hospitals close to Medicare rates, but it pays physicians just 70 percent of what they receive from Medicare, and in some states that figure is much lower. As payments drop, physicians or specialized facilities may refuse to see new Medicaid patients, making it difficult or impossible for those patients to secure needed care. In principle, §30(A) of the Medicaid statute prohibits states from paying providers so little that they abandon the program. Enforcing that obligation has proven challenging, however, as the following case suggests.

■ ARMSTRONG v. EXCEPTIONAL CHILD CENTER, INC.

576 U.S. ___ (2015)

Justice Scalia delivered the opinion of the Court, except as to Part IV.

We consider whether Medicaid providers can sue to enforce §(30)(A) of the Medicaid Act, [which addresses the sufficiency of payments to health care providers].

Medicaid is a federal program that subsidizes the States' provision of medical services to "families with dependent children and of aged, blind, or disabled individuals, whose income and resources are insufficient to meet the costs of necessary medical services." §1396-1. Like other Spending Clause legislation, Medicaid offers the States a bargain: Congress provides federal funds in exchange for the States' agreement to spend them in accordance with congressionally imposed conditions.

In order to qualify for Medicaid funding, the State of Idaho adopted, and the Federal Government approved, a Medicaid "plan," §1396a(a), which Idaho administers through its Department of Health and Welfare. Idaho's plan includes "habilitation services"—in-home care for individuals who, "but for the provision of such services . . . would require the level of care provided in a hospital or a nursing facility or intermediate care facility for the mentally retarded the cost of which could be reimbursed under the State plan," §1396n(c) and (c)(1). Providers of these services are reimbursed by the Department of Health and Welfare.

Section 30(A) of the Medicaid Act requires Idaho's plan to:

> "provide such methods and procedures relating to the utilization of, and the payment for, care and services available under the plan . . . as may be necessary to safeguard against unnecessary utilization of such care and services and to assure that payments are consistent with efficiency, economy, and quality of care and are sufficient to enlist enough providers so that care and services are available under the plan at least to the extent that such care and services are available to the general population in the geographic area. . . .".

Respondents are providers of habilitation services to persons covered by Idaho's Medicaid plan. They sued petitioners—two officials in Idaho's Department of Health and Welfare—in the United States District Court for the District of Idaho, claiming that Idaho violates §30(A) by reimbursing providers of habilitation services at rates lower than §30(A) permits. [In particular, the challengers objected to basing rates on what the state's budget allowed rather than on what the state's own studies indicated that the services actually cost]. They asked the court to enjoin petitioners to increase these rates [by amounts ranging from 105 to 80 percent]. . . .

III

The power of federal courts of equity to enjoin unlawful executive action is subject to express and implied statutory limitations. "'Courts of equity can no more disregard statutory and constitutional requirements and provisions than can courts of law.'" In our view the Medicaid Act implicitly precludes private enforcement of §30(A), and respondents cannot, by invoking our equitable powers, circumvent Congress's exclusion of private enforcement.

Two aspects of §30(A) establish Congress's "intent to foreclose" equitable relief. First, the sole remedy Congress provided for a State's failure to comply with Medicaid's requirements—for the State's "breach" of the Spending Clause contract—is the withholding of Medicaid funds by the Secretary of Health and Human Services. As we have elsewhere explained, the "express provision of one method of enforcing a substantive rule suggests that Congress intended to preclude others." Alexander v. Sandoval, 532 U.S. 275, 290 (2001).

The provision for the Secretary's enforcement by withholding funds might not, by itself, preclude the availability of equitable relief. But it does so when combined with the judicially unadministrable nature of §30(A)'s text. It is difficult to imagine a requirement broader and less specific than §30(A)'s mandate that state plans provide for payments that are "consistent with efficiency, economy, and quality of care," all the while "safeguard[ing] against unnecessary utilization of . . . care and services." Explicitly conferring enforcement of this judgment-laden standard upon the Secretary alone establishes, we think, that Congress "wanted to make the agency remedy that it provided exclusive," thereby achieving "the expertise, uniformity, widespread consultation, and resulting administrative guidance that can accompany agency decisionmaking," and avoiding "the comparative risk of inconsistent interpretations and misincentives that can arise out of an occasional inappropriate application of the statute in a private action." Gonzaga Univ. v. Doe, 536 U.S. 273, 292 (2002) (Breyer,

J., concurring in judgment). The sheer complexity associated with enforcing §30(A), coupled with the express provision of an administrative remedy, §1396c, shows that the Medicaid Act precludes private enforcement of §30(A) in the courts.

Justice BREYER, concurring in part and concurring in the judgment.

. . . I believe that several characteristics of the federal statute before us, when taken together, make clear that Congress intended to foreclose respondents from bringing this particular action for injunctive relief.

For one thing, as the majority points out, §30(A) of the Medicaid Act sets forth a federal mandate that is broad and nonspecific. But, more than that, §30(A) applies its broad standards to the setting of rates. The history of ratemaking demonstrates that administrative agencies are far better suited to this task than judges. More than a century ago, Congress created the Interstate Commerce Commission, the first great federal regulatory rate-setting agency, and endowed it with authority to set "reasonable" railroad rates. It did so in part because judicial efforts to maintain reasonable rate levels had proved inadequate.

Reading §30(A) underscores the complexity and nonjudicial nature of the rate-setting task. That provision requires State Medicaid plans to "assure that payments are consistent with efficiency, economy, and quality of care and are sufficient to enlist enough providers" to assure "care and services" equivalent to that "available to the general population in the geographic area." The methods that a state agency, such as Idaho's Department of Health and Welfare, uses to make this kind of determination may involve subsidiary determinations of, for example, the actual cost of providing quality services, including personnel and total operating expenses; changes in public expectations with respect to delivery of services; inflation; a comparison of rates paid in neighboring States for comparable services; and a comparison of any rates paid for comparable services in other public or private capacities.

At the same time, §30(A) applies broadly, covering reimbursements provided to approximately 1.36 million doctors, serving over 69 million patients across the Nation. And States engage in time-consuming efforts to obtain public input on proposed plan amendments.

I recognize that federal courts have long become accustomed to reviewing for reasonableness or constitutionality the rate-setting determinations made by agencies. But this is not such an action. Instead, the lower courts here . . . required the State to set rates that "approximate the cost of quality care provided efficiently and economically." To find in the law a basis for courts to engage in such direct rate-setting could set a precedent for allowing other similar actions, potentially resulting in rates set by federal judges (of whom there are several hundred) outside the ordinary channel of federal judicial review of agency decisionmaking. The consequence, I fear, would be increased litigation, inconsistent results, and disorderly administration of highly complex federal programs that demand public consultation, administrative guidance and coherence for their success. I do not believe Congress intended to allow a statute-based injunctive action that poses such risks (and that has the other features I mention).

Justice SOTOMAYOR, with whom Justice KENNEDY, Justice GINSBURG, and Justice KAGAN join, dissenting.

Suits in federal court to restrain state officials from executing laws that assertedly conflict with the Constitution or with a federal statute are not novel. To the contrary, this Court has adjudicated such requests for equitable relief since the early days of the Republic. Nevertheless, today the Court holds that Congress has foreclosed private parties from invoking the equitable powers of the federal courts to require States to comply with §30(A) of the Medicaid Act. It does so without pointing to the sort of detailed remedial scheme we have previously deemed necessary to establish congressional intent to preclude resort to equity. Instead, the Court relies on Congress' provision for agency enforcement of §30(A)—an enforcement mechanism of the sort we have already definitively determined not to foreclose private actions—and on the mere fact that §30(A) contains relatively broad language. As I cannot agree that these statutory provisions demonstrate the requisite congressional intent to restrict the equitable authority of the federal courts, I respectfully dissent. . . .

What is the . . . "carefully crafted and intricate remedial scheme" for enforcement of §30(A)? The Court relies on two aspects of the Medicaid Act, but, whether considered separately or in combination, neither suffices.

First, the Court cites 42 U.S.C. §1396c, which authorizes the Secretary of Health and Human Services (HHS) to withhold federal Medicaid payments to a State in whole or in part if the Secretary determines that the State has failed to comply with the obligations set out in §1396a, including §30(A). But . . . §1396c provides no specific procedure that parties actually affected by a State's violation of its statutory obligations may invoke in lieu of [equitable remedies]—leaving them without any other avenue for seeking relief from the State. Nor will §1396c always provide a particularly effective means for redressing a State's violations: If the State has violated §30(A) by refusing to reimburse medical providers at a level "sufficient to enlist enough providers so that care and services are available" to Medicaid beneficiaries to the same extent as they are available to "the general population," agency action resulting in a reduced flow of federal funds to that State will often be self-defeating. See Brief for Former HHS Officials as Amici Curiae 18 (noting that HHS is often reluctant to initiate compliance actions because a "state's non-compliance creates a damned-if-you-do, damned-if-you-don't scenario where the withholding of state funds will lead to depriving the poor of essential medical assistance"). . . .

Second, perhaps attempting to reconcile its treatment of §1396c with this longstanding precedent, the Court focuses on the particular language of §30(A), contending that this provision, at least, is so "judicially unadministrable" that Congress must have intended to preclude its enforcement in private suits. Admittedly, the standard set out in §30(A) is fairly broad. . . . But mere breadth of statutory language does not require the Court to give up all hope of judicial enforcement—or, more important, to infer that Congress must have done so. . . .

Of course, the broad scope of §30(A)'s language is not irrelevant. But rather than compelling the conclusion that the provision is wholly unenforceable by private parties, its breadth counsels in favor of interpreting §30(A) to provide substantial leeway to States, so that only in rare and extreme circumstances could a State actually be held to violate its mandate. The provision's scope may also often require a court to rely on HHS, which is "comparatively expert in the statute's subject matter." When the agency has made a determination with respect to what legal standard should apply, or the validity of a State's procedures for implementing its Medicaid plan, that determination should be accorded the appropriate deference. See, e.g., Chevron U.S.A., Inc. v. Natural Resources Defense Council, Inc., 467 U.S. 837 (1984). . . .

The Court's error today has very real consequences. Previously, a State that set reimbursement rates so low that providers were unwilling to furnish a covered service for those who need it could be compelled by those affected to respect the obligation imposed by §30(A). Now, it must suffice that a federal agency, with many programs to oversee, has authority to address such violations through the drastic and often counterproductive measure of withholding the funds that pay for such services. Because a faithful application of our precedents would have led to a contrary result, I respectfully dissent.

Notes: Enforcing Medicaid

1. *Assuring Access After* Armstrong. The agency charged with administering Medicaid, the Centers for Medicare and Medicaid Services (CMS), believes that *Armstrong* "underscores the need for stronger non-judicial processes to ensure access, including stronger processes at both the state and federal levels for developing data on beneficiary access and reviewing the effect on beneficiary access of changes to payment methodologies." 80 Fed. Reg. 67,579 (2015). But doubts remain as to whether the Medicaid branch of CMS—a small and under-resourced agency—can effectively enforce §30(A).

2. *The Developing Case Law.* Applying and extending *Armstrong*, the federal courts have held that those provisions of the Medicaid statute that establish broad, non-specific guidelines for state Medicaid plans cannot generally be enforced through a private right of action. See, e.g., Davis v. Shah, 821 F.3d 231 (2d Cir. 2016). Although suits under the Administrative Procedure Act may still be brought on the ground that the federal government acted arbitrarily or capriciously in approving a state's Medicaid plan, APA review is highly deferential. See Christ the King Manor v. Burwell, 163 F. Supp. 3d 123 (M.D. Pa. 2016).

Even after *Armstrong*, however, the courts have been receptive to claims that approval of a state's plan will deprive private plaintiffs of specific, unambiguous rights guaranteed under the Medicaid statute. See Planned Parenthood of Gulf Coast v. Gee, 837 F.3d 477 (5th Cir. 2016) (holding that a Medicaid provision "phrased in individual terms and in specific, judicially administrable terms" is privately enforceable); Guggenberger v. Minnesota, 198 F. Supp. 3d 973 (D. Minn. 2016) ("*Armstrong* does not provide a basis for an across-the-board rejection of all private enforcement actions under the Medicaid Act's numerous varied provisions."); Planned Parenthood of Kansas v. Mosier, 2016 WL 3597457 (D. Kan. 2016); but see Does v. Gillespie, 867 F.3d 1034 (8th Cir. 2017) (holding that an apparently specific right is not enforceable through a private cause of action).

3. *Medicaid and Immigration.* Legal immigrants are ineligible for Medicaid until they have been permanent residents for five years. Is that requirement constitutional? It certainly satisfies the rational basis standard under federal law, but at least one state court has ruled that its constitution imposes strict scrutiny of drawing such legislative lines. Finch v. Commonwealth Health Insurance Connector Authority, 459 Mass. 655 (2011). See generally Patricia Illingworth & Wendy E. Parmet, The Health of Newcomers (2017).

4. *Further Reading.* For further discussion of ***Armstrong***, see Henry Paul Monaghan, A Cause of Action, Anyone?, 91 Notre Dame L. Rev. 1807 (2016); Jane Perkins, Pin the Tail on the Donkey: Beneficiary Enforcement of the Medicaid Act Over Time, 9 St. Louis U. J. Health L. & Pol'y 207 (2016); Private Rights of Action—Equitable Remedies to Enforce the Medicaid Act—Armstrong v. Exceptional Child Center, Inc., 129 Harv. L. Rev. 211 (2015).

For discussions on the occasion of **Medicaid's 50th birthday**, Sara Rosenbaum, Medicaid at 50, in The Oxford Handbook of U.S. Health Law (2017); Symposium, The Law of Medicare and Medicaid at 50, 15 Yale J. of Health Pol'y, L. & Ethics 1 (2015); Symposium, The ABCs (Accessibility, Barriers, and Challenges) of Medicaid Expansion. 9 St. Louis U. J. Health L. & Pol'y 179-296 (2016); Commonwealth Fund, Medicare at 50 Years (2015); Symposium, Medicare and Medicaid at 50, 31 JAMA 311 (2015).

4. *Medicare*

REFLECTIONS ON MEDICARE AT 50: BREAKING THE CHAINS OF PATH DEPENDENCY FOR A NEW ERA

Richard L. Kaplan
23 Elder L.J. 1 (2015)

One of the enduring myths surrounding Medicare is that it is a single, integrated program created at one moment in time and largely impervious to change. That is simply not the case. For better or worse, Medicare has evolved since its original enactment in 1965 to encompass several distinct programs, usually denominated Parts A through D, that stand largely separate from one another in terms of their coverages, exclusions, and costs.

ORIGINAL PROGRAM: PART A

Medicare Part A is the original component and represents the height of the social insurance model as applied to health care for older Americans; i.e., it is structured as a mandatory program with its own dedicated source of financing. In both of these aspects, Part A is unique among Medicare's constituent components. Every person who receives income from wages, salaries, or self-employment must pay a "contribution," or tax, to fund this program, and eligibility is based on attaining a specified age—namely, 65 years—that has remain unchanged since the program's original enactment.

Medicare's tax is currently 2.9% of income from earnings, which is collected half from employees and half from employers or paid in its entirety by self-employed persons. An additional 0.9% tax is collected on earnings in excess of $200,000 per year for unmarried persons and $250,000 per year for married couples. This additional Medicare tax, it should be noted, was added only recently by the ACA. But the main point is that Medicare Part A is financed entirely from this dedicated revenue stream, with funds deposited into a "trust fund" that the federal government administers.

The scope of Medicare Part A's coverage consists of four principal components, each with its own limitations, exclusions, and cost-sharing features. Those components pertain to: (1) hospitalization, (2) nursing homes, (3) home health care, and (4) hospice care. . . .

1. HOSPITALIZATION

There is no question that most people's largest medical expenditures are likely to involve hospital stays, but Medicare Part A provides fairly comprehensive coverage for such expenditures. The program covers almost all services incurred during the first 60 days of a "spell of illness." . . . This "spell of illness" determination is important for two independent reasons. First, . . . [a]ny hospital days within a "spell of illness" after the first 60 days are subject to per-day deductibles that are adjusted annually for inflation. . . . Second, each "spell of illness" has a deductible that is also adjusted annually for inflation and [was] $1,260 in 2015. [Because of these cost-sharing obligations,] Medicare enrollees could face substantial out-of-pocket costs from repeated hospital stays. [Those large out-of-pocket costs] illustrat[e] a very important aspect of Medicare Part A—namely, that this program has no "stop loss" provision that limits how much an enrollee is obligated to pay, unlike most private health insurance plans.

For that reason, most Medicare beneficiaries obtain some type of supplemental coverage, often private policies that are usually denominated "Medigap" insurance. . . .

2. NURSING HOMES

No component of Medicare Part A is more misunderstood than its coverage of "skilled nursing facilities," more commonly called nursing homes. Medicare does indeed cover the cost of nursing homes, but under structures that reflect the state of care that such facilities provided when Medicare was first enacted, and are increasingly outdated as Americans live longer and need nursing homes for more extended periods of time. For example, Medicare covers nursing home care only if a patient is admitted to the nursing home within 30 days of that person's being discharged from a hospital. Moreover, the patient must require care in the nursing home for a condition that was treated originally in the hospital or is medically related to that condition. But today, many older people transition from their own home or apartment directly to a nursing facility without needing to go to a hospital first, especially when the underlying ailment is a neurodegenerative condition such as Alzheimer's or Parkinson's disease. . . . Clearly, Medicare's coverage of nursing homes was built on a model of post-hospitalization rehabilitative care and does not encompass the sort of long-term confinement that characterizes many older Americans' nursing home experience today.

3. HOME HEALTH CARE

Medicare Part A covers home health care services subject to three major caveats. First, the recipient of such care must be unable to leave his or her home without assistance from other people or devices such as canes, walkers, or wheelchairs. Second, the home health care services must be provided by a Medicare-certified home health care agency. In other words, help provided by family members, friends, neighbors, or church groups does not qualify for payment by Medicare. Third, home health care services must be provided pursuant to a written plan of care that was prepared by the patient's doctor, and that is reviewed by that doctor every 60 days.

If these requirements are met, Medicare pays for occupational, physical, and speech therapy, along with medical supplies, and "part-time and intermittent" nursing care. . . . Medicare Part A does not, however, cover many home health care services that older patients need to stay in their homes, such as around-the-clock nursing care, meal preparation, or laundry.

4. HOSPICE

One of the less well-known coverages within Medicare Part A is hospice care for persons whose doctors have certified that they have no more than six months to live. Under this coverage, such persons can receive various home care and other benefits, including services that are generally not covered by Medicare, that attempt to mitigate a dying person's pain rather than remedy his or her underlying illness. . . .

OPTIONAL COVERAGE FOR PHYSICIANS' CHARGES: PART B

Medicare Part A excludes many common medical expenses, the most significant being doctors' charges. This exclusion seems unfathomable in today's world, but doctors' fees were apparently not as significant in the pre-Medicare era and were often not covered by the typical private health insurance plans that were marketed as "major medical" policies. In formulating Medicare Part A, its creators consciously tried to replicate those policies, so physicians' charges were not included in Medicare Part A.

Instead, an optional coverage called Medicare Part B was fashioned to cover such charges, as well as other less common expenses, such as ambulance service and durable medical equipment (hospital beds, wheelchairs, scooters, and so forth). Medicare Part B has no relationship to the Medicare payroll tax and is financed strictly on a current-year basis. Premiums are paid by those who have enrolled in Medicare B and are adjusted annually for inflation. In 2015, this premium is $104.90 per month, an amount that was calculated to cover approximately 25% of the program's projected costs for the coming year. The remaining 75% of the program's funding comes from general tax revenues of the federal government, which are paid by all U.S. taxpayers regardless of their age or likely enrollment in Medicare. Most of Part B's financing, in other words, comes from society as a whole, or at least that portion of society that pays income taxes. This arrangement constitutes a substantial subsidization of Medicare Part B for those who elect its coverage.

No one is required to enroll in Medicare Part B, but most eligible persons do so because of this substantial public subsidy. . . .

THE MANAGED CARE ALTERNATIVE: PART C

As managed care plans were introduced into the private health insurance marketplace, this option became available to Medicare beneficiaries on a contractual basis. This approach was formalized in Medicare Part C as "Medicare + Choice" and then re-labeled "Medicare Advantage" as part of the George W. Bush Administration's initiative to boost enrollment in such plans. But regardless of the specific appellation, Medicare's managed care program essentially parallels its private sector counterpart.

For example, Medicare managed care plans promise better coordination of care and simpler paperwork when claiming benefits in exchange for restricting their enrollees to specific doctors, hospitals, home health agencies, and usually pharmacies as well. Older Americans often have established relationships with numerous physicians, so such restrictions may present a difficult dilemma. Perhaps that is why managed care plans represent only a minority of Medicare beneficiaries—approximately three in ten according to the most recent data available.

On the other hand, Medicare managed care represents a major simplification of elders' health care financing by substituting a monthly premium and modest copayments for Medicare's convoluted array of annual deductibles and unlimited coinsurance obligations. Managed care also eliminates the need for supplemental "Medigap" policies and their related claims-filing procedures. Moreover, Medicare managed care plans offer benefits that historically were not available in "traditional" Medicare, such as annual physical examinations and prescription drugs. Indeed, access to such drugs was a major reason that many older Americans enrolled in managed care plans before Medicare Part D became effective in 2006. Even today, managed care plans provide a variety of benefits that Medicare generally does not, including vision and dental care, exercise classes, and other services that are intended to keep enrollees healthy.

ADDING PRESCRIPTION DRUGS: PART D

No single aspect of Medicare better illustrates the ossification of its programmatic development than the failure to provide generally available coverage of prescription medications until Medicare Part D took effect in 2006—four decades after Medicare was enacted! During those intervening years, pharmacological innovations included important maintenance drugs for a wide range of chronic conditions that often affect the Medicare population, such as arthritis, asthma, diabetes, heart disease, and hypertension, among others.

Moreover, when Part D was finally created, it reflected a very different orientation than Medicare Parts A and B regarding the role of government and the appeal of personal choice. Instead, Part D is a quasi-voucher approach that provides subsidies to private prescription drug plans that compete on various parameters including monthly premiums, specific drug coverage, pharmacy location, and other factors. During the annual open enrollment period, new plans become available to Medicare enrollees, though the precise number of different plans that are available to any given enrollee depends upon his or her state of residence. . . . Medicare Part D's plethora of choices has generally been popular with enrollees, despite its inherent complexity and curious financial structure. . . .

Notes: Medicare at 50

1. *Frozen in Time?* Notice the distinct resemblance between Medicare's structure, the basic contours of which were established in 1965, and the structure of the typical, provider-friendly Blue Cross/Blue Shield health plan of the 1960s. The divide between Medicare Part A and Part B resembles the historical divide between Blue Cross (hospital coverage) and Blue Shield (physician coverage), which at the time were often separate companies. Private insurance rarely covered prescription drugs in the 1960s, so neither did Medicare until 2006 (Part D). Later in the chapter, we'll also learn that, originally (until the 1980s), Medicare paid hospitals based on their actual costs and physicians based on their actual charges, similar to how the Blues treated their virtual "owners" at the time. Even to this day, Medicare contracts out most of its day-to-day administrative functions (contracting, claims payment, auditing, etc.) to private, third-party "intermediaries," which often (but not always)

are actual Blues plans. The similarities between Medicare and the Blues were not an accident. The aim was to make Medicare as familiar and non-threatening as possible to the medical establishment, in order to overcome political opposition and the possible boycott of the program. Theodore R. Marmor, The Politics of Medicare (2d ed. 1999). As the story unfolds, consider how influential these historical foundations remain.

2. *The Future of Medicare.* When Medicare was first enacted, Part A was projected to cost only $9 billion a year in 1990. It actually cost $60 billion that year. Government actuaries failed to anticipate the continuing inflationary effects of Medicare's generous payment methods, the increased demand for medical services that resulted from making health insurance much more widespread, and the expanded life expectancy of the elderly. See Steven Hayward & Erik Peterson, The Medicare Monster, Reason, Jan. 1993, at 19. Yet the program remains popular.

> Medicare achieves its highest marks from the millions of elderly beneficiaries who depend on the program to pay for a substantial portion of their medical care, but surveys of public opinion also show wide-spread support for it among people under 65 [as well]. . . . [Nevertheless], given its rapid rate of growth, [Medicare] will remain at the center of government efforts to trim the massive budget deficit. [Previously,] budget-cutting exercises exacted most of their toll from providers, and they remain a prime target now. But providers are scarcely prepared to be the sole stakeholders who accept sacrifice. The only other real options are raising taxes on the general population, reducing Medicare benefits, or asking the elderly to pay more on some income-related basis. However, elected politicians of almost every stripe have shown no disposition to embrace any of these unpopular approaches, suggesting by their inaction that we can somehow have it all. That is indeed a fanciful formula for the future. . . .

John K. Iglehart, The American Health Care System: Medicare, 327 New Eng. J. Med. 1467 (1992). This analysis rings as true today as it did when it was written a quarter-century ago.

In 2016, Medicare consumed about 15 percent of the federal budget, roughly the same amount as was spent on the national defense. That figure will inevitably swell as the costs of medical care continue to increase, the population continues to age, and the baby boomers retire. Budget-conscious policymakers have considered different approaches to reducing Medicare spending, a few of which worked their way into the ACA:

> In its most controversial effort to rein in Medicare cost inflation, the ACA created a new agency known as the Independent Payment Advisory Board (IPAB). Comprising fifteen health-care experts appointed by the President who are removable only for cause, the Board has authority that is nothing short of remarkable. Starting in 2015, the Board must submit to the President and Congress annual "proposals" for cutting Medicare if spending over a five-year period increases faster than preselected targets linked to economy-wide inflation (through 2019) and economic growth (for 2020 and after). IPAB proposals are subject to few constraints: they cannot ration care, modify Medicare eligibility, or increase beneficiary cost sharing.
>
> Eight months after the Board issues a proposal, the Secretary of HHS must implement it—wholesale and without amendment—unless Congress has enacted

(and the President has signed) legislation making different, but equally deep, cuts. The proposal goes into effect "[n]otwithstanding any other provision of law," meaning that Board proposals can override even preexisting congressional statutes with which they conflict. Judicial review of an IPAB proposal or its implementation is prohibited.

The Board's insulation from political influence is both its principal virtue and its biggest vice. To its proponents, the Board's insulation allows it to bring policy expertise to bear on how most effectively to hold down rising Medicare costs. To its detractors, the Board is an antidemocratic abdication of congressional authority to unaccountable green-eyeshade types.

Nicholas Bagley, Bedside Bureaucrats: Why Medicare Reform Hasn't Worked, 101 Georgetown L.J. 520, 569-570 (2013). Medicare spending did not exceed the targets prior to 2018, when Congress abolished IPAB as part of a budget deal in early 2018. The death of IPAB is a testament to the difficulty of following through on the commitment to restrain the growth of health-care spending.

Many policymakers believe that Medicare needs a more fundamental transformation. Premium support—or, more pejoratively, the "voucherization" of Medicare—has received considerable attention, particularly from budget-conscious Republicans.

> In a premium support system, the federal government would provide a payment on behalf of each Medicare beneficiary toward the purchase of a health insurance plan—either a private plan, similar a Medicare Advantage plan, or traditional Medicare. This approach is sometimes called a defined contribution or voucher approach. Under a premium support system, health plans would compete for enrollees and people on Medicare would choose among plans for their coverage—an approach that sounds similar to the current system, but is not the same. A key difference is that payments for services provided to beneficiaries in traditional Medicare would be capitated rather than the current approach that generally ties payments to the specific services that beneficiaries use.
>
> A number of premium support proposals have been introduced in recent years; these proposals are similar in their general approach, but often differ in key policy parameters, and some are more specific than others. Premium support proposals vary in several ways, including: the role of traditional Medicare in the new system, the extent to which benefits would be defined, the rules for health insurers, and the methodology used to set payments to plans, including traditional Medicare. For example, some proposals would base the federal payment to plans on the average bid (the cost to the plan of providing all Medicare-covered services) submitted by plans in a given area while other proposals would base federal payment on the second lowest plan bid. These policy specifications have important implications for federal savings, beneficiaries' costs, the viability of private plans in markets across the country, and the sustainability of traditional Medicare.
>
> Typically, premium support proposals would affect services covered under Medicare Parts A and B, but not Part D.

Gretchen Jacobson & Tricia Neuman, Turning Medicare into a Premium Support System: Frequently Asked Questions, Kaiser Family Foundation (July 2016). Speaker of the House Paul Ryan has expressed interest in adopting a premium support model for Medicare, but those efforts have come to naught so far.

3. *Concierge Medicine.* In general, physicians must accept Medicare's rates as full payment for the services they provide. They cannot charge their patients for the difference between their private rates and what Medicare pays—so-called "balance billing." In recent years, however, some private physicians have begun charging a substantial "retainer" fee of several thousands of dollars a year in addition to Medicare billings. In exchange, patients get "boutique" or "concierge" services, such as 24-hour direct access through cell phones or pagers and a promise that the physician will restrict his practice so as to have more time for each patient.

The legality of this arrangement is still in doubt, with physicians claiming it does not violate balance billing rules since the extra payments are for administrative or non-Medicare-covered services. What about the ethics of these boutique practices? Proponents argue that they allow physicians to regain control of their professional lives and to establish the type of personal and holistic medical practice that has long since disappeared. Critics say that concierge medicine is elitist and exploitative.

4. *Devilish Part D Details.* Enrollment in Part D prescription drug benefit plans is voluntary, i.e., Medicare-eligible individuals choose whether to pay a subsidized premium for coverage offered primarily by competing private insurers. These Part D insurers set their premiums for drug coverage at whatever they think the market will bear. This is in marked contrast to Medicare Part B, with government insurance that has the premium nationwide. For drug coverage, the government subsidizes 75 percent of the Part D premium for most Medicare beneficiaries, but pays 100 percent of the premium for low-income beneficiaries (135 percent of the federal poverty level) who are not covered by another source such as Medicaid. Payments to health plans are adjusted for health status and insurance risk, to counter adverse selection, but premiums to beneficiaries are community rated.

The private companies offering Part D submit plan designs and premium bids to the government for approval. Insurers may offer "alternate" plan designs that are "actuarially equivalent" (or better). Thus, retirees face the following dizzying array of alternatives:

- Several drug plans that provide "standard" benefit plan design
- Several other drug plans that provide "alternate" benefit plan design
- Several Medicare Advantage HMO or PPO plans that include prescription drug coverage

The standard Part D coverage has a $325 deductible and then pays for 75 percent of drug costs up to about $3,000 a year. Then, coverage ceases until total costs reach $4,700 (the "doughnut hole"), at which point 95 percent of drug costs are paid. The ACA has gradually filled the doughnut hole, which is set to disappear as of 2020. The ACA also reduces or eliminates deductibles, co-payments, and gaps in coverage for people who are below 150 percent of the federal poverty level. For the non-poor, however, drug plans are not allowed to cover the deductibles and co-payments in the standard plan.

Controversially, the legislation establishing Part D prohibits the government from regulating or negotiating drug costs. Instead, costs are whatever drug companies charge, subject to negotiation by the private drug plans. Drug plans may also adopt "formularies" that require the use of generic drugs and that refuse to cover more expensive drugs when less expensive ones are equally effective, but beneficiaries may appeal these restrictions in individual cases of medical necessity.

5. *Long-Term Care.* This chapter focuses on conventional medical insurance for hospitals and doctors and so neglects the sources of financing for long-term care insurance that covers nursing homes and home health care. The appropriate source and financing for this type of insurance will be one of the most pressing public health policy issues for decades to come. Two developments are accelerating the rate at which long-term care is increasing its portion of the nation's health care budget: the aging of the baby-boom generation and increasing life expectancy. Private insurance for nursing homes is not very extensive because of its costs. Its costs are high because most people don't consider purchasing it until they anticipate needing it. Mark Pauly, The Rational Nonpurchase of Long-Term-Care Insurance, 98 J. Pol. Econ. 153 (1990). The principal fallback is Medicaid, which requires the elderly to impoverish themselves. Various financial planning techniques are possible for sheltering assets from Medicaid "spend down" rules, but Congress is steadily curbing these techniques. For instance, Medicaid now counts assets that the patient transferred as long as 36 months ago, that are owned jointly by the patient's spouse, or that are in a revocable trust. 42 U.S.C. §1396p. Congress also made it a criminal offense for lawyers or financial advisors to counsel clients in avoiding restrictions.

Policy analysts have explored a number of options for making private financing of nursing homes more feasible (such as "reverse mortgages" and "continuing care retirement communities") or for devising innovative hybrids between public and private financing. The coverage of home health care is somewhat more extensive under private insurance and Medicare because it is seen as an inexpensive alternative to hospital or institutional care.

The Patient Protection and Affordable Care Act was expected to make a major change in long-term care insurance, with a component known as the CLASS Act (for Community Living Assistance Services and Support). This promised to create a public insurance plan that people could contribute to through payroll deductions while they are still working, which then would pay fixed amounts for nursing homes, home care, and related services when the need arose. Before the law took effect, however, CMS actuaries proved critics to be correct, that the premiums allowed by the CLASS Act would not be sufficient to cover the promised benefits due to likely adverse selection (people more likely to contribute if they expect to need long-term care than if they don't). Therefore, Congress, with the Obama administration's support, repealed the CLASS Act in 2013 and created another study commission on long-term care.

6. *Medicare Appeals.* Provider disputes with Medicare are both common and complex. Under Part A, for example, hospitals and other providers submit annual cost reports to one of a dozen private "fiscal intermediaries" known as Medicare Administrative Contractors, or MACs. The MACs review the cost reports, adjust them as necessary to comply with program rules, and issue a "notice of program reimbursement," or NPR, that says what the providers are owed for the year. 42 C.F.R. 405.1803. If a provider believes it is owed more, it can file a request for a hearing before a specialized board within CMS—the Provider Reimbursement Review Board—that adjudicates payment disputes. 42 U.S.C. §1395oo. The Board's decision can then be challenged in court.

The review process can be cumbersome, especially if the provider wishes to raise a legal challenge to a CMS policy. When that happens, the Medicare statute still requires challengers to exhaust their administrative remedies before going to court—even though the PRRB lacks authority to conclude that a CMS policy is unlawful. Although the PRRB can issue a declaration that it lacks authority to decide the issue presented, 42 U.S.C. §1395oo(f)(1), this expedited bypass of futile administrative review is not available for regulatory issues that are unrelated to payment amounts—such as decisions to exclude a provider from the program altogether. Is it sensible to channel claims like that through a lengthy administrative process that lacks authority to decide the ultimate issue? In Shalala v. Illinois Council on Long Term Care, Inc., 529 U.S. 1, 13 (2000), the Supreme Court closed the door on most efforts to bypass administrative review:

> [I]nsofar as [the Medicare statute] demands the "channeling" of virtually all legal attacks through the agency, it assures the agency greater opportunity to apply, interpret, or revise policies, regulations, or statutes without possibly premature interference by different individual courts. . . . But this assurance comes at a price, namely, occasional individual, delay-related hardship. In the context of a massive, complex health and safety program such as Medicare, embodied in hundreds of pages of statutes and thousands of pages of often interrelated regulations, any of which may become the subject of a legal challenge in any of several different courts, paying this price may seem justified. In any event, such was the judgment of Congress.

7. *Further Reading*. For discussions of **Medicare at 50**, see Jonathan Oberlander & Theodore Marmor, Medicare at 50, in The Oxford Handbook of U.S. Health Law (2017); Medicare and Medicaid at 50: America's Entitlement Programs in the Age of Affordable Care (2015) (Alan B. Cohen et al. eds. 2015); Symposium, The Law of Medicare and Medicaid at 50, 15 Yale J. Health Pol'y L. Ethics (2015).

For **historical and political accounts of Medicare** (note 1), see Nicholas Bagley, Bedside Bureaucrats: Why Medicare Reform Hasn't Worked, 101 Georgetown L.J. 520 (2013); Henry Aaron & Jeanne Lambrew, Reforming Medicare: Options, Tradeoffs, and Opportunities (2008); Timothy Stoltzfus Jost, Disentitlement: The Threats Facing Our Public Health-Care Programs and a Rights-Based Response (2003); David Hyman, Medicare Meets Mephistopheles (2006); Jonathan Oberlander, The Political Life of Medicare (2003). The most widely used source for detailed knowledge is the CCH Medicare and Medicaid Guide. See also Terry Coleman, Medicare Law (2d ed. 2006).

For discussion of **concierge medicine** (note 3), see Troyen A. Brennan, Luxury Primary Care: Market Innovation or Threat to Access?, 346 New Eng. J. Med. 1165 (2002); Jeffrey Hammond, Cash Only Doctors: Challenges and Prospects of Autonomy and Access, 80 UMKC L. Rev. 307 (2011); Note, 17 Wash. U. J.L. & Pol'y 313 (2005); Sandra J. Carnahan, Law, Medicine, and Wealth: Does Concierge Medicine Promote Health Care Choice, or Is It a Barrier to Access?, 17 Stan. L. & Pol'y Rev. 121 (2006); Frank Pasquale, The Three Faces of Retainer Care: Crafting a Tailored Regulatory Response, 7 Yale J. Health Pol'y L. & Ethics 39 (2007); Note, 66 Duke L.J. (2017).

For discussions of **Medicare Part D** (note 4), see John B. Kirkwood, Buyer Power and Healthcare Prices, 91 Wash. L. Rev. 253 (2016); Janet Cummings et al., Who Thinks That Part D Is Too Complicated?, 66 Med. Care Res. Rev. 97 (2009); Richard H. Thaler & Cass R. Sunstein, Nudge: Improving Decisions About Health, Wealth, and Happiness, ch. 10 (2008); Jerry Avorn, Part "D" for "Defective": The Medicare Drug-Benefit Chaos, 354 New Eng. J. Med. 1339 (2006); Jonathan Oberlander, Through the Looking Glass: The Politics of the Medicare Prescription Drug,

Improvement, and Modernization Act, 32 J. Health Pol. Pol'y & L. 153 (2007); John K. Iglehart, The New Medicare Prescription-Drug Benefit: A Pure Power Play, 350 New Eng. J. Med. 826 (2004); Thomas R. Oliver et al., A Political History of Medicare and Prescription Drug Coverage, 82 Milbank Q. 283 (2004); Susan Channick, The Medicare Prescription Drug, Improvement, and Modernization Act of 2003, 14 Elder L.J. 237 (2006); Symposium, 23(1) Health Aff. 1 (Jan. 2004).

For discussions of **long-term care** (note 5), see Allison K. Hoffman, Reimagining the Risk of Long-Term Care, 16 Yale J. Health Pol'y, L. & Ethics 239 (2016); Symposium, Health Care Reform, Transition, and Transformation in Long-Term Care, 8 St. Louis J. Health L & Pol'y 1 (2014); Richard Kaplan, Analyzing the Impact of the New Health Care Reform Legislation on Older Americans, 18 Elder L.J. 213 (2011); Joshua M. Wiener et al., Federal and State Initiatives to Jump Start the Market for Private Long-Term Care Insurance, 8 Elder L.J. 57 (2000); Symposium, 29 Health Aff. 6 (2010); Symposium 4 J. Health Care L. & Pol'y 159 (2001); Note, 14 Elder L.J. 485 (2006); Hal Fliegelman & Debora Fliegelman, Giving Guardians the Power to Do Medicaid Planning, 32 Wake Forest L. Rev. 341 (1997); Symposium, 31 McGeorge L. Rev. 703 (2000).

B. INSURANCE AND MANAGED CARE REGULATION

1. The Rise of Managed Care

■ RUSH PRUDENTIAL HMO v. MORAN

536 U.S. 355 (2002)

SOUTER, J., delivered the opinion of the Court, [which was split 5-4].

Illinois's Health Maintenance Organization Act provides . . . a right to independent medical review of certain denials of benefits.[2] The issue in this case is whether the statute . . . is preempted by the Employee Retirement Income Security

2. . . . The Act defines a "Health Maintenance Organization" as "any organization formed under the laws of this or another state to provide or arrange for one or more health care plans under a system which causes any part of the risk of health care delivery to be borne by the organization or its providers." . . . In the health care industry, the term "Health Maintenance Organization" has been defined as "[a] prepaid organized delivery system where the organization *and* the primary care physicians assume some financial risk for the care provided to its enrolled members. . . . In a *pure HMO,* members must obtain care from within the system if it is to be reimbursed." Weiner & de Lissovoy, Razing a Tower of Babel: A Taxonomy for Managed Care and Health Insurance Plans, 18 J. of Health Pol., Pol'y & Law 75, 96 (Spring 1993) (emphasis in original). The term "Managed Care Organization" is used more broadly to refer to any number of systems combining health care delivery with financing. *Id.,* at 97. The Illinois definition of HMO does not appear to be limited to the traditional usage of that term, but instead is likely to encompass a variety of different structures (although Illinois does distinguish HMOs from pure insurers by regulating "traditional" health insurance in a different portion of its insurance laws). Except where otherwise indicated, we use the term "HMO" because that is the term used by the State and the parties.

Act of 1974 (ERISA), 29 U.S.C. §1001 *et seq.*, [which is addressed in the next section]. We hold it is not. . . .

Debra Moran is a beneficiary under [an employee welfare benefit] plan, sponsored by her husband's employer. . . . As the [insurance policy] explains, Rush contracts with physicians "to arrange for or provide services and supplies for medical care and treatment" of covered persons. Each covered person selects a primary care physician from those under contract to Rush, while Rush will pay for medical services by an unaffiliated physician only if the services have been "authorized" both by the primary care physician and Rush's medical director.

In 1996, when Moran began to have pain and numbness in her right shoulder, Dr. Arthur LaMarre, her primary care physician, unsuccessfully administered "conservative" treatments such as physiotherapy. In October 1997, Dr. LaMarre recommended that Rush approve surgery by an unaffiliated specialist, Dr. Julia Terzis, who had developed an unconventional treatment for Moran's condition. Although Dr. LaMarre said that Moran would be "best served" by that procedure, Rush denied the request and, after Moran's internal appeals, affirmed the denial on the ground that the procedure was not "medically necessary." Rush instead proposed that Moran undergo standard surgery, performed by a physician affiliated with Rush.

In January 1998, Moran made a written demand for an independent medical review of her claim. . . . When Rush failed to provide the independent review, Moran sued in an Illinois state court to compel compliance with the state Act. Rush removed the suit to Federal District Court, arguing that the cause of action was "completely preempted" under ERISA, [a federal statute that regulates pension plans and other employee fringe benefits].

While the suit was pending, Moran had surgery by Dr. Terzis at her own expense and submitted a $94,841.27 reimbursement claim to Rush. Rush treated the claim as a renewed request for benefits and began a new inquiry to determine coverage. The three doctors consulted by Rush said the surgery had been medically unnecessary. Meanwhile, the federal court remanded the case back to state court . . . , [and] the state court enforced the state statute and ordered Rush to submit to review by an independent physician. The doctor selected was a reconstructive surgeon at Johns Hopkins Medical Center, Dr. A. Lee Dellon. Dr. Dellon decided that Dr. Terzis's treatment had been medically necessary, based on the definition of medical necessity in Rush's Certificate of Group Coverage, as well as his own medical judgment. Rush's medical director, however, refused to concede that the surgery had been medically necessary, and denied Moran's claim in January 1999. . . . The Court of Appeals for the Seventh Circuit reversed. . . . Because the decision of the Court of Appeals conflicted with the Fifth Circuit's treatment of a similar provision of Texas law in Corporate Health Ins., Inc. v. Texas Dept. of Ins., 215 F.3d 526 (2000), we granted certiorari. We now affirm.

II

To "safeguar[d] . . . the establishment, operation, and administration" of employee benefit plans, ERISA . . . contains an express preemption provision that ERISA "shall supersede any and all State laws insofar as they may now or hereafter relate to any employee benefit plan. . . ." A saving clause then reclaims a substantial amount of ground with its provision that "nothing in this subchapter shall be construed to exempt or relieve any person from any law of any State which regulates insurance, banking, or securities." The "unhelpful" drafting of these antiphonal clauses occupies a substantial share of this Court's time. [See section C and Chapter 2.C.] . . .

As a law that "relates to" ERISA plans, [the Illinois statute] is saved from preemption only if it also "regulates insurance." Rush insists that the Act is not such a law. . . . [I]n deciding whether a law "regulates insurance" under ERISA's saving clause, we start with a "common-sense view of the matter." . . . Rush contends that seeing an HMO as an insurer distorts the nature of an HMO, which is, after all, a health care provider, too. This, Rush argues, should determine its characterization, with the consequence that regulation of an HMO is not insurance regulation within the meaning of ERISA.

The answer to Rush is, of course, that an HMO is both: it provides health care, and it does so as an insurer. Nothing in the saving clause requires an either-or choice between health care and insurance. . . . [I]t would ignore the whole purpose of the HMO-style of organization to conceive of HMOs without their insurance element. . . . The HMO design goes beyond the simple truism that all contracts are, in some sense, insurance against future fluctuations in price, R. Posner, Economic Analysis of Law 104 (4th ed. 1992), because HMOs actually underwrite and spread risk among their participants, a feature distinctive to insurance.

So Congress has understood from the start, when the phrase "Health Maintenance Organization" was established and defined in the HMO Act of 1973, 42 U.S.C. §300 et seq. The Act was intended to encourage the development of HMOs as a new form of health care delivery system, and when Congress set the standards that the new health delivery organizations would have to meet to get certain federal benefits, the terms included requirements that the organizations bear and manage risk. . . . This congressional understanding that it was promoting a novel form of insurance was made explicit in the Senate Report's reference to the practices of "health insurers to charge premium rates based upon the actual claims experience of a particular group of subscribers," thus "raising costs and diminishing the availability of health insurance for those suffering from costly illnesses." The federal Act responded to this insurance practice by requiring qualifying HMOs to [use community rating], and it was because of that mandate "pos[ing] substantial competitive problems to newly emerging HMOs" that Congress authorized funding subsidies [for qualifying HMOs]. . . .

This conception has not changed in the intervening years. Since passage of the federal Act, States have been adopting their own HMO enabling Acts, and today, at least 40 of them, including Illinois, regulate HMOs primarily through the States' insurance departments, see Aspen [Wolters Kluwer], Managed Care Law Manual, although they may be treated differently from traditional insurers, owing to their additional role as health care providers, see, *e.g.*, Alaska Ins. Code §21.86.010 (health department reviews HMO before insurance commissioner grants a certificate of authority); Ohio Rev. Code Ann. §1742.21 (health department may inspect HMO). Finally, this view shared by Congress and the States has passed into common understanding. . . . While the original form of the HMO was a single corporation employing its own physicians, the 1980s saw a variety of other types of structures develop even as traditional insurers altered their own plans by adopting HMO-like cost-control measures. The dominant feature is the combination of insurer and provider, and "an observer may be hard pressed to uncover the differences among products that bill themselves as HMOs, [preferred provider organizations (PPOs)], or managed care overlays to health insurance." Managed Care Law Manual, *supra*. . . . Rush cannot checkmate common sense by trying to submerge HMOs' insurance features beneath an exclusive characterization of HMOs as providers of health care. . . .

On a second tack, Rush . . . [argues] that an HMO is no longer an insurer when it arranges to limit its exposure, as when an HMO arranges for capitated contracts to compensate its affiliated physicians with a set fee for each HMO patient regardless of the treatment provided. Under such an arrangement, Rush claims, the risk is not borne by the HMO at all. . . . The problem with Rush's argument is . . . that capitation contracts do not relieve the HMO of its obligations to the beneficiary. The HMO is still bound to provide medical care to its members, and this is so regardless of the ability of physicians or [other] third-part[ies] to honor their contracts with the HMO. . . .

Nor do we see anything standing in the way of applying the . . . general state definition of HMO [to] include a contractor that provides only administrative services for a self-funded plan. Rush points out that the general definition of HMO under Illinois law includes not only organizations that "provide" health care plans, but those that "arrange for" them to be provided. . . . Rush hypothesizes a sort of medical matchmaker, bringing together [employers] and medical care providers; even if the latter bear all the risks, the matchmaker would be an HMO under the Illinois definition. . . . Even on the most generous reading of Rush's argument, however, it boils down to the bare possibility (not the likelihood) of some overbreadth in the application of [the Illinois statute] beyond orthodox HMOs. . . .

In sum, . . . HMOs have taken over much business formerly performed by traditional indemnity insurers and they are almost universally regulated as insurers under state law. . . . Thus, the Illinois HMO Act is a law "directed toward" the insurance industry, and [so is saved from ERISA preemption]. . . .

MEDICARE AND THE AMERICAN HEALTH CARE SYSTEM: 1996 REPORT TO CONGRESS

Prospective Payment Assessment Commission

The most common managed care models are health maintenance organizations (HMOs), preferred provider organizations (PPOs), and point-of-service (POS) plans. In a traditional HMO plan, subscribers must receive their care from a limited group of providers. PPO and POS subscribers may not be subject to the same level of plan oversight as in HMOs: Generally they may go to any provider, but their out-of-pocket payments are lower if they choose participating providers that give the insurer discounted rates. . . .

Managed care plans use a variety of techniques to control their costs. First, they actively seek providers with lower-cost practice patterns and offer them a defined patient base in exchange for favorable payment rates. By limiting the number of providers or by creating strong financial incentives to choose certain ones, managed care plans influence which providers subscribers will use. Through this selective contracting, managed care plans can substantially affect providers' revenues. Plans' bargaining positions are strongest in areas with excess provider capacity. Providers that choose not to participate or that are not selected by the managed care plan may experience a decline in their patient volume.

In addition, managed care plans often use discounted fee-for-service rates to control their costs. They also use per case, per day, or per person payments to shift some of the financial risk of treating patients to providers. Per case or per day payments are generally made to hospitals, whereas per person payments are more often made to physicians, predominately primary care practitioners. These payment methods reward providers for delivering care efficiently, discouraging unnecessary service use.

A per person, or capitation, payment system is the most comprehensive way to shift financial risk to providers. Under capitation, providers receive a prepaid sum to furnish a defined set of services to a plan's enrollees. This creates a monetary incentive for physicians to limit patients' use of services (or encourage preventive services) because the physician receives the same payment regardless of the volume or intensity of care, or even if no care is provided at all. Many managed care plans also require primary care physicians to act as "gatekeepers" to specialty care or hospital services. Under these arrangements, the primary care physician must preauthorize any services a patient receives. While these physicians usually do not bear the full financial risk for the additional services, delegating the gatekeeping function enables managed care plans to use financial incentives to limit referrals. . . .

Hospitals [And Physicians]

. . . The long-term effects of the changing environment on hospitals are still unclear. . . . Hospitals traditionally have been viewed as the hub of the health care system and often have the capital reserves necessary to finance collaborations with other providers. Those that aggressively pursue such arrangements not only can improve their chances of being the hospital of choice for inpatient services, but also can exert more influence over medical practice decisions. In areas where managed care systems exert more control, however, hospitals may be viewed as cost centers with little input into delivery decisions.

Historically, physicians determined not only which services would be provided, but where those services would be delivered. These decisions generally were made with little accountability for costs. Managed care is changing this. . . . One indication of the level of financial pressure physicians are facing is the [reduced growth] in physician income. . . . Some physicians are responding to the intensified pressures by selling their practices to hospitals or managed care organizations, and becoming employees of those entities. . . . [On the other hand,] [b]ecause physicians generate the demand for hospital services, they have leverage to assume a leadership role in arrangements with other providers. . . .

Notes: Regulation of Health Insurance and Managed Care

1. *What Is Managed Care?* In a traditional indemnity plan, a health insurer reimburses an enrollee for any qualifying medical expenses. As indemnity plans evolved, they began remitting payment directly to physicians and hospitals, eliminating the

need for enrollees to pay up front for their medical care. For patients, the chief advantage of an indemnity-style plan is the flexibility it affords them to choose their own providers. For physicians, indemnity-style plans minimize any intrusion on their medical judgments.

Prepaid medical plans—the original HMOs—operate on a different model. Instead of agreeing to pay for their enrollees' care, they promise to provide that care directly, either through an integrated delivery system controlled by the plan or through tightly affiliated hospitals and physicians. Prepaid medical plans afford patients less freedom to choose their providers and exercise more control over the practice of medicine. In exchange for that loss of flexibility, prepaid medical plans can offer cheaper coverage and may be able to improve the quality of care that their enrollees receive.

Nowadays, few insurers are pure indemnity plans or pure prepaid medical plans. Instead, virtually all insurance falls under the broad umbrella of "managed care." Discussions about managed care can get bogged down in a tangle of acronyms and arcana—closed-panel HMOs, open-panel HMOs, preferred provider organizations (PPOs), exclusive provider organizations (EPOs), and point-of-service plans (POSs) are all types of managed care plans. What really distinguishes these plans from one another, however, is the extent to which they exercise three basic management techniques: cost-containing financial incentives, narrow networks, and utilization review. See Theodore R. Marmor & Jacob S. Hacker, How Not to Think About "Managed Care," 32 U. Mich. J.L. Reform 661 (1999). We will discuss the first two of these techniques in this section, reserving consideration of utilization review until Part D.2.

Despite fierce resistance by many doctors and some patients, managed care remains the dominant form of insurance. However, enrollment has shifted rather dramatically in recent years from tightly managed HMO plans to PPO and other open network plans that give patients more options. Regardless of the form managed care takes, it raises a host of legal, ethical, and regulatory issues. For now, consider these broad inquiries: Are you concerned that insurers are interfering with medical judgment by deciding what treatments to pay for? Would you be more comfortable with a regime that let physicians and patients decide for themselves, but rewarded physicians for saving money or punished them for being excessive? Or is the answer to make patients pay much more out of pocket so that they regulate their own spending decisions?

2. *Conventional Insurance Regulation.* Historically, the states have regulated their own health insurance markets, demanding primarily that insurers maintain large capital reserves for solvency protection and to pay taxes on insurance premiums. States also regulate how insurers invest their funds, the content of insurance policies, the rates insurers charge, and whether insurers engage in fair business practices. See generally R. Jerry, Understanding Insurance Law (4th ed. 2007). States vary a great deal in how or whether they regulate insurers' premium rates.

In what ways does health insurance differ from traditional casualty insurance—say, car insurance? Health insurance does offer protection from unexpected illness or injury. But isn't it also a pooled financing mechanism for predictable medical expenses? Your car insurance doesn't help you finance the cost of automobile maintenance, purchase, and repair. Why should health insurance cover routine doctor visits, preventive care, and the like?

3. *A Brief History of Managed Care.* Precursors of managed care can be traced all the way back into the nineteenth century, mainly as industry-sponsored health clinics for employees. The most prominent early example is Kaiser-Permanente, which was started in the Pacific Northwest by industrialist Henry J. Kaiser in the 1940s to serve the many employees of his different companies. But these prepaid medical plans were fiercely resisted by the American Medical Association, which sought to protect physician independence from corporate control. The AMA went so far as to organize boycotts against prepaid medical plans: physicians were threatened with expulsion from their medical societies and from hospital medical staffs if they participated in prepaid medical plans. The AMA's zealousness attracted the attention of federal antitrust officials, and the Supreme Court eventually sustained a criminal indictment against the AMA under the antitrust laws. See AMA v. United States, 317 U.S. 519 (1943).

Although prepaid medical plans often prevailed in these and other court challenges to their legal authority, the burden of overcoming the persistent hostility of local providers delayed the rise of managed care until the 1980s. Under market pressures, this hostility has given way to resigned acceptance in some parts of the country and open embrace in others.

4. *Financial Incentives.* Although many managed care plans pay providers on a fee-for-service basis, others enter into alternative financial arrangements with providers. Prepaid medical plans like Kaiser, for example, pay a salary to their physicians. In other managed care plans, including the plan at issue in *Rush Prudential,* payments to physicians and hospitals may take the form of complex capitation and "withhold" formulae rather than simple salary:

> Here's how capitation typically works. Say an HMO has 100 enrollees, each covered by a $100 monthly premium. First, the HMO subtracts $20 from each premium to cover its administrative expenses—and pad its profits. It divides the remaining $80 equally between a physician group and a hospital. Of the doctors' $40 payment per member per month, $10 goes to the enrollee's primary care physician. The other $30 is pooled to cover specialty and inpatient care. Half of the doctors' entire capitated payment, $20, is set into a risk pool . . . to pay specialists for care as it occurs. Most groups reimburse specialists on a . . . modified fee-for-service basis, although some groups pay specialists on a capitated basis. The remaining $10 goes into a reserve to cover any unexpectedly high inpatient- or specialty-care costs. [Money left in these pools at year end is returned to the primary care physicians as a bonus, and the physicians make up any deficits.] . . .
>
> [The hospital's portion would amount to $48,000 per year (100 x $40 x 12).] In most capitated environments, the hospital could expect . . . 25 [in]-patient days per 100 enrollees. Given a cost of $1,000 per day, inpatient stays would eat up $25,000 of the hospital's risk pool. Outpatient care would account for another $12,000 of the pool, and out-of-area care $1,000 more. Thus the hospital figures on annual costs of $38,000 against a risk pool of $48,000. The hospital generally splits the resulting $10,000 bonus with the medical group as a reward to doctors for controlling utilization. Conversely, utilization could surge, saddling the hospital with annual expenses of $60,000. This deficit is also split with doctors, who pay for the loss out of the reserve pool they've established for inpatient care.

J. Johnsson, The Whys and Wherefores of Capitation, Am. Med. News, Dec. 6, 1993, at 31. Managed care plans will often mix and match these various approaches to payment. Primary care physicians might receive capitated payments, for example, even as specialists are paid on a fee-for-service basis.

From a patient's perspective, what are the advantages of salaried physicians? Or capitation? What are the risks? For a recent overview of the costs and benefits of different payment approaches, see Robert A. Berenson et al., Payment Methods: How They Work (2016).

5. *Narrow Networks.* Apart from adjusting *how* they pay for care, managed care plans can limit *who* they pay for care. To keep costs low, plans negotiate with physicians, hospitals, and other providers over how much they will pay for medical services. When they cannot reach agreement, plans may exclude providers from their coverage networks. Enrollees must then pay out of pocket if they seek treatment from an out-of-network provider. (Plans will typically include an exception for emergency services outside the coverage area.)

Because managed care plans compete with one another for customers, they have an incentive to exclude providers that demand high prices for their services. Plans use the threat of exclusion to negotiate low rates. At the same time, however, plans that exclude too many providers—or especially popular providers—may not be popular with customers. Especially in areas with a few dominant providers, plans may have little negotiating leverage. Variations in market concentration among providers and insurers explain much of the substantial geographic variation in the cost of insurance across the country. See Eric T. Roberts, Michael E. Chernew & John McWilliams, Market Share Matters: Evidence of Insurer and Provider Bargaining Over Prices, 36 Health Aff. 141 (2017).

Network restrictions are unpopular with physicians, hospitals, and patients. They restrict choice and trigger concerns that only the wealthy, who can afford to purchase gold-plated plans, will have access to the finest medical care, while everyone else will have to make do with second- and third-rate providers. These concerns have fueled particular criticism of the ACA: In response to competitive pressures, many exchange plans have very narrow networks. See Sabrina Corlette et al., Narrow Provider Networks in New Health Plans (Urban Institute, May 2014). Narrow networks, however, are also on the rise in employer-sponsored coverage. Mark Hall & Paul Fronstin, Narrow Provider Networks for Employer Plans (EBRI, Dec. 2016).

Policymakers have responded to frustrations with narrow networks in two principal ways. First, regulators in many states have adopted "network adequacy" rules requiring insurers to demonstrate that their enrollees will have reasonable access to needed services. These rules vary a great deal from state to state, and evidence suggests that compliance is spotty. Although the federal government has adopted a network adequacy rule for plans sold on the exchanges, it has left primary enforcement of the adequacy rule to state insurance regulators. See 82 Fed. Reg. 18372 (2017); Mark Hall & Paul Ginsburg, A Better Approach to Regulating Provider Network Adequacy (Brookings, 2017).

Second, some states have experimented with "any willing provider" statutes, which require managed care plans to include in their network any provider that is willing to accept the plan's standard payment and contracting terms. Interest in these statutes has grown as narrow-network plans have proliferated in the wake of the ACA. See Ashley Nobel, Health Insurers and Access to Health Care Providers: Any Willing Providers (National Conference of State Legislatures, Nov. 2014).

6. *The Managed Care Backlash.* By the late 1990s, the rise of tightly controlled HMOs had precipitated a fierce consumer backlash, stoked in part by an AMA

legislative initiative known as the "Patient Protection Act." The backlash led to the adoption of a spate of laws, mainly at the state level, that attempted to limit what managed care organizations could do to constrain their costs. In addition to the independent review process described in *Rush Prudential,* examples include:

- giving subscribers more information about how HMOs work (prohibiting so-called gag clauses),
- requiring HMOs to include a PPO-type option that allows subscribers to go outside the network,
- giving physicians procedural protections when they are excluded from the network,
- requiring HMOs to pay for emergency care if a "prudent layperson" would have thought it was necessary to go to an emergency room,
- allowing patients with chronic illness to have direct access to specialists, or women to have direct access to obstetricians, without going through the gate-keeping system, and
- mandating minimum coverage provisions such as at least two days in the hospital following childbirth (prohibiting so-called drive-through deliveries).

Frank A. Sloan & Mark A. Hall, Market Failures and the Evolution of State Regulation of Managed Care, 65 Law & Contemp. Probs. 169 (Autumn 2002). The ACA has now adopted a number of these same provisions as federal law—especially for insurers that wish to qualify to sell to individuals and small groups through the new insurance exchanges.

Some commentators have seen in these enactments a broader backlash to market forces in health care:

> The essential message of all the horror stories told by patients is the anguish of abandonment. The howl of doctors, nurses, and other caregivers is moral revulsion at the callousness they are forced to enact. Backlash is a cold shudder against the market paradigm, which taken to its logical endpoint as managed care seems to be doing, respects no human bonds, shows no mercy, and has no use for kindness, loyalty, and other moral qualities of community.

Deborah Stone, Managed Care and the Second Great Transformation, 24 J. Health Pol. Pol'y & L. 1213 (1999). Prof. Stone goes on to criticize these laws for catering to the interests of people with insurance and diverting attention from the plight of those with no insurance.

A similar point is made by Prof. Havighurst, from the other end of the political spectrum. In a provocative essay, he argues that patient protection legislation is being driven by social "elites"—the portion of the public that is "most aware, affluent, influential, and politically active," supported by special interests such as physicians. Therefore, the standards set by this legislation "are designed to suit the preferences of the privileged minority and the interests of health care providers, thereby denying ordinary people the freedom to spend their limited incomes in ways that maximize their welfare." He sees this body of regulation as one of several "mechanisms through which the expensive tastes of upper middle class consumers are invisibly subsidized by persons with either lower expectations or less ability to command attention to their health problems." He concludes:

> It is especially objectionable for academic experts and self-styled "consumer advocates" claiming to represent the interests of all consumers to support the use of the judicial system and state power to deny fellow citizens alternative kinds of health care that would better meet their respective needs—not only for health care but for other things as well. To satisfy their own needs (including their need to demonstrate their symbolic aspirations for others), the political majority, other special interests, and elite movers and shakers of health policy are content to design things so that lower-income consumers have only a Hobson's choice—either pay the high cost of upper-middle-class medical care or go without any health coverage at all.

Clark Havighurst, The Backlash Against Managed Health Care: Hard Politics Make Bad Policy, 34 Ind. L. Rev. 398 (2001). However, many of these "anti-managed care" provisions are ones that HMOs themselves had adopted, under market pressures or after finding that various cost-management strategies were not effective.

7. *Points to Ponder.* What if insurers were to attempt to circumvent these laws by requiring, or encouraging, patients to receive care outside the country (and paying their travel costs for doing so)? Should states or federal exchanges ban such a requirement? See Glenn Cohen, Protecting Patients with Passports: Medical Tourism and the Patient-Protective Argument, 95 Iowa L. Rev. 1467 (2010).

The legal landscape is complicated even more by ERISA preemption. As discussed in more detail in the next section, ERISA broadly preempts any state law that relates to employee benefits, unless the state is regulating the business of insurance. *Rush Prudential* appears to hold that most types of state regulation meet the definition of insurance regulation. See, e.g., Kentucky Ass'n of Health Plans v. Miller, 538 U.S. 329 (2003) (ERISA does not preempt any-willing-provider statute). But states may not regulate employers that self-insure their workers' health care benefits.

8. *Empirical Evidence.* Deciding whether HMOs are the monsters or messiahs of medicine, and the appropriate degree of regulation or encouragement, should be influenced not only by their potential for harm but also by empirical findings on their actual performance. The following notes discuss these findings, first looking at cost containment and then at quality of care.

9. *Do HMOs Harm Quality?* "Reversing the financial incentives in the provision of health care would be dangerous to patients. . . . Incentives for economy can also be incentives for no care or inferior care. . . . The danger that HMOs will provide inferior care is particularly acute when the organization is a profit-making one, when the physician's compensation is based on a percentage of profit rather than a fixed salary, . . . when HMO enrollees have no alternative means of obtaining medical care, and when the HMO population is exclusively poor or aged." Sylvia Law, Blue Cross: What Went Wrong?, 108-109 (2d ed. 1976).

Naturally, there is another side to the story. One reason for optimism about the quality of HMO care is that

> there are countervailing pressures against any tendencies to over-economize. Physicians face the threat of a malpractice suit. . . . Incentives for keeping the subscriber population healthy can be built into the method of rewarding physicians. And competition among pre-paid group practice plans, or between such plans and alternative delivery systems, also limits any potential trend toward unduly low hospitalization rates. Yet the strongest force militating against excessive economizing is the strongly imbued norms of practicing good medicine under conditions of strict professional review.

Developments, The Role of Prepaid Group Practice in Relieving the Medical Care Crisis, 84 Harv. L. Rev. 887, 926 (1971). The HMO industry has developed its own, self-reported measures of quality to assist employers and subscribers in making wise insurance purchasing decisions. These "quality report cards," provide statistics in a comparable format about matters such as the rates of mammography and childhood immunizations, five-year survival rates after cancer, and patient satisfaction. How much confidence do you have that competitive forces will spur HMOs to improve their performance measures? Enough that you think they should be essentially self-regulated for the quality of medical outcomes, like hospitals? Would you expect these measures to be geared more to patients' interest in quality, or employers' interest in cost?

A large and elaborate study by RAND confirmed that low-income enrollees are especially vulnerable in HMOs; those who were sick at the start of the study did worse (under some but not most measures of health status) than comparable patients in fee-for-service insurance. Joseph Newhouse et al., Free for All? Lessons from the RAND Health Insurance Experiment (1993). For most people, however, numerous studies have shown that patient satisfaction and the quality of care overall are as high or higher in HMOs as elsewhere. Yet there is continuing concern over whether patients do as well in HMOs when they suffer from serious chronic illnesses that require ongoing expensive treatment, or from rare conditions that require unusually expensive drugs or special expertise that is not available in the established network.

10. *Do HMOs Save Money?* The cost containment record of HMOs has been mixed. Throughout the 1980s, HMOs engaged in "shadow pricing," namely, tracking their prices close to traditional indemnity insurance and competing instead by offering more comprehensive coverage for the same price, such as reduced patient cost-sharing (deductibles and co-payments). During the 1990s, price competition in some parts of the country (notably California and Minnesota) saw substantial (5 to 10 percent) *declines* in HMO premiums, driven mainly by drastic reductions (30 to 50 percent) in the use of hospitals. Skeptics responded, however, that HMOs achieved lower prices more through "biased" or "favorable" selection than through real efficiencies. HMOs are thought to attract relatively younger and healthier subscribers because their managed care controls are unattractive to patients with chronic illnesses and established provider relationships. Consequently, lower HMO premiums may reflect simply an artificially lower-risk pool of subscribers or "adverse selection" against traditional insurance. The actual extent of this biased selection is in dispute, though, since the lower deductibles and co-payments common in HMOs also tend to attract subscribers who expect substantial medical expenses. One study concluded that HMOs are cheaper than traditional indemnity insurance, but about half the difference is an artifact of HMOs attracting healthier people, and the other half is due to HMOs paying lower prices to hospitals and physicians, not to HMOs delivering less care. Daniel Altman et al., Enrollee Mix, Treatment Intensity, and Cost in Competing Indemnity and HMO Plans, 22 J. Health Econ. 23 (2003).

In any event, HMOs soon lost their price advantages over other kinds of insurance, nor are they offering substantially more generous insurance. Instead, they came to look increasingly like PPOs, with similar levels of cost-sharing and more options to go outside the network or to move within the network without gatekeeping controls. Traditional unrestricted indemnity insurance has all but disappeared from the market, except under Medicare and Medicaid, and even then, managed care is making substantial inroads, as noted in sections A.3 & .4 above. One disenchanted former executive in the managed care industry has this to say about the trajectory of HMOs:

> Conventional wisdom has it that managed care has failed to live up to all but its most brutal promises. Left in the rubble are bewildered consumers, disappointed employers, enraged patients, embittered physicians, and a raft of lawsuits. . . . What once looked like a permanent reduction in health insurance premiums—thanks to a onetime round of severe price competition among managed care organizations—turned out to be an anomaly, a momentary pause in their inevitable rise. . . . In the final analysis, most "managed care" really was "managed cost" all along—but it failed to accomplish even that goal, and the U.S. health care system is worse off for the experiment.
>
> Although it is easy and occasionally fun to pick on the bad manners and various hypocrisies of managed care, it is also unfair. The nation's managed care organizations were asked to do a job that simply cannot be done. . . . As a society, we expected managed care to fix, in a few short years, the disaster in slow motion that is the U.S. health care system. We asked large, organizationally complex insurance companies to reform a century's worth of self-serving professional habits, rein in ever-expanding consumer and patient demands, and fix dysfunctional economic behaviors—all while answering to the taskmasters on Wall Street every quarter. . . . Most of us believed that these insurance companies could do well financially by doing good medically. We were wrong.

J. D. Kleinke, Oxymorons: The Myth of a U.S. Health Care System xi (2001).

11. *Further Reading.* For discussions of the **history of managed care** (note 2), see Developments, supra, 84 Harv. L. Rev. 887 (1971); R. Holley & R. Carlson, The Legal Context for the Development of Health Maintenance Organizations, 24 Stan. L. Rev. 644 (1972); Lawrence Brown, Politics and Health Care Organization: HMOs as Federal Policy (1983); John Iglehart, Physicians and the Growth of Managed Care, 331 New Eng. J. Med. 1167 (1994); Alain C. Enthoven & Laura A. Tollen, Toward a 21st Century Health System: The Contributions and Promise of Prepaid Group Practice (2004); Jan Coombs, The Rise and Fall of HMOs: An American Health Care Revolution (2005).

For discussions of the **managed care backlash** (note 6), see R. A. Dudley & H. S. Luft, Managed Care in Transition, 344 New Eng. J. Med. 1087 (2001); James C. Robinson, The End of Managed Care, 285 JAMA 2622 (2001); Mark A. Hall, The "Death" of Managed Care: A Regulatory Autopsy, 30 J. Health Pol. Pol'y & L. 427 (2005); Thomas Bodenheimer, The HMO Backlash: Righteous or Reactionary?, 335 New Eng. J. Med. 1601 (1996); Symposium, 24 J. Health Pol. Pol'y & L. 873-1257 (1999); Symposium, 16(6) Health Aff. 1 (Dec. 1997).

Both sides of **the debate over managed care patient protection laws** (note 6) are well represented in a series of articles: in favor of these laws, by Marc Rodwin, in 26 Seton Hall L.J. 1007 (1996), 32 Hous. L. Rev. 1319 (1996), and 15 Health Aff. 110 (1996); and against them, by David Hyman, in 73 S. Cal. L. Rev. 221 (2000), 78 N.C. L. Rev. 5 (1999), and 43 Vill. L. Rev. 409 (1998). See generally Russell Korobkin, The Efficiency of Managed Care "Patient Protection" Laws: Incomplete Contracts, Bounded Rationality, and Market Failure, 85 Cornell L. Rev. 1 (1999);

Wendy K. Mariner, Standards of Care and Standard Form Contracts: Distinguishing Patient Rights and Consumer Rights in Managed Care, 15 J. Contemp. Health L. & Pol'y 1 (1998); William Sage, Regulating Through Information: Disclosure Laws and American Health Care, 99 Colum. L. Rev. 1701 (1999); Comment, 28 Cap. U. L. Rev. 685 (2000); Symposium, 47 St. Louis U. L.J. 21 (2003).

For discussions of **the problem of HMO underservice** (note 9), particularly in government programs, see George Anders, Health Against Wealth: HMOs and the Breakdown of Medical Trust (1996); John V. Jacobi, Canaries in the Coal Mine: The Chronically Ill in Managed Care, 9 Health Matrix 79 (1999).

For discussions of the **limited evidence that HMOs harm quality**, see Bruce E. Landon et al., Comparison of Performance of Traditional Medicare vs. Medicare Managed Care, 291 JAMA 1744 (2004); Joseph Gottfried & Frank A. Sloan, The Quality of Managed Care: Evidence from the Medical Literature, 65 Law & Contemp. Probs. 103 (Autumn 2002); Robert Miller & Harold Luft, HMO Plan Performance Update: An Analysis of the Literature, 1997-2001, 21(4) Health Aff. 1 (July 2002); James D. Reschovsky & Peter Kemper, Do HMOs Make a Difference?, 36 Inquiry 374 (2000); Symposium, 30 J. Leg. Stud. 527 (2001).

Exercise: Your Insurance

Investigate your health plan (or your family's health plan) and answer the following questions about your insurance.

- *Cost-sharing.* What is the plan's deductible? For what co-payments and co-insurance are you or your family responsible? Do the out-of-pocket payments vary for inpatient care, outpatient services, or prescription drugs?
- *Networks.* Which physicians and hospitals are in your health plan's network? Can you find an up-to-date provider directory? Are you allowed to visit out-of-network physicians? If so, under what circumstances and at what price?

2. *Consumer-Directed Health Care*

■ TRANSCRIPT OF INTERVIEW WITH JAMIE ROBINSON, Ph.D.*

Lehman Brothers Industry Expert Conference Call Series *May 17, 2002*

As we go into the new decade, the insurance industry is reevaluating whether it wants to be America's method of health care cost control. It's found that this is a very difficult and very unappreciated job. It appears to the public that there is a tradeoff between corporate profits and individual health care, which is a very, very bad image for the industry. The insurers now want to have a completely different image, which is helping the consumer make health care choices. . . .

I think the battle is over and the providers won. The health plans don't really want to get in there and second-guess doctor decision-making. That just proved to

* Reprinted with the permission of Prof. Robinson and the former Lehman Brothers.

be a turf where the providers were very strong, and had the support of the patients and the regulators. . . . There is a lot of lousy medicine being practiced out there that the insurance companies could detect, and could clean up, but they could never convince anybody that they're doing it for the right reasons rather than simply for their own profits.

They've essentially abandoned that role. Increasingly they want to see themselves as a financial services company, like a Fidelity, [which manages investment funds for retirement accounts]. . . . Fidelity offer[s] a stock fund and a bond fund and a mixed fund and employees can allocate their savings across these however they want [with the help of] some decision support tools. . . . The health plans want to do that on the health plan side. "We have our PPO product and our HMO product and our Medical Savings Account product and we're not going to try to force people to pick one or the other. We're going to give them choices. We're going to give them information about the different products, about their prices, about access and about quality. We're going to give them Internet based decision support and tools, and we're going to let them choose. After that, what happens is between the patient and their doctor and their hospital. We, the insurance company, are not going to be responsible for that." . . .

One of the reasons that the insurance industry wants to get out of managed care and go back to being like the financial services industry is that it wants to stop being continually compared to the tobacco industry. It doesn't want to be the second most hated industry in America. The industry needs to re-brand itself as a consumer friendly decision support and information industry rather than something that's trying to save money for corporations.

THE HEALTH CARE CRISIS AND WHAT TO DO ABOUT IT

Paul Krugman & Robin Wells

New York Review of Books, Mar. 23, 2006

. . . [H]eavy reliance on insurance disturbs some economists, who believe that doctors and patients fail to make rational decisions about spending because third parties bear the costs of medical treatment. . . . The 2004 Economic Report of the President [for instance] illustrated the alleged problem with a parable about the clothing industry:[9]

> Suppose, for example, that an individual could purchase a clothing insurance policy with a "coinsurance" rate of 20 percent, meaning that after paying the insurance premium, the holder of the insurance policy would have to pay only 20 cents on the dollar for all clothing purchases. An individual with such a policy would be expected to spend substantially more on clothes—due to larger quantity and higher quality purchases—with the 80 percent discount than he would at the full

9. [See also the similar parable based on insuring food consumption, presented two generations earlier by Judith R. Lave & Lester B. Lave, Medical Care and Its Delivery: An Economic Appraisal, 35 Law & Contemp. Probs. 252 (Spring 1970), which is reprinted on the Web site for this casebook.—Eds.]

> price. . . . The clothing insurance example suggests an inherent inefficiency in the use of insurance to pay for things that have little intrinsic risk or uncertainty. . . .

But it's no use wishing that health care were sold like ordinary consumer goods, with individuals paying out of pocket for what they need. By its very nature, most health spending must be covered by insurance. The reason is simple: in any given year, most people have small medical bills, while a few people have very large bills. . . . [In any given year], health spending roughly follow[s] the "80-20 rule": 20 percent of the population account[s] for 80 percent of expenses. Half the population ha[s] virtually no medical expenses; a mere 1 percent of the population account[s] for 22 percent of expenses. . . . "Most health costs are incurred by a small proportion of the population whose expenses greatly exceed plausible limits on out-of-pocket spending." . . .

So the only way modern medical care can be made available to anyone other than the very rich is through health insurance. . . . [But] the whole system of employer-based health care is under severe strain. We can identify several reasons for that strain, but mainly it comes down to the issue of costs. Providing health insurance looked like a good way for employers to reward their employees when it was a small part of the pay package. [In 2016], however, the annual cost of coverage for a family of four is estimated by the Kaiser Family Foundation at more than [$18,000]. One way to look at it is to say that that's roughly what a worker earning minimum wage and working full time earns in a year. It's [well] more than half the annual earnings of the average Wal-Mart employee. . . . Inevitably, this creates pressure to reduce or eliminate health benefits. And companies that can't cut benefits enough to stay competitive—such as GM—find their very existence at risk. . . . [W]e may well be seeing the whole institution unraveling.

Notice that this unraveling is the byproduct of what should be a good thing: advances in medical technology, which lead doctors to spend more on their patients. This leads to higher insurance costs, which causes employers to stop providing health coverage. . . .

THE "CONSUMER-DIRECTED" DIVERSION

The view that Americans consume too much health care because insurers pay the bills leads to what is currently being called the "consumer-directed" approach to health care reform. The virtues of such an approach are the theme of John Cogan, Glenn Hubbard, and Daniel Kessler's *Healthy, Wealthy, and Wise* [2004]. The main idea is that people should pay more of their medical expenses out of pocket. And the way to reduce public reliance on insurance, reformers from the right wing believe, is to remove the tax advantages that currently favor health insurance over out-of-pocket spending. . . . Instead of raising taxes on health insurance, the [Bush] administration has decided to cut taxes on out-of-pocket spending. . . . The administration's proposals . . . focus[] on an expanded system of tax-advantaged health savings accounts. Individuals can shelter part of their income from taxes by depositing it in such accounts, then withdraw money from these accounts to pay medical bills.

What's wrong with consumer-directed health care? One immediate disadvantage is that health savings accounts, whatever their ostensible goals, are yet another tax break for the wealthy, . . . but little or nothing to lower-income Americans who face a marginal tax rate of 10 percent or less, and lack the ability to place the maximum allowed amount in their savings accounts. A deeper disadvantage is that such accounts tend to undermine employment-based health care, because they encourage adverse selection: health savings accounts are attractive to healthier individuals, who will be tempted to opt out of company plans, leaving less healthy individuals behind.

Yet another problem with consumer-directed care is that the evidence says that people don't, in fact, make wise decisions when paying for medical care out of pocket. A classic study by the Rand Corporation found that when people pay medical expenses themselves rather than relying on insurance, they do cut back on their consumption of health care—but that they cut back on valuable as well as questionable medical procedures, showing no ability to set sensible priorities.

But perhaps the biggest objection to consumer-directed health reform is that its advocates have misdiagnosed the problem. . . . Excessive consumption of routine care, or small-expense items, can't be a major source of health care inefficiency, because such items don't account for a major share of medical costs. Remember the 80-20 rule: the great bulk of medical expenses are accounted for by a small number of people requiring very expensive treatment. When you think of the problem of health care costs, you shouldn't envision visits to the family physician to talk about a sore throat; you should think about coronary bypass operations, dialysis, and chemotherapy. Nobody is proposing a consumer-directed health care plan that would force individuals to pay a large share of extreme medical expenses, such as the costs of chemotherapy, out of pocket. And that means that consumer-directed health care can't promote savings on the treatments that account for most of what we spend on health care. . . .

Notes: Patient Cost-Sharing

1. *The "Consumer-Directed" Movement.* Patients can be sensitized to the costs of treatment options in a variety of ways, loosely referred to as "consumer-directed" health care. One approach is simply to increase substantially the co-payment and deductible amounts, producing what is known as "catastrophic" insurance. "Catastrophic" refers to insurance that kicks in only after a patient has incurred a very large expense; for instance, after paying out of pocket the first $5,000 in a year.

A related idea, mentioned by Krugman and Wells, is to couple catastrophic coverage with a "savings account" that is tax-sheltered, or is subsidized by employers. Money in this account can be used only for medical expenses but is used at the patient's discretion, and unused funds can be rolled forward to future years. Originally called medical savings accounts (MSAs), they are now called health savings accounts (HSAs) or health reimbursement arrangements (HRAs). (In brief, HSA funds belong to the individual account holders whereas HRA funds belong to the employers who fund them for workers.) Under any name, the key is that contributions to these accounts are excluded from income taxation. A federal law promotes the use of health savings accounts by making them available to pay expenses covered by high-deductible "catastrophic" insurance policies—those whose deductibles range anywhere from $1,350 for individuals up to about $13,000 for a family.

Although there is no crisp definition of what counts as "catastrophic" coverage, health plans with very high deductibles have proliferated over the past decade. In 2006, just 4 percent of employees were enrolled in a plan with a deductible of at least $1,000 for an individual or $2,000 for a family. By 2016, that figure stood at 29 percent. See Kaiser Family Foundation, 2016 Employer Health Benefits Annual Survey, Fig. 8.5. These figures can be a bit misleading, however. "[O]ut-of-pocket spending has not increased as a share of total employer-sponsored insurance because the rise in deductibles has been offset by more protection [in the Affordable Care Act] against excessive out-of-pocket costs. There is more focus on the former because more people are affected by the upward pressure on deductibles, but given the extreme concentration of health spending, the latter matters just as much for the total dollars involved." Peter Orszag, U.S. Health Care Reform: Cost Containment and Improvement in Quality, 316 JAMA 493 (2016).

Most of the health plans sold on the Affordable Care Act's exchanges also impose high deductibles: the average "silver" plan in 2017, for example, had a deductible of $3,572 for an individual and $7,474 for families. Cost-sharing protections in the ACA shielded lower-income families from some of these out-of-pocket costs, but high deductibles have still emerged as a source of deep frustration with the ACA. Notwithstanding consumer dissatisfaction, the trend toward greater cost-sharing persists. A few states are even experimenting with limited cost-sharing in their Medicaid programs. See John Z. Ayanian, Michigan's Approach to Medicaid Expansion and Reform, 369 New Eng. J. Med. 1773 (2013).

2. *Every Good Idea Is Flawed.* Krugman and Wells mention several of the grounds for criticizing these initiatives. Consider also this point from a former head of CMS:

> [T]he advocates of increased [leaner insurance] seldom go the further step: inquire just why it is that there is so much health insurance around. . . . Consumers have sought the kinds of health insurance they have, not because they wish to act irrationally in the aggregate economic sense, but precisely because they don't wish to be forced to make rational trade-offs when they are confronted with medical care consumption decisions. No matter how we draw our curves or shape our abstract arguments, the elemental fact is that medical care is about living and dying, something considered by many to be of a rather different character from the purchase of tomatoes. The primary characteristic of most consumers of medical care most of the time is that they are scared. They are scared of dying, or disfigurement, or permanent disability; and these are serious matters. It is hardly fair to expect any of us to make rational decisions about matters of such import. As a society, we may be prepared to pay a substantial economic premium to insulate people from having to make such decisions.

Bruce Vladeck, The Market v. Regulation: The Case for Regulation, 59 Milbank Q. 209 (1981). Professor Robinson flags a related set of concerns:

> [The following] problems will plague a consumer-driven health care system. First, despite the widespread dissemination of information, . . . even the most sophisticated and Internet-enabled consumer . . . will face significant obstacles in understanding the quality and even the true price of health insurance and health care services. . . . [C]onsumers vary enormously in their financial, cognitive, and cultural preparedness to navigate the complex health care system. The new paradigm fits most comfortably the educated, assertive, and prosperous and least comfortably the impoverished, meek, and poorly educated. . . . Finally, the emerging era will make transparent and render difficult the redistribution of income from rich to poor that otherwise results from the collective purchasing and administration of health insurance.

Jamie Robinson, The End of Managed Care, 285 JAMA 2622 (2001).

Which of these arguments is most convincing to you? Even if most people simply follow their physicians' advice about what care they need, is it possible that giving patients more "skin in the game" will make physicians more sensitive to costs, or will make patients more willing to abide by managed care restrictions? In other words, even if patients themselves will not "direct" care, could increased cost-sharing make medical consumers more amenable to cost-based care management? Mark A. Hall & Clark C. Havighurst, Reviving Managed Care with Health Savings Accounts, 24 Health Aff. 1490 (2005).

3. *The Evidence.* Emerging evidence suggests that the critics of consumer-directed health care may have a point. One recent study examined the effect of switching the employees of a large firm into high-deductible health plans. The switch was associated with a substantial reduction (roughly 12 percent or 13 percent) in health-care spending—but not because employees shopped for care or sought out cheaper providers. Instead, "spending reductions were due almost entirely to consumer quantity reductions across a broad range of services, including some that were likely of high value in terms of health and potential to avoid future costs." See Zarek C. Brot-Goldberg et al., What Does a Deductible Do? The Impact of Cost-Sharing on Health Care Prices, Quantities, and Spending Dynamics, Nat'l Bureau of Econ. Research (2015).

The findings echo the conclusions of the famous RAND Corporation study, which was conducted in the late 1970s and placed patients under varying degrees of financial responsibility for their care. The results reveal that cost-sharing indeed has a striking effect on utilization: A catastrophic insurance plan that required the patient to pay 95 percent of the first $1,000 successfully reduced expenditures 31 percent relative to zero out-of-pocket costs, with no discernible differences in health status for most patients. But the lowest-income participants under the cost-sharing plans scored noticeably worse on several measures of health status than did low-income participants under the free plan. Further analysis revealed that most of the cost savings came from patients' reducing their initial visits to their doctors, and that patients cut back both on necessary and unnecessary visits. Once they saw their doctors, patients who paid mostly out of pocket incurred about the same costs as those who paid nothing out of pocket. Joseph Newhouse et al., Free for All? Lessons from the RAND Health Insurance Experiment (1993). These RAND experiments suggest that people in general do not make objectively wise medical spending decisions without the advice of their doctors, but once they consult their doctors, they are inclined to follow medical advice regardless of the financial cost to them (within the $1,000 limit that was studied 30 years ago).

4. *Further Reading.* For additional and more detailed analysis of the entire **debate over consumer-directed health care**, see Timothy S. Jost, Health Care at Risk: A Critique of the Consumer-Driven Movement (2007); Carl Schneider & Mark Hall, The Patient Life: Can Consumers Direct Health Care?, 35 Am. J.L. & Med. 7 (2009); Mark A. Hall, The Legal and Historical Foundations of Patients as Medical Consumers, 96 Geo. L J. 583 (2008); Douglass Farnsworth, Moral Hazard in Health Insurance: Are Consumer-Directed Plans the Answer?, 15 Ann. Health L. 251 (2006); Christopher Robertson, The Split Benefit: The Painless Way to Put Skin Back in the Healthcare Game, 98 Cornell L. Rev. 921 (2013). For analysis of legal issues related to consumer-directed health care, see Haavi Morreim, High-Deductible Health Plans: New Twists on Old Challenges from Tort and Contract, 59 Vand.

L. Rev. 1207 (2006); Timothy S. Jost & Mark A. Hall, The Role of State Regulation in Consumer-Driven Health Care, 31 Am. J.L. & Med. 395 (2005); Mark A. Hall, Paying for What You Get, and Getting What You Pay For, 69 Law & Contemp. Probs. 159 (Autumn 2006).

For further discussions **of health savings accounts** (note 2), see Michael F. Cannon, Health Savings Accounts: Do the Critics Have a Point? (2005); Richard L. Kaplan, Who's Afraid of Personal Responsibility? Health Savings Accounts and the Future of American Health Care, 36 McGeorge L. Rev. 535 (2005); Edward J. Larson & Marc Dettmann, The Impact of HSAs on Health Care Reform: Preliminary Results After One Year, 40 Wake Forest L. Rev. 1087 (2005); Symposium, 19 St. Thomas L. Rev. 1 (2006).

C. ERISA PREEMPTION

This section introduces the broad health policy implications of the Employee Retirement Income Security Act of 1974, a federal statute better known as ERISA, whose primary aim is to regulate private pension plans and other employee fringe benefits. ERISA's main relevance for us is that it preempts certain state laws. While ERISA preemption appears quite technical and perhaps incidental to our main inquiry, it has broad importance for the structure of the health care market and the proper role of state and federal oversight. As one health law scholar has noted, "Although in its text 'hospital' appears only once and 'physician' not at all, ERISA may be the most important law [prior to the Affordable Care Act] affecting health care in the United States." William Sage, "Health Law 2000": The Legal System and the Changing Health Care Market, 15(3) Health Aff. 9 (Aug. 1996).

As you read the main case, pay careful attention to the general purpose that ERISA preemption serves and how its complex preemption provisions are crafted and interpreted. In fact, before you begin, it's a very good idea to read carefully the following statutory language that defines ERISA's scope of preemption:

> (a) Except as provided in subsection (b) of this section, the provisions of [ERISA] shall supersede any and all state laws insofar as they may now or hereafter relate to any employee benefit plan. . . .
>
> (b) (2) (A) Except as provided in subparagraph (B), nothing in [ERISA] shall be construed to exempt or relieve any person from any law of any state which regulates insurance, banking, or securities. (B) Neither an employee benefit plan . . . nor any trust established under such a plan shall be deemed to be an insurance company or other insurer, bank, trust company, or investment company or to be engaged in the business of insurance or banking for purposes of any law of any State purporting to regulate insurance companies, insurance contracts, banks, trust companies, or investment companies. . . .
>
> (c) For purposes of this section, the term *state law* includes all laws, decisions, rules, regulations, or other state action having the effect of law, of any state.

Section 514 of ERISA, 29 U.S.C. §1144.[1]

1. Even these provisions are somewhat an oversimplification because ERISA preemption actually stems from two independent statutory sources, one explicit and the

RETAIL INDUSTRY LEADERS ASSOCIATION v. FIELDER

475 F.3d.180 (4th Cir. 2007)

NIEMEYER, Circuit Judge

On January 12, 2006, the Maryland General Assembly enacted the Fair Share Health Care Fund Act, which requires employers with 10,000 or more Maryland employees to spend at least 8% of their total payrolls on employees' health insurance costs or pay the amount their spending falls short to the State of Maryland. Resulting from a nationwide campaign to force Wal-Mart Stores, Inc., to increase health insurance benefits for its 16,000 Maryland employees, the Act's minimum spending provision was crafted to cover just Wal-Mart. The Retail Industry Leaders Association, of which Wal-Mart is a member, brought suit against James D. Fielder, Jr., the Maryland Secretary of Labor, Licensing, and Regulation, to declare that the Act is preempted by the Employee Retirement Income Security Act of 1974 ("ERISA"), 29 U.S.C. §1144(a). . . . Because Maryland's Fair Share Health Care Fund Act effectively requires employers in Maryland covered by the Act to restructure their employee health insurance plans, it conflicts with ERISA's goal of permitting uniform nationwide administration of these plans. We conclude therefore that the Maryland Act is preempted by ERISA. . . .

[T]he Secretary contends that . . . the Act imposes a payroll tax on covered employers and offers them a credit against that tax for their healthcare spending [rather than mandating an employer's provision of health care benefits]. . . . To resolve the question whether ERISA preempts the Fair Share Act, we consider first the scope of ERISA's preemption provision, and then the nature and effect of the Fair Share Act. . . .

ERISA establishes comprehensive federal regulation of employers' provision of benefits to their employees. It does not mandate that employers provide specific employee benefits but leaves them free, for any reason at any time, to adopt, modify, or terminate welfare plans. Instead, ERISA regulates the employee benefit plans that an employer chooses to establish, setting various uniform standards, including rules concerning reporting, disclosure, and fiduciary responsibility.

The vast majority of healthcare benefits that an employer extends to its employees qualify as an "employee welfare benefit plan," which ERISA defines broadly as:

> any *plan, fund, or program* which . . . was established or is maintained for the purpose of providing for its participants or their beneficiaries, through the purchase of insurance or otherwise, . . . *medical, surgical, or hospital care or benefits, or benefits in the event of sickness, accident, disability,* death or unemployment, or vacation benefits, apprenticeship or other training programs, or day care centers, scholarship funds, or prepaid legal services. . . .

---

other implied. These materials focus on the explicit preemption language in §514 of the Act, which affects primarily regulatory measures. Courts have also recognized a different form of preemption, called complete preemption, emanating from §502 (29 U.S.C. §1132), which gives the federal courts exclusive jurisdiction over actions to enforce rights under ERISA plans. Section 502 is the basis for preempting the tort and contract actions discussed in section D.2 and Chapter 2.C. Unlike the regulatory preemption in §514, there is no "insurance savings clause" for the judicial preemption in §502.

29 U.S.C. §1002(1) (emphasis added).... Because the definition of an ERISA "plan" is so expansive, nearly any systematic provision of healthcare benefits to employees constitutes a plan.

The primary objective of ERISA was to provide a uniform regulatory regime over employee benefit plans. To accomplish this objective, §514(a) of ERISA broadly preempts "any and all State laws insofar as they may now or hereafter *relate to* any employee benefit plan" covered by ERISA. This preemption provision aims "to minimize the administrative and financial burden of complying with conflicting directives among States or between States and the Federal Government" and to reduce "the tailoring of plans and employer conduct to the peculiarities of the law of each jurisdiction." Ingersoll-Rand Co. v. McClendon, 498 U.S. 133, 142 (1990).

The language of ERISA's preemption provision-covering all laws that "relate to" an ERISA plan-is "clearly expansive." N.Y. State Conf. of Blue Cross & Blue Shield Plans v. Travelers Ins. Co., 514 U.S. 645, 655 (1995). . . . [T]he Supreme Court has held, [however,] that not all state healthcare regulations are equal for purposes of ERISA preemption. States continue to enjoy wide latitude to regulate healthcare *providers*. See, e.g., De Buono v. NYSA-ILA Med. & Clinical Servs. Fund, 520 U.S. 806 (1997) (upholding a state tax on gross receipts for patient services at hospitals, residential healthcare facilities, and diagnostic and treatment centers); Travelers, (upholding a state mandate that hospitals charge certain insurers at higher rates than Blue Cross & Blue Shield). And ERISA explicitly saves state regulations of *insurance companies* from preemption. But unlike laws that regulate healthcare providers and insurance companies, state laws that mandate employee benefit structures or their administration are preempted by ERISA. . . . Thus, in *Shaw v. Delta Air Lines, Inc.*, 463 U.S. 85 (1983), the Supreme Court held that ERISA preempted a New York law requiring employers to structure their employee benefit plans to provide the same benefits for pregnancy-regulated disabilities as for other disabilities. . . . On the other hand, a state law that creates only indirect economic incentives that affect but do not bind the choices of employers or their ERISA plans is generally not preempted. . . .

At its heart, the Fair Share Act requires every employer of 10,000 or more Maryland employees to pay to the State an amount that equals the difference between what the employer spends on "health insurance costs" . . . and 8 percent of its payroll. As Wal-Mart noted by way of affidavit, it would not pay the State a sum of money that it could instead spend on its employees' healthcare. This would be the decision of any reasonable employer. . . . An employer would gain from increasing the compensation it offers employees through improved retention and performance of present employees and the ability to attract more and better new employees. In contrast, an employer would gain nothing in consideration of paying a greater sum of money to the State. . . . In effect, the only rational choice employers have under the Fair Share Act is to structure their ERISA healthcare benefit plans so as to meet the minimum spending threshold. . . .

It is a stretch to claim, as the Secretary does, that the Fair Share Act is a revenue statute of general application. When it was enacted, the General Assembly knew that it applied, and indeed intended that it apply, to one employer in Maryland: Wal-Mart. . . . [O]ther States and local governments have adopted or are considering [similar] healthcare spending mandates. . . . If permitted to stand, these laws would force Wal-Mart to tailor its healthcare benefit plans to each specific State, and even to specific cities and counties. This is precisely the regulatory balkanization that Congress sought to avoid by enacting ERISA's preemption provision. . . .

[T]he laws involved in *Travelers* . . . are inapposite because they dealt with regulations that only *indirectly* regulated ERISA plans. In *Travelers,* a New York law required hospitals to add a surcharge to the fees they demanded from most insurance companies, but the law exempted Blue Cross and Blue Shield from having to pay the surcharge. The effect of the law was to make Blue Cross and Blue Shield a cheaper and more attractive option for ERISA-covered healthcare plans to purchase. . . . In short, while the state law in *Travelers* directly regulated *hospitals'* charges to insurance companies, it only *indirectly* affected the prices ERISA plans would pay for insurance policies. . . .

Because the Act directly regulates employers' provision of healthcare benefits, it has a "connection with" covered employers' ERISA plans and accordingly is preempted by ERISA. . . .

MICHAEL, Circuit Judge, dissenting:

Maryland, like most states, is wrestling with explosive growth in the cost of Medicaid. Innovative ideas for solving the funding crisis are required, and the federal government, as the co-sponsor of Medicaid, has consistently called upon the states to function as laboratories for developing workable solutions. In response to this call and its own funding predicament, Maryland . . . require[d] very large employers, such as Wal-Mart Stores, Inc., to assume greater responsibility for employee health insurance costs that are now shunted to Medicaid. I respectfully dissent from the majority's opinion that the Maryland Act is preempted by ERISA. The Act offers a covered employer the option to pay an assessment into a state fund that will support Maryland's Medicaid program. Thus, the Act offers a means of compliance that does not impact ERISA plans, and it is not preempted.

Medicaid is a means-tested entitlement program financed by the states and federal government" that provides medical care for about 60 million Americans. . . . Medicaid was originally intended . . . to serve only as the "payer of last resort." Over time, however, Medicaid has become the payer of first resort for a large percentage of patients. In 2006 state and federal Medicaid spending totaled an estimated $320 billion. Medicaid-the fastest-growing expense for many states-dominates the state budgeting process around the country. . . .

The increase in Medicaid spending is caused in part by the decline in employer-sponsored health insurance. In Maryland's words, Medicaid "has been transformed into a corporate subsidy, with taxpayer-funded employee health care an integral component of [many] an employer's benefits program." Wal-Mart, which is subject to the Maryland Act, is cited as a company that abuses the Medicaid program. "Wal-Mart has more employees and dependents on subsidized Medicaid or similar programs than any other company nationwide." . . . In an internal company memo of fairly recent origin, Wal-Mart acknowledged that "[t]wenty-seven percent of [its employees'] children are on [Medicaid]," and an additional nineteen percent are uninsured. . . . As employers drop or fail to offer affordable family health care coverage, more and more children of low income employees are forced into Medicaid or other taxpayer-funded insurance. . . .

I respectfully dissent on the issue of ERISA preemption because . . . [a]n employer can comply with the Act either by paying assessments into the special fund or by increasing spending on employee health insurance. . . . This choice is real. The assessment does not amount to an exorbitant fee that leaves a large employer with no choice but to alter its ERISA plan offerings. . . . Th[e] choice would simply be a business judgment that Wal-Mart is free to make. Indeed, an employer close to the required statutory percentage, such as Wal-Mart, may find it easier to pay the assessment than to increase health insurance spending. . . . [Therefore,] I would hold that the Act is not preempted.

■ AMERICAN MEDICAL SECURITY, INC. v. BARTLETT

111 F.3d 358 (4th Cir. 1997)

NIEMEYER, Circuit Judge.

. . . This case presents the tension between Maryland's effort to guarantee through its regulation of insurance that employee benefit plans offer at least 28 state-mandated health benefits, and Congress' preemption, through ERISA of any state regulation that "relates to" an employee benefit plan.

ERISA is a comprehensive federal statute regulating [primarily private pension plans, but also covering other employee fringe benefit plans], including plans maintained for the purpose of providing medical or other health benefits for employees. To assure national uniformity of federal law, ERISA broadly preempts state law and assures that federal regulation will be exclusive. Section 514(a) provides that ERISA "shall supersede any and all state laws insofar as they may now or hereafter relate to any employee benefit plan" as defined by ERISA. The courts have interpreted this clause broadly to carry out Congress' purpose of displacing any state effort to regulate ERISA plans. See, e.g., FMC Corp. v. Holliday, 498 U.S. 52, 58 (1990) ("The preemption clause is conspicuous for its breadth"); Shaw v. Delta Airlines, Inc., 463 U.S. 85, 98 (1983) ("The section's preemptive scope [is] as broad as its language"). Thus, any law that "relates to" a plan is preempted by §514(a). . . .

Although ERISA's preemptive scope is broad, the "savings clause" explicitly saves from ERISA's preemption those state laws that regulate insurance. See 29 U.S.C. §1144(b)(2)(A). At the same time, however, the "deemer clause" provides that state insurance laws are not saved from preemption if they deem an employee benefit plan to be an insurance company in order to regulate it. See 29 U.S.C. §1144(b)(2)(B); see also Pilot Life Ins. Co. v. Dedeaux, 481 U.S. 41, 45 (1987). Thus, a preempted law is saved from preemption if it regulates insurance, . . . but at bottom, state insurance regulation may not directly or indirectly regulate self-funded ERISA plans. Accordingly, although plans that provide benefits in the form of insurance may be indirectly regulated through regulation of that insurance, plans that are self-funded or self-insured may not themselves be regulated as insurance companies even if the self-funded or self-insured plan purchases stop-loss insurance to cover losses or benefits payments beyond a specified level. . . .

[Plaintiffs in this declaratory judgment action include three] Maryland employers sponsoring self-funded employee health benefit plans subject to ERISA. Each has purchased stop-loss insurance . . . to cover their plans' benefit payments above an annual $25,000-per-employee level, known as the "attachment point." . . . The employee benefit plans sponsored by these three Maryland employers contained substantially fewer benefits than the 28 mandated by Maryland for health insurance policies regulated by the Maryland Insurance Commissioner. The benefit plans sponsored by these Maryland employers did not, for example, include benefits for skilled nursing facility services, outpatient rehabilitative services, and certain organ transplants, all of which are mandated for inclusion in Maryland health insurance policies. . . .

Stop-loss insurance provides coverage to self-funded plans above a certain level of risk absorbed by the plan. It provides protection to the plan, not to the plan's participants or beneficiaries, against benefits payments over the specified level. . . . Stop-loss insurance is thus akin to "reinsurance" in that it provides reimbursement to a plan after the plan makes benefit payments.

The state of Maryland regulates health insurance, requiring that health insurance policies afford at least 28 specified benefits.[2] Apparently not wishing to be subject to state-mandated health benefits, insurance companies and their ERISA plan clients have entered into arrangements under which plans self-fund benefits and purchase stop-loss insurance to insure themselves against benefits paid beyond designated attachment points. . . . [B]y absorbing a minimal amount of initial risk and insuring the remainder through stop-loss insurance, plans are able to provide health benefits of a kind or at a level different from what state law requires of [regulated] health insurance.

Recognizing that such arrangements bypass Maryland's regulations for health insurance and intending to prevent such arrangements, the Maryland Insurance Commissioner adopted regulations that require plans to absorb the risk of at least the first $10,000 of benefits paid to each beneficiary. . . . Justifying the regulation and explaining how low attachment points permit self-funded ERISA plans to bypass state mandates, the Insurance Commissioner stated in his order: ". . . The goal is obvious: As policies become available with attachment points lower than many deductibles, it became an increasingly attractive option to 'self-insure' a health plan, but to continue to shift the majority of the risk to the insurance carrier by purchasing 'stop loss' coverage." The regulations [that plaintiffs seek to declare invalid] accordingly provide that any stop-loss insurance policy with a specific attachment point below $10,000 is deemed to be a health insurance policy for purposes of Maryland's health insurance regulations and must therefore contain mandated benefits. . . .

2. [Included in this list are: (4) Inpatient mental health and substance abuse services . . . up to a maximum of 25 days per covered person per year in a hospital or related institution; . . . (10) Mammography services for persons ages 40 to 49 once every other calendar year, and for ages 50 and above once per calendar year; . . . (16) Chiropractic services up to 20 visits per condition per year; (17) Skilled nursing facility [and home health] services as an alternative to medically necessary inpatient hospital services up to a maximum of 100 days per year; (18) Infertility [and family planning] services . . . ; (19) Nutritional services for the treatment of cardiovascular disease, diabetes, malnutrition, cancer, cerebral vascular disease, or kidney disease up to a maximum of six visits per year per condition; (20) Autologous and nonautologous bone marrow, cornea, kidney, liver, heart, lung, heart/lung, pancreas, and pancreas/kidney transplants; . . . (25) Pregnancy and maternity services, including abortion; (26) Generic prescription drugs . . . ; (27) Controlled clinical trials. . . .]

In summary, on one side of the issue before us, the Maryland Insurance Commissioner seeks to take advantage of his right under ERISA's savings clause to regulate the business of insurance. And on the other side, the insurance companies seek to take advantage of ERISA's preemption and deemer clauses to remove self-funded plans from the reach of state insurance regulation.

III

We begin the analysis with the question of whether Maryland's regulations "relate to" ERISA employee benefit plans and thus whether they fall within ERISA's preemptive scope. A regulation relates to an employee benefit plan when it has a "connection with or reference to such a plan." *Shaw*, 463 U.S. at 96-97. The Maryland Insurance Commissioner wisely concedes that the regulations at issue do "relate to" ERISA plans. . . .

Even though Maryland's regulations relate to ERISA plans, they nevertheless may be saved from preemption if they constitute a law that "regulates insurance." . . . In determining whether a state law is one that "regulates insurance," it is not enough that it operate only on insurance companies or insurance policies. The regulation must regulate the business of insurance in the sense that the object of its regulation (1) "has the effect of transferring or spreading a policyholder's risk"; (2) "is an integral part of the policy relationship between the insurer and the insured"; and (3) "is limited to entities within the insurance industry." Metropolitan Life Insurance Company v. Massachusetts, 471 U.S. 724, 743 (1985). [That decision held that a state may, consistent with ERISA, require health insurers to include certain mandated mental health benefits in policies they sell to employers.]

In this case, the Maryland Insurance Commissioner can well argue with respect to the first *Metropolitan Life* factor that the setting of attachment points allocates risk. Higher attachment points burden plans with more risk while lower attachment points increase insurance company risk. The Commissioner might also be able to argue successfully on the second *Metropolitan Life* factor that the regulations address a practice integral to the insured-insurer relationship. . . . This factor is, however, complicated by the fact that the intended, stated, and actual effect of the regulations is to reach the relationship between ERISA plans and their participants who are not parties to the insurance contract. The third *Metropolitan Life* factor is complicated in the same way. Although the state's regulation of attachment points is limited to entities in the insurance industry, the stated purpose of the regulations is also to reach the [employer]-participant relationship, a relationship which is outside the insurance industry. . . .

We recognize that the regulations are carefully drafted to focus directly on insurance companies issuing stop-loss insurance and not on the employee benefit plans themselves. . . . The state asserts a need for this regulation because, in its absence, the loophole would allow every self-funded plan to provide coverage for fewer health benefits than state law mandates for health insurance policies. It argues that absorbing a minimal risk is simply a sham to circumvent state insurance regulation, the area carved out by ERISA in which states may act. But in seeking to address this perceived loophole, the state in fact ends up regulating self-funded employee benefit plans that are exclusively subject to ERISA. In seeking to require self-funded plans to offer coverage consistent with state insurance law, Maryland crosses the line of preemption. . . . By aiming at the [employer]-participant relationship, Maryland law violates the ERISA provision that no ERISA plan "shall be deemed to be an insurance company . . . for purposes of any law of any state purporting to regulate insurance companies [or] insurance contracts." 29 U.S.C. §1144(b)(2)(B).

The state's fear that [employers] will circumvent state regulation and offer citizens too few health benefits is understandable. But to state that fear reveals that Maryland is really concerned, not with the business of insurance and its coverage of risks, but with the benefits that ERISA plans can choose to provide their participants and beneficiaries. No matter how understandable this concern may be, only Congress may address it, not the state of Maryland through its insurance regulations. . . . If a self-funded plan insured by stop-loss insurance having an attachment point of $5,000 provided no benefit for organ transplants, the regulations would either raise plan costs by including unwanted, state-mandated insurance coverage for organ transplants or convert the self-funded plan into a fully insured plan contrary to its preference. These effects impermissibly intrude on the relationship between an ERISA plan and its participants and beneficiaries. . . .

When ERISA preempted state law relating to ERISA-covered employee benefit plans, it may have created a regulatory gap, but Maryland is without authority to fill that gap. . . .

Notes: ERISA Preemption; Mandated Benefits

1. *Does Any Law Not "Relate to" Employee Benefits?* Owing to the broad "relates to" language, the potential sweep of ERISA preemption is limited only by the bounds of one's imagination. In these materials, ERISA preemption has major impact primarily in three places (in addition to here): (1) malpractice actions against HMOs, section D.2 and Chapter 2.C; (2) contract claims for the denial of payment under health insurance; and (3) state attempts to encourage employers to offer health insurance. But, ERISA preemption is capable of cropping up almost anywhere. Consider, for instance, whether the following are potentially preempted: physicians' contract actions against managed care plans that drop them from their networks; taxation of firms that assist self-insured employers in administering their health benefits; state laws that limit health insurers' or employers' subrogation rights when employees' tort awards include medical expenses. The answer to each is "potentially, yes" (with certain qualifications). See S. Law & B. Ensminger, Negotiating Physicians' Fees: Individual Patients or Society?, 61 N.Y.U. L. Rev. 1, 80-81 (1986) ("in this judicially constructed Alice in Wonderland world, any state seeking to regulate insurers' arrangements with physicians or providers must be prepared to litigate claims of ERISA preemption").

Broad ERISA preemption was intended to ensure uniform federal regulation of employee benefits. However, ERISA imposes substantive regulation primarily on *pension* benefits, but much less so on *welfare* benefits such as health insurance. It appears that Congress did not realize it was creating such a regulatory vacuum, but subsequent lobbying by vested interests has precluded much alteration of the status quo.

As the *Fielder* case explains, however, courts have begun to adopt a more limited interpretation of "relates to," following the Supreme Court's decision in New York State Conference of Blue Cross & Blue Shield Plans v. Travelers Insurance Co., 514 U.S. 645 (1995). *Travelers* held that ERISA does not preempt a New York statute that requires hospitals to collect surcharges from patients covered by commercial insurers, but not from patients insured by Blue Cross & Blue Shield plans. These surcharges were used to reimburse hospitals for the costs of treating patients without insurance. Blue Cross patients were not charged because Blue Cross's premiums were already more expensive than commercial insurers, due to Blue Cross's policy of accepting both healthy and sick subscribers.

The plaintiffs in *Travelers* argued that the New York statute was preempted by ERISA because it "make[s] the Blues more attractive (or less unattractive) as insurance alternatives and thus ha[s] an indirect economic effect on choices made by insurance buyers, including ERISA plans." The Supreme Court disagreed, holding that statutes that have "only an indirect economic effect on the relative costs of various health insurance packages" available to ERISA plans are not preempted by ERISA. The Court emphasized, though, that it still supports a broad reading of "relates to":

> [W]e do not hold today that ERISA preempts only direct regulation of ERISA plans, nor could we do that with fidelity to the views expressed in our prior opinions on the matter. We acknowledge that a state law might produce such acute, albeit indirect, economic effects, by intent or otherwise, as to force an ERISA plan to adopt a certain scheme of substantive coverage . . . and that such a state law might indeed be preempted under §514. But as we have shown, New York's surcharges do not fall into [that] category; they affect only indirectly the prices of insurance policies, a result no different from myriad state laws in areas traditionally subject to local regulation. . . .

In the subsequent decision mentioned in *Fielder*, the Court found no preemption even though the financial assessment was imposed directly on clinics owned and operated by self-insured employers, since the tax applied generally to all health care facilities and did not target those sponsored by employers. See DeBuono v. NYSA-ILA Medical and Clinical Services Fund, 520 U.S. 806 (1997).

2. *Gobeille.* The scope of *Travelers* remains contested. In Gobeille v. Liberty Mutual Insurance Co., 136 S. Ct. 936 (2016), the Supreme Court heard a challenge to a Vermont law requiring all insurers, public and private, to submit the prices they pay for health care to an "all payer claims database." Eighteen states have moved to establish such databases in the hope of fostering price transparency. "Depending on local policies, that transparency can serve any number of purposes. It can aid state regulators in fashioning new payment models, help researchers better understand the effects of payment and benefits policies, and enable people with high deductibles to comparison shop." Nicholas Bagley & Christopher Koller, Transparency and the Supreme Court—Can Employers Refuse to Disclose How Much They Pay for Health Care?, 373 New Eng. J. Med. 34 (2016).

Vermont argued that the law did not "relate to" benefit plans because it did not require employers to alter their benefit plans or meaningfully intrude on their administration of those plans. By a 6 to 2 vote, the Supreme Court disagreed:

> ERISA's reporting, disclosure, and recordkeeping requirements for welfare benefit plans are extensive. ERISA plans must present participants with a plan description explaining, among other things, the plan's eligibility requirements and claims-processing procedures. Plans must notify participants when a claim is denied and state the basis for the denial. Most important for the pre-emption question presented

here, welfare benefit plans governed by ERISA must file an annual report with the Secretary of Labor. The report must include a financial statement listing assets and liabilities for the previous year and, further, receipts and disbursements of funds. The information on assets and liabilities as well as receipts and disbursements must be provided to plan participants on an annual basis as well. Because welfare benefit plans are in the business of providing benefits to plan participants, a plan's reporting of data on disbursements by definition incorporates paid claims. . . .

It should come as no surprise, then, that plans must keep detailed records so compliance with ERISA's reporting and disclosure requirements may be "verified, explained, or clarified, and checked for accuracy and completeness." . . .

As all this makes plain, reporting, disclosure, and recordkeeping are central to, and an essential part of, the uniform system of plan administration contemplated by ERISA. The Court, in fact, has noted often that these requirements are integral aspects of ERISA. . . .

The State maintains that its program has nothing to do with the financial solvency of plans or the prudent behavior of fiduciaries. This does not suffice to avoid federal pre-emption. . . . In *Travelers*, for example, the Court noted that "[b]oth the purpose and the effects of "the state law at issue "distinguish[ed] it from" laws that "function as a regulation of an ERISA plan itself." 514 U.S., at 658-659. The perceived difference here in the objectives of the Vermont law and ERISA does not shield Vermont's reporting regime from pre-emption. Vermont orders health insurers, including ERISA plans, to report detailed information about the administration of benefits in a systematic manner. This is a direct regulation of a fundamental ERISA function. Any difference in purpose does not transform this direct regulation of "a central matter of plan administration," into an innocuous and peripheral set of additional rules.

136 Sup. Ct. 944-946. The Supreme Court's decision will allow most large employers to withhold price information from the all-payer claims databases. As a result, states will likely struggle to compile a comprehensive picture of medical prices.

3. *The Insurance Savings Clause*. The extent of ERISA preemption depends on the scope of the insurance savings clause, which restores state authority. The three-point test applied in *Metropolitan Life*, which is discussed in *American Medical Security*, pinpoints only the most central core of insurance practice—risk spreading—and only when that practice relates directly to the policyholder. These two limitations exclude a broad array of important activity. In Group Life & Health Insurance Co. v. Royal Drug, 440 U.S. 205 (1979), the Court held that an insurance company's setting the amount it is willing to pay a health care provider does not constitute the business of insurance because it fails to meet either prong of the test. Similarly, in Union Labor Life Insurance Co. v. Pireno, 458 U.S. 119 (1981), the Court excluded from the business of insurance the process of verifying insurance claims, because it occurs only after risk has been transferred.

Subsequent decisions, however, have taken a more relaxed approach to this issue, one that uses a "commonsense" test for what is insurance regulation, a test that does not require that all three parts of the McCarran-Ferguson test be applied in a strict or rigid fashion. For instance, Rush Prudential HMO v. Moran, 536 U.S. 355 (2002), found that a state law that permits an administrative appeal of HMOs' denial of coverage does regulate insurance even though it does not necessarily affect the aspect of insurance that "spreads a policyholder's risk." In Kentucky Ass'n of Health Plans v. Miller, 538 U.S. 329 (2003), the Supreme Court made a "clean break" from its previous reliance on the three-part McCarran-Ferguson definition of insurance regulation. Instead, it adopted the following two-part test to capture the ordinary meaning of insurance regulation: "First, the state law must be specifically directed toward entities engaged in insurance. . . . Second . . . the state law must substantially affect the risk pooling arrangement between the insurer and insured." See also UNUM Life Insurance Co. of America v. Ward, 526 U.S. 358 (1999) (common-law rules regarding interpretation of insurance contracts regulate insurance if they are unique to insurance). Do these subsequent decisions cast doubt on *American Medical Security*'s reasoning? See Russell Korobkin, The Battle over Self-Insured Health Plans, or "One Good Loophole Deserves Another," 5 Yale J. Health Pol'y L. & Ethics 1 (2005) (arguing that this case was wrongly decided).

4. *Self-Insured Employers and the "Deemer Clause."* Owing to ERISA's "deemer clause," employers can avoid all state insurance regulation by self-funding their health care benefits rather than purchasing health insurance. This is one reason that over half of privately insured people are covered by self-funded employer plans. Self-insuring also avoids the state premium taxes that insurers pay, and it potentially reduces the overhead and profits built into insurance premiums. Self-insuring does not entirely eliminate insurers from the equation, however, because most self-insured employers hire insurance companies or other "third-party administrators" to administer claims and to use their networks of providers who have agreed to negotiated discounts. Accordingly, most people cannot tell if their employer plan is self-funded or insured. Under either arrangement, workers have the same insurance card, and they receive care from the same providers under the similar rules.

Conventionally, only large employers take a chance on self-insuring, since even one or two medical problems could bankrupt smaller employers. Although stop-loss insurance protects against that risk, its cost reduces the price advantage being sought. The smaller the employer, the more stop-loss they need to buy, so the equation usually turns negative below about 200 workers.

The ACA may have changed this calculus for small employers, however. Under its community rating rules, small firms with younger and healthier workers have to pay higher premiums in most states if they purchase regulated insurance. By self-insuring, these employers can instead purchase stop-loss coverage that is "experience-rated," meaning that it is priced based on each group's actual, expected claims. Then, if workers or family members develop a serious ongoing health problem, the employer can still jump back into the community-rated market. Imagine what this "adverse selection" would do to community premiums. What can states do to prevent this clear potential for undermining insurance market reforms? In light of *Bartlett*, could they: (1) simply prohibit the sale of stop-loss coverage to small firms, to discourage self-insuring; or (2) require that stop-loss insurance also be community rated?

5. *"Play or Pay" Laws.* The approach to avoiding ERISA preemption attempted by Maryland in its law targeting Wal-Mart is known as "play or pay," meaning that employers can avoid paying the state by "playing" fair regarding their health insurance benefits. Prior to the ACA, the play-or-pay strategy was at the heart of several states' attempts to achieve universal coverage. If ERISA bars either an employer mandate or a play-or-pay law, are states left with no other options than either an individual mandate or a government program funded by a general tax? Could they, for instance, fund universal health care through a general payroll tax that applies to all employers, but give a tax credit to employers that provide insurance?

In Golden Gate Restaurant Association v. City and County of San Francisco, 546 F.3d 639 (9th Cir. 2008), the Ninth Circuit upheld a San Francisco ordinance that required employers either to offer coverage to their employees or pay a tax penalty. The court distinguished *Fielder* on the ground that the penalty would be used to finance a public insurance program for residents whose employers did not offer health coverage. According to the court, that left employers with "a meaningful alternative": they could offer coverage directly (as a fringe benefit of employment) or indirectly (via an earmarked tax). Because an employer that chose the latter approach would have to make no changes at all to its employee benefit plan, the court concluded that ERISA did not preempt the ordinance.

How persuasive is this distinction? Eight of the 27 judges on the Ninth Circuit voted to rehear the case en banc, arguing that it opened a circuit split with *Fielder* and ran counter to the Supreme Court's case law on ERISA preemption. See Golden Gate Rest. Ass'n v. City & Cty. of San Francisco, 558 F.3d 1000 (9th Cir. 2009) (en banc). The restaurant association in *Golden Gate* asked the Supreme Court to review the case, but the ACA was adopted while the association's request was pending. Probably because the ACA obviated the need for state and local play-or-pay laws, the Supreme Court declined to hear the case. If the ACA is partly repealed (its fate remains unclear as of this writing), states and localities may attempt to extend coverage to their uninsured residents—and the legality of play-or-pay laws could again take center stage.

Notably, ERISA does not preempt more incremental state reforms, such as those that make it easier to purchase insurance or that create compensation pools for uncompensated hospital care. See generally Mary Anne Bobinski, Unhealthy Federalism: Barriers to Increasing Health Care Access for the Uninsured, 24 U.C. Davis L. Rev. 255 (1990).

6. *Mandated Insurance Benefits.* Notice in note 2 of the *American Medical Security* case the range of benefits that Maryland requires private health insurance to cover. Which of these mandated benefits are compelled by broad public policy concerns, and which are open to criticism as responses to pressure from particular interest groups? The argument against these mandates is that state legislatures too easily succumb to special interest lobbying by provider groups, thereby increasing the costs of health insurance overall and pricing more people out of the market.

The same tensions exist at the federal level. The Mental Health Parity Act requires that larger employers, including self-insured employers, who offer mental health benefits do so on par with other benefits. Larger employers are not required to offer mental health benefits, but if they do so, those benefits cannot be subject to any different limits (such as cost-sharing, number of treatments, or out-of-network restrictions) than medical benefits. Out of concern that this might prompt employers to drop mental health coverage altogether, however, the law exempts employers for whom this mandate would result in increasing insurance costs more than 1 percent.

The Affordable Care Act greatly expands the federal role in determining which benefits insurance should cover, but it also preserves an important role for the states. Insurers that cover individuals and small groups must offer a comprehensive package of "essential health benefits," including mental health and substance abuse treatment, but each state is permitted to decide what particulars that package should consist of, as long as it is generally consistent with the ACA and with what employers typically cover in that state. Larger employers and those that are self-insured are not required to offer the full set of "essential health benefits."

7. *Accidental Federalism.* Is there any sense or logic in the complicated pattern of state versus federal jurisdiction over the various aspects of health care finance and delivery covered so far in this chapter? Consider not only ERISA but also Medicaid and insurance regulation under the Affordable Care Act. The ACA sets detailed requirements for how states must regulate health insurers if they do not want to turn insurance regulation over to the federal government. Moreover, while federal law leaves most aspects of physician practice to the states, it heavily regulates the privacy of medical information, and it strongly influences hospital regulation through its conditions for Medicare participation.

8. *Further Readings.* On **the history of ERISA's adoption** (note 1), see James A. Wooten, The Employee Retirement Income Security Act of 1974: A Political History (2004); Daniel Fox & Daniel Schaffer, Health Policy and ERISA: Interest Groups and Semiprotection, 14 J. Health Pol. Pol'y & L. 239 (1989).

For discussions of **the *Travelers* decision** (note 1), see Note, 13 Yale L. & Pol'y Rev. 339 (1995); Catherine Fisk, The Last Article About the Language of ERISA Preemption?, 33 Harv. J. on Legis. 35 (1996); Karen Jordan, *Travelers Insurance*: New Support for the Argument to Restrain ERISA Preemption, 13 Yale J. on Reg. 255 (1996). Discussing whether ERISA preempts state-managed care regulation, see Donald T. Bogan, Protecting Patient Rights Despite ERISA: Will the Supreme Court Allow States to Regulate Managed Care?, 74 Tul. L. Rev. 951 (2000); Margaret Farrell, ERISA Preemption and Regulation of Managed Health Care, 23 Am. J.L. & Med. 251 (1997). For discussions of how the ACA might have shifted the ERISA terrain somewhat, see Brendan S. Maher, The Affordable Care Act, Remedy, and Litigation Reform, 63 Am. U. L. Rev. 649 (2014); Katherine T. Vukadin, Hope or Hype?: Why the Affordable Care Act's New External Review Rules for Denied ERISA Healthcare Claims Need More Reform, 60 Buff. L. Rev. 1201 (2012).

For discussions of Gobeille v. Liberty Mutual (note 2), see Erin C. Fuse Brown & Jamie King, The Double-Edged Sword of Health Care Integration: Consolidation and Cost Control, 92 Ind. L.J. 55 (2016); Elizabeth Y. McCuskey, Body of Preemption: Health Law Traditions and the Presumption Against Preemption, 89 Temp. L. Rev. 95 (2016); Edward Zelinsky, Gobeille v. Liberty Mutual: An Opportunity to Correct the Problems of ERISA Preemption, 100 Cornell L. Rev. Online 24 (2015).

For discussions about **employers using stop-loss coverage to take advantage of ERISA** (note 3), see Timothy Jost & Mark Hall, Self-Insurance for Small Employers Under the Affordable Care Act: Federal and State Regulatory Options, 69 N.Y.U. Ann. Surv. Am. L. 539 (2013); K. Caster, The Future of Self-Funded Health Plans, 79 Iowa L. Rev. 413 (1994); J. Lenhart, ERISA Preemption: The Effect of Stop-Loss Insurance on Self-Insured Health Plans, 14 Va. Tax Rev. 615 (1995).

For discussions of **play-or-pay laws** (note 5), see Peter D. Jacobson, The Role of ERISA Preemption in Health Reform: Opportunities and Limits, 37 J.L. Med. & Ethics 88 (2009); Amy B. Monahan, Pay or Play Laws, ERISA Preemption, and Potential Lessons from Massachusetts, 55 Kan. L. Rev. 1203 (2007); Christen Linke Young, Note, Pay or Play Programs and ERISA Section 514: Proposals for Amending the Statutory Scheme, 10 Yale J. Health Pol'y, L. & Ethics 197 (2010).

For discussions of **mandated benefits** (note 6), see the several articles by Amy Monahan at 2007 U. Ill. L. Rev. 1361; 80 U. Colo. L. Rev. 127 (2009); and 2012 U. Ill. L. Rev. 139. See also Nicholas Bagley & Helen Levy, Essential Health Benefits and the Affordable Care Act: Law and Process, 39 J. Heath Pol., Pol'y & Law 441 (2013);

Stacy Tovino, A Proposal for Comprehensive and Specific Essential Mental Health and Substance Use Disorder Benefits, 38 Am. J.L. & Med. 471 (2012).

For discussions of **federalism in health care** (note 7), see Nicholas Bagley, Federalism and the End of Obamacare, 127 Yale L.J. Forum 1 (2017); Patricia J. Zettler, Toward Coherent Federal Oversight of Medicine, 52 San Diego L. Rev. 427 (2015); Brendan S. Maher & Radha A. Pathak, Enough About the Constitution: How States Can Regulate Health Insurance Under the ACA, 31 Yale L. & Pol'y Rev. 275 (2013); Michael Doonan, American Federalism in Practice: The Formulation and Implementation of Contemporary Health Policy (2013); Lars Noah, Ambivalent Commitments to Federalism in Controlling the Practice of Medicine, 53 U. Kan. L. Rev. 149 (2004); Richard P. Nathan, Federalism and Health Policy, 24(6) Health Aff. 1458 (Nov. 2005); John D. Blum, Overcoming Managed Care Regulatory Chaos Through a Restructured Federalism, 11 Health Matrix 327 (2001).

9. *A Path Through the Maze.* Let us recapitulate the complex analysis required to answer an ERISA preemption question: (1) ERISA's preemption clause is extremely broad because so many state laws "relate to" employee benefits. (2) The insurance savings clause would reinstate most relevant state regulation, except for the fact that it sometimes is given a narrow construction. And, (3) regardless, for reasons just explained, self-insured health benefits may never be subjected to state regulation. The confusion surrounding this complicated scheme and the meaning of its various parts has deterred states from asserting more aggressive regulatory jurisdiction, even where that might be possible to do.

ERISA Preemption Quiz

The following questions are supposed to have clear, settled answers for those who understand this complex law. See how you do.

Due to ERISA preemption, are any of the following true? Why or why not?

a. States may not force employers to purchase insurance.
b. States may not require self-insured employers to cover mental health services.
c. States may not regulate the rates that hospitals charge (i) insurers and HMOs, or (ii) self-insured employers.

D. HEALTH INSURANCE COVERAGE

In the previous section, we made the transition from looking at who is covered by what types of insurance, to looking at which benefits are covered. This section explores the latter topic in much greater depth. We start by examining whether it is desirable or permissible to exclude some medical conditions or treatments by assessing which medical needs are most demanding and what treatments work the best. The public policy focus here is on how insurance contracts or statutes might be rewritten, and the legal focus is on disability discrimination. Then, we go on to look at how to interpret and apply insurance contracts and statutes once they are adopted, and how to appeal coverage denials.

As you read this section, realize that, in a world of limited resources, insurance cannot pay for all beneficial medical care that anyone might need. The problem, then, is which approach to limiting insurance benefits makes the most sense, and whether discrimination law and policy allow sensible health care public policy to emerge from either market or political forces.

1. *Rationing and Discrimination*

■ ALEXANDER v. CHOATE

469 U.S. 287 (1985)

Justice MARSHALL delivered the opinion of the Court.

. . . Faced in 1980-1981 with projected state Medicaid costs of $42 million more than the state's Medicaid budget of $388 million, the directors of the Tennessee Medicaid program decided to institute a variety of cost-saving measures. Among these changes was a reduction from 20 to 14 in the number of inpatient hospital days per fiscal year that Tennessee Medicaid would pay hospitals on behalf of a Medicaid recipient. Before the new measures took effect, respondents, Tennessee Medicaid recipients, brought a class action for declaratory and injunctive relief in which they alleged, inter alia, that the proposed 14-day limitation on inpatient coverage would have a discriminatory effect on the handicapped. Statistical evidence, which petitioners do not dispute, indicated that in the 1979-1980 fiscal year, 27.4 percent of all handicapped users of hospital services who received Medicaid required more than 14 days of care, while only 7.8 percent of nonhandicapped users required more than 14 days of inpatient care.

Based on this evidence, respondents asserted that the reduction would violate §504 of the Rehabilitation Act of 1973 . . . [which] provides: "No otherwise qualified handicapped individual . . . shall, solely by reason of his handicap, be excluded from the participation in, be denied the benefits of, or be subjected to discrimination under any program or activity receiving Federal financial assistance." 29 U.S.C. §794. . . .

[The] major thrust of respondents' attack was directed at the use of any annual limitation on the number of inpatient days covered, for respondents acknowledged that, given the special needs of the handicapped for medical care, any such limitation was likely to disadvantage the handicapped disproportionately. . . . [T]he Medicaid programs of only ten states impose such restrictions.[10] Respondents therefore suggested that Tennessee follow these other states and do away with any limitation on the number of annual inpatient days covered. Instead, argued respondents, the state could limit the number of days of hospital coverage on a per-stay basis, with the number of covered days to vary depending on the recipient's illness (for example, fixing the number of days covered for an appendectomy); the period to be covered for each illness could then be set at a level that would keep Tennessee's Medicaid program as a whole within its budget. . . .

10. As of 1980 the average ceiling in those states was 37.6 days. Six states also limit the number of reimbursable days per admission, per spell of illness, or per benefit period.

The first question the parties urge on the Court is whether proof of discriminatory animus is always required to establish a violation of §504 and its implementing regulations, or whether federal law also reaches action by a recipient of federal funding that discriminates against the handicapped by effect rather than by design. . . . Discrimination against the handicapped was perceived by Congress to be most often the product, not of invidious animus, but rather of thoughtlessness and indifference—of benign neglect. . . . For example, elimination of architectural barriers was one of the central aims of the Act, yet such barriers were clearly not erected with the aim or intent of excluding the handicapped. . . .

At the same time, the position urged by respondents—that we interpret §504 to reach all action disparately affecting the handicapped—is also troubling. Because the handicapped typically are not similarly situated to the nonhandicapped, respondents' position would in essence require each recipient of federal funds first to evaluate the effect on the handicapped of every proposed action that might touch the interests of the handicapped, and then to consider alternatives for achieving the same objectives with less severe disadvantage to the handicapped. The formalization and policing of this process could lead to a wholly unwieldy administrative and adjudicative burden. . . .

To determine which disparate impacts §504 might make actionable, . . . [we must strike] a balance between the statutory rights of the handicapped to be integrated into society and the legitimate interests of federal grantees in preserving the integrity of their programs: While a grantee need not be required to make "fundamental" or "substantial" modifications to accommodate the handicapped, it may be required to make "reasonable" ones. . . .

[A]n otherwise qualified handicapped individual must be provided with meaningful access to the benefit that the grantee offers. The benefit itself, of course, cannot be defined in a way that effectively denies otherwise qualified handicapped individuals the meaningful access to which they are entitled; to assure meaningful access, reasonable accommodations in the grantee's program or benefit may have to be made. In this case, the 14-day limitation will not deny respondents meaningful access to Tennessee Medicaid services or exclude them from those services.

The new limitation does not invoke criteria that have a particular exclusionary effect on the handicapped; the reduction, neutral on its face, does not distinguish between those whose coverage will be reduced and those whose coverage will not on the basis of any test, judgment, or trait that the handicapped as a class are less capable of meeting or less likely of having. Moreover, it cannot be argued that "meaningful access" to state Medicaid services will be denied by the 14-day limitation on inpatient coverage; nothing in the record suggests that the handicapped in Tennessee will be unable to benefit meaningfully from the coverage they will receive under the 14-day rule.[22] The reduction in inpatient coverage will leave both handicapped and nonhandicapped Medicaid users with identical and effective hos-

22. The record does not contain any suggestion that the illnesses uniquely associated with the handicapped or occurring with greater frequency among them cannot be effectively treated, at least in part, with fewer than 14 days' coverage. In addition, the durational limitation does not apply to only particular handicapped conditions and takes effect regardless of the particular cause of hospitalization.

pital services fully available for their use, with both classes of users subject to the same durational limitation. . . .

To the extent respondents further suggest that their greater need for prolonged inpatient care means that, to provide meaningful access to Medicaid services, Tennessee must single out the handicapped for more than 14 days of coverage, the suggestion is simply unsound. At base, such a suggestion must rest on the notion that the benefit provided through state Medicaid programs is the amorphous objective of "adequate health care." But Medicaid programs do not guarantee that each recipient will receive that level of health care precisely tailored to his or her particular needs. Instead, the benefit provided through Medicaid is a particular package of health care services, such as 14 days of inpatient coverage. That package of services has the general aim of assuring that individuals will receive necessary medical care, but the benefit provided remains the individual services offered—not "adequate health care." [23] . . .

Section 504 does not require the state to alter this definition of the benefit being offered simply to meet the reality that the handicapped have greater medical needs. To conclude otherwise would be to find that the Rehabilitation Act requires states to view certain illnesses, i.e., those particularly affecting the handicapped, as more important than others and more worthy of cure through government subsidization. Nothing in the legislative history of the Act supports such a conclusion. Cf. Doe v. Colautti, 592 F.2d 704 (3d Cir. 1979) (state may limit covered-private-inpatient-psychiatric care to 60 days even though state sets no limit on duration of coverage for physical illnesses). Section 504 seeks to assure evenhanded treatment and the opportunity for handicapped individuals to participate in and benefit from programs receiving federal assistance. The Act does not, however, guarantee the handicapped equal results from the provision of state Medicaid, even assuming some measure of equality of health could be constructed. . . .

We turn next to respondents' alternative contention . . . that all annual durational limitations discriminate against the handicapped because (1) the effect of such limitations falls most heavily on the handicapped and because (2) this harm could be avoided by the choice of other Medicaid plans that would meet the state's budgetary constraints without disproportionately disadvantaging the handicapped. Viewed in this light, Tennessee's current plan is said to inflict a gratuitous harm on the handicapped that denies them meaningful access to Medicaid services. . . .

On the contrary, to require that the sort of broad-based distributive decision at issue in this case always be made in the way most favorable, or least disadvantageous, to the handicapped, even when the same benefit is meaningfully and equally offered to them, would be to impose a virtually unworkable requirement on state Medicaid administrators. Before taking any across-the-board action affecting Medicaid recipients, an analysis of the effect of the proposed change on the handicapped would have to be prepared. Presumably, that analysis would have to be further broken down by class of handicap—the change at issue here, for example, might be significantly less harmful to the blind, who use inpatient services only minimally, than to other subclasses of handicapped Medicaid recipients; the state

23. . . . [W]e express no opinion on whether annual limits on hospital care are in fact consistent with the Medicaid Act. . . .

would then have to balance the harms and benefits to various groups to determine, on balance, the extent to which the action disparately impacts the handicapped. In addition, respondents offer no reason that similar treatment would not have to be accorded other groups protected by statute or regulation from disparate-impact discrimination.

It should be obvious that administrative costs of implementing such a regime would be well beyond the accommodations that are required. . . . As a result, Tennessee need not redefine its Medicaid program to eliminate durational limitations on inpatient coverage, even if in doing so the State could achieve its immediate fiscal objectives in a way less harmful to the handicapped. . . .

WILL CLINTON'S PLAN BE FAIR?

Ronald Dworkin

New York Review of Books, Jan. 13, 1994

Some critics deny that health-care rationing is really necessary: They argue that if the waste and greed in the American health-care system were eliminated, we could save enough money to give men and women all the medical treatment that could benefit them. But . . . the greatest contribution to the rise in medical costs in recent decades has been the availability of new, high-tech means of diagnosis, like magnetic resonance imaging and new and very expensive techniques like organ transplants and, on the horizon, monoclonal-antibody treatment for cancer. . . . Many politicians and some doctors say that much of the new technology is "unnecessary" or "wasteful." They do not mean that it provides no benefit at all. They mean that its benefit is too limited to justify its cost, and this is an argument for rationing, not an argument that rationing is unnecessary. . . . So we cannot . . . avoid the question of justice: What is "appropriate" medical care depends on what it would be unfair to withhold on the grounds that it costs too much. That question has been missing from the public debate. . . .

For millennia doctors have paid lip service, at least, to an ideal of justice in medicine which I shall call the rescue principle. It has two connected parts. The first holds that life and health are, as René Descartes put it, chief among all goods: Everything else is of lesser importance and must be sacrificed for them. The second insists that health care must be distributed on grounds of equality: that even in a society in which wealth is very unequal and equality is otherwise scorned, no one must be denied the medical care he needs just because he is too poor to afford it. These are understandable, even noble, ideals. They are grounded in a shared human understanding of the horror of pain, and, beyond that, of the indispensability of life and health to everything else we do. The rescue principle is so ancient, so intuitively attractive, and so widely supported in political rhetoric, that it might easily be thought to supply the right standard for answering questions about rationing. . . .

In past centuries, however, there was not so huge a gap between the rhetoric of the rescue principle and what it was medically possible for a community to do. But now that science has created so many vastly expensive forms of medical care, it is preposterous that a community should treat longer life as a good that it must provide at any cost—even one that would make the lives of its people barely worth living. . . .

The rescue principle does have something helpful, though negative, to say about the other question of justice, which is how health care should be distributed. It says that if rationing is necessary, it should not be done, as it now largely is in the United States, on the basis of money. But we need more positive advice: What should the basis of rationing be? The egalitarian impulse of the principle suggests that medical care should be distributed according to need. But what does that mean—how is need to be measured? Does someone "need" an operation that might save his life but is highly unlikely to do so? Is someone's need for life-saving treatment affected by the quality his life would have if the treatment were successful? Does the age of patient matter—does someone need or deserve treatment less at 70 than a younger age? Why? How should we balance the need of many people for relief from pain or incapacity against the need of fewer people for life-saving care? At one point the procedures of an Oregon commission appointed to establish medical priorities ranked tooth-capping ahead of appendectomy, because so many teeth can be capped for the price of one operation. Why was that so clearly a mistake? . . .

■ HEALTH CARE RATIONING AND DISABILITY RIGHTS

Philip G. Peters, Jr.

70 Ind. L.J. 491 (1995)

. . . Any criterion suggested for rationing health care will be controversial. The stakes are high and no popular or ethical consensus has emerged. But allocation decisions are omnipresent and their continuation is inevitable. . . . Americans have never been willing to pay for all the health care that is of any conceivable benefit, nor are they likely to do so in the future. Unfortunately, the existing mechanisms for deciding who receives what care are blunt and often irrational or unfair, reflecting the influence of wealth, employment, habit, cost, and power. . . . Common sense tells us to give priority to services that do the most good. As a result, an approach which would eliminate only the least beneficial or least cost-effective treatments has considerable potential appeal. It offers both the promise of maximizing health care outcomes from limited resources and the surface allure of scientific objectivity and nonpartisan neutrality. . . .

But rationing the least effective care has a dark side beneath its veneer of objectivity. Any health care allocation scheme which attempts to maximize health care outcomes by giving priority to the most effective treatments has the potential to disfavor disabled patients and others, such as the elderly and the frail, whose quality of life is most impaired or whose conditions are most resistant to cure. As a result, the use of effectiveness criteria to allocate health resources may be challenged as violating society's commitment to equality in general, and to protection of those with the greatest need in particular.

The resolution of this conflict between efficiency and equality has dramatic implications for health policy. . . . It arises whenever effectiveness or cost-effectiveness is used by health care providers or insurers to determine which treatments to provide or insure. Those instances range from bedside decisions by clinicians to macroallocation decisions by benefit plans about coverage of conditions such as AIDS, infertility, or mental illness. In each setting, allocations based on medical utility have the potential to disfavor some patients on the basis of their disability. . . .

I. [Effectiveness Measures and the Oregon Experiment]

Health economists have worked for decades on methodologies for calculating both the effectiveness and the cost-effectiveness of health care expenditures.[11] Originally utilized to compare the value of different treatments for the same disease, these methods were later used to compare the cost-effectiveness of treatments for different diseases. Cost-effectiveness calculations have the appeal of incorporating outcomes research, patient preferences, and expected costs into a rational and potentially sophisticated scheme for maximizing health care outcomes from the available resources. . . .

Theoretically, at least, calculating the effectiveness of a medical service is relatively straightforward. This calculation involves both an estimate of the likely outcomes and an assignment of value to those outcomes. The value assigned to an outcome is determined by the impact which the treatment is expected to have on a patient's quality of life. That value is then adjusted to reflect the probability and duration of the expected benefit. The product of this calculus is a single unit which expresses the number and quality of additional years that the treatment is likely to confer. These outcome units have been called both Quality-Adjusted Life Years ("QALYs") and Well Years. . . .

The theoretical value of these calculations cannot be overstated. They provide a common unit of measurement which permits treatments for different diseases to be compared on the basis of their expected benefit or their cost-effectiveness.[16] Using QALYs or their equivalents, comparisons can be made between such disparate treatments as AZT [for AIDS], autologous bone marrow transplants, infertility treatments, mammography screening, early CT scans for head pain, and heroic care for patients in persistent vegetative states. . . .

As the health economist David Hadorn has emphasized, reliable cost-effectiveness data will help health care providers minimize human suffering to the maximum

11. American researchers initially derived the methodology from operations research in engineering and mathematics, using it in the health care setting to measure the tradeoff between survival and quality of life that is implicated by some treatment choices such as conservative care versus aggressive care. The British, most notably Alan Williams, then borrowed the concept as a way of suggesting priorities in their national health care system.

16. . . . John Rawls includes several helpful illustrations of comparisons based on cost-effectiveness:

> For example, a patient with severe arthritis of the hip who is unable to work and is in severe distress scores a quality of life of 0.7. . . . His expectation of life of ten years is reduced to seven quality adjusted life years. Successful hip replacement, by eliminating disability and distress, restores 3 QALYs to his total, at an average cost of pounds sterling 750 per QALY.
>
> Another example is a patient with renal failure undergoing renal dialysis twice a week in hospital for a year. He is unable to work and suffers moderate distress with a quality of life of 0.9. However, hemodialysis is life-saving, so every year adds 0.9 to the number of QALYs he would otherwise enjoy, at a cost of pounds sterling 14000 per QALY.

John Rawls, Castigating QALYs, 15 J. Med. Ethics 143, 144-145 (1989).

extent possible with the resources society allocates to health care.[17] . . . Current insurance and clinical practices often make the same kinds of calculations regarding treatment value and cost, albeit in a more intuitive manner. . . . QALYs can help improve the process, making it more rational and, therefore, more just. . . .

QALYs may also help health decisionmakers to avoid what David Eddy has called "rationing by meat ax." By excluding the least effective treatments for conditions that ordinarily are covered by insurance, savings could be generated to fund more comprehensive coverage of treatments for conditions such as mental health that are typically excluded or restricted. Blanket restrictions on treatments for infertility or mental health, for example, could be replaced by narrower exclusions of only those treatments which are least effective.

In addition, the exclusion of whole groups of uninsured persons from programs such as Medicaid could be replaced by the exclusion of marginally effective care. Oregon, for example, replaced a Medicaid system in which a six-year-old child was eligible when a seven-year-old was not, in which pregnant women had coverage but other women did not, and in which single adults with children were covered but those without children or with a spouse were excluded. In its place, the state has instituted a system [described below] that provides protection for [all people below the poverty line] by prioritizing the treatments covered.[24] . . . This explicit attention to the difficult choices is in marked contrast to current practices, such as those of physicians who use neutral terms such as "futility" to mask intuitive judgments about the value of treatment to the patient. . . .

But measurement of medical effectiveness also presents serious methodological and ethical problems which must be surmounted before its use expands. The methodological problems arise both from the difficulty of obtaining adequate data about outcomes, benefits, and costs and also from predictable issues of study design. Problems of this kind contributed to the failure of Oregon's initial attempt to prioritize medical treatments entirely on the basis of net benefit. . . .

In order to calculate a treatment's medical effectiveness, analysts must estimate its probable outcome and then place a value on that outcome. Both steps could disfavor disabled patients. When outcomes are taken into account, patients with preexisting disabilities, such as diabetes, cancer, or pulmonary disease, could be disfavored because they often have more difficulty fighting unrelated illnesses (comorbidity) than patients who are otherwise healthy.[36] For example, diabetes reduces the probable

17. David C. Hadorn, Setting Health Care Priorities in Oregon: Cost-Effectiveness Meets the Rule of Rescue, 265 JAMA 2218, at 2225 (1991) (describing the original Oregon methodology and the modifications undertaken before submission to the federal government for approval). . . .

24. Compare the approach of Missouri, which spent nearly $1 million keeping Nancy Cruzan alive in a persistent vegetative state, while providing Medicaid for only 40 percent of its citizens below the poverty level. Leonard M. Fleck, Just Health Care Rationing: A Democratic Decisionmaking Approach, 140 U. Pa. L. Rev. 1597, 1611 (1992).

36. See, e.g., David Orentlicher, Rationing and the Americans with Disabilities Act, 271 JAMA 308, 310 (1994) (recognizing that patients with pulmonary disease are poor candidates for coronary bypass surgery). In another example, an HMO denied payment for a $170,000 liver transplant requested by an e-antigen positive hepatitis-B patient due

effectiveness of some treatments for serious heart ailments. Unchecked alcoholism, another disability, could interfere with the success of organ transplantation. . . .

In addition, seriously disabled patients could be disfavored when values are placed on treatment outcomes. For example, QALY use disfavors lifesaving care for patients who are expected to be disabled after treatment, because saving the life of a disabled person with an impaired quality of life will theoretically generate fewer quality-adjusted life years than saving the life of a person whose quality of life after treatment would be better. . . .

The chance that disabled patients will fare unfavorably in QALY calculations is further accentuated by the risk that the scales used to measure quality of life will unfairly underestimate the quality of life of disabled persons. This was precisely the federal government's criticism of the Oregon quality of life measurements. Yet, until the Oregon plan was submitted for federal government approval, no public attention had been called to the discriminatory potential of prioritization on the basis of medical effectiveness. Although the Oregon plan was vilified on other grounds (principally that only poor people would be asked to make sacrifices to help fund an expansion of health care coverage for other poor people), virtually no public debate on disability rights had occurred. As a result, the [first] Bush administration's rejection of the plan because of discrimination against patients with disabilities surprised most observers and caused some speculation that the administration had simply used the disability rights issue to derail a proposal which it found objectionable for other reasons. . . .

Oregon's initial ranking of treatments . . . was based on a pure cost-effectiveness analysis, but problems with that list[44] induced the Oregon Health Services Commission to abandon that list and produce another one . . . using a more intuitive,

---

to the high rate of reinfection of e-antigen positive patients and the liver shortage. Barnett v. Kaiser Found. Health Plan, Inc., Health Care Facility Mgmt. (CCH) ¶22,594 (N.D. Cal. 1993). The HMO's eight-member advisory board had concluded that transplantation was not an appropriate medical treatment for the patient's condition. The federal district court ruled that the HMO had not abused its discretion in considering this factor, even though transplantation might be the patient's only chance of survival. The disability rights laws were apparently not addressed.

44. . . . In David Eddy's view, Oregon's inability to estimate accurately either costs or benefits precluded reliance on its initial list. Categories of services and outcomes were defined too broadly. For example, "trouble speaking" could range from mild lisp to mutism. Duration of treatment benefits was poorly differentiated. Cost data were incomplete or inaccurate. And the list generated serious doubts whether the values assigned to treatment outcomes, especially lifesaving treatments, had been accurately measured. David M. Eddy, Oregon's Methods: Did Cost-Effectiveness Analysis Fail?, 266 JAMA 2135 (1991); David M. Eddy, Oregon's Plan: Should It Be Approved?, 266 JAMA 2439 (1991).

Counter-intuitive rankings resulted from these problems. Reportedly, "burn over large areas of the body" scored the same as an "upset stomach." Michael Astrue, then-general counsel of the Department of Health and Human Services, was startled that treatments for ectopic pregnancies and appendicitis were ranked below some dental caps and splints for temporomandibular joint disorder. . . . Unwillingness to accept the implications of cost-effectiveness analysis, especially for the prioritization of noncritical care over life-extending care, may also partially explain the adverse reaction to this list. . . .

multifactorial methodology. Nonetheless, considerations of effectiveness continued to play a crucial role . . . at three junctures. First, the Commission divided all treatments into one of seventeen different categories and then ranked these categories. A sampling of the categories illustrates the methodology: "acute fatal, treatment prevents death with full recovery" (ranked #1); "maternity care" (#2); "acute fatal, treatment prevents death without full recovery" (#3); "comfort care" (#7); "acute nonfatal, treatment causes return to previous health state" (#10); and "infertility services" (#15). These rankings gave priority to treatments which produced complete cures over those which ordinarily produce only partial recovery. In this way, the Commission retained a blunt measure of effectiveness in its ranking process. The Commission also considered cost-effectiveness as one of many factors used to create and rank these categories.

Second, the Commission used QALYs to rank treatments within the 17 categories.[51] Third and finally, the Commissioners reviewed the resulting list and adjusted some of the rankings using their "professional judgments and their interpretation of the community values." The Commissioners imposed a "reasonableness" test upon themselves, taking into account effectiveness and cost along with other factors such as public health impact, incidence of condition, and social costs. The result was a ranking of 709 treatments of which 587 were to be funded in the first year. . . .

[T]he Department of Health and Human Services ("HHS") announced that Oregon had been denied a waiver [of the usual Medicaid coverage requirements] because its plan violated the Americans with Disabilities Act ("ADA"). . . . HHS specifically identified two instances in which disabilities had been impermissibly taken into account: (1) the ranking of alcoholic cirrhosis of the liver (#690) below other cirrhoses (#366) and (2) the ranking of extremely low birth weight babies (#708) below heavier babies (#22).

Oregon denied that it had violated the ADA, but nevertheless complied with HHS's demands. Approval was not granted until Oregon had eliminated quality of life data from its formal methodology and had abandoned the separate classification of alcoholic cirrhosis and low birth weight babies. In addition, the newly elected Clinton administration insisted that Oregon no longer disfavor infertility treatments. In March, 1993, the Oregon Commission approved a new list which was based first on mortality and then, as a tie-breaker, on cost considerations. It was then adjusted by the Commission to reflect community values, such as a preference for preventive services and a dislike for medically ineffective care. . . .

51. Benefits were measured using Dr. Robert M. Kaplan's Quality of Well-Being ("QWB") scale. Using the results of a random telephone poll of 1,001 Oregon households in which respondents were asked to rank 23 symptoms and 6 levels of functional impairment, the Commission assigned a value to various states of health, such as requiring a wheelchair or having severe burns. The benefits associated with each treatment were then calculated by using the values for the various outcomes provided by the telephone survey and weighting those values to reflect the probability of their occurrence. Expected outcomes were ascertained by polling practitioners. Outcomes (such as death or return to former health) were estimated five years after treatment. Net benefit (QWB) scores were derived by comparing the QWB score without treatment to the QWB score with treatment. The Commission multiplied the expected QWB by the duration of the benefit (thereby obtaining a measure of quality-adjusted life years or QALYs). In most cases, duration was the patient's life expectancy.

This exchange between Oregon and the federal government has dramatic implications for health policy. Oregon's capitulation has cast a shadow over similar endeavors by other states. In its wake, considerable confusion exists about the permissible role of effectiveness in allocating health resources. . . . Alexander Morgan Capron, an . . . advocate of rationing, was . . . dire in his assessment. "As some form of rationing is an inevitable part of all health insurance," he concluded, "the ADA roadblock to rational prioritization of services by their expected benefit should be of grave concern to us all."

Was the federal government correct? Exactly what limits do the disability rights laws place on the use of effectiveness criteria? Answering these questions requires a basic understanding of the disability rights laws.

II. Federal Disability Rights Law

Two federal statutes protect disabled individuals from improper discrimination in health care decisionmaking: The Rehabilitation Act of 1973 and the more recent Americans with Disabilities Act of 1990 ("ADA"). . . . Although the ADA is much more detailed than the Rehabilitation Act and the wording of the various titles of the ADA are slightly different, the basic paradigm of the two federal laws protecting disability rights can be briefly summarized. Section 504 of the Rehabilitation Act bars discrimination by any program receiving federal financial assistance or any executive agency against an "otherwise qualified" individual with a disability "by reason of her or his disability." The ADA extends this prohibition against discrimination "on the basis of" disability to state programs and private entities that do not receive federal funding.

Federal law defines disabled persons as individuals who have a "physical or mental impairment which substantially limits a major life activity," "who have a record of such an impairment," or who are "regarded as having such an impairment." The regulations list examples such as blindness, mental retardation, emotional illness, cancer, heart disease, and HIV infection. . . .

Because functional impairment may affect a person's qualifications for some benefits, the laws governing disability rights permit consideration of a person's disability if the condition legitimately affects that person's ability to meet the essential eligibility requirements. This basic structure is quite different from civil rights legislation governing race because race is presumed to be irrelevant.

While acknowledging that disabilities are sometimes relevant, Congress also recognized that their consideration would often result in the exclusion of disabled persons who could become qualified with modest modifications of policies or practices. To prevent this, Congress required that a reasonable effort be made to accommodate the needs of disabled persons before concluding that they are ineligible. By conferring on people with disabilities this right to affirmative assistance, Congress endorsed, at least in a limited way, an egalitarian approach to distributive justice which allocates extra resources for those persons with the greatest need. . . . To summarize this basic paradigm, a disabled person is qualified to receive health benefits or services if, with reasonable accommodation, she is able to meet the "essential" or "necessary" eligibility criteria. . . .

When the issue is joined, as it was in Oregon, the statutory terms *essential* and *necessary* seem sufficiently elastic to permit courts to consider whether medical utility is a permissible basis for disfavoring disabled patients. In effect, courts would be deciding whether the objective of maximizing health outcomes is an "essential" program objective within the meaning of the equal opportunity laws. . . . HHS did exactly this in responding to the Oregon waiver request. . . .

While the legal status of rationing based on effectiveness is still uncertain, underwriting exclusions based on anticipated cost have express congressional sanction. In the ADA, Congress authorized benefits plans to engage in "the legitimate classification of risk." As a result, plans remain free to consider how various disabilities influence a person's risk of death or illness. This exclusion permits risk-bearing health plans (but not necessarily practicing physicians) to consider the anticipated cost of treating various disabilities. However, the statutory exemption for underwriting practices does not appear to sanction the use of QALYs or other measures of a given treatment's effectiveness. Unlike restrictions based on underwriting risks, eligibility restrictions based on effectiveness are not based on the risk of subscriber illness and its predicted cost. They are based, instead, on predicted outcomes. Patients whose care is relatively ineffective are not necessarily any more costly or financially risky than other patients. . . . As a result, only the cost portion of cost-effectiveness analysis has clear statutory blessing, and even then only when it is part of an underwriting process. . . .

Until the courts rule on this issue, it is possible . . . that employers will be flatly prohibited from adopting health benefits plans that discriminate on the basis of disability for nonunderwriting reasons. . . . [To overcome this objection, employers and insurers will need to establish that] the use of effectiveness criteria is vital to the goal of maximizing health outcomes from fixed resources. . . .

■ MAKING MEDICAL SPENDING DECISIONS: THE LAW, ETHICS, AND ECONOMICS OF RATIONING MECHANISMS*
Mark A. Hall

When we are ill, we desperately want our doctors to do everything within their power to heal us, regardless of the costs. Medical technology has advanced so far, however, that literal adherence to this credo for every human frailty would consume much more than our country's entire economic output,[13] and, in the process, cause economic collapse. . . . Any workable system for financing and delivering health care must face the fundamental problem of how best to allocate limited medical resources among competing beneficial uses. Someone, somewhere must decide which items of potential medical benefit are not worth the cost. . . .

It is sometimes thought that medical advances will eventually reduce medical spending by making people fundamentally healthier, but this assumption is

13. The U.S. gross domestic product per capita is about $23,000. To see how easy it would be to spend this amount each year on maximal health care, consider that it costs about this same amount on average simply to incarcerate a prisoner (not counting the costs of building new prison space). See also Lamm, R.D., "Rationing of Health Care: Inevitable and Desirable," 140 U. Pa. L. Rev. 1511, 1512 (1992) ("[A] French study asked how much it would cost to give all the health care that is 'beneficial' to each citizen. The answer was five-and-one-half times the French gross national product.").

equally flawed. Medical needs are inherently limitless because aging and illness are a permanent feature of the human condition. Much beneficial medical care results in people living to an older age where they are more frail and succumb to more chronic and expensive diseases. This does not mean we should suppress these innovations, only that the drive to conquer all forms of illness is ultimately doomed to failure. The course of history over this century demonstrates that, as medicine advances, so do both medical needs and medical spending.

For these various reasons, most policy analysts recognize that rationing in some form is desirable and inevitable. Every spending decision is necessarily a rationing decision simply because resources devoted to one person or one use are not available for someone or something else. If wants are limitless and resources are finite, it is impossible to maintain that rationing is avoidable in all its forms.

We have always rationed health care resources on a massive scale, only according to irrational and unjust principles.[14] Presently, we ration health care by denying it to those unfortunate individuals who lack insurance either because their employer does not provide it or because their level of poverty has not yet fallen to the desperate level required for Medicaid eligibility. At the same time, we heavily subsidize health insurance for the upper and middle classes through a regressive tax policy that excludes from an employee's income the value of insurance premiums contributed by employers. Moreover, for those who are fully insured, we devote vast resources to save lives and restore health once an illness or accident occurs, but we spend only microscopic amounts in comparison on basic safety, health education, and health prevention measures. . . .

The haphazard and unprincipled basis on which rationing presently occurs effectively rebuts another argument raised by critics of rationing, namely, that rationing should occur only under numerous, morally demanding conditions that presently do not exist. These critics impose unattainably Utopian prerequisites to rationing, such as developing ethically unassailable and scientifically valid rationing criteria, insisting on their strict egalitarian application throughout all strata of society, and first eliminating all wasteful spending, both within medicine and elsewhere in society. These demands ignore the fact that any systematically thought-out rationing scheme, however flawed, is far superior to the thoughtless and inhumane way in which many uninsured people are now treated. A more considered form of resource allocation is the first step, not the last, toward social equity and broad-based reform. Only with some better approach to rationing will minimally acceptable access to health care become affordable for everyone.

Despite these many powerful arguments, it is still controversial to speak in terms of rationing health care. In order to avoid drawing the fire of those who oppose any use of this term, I will instead lean towards the more neutral terminology of resource allocation or spending decisions. I will not entirely refrain from the "R" word, however. Its emotional baggage can help to dramatize the pervasive necessity of making medical spending decisions. Despite their differing emotional content, both rationing and allocation can fairly be used in the generic sense that

14. Fuchs, V.R., "The 'Rationing' of Medical Care," 311 New Eng. J. Med. 1572 (1984); Rosenblatt, R.E., "Rationing 'Normal' Health Care: The Hidden Legal Issues," 59 Texas L. Rev. 1401-1420 (1981).

refers to either implicit or explicit denial of marginally beneficial medical treatment out of consideration for its cost. . . .

[R]egardless of the overall structure of a health care financing and delivery system, [w]hether it is regulatory or competitive, public or private, we are plagued by two basic issues: (1) Who should decide what care is not worth the costs, and (2) what criteria of benefit should be used to make this determination? The second of these problems is the one that has received more attention to date. Numerous volumes have been written on questions such as whether the short supply of transplantable organs should be distributed based simply on random draw or who has been waiting the longest, or instead based on elaborate concepts of medical need or medical benefit.[15] This literature also gives extensive thought to routine medical technologies. It explores whether medical resources generally should be rationed according to age or instead according to some more quantitative formula for effectiveness or value. Others before me have debated at length whether medical benefit should be defined by the number of lives saved, the length of life, the quality of life, or some more intermediate goal such as diagnostic certainty, and whether judgments about people's social worth can be prevented from tainting these concepts.

These are tremendously fascinating and important questions deserving of continuing inquiry, but they avoid what I see as a more fundamental question: Who should be the rationing decisionmaker? . . . [M]edical sociologist David Mechanic [f]irst articulated that health care spending decisions can be made through three fundamentally different mechanisms. Cost-sensitive treatment decisions can be made by patients, by physicians, or by third parties—primarily private and governmental insurers but also various regulatory or review organizations. Elsewhere in our economy, cost/benefit trade-offs are usually made through the purchasing decisions of individual consumers. For example, nutrition resources are allocated at both the macro and micro levels through the aggregation of countless individual decisions of how much food to buy, of what quality, and from what source. This simple market mechanism is not generally available or desirable for health care because of the unpredictability of illness and the complexities of medical judgment. . . . [W]e purchase insurance rather than pay out of pocket because we want to protect ourselves from the uncertain costs of health care and the anxiety of making spending decisions under the strain of serious illness. Moreover, even without insurance, patients make few of their medical decisions themselves because the complexity of treatment compels us to delegate extensive authority to our doctors. . . .

15. Leading general discussions are found in AMA Council in Ethical and Judicial Affairs, "Ethical Considerations in the Allocation of Organs and Other Scarce Medical Resources Among Patients," 155 Archives Internal Med. 29 (1995); R.H Blank, Rationing Medicine (1988); Churchill, L.R., Rationing Health Care in America: Perceptions and Principles of Justice (1987); J.F. Kilner, Who Lives? Who Dies?: Ethical Criteria in Patient Selection (1990); G.R. Winslow, Triage and Justice (1982). An early general discussion is contained in Note, "Scarce Medical Resources," 69 Colum. L. Rev. 620 (1969). A more recent treatment is the cogent and comprehensive analysis by E. Elhauge, "Allocating Health Care Morally," 82 Cal. L. Rev. 1449 (1994). For a thorough discussion of rationing criteria used commonly throughout society, see generally J. Elster, Local Justice: How Institutions Allocate Scarce Goods and Necessary Burdens (1992).

Insurers, either private or governmental, can make medical spending decisions through cost-sensitive rules about what treatment they will pay for. Until recently, this has seldom happened, but in 1994 Oregon became the first state to attempt explicit rule-based rationing for all of medicine. Oregon ranked over 600 condition-treatment pairings (e.g., surgery for appendicitis) according to their medical effectiveness, for purposes of allocating limited Medicaid funding. Elsewhere in this country, efforts are under way to develop a host of much more detailed and nuanced clinical practice guidelines, which could also serve as rule-based tools for third-party resource allocation. In addition to insurers' payment rules, spending decisions can be imposed by other parties who are similarly outside the doctor-patient relationship. Courts, citizen groups or other ideal democratic processes, and physician administrators who review the work of treating doctors are each able to set limits or give directions on how medical resources are spent. . . .

The third fundamental alternative for allocating medical spending authority is for physicians to incorporate cost considerations into their clinical judgment. Authorizing physicians to make cost/benefit trade-off decisions at the bedside differs from centralized, rule-based rationing because it individualizes spending decisions to the circumstances of each patient, and it operates through professional incentives rather than bureaucratic authority. Bedside rationing, however, fundamentally compromises physicians' role-based ethic, which . . . traditionally requires doctors to provide all care that offers any benefit, regardless of its cost. Physician bedside rationing is rendered even more controversial by the use of financial incentives to motivate doctors' performance. . . .

As can be seen from this summary, most of this book is taken up with what Edward Rubin [infra] terms a "microanalysis of social institutions," one that seeks to assess the relative strengths, weaknesses, and characteristics of alternative mechanisms for allocating health care resources, drawing from both political economics and social theory. . . . Accordingly, I will not be wedded to a particular analytical framework or ideological perspective. I will undertake a pragmatic analytical critique, one that seeks to clarify for each rationing mechanism its basic rationale, its inherent limits, the evidence supporting both views, the potential for harm or manipulation, and the accommodations needed to make it work.

RATIONING HEALTH CARE IN BRITAIN AND THE UNITED STATES

Leonard J. Nelson, III

7 J. Health & Biomed. L. 175 (2011)

Rationing is a "dirty word," "a code word for immoral, inappropriate, or greedy," and "a four letter word." And not surprisingly, rationing was at the forefront of the recent debate in the United States over health care reform. Former Governor Sarah Palin's Facebook page allegation that the Democrat's health care reform legislation included "death panels," which would ration care for the sick and elderly, was later named "lie of the year" by the fact checkers at Politifacts.com, but it did garner significant attention. . . .

Although [Sarah Palin's] claims are "sensationalistic," they draw attention to a central truth, i.e., . . . that rationing will have to be a part of any publicly subsidized program for the provision of health care to maintain fiscal sustainability. . . . Dr. [Ezekiel Emanuel, former director of bioethics at the NIH,] identified three levels of health care allocation decisions with respect to government health care decisions. First, macro-allocation decisions determine how much of the gross national product ("GNP") to spend on health care services as opposed to national defense, transportation, etc. Second, there is an intermediate level where a determination will be made as to the basic package of health care services that all citizens are entitled to receive. Third, micro-allocation decisions about which patients are eligible to receive particular services. At the intermediate level, he suggested the need for transparency in the form of "public forums to deliberate about which health services should be considered basic and should be socially guaranteed." . . .

Medicare is already engaged in stealth rationing through the Centers for Medicare and Medicaid Services' the use of National Coverage Determinations ("NCDs"), in which CMS refuses to cover expensive new technologies; CMS nevertheless denies taking cost into account in making decisions relating to coverage. . . . [I]t is unlikely that Congress will give CMS the [express] power to ration health care using a cost-effectiveness analysis. . . . As long as Medicare is a service benefit program, it will be very difficult, politically, to control costs. . . .

[D]uring the debate over health care reform, President Obama spoke of the need for a "very difficult democratic conversation" about health care at the end of life, even expressing doubt about whether his own grandmother should have been given a hip replacement when she was terminally ill. But he also acknowledged that, "It is very difficult to imagine the country making those decisions just through the normal political channels. And that's part of why you have to have some independent group that can give you guidance." . . .

The ongoing debate about the possible role of comparative effectiveness research in health care reform illustrates the political difficulty of rationing health care. . . . The 2009 federal stimulus legislation created [an agency to conduct comparative effectiveness research, which PPACA renamed] the Patient Centered Outcomes Research Institute ("PCORI"). . . . Perhaps in response to concerns about rationing, PPACA expressly precludes the Secretary of the Health and Human Services ("HHS") from relying solely on comparative effectiveness research to deny coverage or from using PCORI sponsored comparative effectiveness research "in a manner that treats extending the life of an elderly, disabled, or terminally ill individual as of lower value than extending the life of an individual who is younger, nondisabled, or not terminally ill." . . . The Secretary is also precluded from using comparative effectiveness "with the intent to discourage an individual from choosing a health care treatment based on how the individual values the tradeoff between extending the length of their life and the risk of disability." . . . [T]hese provisions have been interpreted to prohibit the PCORI "from developing or using cost-per-QALY thresholds," and these provisions have been decried as reflecting "a certain xenophobia toward the kinds of approaches used in Britain, where the National Institute of Health and Clinical Excellence ["NICE"] makes recommendations about technologies and services on the basis of cost-per-QALY thresholds." . . .

[PPACA's] continued reliance on employment-based insurance may make it more difficult to impose rationing in the Medicare program because the standard of care for all is influenced by the care provided through relatively generous employment-based plans. . . . With the exception of "grandfathered" plans, all small group and individual plans offered both within and outside of the exchanges will have to offer at least the "essential health benefits" package. This package is supposed to include the elements of a typical employer plan. [Also, the statute forbids designing "benefits in ways that discriminate against individuals because of their age, disability, or expected length of life" or that are "subject to denial . . . on the basis of the individuals' age or expected length of life or of the individuals' present or predicted disability, degree of medical dependency, or quality of life."] . . .

As noted in the Washington Post, defining the "essential health benefits" is an important and difficult task; "Draw up a package that is too bare-bones and millions of Americans could be deprived of meaningful health coverage when they need it most—undercutting a central goal of the health care law. Add in too many expensive benefits and premiums could spike to unaffordable levels." . . .

PPACA [also] establishes the Independent Payment Advisory Board ("IPAB") for the purpose of reducing the per capita rate of growth in Medicare spending. The board is to be composed of fifteen full-time members who are health care experts drawn from various fields. Beginning in 2014, IPAB is required to make annual recommendations to Congress to reduce per capita growth rates when these costs exceed a targeted per capita growth rate that the Chief Actuary of CMS sets. These recommendations will be implemented unless subsequent congressional action blocks them. Notably, a 3/5 vote in the Senate is required to change the IPAB recommendations. But there are some significant limitations on the nature of these recommendations. PPACA provides that these recommendations, "shall not include any recommendation to ration health care, . . . increase Medicare beneficiary cost-sharing[,] . . . or otherwise restrict benefits or modify eligibility criteria." Prior to 2020, the recommendation also cannot include cuts in payment rates for hospitals and suppliers, which PPACA already targets.

. . . Michael Tanner, a health policy expert at the Cato Institute, [notes] that in light of the restrictions on IPAB, it . . . "will end up as neutered as previous attempts to impose fiscal discipline on government health care programs." With all the constraints on its actions, and the possibilities for Congress to void any cuts proposed, it is unlikely IPAB will be successful in reducing costs in the Medicare program. . . .

Health policy experts customarily refer to the health care "Iron Triangle." . . . The three angles of the triangle or triad are cost, access, and quality. It has been observed that, "increasing the performance of the health care system along any one of these dimensions can compromise one or both of the other dimensions, regardless of the amount that is spent on health care." . . . The debate over the impact of PPACA on Medicare costs illustrates the constraints of the iron triangle. . . . While in theory it may be possible to increase health care access, reduce costs, and improve quality, in practice it is virtually impossible. The reduction of costs in public programs without endangering aggregate quality would have to be based on across the board rigorous application of cost-effectiveness analysis that would result in the denial of beneficial treatments to individuals. It is unlikely that Congress has the political will to impose such a regime. . . . Rationing is certainly the third rail of American politics, and the cost controls in PPACA may not be sufficient to save us from ourselves.

Notes: Health Care Rationing and Disability Discrimination

1. *Medical Effectiveness Measures.* It is important to distinguish among ordinary medical effectiveness, comparative effectiveness, cost-effectiveness, and cost-benefit analysis. Ordinary effectiveness determines simply whether a medical procedure

works at all. Comparative effectiveness asks whether it works better than another method for the same condition. Cost-effectiveness analysis also asks how much it costs to achieve an increment in health improvement. And finally, cost-benefit analysis asks whether an effectiveness improvement is actually worth what it costs.

QALYs were devised so that effectiveness can be judged based on quality of life rather than simply number of lives or years of life saved. A generic unit of health improvement also allows comparisons between totally different treatments and disease conditions, such as determining whether prenatal care yields more medical benefit than liver transplants. That kind of comparative cost analysis can help to determine the best use of limited funds, but it cannot tell us what total health expenditures should be, that is, whether to do *both* prenatal care and liver transplants, or *neither* and instead spend the money on education or housing. If that decision is to be made quantitatively, it requires a cost-benefit analysis, which compares the cost of medical procedures with their benefit in terms of dollars. This is obviously much more controversial since it requires that a value be placed on human life and suffering.

None of the techniques surveyed by Philip Peters goes this far. They only ask, comparatively, whether one benefit is greater than another, not whether the expenditure is worth it at all. But, in adopting the rubric of "comparative effectiveness" rather than "cost effectiveness" in the Affordable Care Act, did Congress mean to say that costs may not be considered at all? For example, it has been estimated that the cost of administering Pap smears, which detect cervical cancer, is roughly $5,000 per additional year of life expectancy for testing every three years but $200,000-400,000 per year of life saved for annual testing. Should insurers, either public or private, be required to fund annual testing? Which would you choose as a patient paying out of pocket? See Sarah Feldman, How Often Should We Screen for Cervical Cancer?, 349 New Eng. J. Med. 1495 (2003) (recommending testing every three years after a series of negative one-year exams).

During the heat of national debate over the Affordable Care Act, political opponents raised yet another storm of controversy over a government blue ribbon panel that happened to issue a recommendation about limiting routine mammography screening to every two years for women over 50, rather than every year and starting at age 40, for women with no prior symptoms or family history of breast cancer. The panel's rationale was to reduce the medical harms from "false positive" results that lead to needless biopsies and surgeries. But, it was also influenced by studies indicating that it would cost $340,000 or more per QALY gained to screen more frequently or at younger ages. See John Schousboe et al., Personalizing Mammography by Breast Density and Other Risk Factors for Breast Cancer, 144 Ann. Intern. Med. 10 (2011).

2. *Comparative Institutional Analysis.* The approach Mark Hall takes to analyzing health care rationing is known as "comparative institutional analysis" or as "legal process theory." It is an approach that is well suited to analyzing numerous legal and public policy issues, in health care and elsewhere, and so it is employed throughout this casebook. Its focus is not so much on what is the correct answer, but on what are the best (or least worst) institutions and processes for arriving at an answer. This approach compares the strengths and weaknesses of various institutions and processes within the judicial system, the private sector, the public sector, the nonprofit sector, and professional groups, among others. For further discussion, see sources cited in note 12.

3. *The Scope of Disability Discrimination Laws.* The potential impact of disability discrimination law on many aspects of medical decisionmaking has come to light only gradually. Here, the primary issue is what constitutes discrimination. How far might courts and agencies actually go in micromanaging medically informed decisions by covered institutions?

Most commentators believe, for example, that it would clearly violate the ADA and §504 for an employer to exclude or limit coverage for AIDS, and this is the interpretation that the EEOC has taken in a number of enforcement actions. But what about other more common, less objectionable restrictions? In *Choate* the Supreme Court cited approvingly a Second Circuit opinion holding that the limitation of mental health coverage does not violate §504. See also Modderno v. King, 82 F.3d 1059 (D.C. Cir. 1996) (disparity in coverage of mental health treatment is not disability discrimination; to rule otherwise would be "to invite challenges to virtually every exercise of the [insurer's or employer's] discretion with respect to the allocation of benefits amongst an encyclopedia of illnesses"). What is the difference between AIDS restrictions and mental health restrictions? Could it be the fact that many mental health patients are not disabled, whereas all AIDS patients are? Then what about the exclusion of experimental cancer treatment? See Henderson v. Bodine Aluminum, 70 F.3d 958 (8th Cir. 1995) (denying expensive new therapy for breast cancer is potentially discrimination where the plan covers this treatment for other cancers and there is evidence it works for breast cancer). But see Lenox v. Healthwise of Kentucky, 149 F.3d 453 (6th Cir. 1998) (no ADA violation in excluding coverage for heart transplants). See Jane Korn, Cancer and the ADA: Rethinking Disability, 74 S. Cal. L. Rev. 339 (2001).

It is also important to realize how many activities and programs the discrimination laws cover. Originally, §504 covered federal government jobs, programs, and contractors. But §1557 of the ACA has extended its reach to any health program or activity that receives federal financial assistance, including plans sold on the ACA's new health insurance exchanges. See 81 Fed. Reg. 31376 (May 18, 2016). The ADA's scope is somewhat different: It covers state and private entities and is divided into several titles, each of which covers different realms of activity— including employment, transportation, and public accommodations. The ADA's prohibition on disability discrimination in connection with the employment relationship extends to employer-sponsored insurance.

Health plans continue to test the limits of these antidiscrimination rules. In 2014, for example, insurers came under attack for designing health plans in a manner that discriminates against people living with HIV/AIDS. By manipulating their drug formularies, the insurers made it excessively costly and bureaucratically difficult for patients to access needed antiretroviral medication. See Douglas B. Jacobs & Benjamin D. Sommers, Using Drugs to Discriminate—Adverse Selection in the Insurance Marketplace, 372 New Eng. J. Med. 399 (2015) (finding evidence of "adverse tiering" on the exchanges). The federal government and state insurance officials have opened investigations into these practices and a number of class-action lawsuits have been filed against major insurers.

4. *Meaningful Access Without Fundamental Alteration.* Does the Supreme Court's "meaningful access to benefits" test provide a good guide for what's permissible? Meaningful access to *which* benefits? To the particular item of treatment being sought or to insurance coverage generally? See Doe v. Chandler, 83 F.3d 1150 (9th

Cir. 1996) (limiting welfare for disabled recipients but not for dependent children does not discriminate against the disabled because states may craft different benefits for different programs).

Choate also speaks in terms of avoiding requirements that would fundamentally alter the nature of the product or program. This is the defense on which Philip Peters rests most of his justification for effectiveness analysis in the remainder of his article. But this issue is also largely untested in the courts. In contrast with *Choate,* see Olmstead v. L.C., 527 U.S. 581 (1999), which found a potential ADA violation where a state Medicaid plan covered long-term hospitalization for mental illness but not less restrictive community placement options, and the Court suggested that it would not be a "fundamental alteration" to require the state to expand its coverage if doing so can be "reasonably accommodated" without straining the budget for other mental health services. Compare Lovell v. Chandler, 303 F.3d 1039 (9th Cir. 2002) (finding an ADA violation where the state expanded eligibility for Medicaid up to three times the poverty level but excluded disabled participants from the increased eligibility parameters, even though the state said this was all it could afford). See Sara Rosenbaum, *Olmstead v. L.C.*: Implications for Medicaid and Other Publicly Funded Health Services, 12 Health Matrix 93 (2002).

For an argument that these distinctions fail to protect adequately against disability discrimination through disparate impact, see D. Orentlicher, Destructuring Disability: Rationing of Health Care and Unfair Discrimination Against the Sick, 31 Harv. C.R.-C.L. L. Rev. 51 (1996). According to another law professor, "the ADA is an inadequate and even inept tool for resolving whether we should tolerate cost-conscious [insurance] policies" because its concepts are so poorly suited for articulating and understanding the underlying social policy debate. Mary A. Crossley, Medical Futility and Disability Discrimination, 81 Iowa L. Rev. 179 (1995).

5. *Tossing Around the Hot Potato.* Against this backdrop of uncertainty, is there clarity in the ACA's legislative language that forbids designing "benefits in ways that discriminate against individuals because of their age, disability, or expected length of life" or that are "subject to denial . . . on the basis of the individuals' . . . present or predicted disability, degree of medical dependency, or quality of life"? As Professor Nelson notes, this appears aimed at prohibiting the government's use of QALYs to define the standard set of "essential health benefits" that private insurers must cover (in the individual and small group markets). However, another statutory provision says that "nothing . . . shall be construed to prohibit . . . [health insurers] from carrying out utilization management techniques that are commonly used as of the date of enactment of this Act." Does that mean that rationing, or cost-effectiveness analysis, is fine as long as the government does not do it?

Partly to avoid grappling with questions like these, the Obama administration adopted a rule deputizing the states to select a "benchmark plan" from among existing health plans in the state. The benefits covered under that benchmark plan would then be considered "essential" within the state. In its rulemaking, HHS explained that a national, uniform definition of essential health benefits would needlessly disrupt the market and thwart state efforts to tailor their insurance rules to local conditions. 78 Fed. Reg. 12834 (Feb. 25, 2013).

6. *Rationing Criteria and Social Values.* QALYs are objectionable on other moral grounds besides disability discrimination. As discussed most forcefully by David Hadorn and John Harris, cited by Peters, the mathematics of QALYs mean that it

is equally as valuable to save ten years from one person's life as it is to save one year of life for ten people. This utilitarian logic does not fit most people's intuitions. See John Taurek, Should the Numbers Count?, 6 Phil. & Pub. Aff. 293 (1977). On the other hand, if we are to avoid use of rationing criteria that contain any controversial value judgments, we would have to adopt completely arbitrary rationing criteria such as a simple lottery, or treating whoever asks first. Most people would view these "neutral" criteria as even more irrational and objectionable. See Einer Elhauge, Allocating Health Care Morally, 82 Cal. L. Rev. 1449 (1994).

The "rescue principle" mentioned by Prof. Dworkin exists in other social arenas such as natural disasters and high-risk recreational activity, where we spend seemingly unlimited amounts responding to crisis situations when people are visibly threatened with death or disability at the same time that we neglect less expensive preventive measures that might avoid a situation in the first place. This is also known as the paradox of "statistical versus identifiable lives." If the thrust of this argument is to spend more on prevention, few would disagree, but if the thrust is to spend less on heroic measures, the argument is met with the following response:

> I will risk my life on the roads to do nothing more than secure a bag of potato chips, not to mention take the risk of eating them simply for fleeting gustatory sensations. But should I come up short in the potato chips v. life lottery, and suffer either a car or a cardiovascular accident, I do not expect society to respond by saying, "Well, tough luck, but you made an open-eyed trade-off here." No, I expect EMTs to rush to the scene and pound on my chest and speed me to the hospital in reckless disregard of the laws set down to reduce the risk faced by other travelers in search of potato chips and other goods. This social response, I am suggesting, can be seen as a way of marking the fact that our lives are shot through with incommensurable values, and that we have to wind our way through them in a way that does its best to acknowledge their separate significance.

J.L. Nelson, Publicity and Pricelessness: Grassroots Decisionmaking and Justice in Rationing, 19 J. Med. & Phil. 333 (1994). In a similar vein, Calabresi and Bobbitt explain that rationing is more socially acceptable when the tragic choices are hidden from view, as they are when the harms are merely statistical, than when identifiable victims of rationing can clearly be seen. G. Calabresi & P. Bobbitt, Tragic Choices (1978). Does this mean that effective rationing can be done only out of public view? If so, is that a legitimate reason to promote or tolerate less explicit or "democratic" forms of rationing?

Prof. Gregg Bloche argues that health care law and policy is in a "confused, even chaotic state" because it assumes that medical resources can be allocated in a "systematically rational manner," which is not feasible or even desirable considering differing values, limitations on human rationality, and inconsistent understandings about what rationality means or requires. Instead, he urges an "inelegant" approach that "defines our aims more modestly, consistent with a picture of rationality as limited by context, discontinuous across different settings, and changeable with time." Gregg Bloche, The Invention of Health Law, 91 Cal. L. Rev. 247 (2003). Does that make things less confused? For further discussion, see sources cited in note 12.

7. *Medicaid Coverage.* Many of the decisions discussed below that require Medicaid to fund controversial procedures such as sex-change operations and liver transplants for former alcoholics are reasoned in terms of disability discrimination,

even though they are based on the Medicaid statute. They reason that the basic standard of rationality and nonarbitrariness required by the Medicaid statute prevents covering a medically beneficial treatment for some conditions but not for others. Therefore, Medicaid must either exclude the treatment altogether or selectively exclude it under generic criteria such as medically necessary or experimental. See, e.g., Salgado v. Kirschner, 878 P.2d 659 (Ariz. 1994) (unreasonable to cover liver transplant only for children; medically relevant factors, not age alone, should determine coverage).

Imagine that you are in charge of allocating limited government health care funds. Where, if anywhere, would you want to set limits? Would you fund a liver transplant for a patient whose recovery is only 50 percent certain? For a patient with only partial liver dysfunction whose life is not at stake? For an alcoholic? Would you support lung transplants for cigarette smokers? Heart transplants for overeaters?

If the legislature appropriated an additional $5 million to use at your discretion, would you choose (1) a large expansion in low-cost prenatal care, which would help decrease the high costs of caring for premature births, or (2) a few expensive organ transplants, or (3) some of both? Which of these decisions would disability discrimination principles allow?

Oregon's adoption of the rationing list reflected an effort to answer some of these difficult questions. The effort was somewhat half-hearted, however. Many of the items eliminated from funding are fairly "small ticket," are requested only rarely, or were not covered in the first place. In other instances, physicians are able to obtain coverage by recharacterizing the patient's condition as especially serious. Accordingly, Oregon's expansion of Medicaid eligibility was financed mostly by increased taxation and legislative appropriations, not by savings from the list. Symposium, 24 J. Health Pol. Pol'y & L. 151 (1999). Does Oregon's experience suggest that saying "no" to particular treatments is impossible? Or does the program's tentativeness merely reflect the novelty of the experiment?

8. *The (Second) Oregon Experiment.* In response to budget cuts during the Great Recession, Oregon turned to a lottery method to keep costs down, enrolling in Medicaid only a fraction of those eligible to join. H. Allen et al., What the Oregon Health Study Can Tell Us About Expanding Medicaid, 29 Health Aff. 1498 (2010). As a method of allocating access to health care, is a random lottery preferable to a rationing list? If so, why?[11]

9. *Hepatitis C.* In 2014, breakthrough anti-viral drugs to treat Hepatitis C came on the market. In contrast to previous therapies, the drugs boast cure rates exceeding 90 percent and have few side effects. The drugs are so effective that prominent clinical guidelines indicate that they should be supplied to nearly everyone who has

11. Unintentionally, Oregon's use of a lottery provided a unique opportunity to study the effects of getting Medicaid coverage. In an ongoing study, researchers are comparing those who won the lottery to those who did not, allowing them to assess Medicaid's effect on utilization, financial security, and health outcomes. Early results indicate that Medicaid leads to less financial strain and reduced levels of depression, but that it also increases use of the emergency room and may do little to reduce hypertension or cholesterol levels. See Katherine Baicker et al., The Oregon Experiment—Effects of Medicaid on Clinical Outcomes, 368 New Eng. J. Med. 1713 (2013).

contracted Hepatitis C. But an estimated 3.2 million people are infected with the disease and the drugs are very expensive: Sovaldi, for example, was initially priced at $84,000 for a twelve-week course of treatment.

Predictably, private insurers and public programs have balked at footing the astronomical bill for these new drugs. States are under particular stress given that a disproportionate number of Hepatitis C patients are poor (and therefore enrolled in Medicaid) or imprisoned. As a result, many private insurers and most states have limited coverage for the drugs to patients whose disease has progressed far enough to lead to severe liver damage.

The coverage limitations have provoked congressional outrage and spurred litigation from patients who argue that they should not have to suffer liver damage before receiving treatment. Only recently—and, not coincidentally, as prices for the Hepatitis C drugs have begun to fall—have payers begun to relent. In 2016, an investigation by New York Attorney General yielded a settlement with seven insurers in which they agreed to cover the drugs for nearly all Hepatitis C patients. Shortly after, a federal judge in Washington State entered a preliminary injunction ordering the state's Medicaid program to pay for the drugs for any beneficiary diagnosed with Hepatitis C. See B.E. v. Teeter, 16-227 (W.D. Wash. 2016). As of this writing, a handful of states—including Massachusetts, New York, and Florida—have voluntarily dropped their Medicaid restrictions. State prison systems, however, remain under enormous strain. Peter Loftus & Gary Fields, High Cost of New Hepatitis C Drugs Strains Prison Budgets, Locks Many Out of Cure, Wall St. J., Sept. 12, 2016.

10. *Race or Gender Discrimination.* Insurance restrictions can be challenged under other discrimination statutes besides disability. Suppose, for instance, that an excluded disease category has a disproportionate impact on blacks. Most commentators conclude that this alone is not illegal without some indication of racial animus or subterfuge. More compelling, however, is the argument that a treatment exclusion has a categorical effect on only one gender. In Newport News Shipbuilding v. EEOC, 462 U.S. 669 (1993), the Court held that an employer violates Title VII's prohibition of sex discrimination by providing more generous pregnancy benefits to female employees than to the wives of male employees. Similarly, would the exclusion of fertility treatment such as in vitro fertilization constitute either gender or disability discrimination? Saks v. Franklin Covey Co., 316 F.3d 337 (2d Cir. 2003) (no, because infertility is not always a disability, and plan excluded fertility treatment for both men and women).

Civil rights discrimination statutes apply to government programs as well, under Title VI. These statutes have had less effect. A series of public interest lawsuits have failed to block cities from closing public hospitals in low-income communities, with courts finding that the disparate impact on minorities does not constitute prohibited discrimination. See, e.g., Bryan v. Koch, 627 F.2d 612 (2d Cir. 1980); NAACP v. Wilmington Medical Center, 657 F.2d 1322 (3d Cir. 1981).

11. *Impotence and Contraception.* Among the various controversies concerning what health insurance should cover, debates about contraception and sexual health have been especially lively. Following the introduction of Viagra, impotence pills for men were covered by traditional health insurance. While Viagra addresses a physical dysfunction often caused by health problems or medication side effects, it is also prescribed in more discretionary situations to enhance sexual performance. Rather than crafting sexual performance indicators or drawing age-based lines, insurers

simply capped the number of Viagra pills permitted per month. (One wonders how they arrived at the cutoff.) See Alison Keith, The Economics of Viagra, 19 Health Aff. 147 (2000).

Insurers' willingness to cover Viagra highlighted the inequities of the then-common practice of not covering contraceptives for women, which are similarly important to sexual health. Although Obama administration rules under the Affordable Care Act at first mandated contraceptive coverage, the Trump administration is expected to rescind or restrict that coverage mandate. Also, the Supreme Court has recognized a right of religiously motivated employers to refuse contraceptive coverage. Burwell v. Hobby Lobby Stores, 573 U.S. ___ (2014). Furthermore, many women encounter obstacles from insurance companies that restrict which types of birth control they make available. See Kaiser Family Foundation, Coverage of Contraceptive Services: A Review of Health Insurance Plans in Five States (2015).

12. *Further Readings.* For further discussions of **moral and public policy dimensions of QALYs** and other criteria for rationing, see Marion Danis et al. eds., Fair Resource Allocation and Rationing at the Bedside (2015); Larry Churchill, Rationing Health Care in America (1987); Frances Kamm, Morality and Mortality (1993); John Kilner, Who Lives? Who Dies? (1990); Paul Menzel, Strong Medicine: The Ethical Rationing of Health Care (1990); Eric Rakowski, Taking and Saving Lives, 93 Colum. L. Rev. 1063 (1993); Matthew D. Adler, QALYs and Policy Evaluation: A New Perspective, 6 Yale J. Health Pol'y L. & Ethics 1 (2006); Sharona Hoffman, Unmanaged Care: Towards Moral Fairness in Health Care Coverage, 78 Ind. L.J. 659 (2003); Norman Daniels & James E. Sabin, Setting Limits Fairly: Can We Learn to Share Medical Resources? (2000); Jennifer Prah Ruger, Health, Capability and Justice: Toward a New Paradigm of Health Ethics, Policy and Law, 15 Cornell J.L. Pub. Pol'y 403 (2006); Amy B. Monahan, Value-Based Mandated Health Benefits, 80 U. Colo. L. Rev. 127-200 (2009); Ani B. Satz, The Limits of Health Care Reform, 59 Ala. L. Rev. 1451 (2008); Symposium, 12 Value in Health S1 (2009). For a harrowing account of hospital rationing in the aftermath of Hurricane Katrina, see Sheri Fink, Five Days at Memorial: Life and Death in a Storm-Ravaged Hospital (2013).

For discussions of **comparative medical effectiveness** (note 1), see Eleanor Kinney, Comparative Effectiveness Research Under the Patient Protection and Affordable Care Act, 37 Am. J.L. & Med. 522 (2011); Richard Saver, Health Care Reform's Wild Care: The Uncertain Effectiveness of Comparative Effectiveness Research, 159 U. Pa. L. Rev. 2147 (2011); Sean Tunis, Reflections on Science, Judgment, and Value in Evidence-Based Decision Making, 26 Health Aff. w500 (2007); Note, 21 Ann. Health L. 329 (2012); Symposium, 31 Health Aff. 2225 (2012); Symposium, 29 Health Aff. 1756 (2010); Govind Persad, Priority Setting, Cost-Effectiveness, and the Affordable Care Act, 41 Am. J.L. & Med. 119 (2015).

For discussions of **Medicare's refusal to explicitly consider costs in making coverage decisions**, see Nicholas Bagley, Bedside Bureaucrats: Why Medicare Reform Hasn't Worked, 101 Geo. L.J. 519 (2013); Jacqueline Fox, The Hidden Role of Cost: Medicare Decisions, Transparency, and Public Trust, 79. U. Cin. L. Rev. 1 (2011); S. Dhruva et al., CMS's Landmark Decision on CT Colonography, 361 New Eng. J. Med. 1316 (2009); Peter Neumann, Medicare's National Coverage Decisions for Technologies, 27 Health Aff. 1620 (2008); Peter J. Neumann et al., Medicare and Cost-Effectiveness Analysis, 353 New Eng. J. Med. 1516 (2006).

For broader discussions of **the use of cost-benefit analyses in legal and regulatory settings generally**, see Matthew Adler & Eric Posner, Cost-Benefit Analysis:

Legal, Economic, and Philosophical Perspectives (2001); Richard L. Revesz & Michael Livermore, How Cost-Benefit Analysis Can Better Protect the Environment and Our Health (2008); Identified versus Statistical Lives: An Interdisciplinary Perspective (I. Glenn Cohen et al. eds. 2015).

An excellent example of **institutional choice analysis** (note 2) applied to problems in health policy is Russell Korobkin, The Efficiency of Managed Care "Patient Protection" Laws: Incomplete Contracts, Bounded Rationality, and Market Failure, 85 Cornell L. Rev. 1 (1999). See also Einer Elhauge, Can Health Law Become a Coherent Field of Law? 41 Wake Forest L. Rev. 365 (2006); William M. Sage, Unfinished Business: How Litigation Relates to Health Care Regulation, 28 J. Health Pol. Pol'y & L. 387 (2003); Ezekiel Emanuel, Choice and Representation in Health Care, 56 Med. Care Res. & Rev. 1 (1999). See generally Neil Komesar, Imperfect Alternatives: Choosing Institutions in Law, Economics, and Public Policy (1995); Edward Rubin, The New Legal Process, The Synthesis of Discourse, and the Microanalysis of Institutions, 109 Harv. L. Rev. 1393 (1996).

For discussions of **ADA issues generally and in insurance coverage and medical care** (note 5), see Leslie Francis & Anita Silvers, Debilitating *Alexander v. Choate*: "Meaningful Access" to Health Care for People with Disabilities, 35 Fordham Urb. L.J. 447 (2008); Alexander Abbe, "Meaningful Access" to Health Care and the Remedies Available to Medicaid Managed Care Recipients Under the ADA and the Rehabilitation Act, 147 U. Pa. L. Rev. 1161 (1999); Mary Crossley, Becoming Visible: The ADA's Impact on Health Care for Persons with Disabilities, 52 Ala. L. Rev. 51 (2000); Mary Crossley, The Disability Kaleidoscope, 74 Notre Dame L. Rev. 521 (1999); Maxwell J. Mehlman et al., When Do Health Care Decisions Discriminate Against People with Disabilities?, 22 J. Health Pol. Pol'y & L. 1385 (1997).

For discussion of the **inevitable difficulties in balancing the ACA's competing goals in light of its various restrictions on rationing** (note 6), see Nicholas Bagley & Helen Levy, Essential Health Benefits and the Affordable Care Act: Law and Process, 39 J. Health Pol., Pol'y & L. 441 (2014); Sara Rosenbaum et al., The Essential Health Benefits Provisions of the Affordable Care Act: Implications for People with Disabilities (2011); Alan Cohen, The Debate over Health Care Rationing: Déjà Vu All Over Again?, 49 Inquiry 90 (2012); Alan Weil, The Value of Federalism in Defining Essential Health Benefits, 366 New Eng. J. Med. 366 (2012); Jesse Hill, What Is the Meaning of Health? Constitutional Implications of Defining "Medical Necessity" and "Essential Health Benefits" Under the Affordable Care Act, 38 Am. J.L. & Med. 445 (2012); Institute of Medicine, Essential Health Benefits: Balancing Coverage and Cost (2011).

For **broader discussions** of how health law addresses disability and discrimination issues more generally, see Jessica Roberts, Health Law as Disability Rights Law, 97 Minn. L. Rev. 1963 (2013); Jessica Roberts & Elizabeth Weeks Leonard, What Is (and Isn't) Healthism, 50 Ga. L. Rev. 833 (2016).

For discussions of **transplant funding** (note 7), see Lisa Deutsch, Medicaid Payment for Organ Transplants: The Extent of Mandated Coverage, 30 Colum. J.L. & Soc. Probs. 185 (1997); Clark Havighurst & Nancy King, Liver Transplantation in Massachusetts: Public Policymaking as Morality Play, 19 Ind. L. Rev. 955 (1986); Note, 79 Minn. L. Rev. 1232 (1995); Note, 89 Nw. U. L. Rev. 268 (1994).

For discussions of **the Oregon scheme and the legality of QALYs under the ADA** (note 8), see Jonathan Oberlander et al., Rationing Health Care: Rhetoric and Reality in the Oregon Health Plan, 164 Canadian Medical Ass'n J. 1583 (2001);

Kevin P. Quinn, Viewing Health Care as a Common Good: Looking Beyond Political Liberalism, 73 S. Cal. L. Rev. 277 (2000); Note, 93 Colum. L. Rev. 1985 (1993); Note, 106 Harv. L. Rev. 1296 (1993).

For discussions of **the Hepatitis C drugs** (note 9), see Judith Graham, Medicaid, Private Insurers Begin to Lift Curbs on Pricey Hepatitis C Drugs, Kaiser Health News, July 5, 2016; Valerie K. Blake, An Opening for Civil Rights in Health Insurance After the Affordable Care Act, 36 B.C. J.L. & Soc. Just. 235 (2016); Hannah Brennan et al., A Prescription for Excessive Drug Pricing: Leveraging Government Patent Use for Health, 18 Yale J.L. & Tech. 275 (2016).

For discussions of **race and gender discrimination** (note 10), see Lisa Kerr, Can Money Buy Happiness? An Examination of the Coverage of Infertility Services Under HMO Contracts, 49 Case W. Res. L. Rev. 559 (1999); Carl Coleman, Conceiving Harm: Disability Discrimination in Assisted Reproductive Technologies, 50 UCLA L. Rev. 17 (2002). For a related issue, see L. Dechery, Do Employer-Provided Insurance Plans Violate Title VII When They Exclude Treatment for Breast Cancer?, 80 Minn. L. Rev. 945 (1996); Christine Nardi, When Health Insurers Deny Coverage for Breast Reconstructive Surgery: Gender Meets Disability, 1997 Wis. L. Rev. 778.

Problem: Allocation Choices in a Public Program

You are CEO of a municipal hospital, funded by the county, looking at next year's budget. This forces you to make tough allocation decisions. Due to your brilliant administrative leadership, the hospital managed to treat all patients who requested service last year, and it still has a $5 million surplus left over. After receiving recommendations from a task force, you have to choose among these three options:

> (1) Return the money to the county to help them avoid an anticipated property tax increase.
>
> (2) Buy one Very Big Fancy Machine (VBFM), which, over the course of its five-year useful life, will treat 100 patients a year, with a 1 percent better chance of saving their life compared with existing technologies. In other words, the machine is expected to save five lives at a cost of $1 million/life. On average, each person saved will live for ten more years. (Imagine a machine that helps resuscitate patients in the emergency room.)
>
> (3) Buy 5,000 Really Simple Little Things (RSLTs), which have a 1 percent chance to extend life one year for each person who uses one. In other words, this will provide one additional year for 50 people, at a cost of $100,000 per person. (Imagine an expensive drug that does a better job of delaying but not avoiding death from cancer.)

Now, suppose you learn that patients treated with the VBFM will be left bed-ridden and debilitated but fully conscious, whereas RSLT patients will be left ambulatory but in pain and with diminished mental capacities. Assuming you were unfettered by the ADA, what do you do? Realizing, however, that the ADA might apply, does it potentially force you to change your mind? What factors determine what effect the ADA might have?

2. *Determining What Is Medically Appropriate*

Once insurance language is written, disputes do not disappear. We still must decide which treatments are actually covered by insurance in effect. The main readings view these issues from a more substantive perspective, and the notes take a more procedural look. The focus in the main readings is on private insurance; the notes include public programs as well. Regardless, the issues remain essentially the same throughout: Who should decide what is medically appropriate, and according to what criteria?

MOUNT SINAI HOSPITAL v. ZOREK

271 N.Y.S.2d 1012 (N.Y. Civ. Ct. 1966)

GREENFIELD, Judge.

One of the most celebrated trials of our literature was the confrontation of Portia and Shylock as they struggled with the problem of the removal of a pound of flesh. Now, once again, the removal of a pound of flesh, or more properly several pounds, has created a weighty legal problem for resolution by the court.

The hopes, despairs, and conflicts of our time, and ultimately every crisis, custom and social neurosis find reflection in the matters brought before the courts, the great mirror of our society. While not of the same magnitude as wars, depressions or the disasters of nature, the problem of obesity has persistently troubled part of mankind, but even more of womankind, ever since man first eked out more than the marginal subsistence required for bare survival, accumulated the luxury of a surplus food supply, and began to live to eat instead of eating to live.

With the plump and fleshy females portrayed by Rubens no longer in vogue, having been supplanted by the ideal of the lithe and willowy high-cheekboned model, the plight of those women whose rotundity does not conform to the ideal has been accentuated. The plaintiff cry "O! that this too too solid flesh would melt Thaw and resolve itself into a dew" is re-echoed today by the plump and portly, and has evoked a burgeoning and varied response from Elizabeth Arden, reducing pills, milk farms, steam baths and slenderizers to No-Cal and the Drinking Man's Diet.

Grace, felicity and beauty are qualities ardently sought after—but aesthetic considerations aside, excess avoirdupois also creates problems of health, vigor, longevity, hygiene and a general state of well-being that call for the arts of the medical practitioner. Obesity is definitely a medical problem. The correlation between overweight and a shortened life-span has been amply demonstrated. What a challenge to a medical Michelangelo, to liberate from beneath mountains of flesh the slender, sylphlike creature yearning to be free!

Doctor John J. Bookman was one who rose to the challenge. Among his patients was Jane Zorek, the wife of the defendant and third-party plaintiff in this action. Mrs. Zorek was 5'2", but could not exactly be described as petite, for she had weighed well over 200 pounds. The doctor had been treating her for a number of medical problems arising from her obesity—including abscesses, cysts, and skin grafts. In 1962, when this had caused sebaceous gland trouble, he had her hospitalized. In the hospital she was put on a rigid reducing diet restricted to 800 calories a day and lost 7 1/2 pounds. The third-party defendant, Associated Hospital Service of New York, with whom Mr. Zorek had a family Blue Cross contract, on that occasion paid the expenses of Mrs. Zorek's hospital stay without a murmur of protest.

Out of the hospital, Mrs. Zorek was unable to maintain her weight loss, and was plagued by recurring boils and cysts. Hence, in May of 1963, Doctor Bookman again concluded that hospitalization was required and had her admitted to the plaintiff Mount Sinai Hospital. This time she was put on what is known as the "Duncan Regime"—a rigid starvation diet, in which the patient receives no calories at all, only fluids, vitamins and minerals. During her three weeks stay in the hospital on this stringent program, Mrs. Zorek lost 17 1/2 pounds without adverse effects.

When pressed by the hospital for payment, Mr. Zorek looked to his Blue Cross policy with Associated Hospital Service of New York for reimbursement. AHS, however, this time refused payment, contending that obesity was not within the coverage of the contract, and that Mrs. Zorek's hospital confinement was not necessary for treatment of her condition. This lawsuit then followed.

[Although] AHS argued that obesity is neither a disease nor an injury, it is clear that Blue Cross coverage is not limited only to those calamities. Since the policy spells out the "condition, disease, ailment or accidental injury" which is *excluded* from coverage, it should be plain that there *is* coverage for hospitalization resulting from any condition, disease, injury or ailment which is not excluded. While it is debatable whether or not obesity is an illness or ailment, certainly it is a "condition," and the test of coverage must be determined on other grounds.

The policy provides:

> Such Hospital Service shall be available to a Subscriber, following his admission to a hospital and during the time he is confined herein as a registered bed patient and while he is under the treatment of a physician, *when such hospital confinement is necessary for his proper treatment*. . . . However, there shall be available only such items of Hospital Service as are necessary and consistent with the diagnosis and treatment of the Condition for which such hospitalization is required. (Italics supplied.)

Under Exclusions appear the following: "A. Hospital Service Shall Not Be Provided: . . . 5. For a hospital stay or that portion of a hospital stay which is primarily for custodial, convalescent or sanitarium type care or for a rest cure."

Associated Hospital Service, the third-party defendant, argues that hospital confinement was not necessary for proper treatment of Mrs. Zorek's obese condition, and that the care rendered to her during her stay in the hospital was convalescent or sanitarium type care which the contract excludes. . . .

The words *necessary for proper treatment* call into play the exercise of judgment. "Proper" in whose eyes? The patient's, the treating physician's, the hospital's, an AHS administrator's, or a court's looking back on the events sometime afterwards? Although no cases have been brought to the court's attention directly dealing with this problem, this court concludes that the applicable standards of judgment as to the treatment prescribed must be those of the treating physician.

Only the treating physician can determine what the appropriate treatment should be for any given condition. Any other standard would involve intolerable second-guessing, with every case calling for a crotchety Doctor Gillespie to peer over the shoulders of a supposedly unseasoned Doctor Kildare. The diagnosis and treatment of a patient are matters peculiarly within the competence of the treating physician. The diagnosis may be insightful and brilliant, or it may be wide of the mark, but right or wrong, the patient under his doctor's guidance proceeds upon his theories and sustains expenses therefor. Can a hospitalization insurer rightfully decline to pay for the expenses incurred on the theory that subsequent events may have proved the diagnosis or the recommended treatment to have been wrong?

Once the treating doctor has decided on the treatment, we may of course review his judgment as to whether or not hospital confinement was necessary for the particular treatment prescribed. The doctor who orders hospital confinement for the removal of a simple splinter or the lancing of a boil has almost certainly exceeded the bounds of proper medical judgment in providing for his patient. The doctor who orders hospitalization for major surgery clearly is correct in concluding that hospital confinement is necessary for that treatment, even though he may be in egregious error in deciding that major surgery is called for. Once the treating doctor has decided on a course of treatment for which hospitalization is necessary, his judgment cannot be retrospectively challenged.

A gall-bladder or a liver condition may be treated by a radical operation or by allowing a healthy regimen and the healing passage of time to work the miracle of regeneration. Who can say with certainty which course of treatment is correct? But if the operation is decided on, can there be a denial of Blue Cross coverage because alternative courses of treatment were available?

In this case doctors might differ as to what treatment should have been given to Mrs. Zorek for obesity and related disorders. The doctor who treated her concluded the appropriate treatment for the condition would be not further home dieting, or intensive exercise, or sanitarium care, but the Duncan regime. Other doctors might disagree as to prescribing the Duncan regime, but they were not treating Mrs. Zorek. . . .

The Duncan regime is a recognized medical treatment for obesity. While there is some controversy about it, and not all doctors would choose to resort to that treatment, many reputable doctors do. Doctor Bookman chose that treatment here. He having determined, within the scope of his medical competence, that the treatment was necessary, the sole question remaining is whether hospitalization was necessary for the treatment decided on.

AHS contends that what was done for Mrs. Zorek in the hospital demonstrates that hospitalization was not necessary. Apart from restricting her intake of food and administering vitamins, the patient was permitted to continue ambulatory and was weighed daily. All these things, AHS contends, were in the nature of custodial care and could have been done at home or in any sanitarium or rest home. Looking back, Mrs. Zorek's stay was indeed uneventful. However, we must measure the necessity for hospitalization by the prospective potentialities for danger inherent in a treatment, and not by fortuitous actuality.

Dr. Bookman testified that the Duncan regime was a dangerous course of treatment, and because of the dangers involved called for careful supervision at all times. The patient's blood pressure, temperature, and body fluids had to be continuously checked to be certain that proper chemical balance was maintained, and he insisted much more than mere custodial care would be required. Indeed, severe shock and even death are known to have ensued for persons following the Duncan regime even under carefully supervised conditions, since the changes which occur may be sudden and drastic. Even the medical expert who testified for Blue Cross stated that while he personally would not recommend the Duncan regime, the reason he would not do so is because of its inherent danger. In fact, he said, it would be foolishness to place someone on a Duncan diet outside of a hospital with facilities for 24 hour supervision and a well-trained medical staff.

Fortunately, there were no adverse developments or complications for Mrs. Zorek during her hospital stay. The possibilities were ever-present however, and in any sensible society penalties are not to be imposed where common-sense precautions are taken. The court concludes that not only was hospitalization necessary once the Duncan regime was decided upon, but that it would have been medically irresponsible to have had anything less. Certainly we must presume that a busy metropolitan hospital complex like Mount Sinai was not going to make one of its much sought-after beds available for three weeks for a person who merely was seeking a "rest cure," and the kind of enforced diet she could otherwise get on a milk farm. It was medical necessity and not cosmetic vanity which dictated the hospital stay. . . .

It is the holding of this Court in construing the Blue Cross contract that when multiple courses of treatment are available, whether for the obese, the alcoholic, or the addicted, if the treating physician chooses that treatment for which hospitalization is required, and rejects those treatments which can be adequately administered in a rest home or sanitarium, then, absent a specific contractual exclusion, there is full coverage for the hospital stay. . . .

The amount of the hospital bill in this case attributed to Mrs. Zorek's treatment for obesity came to $557.90, for which sum the plaintiff, Mount Sinai Hospital, is entitled to judgment. . . .

■ BECHTOLD v. PHYSICIANS HEALTH PLAN OF NORTHERN INDIANA

19 F.3d 322 (7th Cir. 1994)

Coffey, Circuit Judge.

Background

. . . The parties have stipulated to the relevant facts in this case and legal issues only need be determined. Penny Jo Bechtold is a 40-year-old premenopausal adult female. She is employed by Magnavox Electronic Systems which maintains a health plan administered by the defendant Physicians Health Plan of Northern Indiana [PHP]. The plan is an "employee welfare benefit plan" as defined [by ERISA].

In October, 1991, the plaintiff was diagnosed as having breast cancer and underwent a modified radical mastectomy. The surgery disclosed heavy lymph node involvement with the breast cancer cells. After the removal of the tumor she was treated with standard chemotherapy and radiation. Her oncologist recommended that she receive heavy dose chemotherapy with an autologous bone marrow transplant (HDC/ABMT) and referred her to the Cleveland Clinic for this treatment.

HDC/ABMT is a two-step procedure. Physicians first extract ("harvest") the bone marrow cells from the patient's body and place them temporarily in frozen storage. Next, the patient undergoes a cycle of high-dose chemotherapy in hopes of killing the cancer cells. . . . [T]he patient's own ("autologous") stored marrow is [then] reinfused intravenously into the bloodstream to relieve the patient from the toxic effects of the chemotherapy. HDC/ABMT has proven effective in treating certain cancerous blood diseases such as leukemia and Hodgkin's disease but to date it has not been universally accepted treatment for solid-type tumors including breast cancer.

Before Bechtold proceeded with the treatment, PHP advised her that the HDC/ABMT treatment was not a covered service under the plan. . . . [T]he plaintiff . . . appeal[ed] the denial of benefits and received a hearing before a committee [composed of one PHP doctor, one PHP patient, and a representative of PHP management]. The committee recommended that even though the insurer had met its obligations to the plaintiff under the contract, that the insurer should change its policy and authorize payment for the procedure because the treatment was reasonable for a patient of Bechtold's age. PHP did not agree with the committee's recommendation, and refused to pay for the treatment stating that it had "lived up to its Contract obligations" under the "clear and unambiguous language in the Contract." . . .

Discussion

We are aware that Mrs. Bechtold and her immediate family have undoubtedly endured a great deal of heartache, frustration, and depression during her battle with cancer.[2] there is no doubt that the policy questions posed in cases like this are of grave concern to all of us, yet we, as a court of law, are called upon to make legal determinations.[3] The issue in this case is very straightforward: Does the PHP benefit plan authorize coverage of HDC/ABMT? This is a matter of contract interpretation that does not implicate the broader policy issues involved in whether insurers

2. Fortunately for Mrs. Bechtold she has secondary insurance that paid for the treatment and thus this action will merely determine which of two insurers will pay for the treatment.

3. In Harris v. Mutual of Omaha Cos., 1992 WL 421489, 1992 U.S. Dist. LEXIS 21393 (S.D. Ind. Aug. 26, 1992), aff'd, 992 F.2d 706 (7th Cir. 1993), a similar case of a claimant seeking coverage for HDC/ABMT, U.S. District Judge Tinder succinctly summarized the problem facing courts in these difficult claims for medical coverage:

> Despite rumors to the contrary, those who wear judicial robes are human beings, and as persons, are inspired and motivated by compassion as anyone would be. Consequently, we often must remind ourselves that in our official capacities, we have authority only to issue rulings within the narrow parameters of the law and the facts before us. The temptation to go about, doing good where we see fit, and to make things less difficult for those who come before us, regardless of the law, is strong. But the law, without which judges are nothing, abjures such unlicensed formulation of unauthorized social policy by the judiciary. Plaintiff Judy Harris well deserves, and in a perfect world would be entitled to, all known medical treatments to control the horrid disease from which she suffers. In ruling as this court must, no personal satisfaction is taken, but that the law was followed. The court will have to live with the haunting thought that Ms. Harris, and perhaps others insured by the Mutual of Omaha Companies under similar plans, may not ultimately receive the treatment they need and deserve. Perhaps the question most importantly raised about this case, and similar cases, is who should pay for the hopeful treatments that are being developed in this rapidly developing area of medical science?

should cover medical procedures that are presently of unknown medical value and extremely costly.

A claim for benefits under an ERISA-governed plan "is a matter of contract interpretation." . . . The parties have devoted considerable time arguing what the proper standard of review is in this case. In Firestone Tire & Rubber Co. v. Bruch, 489 U.S. 101 (1989), the United States Supreme Court ruled that the denial of benefits by an ERISA plan administrator must "be reviewed under the de novo standard unless the benefit plan gives the administrator or fiduciary discretionary authority to determine eligibility for benefits or to construe the plan." "[I]f a benefit plan gives discretion to an administrator or fiduciary who is operating under a conflict of interest, that conflict must be weighed as a 'facto[r] in determining whether there is an abuse of discretion.' " (quoting Restatement (Second) of Trusts §187, Comment *d* (1959)). The plaintiff argues that because PHP was operating under a conflict of interest (i.e., PHP stood to gain a greater profit if the claim was denied) we should grant less deference to PHP's determination that HDC/ABMT is experimental. We need not decide what level of deference to give to the defendant's interpretation of the contract term because under the facts in this case, even applying de novo review, the clear and unambiguous language of the policy dictates that the defendant, Physicians Health Plan of Northern Indiana, properly denied coverage for the HDC/ABMT treatment.

DENIAL OF COVERAGE

In part, the Plan provides:

> "Experimental or Unproven Procedures" means any procedures, devices, drugs or medicines or the use thereof which falls within any of the following categories: 1. Which is considered by any government agency or subdivision, including but not limited to the Food and Drug Administration, the Office of Health Technology Assessment, or Medicare Coverage Issues Manual to be: a. experimental or investigational; b. not considered reasonable and necessary; or c. any similar finding; 2. Which is not covered under Medicare reimbursement laws, regulations or interpretations; or 3. Which is not commonly and customarily recognized by the medical profession in the state of Indiana as appropriate for the condition being treated. PLAN reserves the right to change, from time to time, the procedures considered to be Experimental or Unproven. Contact PLAN to determine if a particular procedure, treatment, or device is considered to be Experimental or Unproven.

The Medicare Coverage Issues Manual (which is referenced in the PHP Plan) provides in §35-31:

> C. Autologous Bone Marrow Transplantation (Effective for Services Performed on or After 04/28/89). . . . —Insufficient data exist to establish definite conclusions regarding the efficacy of autologous bone marrow transplantation for the following conditions: . . . Acute leukemia in relapse, Chronic granulocytic leukemia or Solid tumors [such as breast cancer] (other than neuroblastoma). In these cases, autologous bone marrow transplantation is not considered reasonable and necessary within the meaning of §1862(a)(1)(A) of the Act and is not covered under Medicare.

The plaintiff does not challenge the language of the Medicare Coverage Issues Manual but argues that the phrase in the Plan that PHP "reserves the right to change, from time to time, the procedures considered to be Experimental or Unproven" creates an obligation on the part of PHP to cover the contested treatment in light of recent medical research endorsing the procedure for solid tumors like breast cancer . . . rather than to hide behind outdated or inapplicable guidelines and therefore if the treatment is no longer experimental—as the plaintiff argues—she is entitled to coverage. . . .

The "right to change" the classification of procedures certainly does not obligate PHP to reclassify hourly, weekly, monthly or annually whether a treatment should be covered on the basis of competing views of medical experts (oncologists). Rather, PHP chose to link the experimental nature of a treatment to the neutral (third party) determination of the medical experts responsible for drafting the Medicare Coverage Issues Manual.[6] Clearly, PHP's intent was to avoid a case-by-case battle of the experts in which PHP would be required to reevaluate covered treatments each time a self-proclaimed "expert" publishes a new article. . . . [The contract] is . . . clear and unambiguous. Heller v. Equitable Life Assur. Soc., 833 F.2d 1253, 1257 (7th Cir. 1987) ("In the absence of a clear, unequivocal and specific contractual requirement [placing a duty on a party,] we refuse to order the same. To hold otherwise and to impose such a requirement would, in effect, enlarge the terms of the policy beyond those clearly defined in the policy agreed to by the parties.").[7] . . .

ERISA . . . does not dictate what a plan such as the PHP plan before us should cover. Hickey v. A.E. Staley Mfg., 995 F.2d 1385, at 1393 (7th Cir. 1993) ("Congress never intended ERISA to dictate the content of welfare benefit plans, much less for the federal courts to determine the content of such plans; . . . the discretion to make decisions concerning the content of the Plan rests with the Plan administrator"). Therefore, we hold that the language of the PHP Plan excludes coverage for HDC/ABMT as a treatment for breast cancer.

FULL AND FAIR REVIEW

Bechtold's second argument is that she was denied full and fair review . . . because PHP refused to accept the recommendation of its own complaints committee and instead denied the benefits based on the Plan Chief Operating Officer's disagreement with the committee's recommendation. We cannot agree with Bechtold's argument on this account because a review of the letter from PHP denying

6. The Medicare Coverage Issues Manual is updated when new medical data becomes available and the updates are published quarterly in the Federal Register. The provision relating to autologous bone marrow transplants for solid tumors (breast cancer) was published in the Federal Register on June 11, 1992, and was in effect at all times relevant to this proceeding (Bechtold was denied coverage in October 1992).

7. In Heller, . . . [w]e [noted] that [t]he insurance company seeking to [limit] coverage . . . need only incorporate a specific requirement to that effect in the policy, and we would not hesitate to enforce the same. On the other hand, insurers who fail to include this express . . . contractual requirement, and who refuse to cover an insured after entering into a binding and enforceable agreement after accepting substantial premiums, in circumstances such as those before us, cause problems not only for the insured, but for the insurance industry as well. Insurance companies, members of a service industry, . . . must conduct themselves accordingly instead of attempting to rely on the courts to correct their own deficiencies in underwriting and/or careless policy drafting.

the benefits makes clear that the committee recognized that the HDC/ABMT treatment was not covered under the plan. The committee, however, recommended a change of policy by the insurer to allow coverage of the procedure because: (1) the procedure was not experimental and PHP has an express intent of providing reasonable care for patients of this type; (2) Medicare supporting claims for this type of noncovered condition, is not that of a patient of Ms. Bechtold's age; (3) supportive data suggests the proposed treatment as very appropriate. . . .

The only authority vested in the committee was to recommend whether a specific claim for benefits had been properly denied based upon the language of the policy; it was not free to cast aside the agreed upon terms of the insurance contract. . . .

Conclusion

As stated above, cases of this nature pose troubling social as well as ethical questions that go well beyond the legal issues. As a court of law we are empowered to decide legal issues presented by specific cases or controversies. The greater social questions must be decided by the political branches of government which can engage in legislative factfinding and benefit from public hearings and constituent expression of opinion. . . . Chesterfield Smith, the former president of the American Bar Association once stated in a Law Day address: "Courts are being asked today to solve problems for which they are not institutionally equipped. . . . The American public perceives the courts as a jack-of-all trades available to furnish the answer to whatever may trouble them." The question of what procedures insurance companies should cover is just the type of problem to which Mr. Smith was referring.

In order to resolve the question of whether health insurance providers should cover treatments like HDC/ABMT, the prudent course of action might be to establish some sort of regional cooperative committees comprised of oncologists, internists, surgeons, experts in medical ethics, medical school administrators, economists, representatives of the insurance industry, patient advocates and politicians. Through such a collective task force perhaps some consensus might be reached concerning the definition of experimental procedures, as well as agreement on the procedures, which are so cost prohibitive that requiring insurers to cover them might result in the collapse of the healthcare industry. While such a committee would in no way be a panacea for our skyrocketing health care costs, it may help to reduce the incidence of suits in which one "expert" testifies that a procedure is experimental and another equally qualified "expert" testifies to the opposite effect. This so called battle of the experts occurs all too frequently in federal court. . . .

Angels

■ RUSH PRUDENTIAL HMO v. MORAN

536 U.S. 355 (2002)

Justice Souter delivered the opinion of the Court [with four justices dissenting].

Petitioner, Rush Prudential HMO, Inc., is a health maintenance organization (HMO) that contracts to provide medical services for employee welfare benefit plans covered by ERISA. Respondent Debra Moran is a beneficiary under one such plan, sponsored by her husband's employer. Rush's "Certificate of Group Coverage," issued to employees who participate in employer-sponsored plans, promises that Rush will provide them with "medically necessary" services. The terms of the certificate give Rush the "broadest possible discretion" to determine whether a medical service claimed by a beneficiary is covered under the certificate. . . .

In 1996, when Moran began to have pain and numbness in her right shoulder, Dr. Arthur LaMarre, her primary care physician, unsuccessfully administered "conservative" treatments such as physiotherapy. In October 1997, Dr. LaMarre recommended that Rush approve surgery by an unaffiliated specialist, Dr. Julia Terzis, who had developed an unconventional treatment for Moran's condition. Although Dr. LaMarre said that Moran would be "best served" by that procedure, Rush denied the request and, after Moran's internal appeals, affirmed the denial on the ground that the procedure was not "medically necessary." Rush instead proposed that Moran undergo standard surgery, performed by a physician affiliated with Rush. [Read the remainder of the facts of this case, excerpted at page 182.]

In January 1998, Moran made a written demand for an independent medical review of her claim, as guaranteed by Illinois's HMO Act, which provides:

> Each Health Maintenance Organization shall provide a mechanism for the timely review by a physician holding the same class of license as the primary care physician, who is unaffiliated with the Health Maintenance Organization, jointly selected by the patient . . . , primary care physician and the Health Maintenance Organization in the event of a dispute between the primary care physician and the Health Maintenance Organization regarding the medical necessity of a covered service proposed by a primary care physician. In the event that the reviewing physician determines the covered service to be medically necessary, the Health Maintenance Organization shall provide the covered service. . . .

When Rush failed to provide the independent review, Moran sued in an Illinois state court to compel compliance with the state Act. . . . [Rush claimed that ERISA preempts the state Act because the Act requires a review mechanism that is inconsistent with ERISA's process for challenging benefit denials.]

[T]his case addresses a state regulatory scheme that provides no new cause of action under state law and authorizes no new form of ultimate relief. While independent review under [the HMO Act] may well settle the fate of a benefit claim under a particular contract, the state statute does not enlarge the claim beyond the benefits available in any action brought under [ERISA]. And although the reviewer's determination would presumably replace that of the HMO as to what is "medically necessary" under this contract, the relief ultimately available would still be what ERISA authorizes in a suit for benefits. . . .

[The Act] does resemble an arbitration provision [which might be preempted] . . . to the extent that the independent reviewer considers disputes about the meaning of the HMO contract and receives "evidence" in the form of medical records, statements from physicians, and the like. But this is as far as the resemblance to arbitration goes, for the other features of review . . . give the proceeding a different character, one not at all at odds with the policy behind [ERISA preemption]. The Act does not give the independent reviewer a free-ranging power to construe contract terms, but instead, confines review to a single term: the phrase "medical necessity," used to define the services covered under the contract. This limitation, in turn, . . . [means that] the independent examiner must be a physician with credentials similar to those of the primary care physician, and is expected to exercise independent medical judgment in deciding what medical necessity requires. Accordingly, the reviewer in this case did not hold the kind of conventional evidentiary hearing common in arbitration, but simply received medical records submitted by the parties, and ultimately came to a professional judgment of his own. Once this process is set in motion, it does not resemble either contract interpretation or evidentiary litigation before a neutral arbiter, as much as it looks like a practice (having nothing to do with arbitration) of obtaining another medical opinion. The reference to an independent reviewer is similar to the submission to a second physician, which many health insurers are required by law to provide before denying coverage. . . . [O]nce [the Act] is seen as something akin to a mandate for second-opinion practice in order to ensure sound medical judgments, the preemption argument that arbitration . . . supplants judicial enforcement runs out of steam.

Notes: Insurance Coverage Disputes

1. *Medicare and Medicaid Coverage.* The coverage of public programs such as Medicare and Medicaid is defined in the same "medically necessary" and "experimental" terms as are commonly used in private insurance contracts. A related body of case law addresses whether novel or alternative treatments are covered under these public programs, reaching similarly mixed results. In favor of coverage, one court held that Medicaid must cover a certain treatment for both early and advanced stages of AIDS, even though FDA approval of the drug was limited to the latter. The court reasoned that "it would be improper . . . to interfere with a physician's judgment of medical necessity" based on FDA drug-labeling requirements because "FDA approved indications [are] not intended to limit or interfere with the practice of medicine; . . . the package insert is only informational." Weaver v. Reagan, 886 F.2d 194, 198 (8th Cir. 1989). In another case, the court found that a sex change operation is medically necessary and nonexperimental under Medicaid. Pinneke v. Preisser, 623 F.2d 546 (8th Cir. 1980). In a third, the court ordered Medicare to cover artificial lens implants for cataract correction despite the fact they were still under research investigation, explaining that

> manufacturers and physicians working to develop [lens implants] need to be assured that they will be reimbursed for their efforts during these investigational periods. Withdrawing Medicare coverage . . . [will likely cause the lens] industry's remarkable level of invention [to] decrease dramatically. . . . [Medicare]'s stultifying regulatory strategy, with its preference for government rules over market-generated innovation, is reminiscent of the central planning apparatuses that other nations are now struggling to leave behind. . . . If this type of thinking were to prevail, the status quo would be frozen and research and development would become a thing of the past. That is not the American way.

American Society of Cataract and Refractive Surgery v. Sullivan, 772 F. Supp. 666 (D.D.C. 1991). For decisions the other way, see Goodman v. Sullivan, 891 F.2d 449 (2d Cir. 1989) (Medicare regulation denying payment for MRI scans does not impermissibly supervise or control the practice of medicine); MacKenzie Medical Supply v. Leavitt, 419 F. Supp. 2d 766 (D. Md. 2006) ("if the Secretary . . . could never deny a claim when the physician had written a prescription, [t]hat would undermine the role of the Secretary in the Medicare system").

Especially controversial have been cases involving major organ transplants (liver, heart, lung, etc.) under Medicaid. In favor of coverage, see Pereira v. Kozlowski, 996 F.2d 723 (4th Cir. 1993); Salgado v. Kirschner, 878 P.2d 659 (Ariz. 1994); Jackson v. Millstone, 801 A.2d 1034 (Md. 2002). Allowing states to limit or refuse coverage, see Dexter v. Kirschner, 984 F.2d 979 (9th Cir. 1992); Shannon v. Jack Eckerd Corp., 113 F.3d 208 (11th Cir. 1997).

2. *Appeal Procedures.* In addition to the *substance* of coverage decisions, *Moran* shows that the proper *procedures* for challenging and reviewing these decisions have been controversial under both public and private insurance. For conventional private insurance, appeal procedures at one time were fairly straightforward: If you were unhappy, you hired a lawyer and sued. Although ERISA preemption complicates which court to sue in and what the standard of review will be, these disputes were resolved essentially like any other contract dispute. But that is true only so far as *judicial* review is concerned. The decision process by the insurer at the initial stage of decision first attracted the attention of state regulators and legislators. This is especially true under managed care because then the denial of coverage does not simply affect who will pay, it often affects whether treatment will be rendered at all. Therefore, it is not sufficient for patients eventually to have their day in court. They need a prompt and fair review process on the spot.

As the *Moran* case illustrates, many states now require prompt external, independent review for all health insurers, but state law still cannot reach self-insured employers. Therefore, the Affordable Care Act implemented a uniform set of external, independent review requirements for all forms of private health insurance, including self-funded employers. These standards require that, under normal circumstances, appeals be sent to an independent physician reviewer within a week, for decision within 45 days. When that length of time would seriously jeopardize health, the review must be completed within three days. 75 Fed. Reg. 43330 (2010). Somewhat surprisingly (or perhaps not), some courts have refused to treat these independent reviews as binding on patients who decide to pursue further appeals in court. See, e.g., Alexandra H. v. Oxford Health Insurance, 833 F.3d 1299 (11th Cir. 2016).

Under Medicare and Medicaid, appeal procedures are even more complex since the analysis varies along each of the following lines, and for each of these categories there are several points of view: There are constitutional, statutory, and regulatory dimensions. Not only do each of these dimensions differ between the two programs, but within Medicare the appeal procedures differ between Part A and Part B, and within Medicaid they vary state by state. Within each program, appeal procedures also differ between fee-for-service and HMO providers. And, appeal issues differ according to what is at stake: basic eligibility or particular covered services. The issues also differ according to whether a patient is challenging a fact-based ruling in an individual case, a general substantive rule or policy decision, or a procedural rule. And, there are various levels of decision, from initial review by "fiscal intermediaries" (insurers under contract with CMS), to administrative review within CMS, to judicial review. To top it all off, a whole different set of procedures and institutions govern appeals by patients over eligibility for coverage than those that govern appeals by providers challenging how much they are paid when services are covered.

3. *Block That Metaphor.* For another court moved to literary heights by an insurance coverage dispute, see Zuckerberg v. Blue Cross & Blue Shield, 464 N.Y.S.2d 678, 683 (1983) (requiring Blue Shield to pay for a course of nutritional cancer therapy of unproven benefit that the plaintiff obtained in Mexico), rev'd on other grounds, 490 N.E.2d 839 (N.Y. 1986), where the court recited:

> A possible path was opened, had it not been taken, what then? At least, it was tried. "For of all sad words of tongue or pen, The saddest are these: 'It might have been!' " (*Maud Muller,* by John Greenleaf Whittier, stanza 53).

For a more somber view, consider the following thoughts from Judge Gladys Kessler in *Salazar v. District of Columbia,* 1996 WL 768038 (D.D.C. 1996):

> This case is about people—children and adults who are sick, poor, and vulnerable—for whom life, in the memorable words of poet Langston Hughes, "ain't been no crystal stair." It is written in the dry and bloodless language of "the law"—statistics, acronyms of agencies and bureaucratic entities, Supreme Court case names and quotes, official governmental reports, periodicity tables, etc. But let there be no forgetting the real people to whom this dry and bloodless language gives voice: anxious, working parents who are too poor to obtain medications or heart catheter procedures or lead poisoning screens for their children, AIDS patients unable to get treatment, elderly persons suffering from chronic conditions like diabetes and heart disease who require constant monitoring and medical attention. Behind every "fact" found herein is a human face and the reality of being poor in the richest nation on earth.

And a more balanced view:

> Coverage litigation has become one of the American health system's Crimeas, a designated battleground for opposing armies. On one side are arrayed individual patients with idiosyncratic needs, and the physicians and hospitals who stand ready to serve them. On the other side can be found employers, insurers and government—in each case claiming to represent the interest of beneficiaries or taxpayers as a whole by denying relief to one member or the group. This is, of course, the core challenge of managed care: creating an efficient system of population-based health management which nonetheless accounts equitably for the interests of individuals.

William Sage, Judicial Opinions Involving Health Insurance Coverage: Trompe L'Oeil or Window on the World?, 31 Ind. L. Rev. 49 (1998).

4. *The Doctor Knows Best.* Returning to the *Zorek* case from 1966, note that three weeks of hospitalization at Mount Sinai Hospital then cost $557.90. Today, this would not even buy *one day's* hospitalization. Should this fact change the outcome in *Zorek*? The *Zorek* court appears quite absolute in its statement that "only the treating physician can determine what the appropriate treatment should be for any given condition." What more prosaic phrase do we usually apply to allowing the one who is paid (or, here, a member of its medical staff) to be the sole judge of the necessity of its services? Consider the contrasting literary viewpoint found in George Bernard Shaw's preface to his play *The Doctor's Dilemma*:

> That any sane nation . . . should . . . give a surgeon a pecuniary interest in cutting off your leg, is enough to make one despair of political humanity. But that is precisely what we have done. And the more appalling the mutilation, the more the mutilator is paid. Scandalized voices murmur that . . . operations are necessary. They may be. It may also be necessary to hang a man or pull down a house. But we take good care not to make the hangman and the house breaker the judges of that.

In *Black & Decker Disability Plan v. Nord,* 538 U.S. 822 (2003), the Court ruled that ERISA does not require employers to defer to the judgment of treating physicians in determining whether a worker is disabled.

5. *ERISA and Medicare.* The seminal decision holding that ERISA governs insurance contract disputes between employers and employees is Pilot Life Insurance Co. v. Dedeaux, 481 U.S. 41 (1987). Thereafter, most of these cases have shifted to the federal courts, where they are decided without a jury and without the possibility of personal injury or punitive damages. ERISA allows recovery of only the monetary value of the treatment at issue. When ERISA does not apply, state court juries have sometimes awarded punitive damages in the range of $50 million to $100 million. Most commentators believe that, although some of the punitive awards were excessive, it is unconscionable to disallow any recovery of basic compensatory damages for bodily injury when there is a clear breach of a contract for medical services.

For private insurers that offer Medicare coverage (known as Medicare Advantage), the Medicare dispute resolution process has a preemptive effect similar to that of ERISA, barring beneficiaries from pursing their grievances under state law. See Uhm v. Humana Health Plan Inc., 573 F.3d 865 (9th Cir. 2009).

6. *In Search of the "Iron Clad" Insurance Contract. Bechtold* demonstrates that the legal landscape has changed considerably since *Zorek.* This is true in several respects. First, coverage decisions under private insurance are now typically decided prior to or during the course of treatment through requests for prior authorization, rather than in the ordinary process of claims review. Second, as the result of ERISA preemption, these cases are now decided in federal court under a potentially more lenient standard of review than that governing garden-variety contract disputes. Third, insurers have rewritten contracts to make their decisions more enforceable. They declare that questions of interpretation are to be determined in the discretion of the insurer, whose decision is binding. And they more frequently exclude specific controversial treatments by name.

None of these changes has dramatically altered the favorable treatment that patients usually receive in court, however. The shift from retrospective to prospective or concurrent utilization review has introduced a different form of hardship. Now, rather than merely risking loss of money, patients risk not getting the treatment at all. As one court noted: "A mistaken conclusion about medical necessity following retrospective review will result in the wrongful withholding of payment. An erroneous decision in a prospective review process, on the other hand, in practical consequences, results in the withholding of necessary care, potentially leading to a patient's permanent disability or death." See Wickline v. State, 239 Cal. Rptr. 810, 812 (Cal. Ct. App. 1986).

Although ERISA allows a more lenient standard of review, *Bechtold* explains that ERISA requires more exacting scrutiny when insurers are under a conflict of interest. The obvious conflict of interest is that insurers usually have already collected their premium and each medical payment comes out of their bottom line.

Moreover, a different part of the *Moran* opinion held that a deferential standard does not apply to reviews by independent physicians, and in Metropolitan Life Ins. Co. v. Glenn, 554 U.S. 105 (2008), the Court held that an insurer administering a self-funded employer plan is under a conflict of interest, even though the insurer spends the employer's money, not its own, when approving claims. Thus, even under ERISA, courts still frequently construe ambiguous terms such as *experimental* and *medically necessary* in favor of patients. See, e.g., Kunin v. Benefit Trust Life Insurance Co., 910 F.2d 534 (9th Cir. 1990) (it is arbitrary and capricious to conclude that autism is excluded as a "mental illness"); Bradley v. Empire Blue Cross & Blue Shield, 562 N.Y.S.2d 908 (N.Y. Sup. Ct. 1990) (patient likely to prevail in showing that HDC/ABMT is not experimental treatment for AIDS, even though his doctor was the only one in the country who had ever used the procedure this way and the patient had signed an informed consent form acknowledging that he was participating in an "experiment").

As for the contract technique used in *Bechtold,* other courts have ruled that incorporation by reference does not give subscribers fair notice of what is excluded, and it is particularly unconscionable to govern young policyholders with rules written for the elderly under Medicare. See, e.g., Waldrip v. Connecticut National Life Insurance Co., 573 So. 2d 1172 (5th Cir. 1991); Hyde v. Humana Insurance Co., 598 So. 2d 876 (Ala. 1992).

The contractual change that has had the most impact is assigning to the insurer the authority to make binding interpretations of ambiguous phrases. Courts have ruled that, in effect, ERISA allows the contract to nullify the usual judicial presumption against the party that drafted the contract (*contra proferentum*). To counter that move, the National Association of Insurance Commissioners proposed a model act to ban such clauses, which several states have adopted. But courts have split on whether ERISA allows this type of regulation. See Standard Insurance Co. v. Morrison, 584 F.3d 837 (9th Cir. 2009).

7. *Conflicts of Interest.* As these cases and notes suggest, various conflicts of interest permeate the arena of insurance coverage determinations. The most obvious conflict is that of the insurer who has to pay. But is an insurer under a conflict of interest if it merely administers claims and does utilization review for a self-insured employer rather than bearing the risk of medical costs itself? In this situation, the insurer is paid a per-case or per-annum administrative fee and the financial risk is borne by the employer. Does this then put the employer under a conflict of interest, or is it accurate to say that the employer has in mind the interests of the employee group as a whole? One interesting case allowed an employer and its workers to sue under ERISA for wrongly *paying out* medical benefits from a self-funded plan under the theory that this depleted the plan's assets, which otherwise would have been available to pay more legitimate claims. IT Corp. v. General American Life Insurance Co., 107 F.3d 1415 (9th Cir. 1997). What about letting committees composed of employees decide these disputes? Are they conflict-free, considering that they may trade off the interests of one patient to favor the interests of the rest of the group?

Various expressions of opinion on these issues can be found in the case law, but suffice it to say that judicial opinions are still inconsistent and evolving. One notable instance of a decision apparently affected by an insurer's conflict of interest occurred in an unreported California trial verdict that was later settled (Fox v. HealthNet). That case also involved HDC/ABMT for breast cancer. There, an HMO refused coverage and the patient later died. The case was tried under state law because her insurance came from her government job, which ERISA does not cover. Therefore, her family was free to seek punitive damages. The jury returned a whopping $89 million verdict. According to press reports, the jury was influenced by two aggravating circumstances: that the HMO's medical director received a bonus determined in part by the amount of money he saved through coverage denials, and that the HMO had recently approved this same procedure for one of its own employees.

A different type of conflict surfaced in another notable case against Health-Net. As discussed in section E.3, HMOs sometimes shift the insurance risk to treating physicians by contracting with them on a fully capitated basis. This in effect tosses the hot potato of making coverage denials to the doctor, because it is the doctor who bears most of the costs. This also minimizes the potential for coverage disputes arising in the first place, since a patient is much less likely to be presented conflicting opinions between her doctor and her insurer if the doctor simply declines to order the treatment. This new dynamic was revealed when the same lawyer who represented Mrs. Fox in the prior case began to investigate a similar case involving Mrs. DeMeurs, also with breast cancer. He found that her doctor initially recommended her for HDC/ABMT but he changed his mind after the HMO medical director called the doctor to question his initial judgment. This case was decided in arbitration, resulting in a $1 million award. In the arbitrators' opinion,

> the [HMO's] actions designed and intended to interfere with an existing doctor/patient relationship constitute extreme and outrageous behavior exceeding all bounds usually tolerated in a civilized society. It is conduct undertaken with reckless disregard of the probability of causing severe emotional distress. This conduct clearly crosses the line of appropriate communication between insurer and doctor.

Do you agree?

8. *Courts, Committees, or Congress?* Suppose we view this situation as one involving two, unavoidably competing conflicts of interest: that of the physician who is to be paid, and that of the insurer/employer who is to pay. Is there any "neutral" third party capable of resolving this conflict? Are the courts themselves neutral, given their tendency, noted by Judge Coffey, to "go about doing good where we see fit"? Is the proper, "unbiased" perspective that of the individual patient who is presently sick and has insurance, or instead that of the pool of subscribers at the point they are deciding how much insurance coverage they can afford? Which perspective are courts more likely to take? Legislatures? Employers? Panels of expert doctors? Panels like those suggested by Judge Coffey composed of various interest groups and expertise? Isn't the hearing committee that actually reviewed Ms. Bechtold's case potentially one such representative panel? See Barnett v. Kaiser Foundation Health Plan, 32 F.3d 413 (9th Cir. 1994) (advisory board composed of HMO's own doctors provides neutral, expert review). If so, why was Judge Coffey so reluctant to accept its recommendation? Which of these various processes do you have the most confidence in, considering the full range of medical conditions and expenditures that are potentially at stake?

9. *Cookbook Medicine.* Why would insurers ever have adopted such broad terms as *medically necessary* and *experimental* in the first place? One could have predicted that it would be impossible to police physicians' decisions by using their own conceptual

norms. One reason contracts might contain such open-ended terms is that health insurance originated from the medical establishment itself, in the form of Blue Cross/Blue Shield. But why has this not changed now that insurers are much more aggressively competitive? Courts frequently urge insurers to make their contracts more specific if they want to reliably exclude coverage. Indeed, it is possible to make coverage terms quite specific using the detailed practice guidelines that are being produced by the health services research community in great numbers. See Clark C. Havighurst, Practice Guidelines for Medical Care: The Policy Rationale, 34 St. Louis U. L.J. 777 (1990). But how realistic is this really? The most extensive effort to date is that in Oregon, described in section D.1, which uses more than 600 treatment-condition pairings (e.g., surgery for appendicitis) to specify Medicaid coverage across the entire range of medical practice.

The difficulty with this approach is aptly captured in Aaron and Schwartz's criticism of the Oregon list as "meat-ax" rationing. All covered treatments are always covered, no matter how mild the condition or how effective the medical intervention, while excluded items are not covered at all no matter how severe the condition or how great the potential is for improvement. To achieve the desirable level of specificity would require rigorous scientific information on each of the almost 10,000 diagnostic entries in the International Classification of Diseases (10th ed.) (known as "ICD-10") and for each of the 10,000 medical interventions listed in the AMA's Common Procedural Terminology (known as "CPT" codes). Moreover, each complication and sequence of events for each of these items would have to be evaluated in all possible combinations. In other words, for two conditions, A and B, we would have to consider A alone, B alone, and AB, as well as A before B and A after B. For even a single, modestly complex disease category (say, heart disease) with only 20 conditions, this analysis would produce some 10 billion different clinical scenarios.

The practical impossibility of adequately capturing the judgmental and nuanced aspects of medical decisionmaking in a detailed, prescriptive fashion has led legal scholars to refer to this as a problem in "relational contracting." Contracts that call for the exercise of professional judgment or that define complex, ongoing service relationships present unique problems as compared with classic contractual settings that simply specify the purchase of identified products. These relational contracts require inventive and flexible contracting tools in order to accomplish their purposes. In health insurance contracts, we see a persistent desire on the part of both subscribers and insurers to use contract terms that invoke broad medical norms rather than precise clinical details. If courts insist on construing these terms against insurers, are they not forcing the parties to adopt suboptimal contracting techniques like the one used in *Bechtold* of simply cross-referencing Medicare rules designed for old people?

Perhaps there is a workable middle ground between hyperspecific contracts and the open-ended discretion conferred by "medically necessary." Consider these thoughtful comments by Prof. Sage:

> The most important thing to appreciate about "medical necessity" is that has always operated at two levels: symbolic and substantive. . . . To many physicians, the phrase "not medically necessary" means "not clinically indicated," which makes them question why a seemingly nonprofessional party such as a health plan has the right to challenge their professional opinion. To many health plans, it means "not covered even though not expressly excluded from coverage," which gives them a degree

> of comfort issuing denials based on established insurance practice even though such decisions outrage physicians. Consequently, decisions involving medical necessity are frequently characterized by inconsistent administration, poor communication, distrust and, if disputes arise, relatively unprincipled, results-oriented judicial resolution. . . .
>
> [M]edical necessity cannot do the heavy lifting of cost control, or of quality assurance, in health care. . . . [H]ealth plans and policymakers have paid too much attention to standardized rules for coverage decisions and too little attention to therapeutic effect. Health care is both an outcome and a process, and all parts of the process, including those involving insurers, need to be caring as well as efficient. Medical necessity determinations should indeed be scientific and equitable, but, like good medicine, should also demonstrate compassion, offer hope, promote trust, and avoid abandonment.

William M. Sage, Managed Care's Crimea: Medical Necessity, Therapeutic Benefit, and the Goals of Administrative Process in Health Insurance, 53 Duke L.J. 597, 600, 650 (2003).

10. *Can Patients Decide?* With both courts and insurers struggling with what is "medically necessary" or "experimental" in any given case, Russell Korobkin has called for putting the choice back into the patient's own hands. Under what Korobkin terms "relative value health insurance," health plans would differ in their depth of coverage. More expensive plans might cover all medically necessary care; other, cheaper plans might exclude from coverage treatments that fail to meet a cost-effectiveness threshold. Patients could select the plans that best suit them. See Russell Korobkin, Relative Value Health Insurance, 39 J. of Health Pol., Pol'y & Law 417 (2014). For a criticism of the Korobkin approach, see Nicholas Bagley et al., Correcting Signals for Innovation in Health Care, Brookings, Oct. 7, 2015.

Another proposal, endorsed by Christopher Robertson, would allow patients to decline treatments in exchange for a cash payment from their insurer:

> Instead of asking patients whether the health care consumption is better than nothing, we should ask patients if health consumption is better than whatever else they may prefer. [T]he potential reform is simple:
>
> 1. Pay a small but substantial part of the insurance benefit as cash directly to the patient-beneficiary.
>
> 2. If the patient chooses to proceed with the treatment, the patient takes the cash payment to the provider (along with any required cost-share obligation), and the insurer matches it with the balance of the insurance benefit. . . .
>
> As such, the patient would receive both a cash benefit (the payment he or she receives) and an in-kind benefit (the payment to the provider), while still perhaps remaining exposed to some portion of the cost out-of-pocket. For patients that choose to spend the money in ways other than the treatment, the insurer saves the remainder of the cost of the procedure. . . .
>
> Patients who receive a split benefit may choose to proceed with the treatment or choose to promote health in some other way, such as consuming some other treatment not covered by the insurer (e.g., acupuncture, an alternative diet regimen, a concierge doctor, or visiting nursing services), paying money to a member of the family to stay home and provide care to the dying patient, or purchasing disability insurance to help cope with the symptoms of the illness. Or patients may use the money to serve other nonmedical values, such as enhancing housing, consuming more of some luxury good, paying off other debts that are causing disutility, paying

for education (for themselves or others), contributing to a charity, or whatever else may appeal to the patient.

Christopher T. Robertson, The Split Benefits: The Painless Way to Put Skin Back in the Health Care Game, 98 Cornell L. Rev. 921 (2013); see also Christopher T. Robertson, Paying for Ourselves: The Ethics, Economics, and Law of Cost-Sharing in Health Insurance (2017).

11. *Paying for Medical Research.* Another important public policy implication of these cases is, who should pay for the necessary costs of medical experimentation? Manufacturers bear most of the costs for clinical trials that test new *drugs* and *devices* subject to FDA approval. Medical *procedures,* in contrast, are not required to be tested and are not owned by anyone. If new medical and surgical techniques are tested at all, the funding usually comes from the National Institutes of Health. Remarkably, its $30 *billion* budget is sufficient only to cover the *research* expenses of clinical trials (patient recruitment, data collection and analysis, etc.), not the *clinical* costs. Conventionally, the clinical costs are paid by patients' private and public insurance. Initially, insurers used "experimental" exclusions to refuse payment only for unscientific, "alternative" medicine. Under pressure from private market forces and public program deficits, insurers also began to refuse payment for some treatments that are rendered in scientific research studies. Despite the explicitly "experimental" setting, insurers have not been uniformly successful. For instance, Medicare decided in the mid-1990s to limit what it pays for treatments during clinical research studies, but following a legal challenge, an executive order, and legislation, Medicare now pays for routine clinical costs involved in NIH-funded or FDA-focused studies, or in studies of medical devices used in life-threatening medical situations. Also, the Affordable Care Act now requires private insurers to cover treatment costs in clinical trials for cancer or "other life-threatening conditions."

12. *Further Reading.* For discussions of **medical necessity** (note 1), see Timothy P. Blanchard, "Medical Necessity" Determinations: A Continuing Healthcare Policy Problem, 37 J. Health L. 599 (2004); Muriel R. Gillick, Medicare Coverage for Technological Innovations: Time for New Criteria?, 350 New Eng. J. Med. 2199 (2004); Janet L. Dolgin, Unhealthy Determinations: Controlling "Medical Necessity," 22 Va. J. Soc. Pol'y & L. 435 (2015).

For those who are interested in **appeals procedures** (note 2), a fairly detailed overview can be found on the Web site for this book, www.health-law.org. There is also substantial scholarly commentary. The most prolific author on these topics is Professor Eleanor Kinney. See Eleanor Kinney, The Accidental Administrative Law of the Medicare Program, 15 Yale J. Health Pol'y L. & Ethics 111 (2015); Eleanor Kinney ed., Guide to Medicare Coverage Decision-Making and Appeals (2002); Eleanor D. Kinney, Medicare Coverage Decision-Making and Appeal Procedures, 60 Wash. & Lee L. Rev. 1461 (2003); Eleanor Kinney, Rule and Policy Making Under the Medicaid Program: A Challenge to Federalism, 51 Ohio St. L.J. 855 (1991). For general and comprehensive overviews, see also Diane Hoffmann & Virginia Rowthorn, Achieving Quality and Responding to Consumers: The Medicare Beneficiary Complaint Process, 5 Ind. Health L. Rev. 9 (2008); Maxwell Mehlman & Karen Visocan, Medicare and Medicaid: Are They Just Health Care Systems?, 29 Hous. L. Rev. 835 (1992).

For in-depth commentary and analysis, with both theoretical and philosophical analyses and numerous suggestions for improvement on the full range of these procedural issues, see Eleanor D. Kinney, Protecting American Health Care Consumers (2002); Aaron Kesselheim, What's the Appeal? Trying to Control Managed Care Medical Necessity Decisionmaking Through a System of External Appeals, 149 U. Pa. L. Rev. 873 (2001); Nan D. Hunter, Risk Governance and Deliberative Democracy in Health Care, 97 Geo. L.J. 1 (2008); Meir Katz, Towards a New Moral Paradigm in Health Care Delivery, 36 Am. J.L. & Med. 78 (2010); Won Bok Lee, Recalibrating "Experimental Treatment Exclusion": An Empirical Analysis, 83 U. Cin. L. Rev. 171 (2014).

For commentary **generally supportive of the *Bechtold* point of view** (note 4), see Mark Hall & Gerard Anderson, Health Insurers' Assessment of Medical Necessity, 140 U. Pa. L. Rev. 1637 (1992); Richard Saver, Reimbursing New Technologies: Why Are the Courts Judging Experimental Medicine?, 44 Stan. L. Rev. 1095 (1992). For **contrasting commentary, supportive of *Zorek***, see David Frankford, Food Allergy and the Health Care Financing Administration: A Story of Rage, 1 Widener L. Symp. J. 159 (1996); Sara Rosenbaum et al., Who Should Determine When Health Care Is Medically Necessary?, 340 New Eng. J. Med. 229 (1999). For **an international perspective**, see Timothy Jost, Health Care Coverage Determinations: An International Comparative Study (2004). For thorough analysis of medical, legal, and health policy issues relating to **bone marrow transplants**, see Richard A. Rettig, False Hope vs. Evidence-Based Medicine: Bone Marrow Transplantation and Breast Cancer (2005); Peter Jacobson et al., Litigating the Science of Breast Cancer Treatment, 32 J. Health Pol. Pol'y & L. 785 (2007). Considering the facts of *Zorek*, it is interesting to note that "stomach-stapling" **surgeries for obesity** constitute a growing area of dispute and litigation. See Mark A. Hall, State Regulation of Medical Necessity: The Case of Weight-Reduction Surgery, 53 Duke L.J. 653 (2004); Manny v. Central States, Southeast and Southwest Areas Pension and Health Welfare Funds, 388 F.3d 247 (7th Cir. 2004) (Posner, J.).

For discussions of **how ERISA shapes the interpretation of insurance contracts** (notes 6 and 7), see John H. Langbein, Trust Law as Regulatory Law: The *UNUM/Provident* Scandal and Judicial Review of Benefit Denials Under ERISA, 101 Nw. U. L. Rev. 1315 (2007); Timothy Jost, "*MetLife v. Glenn*": The Court Addresses a Conflict over Conflicts in ERISA Benefit Administration, 27 Health Aff. w430 (2008); Roy Harmon & A. G. Harmon, Weighing Medical Judgments, 13 Mich. St. U. J. Med. & L. 157 (2009); Maria Hylton, Post-*Firestone* Skirmishes: "Obama Care," Discretionary Clauses and Judicial Review of ERISA Plan Administrator Decisions, 10 Wm. & Mary Pol'y Rev. 1 (2010); Mark Hall et al., Judicial Protection of Managed Care Consumers: An Empirical Study of Insurance Coverage Disputes, 26 Seton Hall L.J. 1055 (1996).

For general analysis of **which institutional actor should make coverage decisions** (note 8), see Mark A. Hall, Making Medical Spending Decisions ch.3 (1997); David Hsia, Benefits Determination Under Health Care Reform: Who Should Decide Coverage Policy?, 15 J. Leg. Med. 533 (1994).

For articles taking a **therapeutic jurisprudence or a legal process approach to analyzing coverage disputes** (note 9), see Kathy Cerminara, Dealing with Dying: How Insurers Can Help Patients Seeking Last-Chance Therapies (Even When the Answer Is "No"), 15 Health Matrix 285 (2005); Nan D. Hunter, Managed Process, Due Care: Structures of Accountability in Health Care, 6 Yale J. Health Pol'y L. & Ethics 93 (2006); Charity Scott, Therapeutic Approaches to Conflict Resolution in Health Care Settings, 21 Ga. St. U. L. Rev. 797 (2005).

For discussions of **paying for clinical medical research** (note 11), see Sandra J. Carnahan, Medicare's Coverage with Study Participation Policy: Clinical Trials or Tribulations?, 7 Yale J. Health Pol'y L. & Ethics 229 (2007); Mark Barnes & Jerald Korn, Medicare Reimbursement for Clinical Trial Services, 38 J. Health L. 609 (2005); Dina Berlyn, Routine Patient Care in Clinical Trials: Whose Cost Is It Anyway?, 16 J.L. & Health 78 (2003); Earl Steinberg et al., Insurance Coverage for Experimental Technologies, 14(4) Health Aff. 143 (Nov. 1995); Mark B. McClellan & Sean R. Tunis, Medicare Coverage of ICDs, 352 New Eng. J. Med. 222 (2005).

Notes: Peer Review Organizations and Utilization Review

1. *Medicare Peer Review.* The very first section of the Medicare statute prohibits any federal "supervision or control over the practice of medicine." 42 U.S.C. §1395. Despite this guarantee of physician autonomy, someone obviously has to scrutinize the necessity of the medical services Medicare pays for. For many years, Medicare used the mechanism of physician peer review—that is, doctors monitoring themselves—to reconcile the principle of noninterference with the need for judging medical necessity. But the peer review organizations (PROs) that Congress established to carry out that function failed to save any money and provoked intense physician blowback. See Timothy Jost, Policing Cost Containment: The Medicare Peer Review Organization Program, 14 Puget Sound L. Rev. 483 (1991).

Over time, PROs have moved away from peer review and refocused their efforts on quality improvement. In 2002, Medicare even began referring to them as Quality Improvement Organizations (QIOs). QIOs serve as government-sponsored consultants that partner with health care organizations—in particular, hospitals and nursing homes—to share data, teach best practices, and offer technical support. The QIOs bear little resemblance to the utilization-review entities that Congress once envisioned. See Nicholas Bagley, Bedside Bureaucrats: Why Medicare Reform Hasn't Worked, 101 Geo L.J. 519, 535 (2013).

2. *UR: Friend or Foe?* In the 1990s, private insurers pursued "utilization review" (UR) much more thoroughly and aggressively than they had in prior decades, leading to a backlash from physicians and patients. Consider the following:

> In the predawn hours of March 27, 1993, Esther Nesbitt was working the night shift at Kaiser's nurse hotline. She had been a nurse for 20 years, working in New York City emergency rooms early in her career. . . . On Nesbitt's desk was a *Manual of Pediatric Protocols,* including a three-page tip sheet entitled "Fever." The tip sheet was arranged much like a set of college notes, with a nine-line definition of fever at the top, an explanation of fever's causes, and only then a series of questions that parents should be asked. Down near the bottom of the first page, ninth in a list of 11 questions, was a question that many emergency-room doctors would pose right away: "Is [the] child having problems breathing?"
>
> From her perch at Kaiser's offices, Nesbitt decided after a few minutes that little James Adams wasn't in respiratory distress. . . . There would be no ambulance called, no authorization for the family to seek the closest hospital. Kaiser had given its instructions. It was up to Lamona Adams to stand in her driveway, holding her baby in the dark, and wait for her husband to come home. [The couple drove 40 miles through a severe rain storm to reach the hospital designated by Kaiser. At that point, their baby had stopped breathing. He turned out to have meningitis, a severe

> but easily treatable infection when caught in time. With aggressive treatment, the doctors saved his life, but they had to amputate all his hands and feet because of damage to his circulatory system.]

George Anders, Health Against Wealth: HMOs and the Breakdown of Medical Trust (1996). And, consider this physician's view:

> To call myself a vascular surgeon, I had to do well in college, then spend the next 12 years working grueling hours, depriving myself of most of the joys of young adulthood and immersing myself in other people's worst misery. . . . I now have an army of vindictive bureaucrats and largely untrained reviewers nipping at my heels, and must spend many hours a week defending myself against their overwhelmingly wrongheaded second-guessing of clinical decisions.

Stephen D. Leonard, M.D., Letter to the Editor, N.Y. Times, Apr. 28, 1992, at A16.

3. *The Legality of Prior Authorization.* Nowadays, utilization review is more often conducted on a prospective basis, prior to treatment, than as part of ordinary insurance claims review. As a result, decisions to deny coverage are likely to result in denial of treatment as well. Those denials of treatment can give rise to tort liability as well as contractual liability. The legality of UR can also be challenged under regulatory and contract law. Because coverage denials affect treatment decisions, utilization review might be characterized as an illegal interference with medical judgment. This might occur, for instance, if the utilization reviewer making a medical necessity determination is not a licensed physician in the relevant state. The usual process is for nonmedical personnel to review coverage requests with screening criteria that flag certain requests for review by a nurse. The nurse then decides which cases to refer for physician review. Usually the request is not denied without physician review, but the physician may be in some central office out of state, and usually is not trained in the particular specialty involved, unless the insurer decides to refer the request for independent review.

Courts generally have upheld this process when challenged based on medical licensure or on general principles of interference with medical judgment. They reason that utilization reviewers do not purport to make medical treatment decisions, only payment decisions. See Morris v. District of Columbia Board of Medicine, 701 A.2d 364 (D.C. 1997) (reviewing medical appropriateness for an insurance company does not constitute the practice of medicine); Association of American Physicians and Surgeons v. Weinberger, 395 F. Supp. 125 (N.D. Ill. 1975) (three-judge court), aff'd mem., 423 U.S. 975 (1975) (medical necessity review under Medicare does not unduly interfere with physicians' judgment). But see Murphy v. Board of Medical Examiners, 949 P.2d 530 (Ariz. Ct. App. 1997) (medical licensing board has jurisdiction over insurance company doctor who allegedly exercised bad medical judgment in denying claims); State Board of Registration for Healing Arts v. Fallon, 41 S.W.3d 474 (Mo. 2001) (same). Might a utilization review requirement that denies coverage unless the patient obtains advance approval be struck down as an illegal forfeiture or penalty clause under contract law? Consider a case where it is clear the request would have been approved if submitted but the insurer denies payment simply because the patient or doctor did not follow the proper channels. Nazay v. Miller, 949 F.2d 1323, 1335 (3d Cir. 1991) (upholding insurer under ERISA, but only where the failure to obtain advance permission cost the patient a 30 percent co-payment, not complete denial of coverage).

Legal oversight of UR has resulted more through legislation than through judicial doctrine. Utilization review regulations now exist in most states. They require insurers and third-party UR firms to maintain proper licensure and expertise of personnel (including M.D.s licensed in the state), to give a prompt response to coverage requests, and sometimes to disclose the screening criteria they use.

5. *Medicaid Appeals.* State Medicaid agencies must supply individuals with a "fair hearing" to challenge the denial of coverage or payment for medical services. (Medicaid beneficiaries who receive benefits through managed care organizations, however, must first proceed through the internal appeals process established by those organizations.) After taking evidence and allowing for cross-examination of witnesses, an administrative law judge will issue a written opinion. If the coverage denial is upheld, the beneficiary can challenge that determination in state court. See Kaiser Family Foundation, A Guide to the Medicaid Appeals Process (2012). Creative litigants have sometimes sought to go straight to court without exhausting their administrative claims. However, since the Supreme Court's 2015 decision in Armstrong v. Exceptional Child Center, Inc., excerpted in Section A.3, the courts have sharply cut back on their willingness to entertain direct challenges by beneficiaries or providers to state Medicaid coverage and payment decisions.

6. *Medicare Appeals.* Under Medicare, judicial review is available only for claims above $1000, and only after administrative remedies are exhausted. 42 U.S.C. §1395ff(b)(1)(E)(i). Because courts give heavy deference to CMS's interpretation of the Medicare statute, however, it tends to be difficult to win on the merits. See Gray Panthers v. Schweiker, 453 U.S. 34 (1981); Atkins v. Rivera, 477 U.S. 154 (1986). See generally Eleanor Kinney ed., Guide to Medicare Coverage Decision-Making and Appeals (2002); Eleanor D. Kinney, Medicare Coverage Decision-Making and Appeal Procedures, 60 Wash. & Lee L. Rev. 1461 (2003). As with Medicaid, litigants have sometimes sought inventive ways to circumvent administrative review. See Mathews v. Diaz, 426 U.S. 67 (1976) (administrative exhaustion waived by agency); Bowen v. Michigan Academy of Family Physicians, 476 U.S. 667 (1986) (under prior version of statute, allowing judicial review of the method for determining reimbursement but not of reimbursement amounts (whatever that means)); City of New York v. Heckler, 476 U.S. 467 (1986) (failure to follow normal appeals route excused by the futility and irreparable injury of strict compliance). Shalala v. Illinois Council of Long Term Care, 529 U.S. 1, however, closed a number of these loopholes and held that the exhaustion requirement is "nearly absolute."

7. *The Success of UR.* Research shows that cost-savings from UR are modest. Utilization review successfully reduces hospitalization expenses, but savings overall are muted by the administrative expense of running these programs. See Uwe Reinhardt, Spending More Through Cost Control: Our Obsessive Quest to Gut the Hospital, 15(2) Health Aff. 145 (May 1996); M. Shapiro & N. Wenger, Rethinking Utilization Review, 333 New Eng. J. Med. 1353 (1995). This anemic performance, coupled with the public and professional backlash UR engenders, has caused health insurers to cut back on the amount of UR they do.

8. *Further Readings.* For **narrative accounts** of the maddening logic and personal impact of medical necessity determinations, see Andrew Batavia, Of Wheelchairs and Managed Care, 18(6) Health Aff. 171 (Nov. 1999); Lisa Iezzoni, Boundaries, 18(6) Health Aff. 171 (Nov. 1999); Margaret Gilhooley, Broken Back: A Patient's

Reflections on the Process of Medical Necessity Determinations, 40 Vill. L. Rev. 153 (1995) (a law professor's personal account of an insurer that "evicted" her from the hospital); Gerald Grumet, Health Care Rationing Through Inconvenience, 31 New Eng. J. Med. 607 (1989) (railing against the "managerial-review process in which armies of claims clerks, administrators, auditors, form processors, peer reviewers, functionaries, and technocrats of every description insinuate themselves into a complex system that authorizes, pays for and delivers medical care"). For a more neutral and academic account of how health insurance medical directors go about their work, see Thomas Bodenheimer & Lawrence Casalino, Executives with White Coats—The Work and World View of Managed-Care Medical Directors, 341 New Eng. J. Med. 1945 (1999). For the view from an actual medical director, see S. D. Boren, I Had a Tough Day Today, Hillary, 330 New Eng. J. Med. 500 (1994).

On the **legal oversight of utilization review** (note 3), see Gail Agrawal, Resuscitating Professionalism: Self-Regulation in the Medical Marketplace, 66 Mo. L. Rev. 341 (2001); Edward P. Richards, The Police Power and the Regulation of Medical Practice: A Historical Review and Guide for Medical Licensing Board Regulation of Physicians in ERISA-Qualified Managed Care Organizations, 8 Ann. Health L. 201 (1999); David L. Treuman, The Liability of Medical Directors for Utilization Review Decisions, 35 J. Health L. 105 (2002).

Problem: Choosing Health Insurance

From what you have learned so far, which of the following insurance plans do you personally prefer, assuming each one costs the same? Defend your choice (both your selection and rejections) with reasons drawn from these readings:

- Plan A: Covers the full range of medical care, subject to standard medical necessity or experimental exclusions, without any deductibles or co-payments, but you must receive all care at an HMO clinic where doctors are paid a bonus for saving money.
- Plan B: Excludes mental health services, but covers the rest of the normal range of medical care, subject to a $250 deductible and 20 percent co-payment up to a maximum of $2,000 per year. Your choice of doctor, but all expensive treatments must be submitted for prior approval by the insurer to determine medical appropriateness.
- Plan C: Covers the full range of medical care, with no major exclusions and your choice of doctor, and no prior authorization requirement, but subject to a $4,000 deductible.
- Plan D: Coverage is defined in an approach similar to the Oregon plan, but using 5,000 specific categories of inclusion and exclusion taken from the latest practice guidelines based on medical research, as selected by a national panel of politically appointed experts. No other restrictions or financial limitations.

E. PROVIDER REIMBURSEMENT

We now shift from patients to providers. Providers are affected by health insurance not only in who and what it covers, but also in how they are paid for services that are covered. The following materials reveal that various methods of provider reimbursement are important in all three arenas of legal practice: litigation, business planning, and public policy.

■ HEALTH PLAN*

Alain Enthoven

1980

Most people think of the need for medical care as an insurable event, very similar to insured hurricane or automobile collision damage. You are either sick or well. If you are sick, you go to the doctor. The doctor diagnoses your illness, applies the standard treatment, and sends the bill for his or her "usual, customary, and reasonable fee," all or most of which is paid by your insurance company. Our entire Blue Cross-Blue Shield and commercial insurance system was built on that view of the problem. Medicare and Medicaid, the public insurance systems for the elderly and poor, were built on the same model. The consequence is a financial disaster. Our society has accepted the casualty insurance model for health care financing, only to find that it contributes to excessive and excessively costly care. . . .

Many people seem to think that medical care is like mechanical engineering—that for each medical condition there is a "best treatment," a "professional standard." It is up to the doctor to know that treatment and use it. People do not fully understand the great uncertainties that pervade medical care and the variety of acceptable treatments. They think of medical care as mostly treatment for acute life-threatening conditions, as if it were accurately represented by the television dramas about the emergency room. Based on these misconceptions, we have applied to medical care a financing system that was developed for casualty (fire and collision) insurance.

The ideal case for casualty insurance is one in which the damage is caused by an act of God and the cost of repair can be determined objectively. In such a case the financial incentives inherent in insurance do not play a significant role in either the incidence of damage or the cost of repair. Insurance of houses against hurricane damage or fires caused by lightning does not bring on more storms. Collision insurance for automobiles fits the model tolerably, but much less well. Most people do not drive less carefully just because they have insurance. But those who do have insurance are likely to demand more and better repairs than those who do not—because someone else is paying the bill. Still, ordinarily, having your collision-damaged car repaired is not an open-ended task.

Medical insurance hardly fits the model at all. The element of judgment and choice in the decision to seek care and in the amount of care provided is too great. Caring for a patient can be open-ended, especially if he or she has a chronic disease. Uncertainty pervades medical diagnosis and treatment. In most cases, there is not one correct or standard treatment. There may be several accepted therapies. Most medical care is not a matter of life and death, but rather of darker or lighter shades of grey concerning the quality of life. . . .

When thinking about medical care, then, we should think in terms of a variety of legitimate treatments for each condition, with their relative merits in a particular case depending on the unique circumstances and values of the people involved. We should remember that there is pervasive uncertainty and that medicine is more an art based on judgment than a science based on calculation. Medical care deals more with the quality of life than with the quantity (length) of life. The "product" does not come in standard units. Medical care is a matter of subtle and complex judgments about more versus less, and more may often not be better. . . .

In view of this, it should not be surprising that the institutional arrangements for providing care, including the financial incentives facing the doctor, are very important. The casualty insurance model does not fit medical care at all well, because making more care free to the patient and remunerative to the doctor leads to more, and more costly, care being demanded and provided. . . .

To observe that financial incentives play an important role in the use of medical services is not to imply that they are the only, or even the most important, factor. Physicians are concerned primarily with curing their sick patients, regardless of the cost. That ethic has been instilled in them through years of arduous training. Many take a failure to cure a sick patient as a personal defeat. When we are sick, we want our doctors to be concerned with curing us and nothing else. Physicians and other health professionals are also motivated by a desire to achieve professional excellence and the esteem of their peers and the public. But their use of resources is inevitably shaped by financial incentives. Physicians who survive and prosper must ultimately do what brings in money and curtail those activities that lose money. . . .

REIMBURSING PHYSICIANS AND HOSPITALS*

Thomas Bodenheimer & Kevin Grumbach

272 JAMA 971 (1994)

During the course of a typical day, many physicians experience four or five distinct types of reimbursement. In this article, we describe the different ways by which physicians and hospitals are paid. Although reimbursement has many facets, from determinations of prices to processing of claims, we focus our discussion on one of its most basic elements: establishing the unit of payment. This unit-of-payment taxonomy is essential for understanding such concepts as managed care and physician-borne "risk," concepts that feature prominently in many health system reform proposals.[[12]]

12. [See also Robert Berenson et al., Payment Methods: How they Work (Urban Institute, June 2016).]

Units of Payment in Order of Least to Most Aggregated

Payee	*Procedure*	*Day*	*Episode of Illness*	*Patient*	*Time*
Physician	Fee for service	Not applicable	Surgical or obstetric fee or physician diagnosis related group	Capitation	Salary
Hospital	Fee for service	Per diem	Hospital diagnosis related group	Capitation	Global budget

Methods of payment lie along a continuum that extends from the least to the most aggregated unit. Under fee-for-service reimbursement, the unit of payment is the visit or procedure. All other reimbursement modes aggregate or bundle together several services into one unit of payment. Reimbursement by episode of illness pays physicians or hospitals one sum for all services delivered during one illness, for example, global surgical fees to physicians and DRGs for hospitals. Per diem payments to hospitals bundle all services delivered to a patient during one day. A further bundling of services is accomplished by capitation payment, in which one payment is made for each patient's treatment during a month or year. Capitation payment is generally associated with managed care. Payment based on all services delivered to all patients within a certain period includes global budget reimbursement of hospitals and salaried payment of physicians. . . .

1. Open-Ended Reimbursement

■ ALLEN v. CLARIAN HEALTH PARTNERS, INC.

980 N.E.2d 306 (Ind. 2012)

RUCKER, Justice.

. . . Abby Allen . . . sought medical treatment at Clarian North Hospital, a hospital owned by Clarian Health Partners, Inc. ("Clarian"). Before receiving treatment Allen, who is uninsured and not covered by Medicare or Medicaid, signed a form contract drafted by Clarian under which she agreed to pay all charges associated with her treatment. The contract did not specify a dollar amount for services rendered, but provided that Allen "guarantees payment of the account." Clarian provided medical treatment to Allen and then billed its "chargemaster" rates* for medical services and supplies in the amount of $15,641.64. [Plaintiffs' class action

* [A chargemaster is a comprehensive list of a hospital's prices for each of its many thousands of different services. See the casebook Web site for examples. —EDS.]

complaint] alleges breach of contract and seeks declaratory judgment, namely, that rates the hospital bills its uninsured patients are unreasonable and unenforceable. According to the complaint, if Allen had been insured then Clarian would have accepted $7,308.78 for the same services and supplies. The complaint alleges that Clarian charges only uninsured patients the chargemaster rates, while "[i]nsured patients and Medicare/Medicaid patients pay significantly discounted rates for the same services and supplies."

[The trial court granted the hospital's motion to dismiss, but the Court of Appeals reversed, holding] that because the contract did not contain a price term the reasonable value of services should be implied, and the issue of reasonableness requires resolution by a fact-finder. We disagree with our colleagues, and . . . we now affirm the [dismissal by] the trial court. . . .

. . . The provision of the contract at issue provides in relevant part: "In consideration of services delivered by Clarian North Medical Center and/or the physicians, the undersigned guarantees payment of the account, and agrees to pay the same upon discharge if such account is not paid by a private or governmental insurance carrier." . . .

We agree that if a contract is uncertain as to a material term such as price then Indiana courts may impute a reasonable price. . . . Restatement (Second) of Contracts §33 (recognizing that in order to give effect to a contract, its terms must be "reasonably certain"). But "[a]n offer which appears to be indefinite may be given precision by usage of trade or by course of dealing between the parties." Id., cmt. a. A contract need not declare a specific a dollar amount for goods or services in order to be enforceable. See id. ("A telephones to his grocer, 'Send me a ten-pound bag of flour.' The grocer sends it. A has thereby promised to pay the grocer's current price therefor.").

In the context of contracts providing for health care services precision concerning price is close to impossible. As the Third Circuit has recognized, omitting a specific dollar figure is "the only practical way in which the obligations of the patient to pay can be set forth, given the fact that nobody yet knows just what condition the patient has, and what treatments will be necessary to remedy what ails him or her." DiCarlo v. St. Mary Hosp., 530 F.3d 255, 264 (3d Cir. 2008). And a leading scholarly article on the subject—while advocating for courts to "shelter" patients in the health care market—recognizes that "courts have generally tolerated low levels of specificity in medical contracts." Mark A. Hall and Carl E. Schneider, Patients as Consumers: Courts, Contracts, and the New Medical Marketplace, 106 Mich. L. Rev. 643, 646, 674 (2008).

In the context of a contract for the provision of and payment for medical services, a hospital's chargemaster rates serve as the basis for its pricing. Each hospital sets its own chargemaster rates, thus each hospital's chargemaster is unique. It is from these chargemaster prices that insurance companies negotiate with hospitals for discounts for their policyholders. . . . Many courts have addressed contracts similar to those of [plaintiffs'] and most have held that price terms in these contracts, while imprecise, are not sufficiently indefinite to justify imposition of a "reasonable" price standard. For example, the Third Circuit held that a patient's promise to pay "all charges and collection costs for services rendered" was not indefinite, and "can only refer to [the hospital's] uniform charges set forth in its Chargemaster." Other courts have reached similar conclusions. But see Doe v. HCA Health Svcs. of

Tenn., Inc., 46 S.W.3d 191, 197 (Tenn. 2001) (holding that a patient's agreement to be "financially responsible to the hospital for charges not covered by" insurance contained an indefinite price term . . .). We align ourselves with those courts that have recognized the uniqueness of the market for health care services delivered by hospitals. . . .

AN AMERICAN SICKNESS

Elisabeth Rosenthal

2017

A Brief History of Medical Coding

Medical coding is a cryptic and constantly evolving numerical language through which the things that are done to you in a hospital or other medical office are expressed on claims and bills. (In one version called Current Procedural Terminology, or CPT, CPT 35476 means "repair venous blockage using a balloon catheter" and CPT 35475 means "repair arterial blockage," for example.)

Medical coding and coders like ours essentially don't exist in any other healthcare system. . . . A detailed itemized bill for a hip replacement in Belgium . . . is not hard to understand, even though it is in Flemish: "Twoopersoonskamer [two-bedded room] = 329 Euro / Implantaten [implant parts] = 1621, 1195 and 209 Euro." An itemized bill for the same operation at many hospitals in the United States would likely total over $100,000 and run dozens of pages, each filled with medical terminology and numerical codes you couldn't possibly comprehend. . . .

In 1948 the World Health Organization took over stewardship . . . [of coding by creating] the International Statistical Classification of Diseases, Injuries and Causes of Death (ICD). The codes became an invaluable tool, a common language for epidemiologists and statisticians to use when tracking the world's afflictions. But in the United States, the codes gradually took on a bedrock financial function as the basis for medical billing. In 1979 the U.S. government decided to use ICD codes in adjudicating Medicare and Medicaid claims, with some modifications added specifically for that business purpose, so the U.S. version is called ICD-CM. Other insurers followed. In multiple volumes, the U.S. version not only categorized and number-coded diagnoses but also introduced codes for procedures.

The financial stakes in coding are high. If you code for "heart failure" (ICD-9-CM code 428) when you could code for "acute systolic heart failure" (code 428.21), the difference is thousands of dollars. According to a coding professional, "In order to code for the more lucrative code, you have to know how it is defined and make sure the care described in the chart meets the criterion, the definition, for that higher number." . . . Submitting a bill using the higher code without meeting those criteria could constitute fraud. The coders who work for hospitals strive to get money. The coders employed by insurers try to deny claims as overreaching. Coders who audit Medicare charts look for abuses that need to be punished.

Suddenly coding meant big bucks and a new industry thrived. For-profit colleges began offering medical coding degrees, and required internships soon followed. There are three different alphanumeric coding languages . . . and each is as different from the other as Chinese is from Russian and Russian is from French. As a result, different degree tracks were necessary, along with professional exams, certifications, and licensure offered by competing professional organizations. . . . Highly skilled coders have contributed to higher costs for patients, because the salaries of this new layer of professionals and their years of education are reflected in our medical bills.

The international ICD system has created codes for novel diseases—Lyme disease, AIDS, and SARS—as well as for conditions like obesity, which was not considered a disease state until 2013. Until obesity was labeled a disease and had codes assigned to it, insurers in the United States could not be obligated to pay for its treatment as a medical condition. Because, in the United States, codes define not just disease states but also the procedures and treatments that the medical profession can sell, providers, insurers, and regulators lobby for and fight over each code rule and revision. Having your code as part of the lexicon matters.

In 1996, Medicare . . . made it clear that certain [procedure] codes couldn't appear on the same bill because they were inherently part of the same procedure. . . . As a rule, an anesthesiologist could not, for example, separately bill for anesthesia and checking your oxygen level during your surgery. One subsumed the other. But the government created modifier 59—a code that could be appended to other codes to allow doctors to take exceptions to that rule in rare cases. Modifier 59 could be deployed to allow for two payments in certain situations, such as when an oncology nurse needed to insert two separate IVs—one to administer chemotherapy and another because the patient appeared to be dehydrated.

And the games began.

An investigation by the HHS OIG in 2005 found massive evidence of modifier 59 abuse. Forty percent of code pairs billed with modifier 59 in 2003 weren't kosher, resulting in $59 million in overpayment. . . .

Instead of resolving the problem, [Medicare's] attempts at clarification simply created a secondary business of even more advanced coding consultants, who advised other coders as well as healthcare providers and taught courses that covered the nitty-gritty of insurers' reimbursement policies. For example, an ER doctor learned that insurers would accept a better-reimbursed code for the examination and treatment of a patient with a finger fracture (usually 99282) if a narcotic painkiller was prescribed (bump up to 99283). With that type of guidance, some surgeons stopped suturing wounds shut after their operations and instead handed off to another doctor, say, a plastic surgeon, who could therefore code and charge separately. . . .

The latest iteration of international disease codes, ICD-10, was completed in 1992 and has been used by the rest of the world for decades. Why did it take the United States until 2015 to fully deploy it? The problem was that the United States' medical billing system, and how to game it, evolved based on ICD-9. . . . Because adopting the new system in the United States would require new billing software and require every coder to go back to class, the medical industry convinced Medicare to delay adopting ICD-10 year after year. Doctors' groups warned that switching to the new system would lead to a "catastrophic" number of "unpaid Medicare claims." When it finally came into use—uneventfully—in late 2015, it created some headaches for doctors and a burst of new business for coding consultants.

Notes: Cost-Based and UCR Reimbursement

1. *Price Discrimination and Sliding Scales.* Are you surprised that Clarian Hospital bills its uninsured patients twice what it agrees to accept from patients with private

insurance? This is also typical for many physicians, especially specialists. In fact, many hospitals (and some specialists) charge uninsured patients or those who are out of network three or four times what they agree to accept from insured patients, for exactly the same services. Hospitals, of course, view the insurance price as a discount, rather than the uninsured price as a mark-up, but either way, the gap between nominal charges and actual payments has widened greatly over recent years.

Based on this gap, some courts, including even the Indiana Supreme Court, have refused to measure the medical costs owed to tort victims based on hospitals' full charges, reasoning that almost no one actually pays these inflated prices. For instance, in *Stanley v. Walker*, 906 N.E.2d 852, 856-857 (Ind. 2009), the court explained:

> As more medical providers are paid under fixed payment arrangements, . . . hospital charge structures have become less correlated to hospital operations and actual payments. The Lewin Group, A Study of Hospital Charge Setting Practices i (2005). Currently, the relationship between charges and costs is "tenuous at best." In fact, *hospital executives reportedly admit that most charges have "no relation to anything, and certainly not to cost."* Hall [& Schneider], Patients as Consumers, 106 Mich. L. Rev. at 665. [Internal Footnote 3: *Indeed, amicus in this case, the Insurance Institute of Indiana, Inc., flatly says "charges billed by health care providers are effectively irrelevant to the value of the services provided. . . ."*] Thus, based on the realities of health care finance, we are unconvinced that the reasonable value of medical services is necessarily represented by either the amount actually paid or the amount stated in the original medical bill. . . .

The *Allen* court, however, held that this tort law precedent should not govern a contract action. In effect, uninsured patients are held to their agreement to pay anything that hospitals care to charge, even if the prices admittedly are unreasonable.

2. *Reasonable Costs.* When Medicare and Medicaid were first adopted in 1965, they aimed to cover hospitals' reasonable costs:

> "Reasonable cost" reimbursement, or reimbursement based on a provider's cost, means simply that the payment made to a hospital for services rendered to Medicare or Medicaid patients is calculated to reimburse the hospital for its expenses, or costs, incurred in providing such services. . . . [B]ecause the approach, as originally employed, contained a guarantee that costs incurred by a hospital would be recouped, hospitals had a clear incentive to expand services and increase costs to meet anticipated new demand, and had no incentives under the reimbursement methodology to control costs. The methodology itself was inherently inflationary in its impact on the payment obligations of the Medicare and Medicaid programs. It substantially increased the pressure to increase costs that was a function of the expanded entitlement to health care created by the programs themselves. [As a result, the annual rate of increase in both charges and costs for hospital rooms doubled in the five years following 1965, compared to the rate of increase in prior years.]
>
> The decision to base Medicare and Medicaid reimbursement on "reasonable cost" reflected congressional concern that hospitals would be unwilling to participate voluntarily in those programs unless adequate reimbursement were assured. The approach did succeed in attracting the voluntary participation of most American hospitals. But the introduction of the Medicare and Medicaid programs stands as an example of the fiscal dangers inherent in a program that rapidly measures entitlement to services without, at the same time, taking strong measures to contain the cost impact of that expansion. . . .

Stephen M. Weiner, "Reasonable Cost" Reimbursement for Inpatient Hospital Services Under Medicare And Medicaid, 3 Am. J.L. & Med. 1 (1977).

3. *Other Litigation, and Historical Practices.* A series of class action lawsuits challenged whether this type of price discrimination is appropriate for tax-exempt "charitable" hospitals. Most courts favored the hospitals, based on a variety of somewhat technical concerns about the appropriateness of a class action and the novelty of the particular theories of liability. Beverly Cohen, The Controversy over Hospital Charges to the Uninsured—No Villains, No Heroes, 51 Vill. L. Rev. 95-148 (2006). However, the Affordable Care Act has an important new provision that requires charitable hospitals to limit charges to low-income uninsured patients eligible to no more than the lowest amounts that insurers pay.

Pharmaceutical companies have also been sued for inflating or misstating their prices. These challenges also sometimes founder on appeal, due to a variety of technical legal deficiencies in the cases. See, e.g., Astra USA v. Santa Clara County, 131 S. Ct. 1342 (2011); AstraZeneca v. Alabama, 41 So. 3d 15 (Ala. 2006). However, at least one large class action has resulted in a multi-million-dollar award. Blue Cross Blue Shield of Massachusetts v. AstraZeneca Pharmaceuticals, 582 F.3d 156 (1st Cir. 2009).

Historically, prior to widespread health insurance, physicians employed much more socially progressive forms of sliding fee scales by charging wealthy patients several times more than middle- or lower-income patients. Courts endorsed and enforced this practice, but it disappeared in the 1960s when insurers began to demand consistent pricing. See Mark A. Hall, Paying for What You Get, and Getting What You Pay For, 69 Law & Contemp. Probs. 159 (Autumn 2006); Spencer v. West, 126 So. 2d 423 (La. Ct. App. 1960); Eagle v. Snyder, 604 A.2d 253 (Pa. Super. Ct. 1992); Annot., 97 A.L.R.2d 1232 (1964).

Economists explain that physicians and hospitals would not be able to vary their charges this widely unless they possessed substantial market or monopoly power over patients without managed care insurance. What do you think is the likely source of this power? Concerns about market power have grown more acute in recent years, which have seen a sharp increase in hospital consolidation. Deploying a widely used economic metric, researchers have demonstrated that roughly half of all hospital markets are highly concentrated and another third are moderately concentrated. See David M. Cutler & Fiona Scott Morton, Hospitals, Market Share, and Consolidation, 310 JAMA 1964, 1969 (2013).

4. *Medical Debt and Bankruptcy.* Widespread practices of charging substantially more than what insurance will pay, and then aggressively pursuing collection of unpaid bills, is one reason medical debt is a leading cause of personal bankruptcies. Even patients with insurance can get stuck with huge bills because, if they seek care out of network, they are not protected by the deep discounts negotiated by insurers and therefore are obligated to pay the portion of full charges that the insurer does not cover. Realize also that, under the common-law "necessaries doctrine," family members might be responsible for a patient's unpaid bills. E.g., Forsyth Memorial Hospital v. Chisholm, 467 S.E.2d 88 (N.C. 1996) (separation does not excuse husband's obligation to pay for wife unless hospital had actual notice at the time).

5. *Surprise Bills.* As network restrictions grow tighter, physicians and other providers have taken steps to retain their ability to charge high prices. Other portions of Elisabeth Rosenthal's book, and her reporting for the New York Times, document one apparently burgeoning practice of "drive-by doctoring," where physicians and other medical professionals assist an in-network physician or hospital in

providing care. When the assisting providers are outside the patient's network, they can charge exorbitant fees for their assistance—without the patient ever realizing that she received out-of-network care. A similar problem arises when a patient goes to an in-network emergency room that is staffed exclusively by out-of-network physicians or arranges surgery with an in-network surgeon and hospital but does not realize that the anesthesiologist has refused to join the network. In specialties where patients have no real ability to pick their doctor (such as anesthesia or emergency care), physicians increasingly are refusing to give insurance plans any substantial discounts, opting instead to remain outside of most or all networks.

Some state legislatures are pushing back. In March 2014, New York passed a law limiting what out-of-network doctors can charge when they work at an in-network facility or where an in-network doctor refers a patient to their care. See N.Y. Pub. Health Law §24. California and Florida enacted similar laws in 2016. See Cal. Assembly Bill No. 72 (2016); Fla. House Bill 221 (2016). Because of ERISA preemption, however, these new state laws do not apply to self-insured employer health plans.

6. *A Rose by Any Other Name.* Rosenthal also documents another anomaly of medical billing: When treatment is at hospital-based outpatient departments, health insurance typically pays both a physician fee and a facility fee, which usually results in a substantially higher payment than if the same service were provided in an ordinary physician's office. "Dr. Ronald Anderson, a Pennsylvania rheumatologist, can inject a bursa with painkillers in his office for about $80. (Bursas are fluid-filled sacs that reduce friction around joints. When they become temporarily inflamed it is called bursitis.) But when one of his patients had the condition treated by an orthopedist at a surgicenter with ultrasound guidance, the bill was almost $5,000, most of which the insurance company paid." Elisabeth Rosenthal, An American Sickness 38 (2017). This disparity has helped to fuel the rapid growth in hospitals' employment of specialists—which not only drives up medical costs, but also exposes patients to more cost burden, since deductibles and co-payments are often substantially higher for treatment at hospital outpatient clinics than at physicians' offices.

7. *Health Insurance Fraud.* More than just inflated prices, health insurance has given rise to fraudulent or abusive billing practices that, under both public and private insurance, are estimated to cost many tens of billions of dollars each year. In the most classic form, consider the following form of Medicaid fraud:

> Nursing facilities represent convenient resident "pools" and make it lucrative for unscrupulous persons to carry out fraudulent schemes. The [Office of Inspector General (OIG)] has become aware of a number of fraudulent schemes . . . by which health care providers, including medical professionals, inappropriately bill Medicare and Medicaid for the provision of unnecessary services and services which were not provided at all. . . . Some examples follow: One physician improperly billed $350,000 over a two-year period for comprehensive physical examinations of residents without ever seeing a single resident. A psychotherapist working in nursing facilities manipulated Medicare billing codes to charge for three hours of therapy for each resident when, in fact, he spent only a few minutes with each resident. . . . The OIG has learned about podiatrists whose entire practices consist of visits to nursing facilities. Noncovered routine care is provided, e.g., toenail clipping, but Medicare is billed for . . . toenail removals, a service that is covered but not frequently or routinely needed. . . . Investigators discovered one resident for whom bills were submitted claiming a total of 11 toenail removals.

DHHS Office of Inspector General, Special Fraud Alert: Fraud and Abuse in the Provision of Services in Nursing Facilities (1996).

In contrast with blatant manufacturing of fictitious patients or procedures, doctors or hospitals accused or convicted of fraud often believe they are doing nothing wrong because they were merely manipulating the complex bureaucratic rules of an underfunded public system in order to do what was right for their patients and receive decent reimbursement. Accordingly, various types of questionable manipulation are commonplace, even by respected doctors, who might exaggerate or fudge diagnoses in order to obtain insurance coverage for treatment they think is proper but that is not actually covered. For instance, a doctor might classify an annual check-up as an office visit for a cold, or he might classify a 15-minute visit as an "extended" office visit. Do these actions deserve felony treatment?

Regardless, fraudulent or abusive billing practices are a matter of sufficient national concern that federal law makes insurance fraud a federal crime and creates a coordinated enforcement effort that has led to a vast increase in the number of prosecutions and settlements (more than $1 billion per year by one estimate). But, this surge in federal fraud prosecution has led to an outcry of protest by physicians and hospitals over abuse of prosecutorial powers. As discussed in Chapter 4.A.2, prosecutors use the federal False Claims Act to charge that incorrect billings under Medicare, or even poor quality of care, constitute criminal fraud. Providers complain that prosecutors are seizing on technical noncompliance with immensely complex Medicare rules and paperwork requirements and relying on vague and ambiguous standards of illegality. Rather than challenge these prosecutions in court, however, providers usually agree to settle, sometimes for very large amounts in the tens or hundreds of millions of dollars, to avoid risking the legal and public consequences of being found guilty of criminal fraud.

8. *Open-Ended Reimbursement: Down but Not Out.* Medicare no longer reimburses hospitals on a reasonable cost basis. However, this is still the basis for paying some nonhospital facilities. It is also the way that Blue Cross and Medicaid historically paid hospitals and in some instances still do. Other private insurers still pay hospitals a negotiated discount from charges. Similarly, as Alain Enthoven notes, doctors traditionally were paid their "usual, customary, and reasonable" (UCR) rates—both by Medicare and Medicaid and by private insurers, although now both types of insurers pay physicians using fee schedules they determine or negotiate. Even though these open-ended forms of reimbursement have been replaced by various forms of "prospective payment," it is still important to understand traditional payment methods, since their incentive effects are what newer payment methods are meant to counteract.

9. *Corporate Structure.* How Medicare measures allowable costs has tremendous influence not only on financial and operational management, but also on basic corporate structure. In particular, repeated waves of hospital mergers have presented regulators and courts with the issue of whether a hospital consolidation is a "bona fide" sale. If not, Medicare reimbursement can be refused either for a loss or for increased depreciation. The casebook's Web site contains further discussion of this complex issue.

10. *Further Readings.* On the **irrationality of medical prices** (note 1), Steven Brill, Bitter Pill: Why Medical Bills Are Killing Us, Time, Feb. 20, 2013; Erin C. Fuse Brown, Irrational Hospital Pricing, 14 Hous. J. Health L. & Pol'y 11 (2014);

George A. Nation III, Healthcare and the Balance-Billing Problem, 61 Vill. L. Rev. 153 (2016).

For **discussions of whether exorbitant contracts should be enforced** (note 1), see Hall & Schneider, supra, 106 Mich. L. Rev. 643; Wendy Epstein, Price Transparency and Incomplete Contracts in Health Care, 67 Emory L.J. (2017); James McGrath, Overcharging the Uninsured in Hospitals: Shifting a Greater Share of Uncompensated Medical Care Costs to the Federal Government, 26 Quinnipiac L. Rev. 173 (2007); George A. Nation III, Obscene Contracts: The Doctrine of Unconscionability and Hospital Billing of the Uninsured, 94 Ky L.J. 101, 121-123 (2006). For general analysis, see Haavi Morreim, High-Deductible Health Plans: New Twists on Old Challenges from Tort and Contract, 59 Vand. L. Rev. 1207 (2006); Comment, 78 Temp. L. Rev. 493 (2005); Government Accountability Office, Health Care Price Transparency (2011); Kelly Kyanko & Susan Busch, The Out-of-Network Benefit: Problems and Policy Solutions, 49 Inquiry 352 (2012).

For discussions of **market power in the health care industry** (note 3), see Martin Gaynor et al., Making Health Care Markets Work, 317 JAMA 1313 (2017); Thomas G. McGuire, Physician Agency, *in* Anthony J. Culyer & Joseph P. Newhouse, Handbook of Health Economics 462, 482, 527 (2000); Martin Gaynor, Issues in the Industrial Organization of the Market for Physician Services, 3 J. Econ. Manag. Strat. 211 (1994); Reuben Kessel, Price Discrimination in Medicine, 1 J.L. & Econ. 20 (1958).

For more on **medical debt and bankruptcy** (note 4), see Melissa B. Jacoby et al., Rethinking the Debates over Health Care Financing: Evidence from the Bankruptcy Courts, 76 N.Y.U. L. Rev. 375 (2001); Melissa B. Jacoby & Elizabeth Warren, Beyond Hospital Misbehavior: An Alternative Account of Medical-Related Financial Distress, 100 Nw. U. L. Rev. 535 (2006); Melissa Jacoby & Mirya Holman, Managing Medical Bills on the Brink of Bankruptcy, 10 Yale J. Health Pol'y L. & Ethics 239 (2010); Symposium, 51 St. Louis U. L.J. 293 (2007); Daniel A. Austin, Medical Debt As a Cause of Consumer Bankruptcy, 67 Me. L. Rev. 1 (2015).

For discussions of **surprise medical bills** (note 5), see Mark A. Hall et al., Solving Surprise Medical Bills (Brookings, 2016); Daryl M. Berke, Drive-by-Doctoring: Contractual Issues and Regulatory Solutions to Increase Patient Protection from Surprise Medical Bills, 42 Am. J.L. & Med. 170 (2016); Erin C. Fuse Brown, Consumer Financial Protection in Health Care, 95 Wash. U. L. Rev. __ (2017).

For discussions of **the extent of medical fraud** (note 7), see Joan Krause, Following the Money in Health Care Fraud, 36 Am. J.L. & Med. 343 (2010); Michael K. Sparrow, License to Steal: Why Fraud Plagues America's Health Care System (1999); Symposium, 51 U. Ala. L. Rev. 1 (1999); Symposium, 3 Quinnipiac Health L.J. 1 (2000); Symposium, 43 St. Louis L. Rev. 1 (1999). For more on **routine, low-level fraud**, see Victor G. Freeman et al., Lying for Patients: Physician Deception of Third-Party Payers, 159 Arch. Intern. Med. 2263 (1999); Matthew K. Wynia et al., Physician Manipulation of Reimbursement Rules for Patients: Between a Rock and a Hard Place, 283 JAMA 1858 (2000).

2. *Prospective Payment*

Open-ended cost-based reimbursement still exists, but both public and private insurance are rapidly moving toward various forms of prospective payment.

Prospective payment systems (PPS) reverse the incentives created by retrospective reimbursement by setting a fixed rate in advance that does not vary as much according to the nature or extent of treatment given. In this regard, prospective payment mimics the incentives created by a competitive market in which, in theory, firms are "price takers," meaning that they are forced to sell at the market rate and cannot unilaterally determine their price. Therefore, providers have a profit/loss-based incentive to cut costs and attract more business. Depending on the form of payment, however, they also have an incentive to manipulate the payment system in socially unproductive ways.

There are huge differences in the degree of prospectivity and the types of manipulation created by different forms of prospective payment. These various forms are defined by the unit of payment and by the methods used to adjust the fixed rate among different patients and providers. The first form we look at is the "DRG" system under Medicare, so named because payment rates are fixed according to "diagnosis-related groups." Although the focus is on Medicare, this payment method, and other types of prospective payment, are in wide use among private insurers and other government programs. Thus, both the details and the general structure of Medicare DRGs have pervasive importance across the landscape of health care financing.

BEDSIDE BUREAUCRATS: WHY MEDICARE REFORM HASN'T WORKED

Nicholas Bagley

101 Geo. L.J. 519 (2013)

[T]o constrain relentless increases in Medicare expenditures, . . . Congress in 1983 adopted the "prospective payment system," still in place today, under which hospital patients are assigned at discharge, depending on their diagnosis, to differently weighted diagnosis related groups (DRGs). To determine how much to pay a hospital for a particular patient stay, the assigned DRG is multiplied by the national average cost of treating a hospital patient (subject to variations for, among other things, high- and low-wage areas).

The shift to prospective payment flipped hospitals' former financial incentives. Under the preexisting "reasonable cost" approach, a hospital earned more for long and resource-intensive stays. Under the prospective payment system, however, a hospital that spends less on a particular patient than the DRG weighted payment can retain the excess, and a hospital that spends more is in the hole. As such, it is generally in a hospital's financial interest to treat patients conservatively and discharge them quickly. Congress's hope was that prospective payment would encourage hospitals to push their physicians to adopt low-cost practice patterns.

Physicians, however, remained free to bill Medicare for their reasonable charges. And during the 1980s, physician payments began spiraling out of control. Alarmed, in 1989 Congress called for the creation of a fee schedule for physician payments. Establishing this fee schedule required estimating the relative "work" (measured with reference to time, stress, and physical and mental effort) for every medical service. Each service was then assigned a relative value unit (RVU) depending on the work that went into the service. A service that required twice as much "work" as another was assigned an RVU twice as high. To calculate what a physician was owed under the fee schedule, the RVU for the service was multiplied by a practice expense adjustment (practices in high-cost areas have a higher adjustment) and a monetary conversion factor that Congress updates each year. The end result, known as the resource-based relative value scale (RB-RVS), went into effect in 1992 and remains in effect today. . . .

More than any other change in Medicare, prospective payment has slowed the rate of cost escalation. The effect has been particularly pronounced for hospital inpatient care. Without denying its successes, however, prospective payment has not enabled Medicare to assert sufficient authority over its [physicians]. . . .

a. Cost Control. Prospective payment for inpatient hospitalizations was supposed to encourage hospitals to adjust the practice patterns of their affiliated physicians. In this respect, it has proven a qualified failure. Although hospitals have successfully encouraged early discharges, they have otherwise only modestly reshaped how physicians practice medicine. This is in large part because physicians are not usually employed by the hospitals in which they work and have a secure source of fee-for-service revenue through Medicare Part B, even for care provided in an inpatient hospital setting. As Mark McClellan observes, "[v]esting the residual rights of production [i.e., treatment] decisions in the physician, and separating physician reimbursement incentives from hospital reimbursement incentives, clearly reduces the strength of the physician-hospital agency relationship." Not only do hospitals often enjoy little leverage over physicians, but hospitals' financial incentives (decrease care intensity) are at loggerheads with those of their medical staffs' (increase care intensity). Further complicating matters, the Medicare statute prohibits hospitals from making any "payment, directly or indirectly, to a physician as an inducement to reduce or limit services provided" to Medicare beneficiaries.

Instead of pushing physicians to practice cost-conscious care, hospitals have instead cut costs in three principal ways. First, they have reduced overhead and eliminated staff, particularly nurses. Second, they have shifted patients from inpatient to outpatient settings. As other institutional providers—skilled nursing facilities, home health-care agencies, and ambulatory surgery centers—have come under prospective payment, the locus of care has lurched toward physician offices. Costs are shifted, not necessarily reduced. Third, some hospitals have inflated Medicare payments by "upcoding" patients—improperly shifting a patient's diagnosis from one DRG code to a more profitable one, [a maneuver known as "DRG creep"]. A functional bureaucracy might police this sort of manipulative behavior, but Medicare lacks a functional bureaucracy.

What's more, and contrary to expectations, prospective payment did not discourage the adoption and use of expensive new technologies of uncertain value. Under the physician fee schedule, such new technologies often involve more "work" and are thus better remunerated. Hospitals in turn compete to attract physicians who, in part for financial reasons, want to use the new technology. Because DRGs are periodically updated whenever a sufficient number of hospitals adopt a new technology, hospitals are too ready to embrace costly medical innovations without regard to their benefits. . . .

Restraining payments to physicians under the fee schedule has posed a particularly vexing challenge. . . . Part of the trouble is that the overstretched CMS bureaucracy cannot itself update the thousands of RVUs that form the backbone of the fee schedule. Out of necessity, the agency has enlisted the help of an AMA panel called the Specialty Society Relative Value Update Committee (RUC), comprising mainly physician specialists, to review codes and recommend updates. Lacking the resources and expertise necessary to push back with any force, CMS approves nine out of every ten RUC recommendations. As Uwe Reinhardt has noted, CMS has de jure authority to adjust rates, but the RUC is the de facto decision maker. The large majority of adjustments increase the RVUs for particular medical services, and most of those adjustments are for specialty services. That encourages [physicians] to provide larger volumes of these often-expensive services.

Even if it had the resources, CMS lacks the timely data it would need to update the fee schedule. As it stands, CMS must wait eighteen months or more for claims data from its carriers. . . . The payment for the service is typically pegged to the initial costs of the treatment, but those costs often decline as the treatment becomes more common. The absence of timely review means that, over time, the new procedure is overcompensated and, hence, overprovided by Medicare's physicians. In the meantime, categories of services that lack new procedures—in particular, primary care—become relatively less remunerative.

b. Quality Improvement. There is little evidence that the shift to prospective payment has pushed physicians to practice higher quality care. To the contrary, prospective payment may exacerbate some quality concerns. In the hospital setting, prospective payment rewards hospitals for providing low-quality care if such care leads to complications that generate higher DRG classifications or rapid readmissions. In addition, hospital encouragement of early discharges poses a risk that patients will be discharged "quicker and sicker," especially where too-early discharges may lead to readmissions. Hospitals have also slashed nursing staff in response to prospective payment. This too is a consequence of Medicare's architecture—the fact that physicians are paid separately from the hospitals in which they practice means that hospital administrators often find it easier to fire nurses than to shift physician practice patterns. But it's problematic. Copious research suggests that reductions in nursing staff contribute to lower quality care.

For physicians, the quality concerns are different. The fee schedule encourages physicians to overuse specialty services, some of which are harmful to patients. Consider imaging services, for example. Because of the fee-for-service incentives baked into the fee schedule, physicians who own or lease their own imaging equipment can bill for each and every scan that they order. The result has been explosive growth in the volume of inappropriate diagnostic imaging services, including CT scans. Yet CT scans involve relatively high doses of radiation and increase cancer risks. To the extent that it encourages intensive medical care of negligible value, the fee schedule is inimical to quality care.

***

When it comes to restraining cost growth, prospective payment remains the most successful reform in Medicare's history. But congressional inattention to the incentives and capacities of hospitals and medical societies, combined with Medicare's rickety administrative structure, has undermined its effectiveness in reshaping how physicians practice medicine. Hospitals often have little capacity to change how physicians with a separate source of revenue do their jobs. Medicare's abiding commitment to compensating for the full costs of care encourages both physicians and hospitals to adopt new and expensive technologies. . . . And a hollow central bureaucracy without access to timely data has struggled, without much success, to restrain growth in payment rates to intensive specialty services.

Notes: DRGs; Relative Value Scales; Rate Regulation

1. *The Structure and Scope of DRGs.* A DRG-type system has been implemented for hospital outpatient services and ambulatory surgical centers, and nursing homes and home health agencies are now paid according to per diem rates fixed by formula rather than through cost-based reimbursement. See generally Rick Mayes & Robert Bereneson, Medicare Prospective Payment and the Shaping of U.S. Health Care (2006).

2. *The Myth of Institutional Control.* The annual adjustment to the standardized hospital rate provides a convenient tool for continuously ratcheting down Medicare outlays: The more economizing effort hospitals exert in response to the incentives of prospective payment, the more leeway Medicare will have each year to tighten up the standardized rate. DRGs thus have the prospect of not only halting future increases in spending (relative to inflation) but also gradually eliminating the system's built-up fat. But this is true only to the extent that hospital managers actually control the costs of treatment. As Professor Bagley observes, physicians control most clinical decisions that drive hospital costs, and they are notoriously independent from institutional control.

This physician independence is not just a matter of professional and institutional culture; it is supported by various legal constraints that protect physicians from outside control. Mark A. Hall, Institutional Control of Physician Behavior: Legal Barriers to Health Care Cost Containment, 137 U. Pa. L. Rev. 431 (1988). Based on the topics covered in Chapters 4.B.1, 4.C.1, and 4.E, imagine what legal objections could be raised if a hospital were to: (1) impose mandatory treatment protocols that physicians must follow (unlicensed, corporate practice of medicine); (2) pay physicians a reward for keeping their patients' costs within DRG limits ("fraud and abuse" fee splitting); or (3) kick off the medical staff any physician who consistently loses money ("economic credentialing"). Responding to Hall's prediction, above, that courts will systematically frustrate cost containment initiatives, Peter Jacobson argues this has not in fact occurred. Peter Jacobson, Strangers in the Night: Law and Medicine in the Managed Care Era (2002).

3. *Hospitalists.* One way that hospitals now assert more administrative control of patient care decisions is by hiring hospital-based physicians called "hospitalists" to take over primary responsibility for case management of hospitalized patients rather than having patients being seen primarily by their regular physicians. So far, hospitalist programs are voluntary, in the sense that primary care physicians can use them at their discretion; but hospitals in theory could start to insist on using their employed staff.

4. *Adjustments to Hospital Rates.* Following the logic that hospitals should bear the brunt of only the costs they control, the Medicare DRG system has been forced to add numerous adjustments other than simply those related to patients' diagnoses. As David Frankford has explained:

> [T]he reimbursement system contains a very complicated set of mechanisms to determine this question. The most important of these adjustments is for geographic variations among hospitals in their cost of labor. . . . [A]ll agree that labor constitutes the most important component of a hospital's operating costs. Accordingly, the statute clearly provides for some type of "wage adjustment." To make this adjustment, [Medicare] divides the country into numerous—and hotly contested—geographic wage areas, and each area is ranked vis-a-vis a national average wage, thereby creating a "wage index"—an indexical ranking of labor costs in different locations. Each hospital is placed into a particular area, and thus its reimbursement for any case is a product of its relevant category of standardized payment amount—rural, large urban, or other urban—weighted to take into account its local labor costs. . . .
>
> There are then "additional payment amounts" made for other factors for which hospitals are not held accountable. Teaching activities in hospitals are thought to generate increased costs indirectly, due to the treatment of more severely ill patients through use of technology and utilization patterns which differ from those prevalent in nonteaching hospitals. Accordingly, payments to teaching hospitals are increased by percentages, called the "indirect medical education adjustment," which vary with the size of the hospital and its teaching program. Somewhat related, but not completely coextensive, is an adjustment made for hospitals which treat a "disproportionate share" of indigent patients. These patients too are thought to generate higher costs because they are more severely ill at admission than the average Medicare beneficiary. Furthermore, treatment of these patients imposes higher costs because post-discharge care is often harder to arrange and because there are generally higher costs associated with operating in areas accessible to the poor. . . . [H]ospitals which are the sole facilities in their respective communities . . . are eligible for designation as a "sole community hospital." . . . [B]oth sole community hospitals and Medicare-dependent, small rural hospitals are given . . . a lump sum payment that is calculated to cover their fixed costs and the costs of maintaining core staff and services. . . . Finally, all hospitals are paid a separate, additional amount for extraordinarily expensive cases—the so-called "outlier cases" which deviate greatly from the average case in a DRG.

David Frankford, The Complexity of Medicare's Hospital Reimbursement System: Paradoxes of Averaging, 78 Iowa L. Rev. 517, 579-584 (1993). See also Southeast Alabama Medical Center v. Sebelius, 572 F.3d 912 (D.C. Cir. 2009) (upholding factors HHS used to determine hospitals' area wage index); Anna Jacques Hospital v. Burwell, 797 F.3d 1155 (D.C. Cir. 2015) (same). Over time, these adjustments have accounted for an increasing portion of total DRG payments. Sam Krinsky, Variation in Payment Rates under Medicare's Inpatient Prospective Payment System, 52 Health Serv. Rev. 676 (2017).

5. *The Ethics of Considering Costs.* A thorny dilemma that DRGs and other forms of prospective payment present is the ethical bind they impose on practicing physicians. Is it morally right for a doctor to be influenced by the inevitable resource constraints placed on hospitals or on society at large, if, as a result of third-party reimbursement, the doctor's patients are sheltered from these constraints? Consider the following hypothetical (but very real) problem:

> Lakeview Hospital's medical director, Jared Lapin, M.D., . . . analyzed a lengthy computer report that matched, for each physician, the revenue the hospital received with the costs incurred for treating patients in each of the DRGs in one month. While studying the 15 DRGs under Major Diagnostic Category number

> 14 (Pregnancy, Childbirth, and the Puerperium), [he] noticed that, . . . across all deliveries, the costs of treating Dr. Weiner's patients exceeded the revenue received from the DRG rates. But the total cost incurred in providing care to the other obstetricians' patients was considerably below revenue and hence the hospital was able to earn a "profit." . . . The reason for Dr. Weiner's comparatively poor overall "financial performance" . . . was that he performed many fewer cesarians than did his colleagues. . . . Dr. Lapin countered that "it's in all our interests to look out for the financial health of the hospital. And since it is unclear which of the two approaches benefits the patient more, I urge you to reconsider the way you handle these cases."

Was it ethical for Dr. Lapin to approach Dr. Weiner if there was no indication he was delivering poor quality care? How should financial considerations, both those related to the hospital and society at large, be weighed against physician judgment? Wasserman, The Doctor, the Patient and the DRG, 13(5) Hastings Center Rep. 23 (Oct. 1983).

6. *Discharging Patients "Quicker and Sicker."* Critics of DRGs have documented that they caused hospitals to discharge patients "quicker and sicker." But is it necessarily wrong that a patient not be allowed to remain in the hospital for the full period of recuperation? Contrast these critics with Katherine Kahn et al., The Effects of the DRG-Based Prospective Payment System on Quality of Care for Hospitalized Medicare Patients, 264 JAMA 1953 (1990) (finding no systematic effects on quality of care). CMS has attempted to prevent premature discharge by requiring that all Medicare patients be given upon admission a written statement of their rights to protest a discharge decision. Patients have a grace period of several days after written notice of discharge to remain in the hospital and appeal the decision to the local Quality Improvement Organization (formerly called Peer Review Organization).

Despite this, a surprising 20 percent of Medicare patients are readmitted to the hospital within 30 days of discharge. Often, this is not so much because of premature discharge, but because hospitals have no financial incentive to manage patients' outpatient care following discharge, such as taking their medications or returning for follow-up visits. To change this, CMS has started penalizing hospitals with excessive readmissions rates. As a result, readmissions have dropped sharply. See Centers for Medicare and Medicaid Services, New HHS Data Shows Major Strides Made in Patient Safety, Leading to Improved Care and Savings, May 7, 2014.

7. *DRG Creep.*

> In New Jersey, a study found that 26.4 percent of the patients had been misclassified [to the wrong DRG]. . . . One of the most publicized examples was the softball player who had injured his finger. He had to be hospitalized for two days so that the bone in his finger could be repaired with a metal pin. The DRG category assigned to this patient was "fracture with major surgery," usually reserved for serious cases such as total hip replacement. While the patient's actual charges would have been less than $1000, the DRG classification resulted in a bill for $5,000.

P. Feldstein, Health Care Economics 296 (2d ed. 1982).

8. *Physicians' Fee Schedules.* It is critical to observe that DRGs only cover hospital costs. What difficulties would be encountered in extending DRGs to physician services? Consider the following explanation by the former head of CMS:

> In view of the generally successful change in Medicare's hospital-payment system, many wonder why we cannot repeat the accomplishment with respect to Medicare payment of physicians. The answer is simple: Paying physicians is far more complicated. When developing a hospital-payment system for Medicare, one must handle 11 million admissions to 7,000 hospitals for 475 diagnosis-related groups. Those numbers pale in comparison to Medicare's 350 million claims from 500,000 physicians for 7,000 different procedure codes. Moreover, whereas hospitals can average their gains and losses under a prospective payment system across many cases, physicians' smaller caseloads and greater specialization make such averaging much more risky for them. These differences mean that improving the way Medicare pays physicians will be vastly more difficult, both analytically and administratively.

William Roper, Perspectives on Physician-Payment Reform, 319 New Eng. J. Med. 865 (1988).

9. *Public Utility Regulation.* The debate over how to slow medical spending tends to pit advocates of market-based reforms against supporters of a single-payer approach. But there is another alternative, one that treats the health care industry as a type of public utility. A public utility approach would retain the architecture of the private financing system while enabling the state to assert control over the medical industry's economic excesses. The approach is not as foreign to the American health care system as it may seem at first glance:

> [I]n the decades following the Second World War, the meteoric growth of the medical industry prompted the enactment of federal and state laws that bore the hallmarks of public utility regulation. Collectively, these laws regulated market entry, imposed service obligations, prohibited certain forms of price discrimination and even fixed prices. In the last decades of the twentieth century, some of this economic regulation gave way in the face of the resurgent belief that market forces, not state control, ought to guide the distribution of health-care services. But a durable strain of the law has always treated modern medicine as a public calling—even today.
>
> The fit is natural. Public utility regulation aims to address the sorts of problems in market ordering—supply imbalances, access restrictions, and abusive and discriminatory pricing—that have long afflicted the medical industry. Now that the [ACA] has eased public concerns about the uninsured, the serious economic challenges facing those with insurance are likely to become more salient. Should the ACA fail to remedy a number of disturbing practices in the medical marketplace, policymakers may find public utility regulation increasingly attractive. Indeed, nascent interest in such regulation suggests that we may already be heading in that direction.

Nicholas Bagley, Medicine as a Public Calling, 114 Mich. L. Rev. 57, 59-60 (2015).

The most comprehensive form of public utility regulation would impose a global budget on hospitals and their employed physicians, as is typical for government-run hospitals. A global budget is difficult to formulate, however, when private hospitals have multiple sources of private sector income. Instead, during the 1970s, about a dozen states instituted comprehensive regulation of hospital rates, regulating what hospitals could charge private or public insurers. The purpose was both to contain costs and to more equitably spread the burden of uncompensated care borne by different hospitals. Since then, however, every one of these states except Maryland has since repealed its "all payer" hospital rate regulation, opting instead to trust in the rise of managed care to restrain medical spending. John McDonough, Tracking the Demise of State Hospital Rate Setting, 16 Health Aff. 13 (1997). The rise of dominant health care systems in many markets has rekindled interest in some quarters in a return to rate-setting.

10. *Hospital Appeals Under Medicare; Constitutionality.* There are few judicial challenges under Medicare to the basic DRG methodology because of provisions in the statute expressly precluding review of the DRG weights and severely limiting the opportunity to challenge individual hospital rates. See Skagit County Public Hospital District v. Shalala, 80 F.3d 379 (9th Cir. 1996); Palisades General Hospital Inc. v. Leavitt, 426 F.3d 400 (D.C. Cir. 2005). Query, then, whether the system has sacrificed accuracy and fairness in order to obtain deceptive legal simplicity. At the administrative level, however, administrative appeals have run so rampant that the Provider Reimbursed Review Board (PRRB) has a backlog of several years. The single matter of adjusting a hospital's rate to accurately reflect geographically determined factors (wages, rural status, etc.) became so burdensome for the PRRB that a separate review board was created for this sole purpose—the Medicare Geographic Classification Review Board. See generally David W. Thomas, Review of Medicare Reimbursement Disputes Under 42 U.S.C. §1395oo: Delineating a Unified Theory of the Provider Reimbursement Review Board's Jurisdiction and Scope of Review, 39 Duq. L. Rev. 287 (2001); Recent Development, 95 N.C.L. Rev. 1293 (2017).

Because participation in Medicare and Medicaid is voluntary, there generally are thought to be no constitutional problems with limiting reimbursement or judicial review. See, e.g., Nazareth Home of Franciscan Sisters v. Novello, 7 N.Y.3d 538 (N.Y. 2006); William Brewbaker, Health Care Price Controls and the Takings Clause, 21 Hastings Const. L.Q. 669 (1994).

11. *Further Readings.* On the **institutional control of physicians** (note 2), see Jessica Mantel, The Myth of the Independent Physician, 64 Case W. Res. 455 (2013); Theodore Ruger, Plural Constitutionalism and the Pathologies of American Health Care, 120 Yale L.J. Online 347 (2011); Robert F. Rich et al., Judicial Interpretations of Managed Care Policy, 13 Elder L.J. 85 (2005).

For more on **"outlier payments" and their manipulation by hospitals** (note 4), see Elizabeth A. Weeks, Gauging the Cost of Loopholes: Health Care Pricing and Medicare Regulation in the Post-Enron Era, 40 Wake Forest L. Rev. 1215 (2005); R. Brent Rawlings & Hugh E. Aaron, The Effect of Hospital Charges on Outlier Payments Under Medicare's Inpatient Prospective Payment System: Prudent Financial Management or Illegal Conduct?, 14 Ann. Health L. 267 (2005).

For further discussion and debate on **Medicare physician payment and relative value scales** (note 8), see Miriam J. Laugesen, Fixing Medical Prices: How Physicians Are Paid (2016); Joseph P. Newhouse, Medicare Spending on Physicians: No Easy Fix in Sight, 356 New Eng. J. Med. 1883 (2007); Paul Ginsburg, Rapidly Evolving Physician-Payment Policy: More Than the SGR, 362 New Eng. J. Med. 172 (2011); Paul B. Ginsburg & Robert A. Berenson, Revising Medicare's Physician Fee Schedule—Much Activity, Little Change, 356 New Eng. J. Med. 1201 (2007); and the annual reports of MedPAC, the Medicare Payment Advisory Commission.

For recent discussions of **rate-setting and the public utility model** (note 9), see Erin C. Fuse Brown, Resurrecting Heath Care Rate Regulation, 67 Hastings L.J. 85 (2015); Robert Murray & Robert A. Berenson, Hospital Rate Setting Revisited

Dumb Price Fixing or a Smart Solution to Provider Pricing Power and Delivery Reform? (2015); David M. Frankford, It's the Prices, Advanced Capitalism, and the Need for Rate Setting—Stupid, 44 J.L., Med. & Ethics (2017).

Problem: Technology Innovation

What effects are DRGs and other forms of prospective payment likely to have on technology acquisition and medical innovation? The answer depends on the type of innovation. Consider: Those that involve greater cost versus lesser costs. Those that increase admissions by finding new things to treat versus those that shorten length of stay for existing diagnoses. And, those that improve diagnostic accuracy versus those that improve treatment. Here are several concrete examples. For each, consider the technology from a perspective of when it was first introduced, that is, assuming that a specific DRG has not yet been created for it or that overall payment rates have not yet been adjusted to reflect the new technology.

1. A procedure known as "balloon angioplasty," (or P.T.C.A. for percutaneous transluminal coronary angioplasty) is an alternative to bypass surgery that involves inserting a small balloon into an artery and inflating it to clear blockage.
2. A PET (positron emission tomographer) scanner, a multi-million-dollar machine that produces images of biochemical activity inside the body, in contrast with an MRI, which depicts soft tissues, or a CAT scan, which depicts bones and hard tissue.
3. Low-osmolality contrast media, used for angiography.
4. Extracorporeal shock-wave lithotripter, a space-age machine that pulverizes kidney stones by concentrating blasts of focused shock (sound) waves, as an alternative to either surgical removal or enduring pain (sometimes excruciating) while waiting to excrete the stones naturally.

4. *Capitation Payment*

PEGRAM v. HERDRICH
530 U.S. 211 (2000)

Justice SOUTER delivered the opinion of the Court.

The question in this case is whether treatment decisions made by a health maintenance organization, acting through its physician employees, are fiduciary acts within the meaning of the Employee Retirement Income Security Act of 1974 (ERISA). We hold that they are not.

Petitioners, Carle Clinic Association . . . , function as a health maintenance organization (HMO) organized for profit. Its owners are physicians providing prepaid medical services to participants whose employers contract with Carle to provide such coverage. Respondent, Cynthia Herdrich, was covered by Carle through her husband's employer, State Farm Insurance Company. The events in question began when a Carle physician, petitioner Lori Pegram, examined Herdrich, who was experiencing pain in the midline area of her groin. Six days later, Dr. Pegram discovered a six by eight centimeter inflamed mass in Herdrich's abdomen. Despite the noticeable inflammation, Dr. Pegram did not order an ultrasound diagnostic procedure at a local hospital, but decided that Herdrich would have to wait eight more days for an ultrasound, to be performed at a facility staffed by Carle more than 50 miles away. Before the eight days were over, Herdrich's appendix ruptured, causing peritonitis.

Herdrich sued Pegram and Carle in state court for medical malpractice, and . . . prevailed [against] both, receiving $35,000 in compensation for her injury. . . . [She also sued in federal court under ERISA, the federal statute discussed in section C and Chapter 2.C that regulates pension plans and other fringe benefits. The ERISA suit alleged that Carle HMO's] rewarding its physician owners for limiting medical care entailed an inherent or anticipatory breach of an ERISA fiduciary duty, since these terms created an incentive to make decisions in the physicians' self-interest, rather than the exclusive interests of plan participants. . . . [This claim was dismissed by the district court but was reinstated by the Seventh Circuit.]

Whether Carle is a fiduciary when it acts through its physician owners as pleaded in the ERISA count depends on some background of fact and law about HMO organizations, medical benefit plans, fiduciary obligation, and the meaning of Herdrich's allegations. . . .

In a fee-for-service system, a physician's financial incentive is to provide more care, not less, so long as payment is forthcoming. The check on this incentive is a physician's obligation to exercise reasonable medical skill and judgment in the patient's interest. . . . The defining feature of an HMO is . . . [that it] assumes the financial risk of providing the benefits promised. . . . Like other risk-bearing organizations, HMOs take steps to control costs, [such as utilization review]. These cost-controlling measures are commonly complemented by specific financial incentives to physicians, rewarding them for decreasing utilization of health-care services, and penalizing them for what may be found to be excessive treatment. Hence, in an HMO system, a physician's financial interest lies in providing less care, not more. The check on this influence (like that on the converse, fee-for-service incentive) is the professional obligation to provide covered services with a reasonable degree of skill and judgment in the patient's interest.

The adequacy of professional obligation to counter financial self-interest has been challenged no matter what the form of medical organization. HMOs became popular because fee-for-service physicians were thought to be providing unnecessary or useless services; today, many doctors and other observers argue that HMOs often ignore the individual needs of a patient in order to improve the HMOs' bottom lines. In this case, for instance, one could argue that Pegram's decision to wait before getting an ultrasound for Herdrich, and her insistence that the ultrasound be done at a distant facility owned by Carle, reflected an interest in limiting the HMO's expenses, which blinded her to the need for immediate diagnosis and treatment.

Herdrich focuses on the Carle scheme's provision for a "year-end distribution" to the HMO's physician owners. She argues that this particular incentive device of annually paying physician owners the profit resulting from their own decisions rationing care can distinguish Carle's organization from HMOs generally, so that reviewing Carle's decisions under a fiduciary standard as pleaded in Herdrich's complaint would not open the door to like claims about other HMO structures. While the Court of Appeals agreed, we think otherwise, under the law as now written.

Although it is true that the relationship between sparing medical treatment and physician reward is not a subtle one under the Carle scheme, no HMO organization could survive without some incentive connecting physician reward with treatment rationing. The essence of an HMO is that salaries and profits are limited by the HMO's fixed membership fees. See Orentlicher, Paying Physicians More to Do Less: Financial Incentives to Limit Care, 30 U. Rich. L. Rev. 155, 174 (1996). This is not to suggest that the Carle provisions are as socially desirable as some other HMO organizational schemes; they may not be. But whatever the HMO, there must be rationing and inducement to ration.

Since inducement to ration care goes to the very point of any HMO scheme, and rationing necessarily raises some risks while reducing others (ruptured appendixes are more likely; unnecessary appendectomies are less so), any legal principle purporting to draw a line between good and bad HMOs would embody, in effect, a judgment about socially acceptable medical risk. A valid conclusion of this sort would, however, necessarily turn on facts to which courts would probably not have ready access: correlations between malpractice rates and various HMO models, similar correlations involving fee-for-service models, and so on. . . . [S]uch complicated factfinding and such a debatable social judgment are not wisely required of courts unless for some reason resort cannot be had to the legislative process, with its preferable forum for comprehensive investigations and judgments of social value, such as optimum treatment levels and health care expenditure. We think, then, that courts are not in a position to derive a sound legal principle to differentiate an HMO like Carle from other HMOs. . . .

C

We turn now from the structure of HMOs to the requirements of ERISA. A fiduciary within the meaning of ERISA must be someone acting in the capacity of manager, administrator, or financial adviser to a "plan." . . . Rules governing collection of premiums, definition of benefits, submission of claims, and resolution of disagreements over entitlement to services are the sorts of provisions that constitute a plan. Thus, when employers contract with an HMO to provide benefits to employees subject to ERISA, the provisions of documents that set up the HMO are not, as such, an ERISA plan, but the agreement between an HMO and an employer who pays the premiums may, as here, provide elements of a plan by setting out rules under which beneficiaries will be entitled to care.

As just noted, fiduciary obligations can apply to managing, advising, and administering an ERISA plan. . . . In general terms, fiduciary responsibility under ERISA is simply stated. The statute provides that fiduciaries shall discharge their duties with respect to a plan "solely in the interest of the participants and beneficiaries." . . . These responsibilities imposed by ERISA have the familiar ring of their source in the common law of trusts: . . . "The most fundamental duty owed by the trustee to the beneficiaries of the trust is the duty of loyalty. . . . It is the duty of a trustee to administer the trust solely in the interest of the beneficiaries." 2A A. Scott & W. Fratcher, Trusts §170, 311 (4th ed. 1987).

Beyond the threshold statement of responsibility, however, the analogy between ERISA fiduciary and common law trustee becomes problematic. This is so because the trustee at common law characteristically wears only his fiduciary hat when he takes action to affect a beneficiary, whereas the trustee under ERISA may wear different hats.

Speaking of the traditional trustee, Professor Scott's treatise admonishes that the trustee "is not permitted to place himself in a position where it would be for his own benefit to violate his duty to the beneficiaries." 2A Scott, §170, at 311. Under ERISA, however, a fiduciary may have financial interests adverse to beneficiaries. Employers, for example, can be ERISA fiduciaries and still take actions to the disadvantage of employee beneficiaries, when they act as employers (e.g., firing a beneficiary for reasons unrelated to the ERISA plan), or even as plan sponsors (e.g., modifying the terms of a plan as allowed by ERISA to provide less generous benefits). . . . ERISA does require, however, that the fiduciary with two hats wear only one at a time, and wear the fiduciary hat when making fiduciary decisions. . . .

The pleadings must also be parsed very carefully to understand what acts by physician owners acting on Carle's behalf are alleged to be fiduciary in nature.[8] It will help to keep two sorts of arguably administrative acts in mind. Cf. Dukes v. U.S. Healthcare, Inc., 57 F.3d 350, 361 (3rd Cir. 1995) (discussing dual medical/administrative roles of HMOs). What we will call pure "eligibility decisions" turn on the plan's coverage of a particular condition or medical procedure for its treatment. "Treatment decisions," by contrast, are choices about how to go about diagnosing and treating a patient's condition: given a patient's constellation of symptoms, what is the appropriate medical response?

These decisions are often practically inextricable from one another. . . . This is so not merely because, under a scheme like Carle's, treatment and eligibility decisions are made by the same person, the treating physician. It is so because a great many and possibly most coverage questions are not simple yes-or-no questions, like whether appendicitis is a covered condition (when there is no dispute that a patient has appendicitis), or whether acupuncture is a covered procedure for pain relief (when the claim of pain is unchallenged). The more common coverage question is a when-and-how question. Although coverage for many conditions will be clear and various treatment options will be indisputably compensable, physicians still must decide what to do in particular cases. The issue may be, say, whether one treatment option is so superior to another under the circumstances, and needed so promptly, that a decision to proceed with it would meet the medical necessity requirement that conditions the HMO's obligation to provide or pay for that particular procedure at that time in that case. . . . In practical terms, these eligibility decisions cannot be untangled from physicians' judgments about reasonable medical treatment, and in the case before us, Dr. Pegram's decision was one of that sort. She decided (wrongly, as it turned out) that Herdrich's condition did not warrant immediate action; the consequence of that medical determination was that Carle would not cover immediate care, whereas it would have done so if Dr. Pegram had made the

8. . . . The fraud claims in Herdrich's initial complaint could be read to allege breach of a fiduciary obligation to disclose physician incentives to limit care, whereas her amended complaint alleges an obligation to avoid such incentives. . . . cf. Varity Corp. v. Howe, 516 U.S. 489, 505 (1996) (holding that ERISA fiduciaries may have duties to disclose information about plan prospects that they have no duty, or even power, to change). But failure to disclose is no longer the allegation of the amended complaint. . . .

proper diagnosis and judgment to treat. The eligibility decision and the treatment decision were inextricably mixed, as they are in countless medical administrative decisions every day. . . .

Based on our understanding of the matters just discussed, we think Congress did not intend Carle or any other HMO to be treated as a fiduciary to the extent that it makes mixed eligibility decisions acting through its physicians. We begin with doubt that Congress would ever have thought of a mixed eligibility decision as fiduciary in nature. At common law, fiduciary duties characteristically attach to decisions about managing assets and distributing property to beneficiaries. Trustees buy, sell, and lease investment property, lend and borrow, and do other things to conserve and nurture assets. They pay out income, choose beneficiaries, and distribute remainders at termination. Thus, the common law trustee's most defining concern historically has been the payment of money in the interest of the beneficiary.

Mixed eligibility decisions by an HMO acting through its physicians have, however, only a limited resemblance to the usual business of traditional trustees. . . . [T]he physicians through whom HMOs act make just the sorts of decisions made by licensed medical practitioners millions of times every day, in every possible medical setting: HMOs, fee-for-service proprietorships, public and private hospitals, military field hospitals, and so on. The settings bear no more resemblance to trust departments than a decision to operate turns on the factors controlling the amount of a quarterly income distribution. Thus, it is at least questionable whether Congress would have had mixed eligibility decisions in mind when it provided that decisions administering a plan were fiduciary in nature. Indeed, when Congress took up the subject of fiduciary responsibility under ERISA, it concentrated on fiduciaries' financial decisions, focusing on pension plans, the difficulty many retirees faced in getting the payments they expected, and the financial mismanagement that had too often deprived employees of their benefits. Its focus was far from the subject of Herdrich's claim.

Our doubt that Congress intended the category of fiduciary administrative functions to encompass the mixed determinations at issue here hardens into conviction when we consider the consequences that would follow from Herdrich's contrary view. . . . Although Herdrich is vague about the mechanics of relief, the one point that seems clear is that she seeks the return of profit from the pockets of the Carle HMO's owners, with the money to be given to the plan for the benefit of the participants. Since the provision for profit is what makes the HMO a proprietary organization, her remedy in effect would be nothing less than elimination of the for-profit HMO. Her remedy . . . might well portend the end of nonprofit HMOs as well, since those HMOs can set doctors' salaries. A claim against a nonprofit HMO could easily allege that salaries were excessively high because they were funded by limiting care, and some nonprofits actually use incentive schemes similar to that challenged here. . . .

It is enough to recognize that the Judiciary has no warrant to precipitate the upheaval that would follow a refusal to dismiss Herdrich's ERISA claim. The fact is that for over 27 years the Congress of the United States has promoted the formation of HMO practices. . . . If Congress wishes to restrict its approval of HMO practice to certain preferred forms, it may choose to do so. But the Federal Judiciary would be acting contrary to the congressional policy of allowing HMO organizations if it were to entertain an ERISA fiduciary claim portending wholesale attacks on existing HMOs solely because of their structure, untethered to claims of concrete harm. . . .

The fiduciary is, of course, obliged to act exclusively in the interest of the beneficiary, but this translates into no rule readily applicable to HMO decisions or those of any other variety of medical practice. While the incentive of the HMO physician is to give treatment sparingly, imposing a fiduciary obligation upon him would not lead to a simple default rule, say, that whenever it is reasonably possible to disagree about treatment options, the physician should treat aggressively. After all, HMOs came into being because some groups of physicians consistently provided more aggressive treatment than others in similar circumstances, with results not perceived as justified by the marginal expense and risk associated with intervention; excessive surgery is not in the patient's best interest, whether provided by fee-for-service surgeons or HMO surgeons subject to a default rule urging them to operate. Nor would it be possible to translate fiduciary duty into a standard that would allow recovery from an HMO whenever a mixed decision influenced by the HMO's financial incentive resulted in a bad outcome for the patient. It would be so easy to allege, and to find, an economic influence when sparing care did not lead to a well patient, that any such standard in practice would allow a factfinder to convert an HMO into a guarantor of recovery. . . .

[T]he defense of any HMO would be that its physician did not act out of financial interest but for good medical reasons, the plausibility of which would require reference to standards of reasonable and customary medical practice in like circumstances. That, of course, is the traditional standard of the common law. Thus, for all practical purposes, every claim of fiduciary breach by an HMO physician making a mixed decision would boil down to a malpractice claim, and the fiduciary standard would be nothing but the malpractice standard traditionally applied in actions against physicians.

What would be the value to the plan participant of having this kind of ERISA fiduciary action? It would simply apply the law already available in state courts and federal diversity actions today, and the formulaic addition of an allegation of financial incentive would do nothing but bring the same claim into a federal court under federal-question jurisdiction. It is true that in States that do not allow malpractice actions against HMOs the fiduciary claim would offer a plaintiff a further defendant to be sued for direct liability, and in some cases the HMO might have a deeper pocket than the physician. But we have seen enough to know that ERISA was not enacted out of concern that physicians were too poor to be sued. . . .

We hold that mixed eligibility decisions by HMO physicians are not fiduciary decisions under ERISA.

■ DIRECT FINANCIAL INCENTIVES IN MANAGED CARE: UNANSWERED QUESTIONS

Henry T. Greely

6 Health Matrix 53 (1996)

The diagnosis was devastating. Joyce—a health-conscious mother of a three-year-old son—had colon cancer. Twenty months and seven operations later, she was dead at age thirty-four. Her husband contends that it was greed that killed [his wife]. In a malpractice suit scheduled for trial this summer, he alleges that the financial incentives in their contracts with the HMO prompted his wife's doctors to place their interests ahead of hers. . . .

What are Direct Financial Incentives?

Direct financial incentives can take many forms, but the key is structuring the physician's compensation in ways that create incentives to practice economically. . . . [F]our general approaches are commonly used: salary, capitation, profit sharing, and bonus. Each can be combined with others in a variety of forms. Under a salaried system, the physician's income is set by the plan, generally annually, through a salary. . . . Under a capitated system, the physician is paid a certain amount, generally on a monthly basis, for each of the managed care plan's patients for whom she is responsible. In its purest form, if the doctor spends less than the capitated amount, she makes a profit on that patient; if she spends more, she takes a loss.

Capitation comes in a dizzying number of forms, with the variations spreading over at least two dimensions. One dimension is the range of services included in the capitation. Capitation to a primary care physician almost always will include primary care services. It may or may not include the costs of specialty or hospital services. It may include or exclude laboratory or radiological services. It could, but rarely does, include mental health services or pharmaceutical costs. If a service is excluded from the capitation agreement, its costs are not charged against the capitated physician, but are paid from some other pool of funds.

The second dimension is the degree to which the physician is at risk even for the capitated services. At the extreme, the risk could be total. A physician receiving ninety dollars per month as "global" capitation (physician services and hospital services) might be held financially responsible for the entire $150,000. . . . More commonly, however, the risk is shared. The physician might be responsible for higher costs only up to a certain point, defined either in terms of dollars per patient or patient pool (through stop-loss insurance) or in terms of a percentage of the capitated amount (through withheld funds). In the alternative, the physician, in turn, may spread the risk through capitated arrangements with other providers, such as hospitals or specialists.

A concrete example might make this more clear. Stanford University offers its employees a choice among three health maintenance organizations. . . . [In one arrangement], the University contracts with three physician groups to provide the HMO-level care. These physician groups would receive approximately ninety dollars per month to cover all physician and hospital services for a middle-aged individual. The physicians then contract with a local hospital to cover all hospital services for about forty dollars per month. The University's plan administrator withholds a percentage of the capitated payment to each physician group. This "withhold" pool is used to pay for services members receive . . . , as well as for unanticipated expenses. At the end of the year, if money remains in the "withhold" pool, it is shared between the physician group, which receives eighty percent of the pool, and the University, which keeps the balance. If no money remains in that pool, the physician group is left with only the payments it has already received, but it is not responsible for any cost overrun.

A third strategy is the bonus. The physicians may be paid during a fixed period under any system: salary, capitation, or fee-for-service. At the end of that period, physicians receive a bonus based on the plan's financial results that year and the physicians' contribution to them. The manner of determining the bonus can vary widely. [Under one] method . . . the physicians receive a negotiated share of the plan's profits. They may receive that share as owners of the plan or otherwise. . . .

In reality, all of these systems can be used and most of them can be combined. . . . For an example, return to the Stanford University [HMO plan]. The university contracts with three local physician groups and a statewide HMO to provide the HMO level of care for this plan. Each of the three physician groups is paid on a capitation basis to cover both the medical and hospital needs of the [HMO] members who come to them, but the contractual negotiations led to somewhat different outcomes. First, the amount paid to the three groups by Stanford to cover its members differs from group to group, depending on the bargains the University struck with each. . . . Then, each of the physician groups in turn contracted with a local hospital, designated by the University, to subcapitate the hospital care of their [HMO] plan members. The amount the groups have to pay the hospital varies, in part because some of the physician groups provided services in their clinics that other groups obtained through the hospital. Third, each of the groups' capitation payments are subject to a percentage withheld to cover member expenses for services obtained outside the HMO. . . .

The result is that each of the four sets of doctors participating in the HMO tier of Stanford's plan, although paid on a capitated basis, is paid differently. Because they are paid differently, the financial incentives they face in making decisions about a patient's care differ. They receive different amounts per patient. . . . Moreover, Stanford's [HMO] plan contracted not with physicians, but with physician groups. In a group practice, each physician does not "eat what he kills," a phrase from other professional organizations that is particularly jarring when used with physicians. Instead, the group as a whole decides how to pay its physician members. Therefore, even if a group has an HMO contract that provides for strict capitation, the group might, in its own compensation scheme, pay the physicians on the basis of any system: salary, profit sharing, capitation, bonus, fee-for-service, or any combination of the above. . . .

Implications for Public Policy

What are the implications of direct financial incentives for patients and for public policy? . . . [A] capitated plan that included diagnostic tests within the capitation might lead a physician not to order an expensive magnetic resonance imaging (MRI) scan for a patient even though there was a small, but nonzero, chance the test would reveal something useful. . . . [Or] direct financial incentives [might] lead physicians to educate asthmatics better about controlling their disease, leading to fewer serious asthma attacks, better health, and fewer expensive emergency room visits and hospital admissions. . . .

To what extent are physicians adopting these [different] methods of lowering costs as a result of direct financial incentives? . . . In the absence of data, we are left with logic and anecdotes, both often misleading when looking at human affairs. . . . [A]t least three important factors will push against a physician's doing "too little." First, truly doing "too little" for a patient often will be more expensive, in the long run, than offering the proper mix of services. . . . Second, by doing too little, for whatever reason, physicians put themselves at risk for malpractice liability. . . . Third, and most important, physicians want to do the right thing for their patients. Faced with a patient who the doctor believes really needs another test, the cost of which will come out of the doctor's income, I am confident that almost all doctors, almost all of the time, will order the test. . . .

We cannot dismiss the possibility that, in some circumstances, direct financial incentives could harm patients. It seems plausible that we could identify some factors or situations that might increase the odds of such bad outcomes. At the same time, the health care world is in the midst of a complicated and rapidly changing revolution in how society buys care. At this point in that revolution, what should be done about direct financial incentives?

One set of at least partial answers has been advanced by the federal government. In the Omnibus Budget Reconciliation Act of 1986, Congress [forbade] hospitals . . . from knowingly making incentive payments to physicians to induce them to reduce or limit services [under Medicare and Medicaid,[11] but] . . . Congress repealed the prohibition [for HMOs]. In its place, Congress substituted three rules governing organizations using such incentives. 42 U.S.C. §1395mm(8). First, [Medicare and Medicaid HMOs] could not have a physician incentive plan that made specific payments to doctors to induce them to limit or reduce medically necessary services to a specific individual. Second, they had to tell [CMS] about their physician incentive plans in detail. Finally, if their plans put physicians or physician groups at "substantial risk," as defined by regulation, they had to provide stop-loss insurance to the physicians and survey their present and past members about the members' access to and satisfaction with the services they received. . . .

[CMS] defined "substantial financial risk" as situations where a physician, or group, would have either more than twenty-five percent (for physicians or groups evaluated annually) or fifteen percent (if evaluated more frequently than annually) of its total compensation from the organization at risk, based at least in part on services the physicians did not provide directly. . . . [These] definitions for "substantial financial risk" [were chosen] solely because those seem to be near the limit of the risk amounts currently used by plans. As the current plans have no proven problems, [CMS] suggests, those percentages should be safe. This, of course, entirely avoids the questions of whether those percentages, or any percentages, are necessary. . . . There seems little reason for substantive regulation when all the regulators can say is that what they propose is consistent with what the industry already does. And, when an industry is evolving as rapidly as this one, such regulation may prove burdensome. . . . If evidence from research made it clear that some combinations of managed care incentives hurt patients, those methods could be banned or discouraged. . . .

In the long run, direct financial incentives may provide a useful solution to the problem of managing care, but only in a context where their risks are shared,

11. [The statute reads: "If a hospital . . . knowingly makes a payment, directly or indirectly, to a physician as an inducement to reduce or limit services provided with respect to [Medicare or Medicaid patients who] are under the direct care of the physician, the hospital . . . shall be subject . . . to a civil money penalty of not more than $2,000 for each such individual with respect to whom the payment is made." 42 U.S.C. §1320a-7a(b)(1).—Eds.]

and, hence, softened. . . . Thus, one way to adjust to direct financial incentives is to reconstruct medicine into a world of fairly large group practices that will be subject to those incentives. . . . I know many physicians who practice under one form of managed care with direct financial incentives: the Kaiser Permanente system. They tell me that they never feel pressure to make a treatment decision for financial reasons, but they also say that they practice differently at Kaiser than they did elsewhere and that their views of what is good medical practice have changed. . . . Physicians may use less expensive but equally effective drugs, or not keep patients in the hospitals longer than studies show is appropriate. All agree that much unnecessary, or unnecessarily expensive, care can be wrung out of the medical system.

At some point, though, when the unnecessary care has been eliminated, society still may be unwilling to pay the bill for all the appropriate care that is technically available. Under a system of care delivered by physician groups, operating under financial incentives, these rationing decisions would be made largely by the physician groups. . . . By burying the decisions in physician groups, one avoids the kinds of express allocation rules that prompt litigation—and accountability. Are physician groups the right bodies to make these rationing decisions? Compared to having them made by managed care groups? Congress? The courts? The "market"? These questions may lurk below the surface of the speculative future outlined above. . . .

Notes: Capitation, Gainsharing, and Other Physician Incentives

1. *The Ethics of Physician Incentives.* Capitation payments and other incentive plans common in HMOs raise a variety of legal and regulatory issues that are considered in other chapters (liability in Chapter 2, and insurance regulation in section B). This section explores only the structure and use of capitation arrangements, and the ethical conflicts of interest they create. The following section covers additional payment innovations targeted more directly to episodes of illness, or to value-based measures of performance.

Regardless of what the law says about capitation, what about professional medical ethics? Should physicians avoid working in settings and contracting with insurers that reward them for reduced care? The following two excerpts give a flavor of this debate. The first is from a prominent physician at Boston University, Norman Levinsky, The Doctor's Master, 311 New Eng. J. Med. 1573 (1984):

> [P]hysicians are required to do everything that they believe may benefit each patient without regard to costs or other societal considerations. In caring for an individual patient, the doctor must act solely as that patient's advocate, against the apparent interests of society as a whole, if necessary. An analogy can be drawn with the role of a lawyer defending a client against a criminal charge. The attorney is obligated to use all ethical means to defend the client, regardless of the cost of prolonged legal proceedings or even of the possibility that a guilty person may be acquitted through skillful advocacy. Similarly, in the practice of medicine, physicians are obligated to do all that they can for their patients without regard to any costs to society.
>
> This [ethic] may become blurred if physicians are pressed to balance the needs of their patients with societal needs. The practitioner may make decisions for economic reasons but rationalize them as in the best interest of the individual patient. . . . It is society, not the individual practitioner, that must make the decision to limit the availability of effective but expensive types of medical care. . . . Society,

> through its elected officials, is entitled to decide that the resources required for [expensive treatment] are better used for other purposes. However, a physician who thinks that his or her patient may benefit from [the treatment] must make that patient aware of this opinion and assist the patient in obtaining the [treatment]. . . .

The contrasting viewpoint is from a well-known economist at MIT, Lester Thurow, Learning to Say "No," 311 New Eng. J. Med. 1569 (1984):

> [From an economic perspective], physicians must stop treatments when marginal benefits are equal to marginal costs. But where lies the point at which marginal costs equal marginal benefits? And who is to make this ethical decision? . . . One answer is that third-party payers can write rules and regulations concerning what they will and will not pay for and can prohibit their clients from buying services that are not allowed under the private or public insurance systems. . . . Such a procedure works, but it works clumsily, since no set of rules can be adjusted to the nuances of individual medical problems. It will be far better if American doctors begin to build up a social ethic and behavioral practices that help them decide when medicine is bad medicine—not simply because it has absolutely no payoff or because it hurts the patient—but also because the costs are not justified by the marginal benefits. . . .
>
> The medical profession now has professional norms concerning what constitutes bad medical practice. Those norms have to be expanded to include cases in which high costs are not justified by minor expected benefits. If such norms are developed and then legally defended against malpractice suits, it just may be possible to build up a system of doctor-imposed cost controls that will be much more flexible than any system of cost controls imposed by third-party payers could be. But if the medical profession fails to do this, sooner or later the United States will move to a system of third-party controls. Something will have to be done.

Which position do you think is more convincing?

Does it make you any more comfortable to know that physicians under financial incentives tend to adjust their practice styles across the board, for both HMO and fee-for-service patients alike? In other words, incentives do affect how physicians behave, but a physician is likely to respond impartially to all his patients rather than differentiate among them based on each patient's particular source of payment. See Rajesh Balkrishnan et al., Capitation Payment, Length of Visit, and Preventive Services, 8 Am. J. Managed Care 332 (2002); Laurence C. Baker, Managed Care Spillover Effects, 24 Annu. Rev. Public Health 435 (2003). Is this the ethical way to respond, or should patients with more generous insurance receive better service?

Commenting broadly on the attempt to regulate physician incentives, consider the following forceful commentary from another prominent health economist, James C. Robinson, Theory and Practice in the Design of Physician Payment Incentives, 79 Milbank Q. 149, 173-174 (2001):

> Physician payment mechanisms are inevitably subject to more public monitoring than compensation systems in other occupations, since we all care more about our doctor's immediate motivation than we do about our accountant's or plumber's. . . . The tendency to overregulate must be recognized, however. The complexity of clinical services, combined with the importance that we all ascribe to what happens between physicians and patients, is conducive to the most egregious manifestations of what legal theorists refer to as the inhospitality tradition. That which cannot be

understood without effort is deemed ipso facto to be designed for fraud, monopolization, or some other antisocial purpose. . . . The contemporary moment in health policy is nothing short of a Dionysian rhapsody of regulation, the inhospitality tradition gone riot, the formal and final enshrinement of the doctrine that everything not mandatory is prohibited. The complexity of physician behavior, the emergence of payment methods that blend fee-for-service and capitation, the interdependence of price mechanisms with nonprice mechanisms, the salience of organization as a support for compensation systems, and the remarkable variety and continual change in all arenas suggest that public policymakers should adopt a stance of intellectual humility and a tone of cautious optimism. In physician payment, as in most other aspects of life, matters are never as good as we might hope but never as bad as we might fear.

See also Thomas P. Stossel, Regulation of Financial Conflicts of Interest in Medical Practice and Medical Research, 50 Perspect. Biol. Med. 54 (2007). Robert Kuttner observes that, "in building adequate risk-adjustment models, there are subtleties of Byzantine complexity. . . . Like so much else about the U.S. health system, [this] seems an astonishingly complex way to achieve some straightforward policy goals." He concludes that "the superior approach would be to cut the increasingly convoluted knot and move to a universal, unfragmented system of health insurance or a neutral form of payment for doctors, such as by salary." Robert Kuttner, The Risk-Adjustment Debate, 339 New Eng. J. Med. 1952 (1999).

2. *Risk Adjustment.* Capitation payments are rarely the same for each patient. Instead, they typically vary according to the patient's age and gender, in order to coarsely reflect how much care different types of patients usually need on average. This kind of calibration is known as "risk adjustment," and how it is done adds another major complication:

The intent of more aggregated payment units, such as capitation, is to encourage providers to make more efficient use of resources for a set bundle of services. However, just as insurance companies and HMOs have discovered an irresistible market logic in skimming off the healthiest subscribers, physicians . . . face a financial incentive to economize under more aggregated payment units by caring for healthier patients. Concern about this undesirable risk-skimming incentive has given rise to attempts to risk adjust reimbursement—that is, to pay at a higher rate for higher-risk patients.

Traditional fee-for-service payment has an intrinsic risk-adjustment factor. The sicker the patient, the more services provided. More services provided means greater reimbursement. In the episode-of-illness mode of payment, risk adjustment has been factored into such payment methods as the Medicare hospital DRG system. . . . Thus, DRG reimbursement is higher for a patient hospitalized for septic shock than for a patient admitted for elective cholecystectomy. . . .

Risk adjustment has been a technically greater challenge in setting capitation payments. The ideal risk-adjustment method for capitation payments would characterize each individual's health status or need for health care services to attach a higher payment rate to the higher-risk patients. For example, [an HMO] could pay a higher capitation rate for . . . HIV patients than for . . . healthy ones. Unfortunately, accurately predicting individuals' need for care is difficult. Data routinely collected during insurance enrollment, such as age, offer only a crude estimate of an individual's likelihood of using services. More accurate predictions necessitate examining an individual's medical history or current level of health, a relatively

> expensive proposition that often still falls short of the desired precision at estimating an individual's future health care expenses. . . . Interest in improving the "science" of risk adjustment is increasing as payers in the United States increasingly turn to capitation and other aggregated units of reimbursement.

Thomas Bodenheimer & Kevin Grumbach, Reimbursing Physicians and Hospitals, 272 JAMA 971 (1994).

Do you see the nightmare of DRGs recurring in the guise of risk adjustment? Medicare has struggled with how to implement risk adjustment for the managed care plans that its beneficiaries can purchase through Medicare Advantage. One approach pays more for patients with a history of designated chronic illnesses. The amount of extra payment is based on days of hospitalization and primary diagnoses in the prior year. Although this creates an incentive for HMOs to hospitalize their patients more in one year to increase payment in the next year, CMS claims there are sufficient checks in place to prevent this incentive from increasing costs. See Lisa Iezzoni et al., Paying More Fairly for Medicare Capitated Care, 339 New Eng. J. Med. 1933 (1998).

3. *Hospital "Gainsharing."* Carefully reread the passage in Prof. Greely's article that discusses the two federal statutes regulating physician incentives under Medicare and Medicaid. Note that the statute governing hospital-created incentives contains a flat prohibition of what has since come to be known as "gainsharing," whereas the HMO regulation is more permissive. Why should the rules about economizing incentives be much stricter for hospitals than for HMOs? The hospital statute was enacted in response to several for-profit hospitals in California that paid each doctor a percentage of the profits the hospital earned under DRGs from the doctor's Medicare patients. But, if Congress did not want money to influence decisions about hospital treatment, why did it adopt the DRG system in the first place?

If it is illegal for hospitals to split cost savings with physicians, then can hospitals not even reward physicians for identifying and eliminating wasteful practice patterns, such as not opening more surgical supplies than are needed for an operation, or using less expensive versions of particularly expensive surgical supplies? Hospital lawyers believed that such worthy purposes would avoid the statutory prohibition by focusing on more aggregate practice patterns among a group of physicians rather than on discrete treatment decisions by particular doctors. At first DHHS broadly pronounced these "gainsharing" efforts illegal, but following an outcry from hospitals and their lawyers, it subsequently declined to prosecute arrangements that contained various safeguards, limits, and oversight mechanisms to guard against abuses, similar to those under the HMO financial incentive statute. Also, regulations now clarify that the gainsharing prohibition applies only to programs that reduce medically necessary care, and the prohibition does not apply to accountable care organizations that participate in Medicare's new "shared savings" program—whose purpose, after all, is essentially the same as the gainsharing plans that DHHS initially disapproved. Still, hospitals and their lawyers often consider the rules to be too restrictive, such that gainsharing arrangements often are not worth the bother or the uncertainty of compliance. See Government Accountability Office, Implementation of Financial Incentive Programs Under Federal Fraud and Abuse Laws (2012).

4. *Disclosing Incentives.* Are you convinced by *Pegram* that it is not a proper judicial function to adjudicate financial conflicts of interest under fiduciary principles?

If this claim were brought under common law, should it still be dismissed? What if the claim involves the failure to *disclose* physician incentives rather than the argument that the incentives *themselves* violate fiduciary duties? Notice in footnote 8 that even *Pegram* says that failing to disclose financial incentives might violate ERISA. See also Shea v. Esensten, 208 F.3d 712 (8th Cir. 2000) (suggesting in dictum that Minnesota would recognize an action against physicians for failing to disclose financial incentives). Prior to *Pegram,* this theory had received only mixed success in the federal courts under ERISA. See Comment, 106 Dick. L. Rev. 415 (2001). Following *Pegram,* at least one court has held that ERISA does not require disclosure of physician incentives unless the patient asks for this information, or unless the HMO knows the patient needed or wanted this information and that it would have avoided harm to the patient. Horvath v. Keystone Health Plan East, Inc., 333 F.3d 450 (3d Cir. 2003). Could this theory of liability be based simply on informed consent law? Compare Mark Hall, A Theory of Economic Informed Consent, 31 Ga. L. Rev. 31 (1997) (arguing no); with Devon C. McGraw, Financial Incentives to Limit Services: Should Physicians Be Required to Disclose These to Patients?, 83 Geo. L.J. 1821 (1995) (arguing yes).

One important decision refused to allow such a suit under state law, citing *Pegram* for support. Neade v. Portes, 739 N.E.2d 496 (Ill. 2000). However, the court held that evidence of physician incentives could be relevant in assessing medical negligence. *Neade* also observed that Illinois, like many other states, has a statute requiring disclosure of incentives but imposes this duty only on the HMO, not on the physician. See Tracy E. Miller & William M. Sage, Disclosing Physician Financial Incentives, 281 JAMA 1424-1430 (1999). Therefore, similar to *Pegram,* the *Neade* court felt that the issue should not be dealt with through common law.

Under either tort law or regulatory law, what is the optimal timing for disclosing physician incentives: when someone is deciding which health insurance to choose, when the person is picking a physician, or when the person is considering a treatment option? Federal rules implementing Medicare's shared savings program for ACOs require primary care physicians to disclose their participation in the incentive program to patients "at the point of care." 42 C.F.R. 425.312(a). How much detail should patients be given? How much is this information likely to really matter to people in making important decisions? See generally Mark A. Hall, The Theory and Practice of Disclosing HMO Physician Incentives, 65 Law & Contemp. Probs. 207 (Autumn 2002).

5. Pegram*'s Importance for Preemption.* Because *Pegram* broadly discusses the purpose and functioning of HMOs, it has importance in a number of other areas of litigation. For instance, consider what this decision has to say about the issue addressed in Chapter 2.C of whether ERISA preempts malpractice claims against HMOs, based on the Court's assumption that Pegram has tort remedies available under state law.

6. *Additional Readings.* For concerns about **global capitation and the role of financial incentives generally** (note 1), see Steffie Woolhandler & David Himmelstein, Extreme Risk: The New Corporate Proposition for Physicians, 333 New Eng. J. Med. 1706 (1995); Christopher Robertson, Effect of Financial Relationships on the Behavior of Healthcare Professionals, 40 J.L., Med. & Ethics 452 (2012).

For more on **the ethics of physicians incentives** (note 1), see Conflicts of Interest in Clinical Practice and Research (Roy Spece et al. eds., 1996); Peter A.

Ubel, Pricing Life: Why It's Time for Health Care Rationing (2000); Christopher Robertson et al., Effect of Financial Relationships on the Behaviors of Health Care Professionals, 40 J.L., Med. & Ethics 452 (2012); Gail Agrawal, Resuscitating Professionalism: Self-Regulation in the Medical Marketplace, 66 Mo. L. Rev. 341 (2001); Mark A. Hall, Rationing Health Care at the Bedside, 69 N.Y.U. L. Rev. 693 (1994); William M. Sage, Physicians as Advocates, 35 Hous. L. Rev. 1529 (1999); Timothy S. Hall, Bargaining with Hippocrates: Managed Care and the Doctor-Patient Relationship, 54 S.C. L. Rev. 689 (2003); Symposium, 40 J.L., Med. & Ethics 436 (2012); and the readings and sources cited in section D.1 and Chapter 1.C.

For general discussion of the methods, purpose, and performance of risk adjustment (note 2), see Mark A. Hall, Risk Adjustment Under the Affordable Care Act, 20 Kan. J.L. & Pub. Pol'y 222 (2011); David Blumenthal et al., The Who, What, and Why of Risk Adjustment, 30 J. Health Pol. Pol'y & L. 453 (2005); Fred Hellinger & Herbert Wong, Selection Bias in HMOs: A Review of the Evidence, 57 Med. Care Res. Rev. 405 (2000); Symposium, Private Employers and Risk Adjustment, 38 Inquiry 242 (2001).

For discussions of **hospital gainsharing** (note 3), see Richard S. Saver, Squandering the Gain: Gainsharing and the Continuing Dilemma of Physician Financial Incentives, 98 Nw. U. L. Rev. 145 (2003); Gail Wilensky, Gain Sharing: A Good Concept Getting a Bad Name?, 26(1) Health Aff. w58 (Jan. 2007); Catherine Martin, Incentive Payment and Shared Savings Programs: The New Gainsharing, 17 BNA Health L. Rep. 1011 (2008); Anne Claiborne et al., Legal Impediments to Implementing Value-Based Purchasing in Healthcare, 35 Am. J.L. & Med. 443 (2009). For discussion of the HMO rules, see M. Hall, Physician Rationing and Agency Cost Theory, *in* Spece, supra; David Orentlicher, Paying Physicians More to Do Less: Financial Incentives to Limit Care, 30 U. Rich. L. Rev. 155, 174 (1996); Stephen R. Latham, Regulation of Managed Care Incentive Payments to Physicians, 22 Am. J.L. & Med. 399 (1996); Douglas Blair, The "PIP" Regulations in Perspective, 29 U. Mem. L. Rev. 137 (1998).

For more on **informed consent and the disclosure of payment arrangements** (note 4), see E. Haavi Morreim, Diverse and Perverse Incentives of Managed Care: Bringing Patients into Alignment, 1 Widener L. Symp. J. 89, 123 (1996); Grant H. Morris, Dissing Disclosure: Just What the Doctor Ordered, 44 Ariz. L. Rev. 313 (2002); Susan M. Wolf, 35 Hous. L. Rev. 1631 (1999); Joan H. Krause, Reconceptualizing Informed Consent in an Era of Health Care Cost Containment, 85 Iowa L. Rev. 261 (1999). For more discussion of **"gag clauses"** (note 5), see Gordon Brand et al., The Two Faces of Gag Provisions: Patients and Physicians in a Bind, 17 Yale L. & Pol'y Rev. 249 (1998); Joan H. Krause, The Brief Life of the Gag Clause, 67 Tenn. L. Rev. 1 (1999).

For a discussion of how **fiduciary law principles** apply to these issues generally, see Peter D. Jacobson & Michael T. Cahill, Applying Fiduciary Responsibilities in the Managed Care Context, 26 Am. J.L. & Med. 155 (2000); Marc A. Rodwin, Strains in the Fiduciary Metaphor: Divided Physician Loyalties and Obligations in a Changing Health Care System, 21 Am. J.L. & Med. 241 (1995).

For general commentary on ***Pegram*** and the issues it raises, see Michael T. Cahill & Peter D. Jacobson, *Pegram*'s Regress: A Missed Chance for Sensible Judicial Review of Managed Care Decisions, 27 Am. J.L. & Med. 421 (2001); Peter J. Hammer, On Peritonitis, Preemption, and the Elusive Goal of Managed Care Accountability,

26 J. Health Pol. Pol'y & L. 767 (2001); Richard A. Ippolito, Freedom to Contract in Medical Care: HMOs, ERISA and Pegram v. Herdrich, 9 Sup. Ct. Econ. Rev. 1 (2001); Arnold J. Rosoff, Breach of Fiduciary Duty Lawsuits Against MCOs, 22 J. Leg. Med. 55 (2001); William Sage, UR Here: The Supreme Court's Guide for Managed Care, 19 Health Aff. 219 (2000); Jeffrey Stempel & Nadia Magdenko, Doctors, HMOs, ERISA, and the Public Interest After Pegram v. Herdrich, 36 Tort & Ins. L.J. 687 (2001); Symposium, 1 Yale J. Health Pol'y L. & Ethics (2001).

4. Value-Based Payment Innovations

REVISITING INCENTIVE-BASED CONTRACTS

Wendy Netter Epstein

17 Yale J. Health Pol'y, L. & Ethics 1 (2017)

Incentive-based compensation has its roots in classic economic theory: rational, selfish actors who are motivated to maximize their own wealth will do their best work if they will get a financial reward for doing so. Material incentives are generally believed to be powerful motivators. The Aztecs rewarded successful warriors with land and better food. Roman warriors were rewarded in the same ways. The use of financial incentives in particular is now pervasive across very different industries, from executive compensation to professional sports and education. Common sense and economic principles both suggest that connecting pay to quality metrics will yield better results.

Incentive pay is a concept that almost everyone seems to be able to get behind. Indeed, incentive regimes are a part of the new ideological hybrid–libertarian paternalism–that encourages behavior by making it attractive without regulating it.[4] The liberal Obama Administration has firmly embraced the idea, arguing that rewarding excellence with pay improves quality. And conservatives generally support incentive pay because it is essentially a private, market-based solution. It remains to be seen if the new Trump Administration will stay the course or not, but there is reason to believe it may not.

It may be right to revisit the move to incentive pay. The history of incentive pay across industries has been mixed. Scholars and policymakers have identified a host of observed and potential mal-effects, from cherry picking easy cases or cheating on the metrics, to excessively focusing on the metrics to the detriment of overall quality of performance. . . .

The issue of how to structure reimbursement agreements is really one of how to draft contracts to maximize party performance. Economists, social scientists, and contracts scholars have contributed to an immense literature addressing the effects of contract drafting strategies on agents' cognition, compliance, and motivation to perform. This literature–theoretical, experimental, and empirical–is complicated, and at times, seemingly conflicting. Financial incentives can motivate, but can also crowd out intrinsic motivation. Contract specificity can inform goals and facilitate

4. *See* Richard Thaler & Cass Sunstein, *Libertarian Paternalism*, 93 Am. Econ. Rev. 175 (2003).

improved performance, while reducing the likelihood that parties will use contractual gaps to justify unethical behavior. But specificity can also cause agents to focus too narrowly and ignore hard cases, decreasing overall performance, among a host of other identified effects.

The literature suggests that the detailed, control-based contracting approach is a better fit for easily measurable, compliance-oriented tasks not requiring creativity or innovation than it is for more difficult-to-define tasks that require motivating the agent's best performance. Experience with incentive-based contracting across industries seems to bear out these predictions. . . .

The health-care industry provides a new lens through which to study this long-standing problem. . . . The general consensus in the industry is that physician financial incentives must be addressed as a part of addressing overall cost and quality concerns. . . . If the problem is that doctors' incentives are out of step with those of payers and patients, then align their incentives; pay physicians for delivering cost-effective, quality care, not for simply delivering more care.

Just as in other industries, the health-care commitment to incentive compensation evidences a commitment to a more detailed contracting approach. In a fee-for-service system, the contracts between physicians and payers are, relatively speaking, unspecific and make only limited use of control elements, such as reporting requirements and financial incentives tied to performance. . . . Importantly, it commits to payment regardless of outcome.

Incentive-based compensation, on the other hand, requires much more detailed contract drafting. The payer provides, *ex ante*, a list of metrics the physician is required to meet. The payer also defines the financial implications of meeting, exceeding, or falling short of those metrics. If fee-for-service contracts tend to be vague in task definition and tend to make limited use of control elements, incentive pay is a move to the other end of the contract-drafting spectrum: detailed task specification and extensive use of contractual control mechanisms such as reporting, monitoring, and financial incentives.

The health-care industry has been focused on how to improve this new payment model–for instance, how to determine the proper amount of the financial incentive and how to choose the correct quality metrics. This Article suggests that focus is misplaced. The key question the health-care industry should be focused on solving is not how to improve this new payment model, although that work may be useful, but rather on where and where not to use the model. The legal, economic, and behavioral literature teaches that an across-the-board approach such as the one currently being hailed in the industry will not be effective. The industry must determine, and then implement, a more nuanced approach that draws the line between tasks where incentive-pay mechanisms will be helpful and those where they will be ineffective at best or harmful at worst. Changing focus in this way is much more likely to yield successful results, even if it requires recognizing that incentive-based compensation cannot solve all of the health industry's problems. . . .

THE HEALTH INDUSTRY'S INCENTIVE-PAY SOLUTION

Linking payment with desired results has been touted by members of Congress as the panacea for health care that can save the United States $700 billion a year, while simultaneously improving quality. . . . In January 2015, the Department of Health and Human Services (HHS) publicly announced a goal of tying fifty percent of payments to alternative payment models, such as ACOs, by the end of 2018 [although the Trump administration is expected to scale back or delay that goal]. . . . The following explains how incentive-based compensation is expected to work.

In the health context specifically, the typical pay-for-performance program provides a bonus to health-care providers (or hospitals or other medical entities) if they meet or exceed agreed-upon metrics, although some are structured to penalize providers that fail to meet defined metrics. . . . Quality and performance measures differ by program, but generally fall into four categories: process, outcome, patient experience, or structure. Process metrics require providers to follow a predefined process to satisfy the metric, such as giving aspirin to heart-attack victims within a certain amount of time after the patient arrives in the emergency room. Outcome measures focus on results. Morbidity and mortality data are the classic examples. More recently, there has been a focus on defining more-specific outcome measures, such as reductions in hemoglobin A1c in diabetic patients. Patient experience measures the patients' perception of the care they receive and is usually collected by compiling the results of patient surveys. Finally, structure considers the inputs into health-care provision, from the facilities and equipment used in treatment, to the adoption of health information technology.

The Affordable Care Act's Commitment to Incentive-Based Compensation

Despite the contentious political debates that surrounded and continue to surround the Affordable Care Act (ACA), there was strong bipartisan support for a key category of reform reflected in the bill: restructuring the Medicare delivery system by tying financial incentives to performance. . . . By some measures, the ACA includes forty five different provisions aimed at reforming health-care delivery to either improve the quality and/or the efficiency of health care in some way.[82] . . . The three largest initiatives are: (1) the establishment of a Shared Savings Program to benefit Accountable Care Organizations; (2) the new incentive-based compensation model for physicians (and hospitals); and (3) a pilot program to test bundled payments, among other initiatives.

A. Accountable Care Organizations

Of all the provisions aimed at reforming the delivery model by aligning incentives, Accountable Care Organizations (ACOs) have received the most attention [and are further discussed in the next reading]. . . . An ACO is a network of care providers committed to improving quality and reducing cost through coordination of efforts. Rather than individual specialists treating one patient without collaboration (thus duplicating tests and procedures, and lacking a cohesive view of the entire patient), ACOs deliver integrated care enabled by shared medical records and other coordination. . . . By giving providers who have at least some control over cost and quality of care a bonus for cost and quality metrics improvement (and

82. This does not include, for instance, the recent enactment of the Medicare Access and CHIP Reauthorization Act of 2015 and its expansion of value-based payment systems for providers.

in some cases a penalty for failing to meet goals), the ACO model aligns provider incentives with governmental priorities.

Both cost savings and quality metrics play a part in determining ACO compensation. First, CMS sets a benchmark of average Medicare expenditures, taking into account a projected growth rate in expenses. CMS also sets a list of [33] quality metrics and associated benchmarks. . . . ACOs receive points on a sliding scale based on level of performance relative to the benchmarks. For instance, ACOs must report on certain preventive health measures administered to patients, such as immunizations for influenza and mammography screenings. ACOs must also report outcome measures for patients with various illnesses. For example, for patients with diabetes, ACOs must document control of Hemoglobin A1c, and for patients with hypertension, ACOs must report on patient blood pressure. . . . The quality metrics differentiate ACOs from HMOs and, in theory, prevent ACOs from saving money by rationing necessary care. . . .

B. INCENTIVE-BASED COMPENSATION FOR PHYSICIANS

The ACA also changes the method of physician [and hospital] payment through the Physician Value-Based Payment Modifier [and the Hospital (In-Patient) Value-Based Purchasing Program]. . . . The modifier adjusts fees paid to physicians [and hospitals] using data reported on quality and resource use. . . . The program started by focusing on measures of clinical processes and results of patient-satisfaction surveys, but over time has come to rely more heavily on outcome measures, such as mortality rates, rather than measures of process compliance. . . .

This new adjustment was first applied in 2015 to [hospitals] group practices with one hundred or more eligible professionals, using quality reporting data from 2013. The program [was expected to] be scaled up to apply to all physicians by 2018 [but has been delayed by the Trump administration]. The program is budget neutral for the government; therefore, some [providers] will see their pay increase while others will see it decrease.

C. BUNDLED PAYMENTS

Finally, [the ACA] establishes a five-year program to test bundled payments [which has now been made ongoing since 2013]. Bundled payments mean that rather than paying per procedure or per test, reimbursement will be based on the expected costs for an entire episode of care (e.g., a single illness or course of treatment). . . . The idea is, if a predefined sum of money will be awarded for patient care and total reimbursement cannot be increased by ordering more tests or procedures, providers will think hard about whether that extra test is likely to yield valuable information before ordering it and will coordinate their efforts to avoid costly and unnecessary duplication. . . . The financial incentive in [the current] model flows directly to the hospital and not the physician, although physician behavior is intended to be targeted as well. . . .

III. INCENTIVE-BASED COMPENSATION: THE EVIDENCE SO FAR

Although incentive-based compensation is, relatively speaking, new to health care, it has long been employed in other industries, such as executive compensation, professional sports, and education. . . .The experience in these three industries . . .

seems to bear out many of the predictions of the literature. While financial incentives do seem to motivate, at least according to some studies, they tend to do so best where easy-to-measure goals are closely associated with the performance the principal wishes to prompt from the agent. But . . . there are other overarching concerns. Financial incentives seem to cause focus on the metric to which compensation is tied, and in particular, promote paying attention to metrics that are easier to move, while ignoring the harder cases. Performance pay can also encourage risk-taking behavior and even cheating.

. . . [P]erformance pay works better in some contexts than others. Key attributes of successful performance pay systems appear to be: (1) easy to define and measure tasks; (2) low ability or need to cheat on the metrics; and (3) a low likelihood of crowding out already strong intrinsic motivation, either because intrinsic motivation is weak to begin with or intrinsic motivation is not particularly necessary to successful execution of the task. . . .

EARLY RESULTS OF INCENTIVE PAY IN HEALTH CARE

. . . A number of studies also assess the extent to which pay for performance can be linked to cost savings. The most salient inquiry is whether cost savings can be achieved while quality metrics are simultaneously maintained or improved. The purpose of incentive-pay models is not to achieve cost savings at the sacrifice of quality. Arguably that was the problem with HMOs. Again, results are mixed. Some are positive. . . . Others actually found that where quality improves as intended, cost increases rather than decreases. . . .

Several studies have also investigated whether incentive pay yields unintended consequences. In other words, some providers might succeed in improving quality and decreasing cost, but might do so in ways that have undesirable effects in other areas.

First, policymakers have been concerned that physician financial incentives will result in adverse selection, where physicians cherry pick the easier cases while harder cases receive less attention. . . . Second, some studies have assessed whether incentive pay tied to certain procedures or categories of care has negative spillover effects on unincentivized procedures. . . . Third, there has been concern over gaming the system or cheating on the metrics. . . . The fourth unintended consequence concerns whether the use of financial incentives affects the intrinsic motivation of providers or provider professionalism. [Studies so far are limited and inconclusive on each of these possibilities]. . . .

Relatedly, some studies have noted that the use of incentive pay has adversely affected the physician-patient relationship.[283] For instance, physicians have reported resentment toward non-compliant patients who negatively impact their compensation. In one study, physicians also reported pressure to convince patients to agree to certain treatments or to bypass the informed-consent process.

283. Note that it is this concern—about the effect of incentive pay on the doctor-patient relationship—that caused Tom Price, President Trump's first Secretary of Health and Human Services, who is also a physician, to come out publicly against the use of incentive pay in health care.

In general, it is hard to draw concrete lessons from this very preliminary and mixed data. But it at least suggests that the predictions of the incomplete contracts literature may bear out in the health industry, as they seem to do in the executive compensation, education, and professional sports examples, and that there may be additional challenges unique to the health-care context. . . . .

Conclusion

The health-care industry has rallied behind a far-reaching implementation of incentive pay, one that applies across delivery models, to generalist and specialty physicians, and to a wide range of procedures and diagnoses. The contracts literature suggests that this is too blunt of an approach. Task specification and control-based contracting that utilizes monitoring and financial incentives tends to work best for ensuring compliance. But it works less well for motivating consummate performance because it can signal distrust and crowd out social and professional norms that would otherwise have operated to improve performance. Task specification coupled with control mechanisms can also lead to gamesmanship and cheating on the metrics to secure increased compensation. The health-care industry should be focusing on where to implement incentive pay to capture its benefits for compliance and standardization, but minimize its negative impact on innovation and the operation of positive norms. The new Trump Administration has an opportunity to study this issue further and to claw back some of the misguided attempts to implement incentive pay where it is likely to have mal-effects. These are lessons to be extrapolated to other industries, as well.

ACCOUNTABLE CARE ORGANIZATIONS IN MEDICARE AND THE PRIVATE SECTOR: A STATUS UPDATE

Robert A. Berenson & Rachel A. Burton (2011)

Why is Everyone Talking About ACOs?

. . . For many [health care policy analysts], the holy grail of health policy-making has been to find a model that aligns health care providers' and patients' interests. In the 1980s and '90s, some thought that health maintenance organizations (HMOs) might be such a model, but patients, encouraged by their physicians, eventually objected to HMOs' perceived intrusion into patient care decisions, causing HMOs to back off from some of their earlier approaches and to now fade from prominence.

Two decades later, the next great hope of many has become accountable care organizations (ACOs). Although known primarily as a Medicare program authorized in the Affordable Care Act (ACA), ACO-style payment arrangements have already been adopted by private insurers, even before the Centers for Medicare & Medicaid Services (CMS) issued its final regulations . . . for the Medicare Shared Savings Program, as it is called. . . . Medicare's ACO approach may influence many more health plans because it provides a model for an intermediary form of delivery: putting providers in a position somewhere between being paid solely through volume-increasing fee-for-service payments and operating within tightly managed, prospectively defined capitated budgets that place providers at full financial risk

Goldilocks

for all spending for their enrolled populations. . . . The ACO's performance on numerous quality metrics is also central to determining whether the ACO is eligible for shared savings and, if so, the amount of shared savings it receives from the sponsoring payer. . . .

In current ACO arrangements, providers generally receive bonuses if their patients' health care costs are below a projected amount based on their own historic spending, regardless of whether the level of their historic spending is high or low. The size of these bonuses depends, in part, on how much savings the ACO produces. Both the [Medicare Shared Savings Program] and private ACO contracts have been layering these bonus payments on top of traditional fee-for-service reimbursement, rather than making the leap to capitation (pre-paid fees paid per patient). . . . Several private ACO contracts [as well as Medicare] are offering providers 50 percent of the savings they generate . . . , and intend to transition their private ACO contracts to some form of capitation in coming years, as in the Pioneer ACO model being pursued by CMS' Innovation Center. . . .

[P]rivate ACO contracts are giving patients added incentives to seek care within their plan's provider network, such as by offering reduced premiums for individuals who receive care from providers taking part in such arrangements. By contrast, Medicare has so far chosen not to offer such financial incentives to Medicare beneficiaries to stay within their ACO's provider network. . . . [Medicare] beneficiaries will retain the freedom to seek care from any health care providers they choose. But if a beneficiary obtains the plurality of their primary care from a provider who belongs to an ACO, that beneficiary's total health care spending, along with care quality metrics, will be measured and used to assess whether their provider's ACO is eligible for shared savings bonus payments. ACOs will be sent lists of beneficiaries they are likely to be held accountable for under CMS' assignment algorithm on a quarterly basis. Then, at the end of the year, CMS will calculate ACOs' shared savings bonus payments based on a re-assessment of where those beneficiaries actually ended up receiving a plurality of their primary care services. CMS calls this approach "preliminary prospective assignment." . . .

WILL ACOs SAVE MONEY?

The results of the only demonstration that directly tested the ACO concept . . . suggest that ACOs will be able to improve the quality of care they deliver (at least as measured by process-oriented clinical quality measures), but will have a harder time generating savings. . . . Only two participants lowered health spending enough to receive bonuses in all five years of the demo, and three of the 10 participants received no bonus in any year of the demo. . . .

Even more disappointing, CMS' independent evaluator questioned whether demo participants generated savings by actually reducing spending or by merely raising the spending targets they had to work within by more thoroughly recording patients' diagnoses. (Under the risk-adjustment model CMS uses, spending and spending targets are adjusted based on patients' diagnoses.) . . .

The bottom line is that the [Medicare] demo does not seem to have succeeded in meaningfully reducing spending growth. However, it should not be surprising that the demo did not cause providers to dramatically alter the way they deliver care to achieve large reductions in health care spending, . . . [g]iven the initial three-year limit on CMS' commitment to the payment approach used in this demo. . . .

WILL QUALITY MEASURES PROTECT PATIENTS AGAINST HARM?

ACO proponents think that publicly available quality measures can go a long way towards protecting patients against the kind of stinting on care that patients perceived HMOs as engaging in during the 1990s. In the [Medicare Shared Savings Program], CMS will monitor ACOs through their reporting on 33 quality measures. ACOs that do not perform at the 30th percentile or percent (depending on the measure) on at least 70 percent of the measures in each of four domains would not be eligible to share in any savings they generate, and would have one year to improve performance before being terminated from the program. . . .

It is unclear whether quality measures currently are up to one of the tasks assigned them, that is, to ensure that cost savings will not be achieved by stinting on care. . . . [The measures] do not cover the full range of areas that an organization responsible for the entire continuum of care for a population of Medicare beneficiaries should address; for example, appropriate referral to specialized centers outside the ACO, when specialized expertise is needed to treat particular forms of cancer. . . .

Notes: Future Directions in Reimbursement

1. *Accountable Care Organizations.* These notes introduce ACOs as a vehicle for payment innovation. As a means to reduce costs, recent evidence suggests that Medicare's ACO program has yielded only small savings. See J. Michael McWilliams et al., Early Performance of Accountable Care Organizations in Medicare, 374 New Eng. J. Med. 2357 (2016). That may be due in part to the weakness of the "shared savings" incentives under Medicare. As discussed more in Chapter 4, ACOs are also designed for use under private insurance, which could opt to use stronger incentives. Or, ACOs might form the nucleus for providers themselves to become insurers, or for them to contract directly with employers, thus acting as virtual insurers.

2. *Value-Based Payment Reform.* In January 2015, CMS announced an ambitious goal of tying at least 90 percent of all Medicare fee-for-service payments to quality or value metrics by the end of 2018. See Sylvia Burwell, Setting Value-Based Payment Goals—HHS Efforts to Improve U.S. Health Care, 372 New Eng. J. Med. 897 (2015). The bipartisan adoption of the Medicare Access and CHIP Reauthorization Act of 2015 (MACRA) should aid the agency's efforts to pay for value instead of quantity.

> This approach incentivizes clinicians to participate in "alternative payment models" (APMs). Examples of APMs could be accountable care organizations, bundled payment models, and medical homes. MACRA establishes specific criteria for "eligible alternative payment entities," which operate under one of these APMs. Essentially, MACRA establishes two paths for payment updates [i.e., increasing the amount that clinicians are paid each year]—a path for clinicians who participate in eligible alternative payment entities and a path for all other clinicians.

Beginning in 2019 and continuing through 2024, clinicians will receive a 5 percent incentive payment if the level of revenue they receive through eligible alternative payment entities meets a certain threshold. In 2025, there will be no update and no incentive payments, and from 2026 on, clinicians meeting the revenue threshold will receive a higher update than clinicians who do not meet that threshold. Thus, how CMS defines eligible alternative payment entities and how clinicians qualify for the incentive payment are of great interest to clinicians.

For clinicians who do not qualify for the APM incentive payment, a separate program exists for assessing clinicians on their performance—the Merit-based Incentive Payment System (MIPS). Performance on MIPS will determine whether clinicians will receive a bonus or a penalty on their fee-for-service (FFS) payments. Although budget neutral in aggregate, these bonuses and penalties could have a large effect on payments for individual clinicians and hence on the attractiveness of the APM and MIPS paths.

Medicare Payment Advisory Commission, June 2016 Report to Congress, at 29-30.

CMS has issued a lengthy and complex set of rules to implement MACRA, which went into effect at the beginning of 2017. See 81 Fed. Reg. 77008 (Nov. 2016). But the law is unpopular among physicians, with the MIPS program attracting particular ire:

> [P]hysicians and their staff currently spend, on average, 785.2 hours ($40,069 per physician) annually simply tracking and reporting quality measures for Medicare, Medicaid, and private health insurers. . . . In spite of the substantial time diverted from patient care and the money ($15.4 billion—roughly the amount of government spending each year on graduate medical education) that could be used for other purposes, most physicians feel that the current measures do not help them improve the care they provide. According to an October 2016 analysis of the current misalignment of health quality measures, the Government Accountability Office concluded that: "Although hundreds of quality measures have been developed, relatively few are measures that payers, providers, and other stakeholders agree to adopt, because few are viewed as leading to meaningful improvements in quality."
>
> Making this huge investment in measure reporting with very little return in quality improvement is wholly inconsistent with the goal of value-based health care. Furthermore, while MIPS is essentially a complex pay-for-performance system that will reward or penalize physicians based on their performance on a range of measures, analyses of pay-for-performance payments systems have shown that they have had little effect on improving the quality of care over the past decade.

John O'Shea, As MACRA Implementation Proceeds, Changes Are Needed, Health Aff. Blog (Apr. 21, 2017). Adding to the confusion is the complexity involved when a given provider or network is subject to multiple different payment methods simultaneously. Robert E. Mechanic, When New Medicare Payment Systems Collide, 374 New Eng. J. Med. 1706 (2016). Based on all of this, the influential Medicare Payment Advisory Commission (MedPAC) has recommended repeal of MIPS, to be replaced with a voluntary approach that bases performance bonuses on measurable patient outcomes. MedPAC, June 2017 Report to Congress.

If paying for performance is so hard, what other approaches could CMS take to assure that it gets good value for its money?

3. *Bundling Payment for Episodes of Care*. Currently, Medicare ACOs receive only a bonus for savings compared to benchmark standard fee-for-service payment

(or possibly a penalty for costing more). But, as Prof. Epstein mentions, some policy analysts hope that ACOs will permit a move away from fee-for-service models entirely, toward paying lump sums for entire episodes of care. Doing that would also depart from having different payment methods for hospitals versus physicians, by bundling payment across all providers for a given episode of treatment, leaving to providers to negotiate how to allocate the bundled payment. Can you start to see the complexities in conducting such negotiations?

> In the early 1990s, Medicare created the Medicare Participating Heart Bypass Center Demonstration, which bundled hospital and physician payments for cardiac bypass graft surgery. The payments covered readmissions within seventy-two hours postdischarge and related physician services for a ninety-day period. Although the demonstration was considered successful, it was not renewed because of opposition from some parts of the hospital industry. . . .
>
> In its June 2008 report, MedPAC [the Medicare Payment Advisory Commission], having studied the issue for more than a year, made [these] unanimous recommendations to Congress regarding bundling [which Congress included in the 2010 health reform law]: . . . Congress should require the Secretary to create a voluntary pilot program to test the feasibility of actual bundled payment for services around hospitalization episodes for select conditions. . . . [T]he commissioners believed . . . that bundling could provide the incentive and opportunity for physicians to reduce the number of hospital visits without harming quality. Second, they intended that a bundled payment pilot would remove legal barriers that currently keep hospitals from compensating physicians for using fewer resources during a hospital stay. Third, depending upon the structure of the bundled payment, physicians would be encouraged to focus on posthospital care and the prevention of [hospital] readmissions. . . .
>
> Whichever model proves to be the best, this type of incentive change is difficult. As noted by [MedPAC's chairman], "[we are] under no illusion that the path of policy change outlined here is easy. . . . But a continuation of the status quo is unacceptable."

Francis J. Crosson & Laura A. Tollen, Partners in Health: How Physicians and Hospitals Can Be Accountable Together (2010).

The CMS Innovation Center is charged with developing demonstration projects to test new payment approaches, including bundled payments. Initially, the Innovation Center's bundled payment initiatives were voluntary: Providers could choose whether or not to participate. The problem with voluntary demonstration projects, however, is that volunteering organizations could be—indeed, they likely are—systematically different from organizations that do not volunteer. What works for volunteers may not work for non-volunteers, making it hard to know whether the demonstration should be scaled up.

To avoid the problems of causal inference, the Innovation Center decided in late 2015 to require providers in 67 geographical areas to accept bundled payments for hip and knee replacements. See 80 Fed. Reg. 73273 (2015). And in January 2017, in the waning days of the Obama administration, the agency announced that it would also require some providers to use bundled payments for hip fractures, heart attacks, and coronary bypass surgery. 82 Fed. Reg. 180 (2017).

Resistance from hospitals and physicians to these "mandatory models" has been intense, however, and Tom Price, President Trump's first Secretary of Health and Human Services (and former physician), has been an especially vocal critic. Shortly after the change in administration, CMS announced that it would delay the newest bundled payment initiatives, perhaps indefinitely. Many in the policy community fear that the abandonment of mandatory models "would eliminate the ability to generate robust evidence on their effectiveness, dealing a severe blow to efforts to use bundled payments to improve care delivery in orthopedics and cardiac care, and to the chances for bringing bundled payments to scale nationally in the coming years." Tim Gronniger et al., How Should the Trump Administration Handle Medicare's New Bundled Payment Programs?, Health Aff. Blog, Apr. 10, 2017.

4. *Staying up to Date.* The following is a sampling of literature on these fast-paced developments, but those wanting the latest should do additional research, since payment reform, like the weather, is subject to rapid change and resists accurate forecasts.

For an overview of **initial ACO performance** (note 1), see Zirui Song & Elliott Fisher, The ACO Experiment in Infancy: Looking Back and Looking Forward, 316 JAMA 705 (2016).

For discussions of **pay for performance** (note 2), see Nita Garg, Hospital Value Based Purchasing and the Bundled Payment Initiative Under the Affordable Care Act: A Good Start, But Is it Good Enough?, 22 Ann. Health L. 171 (2013); Christopher Robertson, Susannah Rose & Aaron S. Kesselheim, Effect of Financial Relationships on the Behaviors of Health Care Professionals: A Review of the Evidence, 40 J.L., Med. & Ethics 452 (2012); Adam Candeub, Contract, Warranty and the Patient Protection and Affordable Care Act, 46 Wake Forest L. Rev. 45 (2011); David M. Cutler, Your Money or Your Life: Strong Medicine for America's Health Care System (2004); Institute of Medicine, Rewarding Provider Performance: Aligning Incentives in Medicare (2006); David Hyman, Follow the Money: Money Matters in Health Care, Just Like Everything Else, 36 Am. J. L. & Med. 370 (2010); David A. Hyman & Charles M. Silver, The Poor State of Health Care Quality in the U.S.: Is Malpractice Liability Part of the Problem or Part of the Solution?, 90 Cornell L. Rev. 893 (2005); Bruce C. Vladeck, If Paying for Quality Is Such a Bad Idea, Why Is Everyone for It?, 60 Wash. & Lee L. Rev. 1345 (2003).

For discussions of **MACRA** (note 2), see Health Policy Brief, Medicare's New Physician Payment System, Health Aff. (April 2016); Eric C. Schneider & Cornelia J. Hall, Improve Quality, Control Spending, Maintain Access—Can the Merit-Based Incentive Payment System Deliver?, 376 New Eng. J. Med. 708 (2017); Peter Hussey et al., The Medicare Access and CHIP Reauthorization Act: Effects on Medicare Payment Policy and Spending, 36 Health Aff. 697 (2016); Jonathan Oberlander & Miriam J. Laugesen, Leap of Faith—Medicare's New Physician Payment System, 373 New Eng. J. Med. 1185 (2015).

For an especially thorough analysis of **paying for episodes of care** (note 3), see William M. Sage, Assembled Products: The Key to More Effective Competition and Antitrust Oversight in Health Care, 101 Cornell L. Rev. 609 (2016). See also Michael E. Porter & Elizabeth Olmsted Teisberg, Redefining Health Care: Creating Value-Based Competition on Results (2006); Karen Davis, Paying for Care Episodes and Care Coordination, 356 New Eng. J. Med. 1166 (2007); Francois de Brantes et al., Building a Bridge from Fragmentation to Accountability: The Prometheus Payment Model, 361 New Eng. J. Med. 1033 (2009); Francois de Brantes et al., Should Health Care Come with a Warranty?, 28(4) Health Aff. w674 (July-Aug. 2009);

Symposium, 28(2) Health Aff. w205 (Jan. 2009); Symposium, 28(5) Health Aff. 1372 (Oct. 2009); Symposium, 29 Health Aff. 1284 (2010); Symposium, 30 Health Aff. 378 (2012).

F. NATIONAL HEALTH INSURANCE

THE HEALING OF AMERICA
T. R. Reid (2009)

. . . [F]or all the local variations, [foreign] health care systems tend to follow [four] general patterns . . . :

THE BISMARCK MODEL

This . . . is named for the Prussian chancellor Otto von Bismarck, who invented the welfare state as part of the unification of Germany in the nineteenth century. Despite its European heritage, the model would look familiar to Americans. In Bismarck countries, both health care providers and payers are private entities. The model uses private health insurance plans, usually financed jointly by employers and employees through payroll deduction. Unlike the U.S. health insurance industry, though, Bismarck-type plans are basically charities: They cover everybody, and they don't make a profit. . . . [T]ight regulation of medical services and fees gives the system much of the cost-control clout that the single-payer Beveridge Model (see below) provides.

THE BEVERIDGE MODEL

This arrangement is named after William Beveridge, a daring social reformer . . . who inspired Britain's National Health Service. In this system, . . . [t]here are no medical bills; rather, medical treatment is a public service, like the fire department or the public library. In Beveridge systems, many (sometimes all) hospitals and clinics are owned by the government [and] some doctors are government employees. . . . These systems tend to have low costs per capita, because the government, as the sole payer, controls what doctors can do and what they can charge. . . .

The Beveridge Model, with government holding almost all the cards, is probably what Americans have in mind when they talk about "socialized medicine." . . . [T]he two purest examples . . . are both found in the Western Hemisphere: Cuba and the U.S. Department of Veterans Affairs. In both of those systems, all the health care professionals work for the government in government-owned facilities, and patients receive no bills.

THE NATIONAL HEALTH INSURANCE MODEL

This system has elements of both Bismarck and Beveridge: The providers of health care are private, but the payer is a government-run insurance program that every citizen pays into. The national, or provincial, insurance plan collects monthly premiums and pays medical bills. . . . As a single payer covering everybody, the national insurance plan tends to have considerable market power to negotiate for lower prices. NHI countries also control costs by limiting the medical services they will pay for or by making patients wait to be treated. The paradigmatic NHI system is Canada's. . . .

The Out-of-Pocket Model

. . . Most of the nations on the planet are too poor and too disorganized to provide any kind of mass medical care. The basic rule in such countries is simple, and brutal: The rich get medical care; the poor stay sick or die. . . .

These four models should be fairly easy for Americans to understand, because we have elements of all of them in our convoluted national health care apparatus. . . . And yet we're like no other country because the United States maintains so many separate systems for separate classes of people. . . .

■ CHAOULLI v. QUEBEC

[2005] 1 S.C.R. 791, 130 C.R.R. (2d) 99, Supreme Court of Canada

Deschamps, J.

Quebeckers are prohibited from taking out insurance to obtain in the private sector services that are available under Quebec's public health care plan. Is this prohibition justified by the need to preserve the integrity of the plan?

As we enter the 21st century, health care is a constant concern. The public health care system, once a source of national pride, has become the subject of frequent and sometimes bitter criticism. This appeal does not question the appropriateness of the state making health care available to all Quebeckers. On the contrary, . . . [o]nly the state can make available to all Quebeckers the social safety net consisting of universal and accessible health care.

The demand for health care is constantly increasing, and one of the tools used by governments to control this increase has been the management of waiting lists. . . . The appellants do not claim to have a solution that will eliminate waiting lists. Rather, they submit that the delays resulting from waiting lists violate their rights under the Charter of Human Rights and Freedoms ("Quebec Charter"), and the Canadian Charter of Rights and Freedoms ("Canadian Charter"). They contest the validity of the prohibition . . . on private insurance for health care services that are available in the public system. . . . In essence, the question is whether Quebeckers who are prepared to spend money to get access to health care that is, in practice, not accessible in the public sector because of waiting lists may be validly prevented from doing so by the state. For the reasons that follow, I find that the prohibition infringes the right to personal inviolability and that it is not justified by a proper regard for democratic values, public order and the general well being of the citizens of Quebec.

The validity of the prohibition is contested by the appellants, George Zeliotis and Jacques Chaoulli [pronounced "shayOOyee"]. Over the years, Mr. Zeliotis has experienced a number of health problems and has used medical services that were available in the public system, including heart surgery and a number of operations on his hip. The difficulties he encountered prompted him to speak out against waiting times in the public health care system. Mr. Chaoulli is a physician who has tried unsuccessfully to have his home delivered medical activities recognized and to obtain a licence to operate an independent private hospital. . . .

The Superior Court dismissed the motion for a declaratory judgment. . . . Piché J. was of the opinion that the purpose of the [the prohibition of private insurance contained in §11 of] the Hospital Insurance Act (s. 11 HOIA) and [§15 of] the Health Insurance Act (s. 15 HEIA) is to establish a public health system that is available to all residents of Quebec. . . . In her opinion, the enactment of these provisions was motivated by considerations of equality and human dignity. She found no conflict with the general values expressed in the Canadian Charter or in the Quebec Charter. She did find that waiting lists are long and the health care system must be improved and transformed. In her opinion, however, the expert testimony could not serve to establish with certainty that a parallel health care system would solve all the current problems of waiting times and access. . . .

In the instant case, s.7 of the Canadian Charter and s.1 of the Quebec Charter have numerous points in common:

Canadian Charter

7. Everyone has the right to life, liberty and security of the person and the right not to be deprived thereof except in accordance with the principles of fundamental justice.

Quebec Charter

1. Every human being has a right to life, and to personal security, inviolability and freedom. . . .

The appellant Zeliotis argues that the prohibition infringes Quebeckers' right to life. Some patients die as a result of long waits for treatment in the public system when they could have gained prompt access to care in the private sector. Were it not for s.11 HOIA and s.15 HEIA, they could buy private insurance and receive care in the private sector.

The Superior Court judge stated [TRANSLATION] "that there [are] serious problems in certain sectors of the health care system" (at p. 823). The evidence supports that assertion. . . . Not only is it common knowledge that health care in Quebec is subject to waiting times, but a number of witnesses acknowledged that the demand for health care is potentially unlimited and that waiting lists are a more or less implicit form of rationing. Waiting lists are therefore real and intentional. The witnesses also commented on the consequences of waiting times. Dr. Daniel Doyle, a cardiovascular surgeon, testified that when a person is diagnosed with cardiovascular disease, he or she is [TRANSLATION] "always sitting on a bomb" and can die at any moment. In such cases, it is inevitable that some patients will die if they have to wait for an operation. . . .

In the opinion of my colleagues Binnie and LeBel JJ., there is an internal mechanism that safeguards the public health system. According to them, Quebeckers may go outside the province for treatment where services are not available in Quebec. This possibility is clearly not a solution for the system's deficiencies. The evidence did not bring to light any administrative mechanism that would permit Quebeckers suffering as a result of waiting times to obtain care outside the province.

The possibility of obtaining care outside Quebec is case specific and is limited to crisis situations. . . .

[Justice Deschamps concluded that the prohibition of private insurance, coupled with long waiting times, constitutes a prima facie deprivation of the rights protected by §1 of the Quebec Charter.]

Justification for the Prohibition

Section 9.1 of the Quebec Charter sets out the standard for justification. It reads as follows: "In exercising his fundamental freedoms and rights, a person shall maintain a proper regard for democratic values, public order and the general well being of the citizens of Québec." In this respect, the scope of the freedoms and rights, and limits to their exercise, may be fixed by law. . . . First, the court must determine whether the objective of the legislation is pressing and substantial. Next, it must determine whether the means chosen to attain this legislative end are reasonable and demonstrably justifiable in a free and democratic society. For this second part of the analysis, three tests must be met: (1) the existence of a rational connection between the measure and the aim of the legislation; (2) minimal impairment of the protected right by the measure; and (3) proportionality between the effect of the measure and its objective. . . .

Even if it were assumed that the prohibition on private insurance could contribute to preserving the integrity of the system, . . . prohibiting insurance contracts is by no means the only measure a state can adopt to protect the system's integrity. . . . The regimes of the provinces where a private system is authorized demonstrate that public health services are not threatened by private insurance. It can therefore be concluded that the prohibition is not necessary to guarantee the integrity of the public plan. . . .

In a number of European countries, there is no insurance paid for directly out of public funds. In Austria, services are funded through decentralized agencies that collect the necessary funds from salaries. People who want to obtain health care in the private sector in addition to the services covered by the mandatory social insurance are free to do so, but private insurance may cover no more than 80 percent of the cost billed by professionals practising in the public sector. The same type of plan exists in Germany and the Netherlands, but people who opt for private insurance are not required to pay for the public plan. Only nine percent of Germans opt for private insurance. . . . C. H. Tuohy, C. M. Flood and M. Stabile, "How Does Private Finance Affect Public Health Care Systems? Marshaling the Evidence from OECD Nations" (2004), 29 J. Health Pol. 359. . . .

The United Kingdom does not restrict access to private insurance for health care. Nor does the United Kingdom limit a physician's ability to withdraw from the public plan. However, physicians working full-time in public hospitals are limited in the amounts that they may bill in the private sector to supplement income earned in the public sector. Only 11.5 percent of Britons had taken out private insurance in 1998, and only eight percent of hospital beds in the United Kingdom are private. New Zealand has a plan similar to that of the United Kingdom with the difference that 40 percent of New Zealanders have private insurance. . . .

As can be seen from the evolution of public plans in the few [European] countries that have been examined in studies produced in the record, there are a wide range of measures that are less drastic, and also less intrusive in relation to the protected rights. . . . A measure as drastic as prohibiting private insurance contracts appears to be neither essential nor determinative. . . .

Governments have promised on numerous occasions to find a solution to the problem of waiting lists. Given the tendency to focus the debate on a sociopolitical philosophy, it seems that governments have lost sight of the urgency of taking concrete action. The courts are therefore the last line of defence for citizens. . . .

[Justice Deschamps concluded that the violation of the provincial Quebec Charter was not justified. Therefore, she declined to consider whether the prohibition also violates the national Canadian Charter. The concurring opinion, however, which follows, did address the Canadian Charter.]

McLachlin, the Chief Justice, and Major, J. (concurring)

We concur in the conclusion of our colleague Deschamps J. that the prohibition against contracting for private health insurance violates s. 1 of the Quebec Charter of Human Rights and Freedoms. . . . [We go further and find] that the anti-insurance provision also violates s. 7 of the Canadian Charter of Rights and Freedoms ("Charter"). . . .

The [Canadian Charter] does not confer a freestanding constitutional right to health care. However, where the government puts in place a scheme to provide health care, that scheme must comply with the Charter. . . . The Canada Health Act, the Health Insurance Act, and the Hospital Insurance Act do not expressly prohibit private health services. However, they limit access to private health services by removing the ability to contract for private health care insurance to cover the same services covered by public insurance. The result is a virtual monopoly for the public health scheme. The state has effectively limited access to private health care except for the very rich, who can afford private care without need of insurance. This virtual monopoly, on the evidence, results in delays in treatment that adversely affect the citizen's security of the person. Where a law adversely affects life, liberty or security of the person, it must conform to the principles of fundamental justice. This law, in our view, fails to do so. . . .

The government defends the prohibition on medical insurance on the ground that the existing system is the only approach to adequate universal health care for all Canadians. The question in this case, however, is not whether single-tier health care is preferable to two-tier health care. . . . The mere fact that this [case] may have policy ramifications does not permit us to avoid [deciding] it. . . .

Given the ban on insurance, most Quebeckers have no choice but to accept delays in the medical system and their adverse physical and psychological consequences. Delays in the public system are widespread and have serious, sometimes grave, consequences. There was no dispute that there is a waiting list for cardiovascular surgery for life-threatening problems. . . . Inevitably, where patients have life-threatening conditions, some will die because of undue delay in awaiting surgery. The same applies to other health problems. . . . Dr. Eric Lenczner, an orthopaedic surgeon, testified that the one-year delay commonly incurred by patients requiring ligament reconstruction surgery increases the risk that their injuries will become irreparable. Dr. Lenczner also testified that 95 per cent of patients in Canada wait well over a year, and many two years, for knee replacements. . . . Even though death may not be an issue for them, these patients "are in pain," "would not go a day without discomfort" and are "limited in their ability to get around," some being confined to wheelchairs or house bound. . . .

In addition to threatening the life and the physical security of the person, waiting for critical care may have significant adverse psychological effects. . . . Studies confirm that patients with serious illnesses often experience significant anxiety and depression while on waiting lists. . . . This adverse psychological impact can have a serious and profound effect on a person's psychological integrity, and is a violation of security of the person. . . .

The principle of fundamental justice implicated in this case is that laws that affect the life, liberty or security of the person shall not be arbitrary . . . in the sense of bearing no real relation to the [government's] goal and hence being manifestly unfair. The more serious the impingement on the person's liberty and security, the more clear must be the connection. Where the individual's very life may be at stake, the reasonable person would expect a clear connection, in theory and in fact, between the measure that puts life at risk and the legislative goals. . . .

The government argues that the interference with security of the person caused by denying people the right to purchase private health insurance is necessary to providing effective health care under the public health system. It argues that if people can purchase private health insurance, they will seek treatment from private doctors and hospitals, which are not banned under the Act. According to the government's argument, this will divert resources from the public health system into private health facilities, ultimately reducing the quality of public care. . . .

This brings us to the evidence called by the appellants at trial on the experience of other developed countries with public health care systems which permit access to private health care. The experience of these countries suggests that there is no real connection in fact between prohibition of health insurance and the goal of a quality public health system. . . . [M]any western democracies that do not impose a monopoly on the delivery of health care have successfully delivered to their citizens medical services that are superior to and more affordable than the services that are presently available in Canada. . . .

In Sweden, the availability of private health care insurance appears not to have harmed the public health care system. In Germany, public health care insurance is administered by 453 Sickness Funds—private non-profit organizations structured on a regional task or occupational basis. Sickness Fund membership is compulsory for employees with gross incomes lower than approximately [$50,000], and voluntary for those with gross incomes above that level. . . . In Germany, as in Sweden, private health insurance is available to individuals at a certain income level who may voluntarily opt out of the Sickness Funds. . . . Despite the availability of alternatives, 88 per cent of the German population are covered by the public Sickness Funds. . . .

It is compelling to note that not one of the countries referred to relies exclusively on either private insurance or the public system to provide health care coverage to its citizens. Even in the United States, where the private sector is a dominant participant in the field of health care insurance, public funding accounts for 45% of total health care spending. . . .

The government undeniably has an interest in protecting the public health regime. However, given the absence of evidence that the prohibition on the purchase and sale of private health insurance protects the health care system, the rational connection between the prohibition and the objective is not made out. . . .

In sum, the prohibition on obtaining private health insurance, while it might be constitutional in circumstances where health care services are reasonable as to both quality and timeliness, is not constitutional where the public system fails to deliver reasonable services. Life, liberty and security of the person must prevail. . . .

BINNIE and LEBEL, J.J. (Dissenting)

. . . The Quebec government views the prohibition against private insurance as essential to preventing the current single-tier health system from disintegrating into a de facto two-tier system. The trial judge found, and the evidence demonstrated, that there is good reason for this fear. . . . It would be open to Quebec to adopt a U.S.-style health care system. No one suggests that there is anything in our Constitution to prevent it. But to do so would be contrary to the policy of the Quebec National Assembly, and its policy in that respect is shared by the other provinces and the federal Parliament. As stated, Quebec further takes the view that significant growth in the private health care system (which the appellants advocate) would inevitably damage the public system. Our colleagues the Chief Justice and Major J. disagree with this assessment, but governments are entitled to act on a reasonable apprehension of risk of such damage. . . . We now propose to review briefly some of the evidence supporting the findings of the trial judge. . . .

(II) THE IMPACT OF A PARALLEL PRIVATE REGIME ON GOVERNMENT SUPPORT FOR A PUBLIC SYSTEM

The experience in [European] countries shows that an increase in private funding typically leads to a decrease in government funding. At trial, Dr. Bergman explained that a service designed purely for members of society with less socio-economic power would probably lead to a decline in quality of services, a loss of political support and a decline in the quality of management. . . .

(III) PRIVATE INSURERS MAY "SKIM THE CREAM" AND LEAVE THE DIFFICULT AND COSTLY CARE TO THE PUBLIC SECTOR

The evidence suggests that parallel private insurers prefer to siphon off high income patients while shying away from patient populations that constitute a higher financial risk, a phenomenon known as "cream skimming." The public system would therefore carry a disproportionate burden of patients who are considered "bad risks" by the private market by reason of age, socio-economic conditions, or geographic location. . . .

(IV) THE U.S. TWO-TIER SYSTEM OF HEALTH COVERAGE

Reference has already been made to the U.S. health care system, which is the most expensive in the world, even though by some measures Americans are less healthy than Canadians. The existence of a private system has not eliminated waiting times. The availability, extent and timeliness of health care is rationed by private insurers, who may determine according to cost, not need, what is "medically necessary" health care and where and when it is to occur. Whether or not the private system in the U.S. is better managed is a matter of debate amongst policy analysts.

The point here is simply that the appellants' faith in the curative power of private insurance is not borne out by the evidence put before the Court. . . .

[One additional justice concurred in each of the two secondary opinions, producing a vote of 1+3 vs. 3. Because of the difference among the majority justices over whether only the Quebec Charter was violated, or also the Canadian Charter, only the authoring Justice Deschamps signed the "majority" opinion. Therefore, this case controls only in Quebec. Another unusual aspect is that two of the Court's nine justices did not participate because they were appointed after the case had been argued.]

■ STATEMENT INTRODUCING THE U.S. NATIONAL HEALTH INSURANCE ACT

Marcia Angell, M.D.*

Feb. 4, 2003

Americans have the most expensive health care system in the world. We spend about twice as much per person as other developed nations, and that gap is growing. That's not because we are sicker or more demanding (Canadians, for example, see their doctors more often and spend more time in the hospital). And it's not because we get better results. By the usual measures of health (life expectancy, infant mortality, immunization rates), we do worse than most other developed countries. Furthermore, we are the only developed nation that does not provide comprehensive health care to all its citizens. . . .

The underlying problem is that we treat health care like a market commodity instead of a social service. Health care is targeted not to medical need, but to the ability to pay. Markets are good for many things, but they are not a good way to distribute health care. . . . It's instructive to follow the health care dollar as it wends its way from employers toward the doctors and nurses and hospitals that actually provide medical services.

First, private insurers regularly skim off the top a substantial fraction of the premiums—anywhere from 10 to 25 percent—for their administrative costs, marketing, and profits. The remainder is then passed along a veritable gauntlet of satellite businesses that feed on the health care industry, including brokers to cut deals, disease-management and utilization review companies, drug-management companies, legal services, marketing consultants, billing agencies, information management firms, and so on and so on. Their function is often to limit services in one way or another. They, too, take a cut, including enough for their own administrative costs, marketing, and profits. I would estimate that no more than 50 cents of the health care dollar actually reaches the providers—who themselves face high overhead costs in dealing with multiple insurers. . . .

The program [that Physicians for a National Health Program] are introducing today is the very soul of simplicity and efficiency, compared with our private health care system. It is a single-payer system, that is, health care funds would be

* Former Editor-in-Chief, *New England Journal of Medicine.*

distributed by a single, public entity, so that health care could be coordinated to eliminate both gaps and overlap. In many ways, our program would be tantamount to extending Medicare to the entire population. Medicare is, after all, a government-financed single-payer system embedded within our private, market-based system. It's by far the most efficient part of our health-care system, with overhead costs of less than 3 percent, and it covers virtually everyone over the age of 65, not just some of them. Medicare is not perfect, but it is by far the most popular part of the U. S. health care system. . . .

What are the usual objections to the sort of national program we are calling for today? They are mostly based on a number of myths. Myth #1 is that we can't afford a national health care system, and if we try it, we will have to ration care. My answer is that . . . [a] single-payer system would be far more efficient, since it would eliminate excess administrative costs, profits, cost-shifting and unnecessary duplication. . . .

According to Myth #2, innovative technologies would be scarce under a single-payer system, we would have long waiting lists for operations and procedures, and in general, medical care would be threadbare and less available. This misconception is based on the fact that there are indeed waits for elective procedures in some countries with national health systems, such as the U. K. and Canada. But that's because they spend far less on health care than we do. (The U. K. spends about a third of what we do per person.) If they were to put the same amount of money as we do into their systems, there would be no waits and all their citizens would have immediate access to all the care they need. For them, the problem is not the system; it's the money. For us, it's not the money; it's the system. . . .

Myth #3 is that a single-payer system amounts to socialized medicine, which would subject doctors and other providers to onerous, bureaucratic regulations. But in fact, although a national program would be publicly funded, providers would not work for the government. That's currently the case with Medicare, which is publicly funded, but privately delivered. As for onerous regulations, nothing could be more onerous both to patients and providers than the multiple, intrusive regulations imposed on them by the private insurance industry. . . .

Myth #4 says that the government can't do anything right. Some Americans like to say that, without thinking of all the ways in which government functions very well indeed, and without considering the alternatives. I would not want to see, for example, the [National Institutes of Health], the National Park Service, or the IRS privatized. We should remember that the government is elected by the public and we are responsible for it. An investor-owned insurance company reports to its owners, not to the public.

Some people say that a single-payer system is a good idea, but politically unrealistic. That is a self-fulfilling prophecy. In my opinion, the medical profession and the public would be enthusiastic about a single-payer system if the facts were known and the myths dispelled. Yes, there would be powerful special interests opposing it and I don't underestimate them, but with courageous leadership . . . and the support of the medical profession and public, I believe there is nothing unrealistic about a National Health Insurance Program.

I want to mention one final and very important reason for enacting a national health program. We live in a country that tolerates enormous disparities in income, material possessions, and social privilege. That may be an inevitable consequence of a free market economy. But those disparities should not extend to denying some of our citizens certain essential services because of their income or social status. One of those services is health care. Others are education, clean water and air, equal justice, and protection from crime, all of which we already acknowledge are public responsibilities. We need to acknowledge the same thing for health care. Providing these essential services to all Americans, regardless of who they are, helps ensure that we remain a cohesive and optimistic country. . . .

■ THE GRASS IS NOT ALWAYS GREENER: A LOOK AT NATIONAL HEALTH CARE SYSTEMS AROUND THE WORLD

Michael Tanner*

2008

Critics of the U.S. health care system frequently point to other countries as models for reform. They point out that many countries spend far less on health care than the United States yet seem to enjoy better health outcomes. . . . In his movie *SiCKO*, Michael Moore . . . compares the U.S. system unfavorably with those of Canada, Great Britain, and France. Economist and New York Times columnist Paul Krugman also thinks the health care systems of France, Britain, and Canada are better than that of the United States. . . .

These critics contend that by adopting a similar [single-payer, national health care] system the United States could solve many of [its] problems. . . . Under such a system, health care would be financed through taxes rather than consumer payments or private insurance. Direct charges to patients would be prohibited or severely restricted. Private insurance, if allowed at all, would be limited to a few supplemental services not covered by the government plan. The government would control costs by setting an overall national health care budget and reimbursement levels.

However, a closer look at countries with national health care systems shows that those countries have serious problems of their own, including rising costs, rationing of care, lack of access to modern medical technology, and poor health outcomes. Countries whose national health systems avoid the worst of these problems are successful precisely because they incorporate market mechanisms and reject centralized government control. . . . Health care reform should be guided by the Hippocratic Oath: First, do no harm. Therefore, before going down the road to national health care, we should look more closely at foreign health care systems and examine both their advantages and their problems. . . .

TYPES OF NATIONAL HEALTH CARE SYSTEMS

National health care, or universal health care, is a broad concept and has been implemented in many different ways. There is no single model that the rest of the world follows. Each country's system is the product of its unique conditions, history, politics, and national character, and many are undergoing significant reform. . . .

* Director of Health and Welfare Studies, Cato Institute.

Some countries, such as France and Japan, impose significant cost sharing on consumers in an effort to discourage overutilization and to control costs. Other countries strictly limit the amount that consumers must pay out of pocket. Some countries permit free choice of providers, while others limit it. In some countries there is widespread purchase of alternative or supplemental private insurance, whereas in others, private insurance is prohibited or used very little. Resource allocation and prioritization vary greatly. Japan spends heavily on technology but limits reimbursement for surgery, while France has exceptionally high levels of prescription drug use. . . .

With all of that in mind, consider the following prominent national health care systems.

FRANCE

Some of the most thoughtful proponents of national health care look to France as a model of how such a program could work. . . . Ezra Klein of the *American Prospect* calls France "the closest thing to a model structure out there." The French system ranks at or near the top of most cross-country comparisons and is ranked number one by the [World Health Organization].

Although the French system is facing looming budgetary pressures, it does provide at least some level of universal coverage and manages to avoid many of the problems that afflict other national health care systems. . . . France provides a basic level of universal health insurance through a series of mandatory, largely occupation-based, health insurance funds. These funds are ostensibly private entities but are heavily regulated and supervised by the French government. Premiums (funded primarily through payroll taxes), benefits, and provider reimbursement rates are all set by the government. In these ways the funds are similar to public utilities in the United States. . . .

Payroll taxes provide the largest source of funding. Employers must pay [13.55] percent of wages for every employee. . . . In addition, there is a 5.25 general social contribution tax on income. . . . Thus, most French workers are effectively paying 18.8 percent of their income for health insurance. Finally, dedicated taxes are assessed on tobacco, alcohol, and pharmaceutical company revenues. . . .

Most services require substantial copayments, ranging from 10 to 40 percent of the cost. As a result, French consumers pay for roughly 13 percent of health care out of pocket, roughly the same percentage as U.S. consumers. Moreover, because many health care services are not covered, and because many of the best providers refuse to accept the fee schedules imposed by the insurance funds, more than 92 percent of French residents purchase complementary private insurance, [which] . . . makes up roughly 12.7 percent of all health care spending in France. . . .

Although reimbursement levels are set by the government, the amount physicians charge is not. The French system permits providers to charge more than the reimbursement schedule, and approximately one-third of French physicians do so. . . . [P]hysicians employed by hospitals, as opposed to those in private practice, do not have the same ability to charge more than the negotiated rate. The government also sets reimbursement rates for both public and private hospitals, which are generally not allowed to bill beyond the negotiated fee schedules. . . .

A 2004 poll showed that the French had the highest level of satisfaction with their health care system among all European countries. This is partly because their hybrid system has avoided many of the biggest problems of other national health care systems. Yet it also stems from French social character. For example, by a three-to-one margin, the French believe the quality of care they receive is less important than everyone having equal access to that care. This means the French experience may not be easily transferable to the United States, which has a far less egalitarian ethic. . . .

GREAT BRITAIN

Almost no one disputes that Britain's National Health Service faces severe problems, and few serious national health care advocates look to it as a model. Yet it appears in Moore's movie *SiCKO* as an example of how a national health care system should work, so it is worth examining.

The NHS is a highly centralized version of a single-payer system. The government pays directly for health care and finances the system through general tax revenues. Except for small copayments for prescription drugs, dental care, and optician services, there are no direct charges to patients. Unlike many other single-payer systems such as those in Canada and Norway, most physicians and nurses are government employees.

For years, British health policy has focused on controlling spending and in general has been quite successful, with the system spending just 7.5 percent of GDP on health care. . . . And that level of services leaves much to be desired. Waiting lists are a major problem. As many as 750,000 Britons are currently awaiting admission to NHS hospitals. These waits are not insubstantial and can impose significant risks on patients. For example, by some estimates, cancer patients can wait as long as eight months for treatment. Delays in receiving treatment are often so long that nearly 20 percent of colon cancer patients considered treatable when first diagnosed are incurable by the time treatment is finally offered. . . .

Explicit rationing also exists for some types of care, notably kidney dialysis, open heart surgery, and some other expensive procedures and technologies. Patients judged too ill or aged for the procedures to be cost-effective may be denied treatment altogether. . . .

A small but growing private health care system has emerged in the UK. About 10 percent of Britons have private health insurance. Some receive it through their employer, while others purchase it individually. In general, the insurance replicates care provided through the [national health system] and is purchased to gain access to a wider choice of providers or to avoid waiting lists. . . .

The British public is well aware of the need for reform. Nearly two-thirds of Britons (63 percent) say that the need for reform is "urgent." . . . Yet Britons are also extremely proud of their health care system and wary of any reforms that would "Americanize" it. . . .

SWITZERLAND

Of all the countries with universal health care, Switzerland has one of the most market-oriented systems. Indeed, the Swiss government actually pays for a smaller amount of total health care expenditures than the U.S. government, 24.9 percent versus 44.7 percent.

The Swiss system is based on the idea of managed competition, the same concept that underlay . . . [t]he 1993 Clinton health plan, . . . Mitt Romney's reforms in Massachusetts, and most of the proposals advocated by the current Democratic presidential candidates. Managed competition leaves the provision of health care and health insurance in private hands but creates a highly regulated artificial marketplace as a framework within which the health care industry operates. . . . Individuals have a choice of insurers within the regulated marketplace and a choice of providers. Although the government sets a standard benefits package, insurers may compete on price, cost sharing, and additional benefits. . . .

Swiss law requires all citizens to purchase a basic package of health insurance, an individual mandate. . . . Insurance is generally purchased on an individual basis. Few employers contribute to the purchase or provide insurance. . . .

Individuals can purchase expensive policies with very low deductibles and copayments, or far less expensive policies with high deductibles or extensive copayments. Thus, premiums vary according to their cost-sharing attributes and plan type. . . . Because employers do not pay for workers' health insurance, the Swiss are exposed to the full cost of their insurance purchases. As a result, many Swiss have opted for high-deductible insurance. Thus, with high deductibles and extensive copayments, the Swiss pay out of pocket for 31.5 percent of health care, twice as much as in the United States. . . .

The Swiss government offers subsidies to low-income citizens to help them purchase a policy. . . . These subsidies are designed to prevent any individual from having to pay more than 10 percent of income on insurance. . . .

Swiss insurers operate as cartels to negotiate provider reimbursements on a [regional] basis. Providers must accept the negotiated payment, and balance-billing is prohibited. If insurers and providers are unable to reach agreement on a fee schedule, canton governments are empowered to step in and impose an agreement. . . . Private hospitals negotiate reimbursement with insurance cartels and physicians in the same manner. Public hospitals are operated by cantons, which negotiate reimbursement rates with insurers and provide subsidies to the hospitals. In some cantons, individuals with only the basic insurance plan must use public hospitals; supplementary insurance is required for admission to private hospitals. . . .

The Swiss do not impose a global budget on their health care system and have therefore avoided the waiting lists common in other systems. In addition, the Swiss have a high degree of access to modern medical technology, but it has come at a cost. The Swiss spend 11.5 percent of GDP on health care, second only to the United States.

Since Swiss health care consumers are exposed to the cost consequences of their health care decisions, this trade-off between access and cost can be presumed to reflect the desires of Swiss patients. They have chosen high quality care even though it costs them more. Given that . . . Switzerland is a wealthy nation, such a decision seems entirely reasonable.

At the same time, it is notable that Swiss health care spending remains below that of the United States for nearly comparable care. Strong evidence suggests that the exposure of Swiss consumers to the cost consequences of their health care decisions has made them more conscious consumers and helped limit overall health care costs. . . .

The Swiss generally seem pleased with their system. Earlier this year, Swiss voters overwhelmingly rejected a proposal to replace the current system with a single-payer plan. . . .

CONCLUSION

. . . [It is] important to realize that no country's system would translate directly to the United States. Americans are unlikely to accept the rationing or restrictions on care and technology that many countries use to control costs. Nor are U.S. physicians likely to accept a cut in income to the levels seen in countries like France or Germany. The politics, economics, and national cultures of other countries often vary significantly from those of the United States. Their citizens are far more likely to have faith in government actions and to be suspicious of free markets. And polling suggests that citizens of many countries put social solidarity and equality ahead of quality and choice when it comes to health policy. American attitudes are quite different. . . . Even so, some important lessons can be drawn from the experiences of other countries: . . .

Those countries that have single-payer systems or systems heavily weighted toward government control are the most likely to face waiting lists, rationing, restrictions on the choice of physician, and other barriers to care. Those countries with national health care systems that work better, such as France, the Netherlands, and Switzerland, are successful to the degree that they incorporate market mechanisms such as competition, cost-consciousness, market prices, and consumer choice, and eschew centralized government control. . . .

Although no country with universal coverage is contemplating abandoning a universal system, the broad and growing trend in countries with national health care systems is to move away from centralized government control and introduce more market-oriented features. . . . Thus, even as Americans debate adopting a government-run system, countries with those systems are debating how to make their systems look more like that of the United States. . . . Therefore, if U.S. policymakers can take one lesson from national health care systems around the world, it is not to follow the road to government-run national health care, but to increase consumer incentives and control. . . .

Notes: Foreign and Single-Payer Health Care Systems

1. Chaoulli. How consistent is the *Chaoulli* decision with U.S. constitutional law? In Canada, this decision generated a great deal of criticism and controversy, much of which is addressed in the excellent anthology, Colleen M. Flood et al. eds., Access to Care, Access to Justice: The Legal Debate over Private Health Insurance in Canada (2005).

Somewhat surprisingly, the Canadian Supreme Court's decision has not led to the wholesale repeal of the private insurance prohibition in Quebec, much less in other provinces. Instead, these governments have worked to shorten waiting lists and to provide targeted funding for those who are forced to seek private care outside the system for critical surgeries when waits become too long. Quebec also now allows the sale of insurance covering only select surgeries.

2. *Is Health Care Special?* Consider these thoughts on the role of government generally in health care financing and delivery:

> We must apply some modest degree of scrutiny to the proposition that health care is special: surely it is important, but so is food, clothing, shelter, education, entertainment, and all the other goods and services that are necessary to sustain life and to make the life sustained worth living. Importance, however, is not an argument for

> government subsidy or support, for if it were then socialism would apply to things where it matters most, and lead to the most ruinous of consequences. Instead the importance, so to speak, of importance is simple: It is important to get the right set of solutions, be it private or public, to the problem at hand. Importance does not create a presumption in favor of government, or for that matter against it. It only raises the stakes for making a correct decision in the matter at hand.

Richard A. Epstein, Why Is Health Care Special?, 40 U. Kan. L. Rev. 307 (1992).

3. *The AMA's Opposition.* Although the AMA endorsed the ACA, it has steadfastly opposed national health insurance throughout the past century. As Dr. Marcia Angell demonstrates, however, other medical groups support single-payer reforms. Why doesn't the AMA see it in its interest for the government to provide universal insurance so that everyone can pay for medical services? If you were a doctor, would you prefer the restrictions as well as the protections of a government-run system over the ravages of the unregulated managed care marketplace? Realize that the unregulated market was much more attractive in the 1950s when organized medicine controlled health insurance through Blue Cross, when there was little antitrust scrutiny of physician collusion, and when the corporate practice of medicine doctrine more actively preserved physicians' independence from medical institutions—topics that are discussed in Chapter 4.

4. *Socialized Medicine.* Critics of government involvement in health care frequently lump all forms of involvement together as "socialized medicine." It is important, however, to distinguish whether government is merely paying for health care, or also directly delivering health care. Canada (like Medicare) does only the first, which is more accurately labeled "socialized *insurance.*" As T. R. Reid notes, the U.S. analogue for true British-style socialized medicine is the Veterans Administration (VA) health care system, which covers veterans' service-related health problems. Rather than this giving the idea a bad name, many observers point to the VA as a model for efficient delivery of high-quality care:

> [The VA] runs its own hospitals and clinics, and provides some of the best-quality health care in America at far lower cost than the private sector. How does the VA do it? It turns out that there are many advantages to having a single health care organization provide individuals with what amounts to lifetime care. For example, the VA has taken the lead in introducing electronic medical records, which it can do far more easily than a private hospital chain because its patients stay with it for decades. The VA also invests heavily and systematically in preventive care, because unlike private health care providers it can expect to realize financial benefits from measures that keep its clients out of the hospital.

Paul Krugman & Robin Wells, The Health Care Crisis and What to Do About It, New York Review of Books, March 23, 2006.

Is there any reason state or federal governments couldn't do a decent job delivering care directly to people who can't afford insurance? What if government health care were as good (or bad) as student health services? Would that be "good enough for government work"?

5. *Single-payer?* During the primary campaign of 2016, Senator Bernie Sanders's proposal for a single-payer program—what he termed "Medicare for All"—generated considerable enthusiasm on the political left. Sanders's proposal called for replacing the complexities of the current system with a single, government-run program

that would cover the entire range of medically necessary care for the entire population. Pointing to international experience, where state-run coverage of this sort is common, many members of the public and some influential voices in the medical community argue that single-payer would reduce administrative costs, enable government to bargain effectively for low prices, and improve coverage for the uninsured and the underinsured.

Despite this enthusiasm, most experts—even those sympathetic to single-payer—believe that it is unrealistic to hope for its adoption. The price tag for a single-payer scheme far exceeds that of the ACA and there is little appetite in Congress to support the tax increases that would be necessary to finance a vast expansion of public coverage. See John Holahan et al., Urban Institute, The Sanders Single-Payer Health Care Plan: The Effect on National Health Expenditures and Federal and Private Spending (2016). Any such proposal would also face fierce opposition from existing health insurers (which could be put out of business), the health care industry, and much of organized medicine.

6. *The Public Option.* Given the bleak political outlook for Medicare for All, some have suggested a slower, long-term effort to move toward a single-payer scheme, perhaps by incorporating a "public option" into the ACA. Glenn Hackbarth, Today's Medicare Is Built on 50 Years of Robust Compromise. Now What? Health Affairs Blog (March 8, 2016). Under the public option, the government would operate a health plan that it would then sell on the exchanges. If consumers preferred the public plan to private plans, the public option could come to dominate the market, displacing private insurance and perhaps paving the road to single-payer.

A public option appeared likely early in the congressional deliberations over the ACA, but it was dropped as part of a political compromise. Hillary Clinton resurrected the idea in her 2016 presidential run. The idea is straightforward: The government (either state or federal) would run a plan that would pay rates based on Medicare's payment schedules. The hope is that the public option would have enough bargaining leverage to entice providers to participate, even if the public option paid less than private insurers. Low payment rates would mean low premiums for the public option, and competition between the public option and private insurers would restrain prices in the private market.

Opposition to the public option is intense. Critics question whether private insurers stand a chance of competing with the government on an even footing and believe that the public option's supporters wish to use it as a Trojan horse to achieve single-payer reform. Supporters point to Medicare Advantage as proof that a public option and private insurance can coexist. They also argue that the public option may be critical in those states with limited competition among private insurers.

7. *Crowd-Out and Sliding Scales.* A major difficulty of offering a government program alongside privately purchased insurance, in order to cover people who are uninsured, is that, if the government system is halfway decent, many people who otherwise might or do purchase insurance would simply drop it in favor of the free (or greatly discounted) government program. This drop-out problem—which is also known as "crowd-out," meaning the public provision crowds out private provision—has happened at least to some extent, for instance, when states expanded Medicaid to cover children above poverty. Then, some parents with family policies through work switched to less expensive single coverage, or employers stopped offering to pay as much for family members.

Do crowd-out problems necessarily mean that a comprehensive insurance system must be either all private or all public? In theory, it is possible to construct sliding-scale eligibility and subsidy rules that reduce incentives to switch from one to the other, but doing that is substantially more complicated. This smoothing of the boundaries also confronts the basic problem encountered by any sliding scale subsidy: The more that basic needs are subsidized, the more that people stand to lose when they earn more income. Thus, income-based subsidies function like a tax, in reverse: It costs to earn more, which means there is less incentive to work. This work disincentive also exists in any kind of income tax, so it isn't necessarily crippling, but adding expensive social programs on top of income tax rates compounds the disincentive. Thus, if the scale slides too steeply, for a benefit as expensive as health insurance, people in some lower-income brackets might stand to lose almost all of any increased income, when tax effects are combined with social support. The only way to avoid this incentive at the margin is to make the social support scale up or down more gradually, but that means extending it to much greater portions of the population.

8. *Beware of What You Wish For.* Do you think national health insurance is politically feasible in the United States—at least in your lifetime? What social, economic, and political conditions might give rise to this sort of comprehensive reform? Consider these thoughts from two eminent health policy scholars:

> Any comprehensive change in the health care system is likely to result in winners and losers. Prospective losers are likely to be much more involved and effective in blocking change than prospective winners will be in promoting it. As Machiavelli, one of the shrewdest political analysts of all time, noted, "There is nothing more difficult to carry out, nor more the reformer has enemies in all those who profit by the old order, and only lukewarm defenders in all those who would profit by the new order." . . . What might set the stage for comprehensive reform of health care? A major war, a depression, or large-scale civil unrest might well set in motion a change in the political climate that would overpower the obstacles that prevail in normal times. A national health crisis, such as a flu pandemic, might also light the fuse of change.

Victor R. Fuchs & Ezekiel J. Emanuel, Health Care Reform: Why? What? When?, 24(6) Health Aff. 1399 (Nov. 2005).

9. *Managed Competition.* Rather than adopting a cohesive single-payer system, the United States is more likely to continue developing a "managed competition" or "voucher" approach to purchasing coverage. The health insurance exchanges created by the ACA, for instance, are a leading example of this approach, which, as Michael Tanner describes, is also used in Switzerland. As Tanner notes, the idea is widely adaptable. Republicans advocate using a managed competition voucher approach to privatizing both Medicare and Medicaid, and Medicare currently uses this approach for Part D drug coverage.

One major difficulty that exists in any managed competition framework is making surc that market forces focus on efficient delivery of quality care rather than on selecting the healthiest people and avoiding the sickest. For that to happen, competing insurers must be paid proportionately to each subscriber's actuarial risk. Otherwise, insurers will find ways to engage in covert or overt risk selection—for instance, by tailoring their marketing or plan designs and operations to attract healthier subscribers or discourage sicker ones. Unless older and sicker people are required to pay more, the only obvious way to fix this problem is to "risk adjust" the subsidized "voucher" amounts to accurately reflect each subscriber's health risk.

10. *Further Readings.* For additional readings on **foreign health care systems generally**, see Sarah Thomson et al., International Profiles of Health Care Systems (2012); David A. Rochefort & Kevin P. Donnelly, Foreign Remedies: What the Experience of Other Nations Can Tell Us About Next Steps in Reforming U.S. Health Care (2012); David Squires, The U.S. Health System in Perspective: A Comparison of Twelve Industrialized Nations (Commonwealth Fund, 2011); Daniel Callahan & Angela Wasunna, Medicine and the Market: Equity v. Choice (2006) (focusing on developing countries); Nathan Cortez, International Health Care Convergence, 26 Wis. Int'l L.J. 646 (2008); Timothy Jost, Private or Public Approaches to Insuring the Uninsured: Lessons from International Experience with Private Insurance, 76 N.Y.U. L. Rev. 419 (2001); Symposium, 30 J. Health Pol. Pol'y & L. 1 (2005); Symposium, 23(3) Health Aff. 7 (June 2004); Symposium, 28 J. Health Pol. Pol'y & L. 575 (2003). For the developments in the British NHS, see Henry J. Aaron & William B. Schwartz, Can We Say No? The Challenge of Rationing Health Care (2005); Rudolf Klein, Britain's National Health Service Revisited, 350 New Eng. J. Med. 937 (2004). On **Canada**, see Colleen Flood ed., Just Medicare (2006); Allan S. Detsky & C. David Naylor, Canada's Health Care System: Reform Delayed, 349 New Eng. J. Med. 804 (2003).

For analysis of the **implications of the *Chaoulli* case for U.S. constitutional law and public policy** (note 1), see Roy G. Spece Jr., A Fundamental Constitutional Right of the Monied to "Buy Out Of" Universal Health Care Program Restrictions Versus the Moral Claim of Everyone Else to Decent Health Care, 3 J. Health & Biomed. L. 1 (2007); Mary Anne Bobinski, The Health Insurance Debate in Canada: Lessons for the United States?, 14 Conn. Ins. L.J. 341 (2008).

For further criticism of a **government takeover of the health care finance and delivery** (note 2), see John C. Goodman et al., Lives at Risk: Single-Payer National Health Insurance Around the World (2004).

For discussions of **the AMA's resistance to government regulation** (note 2), see George Lundberg, Severed Trust: Why American Medicine Hasn't Been Fixed (2000); Robert Berenson, Do Physicians Recognize Their Own Best Interests?, 13(2) Health Aff. 185 (Apr. 1994) (critiquing as inconsistent and shortsighted the AMA's historical antipathy to government regulation).

For readings on the **socialized medicine and the Veterans Health Administration** (note 4), see Phillip Longman, The Best Care Anywhere (2d ed. 2010); Adam Oliver, The Veterans Health Administration: An American Success Story?, 85 Milbank Q. 1 (2007). For an argument to expand access to government clinics and hospitals, see Donald W. Moran, Whence and Whither Health Insurance? A Revisionist History, 24(6) Health Aff. 1415 (Dec. 2005); Mark A. Hall, Approaching Universal Coverage with Better Safety Net Programs for the Uninsured, 11 Yale J. Health Pol'y L. & Ethics (2011).

For arguments **in favor of single-payer** (note 5), see Dominic F. Caruso, David U. Himmelstein & Steffie Woolhandler, Single-Payer Health Reform: A Step Toward Reducing Structural Racism in Health Care, Harvard Public Health Review (July 2015); Adam Gaffney et al., Moving Forward from the Affordable Care Act to a Single-Payer System, 106 Am. J. Public Health 987 (2016).

For articles **questioning the political viability of single-payer** (note 5), see Jonathan Oberlander, The Virtues and Vices of Single-Payer Health Care, 374 New

Eng. J. Med. 1401 (2016); Harold Pollack, Medicare for All—If It Were Politically Possible—Would Necessarily Replicate the Defects of Our Current System, 40 J. Health Politics, Policy and Law 921, 924 (August 2015).

For debate over **the public option** (note 6), see John Z. Ayanian & Richard Hirth, Going Public: Could Clinton's Health Care Proposals Work? The Conversation (2016); Jacob Hacker, There's a Simple Fix for Obamacare's Current Woes: The Public Option, Vox.com (2016); Susan Jaffe, A Public Health Insurance Plan, Health Policy Brief, Nov. 10, 2009; Victor R. Fuchs, The Proposed Government Health Insurance Company, 360 New Eng. J. Med. 2273 (2009); Michael F. Cannon, Fannie Med? Why a "Public Option" Is Hazardous to Your Health (2009); John Holahan & Linda J. Blumberg, Is the Public Plan Option a Necessary Part of Health Reform? (2009).

For more on **crowd-out** (note 7), see Jonathan Gruber & Kosali Simon, Crowd-Out Ten Years Later: Have Recent Public Insurance Expansions Crowded Out Private Health Insurance?, 27 J. Health Econ. 201 (2008); John V. Jacobi, Medicaid Expansion, Crowd-Out, and Limits of Incremental Reform, 45 St. Louis U. L.J. 79 (2001).

The original work of the Stanford economist who first articulated the idea of **managed competition** (note 9) can be found at Alain Enthoven, Consumer Choice Health Plan: A National Health Insurance Proposal Based on Regulated Competition in the Private Sector, 298 New Eng. J. Med. 650, 709 (1978); Jackson Hole Group, Managed Competition II: A Proposal, 46 Wash. U. J. Urb. & Contemp. L. 33 (1994). See generally Paul Starr, The Logic of Health-Care Reform (1992); Walter Zelman, The Changing Health Care Marketplace (1996); Alain Enthoven, The History and Principles of Managed Competition, 12 (Supp. 1) Health Aff. 24 (Jan. 1993).

Problem: Universal Access to Health Care

Be prepared to either defend or attack each of the following propositions, using analysis and facts from the readings in this chapter.

1. A two-tier health care system—one that tolerates different standards of access and care according to wealth and social position—is morally unjustified because health care is a basic human right of fundamental importance.
2. A system of socialized medicine like that in Canada is distinctly un-American and will lead to massive rationing of services.
3. In order to have a coherent health care financing system, it is essential to sever the link between employment and insurance.
4. The best feasible way to guarantee everyone access to a decent minimum level of health care is to fund a comprehensive network of public hospitals and outpatient clinics as a safety net for those without health insurance.

Exercise: Negotiating Health Care Reform

Assume you represent the interests of one of the following groups: physicians, low-income public, upper- and middle-income public, large insurance companies and HMOs, small employers, or large employers. Now, develop your legislative lobbying position with respect to each of the following reform ideas:

1. A British-type system
2. A Canadian-type system
3. An entirely privatized system that gives each person a voucher, funded by the government, sufficient to pay for 60 to 100 percent (depending on income) of the cost of the lowest-priced insurance policy in the market, and then leaving it entirely to individual choice whether and what to buy.

Meet with representatives from the other interest groups and attempt to negotiate comprehensive health care reform.

G. ECONOMIC AND REGULATORY THEORY

As an interlude between this and the next chapter, this section addresses economic and regulatory theory in more depth, as it applies to health care public policy. In Chapter 1, we learned that American medicine is thought to be in a crisis, both because of the number of people without either public or private health insurance coverage and because of steeply escalating medical costs. This chapter has helped us to understand why this crisis arose and some of the public policy responses; the next chapter considers additional responses to the crisis in spending. These responses are sometimes focused on activating market forces and at other times on regulatory controls; often, reforms contain a mix of these objectives.

It is obvious, then, that a full understanding of these issues requires some appreciation of economic and regulatory theory. Economic theory also helps us to better understand the root of the problems that cost containment measures are designed to correct, so we can better assess how well they are likely to work. Specifically, we must be able to intelligently discuss the extent to which health care delivery should be left to market forces, whether government regulation should displace market mechanisms because of the unique attributes of medicine, or whether government should try to make the market work better. Do not expect to be able to resolve these issues. Instead, as you read these selections, focus your thoughts on the legal and public policy positions you have seen so far and ask yourself which are supported or undermined by each of the points the authors make.

For additional readings on economics versus regulation in health care, see Glenn Cohen, Holly Lynch & Christopher Robertson eds., Nudging Health: Health Law and Behavioral Economics (2016); Michael F. Cannon & Michael D. Tanner, Healthy Competition (2005); David Hyman, Improving Healthcare: A Dose of Competition (2005); Handbook of Health Economics (Anthony Culyer & Joseph P. Newhouse eds., 2000); Joseph White, Markets and Medical Care, 85 Milbank Q. (2007); Robert Field, Government as the Crucible for Free Market Health Care, 159 U. Penn. L. Rev. 1669 (2011); Ronen Avraham & K. A. D. Camara, The Tragedy of the Human Commons, 29 Cardozo L. Rev. 479 (2007); H. E. Frech, Competition and Monopoly in Medical Care (1996); Gregg Bloche, The Invention of Health Law, 91 Cal. L. Rev. 247 (2003); Symposium, Kenneth Arrow and the Changing Economics of Health Care, 26 J. Health Pol. Pol'y & L. 823 (2001); Symposium, 31 J. Health Pol. Pol'y L. 417 (2006); Symposium, 22 J. Health Pol. Pol'y & L. 382 (1997); Symposium, 13 J. Health Pol. Pol'y & L. 223-364 (1988); Symposium, 34 Vand. L. Rev. 849 (1981).

HEALTH PLAN*

Alain Enthoven

1980

The fundamental strategic choice for public policy on health care costs is competition or regulation. . . .

The choice between competition and regulation is a choice about the role of government. In the strategy of competition the government takes a much simpler and less intrusive role than in the regulatory approach. It seeks to set the basic framework of rules and incentives in such a way that the market (that is, the interaction of people making transactions in their own best interests) will produce the desired result. In the regulatory approach applied to health care, the government takes on a much more complex and demanding role, a role in which, in my view, it is bound to fail. In the regulatory approach government would leave today's cost-increasing incentives in place and then try to stop them from having their natural effect by direct detailed controls such as telling doctors how much they can charge for each service. In this approach direct controls are intended to substitute for rational economic incentives. In my view, the regulatory approach is like trying to make water run uphill, whereas in the competitive market approach the government is merely trying to channel the stream in its downhill course.

Procompetitive regulation is likely to be much simpler and more effective than direct controls on prices, capacity, and use of services, which act in opposition to the financial incentives. For in this case the basic incentives are pointing people in about the right direction. The regulators are attempting merely to modify the behavior of the regulated at the margin. . . .

On the other hand, under the regulatory approach, the regulators are attempting to make regulated entities behave in ways that are directly opposed to their financial interests, possibly even threatening their survival. Therefore, the incentive to attempt to bend, fight, or evade the regulations is much stronger. . . .

Regulation often raises costs to consumers. Regulators become responsible for the economic survival of the regulated. If they let a regulated entity fail, they will be blamed for denying society a needed service and for causing a loss of jobs. So they cannot force the regulated to sustain losses or even to live with less than some target rate of return on investment. So cost increases have to be "passed through" to consumers, and price controls become cost reimbursement, with all of its cost-increasing incentives.

Regulators are often "captured" by the regulated. They must get their information about the regulated industry from the regulated. The regulated firms hire high-priced lawyers and lobbyists who exert a constant pressure in their favor. The consumer interest in lower prices or better service is too diffused to allow for an effectively organized counterpressure. The formal procedures of regulation also make it very costly and time-consuming. This is especially true if there are many entities to be regulated, with many special circumstances to be considered, as is the case with physicians and hospitals. . . .

Competition, on the other hand, sets up an inexorable force for cost reduction. If company *B* can make a product of equal quality to company *A*'s, but for less cost, it can sell it for a lower price and take the business away from company *A*. If company *A* cannot match the cost reduction, it will lose profits in the short run and risk being driven out of business in the long run. Survival demands that it cut costs. It has no regulators to appeal to for protection. . . .

Competition rewards innovation and often channels it in socially desirable directions. Fortunes are made on new products and services, so innovations that lead to better services or reduced costs are encouraged. Firms that do not match their competitors' innovations often do not survive.

Market economies are the most effective in improving productivity and raising living standards. There are good reasons for this. People accept efficiency-improving changes such as closing unneeded plants or hospitals produced by impersonal market forces in the private sector. The people directly affected may not like them, but there is not much they can do about them. In the long run the whole economy benefits. But when such changes are imposed by government, those who would be harmed resist them, usually successfully, through legal and political action. . . .

In market systems producers and consumers adapt continuously and gradually to changing conditions, even in anticipation of future events. The expectation of higher gasoline prices in the future motivates people to buy cars with good mileage now. In regulatory systems the rules themselves create vested interests which make the rules very difficult to change. These factors make for great rigidity in regulated industries, in contrast to flexible adaptation in markets.

Government often responds to well-focused producer interests; competitive markets respond systematically, if imperfectly, to consumer interests. Voters base their choices on issues of decisive personal importance, on their pocketbooks if they see their livelihoods at stake. People specialize in production and diversify in consumption. To a dairy farmer, a rise in coffee prices is a minor irritant, but an increase in the price of milk (supported by government) is a "make-or-break" issue. People are therefore much more likely to pressure their representatives about the issues that affect their livelihoods than on their interests as consumers, and their companies and unions provide natural organizations for doing so. In competitive markets companies get their revenues from satisfied customers who have alternative choices. So in product and pricing decisions, business must seek to serve the desires of consumers. Thus the choice between a regulated and a competitive market system of health care services is a choice between service that responds mainly to the interests of providers or to those of consumers.

Regulation depends on coercion, on forcing people to behave in ways they consider opposed to their own best interests. The decentralized competitive market, on the other hand, leaves maximum freedom to individual providers and consumers consistent with achievement of society's purposes. As Charles Schultze put it:

Relationships in the market are a form of unanimous-consent arrangement. When dealing with each other in a buy-sell transaction, individuals can act voluntarily on the basis of mutual advantage. . . . Market-like arrangements not only minimize the need for coercion as a means of organizing society; they also reduce the need for compassion, patriotism, brotherly love, and cultural solidarity as motivating forces behind social improvement.

The development of these desirable virtues is more likely to be encouraged if we do not place too heavy a burden on people who practice them.

Moreover, the market encourages the pluralism and diversity that is valued by the American people. The regulatory approach works on the basis of uniform numerical standards. . . . [It thus tends to ignore individual differences in] a patient's needs, preferences, and lifestyle. Consider a woman who likes to ski and ride horseback and who has a partially detached retina in one eye. One ophthalmologist believes in an operation that does a minimum amount of "welding" (photocoagulation) and would minimize her loss of vision. Although that might satisfy the physician's criterion of technical excellence, it does not allow the woman to resume her athletic pursuits safely. Another ophthalmologist might propose to coagulate a complete circle around her retina. In this case the patient would lose some vision, but would have more of a guarantee that the retina will not detach again, and she could ski and ride again.

Patients suffering from severe angina pectoris (chest pain thought to be due to a lack of oxygen supply to the heart) pose another therapeutic dilemma. One doctor may recommend heart surgery; another, treatment with drugs such as nitroglycerine. For most such patients, there is no consensus among physicians today as to which is the best treatment. What is "best" in a particular case will depend on the values and needs of the patient, the skills of the doctor, and the other resources available. . . .

HEALTH CARE INTO THE 21ST CENTURY

Mark A. Peterson

22 J. Health Pol. Pol'y & L. 291 (1997)

What are we to make of the market transformation of health care in the United States, the core legacy of the current decade? Should we favor the dynamics of markets, standing alone, as a vehicle for reform? What are the limitations? What has motivated the restructuring of the private insurance system? What happens when the market transformation extends from private insurance to the publicly financed programs for the elderly and poor? . . . Before launching into that analysis, it is imperative to . . . [ask] what do we mean when we speak of markets in the health care setting? . . . [R]elatively few people, beyond some libertarian and right-wing politicians, believe that all matters pertaining to the delivery of medical care services should be left to the marketplace, however conceived. Some individuals may believe that health care is no different from toothpaste, but that view is shared by few analysts and citizens.

Most market advocates, such as health economists Alain Enthoven and Mark Pauly, support major interventions by the government to subsidize insurance coverage and promote improved rules of the game for an otherwise inefficient market. Analysts across the spectrum of opinion reject the simplistic dichotomies of government versus the market, or regulation versus competition. More pertinent are questions about where, when, in what form, and under what conditions both markets and government have a role.

In the health care setting, the market is more typically a reference to a set of market-like instruments or arrangements. These include privately owned or managed institutions, which can range from stockholder-owned insurance companies to nonprofit sickness funds in the German tradition. They often refer to the use of incentives embedded within institutions of whatever sort (private or public) that are designed to promote more efficient individual-level behavior. Fully capitated payments to physicians by corporate HMOs, which shift risk to the doctor and reward the utilization of fewer services, would certainly be included. But one would also have to consider the hospital payment methodology of diagnosis-related groupings (DRGs) used by a public program like Medicare. The market frequently is taken to refer to a process of decision making; for example, using competition among substitutable entities to identify and select the best choice according to some measure of utility. That competition, however, can be among private firms, nonprofit institutions, or even public agencies or employees. It can occur within an unregulated marketplace or within the bowels of the public sector. The same can be said of another market-like arrangement: contracting between relevant parties.

■ CALIFORNIA DENTAL ASS'N v. FEDERAL TRADE COMMISSION
526 U.S. 756 (1999)

Souter, J.

[The issue in this case is] whether a "quick look" sufficed to justify finding that certain advertising restrictions adopted by the California Dental Association violated the antitrust laws. . . . The CDA is a voluntary nonprofit association of local dental societies to which some 19,000 dentists belong, including about three-quarters of those practicing in the State. . . . [These dentists] agree to abide by a Code of Ethics (Code) including the following:

> Although any dentist may advertise, no dentist shall advertise or solicit patients in any form of communication in a manner that is false or misleading in any material respect. In order to properly serve the public, dentists should represent themselves in a manner that contributes to the esteem of the public. . . .

The CDA has issued a number of advisory opinions interpreting this section, and through separate advertising guidelines intended to help members comply with the Code and with state law the CDA has advised its dentists of disclosures they must make under state law when engaging in discount advertising. . . .

The FTC brought a complaint against the CDA, alleging that . . . the CDA had unreasonably restricted two types of advertising: price advertising, particularly discounted fees, and advertising relating to the quality of dental services. An Administrative Law Judge (ALJ) . . . found a violation of §5 of the FTC Act, [which prohibits "unfair competition and deceptive acts or practices." 15 U.S.C. §45(a)(1). We reverse and remand.] . . .

The restrictions on both discount and nondiscount advertising are, at least on their face, designed to avoid false or deceptive advertising in a market characterized by striking disparities between the information available to the professional and the patient.[10] In a market for professional services, in which advertising is relatively rare and the comparability of service packages not easily established, the difficulty for customers or potential competitors to get and verify information about the price and availability of services magnifies the dangers to competition associated with misleading advertising. What is more, the quality of professional services tends to resist either calibration or monitoring by individual patients or clients, partly because of the specialized knowledge required to evaluate the services, and partly because of the difficulty in determining whether, and the degree to which, an outcome is attributable to the quality of services (like a poor job of tooth filling) or to something else (like a very tough walnut). Patients' attachments to particular professionals, the rationality of which is difficult to assess, complicate the picture even further. The existence of such significant challenges to informed decisionmaking by the customer for professional services immediately suggests that advertising restrictions arguably protecting patients from misleading or irrelevant advertising call for more than cursory treatment as obviously comparable to classic horizontal agreements to limit output or price competition.

WHERE YOU STAND DEPENDS ON WHERE YOU SIT: MUSINGS ON THE REGULATION/COMPETITION DIALOGUE*

Donald R. Cohodes

7 J. Health Pol. Pol'y & L. 54 (1982)

An analysis of alternative approaches to containing medical care costs—especially an analysis oriented toward market approaches—must be firmly based on an understanding of the medical care market: why medical care is different from other products; why the nature of medical care leads to institutional factors that do not exist in other markets; why institutional arrangements that do exist and work well in other markets cause problems in the market for medical care; why governmental attempts to deal with the medical care market often have perverse or inflationary effects; and why the interaction of all these factors tends to undermine the means and the incentives for an efficient, cost-effective market for medical care.

Medical care has a number of characteristics that distinguish it from most other products in important ways:

10. "The fact that a restraint operates upon a profession as distinguished from a business is, of course, relevant in determining whether that particular restraint violates the [antitrust laws]. It would be unrealistic to view the practice of professions as interchangeable with other business activities, and automatically to apply to the professions antitrust concepts which originated in other areas. The public service aspect, and other features of the professions, may require that a particular practice, which could properly be viewed as a violation of [antitrust laws] in another context, be treated differently." Goldfarb v. Virginia State Bar, 421 U.S. 773, 788-789, n. 17, 95 S. Ct. 2004, 44 L. Ed. 2d 572 (1975).

1. *Demand for health.* Medical care services are not purchased from any desire for such services in themselves. The demand for medical care services is derived from the "demand" for good health.
2. *Medical care and health.* Medical care is only one determinant of health status, and for most people at most times it is not even a very important determinant. Environment, exercise, nutrition, and personal habits also are important factors affecting health status.
3. *Risk.* The need for medical care is unpredictable, requiring expenditures that are irregular and of uncertain magnitude.
4. *Immediacy.* The need for medical care is often immediate, allowing little time for shopping around and seeking advice or alternatives.
5. *Lack of information.* Consumers are usually ignorant of their medical care needs. They cannot possibly obtain the knowledge and training to diagnose their own medical care needs and "demand" the required services.
6. *Uncertainty.* Physicians, though highly trained and better able to diagnose needs and prescribed treatment, also are often uncertain about the appropriate services to provide.

These factors clearly hamper the operation of a normal market. . . .

Certain institutional developments and responses to the unique characteristics of medical care have further aggravated the problem. These include:

1. *Physician as agent.* Because of the consumer's uncertainty about the medical services he needs, the physician serves a dual role. Once the consumer has decided to seek care and select a physician, the physician diagnoses problems and decides on the course and place of treatment. The physician thus acts as agent for the consumer. But the physician provides more than advice; he also provides medical services. Unlike most producers, the physician may control the demand for his services. The more services he prescribes, the more fees he collects. It is this factor that makes fee-for-service pricing of physician services a concern to those who would like to see a more competitive medical care market. The problem is compounded by the uncertainty of medical science. The physician may not know exactly what the patient needs. The lack of accepted standards of medical practice, and the consequent fear of malpractice claims, leads to "[defensive] medicine"—the provision of services that may be neither warranted nor efficient. When the physician makes decisions for the consumer, there is little incentive for efficient use of resources.
2. *Third-party payment.* Due to the risk and uncertainty of incurring medical expenses, consumers purchase insurance to regularize their expenses. The predominant form of insurance purchased today is characterized by direct third-party payments of some or all medical expenses. The consequent reduction or absence of direct consumer payment for services has been found to be a significant factor affecting consumer and provider decision-making. The insulation of the consumer from direct payment for care has been shown to undermine incentives for cost-conscious consumer behavior. When a consumer pays little or nothing out-of-pocket for the

services he is receiving, economic theory and empirical evidence indicate that more service will be demanded than if out-of-pocket expenses reflect the full cost of care.

3. *Retrospective cost reimbursement.* Not only are payments made by a third party, but payments are generally based on incurred costs. This rewards physicians and hospitals with more revenues for generating more costs. In contrast to the competitive theory of economic efficiency, where producers are rewarded for lowering costs, providers of medical services are rewarded for raising costs.

Table 1. The Market for Medical Care

Assumptions Underlying a Perfectly Competitive Market	*Match with Market for Medical Care*	*Specific Differences*
Market Structure		
Large number of buyers and sellers	Mixed	Many consumers and physicians; few hospitals
Complete information (absence of uncertainty)	No	Consumer ignorance of the product risk and uncertainty of need
Firms operate independently (no one seller can influence price)	No	Price fixing (physician fee schedules); Cost reimbursement for hospitals
Free entry and exit of all producers	No	Barriers to entry (personnel licensure, hospital accreditation, certificate-of-need programs, a limited number of medical schools)
The product is homogeneous	No	Multiple, undefined products; varied quality
The consumer is the key decision-maker	No	Physicians act as agents on behalf of consumers
Market Conduct		
Firms are price-takers	No	Hospitals and physicians are price setters
Firms maximize their profits	No	In general, hospitals are nonprofit organizations which seek to maximize other objectives (growth, prestige) Similarly, physicians may have noneconomic motives, such as intellectual curiosity, esteem of peers

Together, these factors undercut virtually all normal incentives for market efficiency. Consumers trust providers to make consumption decisions; and since they often pay little or nothing *directly* for medical services, consumers have little incentive to economize. Providers are generally paid by a third party; and since they are reimbursed for their fees and incurred costs, providers have little incentive to economize. Insurers spread the costs among all subscribers, who in the end pay for this inefficiency in the *indirect* costs of their premiums. No one in this triangular flow of dollars has sufficient incentives to make economizing choices; indeed, the predominant incentives are for more and more spending.

Other institutional and attitudinal factors compound the cost-inflating incentives described above:

1. *Medical ethic.* Physicians are generally unconcerned with, and unaccountable for, the costs of services recommended and rendered. This is especially true of hospital costs. Physician training emphasizes thoroughness and the use of all available resources to help the patient, rather than the management of health care resources and the trade-off of cost and effectiveness. While difficult to change, this attitude has serious efficiency implications in a system where resources are allocated by physicians.
2. *Medical mystique.* Physicians are among the most respected members of society, and in the medical marketplace few consumers question the wisdom of physician recommendations. Moreover, the idea that "money is no object" in medical care decisions is widespread among consumers as well as physicians. Few consumers even ask about the prices of medical care. Again, these attitudes have serious implications in a system where individual consumers do not bear much of the direct costs of resource consumption.
3. *Nonprofit institutions.* In a society where health has no price, institutions are not expected to profit from illness. Large segments of the medical care industry are nonprofit, and the response to financial incentives differs from that of a profit-making industry. While profit-making firms strive to maximize earnings and thus to minimize cost per unit of output, nonprofit hospitals place more emphasis on maximizing quality of service or capital investment. The growth-with-quality imperative creates incentives for greater costs. This must be a concern in a financing system based on cost reimbursement.

These societal and institutional attitudes—that cost should not be a factor in medical decisions, that health has no price, that quality is of paramount concern—are unique to the medical care market. They create strong pressures for spending. The institutional and financing arrangements in the market offer little resistance to cost increases and little incentive for efficient resource allocation.

Some government policies also contribute to the incentives for cost-increasing behavior in the medical care sector. This happens at both the federal and state levels through direct and indirect subsidies, health care financing programs, and extensive regulation:

1. *Tax subsidies.* By exempting from taxation employer contributions to health care plans, the federal income and payroll tax structures provide an enormous ($[200 billion in 2006]) subsidy for private insurance coverage. This,

in effect, allows employees to purchase insurance with pre-tax dollars rather than after-tax dollars, an average subsidy of 30 percent of the employer's contribution. This subsidy distorts the employee's incentive for efficient health care expenditures by encouraging the purchase of more expensive, first-dollar coverage.

2. *Hidden premium costs.* The tax incentive to pay for medical insurance through employers results in substantial consumer ignorance of full premium costs. Approximately 80 percent of health insurance premiums are paid through employment-related group insurance plans. Under these group plans, on average, the employer pays two-thirds of the total premium. . . . These institutional and consumer responses to the government subsidy provide further incentives for consumers to seek more comprehensive, cost-inflating coverage than if the premium costs were paid directly.
3. *Medicare and Medicaid.* These two health care financing programs rely almost entirely on third-party, fee-for-service, and cost-reimbursement financing. They pay more on behalf of people who choose more costly systems of care, and they pay more to providers that cost more.
4. *Regulatory barriers to efficiency.* Federal and state legislatures and regulatory agencies, often with the advice of medical associations, have adopted regulations that in many respects serve as barriers to cost-reducing innovation. The use of supervised para-professionals and physician extenders for routine services, for example, has been severely restricted by regulation. Restrictive laws and practices have also inhibited the growth of alternative, more efficient health delivery systems. Even the Health Maintenance Organization Act, which was intended to spur the growth of HMOs, encumbered developing HMOs with enough restrictive "quality controls" to raise the cost of their operation and make them less competitive than they could be.

While some government policies have attempted to contain medical costs through direct economic regulation, other policies have exacerbated the inflationary pressures within the market.

A brief sketch of the medical care market cannot provide a definitive background for understanding the regulation/competition debate. However, it is essential to begin an assessment of the debate with an examination of intrinsic market characteristics. Only by distinguishing those elements that are intrinsic and cannot be changed (e.g., risk, uncertainty) from those elements that are institutional responses and may be changed (e.g., third-party cost reimbursement), and by distinguishing both from the symptoms (e.g., excess bed capacity), can the true sources of the problem be identified and effective policy alternatives be developed.

HEALTH CARE CHOICES: PRIVATE CONTRACTS AS INSTRUMENTS OF HEALTH REFORM

Clark C. Havighurst

1995

The nature of the challenge posed by health care costs can be appreciated best by seeing the graphic demonstration in Figure 9.4.

FIGURE 3.4 Targets in the War on Health Care Costs

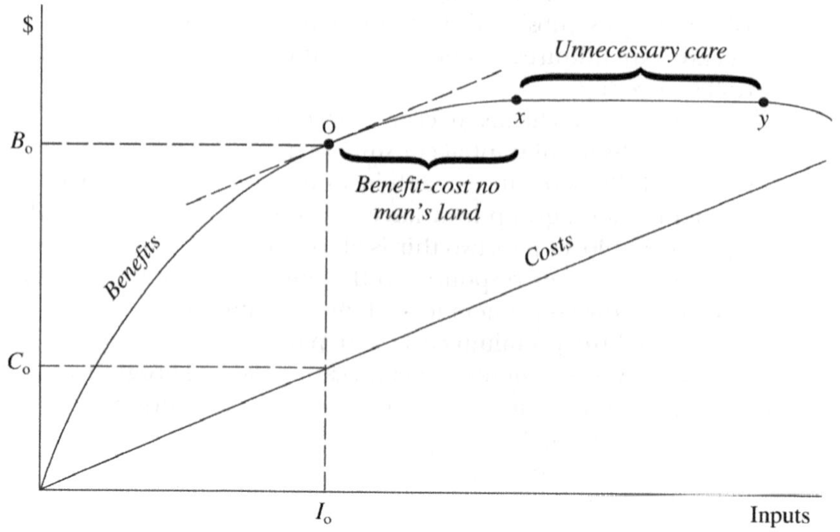

The "benefits" curve in Figure 3.4 shows heuristically the probable relationships between the benefits of health care (measured in dollars on the vertical axis) and the inputs needed to obtain them. It is assumed that "inputs" are all uniform and that they will be added in a sequence dictated by their ability to yield benefits. Thus, at low input levels, the benefits curve rises steeply, reflecting the true miracles of modern medical science. The curve rises more and more gradually, however, as the inputs being added yield either cures at increasingly higher cost or benefits of increasingly equivocal kinds. The curve is flat after point *x*, as added inputs yield no benefit, illustrating the notion of unnecessary care. (The curve actually falls after point *y*, showing that some medical care is positively harmful.)

The benefits curve alone cannot reveal where society or any given purchaser should stop adding inputs. Although no care should be purchased beyond point *x*, cost-containment efforts that stop there would not ensure an efficient level of consumption. Efficiency demands that costs be taken into account. The diagram therefore introduces a cost curve, a straight line illustrating the cumulative dollar cost of adding uniform inputs. The critical feature of this line for present purposes is its slope (rate of increase), which is reflected in the dotted parallel line having a point of tangency with the benefits curve at point *o*. At that point, the benefits curve is rising at exactly the same rate as the cost line. Up to that point, the inputs added yield benefits that exceed the costs incurred. Beyond point *o*, however, the benefits obtainable by adding additional inputs are no longer as great as the cost of those inputs. In other words, marginal costs exceed marginal benefits. *Io* then represents . . . the optimal (efficient) level of inputs, and *Co* represents the (provisionally) optimal level of spending.

The first crucial point in this demonstration is that even though adding inputs and expenditures beyond point *o* would improve aggregate health, that fact does not justify such additional spending; employing the same resources in other ways, dedicating them to nonhealth purpose, would increase welfare even more. This conclusion, while theoretically correct, may be hard to accept because of doubts about valuing the health benefits of individuals in dollars and trading them off against other things beneficial to other individuals. It is not proposed, however, to operationalize this calculus in making social decisions or in rationing care. Instead, the analysis here is offered simply to make the point that it is almost certainly socially wrong—in the sense that it reduces aggregate welfare—to pay for every health service that yields some benefit. This point, however, is the beginning, not the end, of the discussion.

An equally important implication of the foregoing demonstration is the obvious practical difficulty of deciding what specific services to omit and of preventing them from being rendered in particular cases. This difficulty will be encountered at whatever level the requisite actions must be taken, whether by society as a whole acting through government, by financing intermediaries, by providers of care, or by individual patients. To highlight this aspect of the problem we are setting for ourselves, the diagram labels the portion of the benefits curve between point *o* and point *x* as the benefit-cost no man's land. In this area, health care, being beneficial, will seem desirable as long as the decisionmaker—public or private, as the case may be—does not consider the true cost of providing it. The potential for conflict is clear. Precisely because anyone venturing to fight the battle for cost containment in this range is likely to draw criticism of the most intense kind, including lawsuits, the no-man's-land metaphor seems apt. Again and again in the discussion ahead, there will be occasions to ask whether the cost-containment weapons being used are capable of fighting the battle in the benefit-cost no man's land. We will discover that virtually all of the cost-containment measures in use today seek to eliminate only flat-of-the-curve care and not to take on the more dangerous challenge.

HEALTH CARE, MARKETS, AND DEMOCRATIC VALUES*

Rand E. Rosenblatt

34 Vand. L. Rev. 1067 (1981)

Market advocates attempt to structure the patient's relationship to health care as an economic transaction, namely, as an exchange of a commodity for money in a competitive market setting. A primary justification for increasing market competition in health care is to promote efficiency in the use and delivery of services. Some proponents argue that market competition also has value in its own right as a uniquely legitimate method of defining and promoting efficiency. It is argued that collective social decisions, however made, are inherently coercive and inevitably inefficient. Market mechanisms are said to promote only the value of individual liberty, which enables consumers to express their own preferences by their economic "votes"; otherwise, these mechanisms are considered to be value-neutral.

Despite its considerable superficial appeal, this position is misguided. The distribution of health services through competitive markets promotes at least three major and related nonneutral values. First, in a competitive market individuals are encouraged to make decisions about health care primarily from an economic perspective, as opposed to a broader, more realistic view. Second, individuals also are encouraged to perceive health care choices and health itself as an individual matter, rather than as a matter based upon a close interrelationship between individual decisions and social patterns concerning nutrition, work, environmental quality, economic opportunity, and many other factors. Last, in a competitive market, individuals in their role as citizens or government officials are encouraged to believe that the proper goal of most government policy is to encourage voluntary market transactions. As a result, issues of equality become confined to the special and limited sphere of redistributing purchasing power, the purpose of which is to permit deserving low income persons to participate in the free market. These three values may be defensible, but they certainly are not neutral, at least not in the sense of simply allowing individuals to express their own preferences. On the contrary, they are designed to exert influence over what those preferences might be, as well as to limit the kinds of social settings in which preferences can be expressed and satisfied. . . .

Health can be understood rather simply as the absence of disease and death, and health care as a "curative defense" against both. Health care, . . . however, also must be understood as a caring rather than purely a curative activity, the goal of which is to reduce pain and anxiety and increase the patient's sense of self-determination and quality of life. . . . From this perspective, a central need of health care reform is not more refined quantitative cost-benefit analyses, but rather a restructuring of the patient-provider relationship that ideally could increase the sense of self-determination and satisfaction for both. . . .

A question of great importance about the market approach to health care delivery is how it will affect people with low incomes. By their very nature, markets respond to those consumer preferences that are expressed with money, and people with the least money, therefore, tend to have their preferences given the least attention. Market advocates are aware that some number of low income people could not afford to pay for services or insurance in a competitive health care market. Consequently, they usually propose the simple solution of income transfers—typically effected through a voucher for medical care—that would be sufficient to purchase "basic or necessary" services. . . .

Despite this apparently benign intention of the market advocates, there are strong reasons to believe that poor and low income persons will suffer grievously. A society that embraces a market approach to most of its daily economic life, including the socially sensitive area of health care, is unlikely to redistribute adequate purchasing power to people in economic need. Whether it is theoretically possible for a market society to be strongly egalitarian as well need not be definitively resolved; it is sufficient to note the major reasons why the market perspective is often inconsistent with egalitarian redistribution. First, such a society, or the dominant groups within it, are likely to have a strong belief that the income distribution produced by the market is just. Moreover, they are likely to see unequal economic rewards as necessary incentives for socially desirable qualities such as hard work, risk taking, and enterpreneurial initiative. Income redistribution—even in the form of in-kind vouchers for medical care—probably will be viewed as threatening work incentives and efficient allocation of resources.

4

Regulation of Health Care Facilities and Transactions

There was a time, prior to the 1980s, when the only legal representation most hospitals and doctors required, aside from malpractice defense, was occasional tax advice. It was once common for even large hospitals to rely solely on sporadic pro bono counsel. These idyllic days are now long past. Health care law has been one of the most rapidly growing areas of legal specialization for over two decades. Despite its focus on a single industry, health care law calls on a broad array of legal talents and requires sophistication in subjects as diverse as antitrust, corporate and tax law, administrative law, and securities regulation.

This transformation in the legal climate has resulted from the strong winds of economic and organizational change that are buffeting the health care delivery system. What was once a tranquil service industry dominated by religious orders is now a dynamic sector of the economy driven by a new-found entrepreneurial fervor. "Vertical integration," "diversification," "joint venturing," and "strategic aligning" are the buzzwords that fill today's health care trade press and boardrooms. The days of solo physician practice, freestanding hospitals, and bright-line divisions among doctors, hospitals, and insurers are giving way to various forms of joint ventures, complex corporate structures, and integrated alternative delivery systems.

The driving force behind this massive restructuring is the fear that unless individual providers are affiliated with larger institutions, alliances, or ventures, their business will dwindle under intensified competition or they may be forced out of business entirely. The feeling is that the stakes are high, and the time is now, so few providers have failed to act. See generally Einer Elhauge ed., The Fragmentation of U.S. Health Care: Causes and Solutions (2010); James C. Robinson, The Corporate

Practice of Medicine (1999); Jessica Mantel, The Myth of the Independent Physician: Implications for Health Law, Policy, and Ethics, 64 Case W. Res. L. Rev. 455 (2013); Abbe R. Gluck, The New Health Care Industry: Consolidation, Integration, Competition in the Wake of the ACA, Health Aff. Blog (Feb. 24, 2016); Symposium, 36 Health Aff. 1527 (2017); Symposium, 29 Health Aff. 1284 (2010); Symposium, 5(6) J. Gen. Intern. Med. 584 (June 2010); Symposium, 67(4) Med. Care Res. Rev. (Aug. 2010); Symposium, 27 Health Aff. 1218 (2008).

Corporate Structure and Integration

It is easy enough to draw in broad outline the forces that are restructuring health care financing and delivery. It is much more difficult to classify all of the variety of forms in which these restructurings can take shape. This difficulty arises in part from the lack of a settled vocabulary of consistent usage, in part from the still developmental nature of the market, and in part from the vast complexity that is inherent in the field.

An "integrated delivery system" (IDS) is the broadest construct, including, at a minimum, a full array of hospital and physician services in both inpatient and outpatient settings. It may also include long-term-care facilities and specialized services such as mental health or physical therapy. Most important, an integrated system incorporates some form of insurance risk, either by selling insurance directly, or contracting with insurers or employers on a capitated basis.

In the simplest manifestation, this would be an ordinary staff-model HMO that owns its own hospitals, employs its own physicians, and markets its own insurance. A contrasting model is one in which physicians and hospitals remain in separately governed entities but affiliate with each other and the insurer by some commonality of ownership or contract. A holding company might tie the components together, or one of the components—usually the insurer or the hospital—might be the dominant party. A structure in which the insuring entity is the dominant party is a group- or network-model HMO. A structure in which a nonprofit hospital or its nonprofit parent is the dominant party has come to be known as the "Foundation model."[1] When hospitals and physicians stand on approximately equal footing, as in a partnership, the structure is sometimes known as a "physician-hospital organization" (PHO).

Short of full integration, affiliations between and among hospitals, doctors, and insurers can take place through a variety of contracting or partnership arrangements, in both horizontal and vertical dimensions—that is, among similar providers or between different delivery-system components. To make things even more confusing, the same term sometimes applies to substantially different arrangements. For instance, a group of physicians that contract with each other in order to negotiate with insurers can be called an "independent practice association" (IPA),

1. This terminology arose in California, the first state to be swept by integrated networks, so as to take advantage of a provision in the California statutes that exempts so-called foundations from a certain legal restriction that otherwise precludes the employment of physicians. Although a "foundation" is not actually any particular type of legal entity, here it is interpreted to mean a nonprofit corporation.

but this term applies to the type of HMO that contracts with a large number of physicians on a nonexclusive basis. When insurers other than HMOs do this on a fee-for-service rather than capitated basis, the structure is usually called a PPO, for preferred provider organization.

Similarly, a hospital or insurer "acquiring" a physician practice has a number of still unsettled meanings. Aside from actually employing physicians, networks can contract with them or make them equity partners (i.e., investors). One common arrangement, referred to above as a "management services organization" (MSO), is for the network to acquire the tangible assets of a physician practice—the office building, files, medical records, etc.—for a lump sum price but for the physicians themselves to remain independent contractors. They agree to treat network patients under a predetermined compensation arrangement, and the network agrees to manage their office practice (staffing, billing, etc.).

This description should not be taken as a fixed categorization, much less a "how-to" guide. The variety of organizational techniques are far too numerous, and the field of activity is far too fluid, for any such codification. Many of the structures in use are fairly conventional forms of HMOs and hospital holding companies. Others are hybrids whose names seem to change every year or two, and many of the terms just defined are used by others in different and inconsistent ways. Accountable care organizations (ACOs), for instance, were not heard or thought of before about 2008, and we still lack a fixed definition of what they are. Once defined, it may be hard to distinguish ACOs from other similar constructs that were once in vogue but have receded from prominence. What happens next is anyone's guess. The only thing that is certain about the future is that things will not stay the same.

The Scope of This Chapter

The result of this cauldron of activity, aside from a never-ending stream of new acronyms and buzz phrases, is a tremendous surge in legal work. Each of these innovative ventures must be examined against the backdrop of both traditional legal doctrine and new bodies of health care regulation. This chapter covers a range of issues that modern health care attorneys must contend with at the cutting edge of their practice field. This is necessarily a grab bag of legal issues. Because we cannot hope to convey the universe of law relevant to the multitude of organizational and operational activities of health care business, we will set aside the areas of doctrine that have more general applicability—such as contract law and securities regulation—and focus instead on the doctrinal areas of unique importance to health care. Those who desire greater detail or depth might consult one of the following multivolume treatises: Wolters Kluwer's Hospital Law Manual and Managed Care Law Manual; Carol Colborn-Loepere et al., Health Care Financial Transactions Manual; Hooper Lundy & Bookman, Treatise on Health Care Law; American Health Lawyers Association, Health Law Practice Guide.

This chapter progresses through the layers of complexity in the health care industry as follows. The chapter begins with the regulation, corporate structure, and taxation of hospitals and other facilities as discrete, freestanding institutions. It then explores how these institutions relate with physicians. Then the chapter addresses the application of antitrust law to a range of key activities and organizations. The chapter concludes with the topic of greatest complexity: the regulation of financial relationships among all components of the health care financing and delivery system. Throughout, there are two central questions: What are the motivating concerns and concepts of each discrete body of law? Are they still relevant in the rapidly changing environment in which health care institutions currently find themselves? This inquiry is not simply whether courts correctly discern the technical aspects of each separate body of law; it is whether health care law more generally suffers from a "pathology" of viewing each topic too parochially and dissecting problems too narrowly. The risk is that courts will fail to see the overall, interactive effects of the many strands of legal doctrine that determine how medical institutions are formed and operated and that have a major impact on our nation's health care public policy.

■ PARTNERS IN HEALTH: HOW PHYSICIANS AND HOSPITALS CAN BE ACCOUNTABLE TOGETHER

Francis J. Crosson & Laura A. Tollen (2010)*

Any approach to sustained cost reduction in health care must involve hospitals and physicians. Hospitalizations are the costliest form of care delivery, and conventional wisdom is that physician care decisions directly drive over 80 percent of total health care costs. Accordingly, there is a growing consensus that changes in payment incentives to hospitals and physicians are required, and that such changes must be more than superficial. Most such payment reforms involve either prepayment for services to be rendered, with some form of risk sharing, or episode-based payments such as case payments to physicians and hospitals together.

But there is a problem. As seen in [the figure below], advanced payment methodologies are most feasible in an environment of highly organized providers. Such payment methodologies are much less feasible in the disaggregated delivery model that exists in much of the United States today. . . .

The solution to the problem is a coordinated set of delivery system reforms that involve changes in both payment and incentives and in the structure of how hospitals and physicians are organized to provide care. The changes must address the chicken-or-the-egg dilemma that has impeded progress in delivery system integration in many parts of the country. Without payment reform, there is little motivation for disaggregated physicians to do the hard work of forming larger organizations and to work with hospital administrators. Conversely, without the existence of greater numbers of integrated organizations, payers (including Medicare) have gained little traction in developing advanced payment methodologies because so few entities are capable of receiving them and succeeding with them.

Over the past eighty years, there have been a number of carefully constructed calls for delivery system integration. In 1933, the Committee on the Costs of Medical Care recommended that the United States seek to create many more group practices (modeled after the Mayo Clinic), because such practices were more

FIGURE 4.1 Organization and Payment Methods

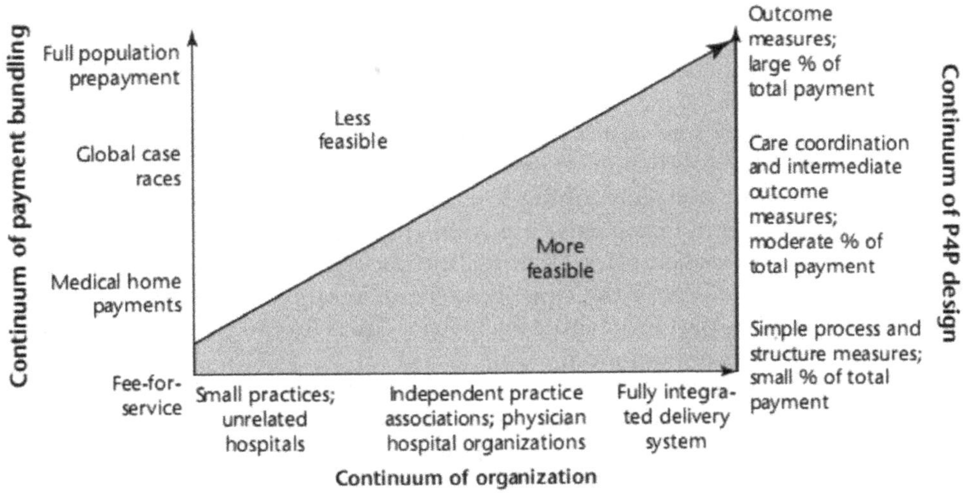

efficient and less costly than solo practices. More recently, . . . in its landmark report in 2007, *A High Performance Health System for the United States,* The Commonwealth Fund Commission on a High Performance Health System called for "the U.S. [to] embark on the organization and delivery of health care services to end the fragmentation, waste, and complexity that currently exist. Physicians and other care providers should be rewarded, through financial and non-financial incentives, to band together into traditional or virtual organizations that can provide the support needed for physicians and other providers to practice 21st century medicine."

The goal then, in the context of [the figure above], is to move through both payment changes and delivery system changes over time from the "southwest" corner of the figure to somewhere closer to the "northeast" corner. There are many ideas about how to do this, discussed throughout this book. Virtually every one of these ideas for change will require increased collaboration or integration between hospitals and physicians. . . .

Clinical Integration

Most U.S. physicians practice medicine, at least in part, within a hospital setting but without a direct legal or financial relationship with the hospital. There are some exceptions to this model. In integrated delivery systems, such as Kaiser Permanente, . . . most physicians are employed by the group practice, which either owns or has a financial arrangement with the hospital or hospitals. Similarly, in physician hospital organizations (PHOs), the hospital and its associated physicians create a joint financial entity through which revenue is distributed. Recently, hospitals have begun to employ physicians directly in a variety of specialties. . . . In each of these settings, there is usually a sound structural, financial, and legal basis for physicians to work closely together to improve care quality and reduce unnecessary costs. . . .

In the more common setting, where the physicians and hospitals are not part of a single economic entity, the situation is quite different. In some states, the "corporate practice of medicine bar" prevents hospitals from hiring physicians. . . . In addition, a broad range of federal laws and regulations inhibits physician-hospital interrelationships, including antitrust provisions, tax-exempt organization regulations, laws intended to prevent limitation of services to Medicare beneficiaries, and "anti-kickback" and "Stark" provisions.

These regulations, as well as possible mitigation approaches, are discussed in detail [throughout this] chapter. Were there to be a significant "relaxation" of the laws and regulations that now inhibit financial arrangements between otherwise separate physicians and hospitals, it is possible that more formal integrated structures . . . might be less necessary. However, the pace of such regulatory changes is likely to be too slow to foster the type of systematic reorganization that appears to be called for now, as part of health care reform. Therefore, other, more complex proposals are under consideration. . . .

Whether . . . integration driven by a more widespread use of bundled payments, or the evolution of [Accountable Care Organizations], becomes the predominant reform dynamic in the next five or so years, there is little question that change is coming. . . . There are really only two ways to reduce [costs], either through progressive fee-for-service payment reductions to physicians and hospitals or through reorganization of care delivery and changes to payment and incentives. It is likely that only the latter choice has a simultaneous chance to improve quality. So the best hope is the most radical—to restructure and integrate. . . .

But are U.S. physicians and hospitals capable of proceeding successfully through such changes? . . . Some remember all too well the failed attempts to "integrate" in the mid-1990s to prepare for managed care prepayment, which never materialized. Many nascent organizations failed or disbanded as a consequence. Hard feelings and financial losses were the result. Currently, in many institutions, physicians and hospitals are at loggerheads over control issues or are in frank competition for patients needing complex, profitable procedures. A first step in breaking down this negative environment is to analyze what is wrong and how it could be different. . . .

Notes: Innovation Without End

1. *ACOs: Here We Go Again.* It is expected that ACOs will take multiple forms, similar to previous managed care organizations and alternative delivery structures reviewed in this and the previous chapter. Many of these existing templates are being dusted off and buffed up to respond to the new buzz. According to one astute observer, the "problem with this movie is that we've actually seen it before, and it was a colossal and expensive failure." Jeff Goldsmith, The Accountable Care Organization: Not Ready for Prime Time (Health Affairs Blog, Aug. 17, 2009). Initial reactions to Medicare's ACO rules were often negative, claiming that the potential rewards did not outweigh the business risks and administrative costs. Others, however, are more optimistic. Also, this time around, perhaps physicians will take the lead, rather than hospitals or insurers. E. J. Emanuel, Why Accountable Care Organizations Are Not 1990s Managed Care Redux, 307 JAMA 2263 (2012). But, the skeptics point out that many physician-led organizations also failed in the 1990s, and that hospitals are better able to shoulder the considerable capital costs entailed

in forming new delivery system structures. See Chapter 4.E.3 for further discussion concerning ACA performance. Various legal issues raised by ACOs are covered throughout this chapter.

2. *Medical Homes vs. Retail Clinics.* Short of full-scale integration across the spectrum of care, "medical homes" provide better integration of primary care and other outpatient services, especially for people with chronic illness. Medical homes are primary care physicians or clinics that provide a fuller spectrum of services, including a comprehensive medical record and coordinated referrals to necessary specialists. From one vantage, these are kinder and gentler versions of the primary care "gatekeepers" much reviled under the first generation of managed care. It is not clear, however, whether they have potential to save money since, at least initially, medical homes require more payment than ordinary primary care, in order to support their broader range of supporting services. As with other practice innovations, the Affordable Care Act called for medical homes to be studied and encouraged, but it failed to set a firm course. At the other end of the integration spectrum, retail medical clinics are an emerging development implicating licensure, reimbursement, and corporate laws. Located in drugstores and megastores such as Walmart, they are staffed by nurse practitioners to provide simple and routine urgent care and medical screening services.

3. *Milking the System.* One reason for the huge upsurge in hospitals employing physicians is the disparity in payment rates between office-based and facility-based procedures. For exactly the same procedure, such as a colonoscopy, Medicare and private insurance typically pay considerably more when it is done at a facility, such as a hospital outpatient department, than at a physician's office. The main reason for the greater payment is that physicians practicing in office settings receive only a "professional fee," whereas at a facility the insurer also pays a facility fee. Thus, payment rates can double or triple simply by moving procedures from offices to facilities—an economic gain that strongly incentivized employment of previously independent physicians.[2] See Caroline S. Carlin, Roger Feldman & Bryan Dowd, The Impact of Provider Consolidation on Physician Prices, __ Health Econ. __ (2017).

4. *Sobering Thought of the Day.* According to one astute observer:

> [A]lmost any fix for what ails the U.S. health care system, be it a private market initiative or act of public legislation, every "solution" an entrepreneur or politician can dream up, runs headlong into the utter complexity of the system, the uncanny ability of those working in it to defend their precious turf against the solution, and the constant disconnect between what people in health care say they are going to do and what they actually end up doing. . . . The long view of our industry's history shows that health care is not changing so much as running in place, faster and faster, consuming more and more dollars as it tries to "re-engineer" itself out of its own realities.

2. Even more stimulus came from the fact that, for a while, hospitals could simply designate a physician's clinic as part of its facilities, thus escalating reimbursement without making any changes in the site of service (other than the signage). Starting in 2017, however, Medicare does not allow hospitals to claim facility fees for services performed off campus. However, the fundamental payment disparity still exists.

J.D. Kleinke, Oxymorons: The Myth of a U.S. Health Care System xii (2001).

5. *Further Readings.* On **ACOs** (note 1), see Stephen Shortell et al., A Taxonomy of Accountable Care Organizations for Policy and Practice, 49(6) Health Serv. Res. 1883 (2014); Bruce Fried et al., Accountable Care Organizations: Navigating the Legal Landscape, 4 J. Health & Life Sci. L. 88 (2010); Douglas A. Hastings, Constructing Accountable Care Organizations: Some Practical Observations at the Nexus of Policy, Business, and Law, 19 BNA Health L. Rep. 883 (2010); John Hoff, How CMS's Final Regulations for Accountable Care Organizations Fall Flat (2012); Sara Kreindler et al., Interpretations of Integration in Early Accountable Care Organizations, 90 Milbank Q. 457 (2012); State Actions to Promote and Restrain Commercial Accountable Care Organizations (UC Berkeley, Oct. 2015); Symposium, 73(6) Med. Care Res. & Rev. 643 (2016); Symposium, 40(4) J. Health Pol. Pol'y L. 637 (2015); Symposium, 28 J. Contemp. Health L. & Pol'y 224 (2012); Symposium, 31 Health Aff. 2362 (2012); Symposium, 42 Seton Hall L. Rev. 1371 (2012).

On **medical homes** (note 2), see generally Anna D. Sinaiko et al., Synthesis of Research on Patient-Centered Medical Homes Brings Systematic Differences Into Relief, 36 Health Aff. 500 (2017); Symposium, 25(6) J. Gen. Intern. Med. 584 (June 2010); Symposium, 67(4) Med. Care Res. Rev. (Aug. 2010). On **retail clinics** (note 2), see William Sage, The Wal-Martization of Health Care, 28 J. Leg. Med. 503 (2007); William Sage, Out of the Box: The Future of Retail Medical Clinics, 3 Harv. L. & Pol'y Rev. 1 (online) (2009); Kaj Rozga, Retail Health Clinics: How the Next Innovation in Market-Driven Health Care Is Testing State and Federal Law, 35 Am. J.L. & Med. 205 (2009); Julie Muroff, Retail Health Care: "Taking Stock" of State Responsibilities, 30 J. Leg. Med. 151 (2009); Kristin Schleiter, Retail Medical Clinics: Increasing Access to Low Cost Medical Care Amongst a Developing Legal Environment, 19 Ann. Health L. 527 (2010); Symposium, 27(5) Health Aff. 1271 (Oct. 2008).

Problem: The History of Florence Nightingale Hospital and How It Grew*

This hypothetical serves as the basis for several of the discussion problems later in this chapter. It illustrates the profound transformations that have occurred in the health care sector over the last half century. It might be helpful in reviewing this to chart the legal measures that appear to prompt or support these organizational changes.

Florence Nightingale Hospital (FNH) is a private, nonprofit 400-bed facility employing more than 2,000 workers, with more than $100 million in annual revenues. It is located on the outskirts of a metropolitan area of one million people that contains three other major tertiary care hospitals of 300 beds or more and four

*This fact scenario and many of the problems in this chapter that grow from it are based on ones originally developed by Prof. Phyllis Bernard at Oklahoma City University School of Law. The editors appreciate her permission to adapt them for use in this book.

smaller, community hospitals of 100 to 150 beds. Currently, 38 percent of FNH's gross revenues are from Medicare, 12 percent are from Medicaid, and 40 percent from private insurance or out-of-pocket payments. The remaining 10 percent is bad debt or charity care.

Florence Nightingale Hospital was born in the 1950s as a small community hospital. It began as an effort by persons from the local church and medical communities joining forces with local business leaders to provide convenient hospital care in the growing suburbs. When the federal Hill-Burton program created a reservoir of construction loan money in the 1950s, the group of town boosters chose to apply for a construction loan to build a 100-bed facility. Its affiliation with the religious denomination has never been formalized through ownership, and the church no longer provides any significant financial support. Nevertheless, the charitable role of the hospital is taken seriously by the board of directors, which always includes one or two members of the denomination.

In the latter 1960s, increased revenues through the Medicare program enabled the hospital to obtain further construction loans, and the hospital expanded to add 100 more beds and more sophisticated inpatient services. Another wave of change swept through the health care industry in the 1980s, in response to a fundamental alteration in the way Medicare pays hospitals. Some hospitals consolidated, whereas Florence Nightingale sought to diversify operations and increase its patient base by providing a wider range of services and much larger bed capacity. Using a bond issue financed through the state, the hospital doubled in size to 400 beds. In addition, the hospital reorganized as the Florence Nightingale Healthcare Corporation in order to expand into nursing home, home health, and other related ventures.

In the 1990s the city had grown to reach Florence Nightingale Hospital's doorstep. FNH was no longer merely a suburban hospital. It became a major tertiary hospital serving the metroplex. However, revenues were beginning to dip due to the advent of managed care systems. Its average occupancy rate dropped from 85 to 70 percent.

In response, the hospital merged in 2000 with two other hospitals on the same side of town and formed the Florence Nightingale Network. The objective was to curb the loss of patients to other managed care networks by signing up a number of physicians, mainly in primary care but also in common specialties, and then marketing this network directly to employers and also to large insurance companies who would then offer the network to their customers. This effort was partially a bust, but in other ways was a great success. The idea of marketing directly to employers did not work because the network does not cover a broad enough geographic area to appeal to the largest employers, and smaller employers prefer a network that includes most of the physicians in town so they don't have to force their employees to switch doctors.

The network was a great advantage, however, in contracting with insurers. Because of employers' demands for broad networks, and regulators' requirements that managed care insurers provide adequate network capacity, insurers feel they have to include Florence Nightingale's facilities and physicians in their networks if they want to sell insurance in the region. Therefore, over the past few years, Florence Nightingale has been able to insist on double-digit increases in the payment rates from managed care plans.

Recently, however, Florence Nightingale is starting to lose some of its most profitable business to physicians on its medical staff who have opened outpatient surgery and radiology clinics. There are rumblings that some doctors might even open a competing hospital that refuses to take Medicaid or uninsured patients. And, there is talk among area physicians of starting their own ACO, in order to benefit from enhanced Medicare payments. Florence Nightingale is now considering what its next moves should be.

A. PROFESSIONAL AND FACILITY REGULATION

1. *Professional Licensure*

During the nineteenth century, snake oil salesmen and other quacks roamed the countryside preying on the gullible public with unfounded promises of miracle cures. To eliminate such practices, around the turn of the twentieth century every state began to license medical practitioners. The typical Medical Practice Act makes it a criminal offense to practice medicine without a physician's license and establishes the grounds for revocation or suspension of a license. The job of medical licensure and discipline is entrusted to a Board of Medical Examiners, which usually consists predominantly of physicians. Some alternative practitioners, such as osteopaths, chiropractors, and podiatrists, have likewise been successful in petitioning the legislature for recognition and protection through professional licensure and self-regulation. Thus, professional licensure serves a "fencing" function, one that keeps some persons from providing health care services altogether and that separates providers into different categories of professionals with at least somewhat distinct areas of permissible practice. And licensure also serves a policing function that investigates and disciplines allegedly errant providers.

■ STATE v. MILLER
542 N.W.2d 241 (Iowa 1995)

ANDREASEN, Justice.

Albert C. Miller appeals from his convictions for practicing medicine without a license. He urges . . . that the record contains insufficient evidence to support his convictions. We affirm the judgment of the district court.

Miller was charged by a trial information with seven counts of practicing medicine without a license. [This prosecution was brought after Mr. Miller repeatedly violated injunctions to cease treated patients as described below. Most of the offenses charged were Class D felonies.] . . .

Several persons testified at trial describing treatments they received from Miller in his home for various ailments. His usual method of treatment was to put a lock of the person's hair or a photograph of the person into a machine called a radionics device. After recording numerous readings from the device on a chart, he would treat the person by administering mild electric shocks from a "function generator," massaging the person's feet or neck, or placing large magnets next to the person. In addition, he often sold or recommended natural vitamins or nutrients to the people who visited him. Although Miller did not charge for the treatments, he consistently accepted donations of $10 for each treatment. He did not have any license to practice medicine, osteopathy, or surgery.

Dr. John Renner, M.D., Director of the Consumer Health Information Research Institute, testified as an expert witness for the state. He found the various treatments and vitamins given by Miller to his patients, while not necessarily harmful, were generally not medically useful. In his opinion the primary danger was not from the medicine itself, but from the fact it delayed appropriate, potentially beneficial, medical treatment.

On July 14, 1994, the jury returned verdicts finding Miller guilty on all seven counts. He was sentenced to a term of incarceration not to exceed five years on six counts. On the seventh count, he was sentenced to four months in the county jail. All the sentences were suspended and Miller was placed on probation for five years. . . .

We must uphold the jury's verdict unless the record lacks substantial evidence to support the charges. Substantial evidence is evidence which could convince a rational jury the defendant is guilty of the crimes charged beyond a reasonable doubt. . . .

Miller was charged with practicing medicine and osteopathic medicine in violation of Iowa Code §147.2. Two separate instructions were given to the jury defining the practice of medicine and osteopathic medicine. One instruction . . . provided the following definition:

> The practice of medicine and osteopathic medicine means holding one's self out as being able to diagnose, treat, or prescribe for any human disease, pain, injury, deformity, or physical or mental condition and who shall either offer or undertake, by any means or methods, to diagnose, treat, or prescribe for any human disease, pain, injury, deformity or physical or mental condition.

The other instruction provided that the following "persons shall be deemed to be engaged in the practice of medicine and osteopathic medicine":

> 1. Persons who publicly profess to be physicians or who publicly profess to assume the duties incident to the practice of medicine and osteopathic medicine.
> 2. Persons who prescribe, or prescribe and furnish medicine for human ailments. . . .

Miller argues that he did not publicly profess to be a physician or publicly profess to assume the duties incident to the practice of medicine and osteopathic medicine. He emphasizes that he never advertised nor described himself as a doctor; he would sometimes recommend that his customers consult a licensed physician or chiropractor; and he only met people in his home, not in an office.

We conclude there is sufficient evidence to conclude that Miller publicly professed to assume the duties incident to the practice of medicine and osteopathic medicine. We have defined the "duties incident to the practice of medicine" to include diagnosing patients' ailments and prescribing the proper treatment.

Witnesses testified that they were treated by Miller for various ailments including arthritis, rash, infection, headaches, constipation, and neck, shoulder, and back pain. Although he may not have referred to himself as a doctor, he led his customers to believe that he could diagnose and treat their ailments. Even though Miller did not formally advertise his treatments, he gained a large local customer base by means of referral from one customer to another. The fact that Miller would sometimes recommend that his customers consult a licensed physician or chiropractor does not detract from the fact that he would diagnose and treat their physical conditions, at least up to a certain point.

We also conclude there was sufficient evidence that Miller routinely prescribed and furnished medicine. Miller argues that he sold or recommended only natural vitamins or nutrients. His defense, through the testimony of a witness, was that vitamins and nutrients were not medicines, but food.

We have broadly construed the statutory words "prescribe and furnish medicine" to include administering any substance or remedy in the treatment of an ailment or disease. The fact that a substance may also have value as a food "will not deprive of its character as a medicine if it be administered and employed for that purpose." State v. Bresee, 114 N.W. 45, 47 (1907).

> It is evident [the defendant] was catering to patronage of the sick who were asking relief from their ills, and, if [he] listened to their statements, assured them of [his] ability to help them out, and supplied them with [his] alleged appropriate remedies giving instructions for their application or use, this would seem to come . . . within the ordinary and usual signification attached to the words "prescribing" or "prescribing and furnishing medicines," as they are commonly used and understood. Id.

We believe Miller's actions of selling or recommending natural vitamins to his customers constitutes furnishing a substance or remedy for treating their ailments.

We conclude there is sufficient evidence to convince a rational jury beyond a reasonable doubt that Miller was guilty of practicing medicine and osteopathic medicine without a license.

[On an ironic note, the court also rejected Miller's appellate lawyers' claim that the district court had erred in permitting him to represent himself at trial. Miller had initially sought to appoint "unlicensed" counsel to represent him at trial and chose to represent himself when his request was rejected. The court held that Miller knowingly and intelligently waived his right to licensed representation.]

■ CHARACTER, COMPETENCE, AND THE PRINCIPLES OF MEDICAL DISCIPLINE

Nadia N. Sawicki

13 J. Health Care L. & Pol'y 285 (2010)

As the state agencies responsible for the licensure and discipline of physicians, medical boards serve as the gatekeepers of the medical profession. However, critics frequently question whether boards have, in fact, been living up to their potential in this regard, particularly in the context of professional discipline. Since the 1970s, state medical boards have faced criticism from a variety of sources for inappropriately screening applicants for medical licensure,[3] failing to discipline dangerous physicians, and generally being lax in their oversight duties at the expense of a vulnerable public.[7] . . .

[A] common explanation for medical boards' lax approach to professional discipline is that the boards are "captured" by professional interests or otherwise lack meaningful public oversight. Indeed, one of the most prominent criticisms of the medical profession in the 20th century has been that it is self-protective, monopolistic, and more attuned to the economic security of its members than to the welfare of the public at large. . . .

While there is likely some element of truth to the argument that medical boards discipline physicians too infrequently, this Article identifies a more substantive problem—namely, that when boards do choose to exercise their disciplinary discretion, they often focus on character-related misconduct, including criminal misconduct, that bears only a tangential relation to clinical quality and patient care. . . . In recent years, medical providers have been disciplined on grounds as varied as tax fraud, failure to facilitate review of child support obligations, soliciting sex in a public restroom, possession of marijuana for personal use, and reckless driving involving alcohol, as well as other conduct allegedly bringing the medical profession into disrepute. While these are not commendable activities by any stretch of the imagination, this Article questions whether, in light of the traditional goals of professional discipline, sanctioning physicians on these grounds (as opposed to grounds more clearly linked to clinical practice) is the most effective or efficient use of medical boards' resources. . . .

A. Medical Board Authority: History and Practice

Among the unenumerated powers reserved to each state under the Tenth Amendment is the power to protect the health, safety, and welfare of its citizenry, commonly known as the police power. . . . As explained by the Supreme Court in *Dent v. West Virginia*, 129 U.S. 114 (1889), . . . [i]t is pursuant to their police powers that states are authorized to regulate law, medicine, and other professions, which they typically do by delegating authority to professional licensing boards.

. . . The first state medical boards were created in the late 1800s when private medical associations pushed state legislators to adopt laws regulating the practice of medicine. These efforts were driven by physicians who, fearful of incursions on

3. *See* Marc T. Law & Zeynep K. Hansen, *Medical Licensing Board Characteristics and Physician Discipline: An Empirical Analysis*, 35 J. Health Pol. Pol'y & L. 63, 66 (2010).

7. Economists, in particular, have long made similar arguments, questioning the value of licensure and self-regulation in highly insulated and self-protective professions, like medicine. These authors and others suggest that medical quality and patient safety could be better safeguarded through market-based solutions that close the information gap between physicians and consumers. *See generally* Walter Gellhorn, *The Abuse of Occupational Licensing*, 44 U. Chi. L. Rev. 6, 16-18, 22, 25 (1976) (arguing that occupational licensing impedes access to needed services and serves only to protect those who have already been licensed, rather than protect the public from incompetent professionals); Anthony Ogus, *Rethinking Self-Regulation*, 15 Oxford J. Legal Stud. 97 (1995) (offering general criticism of the self-regulatory model). . . .

their territory by "irregulars" and "quacks," were convinced that well-drafted legislation—far from being self-defeating—could serve an important role in protecting their professional interests. Though some historians suggest that professional self-protection, rather than concern for patient safety, was the driving force behind these lobbying efforts, the medical practice acts that resulted were, as a matter of law, clearly adopted pursuant to the legislative authority to protect public health and safety.

At a minimum, modern medical practice acts define the practice of medicine, establish the requirements for medical licensure, and set forth procedures for disciplinary action against licensees. . . . Modern medical boards generally include some public members but are dominated by physicians appointed by the governor.

American licensure laws are exclusive in that they grant qualified individuals the right to engage in the lawful practice of medicine and prohibit the practice of medicine by unlicensed persons. The requirements for obtaining a medical license are relatively consistent from state to state—generally, the applicant must be a graduate of an approved medical school, have completed at least one year of an approved graduate medical education program (residency or fellowship), and have passed the United States Medical Licensing Examination (USMLE). Beyond imposing educational and training requirements, many medical practice acts also require that applicants for medical licensure demonstrate good moral character. . . .

Medical boards' ongoing duties include periodic re-registration of licensees, which is typically contingent on completion of specified hours of Continuing Medical Education training. However, medical boards rarely impose additional requirements intended to ensure the quality of care, such as mandatory recertification or random practice audits, upon physicians who have already received their licenses. As a result, the most important of state medical boards' oversight responsibilities with respect to medical quality is the discipline of professional licensees.

The medical disciplinary process is generally reactive, rather than proactive. It begins when a member of the public files a complaint, or, in the case of discipline on the grounds of criminal or civil liability, when a court or law enforcement agency files a report with the medical board. The board screens, and, if appropriate, investigates the complaint; if the board finds the complaint is valid, it may exercise its discretion to pursue disciplinary action against the physician, which can range from oral or written reprimand to license revocation or suspension.

Although the substantive grounds for professional discipline vary from state to state, most state medical practice acts authorize discipline for gross incompetence, physical or mental impairment, alcohol or drug abuse, practicing without a license or aiding the unlicensed practice of medicine, as well as reciprocal discipline against those providers who have been subject to disciplinary action in other states. Moreover, most states authorize discipline under a broad category of "unprofessional conduct," which may include violations of codes of medical ethics, conduct that brings the medical profession into disrepute, or other unspecified forms of "dishonorable conduct," including criminal acts (typically felonies or crimes of "moral turpitude"). . . .

In foundational cases such as *Dent* [*v. West Virginia*] and *Schware v. Board of Bar Examiners*, 353 U.S. 232 (1957), the Supreme Court held that the criteria for licensure and discipline may not be vague, arbitrary, or unattainable, and "must have a rational connection with the applicant's fitness or capacity to practice" his profession. However, because no fundamental rights are implicated in the loss of a professional license, courts review boards' disciplinary determinations under a highly deferential standard. . . .

[T]he medical board's disciplinary authority is aimed at protecting medical consumers from the harms they may incur at the hands of incompetent or dishonest physicians. This is reflected in the sanctions that may be imposed on physicians, which range from alerting the medical board and community of a potential for harm (via a public letter of reprimand) to withdrawing the physician's right to practice (delicensure). Unlike criminal law, which is aimed at punishing wrongdoers, or civil law, which is aimed at victim compensation, professional discipline seeks to protect public welfare by incapacitating or rehabilitating dangerous physicians. . . .

A final, and related, insight . . . is [that] professional licensure and discipline standards are established to ensure a minimal level of competence, rather than to identify aspirational standards of professional conduct. . . . The appropriate view of professional licensure, then, is as a floor beyond which practitioners may not drop, rather than an ideal towards which they must strive. In other words, though we view a medical license as evidence that a physician possesses the basic tools necessary to practice medicine safely, the license does not ensure that he will actually use these tools correctly going forward. Moreover, a medical license does not distinguish the merely competent provider from the excellent provider—that distinction takes place at the marketplace level. . . .

C. Quantitative and Qualitative Concerns

Despite the fact that the theoretical underpinnings of the American medical disciplinary regime are sound, the system as it is being practically implemented boasts few supporters. . . . The most common criticism that has been traditionally levied against medical boards is that they simply do not discipline physicians often enough to have a substantial impact on patient safety and public health. . . . [E]stimates suggest that less than one-half of one percent of licensed physicians face serious discipline annually. . . .

While there may be some truth to [these] claims, . . . [t]he rate at which medical professionals face serious discipline annually is comparable to the rate of serious professional discipline in other professions, including law. It is also comparable to the rate of felony convictions among the American public. While professional boards and prosecutors certainly could be doing more to pursue those who violate professional standards or break the law, given the parallels between the rates of professional discipline and criminal conviction, the degree of invective levied at medical boards by public advocates seems disproportionate. . . .

Arguably more important in determining whether medical boards are likely to be successful in protecting the public is the qualitative issue of which physicians are being disciplined and on what substantive grounds. That is, if medical boards can pursue only 3,000 serious disciplinary actions against physicians each year, boards . . . ought to ask which is likely to have the greatest impact on patient protection, which [complaints have] the closest link to fitness to practice, and where each [case] falls on the spectrum from minimal competencies to aspirational standards. . . .

[M]edical boards rarely take disciplinary action on the basis of incompetent medical practice or poor quality of care. . . . [F]ewer than 15% of professional disciplinary actions taken between 1999 and 2008 appear to have been taken on grounds clearly related to clinical competence. . . . Although the majority of disciplinary actions are taken on unspecified grounds, the ones that are categorized tend to fall within three broad categories—drug or alcohol abuse, criminal convictions, and unspecified unprofessional conduct. . . . [B]etween 1994 and 2002, unspecified "unprofessional conduct" was the single most frequently cited ground for discipline, appearing in approximately a third of all cases. . . .

Often, when boards take serious disciplinary action on the basis of unprofessional behavior or criminal conduct, the sanctioned physicians challenge their suspensions on due process grounds, arguing that their behavior, while possibly indicative of poor personal judgment or character, is simply not relevant to their fitness to practice medicine. . . .

[D]. An Imperfect Fit with the Principles of Professional Discipline

The fact that physicians are frequently sanctioned for engaging in character-related or criminal misconduct is troubling in light of the [principle] . . . that boards ought to be primarily concerned with enforcing minimal standards of fitness to practice in an effort to protect consumers of medical services. It hardly seems obvious why . . . boards should be using their scarce resources to discipline physicians for character-related misconduct occurring outside the clinical sphere, particularly where such behavior is already subject to criminal or civil sanctions. . . . [M]ost state court decisions in disciplinary matters simply conclude that moral character broadly defined is a necessary component of fitness to practice without providing adequate support for this assertion. . . . Even Hawker v. New York, 170 U.S. 189 (1898), the case that speaks most directly to the issue of character-related criteria for professional licensure and discipline, offers little guidance. In *Hawker*, the Supreme Court upheld a New York state law prohibiting the practice of medicine by those who have been convicted of a felony, but provided little support for its conclusion that personal "[c]haracter is as important a qualification as knowledge" for professional practice and is therefore subject to discipline. In two brief sentences, the Court offered the following meager explanation of its conclusion: "The physician is one whose relations to life and health are of the most intimate character. It is fitting, not merely that he should possess a knowledge of diseases and their remedies, but also that he should be one who may safely be trusted to apply those remedies." . . .

Trust theorists posit that misconduct outside the clinical sphere is a legitimate subject for professional discipline if it is likely to cause public distrust of the medical profession. . . . [But] [p]atients may place faith in their physicians for any number of reasons—their religion, their affiliation with a particular hospital, their personal appearance—and it is by no means clear why a state should facilitate patient decisions that are based on non-clinical, irrelevant, or potentially discriminatory factors that have no clear link with fitness or competency to practice medicine. . . .

Much like criminal law, professional discipline serves an important signaling function for the medical community. It is the rare doctor who, in an effort to understand the boundaries of permissible professional behavior, turns first to the local law library to brush up on recent state legislation and case law. More likely, he receives periodic disciplinary updates from his state medical board, reads about cases of professional discipline in the media, and hears about the experiences of colleagues and friends. Given that some of the most public and visible cases of professional discipline deal with cases of misconduct that bear little connection to the practice of medicine, I argue that modern medical boards that discipline on character-related grounds may not be sending the most constructive signals to physicians trying to conform their behavior to the law. . . .

Notes: Professional Licensure

1. *Criminal Prosecution.* Note that the unlicensed practice of medicine is a criminal offense; persons convicted of the offense can be fined and imprisoned. Suppose that the patient of an unlicensed provider is injured in the course of receiving care. Is the provider liable in tort under a negligence per se theory? Jurisdictions may also criminalize "assisting" in the unlicensed practice of medicine. This criminal offense can have civil law implications as well. Physicians and other licensed health care professionals are subject to professional disciplinary action, such as license revocation or suspension, for assisting in the unlicensed practice of medicine. Annot., 99 A.L.R.2d 654 (1965).

2. *Physician Supply.* Most states require M.D.s to graduate from an AMA-accredited medical school (or, for foreign medical graduates, certification by the Educational Commission for Foreign Medical Graduates (ECFMG) and an internship in an AMA-approved residency program). As a result, medical licensure essentially cedes to the medical profession control of how many doctors can enter practice, since the AMA can control the size of medical school classes through the accreditation process and the ECFMG can control the certification process. Mark A. Peterson, From Trust to Political Power: Interest Groups, Public Choice, and Health Care, 26 J. Health Pol. Pol'y & L. 1145 (2001).

Allowing the medical profession to control entry into its own market creates the anticompetitive risk that the AMA will act out of economic self-interest to maintain artificial shortages. Barriers to entry into service professions tend automatically to drive up prices by creating a supply shortage. Reuben Kessel, Price Discrimination in Medicine, 1 J.L. & Econ. 20 (1959); Reuben Kessel, The A.M.A. and the Supply of Physicians, 35 Law & Contemp. Probs. 267 (Spring 1970).

Concern about physician shortages seems misplaced these days, when we are much more apt to hear about the "glut" of physicians, particularly of specialists. The ratio of physicians to citizens in the United States has been steadily increasing, rising from 146 physicians/100,000 in 1950 to 233/100,000 in 1990, to 277/100,000 in the year 2008. Some experts argue that the ideal ratio lies somewhere between 160 and 200 physicians per 100,000. More important than the total number, however, is their distribution. Policymakers are concerned that there are too few primary care physicians, who are less expensive, and too many specialists, who drive up the cost of care by providing services that could be more cheaply provided by family practitioners or other generalists. Also, the geographic distribution of physicians clearly remains problematic. Many rural areas have found it difficult to attract physicians. A similar problem can be found in some urban centers, where physicians have not been willing to establish practices that serve low-income populations. Tracy Hampton, US Medical School Enrollment Rising, But Residency Programs Too Limited, 299 JAMA 284 (2008).

3. *Defining Medical Practice.* The legislative definition of the "practice of medicine" typically is quite broad, as can be seen by examining the jury instructions in *Miller.* The breadth of the definition is important because persons who engage in the specified activities without an appropriate license are subject to criminal penalties. How far can the definition of medical practice be stretched?

The various exotic and peripheral ministrations successfully attacked under the medical licensure statutes range from the sublime to the ridiculous. Magnetism, mental suggestion, faith healing, color wave therapy, reflexology, massage, hypnotism, tattooing, and electrical hair removal all have been held to constitute the practice of medicine. See, e.g., State v. White, 560 S.E.2d 420 (S.C. 2002) (state statute restricting tattooing to licensed physicians for cosmetic or reconstructive purposes does not violate free speech and is valid exercise of police power.) Even the commonplace practice of offering nutritional advice might subject the advisor to criminal prosecution, as in *Miller.* Courts have found that some activities, such as ear piercing and cosmetic hair removal, lie outside the sometimes seemingly unlimited scope of medical practice.

The very breadth of the typical medical practice act definition suggests a trap for the unwary, who might unexpectedly confront criminal liability for engaging in seemingly innocuous activities. Do the instructions given to the jury in *Miller* provide appropriate guidance for their decision? Defendants have challenged these statutes on vagueness grounds; however, courts have been understandably reluctant to agree and have upheld the statutes by artfully using a number of different techniques of statutory construction. See People v. Rogers, 641 N.W.2d 595 (2001) (statutory definition not facially overbroad or unconstitutionally vague).

4. *Licensure vs. Credentialing.* Thinking about both the broader purposes and criticisms of licensing health care professionals, what benefits does professional licensure have over a system of accreditation or certification? Under the latter, patients would be given clear notice about who does and does not have recognized credentials, but they would be permitted to choose whether to seek care from an unaccredited or uncertified person. Health care payers, such as insurance companies, might be empowered to reject payment claims made by those lacking certification. Licensure schemes are preferred where there is a risk that consumers might not be able to exercise reasoned judgment about the qualifications of their health care providers, perhaps because of lack of knowledge, the decisionmaking deficits created by disease, or financial distress. See Timothy Stoltzfus Jost, Oversight of the Quality of Medical Care: Regulation, Management, or the Market, 37 Ariz. L. Rev. 825 (1995); Randall G. Holcombe, Eliminating Scope of Practice and Licensing Laws to Improve Health Care, 31 J.L. Med. & Ethics 236 (2003).

5. *A Right to Receive Treatment?* Do patients have any constitutionally protected interest in being able to choose to receive health care services of one type or another, from one type of provider or another? The issue was not raised in *Miller* but has been litigated elsewhere. Most courts have found that there is no fundamental right of access to treatment by unlicensed providers. See, e.g., Mitchell v. Clayton, 995 F.2d 772, 775-776 (7th Cir. 1993). The Supreme Court's ruling in the physician-assisted suicide cases suggests that the Constitution does not give patients a protected interest in obtaining particular types of medical treatment. What if, however, a case could be made that the particular treatment is the only one that might work?

6. *A Right to Provide Care?* Medical practitioners have been equally unsuccessful in their attempts to claim a constitutional right to provide care. Courts uniformly have upheld state licensing regulations so long as they are rationally related to serving some legitimate state interest. In Williamson v. Lee Optical of Oklahoma, Inc., the plaintiff challenged the constitutional validity of Oklahoma's licensure provisions that made it "unlawful for any person not a licensed optometrist or ophthalmologist to fit lenses to a face or to duplicate or replace into frames lenses or other optical appliances, except upon written prescriptive authority of an Oklahoma licensed ophthalmologist or optometrist." 348 U.S. 483, 485 (1955). The district court had held a portion of the statute unconstitutional, finding in part that it unreasonably prohibited opticians from making duplicate lenses for persons whose glasses were lost or broken. The Court upheld the statute, using classic rational basis review:

> The Oklahoma law may exact a needless, wasteful requirement in many cases. But it is for the legislature, not the courts, to balance the advantages and disadvantages of the new requirement. It appears that in many cases the optician can easily supply the new frames or new lenses without reference to the old written prescription. . . . But the law need not be in every respect logically consistent with its aims to be constitutional. It is enough that there is an evil at hand for correction, and that it might be thought that the particular legislative measure was a rational way to correct it.
>
> The day is gone when this Court uses the due process clause of the Fourteenth Amendment to strike down state laws, regulatory of business and industrial conditions, because they may be unwise, improvident, or out of harmony with a particular school of thought. . . . Id. at 487-488.

The Court also rejected an equal protection claim, again stating the applicable rational basis test in classic terms:

> The problem of legislative classification is a perennial one, admitting of no doctrinaire definition. Evils in the same field may be of different dimensions and proportions, requiring different remedies. Or so the legislature may think. Or the reform may take one step at a time, addressing itself to the phase of the problem which seems most acute to the legislative mind. The legislature may select one phase of one field and apply a remedy there, neglecting the others. The prohibition of the equal protection clause goes no further than the invidious discrimination. We cannot say that that point has been reached here. . . . Id. at 489.

The rational basis approach adopted in *Lee* has been applied in nearly every case since. See, e.g., National Ass'n for the Advancement of Psychoanalysis v. California Board of Psychology, 228 F.3d 1043 (9th Cir. 2000) (upholding state's mental health licensing scheme under rational basis test); Sherman v. Cryns, 786 N.E.2d 139 (Ill. 2003) (state midwifery licensing statute is rationally related to a legitimate state interest).

States often provide an exception to the normal rules governing the practice of medicine for religious practitioners. See, e.g., Cal. Bus. & Prof. Code §2063 ("Nothing in this chapter shall be construed . . . [to] regulate, prohibit, or apply to any kind of treatment by prayer, nor interfere in any way with the practice of religion."). Is this religious exemption required by the First Amendment? Does an exemption for religious practitioners violate the First Amendment's prohibition of state establishment of religion? Does the exemption for religious practitioners undercut the rationale for general licensure requirements—if the public health is at risk from "unscientific" practitioners, then shouldn't the public be protected from religious practitioners? Most academic attention focuses on the liability of parents for child neglect for the use of religious or spiritual healers. See, e.g., Jessie Hill, Whose Body, Whose Soul?, 32 Cardozo L. Rev. 1857 (2011).

7. *Alternative Healing Techniques.* Why did Miller's patients seek his assistance? Why are alternative practitioners so popular? First, of course, critics of the medical system note that the appeal can be directly related to the "ills" of traditional medicine. Medical practice is expensive, impersonal, and bureaucratic. Second, alternative therapies apparently work, at least some therapies for some people. The National Institutes of Health (NIH) created the Center for Complementary and Alternative Medicine (CAM) in 1992 to fund research designed to test the efficacy of a wide range of alternative therapies. Even if the alternative therapy is scientifically worthless, a significant percentage of people given a placebo will experience relief from their symptoms and even an improvement in their condition. Given all of this, perhaps licensure requirements keep people from seeking out potentially effective care. Does that mean alternative healers should be exempted from licensure, or should instead petition legislatures for their own licensure schemes? See John Lunstroth, Voluntary Self-Regulation of Complementary and Alternative Medicine Practitioners, 70 Alb. L. Rev. 209 (2006).

8. *Interprofessional Disputes.* Rules prohibiting the unlicensed practice of various professions also serve to establish boundaries between particular classes of health care providers. Persons providing health care services pursuant to statutory authorization are not guilty of the unlicensed practice of medicine. Thus a nurse is not engaging in the unlicensed practice of medicine when she or he makes a nursing diagnosis or provides nursing services to a patient.

Still, interprofessional turf battles are waged, particularly where nonphysician health care providers have attempted to expand their scope of practice. See, e.g., Brown v. Belinfante, 557 S.E.2d 399 (Ga. Ct. App. 2001) (oral surgeon violates dental practice act by performing facelift); Connecticut State Medical Society v. Connecticut Board of Examiners of Podiatry, 546 A.2d 830 (Conn. 1988) (litigation to determine whether podiatrists can treat ankles).

9. *Physician Extenders.* Physicians often delegate functions to other types of health care practitioners, such as nurses or physician assistants. The educational training of these other health care providers can vary widely. Traditionally, nurses have performed a wide range of functions within the health care system, sometimes under the control of physicians and sometimes exercising independent, nursing judgment. Physician assistants, in contrast, have traditionally been characterized as "dependent" practitioners, who perform only tasks delegated by physicians. Many states now certify or otherwise regulate physician assistants to ensure that they are appropriately supervised.

Can physicians delegate tasks to assistants who are not independently licensed, without assisting in the unlicensed practice of medicine? Some legislatures have been extremely active in attempting to mark the bounds of appropriate delegation. Others provide physicians broad discretion to delegate tasks however they want as long as they do so consistent with proper medical standards, they supervise and retain responsibility, and the person doing the tasks does not purport to be practicing medicine. See, e.g., Tex. Occ. Code Ann. §157.001.

Nurse practitioners and physician assistants play a particularly important role in providing medical services in rural and central urban areas, where physicians are rare. Residents of these areas will often not have access to any health care unless they can be treated by "physician extenders." As a consequence, many states permit physicians to delegate more tasks, such as signing certain prescriptions, in "medically underserved" areas of the state.

Physician assistants or nurses performing delegated tasks generally do so pursuant to physician's orders, standing medical orders, standing delegation orders, or written protocols. Courts, administrative agencies, and legislatures have struggled to define when a physician's degree of supervision is inadequate. Some jurisdictions have at least partially defined the degree of required supervision by establishing periodic physician reviews (e.g., daily status reports, once a week on-site direction, etc.) and limiting the number of persons whom the physician can supervise. Should surgeons be permitted to delegate some tasks during surgery to persons not licensed to practice medicine?

10. *Telemedicine and "Mobile" Medicine.* Health care provider licensure is a matter of state law. How should this state-level system respond to the growing nationalization of health care practice, in which physicians in other states may use telemedicine or Internet technology to diagnose and recommend treatment for patients from afar? Many states have amended their licensing statutes or regulations in recent years to respond to this issue, some by tightening rules that prohibit out-of-state physicians from providing regular and ongoing direct care to patients, and others by specifying under which conditions this may be done. See note 13 below.

A related, but potentially even more revolutionary, development is "mobile medicine" in the form of small devices and apps that monitor health, facilitate self-help measures, and connect people with care advisors potentially anywhere in the world, or perhaps only through artificial intelligence. At the federal level, the FDA has indicated its intent to assert its jurisdiction over medical devices. Nathan Cortez, The Mobile Health Revolution?, 47 U.C. Davis L. Rev. 1173 (2014). At the state level, there are potential issues, not yet widely asserted, regarding whether these apps constitute diagnosis or prescription that amounts to the practice of medicine. Fazal Khan, The "Uberization" of Healthcare: The Forthcoming Legal Storm over Mobile Health Technology's Impact on the Medical Profession, 26 Health Matrix 123 (2016).

11. *Grounds for Discipline.* Despite Prof. Sawicki's criticisms, medical boards sometimes do discipline physicians who have delivered substandard, incompetent, or negligent care. When they do, boards are generally not required to prove that any patients were actually harmed. See Annot., 93 A.L.R.2d 1398 (1964); Annot., 28 A.L.R.3d 487 (1969); Annot., 22 A.L.R.4th 668 (1983).

As Prof. Sawicki notes, however, professional discipline often targets purely economic misbehavior. For instance, licensure codes often attempt to restrict the range of permissible advertising or solicitation that practitioners may use. One rationale for these restrictions is that they prevent consumer fraud and abuse. Another is that they insulate the profession from the demands of competition, which might result in price wars and lost income. States generally may not restrict truthful, non-misleading professional advertisements without violating the First

Amendment's protection of free speech. See, e.g., Virginia State Board of Pharmacy v. Virginia Citizens Consumer Council, Inc., 425 U.S. 748, 762 (1976) (striking down ban on price advertising by pharmacists); Culpepper v. Arkansas Board of Chiropractic Examiners, 36 S.W.3d 335 (Ark. 2001) (ban on direct contact by chiropractors with potential patients is unconstitutional).

What of professional disciplinary rules that forbid certain business arrangements, such as assisting in the corporate practice of medicine? See section B.3. Viewed in one light, these provisions indirectly protect patients by reducing the threat that economic motivations will override patient interests in the provider-patient relationship. Once again, however, it could readily be argued that these prohibitions serve to protect professional autonomy, regardless of the impact on patients.

12. *An Administrative Law Primer.* Complaints against medical practitioners are adjudicated initially by "hearing officers," who determine if a violation has occurred and recommend an appropriate sanction. The agency typically has an internal appeals process with the final agency determination rendered by the relevant board itself. The agency's procedures are likely to be established within its enabling legislation and within the state's Administrative Procedure Act. Alleged flaws in this process are often the main focus of any court challenges, giving rise to constitutional and statutory issues that are studied at length in Administrative Law. Some of these issues are also addressed briefly in section C.2 below, dealing with disciplinary actions by hospitals against physicians. For additional discussion, see materials on the Web site for this book, www.health-law.org, and note 13.

13. *Additional Readings.* On the *history of medical licensure,* see Lewis Grossman, The Origins of American Health Libertarianism, Yale J. Health Pol'y L. & Ethics 76 (2013).

On **scope of practice issues** (notes 8 and 9), see Barbara J. Safriet, Closing the Gap Between *Can* and *May* in Health-Care Providers' Scopes of Practice: A Primer for Policymakers, 19 Yale J. on Reg. 301 (2002); Lori B. Andrews, The Shadow Health Care System: Regulation of Alternative Health Care Providers, 32 Hous. L. Rev. 1273, 1275 (1996); Laura Hermer & William Winslade, Access to Health Care in Texas: A Patient-Centered Perspective, 35 Tex. Tech L. Rev. 33 (2004); Joy L. Delman, The Use and Misuse of Physician Extenders, 24 J. Leg. Med. 249 (2003); Symposium, 32(11) Health Aff. 1870 (2013).

On **telemedicine and mobile apps/devices** (note 10), see Roundtable on Legal Impediments to Telemedicine, 14 J. Health Care L. & Pol'y 1-117 (2011); Amar Gupta & Deth Sao, The Constitutionality of Current Legal Barriers to Telemedicine in the United States, 21 Health Matrix 385 (2011); John Blum, Internet Medicine and the Evolving Legal Status of the Physician-Patient Relationship, 24 J. Leg. Med. 413 (2003); Symposium, 33(30) Health Aff. 194 (2014); Symposium, 14 J. Health Care L. & Pol'y 1 (2011); Symposium, 46 St. Louis U. L.J. 1-110 (2002).

On **First Amendment issues** (note 11), see Jess Alderman, Words to Live By: Public Health, the First Amendment, and Government Speech, 57 Buff. L. Rev. 161 (2009); Paula Berg, Toward a First Amendment Theory of Doctor-Patient Discourse and the Right to Receive Unbiased Medical Advice, 74 B.U. L. Rev. 201, 241-243 (1994).

On **administrative and due process issues** (note 12), see Eleanor Kinney, Administrative Law of Health Care in a Nutshell (2016); J. Bruce Bennet, The Rights of Licensed Professionals to Notice and Hearing in Agency Enforcement Actions, 7 Tex. Tech Admin. L.J. 205 (2006); Annot., 10 A.L.R.5th 1 (1993); Annot., 74 A.L.R.4th 969 (1989).

Problem: Professional Licensure

Dr. Alicia Chuanski lives in an urban area in a state that has many underpopulated, rural areas. She has established a thriving family practice in the city. She is interested in expanding her practice into a rural area about 90 miles from her office. She hopes to set up a satellite office, staffed with a nurse and a physician assistant. Dr. Chuanski plans to supervise the satellite office in several ways:

1. She will establish detailed protocols for the nurse and physician assistant. They both will meet with patients, take patient histories and record patient symptoms, and establish baseline heart rates, blood pressures, and temperatures. The protocols will establish diagnostic or other procedures that should be followed for patients with particular symptoms. The protocols also will establish "opt-out" points: symptoms or complaints that indicate the need to refer patients to the nearest emergency room, which is about 20 miles away. Dr. Chuanski will leave a presigned prescription pad at the satellite for the use of the nurse and physician assistant (pursuant to the protocols); prescriptions will be reviewed on a daily basis.
2. Dr. Chuanski will attempt to establish a backup relationship with a nearby physician, perhaps one who maintains an office near the hospital mentioned above.
3. Dr. Chuanski will be available for phone consultations from 12 to 1:00 P.M. and from 4:30 to 5:30 P.M. every work day. Summary reports on the day's patients will be faxed to her each evening.
4. As the price of technology decreases, Dr. Chuanski will consider establishing a video link to the satellite so that she could "see" and "examine" patients from her office in the city.
5. Dr. Chuanski will visit the satellite once every ten days or so.

Evaluate Dr. Chuanski's plans. Will the nurse and/or physician assistant be engaged in the unlicensed practice of medicine? Is Dr. Chuanski assisting in the unlicensed practice of medicine? Is Dr. Chuanski engaged in unprofessional conduct that could lead to disciplinary action? Where would you look to answer these questions? What additional information might you need to answer the questions? Can you suggest any improvements to Dr. Chuanski's plans?

2. *Facility Licensure and Accreditation*

PATIENT POWER: SOLVING AMERICA'S HEALTH CARE CRISIS
John C. Goodman & Gerald L. Musgrave
(1992)

In terms of rules, restrictions, and bureaucratic requirements, the health care sector is one of the most regulated industries in our economy. Consider Scripps Memorial Hospital, a medium-sized acute care facility in San Diego, California. As [the following] table shows, Scripps must answer to 39 governmental bodies and 7 nongovernmental bodies, and must periodically file 65 different reports, about one report for every four beds.[1] . . . Regulatory requirements intrude in a highly visible way on the activities of the medical staff and affect virtually every aspect of medical practice. Another California hospital, Sequoia Hospital in the San Francisco Bay area, has attempted to calculate how many additional employees are required as a result of government regulations. Sequoia's [administrative and nursing] staff increased by 163.6 percent [from 450 to 736] between 1966 and 1990, even though the average number of patients per day (250) did not change. . . .

Regulatory Agencies Over Scripps Memorial Hospital, 1989

Agency
Government
Occupational Safety and Health Administration
San Diego County Health Department
State Board of Equalization (hazardous waste tax return)
Internal Revenue Service
Franchise Tax Board
Secretary of State
Medicare
State Board of Equalization (sales tax return)
California Hospital Facilities Commission
State Board of Health
Environmental Protection Agency
Department of Transportation
Department of Health Services
Air Resources Board
Office of Emergency Services
Health and Welfare Agency
Air Pollution Control/Air Quality Management District
Regional Water Quality Control Board
Local Sewering Agencies
San Diego Department of Health Services

1. The hospital association in New York once claimed that its members were subject to 174 regulatory bodies, and another survey found that hospitals have to submit themselves to over 50 different inspections and reports each year, often requiring into similar matters. B. Gray, The Profit Motive and Patient Care 112 (1991). [The American Hospital Association claims that, for every hour of patient care, hospitals engage in 30 to 60 minutes of paperwork. Patients or Paperwork? The Regulatory Burden Facing America's Hospitals (2001). See also John Braithwaite & Valerie Braithwaite, The Politics of Legalism: Rules Versus Standards in Nursing-Home Regulation, 4 Soc. Leg. Stud. 307, 320 (1995) ("the people who inspect U.S. nursing homes are checking compliance with over a thousand regulations"); Christopher J. Conover, Health Care Regulation: A $169 Billion Hidden Tax (Cato Institute, 2004) (finding that health care regulation costs twice as much as its benefits are worth). See generally Robert I. Field, Health Care Regulation in America: Complexity, Confrontation and Compromise (2007).]

Agency
State Licensing Board
Board of Registered Nursing
Licensed Vocational Nursing Board
U.S. Department of Labor
Industrial Welfare Commission
Fair Employment Practice Commission
National Labor Relations Board
Immigration and Naturalization Service
Employment Development Department
Social Security Administration
Employee Retirement Income Security Requirements
State Board of Pharmacy
Drug Enforcement Agency
Food and Drug Administration
Bureau of Narcotic Enforcement
California Department of Health, Radiologic Health Branch
Nongovernment
Joint Commission on Accreditation of Hospitals
American Hospital Association
American Conference of Governmental Industrial Hygienists
California Medical Association
Radiation Safety Organization (Syncor, Inc.)
National Association of Social Workers
American College of Surgeons
San Diego and Imperial Counties Organization for Cancer Control

Note: Facility Licensing, Accreditation, and Certification

Three terms are commonly used to describe the multilevel process for inspecting and approving health care facilities by state, federal, and private agencies: licensure, accreditation, and certification. Each of these terms has a specific meaning, and each represents a different level of significance for operation within the health care community. The requirements for licensure, accreditation, and certification exert a strong regulatory force on the organization and operation of health care facilities.

Licensure is the mandatory governmental process whereby a health care facility receives the right to operate. In the United States, licensure operates on a state-by-state basis. A health care facility (as that term is defined in the statute) cannot open its doors lawfully without a license from the appropriate state agency. Licensed health care facilities include hospitals, nursing homes, ambulatory surgery centers, freestanding emergency centers, pharmacies, and, in some instances, diagnostic centers. State licensing schemes also exist for various financing systems, both for ordinary health insurance and for innovative delivery systems such as HMOs, PPOs, and utilization review systems.

Accreditation is a private voluntary approval process through which a health care organization is evaluated and can receive a designation of competence and quality.

Most private accreditation for health care organizations today is done under the auspices of the Joint Commission for the Accreditation of Healthcare Organizations (called "JCAHO," "Jayco," or "Joint Commission," formerly known as the Joint Commission for the Accreditation of Hospitals). The Joint Commission is governed by the major trade associations, primarily the American Medical Association, the American Hospital Association, the American College of Surgeons, and the American College of Physicians, and its accreditation programs serve all sorts of health care organizations, although its primary participants are hospitals. Although the Joint Commission is private and purely voluntary, historically it has wielded enormous power and influence because virtually no hospital of respectable size risks the business consequences of jeopardizing its accreditation status. However, the Joint Commission's dominance of facility accreditation is starting to wane somewhat in the face of increasing competition from other accrediting bodies for nonhospital facilities.

Certification is a voluntary procedure for health care organizations to meet the qualifications for participation in government funding programs, specifically Medicare and Medicaid. Although certification is voluntary, more often than not Medicare and Medicaid certification are necessary to the economic survival of a health care organization.

The three functions of licensure, accreditation, and certification are intertwined to a considerable extent. Joint Commission accreditation, for example, frequently satisfies the requirements for both state licensing and Medicare/Medicaid certification. Where this is not the case, Medicare/Medicaid certification surveys are often performed by the same agency and personnel that conduct state licensing surveys. Not only are the three functions intertwined, but there is also a high level of congruence among the various standards and processes employed in each function. Therefore, these materials will examine all three systems interchangeably.

■ ESTATE OF SMITH v. HECKLER

747 F.2d 583 (10th Cir. 1984)

McKay, Circuit Judge.

Plaintiffs . . . brought this class action on behalf of Medicaid recipients residing in nursing homes in Colorado. They alleged that the Secretary of Health and Human Services (Secretary) has a statutory duty . . . to develop and implement a system of nursing home review and enforcement designed to ensure that Medicaid recipients residing in Medicaid certified nursing homes actually receive the optimal medical and psychosocial care that they are entitled to under the Act. The plaintiffs contended that the enforcement system developed by the Secretary is "facility oriented," not "patient oriented" and thereby fails to meet the statutory mandate. . . .

[P]laintiffs instituted the lawsuit in an effort to improve the deplorable conditions at many nursing homes. They presented evidence of the lack of adequate medical care and of the widespread knowledge that care is inadequate. Indeed, the district court concluded that care and life in some nursing homes is so bad that the homes "could be characterized as orphanages for the aged." . . . [Nevertheless] [t]he trial court denied relief. This appeal is from that judgment. . . .

An understanding of the Medicaid Act (the Act) is essential to understand plaintiffs' contentions. The purpose of the Act is to enable the federal government to assist states in providing medical assistance to "aged, blind or disabled individuals, whose income and resources are insufficient to meet the costs of necessary medical services, and . . . rehabilitation and other services to help such . . . individuals to attain or retain capabilities for independence or self care." To receive funding, a state must submit to the Secretary and have approved by the Secretary a plan for medical assistance which meets the requirements of 42 U.S.C. §1396a(a). . . . The plan must include descriptions of the standards and methods the state will use to assure that medical or remedial care services provided to the recipients "are of high quality." . . . The appropriate state agency must determine on an ongoing basis whether participating institutions meet the requirements for continued participation in the Medicaid program. . . . In conducting the review, however, the states must use federal standards, forms, methods and procedures. . . .

Among other things, the regulations provide for the frequency and general content of patients' attending physician evaluations, nursing services with policies "designed to ensure that each patient receives treatments, medications, . . . diet as prescribed . . . rehabilitative nursing care as needed, . . . is kept comfortable, clean, well-groomed, [is] protected from accident, injury, an infection, and [is] encouraged, assisted, and trained in self-care and group activities." The rehabilitative nursing care is to be directed toward each patient achieving an optimal level of self-care and independence. The regulations require a written patient care plan to be developed and maintained for each patient. . . . Finally, the regulations provide for treatment of the social and emotional needs of recipients.

The Secretary has established a procedure for determining whether state plans comply with the standards set out in the regulations. This enforcement mechanism is known as the "survey/certification" inspection system. Under this system, the states conduct reviews of nursing homes. . . . The Secretary then determines, on the basis of the survey results, whether the nursing home surveyed is eligible for certification and, thus, eligible for Medicaid funds. . . .

The plaintiffs do not challenge the substantive medical standards, or "conditions of participation," which have been adopted by the Secretary and which states must satisfy to have their plans approved. Rather, plaintiffs challenge the enforcement mechanism the Secretary has established. The plaintiffs contend that the federal forms . . . which states are required to use, evaluate only the physical facilities and theoretical capability to render quality care. They claim that . . . out of the 541 questions contained in the Secretary's form which must be answered by state survey and certification inspection teams, only 30 are "even marginally related to patient care or might require any patient observation. . . ." Plaintiffs contend that the enforcement mechanism's focus on the facility, rather than on the care actually provided in the facility, results only in "paper compliance" with the substantive standards of the Act. Thus, plaintiffs contend, the Secretary has violated her statutory duty to assure that federal Medicaid monies are paid only to facilities which meet the substantive standards of the Act—facilities which actually provide high quality medical, rehabilitative and psychosocial care to resident Medicaid recipients. . . .

Congress intended the Secretary to be responsible for assuring that federal Medicaid money is given only to those institutions that actually comply with Medicaid requirements. The Act's requirements include providing high quality medical care. . . . Being charged with this function, we must conclude that a failure to promulgate regulations that allow the Secretary to remain informed, on a continuing basis, as to whether facilities receiving federal money are meeting the requirements of the Act, is an abdication of the Secretary's duty. . . .

■ COSPITO v. HECKLER

742 F.2d 72 (3d Cir. 1984)

GARTH, Circuit Judge.

Appellants Douglas Cospito, et al., ("the Patients") are or have been patients at the Trenton Psychiatric Hospital (TPH). In 1975, TPH lost its accreditation from codefendant Joint Commission on Accreditation of [Healthcare Organizations (JCAHO or JCAH)]. As a result, codefendant Secretary of the Department of Health, Education, and Welfare (now the Department of Health and Human Services) terminated various federal benefits which were conditioned upon the beneficiaries being treated at a qualified psychiatric hospital. . . . The Patients brought this action in district court challenging the loss of their federal benefits on several constitutional grounds. . . .

Beginning in 1973, TPH was surveyed under the standards for "psychiatric facilities" recently promulgated under the auspices of JCAH. Following the 1973 survey, major deficiencies were disclosed in several areas, including patient treatment, staffing, environment, and fire safety. TPH was accredited for only one year, and was notified that these deficiencies must be corrected to maintain accreditation. In 1974, however, many of the same deficiencies were found again. A preliminary decision was made by JCAH not to accredit. At TPH's request, a resurvey was conducted in May, 1975, which again resulted in a preliminary decision not to accredit. TPH did not appeal from that decision, and the deaccreditation became final. . . .

JCAH is an Illinois not-for-profit corporation formed in 1951 for the purpose of creating and maintaining professional standards for evaluating hospital performance. The body is governed by a 22-member Board of Commissioners. Its constituent members consist of the American College of Physicians, the American College of Surgeons, the American Dental Association, the American Hospital Association, and the American Medical Association. . . .

The survey itself consists of an on-site visit conducted by a team of surveyors designated by JCAH. The surveyors evaluate the quality of the facility's environment and review its administrative records to determine whether they conform to applicable standards. . . .

JCAH accreditation, however, must be distinguished from certification by the Secretary for eligibility in federal assistance programs. While JCAH accreditation may, depending on the circumstances, be a component of certification, the two are not necessarily coextensive, and at least as a matter of terminology, we will refer to the two separately. . . .

The Patients at TPH had, before decertification by the Secretary, been the beneficiaries of three types of federally funded benefits: (1) Medicare, (2) Medicaid, and (3) Supplemental Social Security Income. . . . When TPH was decertified in 1975, all of the benefits described above were terminated, since TPH was no longer an institution eligible under Medicare and Medicaid. . . . The Patients brought suit in district court alleging that deprivation of their Medicare, Medicaid, and Social Security benefits was unconstitutional. They alleged lack of procedural due process, lack of substantive due process, lack of equal protection, and unconstitutional delegation of authority to JCAH. . . .

Our analysis of the procedural due process aspects of this case is guided by the Supreme Court's decision in O'Bannon v. Town Court Nursing Center, 447 U.S. 773 (1980), which involved facts comparable to those presented here. In *Town Court,* residents of a nursing home claimed a violation of due process when they lost federal benefits as a result of the decertification of their facility. Like the Patients here, they claimed a right to a pretermination hearing.

The Supreme Court found as a threshold matter, however, that the residents of the nursing home had not been deprived of any protectable property interest, and thus, absent this foundation, no due process right was triggered. Writing for the Court, Justice Stevens found that patients did not have a settled interest in receiving benefits at any [particular] facility, including a decertified one, and therefore there had been no deprivation of "property." . . .

[T]he only factor which even arguably distinguishes this case from *Town Court* is the fact that the Patients are unable to transfer out of TPH [because they were involuntarily committed under state mental health law]; [therefore], they are barred from receiving federal benefits at another qualified institution. Thus, they contend that there has been an actual "deprivation" of a protectable interest. Even accepting that contention, however, . . . [b]ecause any loss of benefits to the Patients was only "indirectly" caused by the Secretary's decision to decertify TPH, whatever deprivation which was suffered [by virtue of the state-law psychiatric commitment] was not the result of any [federal] governmental action. The Patients are therefore not in a position to claim any Fifth Amendment due process protection, even if they alleged a "deprivation."[17] . . .

Finally, we turn to the Patients' argument that the Medicare (and thus Medicaid) provisions improperly delegate authority to JCAH, in derogation of Congress' ultimate responsibility to establish federal policy. . . . We need not reach the question of whether delegation of such authority to a private entity breaches the constitutional barrier, since our reading of the Medicare statute, which in turn is applicable to the Medic[aid] and Social Security programs, convinces us that the Secretary retains ultimate authority over decertification decisions, through the ability to engage in a "distinct part" survey. . . .

While JCAH accreditation may, under certain circumstances, independently satisfy the statutory requirements for participation in Medicare, the Secretary is free to prescribe standards which are higher than those of the Commission, in which case JCAH accreditation would not be effective. Moreover, if the Secretary determines that, despite JCAH accreditation, a particular hospital nevertheless has serious deficiencies, he may, after appropriate notice, decertify the institution. On the other hand, if the Secretary chose to promulgate a standard lower than that of JCAH, a general hospital could presumably be certified by meeting only that lesser standard, even if it did not meet the requirements imposed by the Commission.

17. The district court granted summary judgment on the procedural due process claim for the reason that, in its opinion, the procedures used adequately safeguarded the Patients' interests, [a]pplying the tests of Mathews v. Eldridge, 424 U.S. 319 (1976). . . . Without disagreeing with the district court's reasoning, we note that our analysis makes it unnecessary to reach the issues addressed by the court below. . . .

The Patients argue, however, that in the case of psychiatric hospitals, the statute places JCAH accreditation in a position of ascendancy over approval by the Secretary, thus leading to the question of unconstitutional delegation to a private group. Our reading of the statute leads us to disagree. While Congress did choose to give special attention to JCAH accreditation in the context of psychiatric hospitals,[27] it still provided the "distinct part" survey as a mechanism whereby the Secretary could independently determine whether a particular institution was qualified for participation. Through consecutive or simultaneous distinct part surveys, therefore, it is possible to obtain a de novo evaluation by the Secretary on the adequacy of a hospital's facilities. . . .

Since, in effect, all actions of JCAH are subject to full review by a public official who is responsible and responsive to the political process, we find that there has been no real delegation of authority to JCAH.[29] . . .

BECKER, Circuit Judge, dissented.

Notes: Facility Regulation and Accreditation

1. *Which Facilities Are Covered?* The first question under any licensing scheme is its jurisdiction. Jurisdictional issues arise with increasing frequency as the result of innovative service delivery and ownership arrangements in the medical industry. One common issue is whether a license for a central facility such as a hospital covers satellite facilities such as urgent care centers, or whether they must be separately licensed. Another issue is whether a specialty clinic, say for abortions or for expensive diagnostic scans, can be treated as simply a physician's office, which does not require a facility license. See RIH Medical Foundation v. Nolan, 723 A.2d 1123 (R.I. 1999) (physician-owned corporation that operates physician offices is exempt from health facility licensing); Ex parte Sacred Heart Health System, 155 So. 2d 980 (Ala. 2012) (announcing five-part test to determine when a physician's office is not a regulated facility); Covenant Healthcare System, Inc. v. City of Wauwatosa, 800 N.W.2d 906 (Wis. 2011) (urgent care center is not just an expanded doctor's office, but functions more like a "hospital," for purposes of tax-exempt status). A third issue is whether an existing license covers the buyer or lessor of a health facility, and whether turning the facility's operation over to a management company requires applying for a formal transfer of the license. Often, the same questions apply generally to accreditation and certification. Usually, the only way to know the answer is to simply ask the governing authorities, since statutes and regulations frequently

27. The legislative history reveals that Congress intended "to support the efforts of the various professional accrediting organizations sponsored by the medical and hospital associations. . . ."

29. Our resolution of this issue renders somewhat academic the Patients' contention that it was improper for JCAH to "subdelegate" the responsibility for evaluating psychiatric hospitals to the various accreditation councils. Since we have found that no real authority was actually vested in JCAH, it follows that there could be no improper "subdelegation" of authority to divisions of the Commission. . . .

fail to flesh out these details. The consequences for wrongly interpreting licensing jurisdiction can be severe. In one case, the court refused to enforce any of the contracts entered into by an unlicensed nursing agency. U.S. Nursing Corp. v. St. Joseph Medical Center, 39 F.3d 790 (7th Cir. 1994). See also section B.3 discussing the corporate practice of medicine doctrine.

2. *Regulation Run Amok?* One possible result of excess regulation may be to spur the increasing trend, known as "medical tourism," of traveling overseas to receive medical care much more cheaply in foreign countries. On health care regulation generally, see Robert Field, Health Care Regulation in America: Complexity, Confrontation, and Compromise (2007); Symposium, Rethinking Regulation in an Era of Reform, 32 Hamline J. Pub. L. & Pol'y 301 (2011).

3. *Measuring Quality Through Structure or Outcomes.* The next question under any of these regulatory or quasi-regulatory schemes is their content. A detailed understanding is beyond the scope of this book. However, it is possible to convey the gist of this content by distinguishing among structural, process, and outcome measures of quality. State licensing authorities, like the Medicaid nursing home requirements in *Estate of Smith,* do not inquire into the actual outcomes of patient treatment. Instead, facility licensure provisions typically read like a gigantic building code for the industry, specifying a host of architectural, safety, and sanitation minutiae. Similarly, the Joint Commission accreditation standards traditionally have addressed only the organizational and structural aspects of each hospital department—issues such as whether bylaws are properly drafted, whether proper committees are established, and whether administrative structures contain proper monitoring and documentation—rather than attempting any direct assessment of the actual outcomes of medical care in the hospital. This point was articulated in an Internet discussion group by someone who worked as a hospital therapist and department manager for 13 years:

> We never worried about JCAHO until the three months prior and the two days of the inspection. In the three months prior, we backdated all the documentation that we needed to get through the inspection, and in the two days they were there we spent telling them how focused we were on quality, etc. As long as the paperwork is in order, people can be dying in the halls and there could be guppies in the IV fluids; the JCAHO wouldn't notice.

For an extensive critique of the traditional structural and process measures of institutional quality and an argument for adopting outcomes measures, see Troyen Brennan & Donald Berwick, New Rules: Regulation, Markets and the Quality of American Health Care (1996), which also contains an excellent overview and historical account of licensure and accreditation. Assessing regulatory approaches in light of vastly expanded sources of information about quality and costs, see Kristin Madison, Regulating Health Care Quality in an Information Age, 40 U.C. Davis L. Rev. 1577 (2007).

More generally, "new governance" is an important intellectual movement in administrative law, which considers from an empirically informed behavioral perspective a more diverse set of tools to accomplish regulatory goals than traditional "command and control" regulation. For a review of applications to hospital, insurance, and health care regulation, see Nan D. Hunter, Risk Governance and

Deliberative Democracy in Health Care, 97 Geo. L.J. 1-60 (2008); John Blum, The Quagmire of Hospital Governance: Finding Mission in a Revised Licensure Model, 31 J. Leg. Med. 35 (2010); Symposium, 2 Regulation & Governance 1 (2008).

4. *Process and Outcomes Measures.* The *Smith* case presaged a move away from purely structural measures of quality. That decision resulted in a statutory amendment (known as OBRA '87) and an extensive set of regulations (updated in 2016) that govern in considerable detail the treatment plans, living environment, legal rights, and human dignity of nursing home patients. 42 C.F.R. §§483 et seq. These regulations are focused primarily on the process of care. In a controversial decision, the Third Circuit ruled that Medicaid's nursing home standards can form the basis for a personal injury suit against the nursing home, by the estate of a deceased patient. Grammer v. John J. Kane Regional Centers, 570 F.3d 520 (3d Cir. 2009). See generally David Bohm, Striving for Quality Care in America's Nursing Homes, 4 DePaul J. Health Care L. 317 (2001); Jennifer Brady, Long-Term Care Under Fire: A Case for Rational Enforcement, 18 J. Contemp. Health L. & Pol'y 1 (2001); Comment, 73 U. Colo. L. Rev. 1013 (2002); Symposium, 26 J. Leg. Med. 1 (2005).

Reformers have tried to move even further toward evaluating institutions based on the outcomes of treatment. For instance, CMS at one point (in 1997) proposed fundamentally revising the standards for hospital participation in Medicare and Medicaid to focus much more extensively on outcomes of care and systems for continuous quality improvement. The proposed standards would have required each patient to receive a comprehensive assessment of care needs and a coordinated plan of care within 24 hours of admission. However, the final rule (adopted in 2003) falls back on general process requirements of having "data-driven quality assessment and performance improvement" systems that "measure, analyze, and track quality indicators," and then taking unspecified "actions aimed at performance improvement" that "track performance to ensure that improvements are sustained." 42 C.F.R. §482.

The Joint Commission has also attempted to streamline accreditation standards and focus more on patient safety issues. One key feature is a self-assessment and a "sentinel event" policy that requires hospitals to take the following actions whenever there is an unexpected death or serious injury resulting from treatment: inform the patient or family, conduct a "root cause" analysis, and institute a corrective action plan. However, hospitals do not have to report these events to the Joint Commission, since doing so might compromise the hospital's ability to protect the information from discovery in lawsuits. Symposium, 35 J. Health L. 179 (2002). As a result, the Joint Commission's outcomes initiative has become simply another process measure, one that requires institutions to assess internally their bad outcomes rather than enforcing mandatory outcomes standards.

Outcomes measures of quality may find their purest expression in the accreditation of HMOs and other types of integrated delivery systems. The National Committee for Quality Assurance (NCQA) is the leading accreditation organization for these new comprehensive financing and delivery systems. From the start, it has spearheaded a focus on outcomes measures in the form of the quality report cards. These report cards adopt a standard reporting format about matters such as patient satisfaction, childhood immunization rates, and other broad indicators of health status (not just medical treatment) in the covered population. The aim is to provide this information as a basis on which subscribers and employers can comparison shop based on both price and quality, thereby substituting more market-based forces for regulatory oversight.

5. *Challenging Adverse Decisions.* The third major area of concern under licensure, accreditation, and certification programs is the processes for determining compliance and challenging adverse decisions. Space limitations preclude us from covering these important aspects of public oversight and legal practice. In brief summary, substantial procedural protections are usually built into these regulatory schemes, so challenges for denial of due process usually fail. The most intense disputes arise when licensing inspectors find such glaring safety concerns that the facility is shut down immediately without a chance for correction or rebuttal. These shutdowns have been challenged as unconstitutional, but usually without success considering the patient protection concerns at stake and the ample procedural rights following a temporary shutdown.

Constitutional challenges depend on the presence of state action, which usually does not exist for private accreditation. McKeesport v. Accreditation Council for Graduate Medical Education, 24 F.3d 519 (3d Cir. 1994). Contra St. Agnes Hospital v. Riddick, 668 F. Supp. 478 (D. Md. 1987) (state action exists where private accreditation affects state licensure). Therefore, suit against accreditation organizations depends on somewhat obscure common-law theories of fairness in business dealings. There are only a few such cases, the leading ones arising in connection with physician accreditation and membership in professional societies. They reason, similar to Greisman v. Newcomb Hospital, page 457, that when membership organizations control important economic and public interests, they must provide rational reasons and a fair process for their exclusion decisions. See Pinsker v. Pacific Coast Society of Orthodontists, 526 P.2d 253 (Cal. 1974); Falcone v. Middlesex County Medical Society, 170 A.2d 791 (N.J. 1961). See generally Robert Trefney, Judicial Intervention in Admissions Decisions of Private Professional Associations, 49 U. Chi. L. Rev. 840 (1992).

6. *The Public Role of Private Accreditation. Cospito* raises the important public policy question of whether public regulatory authorities cede too much control to private accreditation organizations that are controlled by the regulated industry. State licensure of health care facilities, like federal certification, sometimes defers to the Joint Commission, either by using its accreditation as a proxy for licensure or by incorporating many of its standards. Even if this passes constitutional muster, it still deserves critique for whether this essentially self-regulatory approach is good public policy. See generally Symposium, Private Accreditation in the Regulatory State, 57 Law & Contemp. Probs. 4 (Autumn 1994) (exploring this and a number of other important legal and public policy issues concerning accreditation). It is worth observing that, although the Joint Commission arose from the hospital industry, it has long been sufficiently independent that it sometimes receives harsh criticism from hospitals for the expense and intrusiveness of its inspections. At the same time, consumer groups lash out against the Joint Commission for its relationship with the hospital industry.

7. *Occupational Hazards and Medical Wastes.* These are not the only regulatory authorities affecting health care facilities. Because of the size, complexity, and public importance of hospitals, they are subject to numerous specialized regulatory laws and generalized laws that have special importance in the hospital setting. Two

prime examples are the laws governing workers' exposure to infectious diseases and the disposal of medical waste.

The federal Occupational Safety and Health Administration (OSHA) is quite involved in regulating health care facilities to ensure that health care workers are protected from occupational hazards. Some of the hazards confronted by health care workers are identical to those found in other job settings: dangerous machinery, exposure to chemicals, and so forth. See generally Mark Rothstein, Occupational Safety and Law (2017). The health care environment also creates unique risks, particularly through potential exposure to communicable diseases. In 1991, OSHA enacted regulations designed to reduce the risk of workplace exposure to disease, particularly to HIV and hepatitis. Under the "Bloodborne Pathogen" rule, employers must develop an exposure control plan, which means that they must identify workers whose jobs create a "reasonably anticipated" exposure to infectious body fluids and they must develop a training and protection program to reduce the risk of exposure. 29 C.F.R. §1910.1030. Health care facilities must also provide employees with protective equipment, establish safe workplace practices, and employ "engineering controls" (such as use of puncture-resistant containers for used needles). Employers are required to monitor exposures and to keep records of incidents. Each of these requirements imposes significant costs and administrative burdens on health care facilities. See, e.g., American Dental Association v. Martin, 984 F.2d 823 (7th Cir. 1993). See also Paula E. Berg, When the Hazard Is Human: Irrationality, Inequity, and Unintended Consequences in Federal Regulation of Contagion, 75 Wash. U. L.Q. 1367 (1998). Health facilities in violation of OSHA standards can face significant fines.

Most people do not think of health care facilities as producing hazardous waste. Yet the point can be driven home—literally—when medical waste, including used needles and bloody refuse, washes up on our nation's beaches. Chryssa V. Deliganisa & Steve P. Calandrillo, Syringes In The Sea: Why Federal Regulation Of Medical Waste Is Long Overdue, 41 Ga. L. Rev. 169 (2006). In 1990, the EPA estimated that hospitals, medical offices, and other facilities produced about a half million tons of medical waste that "contains pathogens with sufficient virulence and quantity so that exposure to the waste by a susceptible host could result in an infectious disease." States have been the primary regulators of the disposal of medical waste produced by health care facilities. States regulate the ways in which the waste is transported, stored, and decontaminated or destroyed. See 86 A.L.R.4th 401 (1991).

The EPA has not specifically regulated medical waste—only issued model guidelines. Attempts to assert more federal control over medical waste under the various environmental statutes have been largely unsuccessful.

Research Exercise: Medicare/Medicaid Certification*

Your client is a hospital that has recently undergone a series of layoffs. A disgruntled former employee, a nurse, has complained to the state health department

*The editors are grateful to Prof. Phyllis Bernard for permission to use this problem, which she devised.

that the quality of patient care has suffered significantly. The hospital has had reason to be concerned about high rates of nosocomial infections (infections acquired in a hospital). There is also concern about bedsores and soiled linen. One patient's open wound was infected by maggots. The nurse's call to the state health department triggered a surprise inspection by the unit charged with overseeing certification for participation in the Medicare and Medicaid programs. It appears likely that the state Department of Health will seek summarily to terminate the hospital's status under these programs as a "participating provider" (also known as the "provider agreement"). Consult the Code of Federal Regulations or one or more of the relevant practitioner treatises (e.g., Wolters Kluwer's Medicare and Medicaid Guide or Hospital Law Manual) to determine what this means and what can be done about it.

UNIVERSAL HEALTH SERVICES v. UNITED STATES, ex rel. ESCOBAR AND CORREA

136 S. Ct. 1989 (2016)

Justice THOMAS.

The [federal] False Claims Act imposes significant penalties on those who defraud the Government. This case concerns a theory of False Claims Act liability commonly referred to as "implied false certification." According to this theory, when a defendant submits a claim, it impliedly certifies compliance with all conditions of payment. But if that claim fails to disclose the defendant's violation of a material statutory, regulatory, or contractual requirement, so the theory goes, the defendant has made a misrepresentation that renders the claim "false or fraudulent." This case requires us to consider this theory of liability and to clarify some of the circumstances in which the False Claims Act imposes liability.

We first hold that . . . [a] misrepresentation about compliance with a statutory, regulatory, or contractual requirement must be material to the Government's payment decision in order to be actionable under the False Claims Act. We clarify below how that rigorous materiality requirement should be enforced. . . .

I

Enacted in 1863, the False Claims Act "was originally aimed principally at stopping the massive frauds perpetrated by large contractors during the Civil War." . . . Congress responded by imposing civil and criminal liability for 10 types of fraud on the Government, subjecting violators to double [and now triple] damages, forfeiture, and up to five years' imprisonment. . . . The Act's scienter requirement defines "knowing" and "knowingly" to mean that a person has "actual knowledge of the information," "acts in deliberate ignorance of the truth or falsity of the information," or "acts in reckless disregard of the truth or falsity of the information." And the Act defines "material" to mean "having a natural tendency to influence, or be capable of influencing, the payment or receipt of money or property." . . .

The alleged False Claims Act violations here arose within the Medicaid program . . . . [The complaint alleges that, for] five years, Yarushka Rivera, a teenage beneficiary of Massachusetts' Medicaid program, received counseling services at Arbour Counseling Services, . . . owned and operated by a subsidiary of petitioner Universal Health Services. . . . In May 2009, Yarushka had an adverse reaction to a medication that a purported doctor at Arbour prescribed after diagnosing her with bipolar disorder. Her condition worsened; she suffered a seizure that required hospitalization. In October 2009, she suffered another seizure and died. She was 17 years old.

Thereafter, an Arbour counselor revealed to respondents Carmen Correa and Julio Escobar—Yarushka's mother and stepfather—that . . . of the five professionals who had treated Yarushka, only one was properly licensed. The practitioner who diagnosed Yarushka as bipolar identified herself as a psychologist with a Ph. D., but failed to mention that her degree came from an unaccredited Internet college and that Massachusetts had rejected her application to be licensed as a psychologist. Likewise, the practitioner who prescribed medicine to Yarushka, and who was held out as a psychiatrist, was in fact a nurse who lacked authority to prescribe medications absent supervision . . . . And the problem went beyond those who treated Yarushka. Some 23 Arbour employees lacked licenses to provide mental health services . . . .

When submitting reimbursement claims, Arbour used payment codes corresponding to different services that its staff provided to Yarushka, such as "Individual Therapy" and "Family Therapy." Staff members also misrepresented their qualifications and licensing status to the Federal Government to obtain individual National Provider Identification numbers, which are submitted in connection with Medicaid reimbursement claims . . . .

In 2011, respondents filed a *qui tam* suit[3] in federal court alleging that Universal Health . . . submitted reimbursement claims that made representations about the specific services provided by specific types of professionals, but that failed to disclose serious violations of regulations pertaining to staff qualifications and licensing requirements for these services. . . . Universal Health thus allegedly defrauded the program, which would not have reimbursed the claims had it known that it was billed for mental health services that were performed by unlicensed and unsupervised staff. The United States [initially] declined to intervene [but then briefed the case when it reached the Supreme Court].

The District Court granted Universal Health's motion to dismiss the complaint . . . [because] none of the regulations that Arbour violated was a condition of payment. The United States Court of Appeals for the First Circuit reversed in relevant part and remanded. The court observed that each time a billing party submits a claim, it "implicitly communicate[s] that it conformed to the relevant program [participation] requirements, such that it was entitled to payment." . . . In the court's view, a statutory, regulatory, or contractual requirement can be a condition of payment either by expressly identifying itself as such or by implication. The court then held that . . . the [state licensure] regulations themselves "constitute[d] dispositive evidence of materiality" because they identified [proper licensure] as an "express and absolute" condition of payment . . . .

3. [This is a suit in which a private "bounty hunting" party or "whistleblower" (referred to as the "relator") sues on behalf of the federal government to recoup falsely paid amounts. If successful, the court can award the relator up to 30 percent of the recovery. If the government chooses to intervene, it then conducts the litigation, but the relator still receives 15-25 percent of the recovery. See Section E for further discussion.]

We granted certiorari to resolve the disagreement among the Courts of Appeals over the validity and scope of the implied false certification theory of liability. The Seventh Circuit has rejected this theory, reasoning that only express (or affirmative) falsehoods can render a claim "false or fraudulent" . . . . Other courts have accepted the theory, but limit its application to cases where defendants fail to disclose violations of expressly designated conditions of payment [rather than more general "conditions of participation" in the government program]. Yet others hold that conditions of payment need not be expressly designated as such to be a basis for False Claims Act liability.

II

We first hold that the implied false certification theory can, at least in some circumstances, provide a basis for liability. By punishing defendants who submit "false or fraudulent claims," the False Claims Act encompasses claims that make fraudulent misrepresentations, which include certain misleading omissions. When, as here, a defendant makes representations in submitting a claim but omits its violations of statutory, regulatory, or contractual requirements, those omissions can be a basis for liability if they render the defendant's representations misleading with respect to the goods or services provided. . . .

We need not resolve whether all claims for payment implicitly represent that the billing party is legally entitled to payment. The claims in this case do more than merely demand payment. They fall squarely within the rule that half-truths—representations that state the truth only so far as it goes, while omitting critical qualifying information—can be actionable misrepresentations. . . . [For example], an applicant for an adjunct position at a local college makes an actionable misrepresentation when his resume lists prior jobs and then retirement, but fails to disclose that his "retirement" was a prison stint for perpetrating a $12 million bank fraud.

So too here, by submitting claims for payment using payment codes that corresponded to specific counseling services, Universal Health represented that it had provided individual therapy, family therapy, preventive medication counseling, and other types of treatment. Moreover, Arbour staff members allegedly made further representations in submitting Medicaid reimbursement claims by using National Provider Identification numbers corresponding to specific job titles. And these representations were clearly misleading in context. Anyone informed that a social worker at a Massachusetts mental health clinic provided a teenage patient with individual counseling services would probably—but wrongly—conclude that the . . . social worker possesses the prescribed qualifications for the job. . . . .

Accordingly, we hold that the implied certification theory can be a basis for liability, at least where two conditions are satisfied: first, the claim does not merely request payment, but it also makes specific representations about the goods or services provided; and second, the defendant's failure to disclose noncompliance with material statutory, regulatory, or contractual requirements makes those representations misleading half-truths.

The second question presented is whether, as Universal Health urges, a defendant should face False Claims Act liability only if it fails to disclose the violation of a contractual, statutory, or regulatory provision that the Government expressly designated a condition of payment. We conclude that the Act does not impose this limit on liability. But we also conclude that not every undisclosed violation of an express condition of payment automatically triggers liability. Whether a provision is labeled a condition of payment is relevant to but not dispositive of the materiality inquiry. . . .

A defendant can have "actual knowledge" that a condition is material without the Government expressly calling it a condition of payment. If the Government failed to specify that guns it orders must actually shoot, but the defendant knows that the Government routinely rescinds contracts if the guns do not shoot, the defendant has "actual knowledge." . . .

We now clarify how that materiality requirement should be enforced. . . . The materiality standard is demanding. The False Claims Act is not . . . a vehicle for punishing garden-variety breaches of contract or regulatory violations. A misrepresentation cannot be deemed material merely because the Government designates compliance with a particular statutory, regulatory, or contractual requirement as a condition of payment. . . . [If that were so, the] Government might respond by designating every legal requirement an express condition of payment. But billing parties are often subject to thousands of complex statutory and regulatory provisions [that are conditions of participation.] . . . . Materiality, in addition, cannot be found where noncompliance is minor or insubstantial. . . .

[P]roof of materiality can include, but is not necessarily limited to, evidence that the defendant knows that the Government consistently refuses to pay claims in the mine run of cases based on noncompliance with the particular statutory, regulatory, or contractual requirement. Conversely, . . . if the Government regularly pays a particular type of claim in full despite actual knowledge that certain requirements were violated, and has signaled no change in position, that is strong evidence that the requirements are not material.

These rules lead us to disagree with the Government's and First Circuit's view of materiality: that any statutory, regulatory, or contractual violation is material so long as the defendant knows that the Government would be entitled to refuse payment were it aware of the violation. At oral argument, the United States explained the implications of its position: If the Government contracts for health services and adds a requirement that contractors buy American-made staplers, anyone who submits a claim for those services but fails to disclose its use of foreign staplers violates the False Claims Act. To the Government, liability would attach if the defendant's use of foreign staplers would entitle the Government not to pay the claim in whole or part—irrespective of whether the Government routinely pays claims despite knowing that foreign staplers were used. Likewise, if the Government required contractors to aver their compliance with the entire U.S. Code and Code of Federal Regulations, then under this view, failing to mention noncompliance with any of those requirements would always be material. The False Claims Act does not adopt such an extraordinarily expansive view of liability. . . .

We emphasize . . . that the False Claims Act is not a means of imposing treble damages and other penalties for insignificant regulatory or contractual violations. This case centers on allegations of fraud, not medical malpractice. Respondents have alleged that Universal Health misrepresented its compliance with mental health facility requirements that are so central to the provision of mental health counseling that the Medicaid program would not have paid these claims had it known of these violations. Respondents may well have adequately pleaded a violation of [the False Claims Act]. But we leave it to the courts below to resolve this in the first instance.

Notes: Medicare Conditions of Participation; Health Care Fraud

1. *What's in a Name?* Note the distinction that previous courts had drawn between "conditions of *participation*" and "conditions of *payment*." The former refers to all regulatory requirements that providers must meet to join the program and remain in good standing. The latter refers to requirements for paying particular claims to participating providers. Other courts (and the district court in *Escobar*) had previously drawn a line between these two sets of conditions—in part because participation conditions are so numerous, technical, and potentially ambiguous. Although *Escobar* eliminates this line, it emphasizes the materiality line; conditions of either payment or participation are actionable, but only if the provider has reason to know that they actually matter to the program's reimbursement policies and practices. It remains unclear whether, on balance, the decision will end up being more restrictive or more enabling to false claims suits.

2. *Fraud on Steroids.* Expansive interpretations of what constitutes a "false" claim, and when such claims are submitted "knowingly," have led to a spate of both private and government enforcement actions. Use of *qui tam* actions by private "bounty hunting" parties have proliferated, as further discussed in Section E. Direct government enforcement actions are also numerous, resulting in several billions of dollars in recoveries each year. Most of these are not for what one would call typical "fraud," however. Instead, usually they are for legitimate services that are inappropriately billed. As further illustrated in Section E, because a single error in procedures or documentation for submitting claims can be replicated in countless numbers of claims until noticed and rectified, false claims damages can be enormous, even ruinous. Therefore, hospitals and other providers have complained bitterly that they have no choice but to agree to very large settlements, sometimes in the tens or hundreds of millions of dollars, for what they consider to be innocent behavior, honest differences of opinion, or at most only careless mistakes rather than criminal fraud.

3. *Food for Thought.* Various scholars have considered, with mixed support in the case law, whether the False Claims Act can be used to **police low quality or unnecessary care**, or even failure to obtain informed consent. See, e.g., Isaac D. Buck, Overtreatment and Informed Consent: A Fraud-Based Solution, 43 Fla. St. U. L. Rev. 901 (2016); Isaac D. Buck, Breaking the Fever: A New Construct for Regulating Overtreatment. 48 UC Davis L. Rev. 1261 (2015); Isaac D. Buck, Caring Too Much: Misusing the False Claims Act to Target Overtreatment, 74 Ohio St. L.J. 463 (2013); Joan H. Krause, Medical Error as False Claim, 27 Am. J L. & Med. 181 (2001).

For additional commentary and critique of **medical fraud enforcement generally**, see David Hyman, Health Care Fraud and Abuse: Market Change, Social Norms, and "The Trust Reposed in the Workmen," 30 J. Legal Stud. 531 (2002); Joan H. Krause, "Promises to Keep": Health Care Providers and the Civil False Claims Act, 23 Cardozo L. Rev. 1363 (2002); Kathleen Boozang & Simone Handler-Hutchinson, "Monitoring" Corporate Corruption: DOJ's Use of Deferred Prosecution Agreements in Health Care, 35 Am. J.L. Med. 89 (2009); Isaac D. Buck,

Enforcement Overdose: Health Care Fraud Regulation in an Era of Overcriminalization and Overtreatment, 74 Md. L. Rev. 259 (2015); Anthony Kyriakakis, The Missing Victims of Health Care Fraud, 2015 Utah L. Rev. 605.

3. Certificate of Need Regulation

Certificate of need (CON) laws are another important type of facility regulation, one that operates essentially like a building permit for hospitals and other medical facilities, but with a focus on costs rather than on quality. Medical facilities must show that a need exists in the community, and that they satisfy financial feasibility and other criteria, before undertaking any of several enumerated new activities. These typically include substantial new construction, the purchase of major new equipment, the initiation of important new services, or a change in ownership. Hospitals, nursing homes, and outpatient clinics are all usually covered by this legislation, but physician offices are frequently excluded.

These laws are an outgrowth of community health planning efforts that began in the 1940s, when the country first recognized a shortage and maldistribution of hospitals. At that time, planning efforts were attached to federal grants and loans for hospital construction under the Hill-Burton Act of 1946 to make sure new hospitals were placed where they were most needed. In 1964, New York State adopted the first state CON law. It made health planning mandatory for all facilities and it was concerned with both hospital excess capacity as well as hospital shortages. The American Hospital Association quickly embraced this mandatory planning philosophy and began lobbying other states to follow suit.

CON laws became widespread after the federal government enacted the National Health Planning and Resources Development Act (NHPRDA) of 1974, 42 U.S.C. §§300k-300t-14 (repealed). NHPRDA required states to follow a model CON process in order to continue receiving certain federal funding for public health activities, and to continue participating in Medicaid. By 1980, all states had enacted some version of CON legislation. This federal initiative quickly came to an end when President Reagan signed the Omnibus Health Package of 1986 repealing NHPRDA. About a dozen states thereafter repealed their CON laws, but most states still retain this regulation and many have expended it (for instance, to cover more outpatient services). The old federal law thus remains influential on the interpretation of the state laws because it served as the model enacted by most states.

The following materials provide a glimpse of how this regulatory scheme functions in the three dozen states in which it is still active. As you read the next case, consider whether the rationale for this regulation was sound when it was first enacted, and whether it remains sound today.

■ OVERLAKE HOSPITAL ASSOCIATION v. DEPARTMENT OF HEALTH

239 P.3d 1096 (Wash. 2010)

ALEXANDER, J.

Swedish Health Services (Swedish) and the Washington State Department of Health (Department) seek review of a decision of the Court of Appeals, in which that court concluded that the Department used flawed methodology in determining that there was need for an additional ambulatory surgical facility (ASF) in East King County. . . . We agree with Swedish and the Department and, consequently, reverse the Court of Appeals.

In 1979, the legislature created the certificate of need [CON] program, which authorizes the Department to control the number and types of health care services and facilities that are provided in a given planning area. The purpose behind this legislation was to ensure that such services and facilities are developed in a manner consistent with identified priorities and without unnecessary duplication. Under this statutory regime, in order for certain health care providers to establish or expand health care facilities within this state, including [ambulatory surgical facilities], they must obtain a [CON] from the Department.

In determining whether there is need for an additional ASF in a given area, the Department employs the three-step methodology . . . designed to determine: (a) the existing capacity of operating rooms in the planning area, (b) the anticipated number of surgeries in the area three years into the future, and (c) whether existing operating room capacity is sufficient to accommodate the projected number of future surgeries.

Facilities in the offices of private physicians or dentists, whether for individual or group practice, are exempt from the definition of an ASF. . . . Historically, and in the instant case, the Department excludes exempt surgical facilities in calculating step one of the methodology—existing capacity. It does, however, include surgeries performed in the exempt facilities in calculating step two-projected future need.

In November 2002, Swedish applied for a [CON] to establish a new ASF in Bellevue, Washington. Overlake Hospital Association (Overlake) and Evergreen Healthcare (Evergreen) each obtained "affected part[y]" status and submitted comments to the Department in opposition to Swedish's application. Using the methodology described above, the Department determined that there was need in East King County for an additional ASF with 5.39 outpatient operating rooms. Accordingly, it issued a [CON] to Swedish to build a five-room ASF in Bellevue.

Overlake and Evergreen requested an adjudicative proceeding before a health law judge to determine whether the Department erred. . . . In upholding the Department's decision, . . . the health law judge determined that exempt facilities should be excluded from the calculation of existing capacity, but included in the calculation of future need. . . . In holding that Swedish established need for an additional five operating room ASF in Bellevue, the health law judge took particular note of the legislature's emphasis on assuring "that all citizens have accessible health services" and indicated that "[i]f the more inclusive approach were followed, the calculation of available operating rooms would include [exempt facilities] that would not be available to many of the individuals within the health planning area." . . .

In determining whether to issue a [CON] for a new health care facility, the Department is to consider the following factors: (1) need, (2) financial feasibility, (3) structure and process of care, and (4) cost containment. Factors two, three, and four have not been at issue in this case. Rather, the focus has been on factor one—whether the Department used the proper methodology for calculating need. More specifically, the question before us is whether the Department erred in the manner in which it factored exempt facilities in its calculation of existing capacity and future need. . . . For future need, [the Department, under its rules,] must

> [p]roject number of inpatient and outpatient surgeries performed within the hospital planning area for the third year of operation. This shall be based on the current number of surgeries adjusted for forecasted growth in the population served and may be adjusted for trends in surgeries per capita. . . .
>
> Subtract the capacity of dedicated outpatient operating rooms from the forecasted number of outpatient surgeries. . . .
>
> Determine the average time per inpatient and outpatient surgery in the planning area. . . .
>
> Calculate the sum of inpatient and remaining outpatient . . . operating room time needed in the third year of operation.
>
> Net need, the ultimate question for the Department, is determined by calculating the difference, if any, between existing capacity and future need.

. . . [T]he Court of Appeals concluded that the Department acted arbitrarily and capriciously by employing the methodology it did for calculating net need, i.e., excluding exempt facilities in calculating existing capacity, while at the same time including surgeries performed at those facilities in calculating future need. . . .

We are satisfied that the public policy rationale behind the [CON] program, which convinced the health law judge that the regulation meant that exempt facilities should be excluded from existing capacity but included in future need, resolves the ambiguity. As noted above, the legislature has made clear its intent to "promote, maintain, and assure the health of all citizens in the state, provide accessible health services, health manpower, health facilities." That, in our judgment, is the overriding purpose of the [CON] program. While we agree with Overlake and Evergreen that controlling the costs of medical care and promoting prevention are also priorities, we believe that these goals are of secondary significance because, to a large extent, they would be realized by promotion and maintenance of access to health care services for all citizens. . . .

In sum, we are satisfied that the Department's interpretation of the regulation is consistent with the goal of assuring a sufficient supply of publicly available ASFs, in that the approach "does not rely on unregulated exempt [facilities] to meet any part of the public demand for the service." The Department's reasoning, we believe, was well described by a Department analyst . . . at the hearing before the health law judge as follows:

> . . . The facilities that are described as exempt facilities, the use of those facilities is limited only to members of those group practices. And very frequently, we see that the use of these facilities is limited to one, sometimes two, different specialties of medicine, such as ENT [ear, nose, and throat] surgery or oral surgery or something like that. So those operating rooms are not really analogous to a generally available ambulatory surgery center, operating room, where a multitude of various services could be performed by a number of different physicians.

. . . [W]e conclude that the Department properly considered the competing policy rationales . . . and that its decision was not arbitrary or capricious. . . .

CERTIFICATE OF NEED IN THE POST-AFFORDABLE CARE ACT ERA

Emily Whelan Parento[4]

105 Ky. L.J. 201 (2017)

I. The Evolution of Certificate of Need programs

CON programs are a powerful force in the majority of states, serving as a gatekeeper to the supply of healthcare facilities. Under CON laws, healthcare facilities are required to obtain a permit from state health planning entities before offering new services, constructing new buildings, or purchasing new medical equipment. For example, if a hospital wishes to add additional beds to its facility, it must seek approval from the state, which will evaluate the request based on a determination of, at minimum, whether there exists sufficient public "need" for the new beds. . . . Beyond need, which is usually determined either in whole or in part by reference to a numeric formula, additional review criteria may exist, including accessibility, costs, feasibility, available economic resources, quality, and others. . . .

[A]n understanding of the underlying rationale for CON and changes in the programs over time is essential to understanding their place in the modern healthcare delivery system. In most instances, the government allows market forces to determine the appropriate supply of a product, and for consumers to purchase the amount of that product that meets their needs. However, the market for healthcare services is not a normal market, and it is this recognition that led to the development of health planning authorities and ultimately to CON programs.

Following the end of World War II, "faced with the aging infrastructure of a healthcare system ill-equipped to accommodate the needs of returning soldiers and the inevitable baby boom that followed," Congress passed the Hospital Survey and Construction Act (the "Hill-Burton Act," or the "Act"), which was designed to promote public and nonprofit hospital construction and modernization . . . . As Nicholas Bagley recently observed, although the scope of the Hill-Burton Act increased rapidly throughout the 1960s, the health planning in this era "lacked regulatory bite," as planning agencies could advocate for particular facilities and services to be provided, but could not compel the private sector to build facilities or provide the needed services.[5]

. . . . [I]ncreasing health sector costs led government officials to look to additional strategies to regulate costs, including by instituting CON programs to constrain facility supply as a cost control mechanism, an approach heavily influenced by the theory of Milton Roemer that "[a] built bed is a filled bed." Under Roemer's Law, there exists a direct correlation between capacity and utilization; when combined with the availability of third-party reimbursement, oversupply of resources will create its own demand for excessive use. . . .

4. [Before joining the faculty of the University of the Pacific McGeorge School of Law, Prof. Parento was head of the Office of Health Policy in Kentucky, where she oversaw Kentucky's certificate of need program.]

5. Nicholas Bagley, Medicine as a Public Calling, 114 Mich. L. Rev. 57, 88 (2015).

Congress passed the National Health Planning and Resources Development Act of 1974 ("NHPRDA"). NHPRDA provided significant funding for state health planning activities and "effectively required states to adopt certificate of need laws conforming to federal standards." By 1980, every state except Louisiana had a CON program. . . . [By] preventing more beds from being built, and later by preventing proliferation of other services deemed "unnecessary," states–and, for a time, the federal government–hoped to slow the alarming rise in healthcare expenditures. Later, and perhaps in response to criticisms that the programs were proving ineffective at achieving meaningful cost containment, additional justifications for the programs became prevalent, such as ensuring an adequate distribution of healthcare services across geographic areas and socioeconomic groups, providing states a regulatory lever to require that healthcare providers deliver sufficient and quality care for the indigent. . . .

At first glance, it is not apparent how a supply constraint mechanism can result in lower costs for a product. Conventional economic theory suggests that restricting supply of a product does not result in reduced prices–rather, assuming constant demand, prices would increase in the face of decreased supply as more people competed to purchase a product in limited supply. However, healthcare is not a normal product and the market for health services has a number of factors that render it far from efficient. Thus, the theory for the ability of CON programs to contain costs, as noted above, is that by restricting the arms race among healthcare providers to build ever newer and more expensive facilities (e.g., new hospital buildings when an older one will suffice) and to offer newer and more expensive services even when those services are not demonstrably more effective than older treatments (e.g., MRI and CT scans instead of X-rays), CON programs prevent providers from raising prices to reflect the costs of these newer facilities and treatments. This theory was reasonable at the time it was first conceived–when providers were often paid an amount equal to their cost plus a small percentage of that cost, there was no incentive for providers to keep costs low. Thus, it stood to reason that restricting the ability of providers to increase their costs via capital expenditures would result in a more reasonable rate of increase in healthcare expenditures. . . .

While laudable in intent, CON programs were largely perceived as falling short of expectations by the early 1980s, particularly as a deregulatory political climate prevailed. Costs continued to escalate, and a number of studies found that CON programs did not help contain healthcare expenditures. Moreover, as larger and more influential healthcare entities learned to navigate the often complicated and bureaucratic programs, perceptions of protectionism of incumbents further undermined support for CON. Congress, too, became skeptical of the benefits of CON and repealed NHPRDA in 1987. By 1990, eleven states repealed their programs, and by 2000, a total of fourteen states had repealed their CON laws.

Although many states repealed their programs following the repeal of the federal mandate, the trend toward full repeal has stalled. . . . While CON remains prevalent, there continues to be vigorous debate over the wisdom of these programs in states at all points along the political spectrum. In recent years, several states have reexamined the efficacy of the CON system and proposed modifications to existing CON programs. In 2009, half of the thirty-six states with CON programs had bills to repeal or reform these programs introduced in their state legislatures. . . . These efforts at CON reform have continued in the post-Affordable Care Act era. . . .

II. Skepticism Toward Certificate of Need from All Quarters

. . . [F]or at least the past fifteen years, the FTC and the DOJ Antitrust Division have taken an active position against the continuance of CON programs. . . . In [various] statements, the agencies opine that CON laws impede the efficient performance of healthcare markets by creating barriers to entry and expansion, to the detriment of healthcare competition and consumers. The agencies cite economic research on the effects of CON laws, as well as some of the well-known risks that CON laws entail. For example, the agencies observe that in addition to limiting entry, CON laws create opportunities for existing competitors to exploit the CON process to thwart or delay new competition; they can facilitate anticompetitive agreements among providers; and, as noted by a number of researchers who interviewed former state CON officials, the CON process itself may be susceptible to corruption. . . .

Most recently in 2015, current FTC Commissioner Maureen K. Ohlhausen characterized certificate of need programs as a "prescription for higher costs." Ohlhausen observed that CON programs were particularly unhelpful to achieving the goals of healthcare market regulation in that they "stand out as an example of regulation that squelches the beneficial effects of competition in healthcare markets without delivering valuable public benefits in return." Noting that the cost-plus payment methodology that was in existence at the time programs began has been largely abolished in favor of negotiated rates between insurers and providers, Ohlhausen argued that as the "purported market failure that CON laws were designed to fix no longer exists," it should surprise no one that "it has proven difficult to demonstrate the benefits of a legislative scheme designed to fix an issue overtaken by subsequent events." She further explained that although the benefits of CON have been difficult to quantify, the negative results are readily apparent–CON laws operate to insulate healthcare providers from "socially beneficial" competition.

[Ohlhausen] correctly raises the question as to why CON laws are still on the books in thirty-five states even in the absence of demonstrable success at achieving their original cost containment objectives. The answer, it seems, is a combination of legislative inertia and shifting policy rationales of CON proponents to justify the continued existence of the programs. Ohlhausen observes that CON laws "insulate politically powerful incumbents from market forces, and those providers naturally are loathe to give up the special government preferences that CON laws bestow." However, she writes, incumbents cannot directly espouse to legislators that they deserve special protection at the expense of the public interest–so, instead, providers have adopted new rationales for the continued existence of CON, among them that the programs allow for improved care of the indigent.

This argument must be deconstructed to be understood, because it is not readily apparent how insulation from competition leads to better care for the poor. In essence, incumbents argue that the guarantee of restricted competition allows them to negotiate higher prices with private insurance companies, thereby conferring a larger profit margin, which allows for more resources to provide care to poorer patients without insurance. So, there is a cross-subsidization whereby providers, usually hospitals, will charge higher rates to wealthier patients and retain profitable procedures that might otherwise migrate to lower-cost venues (e.g., imaging, outpatient surgical procedures) to subsidize unprofitable areas of the business, including indigent care. The trouble, as Ohlhausen notes, is that this argument has not been proven to be correct; studies have not shown a marked difference in the provision of indigent care by hospitals in CON states as compared to those in states without the programs. . . . . Thus, she surmises that . . . arguments by CON proponents that the programs support indigent care claims "appear to be little more than an argument of convenience by politically powerful special interests attempting to protect their historical government perquisites." . . . .

Among academic scholars, it is rare to find ardent, or even lukewarm defenders of CON programs. Although the arguments for the effectiveness of CON have not been conclusively disproven, the prevailing view reflects considerable skepticism about the ability of CON programs to achieve any of their intended aims. . . . [T]here appears to widespread acknowledgement that CON programs as administered are essentially unable to be insulated from political influence. Arguing in 2010 in favor of a more evolved model of state health planning rather than turning the healthcare delivery system over to market forces, John Blum acknowledged the marked distinction between the intent and reality of CON programs:

> Somewhere along the journey of C.O.N. laws, these statutes became dominated by process review and evaluation, and the core function of creating state and regional health plans dropped from the agenda of these agencies, or planning was turned over to state bureaucrats whose best efforts were foiled by political realities.[6] . . .

III. The Ability of CON Programs to Survive Constitutional Challenge

It is not for lack of legal challenge that CON programs remain in place. Opponents have attempted a number of constitutional and other challenges to the laws, but courts have refused to overturn them.

The most obvious and common line of challenge to CON laws is under the Commerce Clause. In *Colon Health Centers of America v. Hazel*, 813 F.3d 145 (4th Cir. 2016), out-of-state providers of medical imaging services challenged Virginia's CON law under the dormant aspect of the Commerce Clause. The Fourth Circuit rejected the challenge and affirmed the district court, which found that the law neither discriminated nor placed an undue burden on interstate commerce. The court first reiterated the well-known standard that a statute that is facially discriminatory, or discriminatory in purpose or effect, may survive strict scrutiny only if it "advances a legitimate local purpose that cannot be adequately served by reasonable nondiscriminatory alternatives." While the parties agreed the statute was not facially discriminatory, plaintiffs argued that it was discriminatory in purpose, with a primary goal to shelter existing providers (all of whom were, by definition, in state) from competition at the expense of out-of-state businesses seeking entry into the market. Rejecting this argument, the court noted that Virginia's CON law served a number of "legitimate public purposes: improving healthcare quality by discouraging the

6. John D. Blum, *Finding a New Regulatory Pathway for the Old Labyrinth of Health Planning*, 19 Annals of Health L. 213, 216 (2010).

proliferation of underutilized facilities, enabling underserved and indigent populations to access necessary medical services, and encouraging cost-effective consumer spending." Accordingly, the court said it could not "discern a sinister protectionist purpose in this straightforward effort to bring medical care to all the citizens of the Commonwealth in the most efficient and professional manner."

Turning to the question of whether the law was discriminatory in effect, the court was equally unconvinced. Plaintiffs alleged that Virginia's law "systematically advantage[d] established in-state providers at the expense of new, primarily out-of-state firms," by impermissibly granting current providers "the authority to thwart the market entrance of out-of-state providers" through participation in the adversarial process as applications were evaluated (existing providers could oppose applications by new entrants at a hearing) and by allowing existing providers to file competing applications to block the approval of new entrants. The court evaluated these claims with regard to whether the plaintiffs demonstrated that Virginia's CON law, "if enforced, would negatively impact interstate commerce to a greater degree than intrastate commerce," in considering whether the CON law "erects a special barrier to market entry by non-domestic entities," but concluded that plaintiffs had not shown that they faced a special hardship compared to instate providers. The court noted repeatedly that CON programs are generally policy decisions that are properly the purview of legislators, and although the plaintiffs were frustrated by legislative policy, the court declined to take the "potentially limitless step of striking down every state regulatory program that has some alleged adverse effect on market competition." As the court observed, "[w]e live in such an interconnected economy that for any regulation some effects are almost bound to be felt out of state. To accept appellants' arguments 'would broaden the negative Commerce Clause beyond its existing scope.' "

Having rejected the plaintiffs' argument, the court determined that the law survived a rational basis review by balancing the putative local benefits against the incidental burdens on state commerce, as required by the Supreme Court in Pike v. Bruce Church, Inc., 397 U.S. 137 (1970). Virginia had put forth a number of rational reasons in support of its CON program, among them the many justifications described above–improvement in healthcare quality, indigent care, ensuring appropriate distribution of services across geographic areas, and even healthcare cost reduction. Fundamentally, the court believed that the decision over the merits of CON was a legislative one, observing that while "[t]he battle between laissez fairists and regulators is as old as the hills," these disputes are "more often over economics and politics than over law." Moreover, the court noted, "[l]egislators, not jurists, are best able to compare competing economic theories and sets of data and then weigh the result against their own political valuations of the public interests at stake."

. . . .

In short, the post-ACA healthcare market looks very different. This is true whether a state has embraced healthcare reform or resisted it. Accordingly, the historic rationale for CON programs, much of which rested on a foundation of (1) a large uninsured population requiring significant uncompensated care from providers and (2) a market in which providers were reimbursed under a FFS payment structure, must now be reexamined in view of the shifted coverage and payment landscape. Policy objectives such as cost containment via supply restrictions (on the theory that a bed built is a bed filled) and preventing overutilization of high-cost services are significantly less relevant when payment is based on the value of the service delivered rather than the quantity of services provided. Similarly, enabling cross-subsidization of profitable services to support the provision of indigent care becomes less necessary when the uninsured population is significantly reduced. . . .

The call for full-scale repeal of CON programs has largely been unsuccessful and seems likely to continue to fall on deaf ears among legislators in the states that retain CON laws. A more successful strategy for health-oriented policymakers and stakeholders is to embrace CON programs as an additional regulatory tool to drive systematic change in healthcare delivery systems, [such as preferential treatment for those who adopted interconnected electronic health records, meet objective quality metrics, or participate in value-based payment programs, as Kentucky was the first to do.]. . . .

Notes: Certificate of Need Regulation

1. *Incomplete Public Utility Regulation.* "Certificate-of-need laws establish entry controls which are similar in intent and impact to the certificate-of-public-convenience-and-necessity device widely employed in public utility and common carrier regulation." Clark Havighurst, Regulation of Health Facilities and Services by "Certificate of Need," 59 Va. L. Rev. 1143, 1153 (1973). As such, they appear to be an aggressive regulatory approach to containing health care costs. Yet it is hard to see why they might ever succeed. CON laws address primarily capital investment, not operating expenses. Thus, CON programs may slow the increase in numbers of beds, but the funds saved are simply moved to new services and equipment. Moreover, CON laws constrain only what hospitals *spend,* not what they *charge.* In the latter respect, CON programs constitute incomplete public utility regulation. Most such regulation imposes *price* controls in addition to *entry* controls. Indeed, price control would seem essential since restricting entry tends to create monopoly power. In contrast with the Fourth Circuit decision noted by Prof. Parento, one court relied on this effect of conferring state-sanctioned monopolies without controlling for monopolistic abuse to support its holding that the original North Carolina CON statute was unconstitutional. In re Certificate of Need for Ashton Park Hospital, 193 S.E.2d 729 (N.C. 1973). Other courts to consider the issue, though, have upheld the constitutionality of CON regulation.

2. *Needs vs. Wants.* When CON laws were first adopted, the CAT scanner was one of the primary examples cited of a technology much in need of centralized planning. Ironically, the capital expenditure threshold for CON review of equipment purchases has risen to the extent that CAT scanners usually require no approval. A greater irony is that the CON laws have proven inadequate for controlling even far more expensive technological devices. How has this happened? Consider the following explanation:

> Need is a medical concept, largely defined by professionals. It is subjective, rather than objective, and consequently is not a limiting, but an expansive concept. Unlike economic "demand" for goods and services, which reflects both consumers' wants and their resource limitations, medical need reflects what professionals deem desirable, rather than what patients can afford. Professionals decide what is needed according to their concept of what constitutes good care, which tends

> to be established according to the state of the art—what is medically possible at a given time. Virtually any medical benefit is seen as a need; medical professionals are generally guided by a more-is-better philosophy, which has been characterized as a "technological" or a "quality imperative." . . . The most obvious way to judge future need is to extrapolate from past patterns of growth for the institution or area under consideration. Historically, such projections have been the major quantitative tool of health planners. Simply applied, such methods perpetuate past patterns—including presumably inappropriate growth. . . . [T]he appropriateness of current utilization is not challenged. . . .

Randall Bovbjerg, Problems and Prospects for Health Planning: The Importance of Incentives, Standards, and Procedures in Certificate of Need, 1978 Utah L. Rev. 83. See also H. Aaron & William Schwartz, The Painful Prescription (1984) ("the prevention of all duplication would achieve only modest, one-time savings, which would not affect the subsequent rate of increases in cost."). Consider, for example, that even if CON laws can limit the number of X-ray or CAT scan machines, they do not limit the further development of different types of scanners. X-rays show bones and harder tissue in two dimensions. CAT scans do the same in three dimensions. MRIs show muscle and other soft tissue in much finer detail. PET scans reveal how organs are functioning, by identifying blood flow and metabolism. Each technology costs progressively more than the next, with PET scanners topping out at a several million dollars. Consider also proton beam therapy for cancer—which is much more precise than standard radiation therapy, but currently costs in the vicinity of $100 million per machine.

3. For review of the substantial case law challenging CON decisions, see Annot., 61 A.L.R.3d 278 (1994).

IRVINGTON GENERAL HOSPITAL v. DEPARTMENT OF HEALTH

374 A.2d 49 (N.J. Super. 1977)

Irvington General Hospital submitted an application for a certificate of need in November 1973. It sought permission to construct an addition to the hospital and to add . . . 19 medical/surgical beds. After several delays attributable both to the Department [of Health] and the applicant, hearings were held in September and October 1975. The hearing officer recommended that the application be approved. . . .

Between the time of the hearing and the time when the Health Care Administration Board considered the hearing officer's recommendation, the Board reclassified 150 long-term care beds at Clara Maas Hospital as medical/surgical beds, thereby creating an excess of medical/surgical beds in Essex County, the county in which Irvington General Hospital is located. . . . [O]n May 6, 1976 the Board remanded this application to the hearing officer, instructing him to make additional findings of fact "particularly pertinent to the current effect of the reclassification of the beds in the area."

The remand hearing was held, and thereafter the hearing officer recommended that the application be denied solely on the ground that Department of Health statistics now showed an excess of medical/surgical beds in the county. . . .

We agree with plaintiff's contention that the Board erred in giving conclusive weight to the[se] Department of Health statistics. . . . [T]he Legislature has required the Health Care Administration Board to take into account several factors:

> (a) the availability of facilities or services which may serve as alternatives or substitutes, (b) the need for special equipment and services in the area, (c) the possible economies and improvement in services to be anticipated from the operation of joint central services, (d) the adequacy of financial resources and sources of present and future revenues, (e) the availability of sufficient manpower in the several professional disciplines, and (f) such other factors as may be established by regulation.

It is clear, therefore, that in light of those established considerations and the general policy of providing the highest quality health care, it is not sufficient for the Board to consider only the number of beds available in the area, particularly where the area designated by the Department as the "area to be served" may not, in fact, coincide with the area for which the services will, in fact, be provided. Total reliance upon bed statistics would permit the Board to make its decision solely on the basis of the first factor noted in N.J.S.A. 26:2H-8: "the availability of facilities, or services which may serve as alternatives or substitutes." It would permit the Board to ignore the remaining factors, notably, in this case, the second one: "the need for special . . . services in the area."

The extensive record compels the conclusion that Irvington General Hospital primarily serves the population of the Town of Irvington. That town has the largest density of citizens over 65 of any municipality in this State. Testimony of various experts establishes that the elderly patients who make up the largest portion of the Hospital's population have a greater need than other patients for the support of relatives and friends during their illnesses, and that the knowledge that they and their families are secure is a significant factor in their successful medical treatment.

The testimony also shows that public transportation to other hospitals in Essex County is poor and that many elderly patients are at least reluctant to go to those hospitals because they are located in a high crime area. Moreover, their elderly spouses and friends are unable to visit them at other locations because of the lack of transportation and threats to their safety. . . .

[W]e believe that the Board, in deciding whether to grant a certificate of need, may not, as it did here, rely solely on bed need statistics. Unquestionably, it must also take into account all of the factors set out in N.J.S.A. 26:2H-8 and must, if appropriate, recognize and accept a need for special services in any local area smaller than the larger health care area established by the Department.

Because the Board failed to make those considerations a remand is required. On remand we direct that the Board take into account an additional factor: At the time of the original hearing the Department statistics showed that Essex County needed 73 more medical/surgical beds. By the time of the remand hearing 150 beds at Clara Maas Hospital had been reclassified to medical/surgical. That fact created an excess of beds in the county. The reclassification had been made upon application by Clara Maas suggested by the Department. We cannot tell from the record when the Clara Maas application was made. If, in fact, it was made after the application by Irvington General, we direct that the Irvington General application be considered first, since it was submitted first. In other words, on remand the

Irvington General application should be considered as if the Clara Maas application had not yet been determined. . . .

CERTIFICATE OF NEED FOR HEALTH CARE FACILITIES: A TIME FOR REEXAMINATION

Roberta M. Ross

7 Pace Law Review 491 (1987)

A. The Scope of CON Laws

[The model federal act, the National Health Planning and Resources Development Act (NHPRDA) of 1974,] required . . . CON review prior to:

> 1) acquisition of major medical equipment costing in excess of $400,000;
> 2) other obligations of capital expenditures in excess of $600,000, indexed for inflation;
> 3) capital expenditures resulting in a substantial change in bed capacity;
> 4) capital expenditures resulting in a substantial change in health services provided by a health care facility; and
> 5) offer[ing] of a new health service or reinstatement of a discontinued health service.

Institutional health care providers, such as hospitals or nursing homes, were subject to CON review [but doctors' offices were not]. Federal regulations defined "health care facilities" as hospitals, skilled nursing facilities, kidney disease treatment centers, intermediate care facilities, rehabilitation facilities, and ambulatory facilities. Health maintenance organizations (HMO's) were largely exempt from CON review.

NHPRDA's focus on institutional health care providers created a loophole that permitted private physicians to purchase equipment for their offices without CON review, while hospitals could purchase the same equipment only after going through CON review. . . . In response to this concern, an amendment . . . broadened NHPRDA's scope to include noninstitutional health care providers, such as individual physicians or groups of physicians, to the extent that they acquired expensive equipment located outside of a hospital but used to service inpatients of a hospital. Another provision of the 1979 amendment brought within the scope of CON acquisitions made "on behalf of a health care facility" as well as acquisitions made "by" the health care facility itself. . . .

B. Burdens Encountered in Complying with Requirements

Once a health care facility decides to make an application for a Certificate of Need, there are many potential sources of delay. The actual application can take months to prepare and, regardless of how lengthy it is, additional information is frequently requested. For example, the CON application filed by a group of Connecticut hospitals for a magnetic resonance imaging (MRI) center was over 1400 pages, and the required supplement exceeded 1700 pages. From conception until final approval, Greenwith Hospital's noncontroversial and unopposed request for a

CON to replace its telephone system took one year, and that period was "brief" only because the hospital agreed to waive its right to a hearing.

Review of an application may also be delayed by "batching," which requires applications for similar facilities or services to be evaluated contemporaneously and measured against each other. . . . Further delays may be caused by declarations of moratoria on review of CON applications.

The cost of applying for a CON can be considerable, exceeding $100,000 for major projects. If litigation is required, the cost may reach $350,000. . . .

C. Circumventing the Requirements

The burdens imposed by CON review have prompted health care facilities to seek ways of avoiding the requirement. Among the approaches they have taken are: piecemeal acquisition of major equipment where the components are below the monetary threshold for CON review; use of parent corporations and their subsidiaries to provide benefits to health care facilities; and arrangements between health care facilities and private physicians whereby the private physicians obtain major medical equipment, the benefits of which are made available to the health care facility. . . .

The first of the circumvention devices, piecemeal acquisition, is illegal in most instances. . . .

There is a paucity of cases involving the use of parent corporations to avoid review. This method, however, is not uncommon, and is openly employed. In a typical situation, a hospital seeks to construct a parking garage for the convenience of its patients and staff. Because the hospital is a health care facility, and because the garage may involve a capital expenditure in excess of the threshold, the hospital must apply for a CON. To avoid this, the hospital creates a parent corporate entity with two subsidiary corporations, one of which is the hospital. The second subsidiary is not a health care provider and, arguably, not subject to the CON statute. It builds and operates the garage with the result that the hospital has the parking facilities it requires, without subjecting the project to CON review.

. . . The use of creative corporate structuring devices to avoid review depends upon whether the state statute includes a CON requirement for acquisitions "on behalf of" a health care facility and, where it does have this requirement, how the phrase on behalf of is interpreted. For example, a Washington, D.C., court read this language to include the benefit to a hospital of a parking garage developed by a subsidiary of the hospital's corporate parent. An injunction was granted, halting the construction of a four and a half million dollar garage. . . . District of Columbia v. Washington Hosp. Center Health Sys., No. 6970-83 (D.C. Super. Ct. Jul. 25, 1983). . . . A Nebraska court, on the other hand, has interpreted "on behalf of" more narrowly, holding that a separate tax entity that constructs a physicians' office building adjacent to a hospital is not subject to CON, because on behalf of does not necessarily mean for the benefit of. State v. Coleman, No. 354-194 (Lancaster County Dist. Ct. Sept. 24, 1982). . . .

The third device, arrangements between health care facilities and private physicians, has been possible in states that failed to extend their CON statutes to physicians' offices in accordance with the federal amendment. Challenges to such arrangements have occurred in New York and New Jersey. . . . Using private funds, Clifton Springs Sanitarium purchased a trailer which it installed on its grounds eight feet from its hospital building. A walkway and electrical lines connected the trailer to the hospital building. The trailer was leased to a staff radiologist who leased, and later purchased, a CAT scanner. The radiologist performed CAT scans on inpatients of Clifton Springs Sanitarium, inpatients of other hospitals, and outpatients in the area. No CON was obtained. . . . The Administrative Law Judge concluded that the hospital had violated the law, and the state then ordered the doctor to discontinue performing CAT scans on patients of Clifton Springs Sanitarium. The Appellate Division annulled the determination, holding that a CON was not required because the CAT scan services were provided by a private physician and not by the hospital. Clifton Springs Sanitarium Co. v. Axelrod, 115 A.D.2d 949, 497 N.Y.S.2d 525 (4th Dep't 1985). The court took note that the trailer was purchased with private money and was not part of the hospital or constructed according to the hospital building code; that the scanner was the property of the doctor; that the doctor was not required to perform scans on the hospital's patients; and that the radiologist paid the staff and billed the patients directly. . . .

Conversely, a New Jersey court, deciding Radiological Society of New Jersey v. New Jersey State Department of Health, Hospital Rate Setting Commission, 208 N.J. Super. 548, 506 A.2d 755 (1986), read that state's CON statute as being applicable to private physicians who provide services to inpatients of a hospital. Despite the New Jersey statute's private physician exclusion, the Radiological court held that a physician who acquires a CAT scanner and magnetic resonance imaging (MRI) equipment must first obtain a CON. . . .

Whether it is desirable to close the loopholes that permit circumvention of the CON process is a policy decision that should be made only after an evaluation of the efficacy of the process. If the process does not make a significant contribution toward cost containment and equitable distribution of health care resources and if it provides, as some critics suggest, an obstacle to improved health care, it may be that the CON requirement should be abandoned.

D. The Impact of CON Laws

. . . The enormous expenditure of time and money by both administrative agencies and health care providers in complying with the CON process substantially reduces any savings that might be attributable to it. For all its promise, CON review has resulted in the elimination of few projects. Of over 20,000 CON applications reviewed throughout the country between 1979 and 1981, only ten percent were ultimately disapproved. Such statistics prompt understandable concern as to the wisdom of continuing to invest significant amounts of time, money, and effort on the CON process. . . .

Notes: Certificate of Need Review Criteria and Process

1. *Competing Criteria.* How is an agency to "take into account all of the factors set out in [the CON statute]" as required by *Irvington* when those factors are as diverse and opposed as quality, cost, and access?

> Most CON programs . . . have one stated goal: the promotion of equal access to quality health care at reasonable cost. The problem is that this single, seemingly unimpeachable goal is in reality three goals that compete and are often mutually

> irreconcilable: quality, accessibility, and cost control. How these three goals are interpreted and implemented varies directly with who is doing the interpreting and for what purpose. Health care providers, for example, tend to perceive need from the quality side of the spectrum. . . . Consumers, while also oriented to issues of quality, tend to view accessibility as a major goal of CON. . . . As for the regulators, there can be little doubt that CON has one essential purpose: to keep costs down.

Medicine in the Public Interest, Certificate of Need: An Expanding Regulatory Concept (1978).

2. *Difficulties Associated with Health Planning.* "Perhaps the chief source of discouragement about health planning is the complexity of the task. Among the factors relevant in the planning effort are [the nature of existing facilities and their service areas, population size and characteristics, and current use patterns]. Even this list fails to convey the difficulty of projecting changes in population, technology, . . . and patterns of utilization. . . . The complexity is such that the agencies themselves lack confidence in their ability to make hard-and-fast judgments, and the result is a lack of firm standards for decision making. In such circumstances, the pressures of politics necessarily become dominant." Clark Havighurst, supra, 59 Va. L. Rev. 1202-1204.

3. *The Scope of CON Laws.* States have departed from the federal model in several ways. About a dozen states have entirely repealed their CON laws. Many others have modified their laws to narrow the range of health care facilities and projects subject to review. For instance, many states have raised the dollar thresholds to double or more the original federal levels. A few states have reinvigorated this regulation by adopting an entirely different approach to defining the scope of their CON laws. These states cover specified new health services regardless of their capital or operating cost and regardless of whether a "health care facility" undertakes the expenditure. This approach is typical for organ transplant and heart surgery programs and for expensive diagnostic machinery.

4. *Circumvention Techniques.* The doctor's office exemption has proven to be quite a large loophole. For instance, the exemption has been used frequently to purchase magnetic resonance imagers (MRIs) without CON approval. MRIs are highly sophisticated diagnostic scanning devices that cost over $1 million to $2 million installed. Although they originally were found only in major medical centers, the majority of MRIs are now located outside the hospital setting, in part because of the CON laws. As Ross summarizes, a number of states have attempted to close this loophole by extending CON laws to outpatient facilities intended primarily to treat inpatients, while others apply CON review to specified equipment and services regardless of institutional sponsorship.

Health care facilities have found various other inventive techniques for circumventing the CON laws. One is suggested by Irvington's willingness to "recognize and accept a need . . . in [a] local area smaller than the larger health care area established by the Department." For instance, an applicant in an overserved metropolitan area may try to carve out an unserved area in the affluent, growing suburbs, as suggested by the *Overlake* case. Whether this technique is successful turns on whether the suburbs are considered to be within the service area of the existing "downtown" facilities. States vary in their methodologies for defining service areas. Without entering into the full complexities of service area gerrymandering, consider what the policy implications are of (a) refusing local medical facilities to newly emerging communities and (b) locating new construction in affluent white suburbs to the detriment of patient census in older, city-center hospitals.

Another technique for circumventing numerical service-need limitations is for an existing hospital to construct a new facility that "replaces" older beds, sometimes in an entirely different location. This technique of trading in old beds for new ones has created a lively market in the sale of older hospitals. In some cases, the replaced capacity consists of only "paper beds," i.e., licensed bed capacity that has long since been taken out of operation to make room for other uses and services.

5. *Review Procedures.* Irvington required the earlier CON application to be considered first. But what if both applications were filed at approximately the same time? In such circumstances, courts require the applications to be considered in a comparative hearing, which seeks to determine not only whether there is a need for the service or facility, but, if so, who among many hospitals will best serve that need. Comparative hearings can turn into surprisingly complex affairs that last for weeks. Once one application is filed, it is usually followed by several other competing ones that are batched together in the same review cycle. In the experience of one of your authors, these contests quickly degenerate into disputes over trivia such as who has the superior parking lot design or who is cutting down the most trees. See generally Annot., 61 A.L.R.3d 278 (1994).

B. CORPORATE FORM

1. Nonprofit and Public Entities

Regulatory constraints on medical institutions are not always imposed from external sources. Some derive from their own internal organization. For instance, because most hospitals and some HMOs are organized as nonprofit corporations, they are subject to a special set of corporate governance and tax rules, which the next case introduces. Public hospitals are subject to similar restrictions. These ancient rules, derived from the law of charitable trusts, are becoming increasingly relevant as various health care facilities contemplate expanding their range of activities or converting to a more commercialized corporate form.

■ QUEEN OF ANGELS HOSPITAL v. YOUNGER
136 Cal. Rptr. 36 (Cal. 1977)

KAUS, Presiding Justice.

[Queen of Angels Hospital (Queen) was founded in 1927 in connection with the Catholic church. The Franciscan Sisters of the Sacred Heart, known as "the Motherhouse," is a large religious order that, for 30 years, has staffed an outpatient clinic in the hospital.] . . . In April 1971—the details will be supplied in the discussion—Queen's board of directors approved a lease to be effective May 1, 1971, between Queen as lessor and W.D.C. Services, Inc., hospital entrepreneurs, as lessee. Queen leased the hospital, excepting the outpatient clinic and a convent house, to W.D.C. for 25 years with two options for ten additional years each. The minimum annual rental guaranteed Queen was $800,000 for the first two years and one million dollars a year thereafter.

Queen intends to use a substantial portion of the lease proceeds to establish and operate additional medical clinics in East and South Central Los Angeles, which clinics will dispense free medical care, aid and advice to the poor and needy. It is not disputed that an outpatient clinic is not functionally equivalent to a hospital.

In June 1971, the Motherhouse submitted a claim for 16 million dollars for the value of the Sisters' past services to Queen's board of directors. . . . [A]n agreement was executed between Queen and the Motherhouse, effective May 1971, settling and compromising the claim for the Sisters' past services by agreeing that Queen should pay to the Motherhouse $200 per month for each Sister in the Order over the age of 70 years, . . . whether or not the particular Sister performed services at Queen of Angels Hospital. The initial annual cost of the agreement would be $309,600—in July 1971, there were 129 Sisters over the age of 70. . . .

[Queen and Motherhouse] filed a declaratory relief action against the Attorney General to determine the validity of [the] lease agreement . . . and the . . . retirement pay. . . . [The trial court ruled in favor of the plaintiffs on the issue of the lease but against the plaintiffs on the issue of the retirement pay, and so both parties appealed.]

1. The Hospital [Lease]

The Attorney General contends that under its articles of incorporation, Queen held its assets in trust primarily for the purpose of operating a hospital, and the use of those assets exclusively for outpatient clinics would constitute an abandonment of Queen's primary charitable purpose and a diversion of charitable trust assets. . . .

The rules governing the use of the assets of a nonprofit charitable organization are well established: "(A)ll the assets of a corporation organized solely for charitable purposes must be deemed to be impressed with a charitable trust by virtue of the express declaration of the corporation's purposes. . . . It follows that . . . (a nonprofit corporation cannot) legally divert its assets to any purpose other than charitable purposes. . . ." Pacific Home v. County of Los Angeles, 41 Cal. 2d 844, 852, 264 P.2d 539, 543. "Since there is usually no one willing to assume the burdens of a legal action, or who could properly represent the interest of the trust or the public, the Attorney General has been empowered to oversee charities as the representative of the public." Holt v. College of Osteopathic Physicians & Surgeons, 61 Cal. 2d 750, 754, 40 Cal. Rptr. 244, 247, 394 P.2d 932, 935. . . .

With this apparent agreement in principle we turn to an examination of the articles of incorporation and the relevant undisputed facts. The articles of incorporation, as amended in 1941, provides in relevant part as follows:

> . . . the purposes for which said corporation is formed are:
>
> (1) To establish, . . . own, . . . maintain, . . . and operate a hospital in the City of Los Angeles, . . . to furnish, . . . hospital care, . . . and medical and surgical treatment of every kind and character, and to receive, treat and care for patients, invalids, the aged and infirm, and generally to conduct and carry on, and to do all things necessary or advisable in conducting and carrying on a hospital;

> (2) To perform and to foster and support acts of Christian charity particularly among the sick and ailing; to practice, foster and encourage religious beliefs and activities, particularly those of the Holy Roman Catholic Church; to house and care for unprotected and indigent sick, aged and infirm persons regardless of race, creed, sex or age;
>
> (3) To educate, . . . nurses and medical students, and to provide facilities for the same;
>
> (4) That it is a corporation which is not formed for pecuniary gain . . . and any revenue received . . . from the operation and carrying on of said hospital shall be used in improving the same . . . or shall be used in enlarging and improving said hospital and in enlarging the field and scope of its charitable, religious and educational activities;
>
> (5) To lease or purchase any real estate, . . . which may be necessary, proper or useful in carrying out the purposes or for the benefit of the hospital, or as may be deemed to be conducive to the welfare of this corporation; . . .[2]

[W]hat is most apparent in the articles of incorporation is that . . . the framework of those multiple purposes is the operation of a hospital. Clinics are not even mentioned. . . . [A]lthough Queen did operate a clinic from 1932 to the present time, that clinic was physically housed within the hospital and drew on hospital resources. . . .

Queen also represented to the public that it was a hospital. In its statement to the Franchise Tax Board, it stated that it was in the "business of running a hospital." Similar statements were made to the Internal Revenue Service and Los Angeles county tax authorities. Funds were solicited from the public for the hospital or hospital purposes. Such acts further bind Queen to its primary purpose of operating a hospital. In brief, whatever else Queen of Angels Hospital Corporation may do under its articles of incorporation, it was intended to and did operate a hospital and cannot, consistent with the trust imposed upon it, abandon the operation of the hospital business in favor of clinics.

Queen's argument in response does not meet the issue. Plaintiffs point out, as we have noted, that the corporation has multiple "purposes"; that the purpose "to furnish, . . . medical and surgical treatment" is broad enough to authorize the operation of a clinic or clinics and that acts of "Christian charity" encompass all forms of medical aid, care, and advice to the poor and needy. None of the foregoing is disputed. The question is not whether Queen can use some of its assets or the proceeds from the operation of the hospital for purposes other than running a hospital; it certainly can and has. The question is whether it can cease to perform the primary purpose for which it was organized. That, we believe, it cannot do.

Moreover, the issue is not, as plaintiffs contend, whether the operation of clinics serving the poor in the areas in which they live is as worthy a use of charitable funds. . . . This corporation is bound by its articles of incorporation. Queen may maintain a hospital and retain control over its assets or it may abandon the

2. The articles also contain a "parity clause" which provides that the corporation may generally "do all acts and things which may be necessary, proper, useful or advantageous to the full carrying out of the purposes of this corporation." . . .

operation of a hospital and lose those assets to the successor distributees, but it cannot do both. . . .

2. The Retirement Plan

The trial court made the following relevant findings: . . . The property of Queen does not belong to either the Motherhouse or the Roman Catholic Church. From the inception of the hospital through 1971, services . . . provided Queen by the [M]otherhouse . . . were considered donated to Queen by both parties. Neither the Motherhouse nor the Sisters expected any further or future compensation for those services. Although the claim for compensation for past services was made in good faith and was not a dishonest claim, "there was no basis for such claim and neither the Motherhouse nor Queens had a reasonable basis for believing in the validity of the claim." The compromise of the claim—e.g., the retirement plan—"was not a proper exercise of sound business judgment or of the fiduciary duties of Queens' Board." The court concluded that . . . the retirement plan was invalid and that, if implemented, it would constitute a diversion of charitable assets.

First, although plaintiffs make much of the relationship between Queen and the Motherhouse and attempt to present this relationship in terms of Roman Catholic Canon Law, the trial court properly rejected this approach. Plaintiffs' assertion that such evidence is material reflects an attempt to bootstrap a First Amendment argument by citing . . . moral and ecclesiastic duties of Queen and the Motherhouse, and then arguing that whether the retirement plan accords with church doctrine is an internal ecclesiastic matter. Throughout, plaintiffs have sought the benefits of and conformed to the general requirements of civil law; they cannot now decline to be ruled by the principles which Queen has itself invited.

Applying neutral principles, . . . there was no reasonable basis for compromising the 16 million-dollar claim submitted by the Motherhouse for past services. Although plaintiffs attempt to analogize the pension plan to a—sometimes—enforceable promise to pay for past services, as the Attorney General points out, the compromise "bore no relationship whatsoever to a traditional retirement plan as it provided payments to all of the Sisters of the Order over the age of 70 wherever situated, regardless of whether they had ever served at Queen of Angels, or if so, how long, or when, and regardless of any other provisions being made for such Sisters through retirement plans at any of the other ten hospitals established by the Franciscan Sisters." . . .

3. [Legal and Business] Fees

[The lease was negotiated by an attorney, John Brandlin, who was also a member of Queen's board of directors.] The Attorney General contends that Queen's agreement to pay [Brandlin and his business partners] 3 percent of the annual rentals for the first five years of the lease and 2 percent of the annual rentals for each year thereafter as fees for negotiating the lease is, in fact, an agreement to pay real estate brokers' fees and, since none of the recipients is licensed, the agreement is invalid. . . .

The underlying facts are as follows: During the time in which this lease was negotiated, prepared and executed, Brandlin was Queen's attorney and also a member of Queen's board of directors. The hospital was in financial difficulties and Brandlin was authorized to find out what could be done about leasing the hospital, an idea he had proposed informally. Another of Brandlin's clients was John L. Donovan, a stockbroker, through whom Brandlin met Glenn Thomason, "a kind of hospital entrepreneur" who "deals in hospitals." None of the three was licensed as a real estate broker. In late 1969, Brandlin, Donovan and Thomason had contemplated the formation of a corporation—"American Hospital Administrators"—to acquire or lease hospitals and go "public" with them, but the project never got off the ground.

In July 1970, after preliminary discussions, Brandlin was told by Sister Timothy Marie that Queen was interested in pursuing the possibility of a lease. . . . After further discussions with W.D.C. and with the Order's headquarters in Illinois, Brandlin began preparing the documents. Brandlin did all of the legal work.

The agreement presented to the Board covering the services of Thomason, Donovan and Brandlin states that the three "are entitled to reasonable compensation" for their "services." . . . Brandlin was employed on a retainer basis by Queen until about April 1971, and thereafter he billed his legal services—other than the fee in dispute—based upon an hourly rate. . . .

That Brandlin's involvement in three capacities—lawyer, trustee and frustrated entrepreneur—was legal and professional dynamite is obvious. Nevertheless, professional protocol—such as disclosure [and] disqualification as trustee when called for—appears to have been scrupulously observed. . . .

In essence, this is what happened: Brandlin rendered legal services to Queen's. These were undoubtedly of such a nature that a layman would have been required to be a licensed real estate broker. Brandlin, however, was an attorney and, as such, came within [an] exception. . . . The Attorney General claims that Queen could not obligate itself to pay Donovan and Thomason anything because they were more than mere finders [and thus were seeking a sales commission without a real estate license]. To be brief and blunt, we disagree on the facts. . . .

The judgment is reversed.

COLUMBIA/HCA AND THE RESURGENCE OF THE FOR-PROFIT HOSPITAL BUSINESS*

Robert Kuttner**

335 New Eng. J. Med. 362 (1996)

This two-part article addresses the medical, ethical, and public-policy issues posed by the resurgence of for-profit chains and their acquisition of nonprofit community hospitals. The prime case in point is Columbia/HCA Healthcare Corporation, the largest and most aggressive of the for-profit chains, the product of three large and several smaller mergers. With 340 hospitals, 135 outpatient-surgery offices, and 200 home health care agencies in 38 states, Columbia/HCA

*Excerpted with permission of the publisher. Copyright © 1992, Massachusetts Medical Society.

**The author is a respected journalist and social critic.

now controls nearly half the for-profit beds, and 7 percent of all hospital beds, in the United States. The company's gross earnings exceed 20 percent of revenues, and its 1995 profits were just under $1 billion, with $20 billion in assets. . . .

Columbia's founder, Richard Scott, bought his first two hospitals in El Paso, Texas, from Healthtrust in 1988. From a base of 12 hospitals in 1991, Columbia acquired Basic American Medical (1992, 8 hospitals), Galen (1993, 71 hospitals), HCA (1994, 97 hospitals), Medical Care America (1994, 96 ambulatory surgical centers), and the rest of Healthtrust (1995, 117 hospitals) after a bidding war with NME. . . . In 1995 alone, Columbia/HCA acquired or negotiated joint ventures with 32 nonprofit hospitals. . . .

The company has targeted and achieved a formidable corporate goal of a 20 percent gross return on revenues. I was told by a Columbia/HCA executive that chief executives of company hospitals who fall short of this goal are regularly called to corporate headquarters in Nashville to explain and are ordered to redouble their efforts. Further economies at the local hospital usually follow. . . .

Columbia/HCA's most audacious recent foray [is] in Ohio. . . . In March, Blue Cross and Blue Shield of Ohio, the state's largest insurer, with annual revenues of some $2 billion, agreed to sell 85 percent ownership to Columbia for $299.5 million through a complex venture called BlueCo, legally crafted to avoid the form of a conversion, thus eliminating a payout obligation to policyholders or a charitable foundation. Because $223 million of Blue Cross and Blue Shield reserves would go to the new venture, Columbia/HCA would be buying Blue Cross and Blue Shield largely with the latter's own assets. . . . Under the proposed acquisition, Columbia/HCA will pay three top executives of Ohio Blue Cross and Blue Shield over $15 million in severance payments characterized as consulting fees and agreements not to compete, with millions more going as a consulting fee to the Blues' outside lawyer. . . .

[T]he big nonprofits are now in many ways defensively emulating Columbia/HCA and other for-profits. . . . A market culture and market idiom are becoming pervasive, even among nonprofits. Within living memory, service areas were not called markets; heads of hospitals were administrators, not chief executive officers; hospitals did not advertise for patients; and few hospital administrators spoke of market share, let alone EBITDA (earnings before interest, taxes, depreciation, and amortization). All this has changed, perhaps irrevocably. . . .

[A year after this was written, Richard Scott, who subsequently became governor of Florida, was ousted by Columbia/HCA's board of directors, in part because the company's image had become so tarnished by his management style. This occurred amid a sweeping federal probe of billing practices at several of Columbia's hospitals, and was followed by criminal fraud indictments against several of Columbia's managers. The company has since dropped Columbia from its name and returned to HCA, for Hospital Corporation of America. To settle the government's fraud investigation and associated lawsuits, HCA agreed to pay a record $1.7 *billion*. See Symposium, 17(2) Health Aff. 1 (Mar.–Apr. 1998). It is still the largest hospital chain in the country.

Similar controversy subsequently erupted for another for-profit hospital chain, Tenet Healthcare, which also agreed to a very large settlement, of nearly $900 million. See Elizabeth A. Weeks, Gauging the Cost of Loopholes: Health Care Pricing and Medicare Regulation in the Post-Enron Era, 40 Wake Forest L. Rev. 1215 (2005).]

Notes: Charitable Trust Law; Public and Religious Hospitals; For-Profit Conversions

1. Queen of Angels, the hospital, was located near Hollywood and, at one time, was the birthplace for the vast majority of L.A. residents, including many movie stars. In 1985, it merged with Hollywood Presbyterian Medical Center, and was then purchased by the for-profit Tenet Health System in 1998, and sold in 2005 to Dr. Kwang Yul Cha, a Korean fertility specialist. The new management team borrowed from the hotel industry to provide concierge-type services such as valet parking and bellhop attendants. In 2007, the hospital agreed to pay a $1 million fine resulting from a federal investigation into its allegedly dumping an uninsured paraplegic patient on skid row wearing nothing more than a soiled gown and a broken colostomy bag. Richard Winton, Skid Row Dumping Suit Settled, L.A. Times, May 31, 2008.

Queen of Angels, the case, succinctly applies three distinct doctrines of nonprofit and charitable trust law: (1) *ultra vires* or charitable purpose; (2) duty of care or the business judgment rule; and (3) duty of loyalty and conflict of interest. These notes will explore each in turn.

2. *Ultra vires* ("beyond its powers") is the term sometimes used to describe the court's first holding. How would you revise the articles of incorporation to avoid this holding? Where bylaws are worded differently, courts are usually not nearly such sticklers about modifying corporate purposes, as long as the new purpose still pursues the same general charitable aims. See, e.g., Attorney General v. Hahnemann Hospital, 494 N.E.2d 1011 (Mass. 1986) (allowing hospital to devote proceeds of its sale to other health care institutions but not to "any activity that promotes the health of the general public" such as research or education). Restrictions can be even more stringent than in *Queen of Angels,* however, if the hospital has received gifts with specific strings attached. Especially troubling are gifts limited to a particular facility's location or ownership, not just to the facility type. One commentator explains:

> Unrestricted gifts received by a charitable corporation must be used for a purpose for which the charitable corporation exists generally; gifts which have certain terms or conditions attached must be used in accordance with such specifications. These restrictions can be extraordinarily burdensome to the sale or lease of an entire facility, particularly since the facility might be constructed with gifts from thousands of individual donors. As an example, Professor Bloche [infra] recounts the difficulty faced by Creighton University when it sold its primary teaching hospital to American Medical International. . . . The University had to consider whether the sale of the hospital was consistent with [a] single [restricted] gift, even though it constituted only a tiny fraction of the hospital's original construction costs.

Jeffrey Heidt, Conversion of Status and Facility Closure, *in* Health Care Corporate Law: Facilities and Transactions (M. Hall & W. Brewbaker eds., 1996).

3. *Public and Religious Hospitals.* Public hospitals, those owned by government and chartered by statute, are subject to similar limitations on their powers, depending on how their corporate purposes are stated in the governing statutes. See, e.g., New York City Council v. Giuliani, 93 N.Y.2d 60 (1999) (public hospital not authorized to enter long-term sublease agreement). But see In re University Hospitals

Authority, 953 S.W.2d 314 (Okla. 1997) (approving a state university hospital's long-term lease and management agreement with a for-profit company).

Queen of Angels Hospital also highlights another source of restriction for corporate transactions—religious law—which is particularly important for Catholic hospitals because of the formality of canon law. Although the court found that canon law does not *supersede* secular law, it does *supplement* secular law in practical effect. Before undertaking a major corporate transaction, a Catholic institution must receive approval from the Holy See that it satisfies the Ethical and Religious Directives for Catholic Health Facilities. This requirement stopped another effort by the Queen of Angels board to sell its hospital. The archbishop of Los Angeles refused approval, and the state attorney general ruled that the hospital's bylaws make this decision binding on the corporation. But see Kansas East Conference of the United Methodist Church v. Bethany Medical Center, 969 P.2d 859 (Kan. 1998) (Methodist church is not entitled to the proceeds from the sale of a hospital it helped to found.).

4. Cy Pres. As the court briefly notes, the *ultra vires* doctrine does not require a nonprofit board to continue running a money-losing hospital until it goes bankrupt. The board is permitted to wind up operations and transfer ownership entirely to a new corporation. In such an event, another trust law doctrine, *cy pres* ("as near as possible"), determines what alternative use to make of the proceeds from the sale. *Cy pres* precedents allow considerably more flexibility in selecting alternate charitable purposes of the same general type when the original purpose is no longer possible or practical. Should a long-term lease be treated so differently than a complete sale, especially when the lease was approved by the same religious order that founded the hospital? Should courts give nonprofit hospitals greater managerial leeway today as a result of the greatly increased competition caused by the rapid infiltration of managed care? One commentator has opined in the context of teaching hospitals that "courts should give considerable weight to the argument that intensified competitive pressures in the hospital industry are 'circumstances not . . . foreseen' by a donor and [thus a gift to a medical school would be rendered] more effective in advancing teaching and research if applied to some activity other than hospital operations." M. Gregg Bloche, Corporate Takeover of Teaching Hospitals, 65 S. Cal. L. Rev. 1035 (1992).

Where circumstances justify invoking the *cy pres* doctrine, then the alternative uses for the proceeds are usually quite broad. As Heidt, supra, explains:

> Nonprofit hospitals that sell or lease their facilities will usually attempt to comply with these restrictions in one of three ways. First, they might use the proceeds to operate a different type of health care facility such as an outpatient clinic or long-term care facility. Second, the nonprofit can consider converting to a funding agency that supports other health care facilities or activities. For instance, the proceeds from the sale or lease of a teaching hospital might be used to fund medical research. Third, the proceeds might be used to support charitable activities at the very facility being sold or leased. Such activities include not only medical education and research, but also charity care. In structuring this latter arrangement, however, care must be taken to avoid the characterization that the nonprofit is paying a rebate to the for-profit buyer by helping the buyer to reduce its bad debt.

5. *Conversions to For-Profit.* As Kuttner explains, nonprofit health care entities, including hospitals and HMOs, are increasingly converting to for-profit status by

selling out to investor-owned corporations—not so much because they are losing money but because they can make more if they have better access to capital. In one of the most notable instances, Blue Cross of California created a for-profit HMO subsidiary called WellPoint Health Networks. WellPoint was a big success, and its stock became very valuable. In 1993, California Blue Cross folded itself into WellPoint, thereby giving up its nonprofit status, but California regulators required Blue Cross to leave $3 billion of assets behind in a nonprofit foundation to support medical research and care for the poor.

In such cases, the difficult legal issue is not only what alternative uses to make of the charitable proceeds, but also whether the buyer is paying sufficient value for the business and its assets so that the past support from donors and from tax exemption is not dissipated. The bargained-for price is often not reliable because the purchasing corporation is often not at arm's length, especially when it is simply part of an internal corporate reorganization, as in the Blue Cross example. These concerns have prompted state attorneys general to assert jurisdiction over these transactions by invoking their authority under either common law or under newly enacted statutes in many states designed to regulate (or perhaps discourage) these transactions. Also, consumer advocates have sued to enforce charitable trust principles. In some cases, converting hospitals and insurers have been required to turn over to a foundation only a relatively modest sum ($50 million to $150 million), based on the net asset value of the company. In other instances, however, such as the California Blue Cross conversion, the foundation has been given full stock ownership of the new company, which avoids the need to agree to a valuation. When the foundation divests the stock, it is usually worth many times more than the company's asset value. Which measure of value is more appropriate: the historical asset value while the company was still a nonprofit, or the new equity value created by the conversion to for-profit status? See In re Manhattan Eye, Ear & Throat Hospital, 715 N.Y.S.2d 575 (Sup. Ct. 1999) (blocking a transaction similar to that in *Queen of Angels* because the sales price failed to account for the goodwill value of the hospital's name and its value as an ongoing business).

Should these conversions concern us? Perhaps the incentive that insurers and HMOs have to compromise care is much more tolerable if the nonprofit form meant that denying care to one patient is likely to help another patient who is in greater need. Because nonprofit insurers may not distribute earnings to owners, perhaps there is a greater chance their earnings will be devoted to patient care. One indication this is true is that the "medical loss ratio" (the amount of premium dollars devoted to medical care rather than to overhead) is generally higher for nonprofit HMOs than for for-profits. Also, some research studies have found that nonprofit HMOs perform notably better than for-profits on a number of measures of quality of care. Ha T. Tu & James D. Reschovsky, Assessments of Medical Care by Enrollees in For-Profit and Nonprofit Health Maintenance Organizations, 346 New Eng. J. Med. 1288 (2002). Based on these factors, Minnesota requires all HMOs to be nonprofit. See also Premera v. Kreidler, 131 P.3d 930 (Wash. App. 2006) (upholding a regulator's refusal to allow a Blue Cross plan in Washington State to convert to for-profit status).

6. *Business Judgment.* The Motherhouse pension plan was struck down as an improper "exercise of sound business judgment," which the board members are required to exercise as part of their fiduciary duty of care. Again, this appears to be

an especially strict application of fiduciary rules. In contrast, the business judgment rule that applies to for-profit directors is considerably more forgiving. Other courts have rejected the stricter charitable trust scrutiny and ruled that the same leniency should be given to nonprofit as to for-profit directors, considering that they often serve for free and they increasingly are functioning in a more commercial business climate that requires broader business discretion. The leading case to this effect was decided in relation to another hospital, one whose board members were sued for investing its funds in low-interest accounts at banks affiliated with board members. Stern v. Lucy Webb Hayes National Training School for Deaconesses & Missionaries, 381 F. Supp. 1003 (D.D.C. 1974) (holding, despite the more lenient scrutiny, that fiduciary duties were violated by the conflict of interest). This liberalized business judgment rule is adopted by the Revised Model Nonprofit Corporation Act §8.30.

7. *Conflicts of Interest.* Brandlin, the Queen of Angels lawyer, ran a serious risk of violating his duty of loyalty because of the conflict of interest between his board position and his own law practice and entrepreneurship. He was saved by full disclosure and because his terms were reasonable. But for that, the transaction might have been declared void and Brandlin held liable for damages to the corporation. In Boston Children's Heart Foundation v. Nadal-Ginard, 73 F.3d 429 (1st Cir. 1996), the court upheld a $6.5 million award against a physician board member and employee who failed to disclose he was being paid to work for a competing hospital and research center at the same time.

Is it appropriate for existing board members and top management to participate in the profits realized by a conversion to for-profit status? This might occur if they take an ownership position in the new for-profit corporation, or if they are given stock as part of a severance bonus. Although the initial ownership share or severance bonus might be valued only modestly, when the for-profit decides to "go public" (sell shares in the stock market), the initial directors and managers might find themselves suddenly wealthy, as happened with Blue Cross of California and with many other recent hospital and HMO conversions like those described by Kuttner. The usual remedy for a conflict of interest is disclosure and ratification by the board, but this does not work where most or all of the board is subject to the same conflict. As a result, a state court may be asked to evaluate the fairness of the transaction to the nonprofit entity under common-law principles of fiduciary responsibility. Also, these transactions raise dangerous red flags of "private inurement" under principles of tax exemption discussed below.

8. *Further Readings.* On **religious hospitals** (note 3), see Kathleen Boozang, Deciding the Fate of Religious Hospitals in the Emerging Health Care Market, 31 Hous. L. Rev. 1429 (1995); Lisa C. Ikemoto, When a Hospital Becomes Catholic, 47 Mercer L. Rev. 1087 (1996); Lawrence Singer, Realigning Catholic Health Care: Bridging Legal and Church Control in a Consolidating Market, 72 Tulane L. Rev. 159 (1997); Comment, 17 St. Louis U. Pub. L. Rev. 157 (1999).

On **conversion to for-profit status** (note 5), see Mark A. Hall & Christopher Conover, Privatization of Blue Cross Plans: Public Benefit or Public Harm?, 27 Annu. Rev. Public Health 443 (2006); David Hyman, Hospital Conversions: Fact, Fantasy, and Regulatory Follies, 23 J. Corp. L. 741 (1998); Mark Krause, "First, Do No Harm": An Analysis of the Nonprofit Hospital Sale Acts, 45 UCLA L. Rev. 503 (1997).

On the **business judgment rule** (note 6), see Michael Peregrine & James Schwartz, The Business Judgment Rule and Other Protections for the Conduct of Not-for-Profit Directors, 33 J. Health L. 455 (2000); Mary O'Byrne, Directors' Duty of Care to Monitor Information Systems in HMOs: Some Lessons from the Oxford Health Plan, 14 J.L. & Health 45 (2000).

For discussion of the post-Enron corporate governance issues raised by **the Sarbanes-Oxley Act**, see Robert W. Friz et al., The Sarbanes-Oxley Act: Considerations for Nonprofit Health Care Organizations, 18(5) The Health Lawyer 1 (June 2006); Michael J. Myers, Juxtaposing Sarbanes-Oxley with JCAHO Governance Standards: A Shortcut to Auditable Health System Compliance?, 51 S.D. L. Rev. 465 (2006); Glenn T. Troyer et al., Governance Issues for Nonprofit Healthcare Organizations and the Implications of the Sarbanes-Oxley Act, 1 Ind. Health L. Rev. 175-211 (2004); James G. Wiehl, Roles and Responsibilities of Nonprofit Health Care Board Members in the Post-Enron Era, 25 J. Leg. Med. 411 (2004); Symposium, 3 Seattle J. Soc. Justice 205 (2004); Note, 2011 U. Ill. L. Rev. 229.

Problem: For-Profit Joint Venture

To seek shelter from the competitive storm, Florence Nightingale Hospital (FNH) is considering forming a joint venture with an existing for-profit HMO. FNH would be given 30 percent ownership of the privately held HMO, and each of its five board of trustee members would be given 1 percent ownership, in exchange for FNH contributing $10 million in capital funds, which is 35 percent of the HMO's appraised net worth. Since the HMO already owns its own nursing home, FNH will raise the capital by selling its nursing home. FNH will receive 30 percent of whatever profit distributions the HMO board chooses to make from time to time and the trustees will receive their 1 percent shares. FNH also hopes to increase its patient base for hospital admissions and to secure a better bargaining position for reimbursements from the HMO, but the HMO is making no promises about where its subscribers will be sent for hospital care, nor how it will pay FNH for hospital services to its subscribers.

Assume that FNH has articles of incorporation similar to Queen of Angels', only covering nursing home as well as hospital services, and that it has received only general, unrestricted gifts from donors. Also, assume there is no other management or personal connection between FNH and the HMO. What issues would you want to alert the hospital board to concerning whether this is a permissible venture and how the HMO can use its capital funds? Would these parties be advised to have the HMO pledge some portion of its revenues to pay for charity care services at FNH?

2. *Charitable Tax Exemption*

This section explores the fundamental justification for classifying various medical institutions as charitable for purposes of tax exemption. The question you should ask yourself is how nonprofit hospitals differ from their for-profit counterparts, and whether those characteristics also allow others in the health care sector to qualify for exemption. These readings then explain the detailed organizational and operational constraints that must be met in order to maintain charitable status.

EASTERN KENTUCKY WELFARE RIGHTS ORGANIZATION v. SIMON

506 F.2d 1278 (D.C. Cir. 1974)

JAMESON, Senior District Judge:

. . . Sections 501(a) and (c)(3) of the Internal Revenue Code of 1954 exempt from federal income tax: "(3) Corporations, and any community chest, fund, religious, or foundation, organized and operated exclusively for charitable . . . purposes, . . . no part of the net earnings of which inures to the benefit of any private shareholder or individual." . . . Other related sections of the Code provide that contributions to such tax exempt charitable organizations are deductible for purposes of computing federal income tax and estate and gift taxes.

Hospitals and other health organizations have never been expressly categorized as tax exempt organizations and have achieved that status only by qualifying as "charitable" organizations under the Code. Long established Internal Revenue Service (I.R.S.) policy held that hospitals qualified as charitable organizations under §501(c)(3) only if they provided free or below cost service to those unable to pay. This policy was articulated in Revenue Ruling 56-185, which held that a hospital could qualify for tax exempt status only if it was "operated to the extent of its financial ability for those not able to pay for the services rendered and not exclusively for those who are able and expected to pay."[2]

The I.R.S. modified this position in 1969 with the issuance of Revenue Ruling 69-545. The new ruling broadly defines "charitable" in terms of community benefit and holds that the promotion of health constitutes a "charitable purpose" in the "generally accepted legal sense of that term" and within the meaning of §501(c)(3) of the Code. According to the ruling, "The promotion of health . . . is one of the purposes in the general law of charity that is deemed beneficial to the community as a whole even though the class of beneficiaries eligible to receive a direct benefit from its activities does not include all members of the community, such as indigent members of the community." . . .

Based on this community benefit concept, a nonprofit hospital can qualify as a charitable organization under §501(c)(3) "by operating an emergency room open to all persons and by providing hospital care for all those persons in the community able to pay the cost thereof either directly or through third party reimbursement . . ." (e.g. private health insurance, Medicare, or Medicaid). Thus, for a hospital to qualify as a tax-exempt organization, the provision of free or below cost service to those unable to pay is no longer essential.

Alleging harm from this new ruling, the plaintiffs-appellees, a group of health and welfare organizations and indigent persons, brought this action seeking to

2. Other pertinent parts of Revenue Ruling 56-185 state: "It is normal for hospitals to charge those able to pay for services rendered in order to meet the operating expenses of the institution without denying medical care or treatment to others unable to pay. . . . It may furnish services at reduced rates which are below cost, and thereby render charity in that manner. . . . It must not, however, refuse to accept patients in need of hospital care who cannot pay for such services."

declare Revenue Ruling 69-545 invalid and to enjoin its implementation. They submitted affidavits recounting incidents in various parts of the country involving the denial of hospital services to indigents by institutions enjoying tax exempt status as "charitable" organizations. . . .

We conclude that Revenue Ruling 69-545 is not inconsistent with 26 U.S.C. §501(c)(3) and that the modification of the prior ruling was authorized. The definition of the term *charitable* has never been static and has been broadened in recent years. . . . In promulgating Revenue Ruling 69-545, the Commissioner [relied] on an analogy to the law of charitable trusts. [T]he Commissioner cited both the Restatement (Second) of Trusts, §368 and §372,[16] and IV Scott on Trusts (3rd ed. 1967) §368 and §372 in holding that the promotion of health is a charitable purpose within the meaning of §501(c)(3).

The term *charitable* is thus capable of a definition far broader than merely the relief of the poor. The law of charitable trusts supports the broader concept. . . . While it is true that in the past Congress and the federal courts have conditioned a hospital's charitable status on the level of free or below cost care that it provided for indigents, there is no authority for the conclusion that the determination of "charitable" status was always to be so limited. Such an inflexible construction fails to recognize the changing economic, social and technological precepts and values of contemporary society.

In the field of health care, the changes have been dramatic. Hospitals in the early part of this nation's history were almshouses supported by philanthropy and serving almost exclusively the sick poor. Today, hospitals are the primary community health facility for both rich and poor. Philanthropy accounts for only a minute percentage of the hospital's total operating costs. Those costs have soared in recent years as constant modernization of equipment and facilities is necessitated by the advances in medical science and technology. The institution of Medicare and Medicaid in the last decade combined with the rapid growth of medical and hospital insurance has greatly reduced the number of poor people requiring free or below cost hospital services. Much of that decrease has been realized since the promulgation of Revenue Ruling 56-185. Moreover, increasingly counties and other political subdivisions are providing nonemergency hospitalization and medical care for those unable to pay. Thus, it appears that the rationale upon which the limited definition of "charitable" was predicated has largely disappeared. To continue to base the "charitable" status of a hospital strictly on the relief it provides for the poor fails to account for these major changes in the area of health care. . . .

It is important to note also that Revenue Ruling 69-545 . . . entails the operation of an emergency room open to all regardless of their ability to pay and providing hospital services to those able to pay the cost either directly or through third party reimbursement. Thus, to qualify as a tax exempt charitable organization, a hospital must still provide services to indigents.

16. The Restatement (Second) of Trusts §368 (1959) states: "Charitable purposes include: (a) the relief of poverty; (b) the advancement of education; (c) the advancement of religion; (d) the promotion of health; (e) governmental or municipal purposes; (f) other purposes the accomplishment of which is beneficial to the community."

The required provision of emergency room services is of great import to the indigent. Emergency room service is often the only means of access that the poor have to medical care. Furthermore, the fact that hospitals seeking to qualify as charities pursuant to Revenue Ruling 69-545 must accept Medicare and Medicaid patients is also significant. A large percentage of the indigent populace of the nation is now covered by either Medicare or Medicaid. In the final analysis, Revenue Ruling 69-545 may be of greater benefit to the poor than its predecessor Ruling 56-185. . . .

[On appeal, the Supreme Court dismissed this case for lack of standing under the reasoning that, even if the plaintiffs won, they may not be any better off since nonprofit hospitals would be free to relinquish their charitable status rather than agreeing to treat more indigent patients. Eastern Kentucky Welfare Rights Organization v. Simon, 426 U.S. 26 (1976).]

■ PROVENA COVENANT MEDICAL CENTER v. DEPARTMENT OF REVENUE

925 N.E.2d 1132 (Ill. 2010)

KARMEIER, J.

The central issue in this case is whether Provena Hospitals established that it was entitled to a charitable exemption under . . . the Property Tax Code . . . for various parcels of real estate it owns in Urbana, [Illinois]. The Director of Revenue determined that it had not and denied the exemption. . . . Following a hearing, the circuit court determined that Provena Hospitals was entitled to both a charitable and religious exemption. . . . [We uphold] the decision by the Department of Revenue to deny the exemption.

BACKGROUND

. . . Provena Hospitals was formed through the consolidation of four Catholic-related health-care organizations and is organized as a not-for-profit corporation under the laws of Illinois. . . . Provena Hospitals is exempt from federal income tax under section 501(c)(3) of the Internal Revenue Code. The Illinois Department of Revenue has also determined that the corporation is exempt from this state's retailers' occupation tax, service occupation tax, use tax, and service use tax. In addition, the Illinois Attorney General has concluded that the corporation "meets the qualifications of 'An Act to Regulate Solicitation and Collection of Funds for Charitable Purposes' . . . and constitutes a religious organization exempt from filing annual financial reports under those statutes."

Provena Hospitals owns and operates six hospitals, including Provena Covenant Medical Center (PCMC), a full-service hospital located in the City of Urbana . . . [serving] a 13-county area in east central Illinois. . . . Just as PCMC relies on private physicians to fill its medical staff, it utilizes numerous third-party providers to furnish other services at the hospital. . . . The company providing lab services is one of the businesses owned by Provena Enterprises, a Provena Health subsidiary. It is operated for profit. Provena Hospitals' employees do not work gratuitously.

Everyone employed by the corporation, including those with religious affiliations, are paid for their services. . . .

PCMC has agreements with some private third-party payers which provide for payment at rates different from "its established rates." The payment amounts under these agreements cover the actual costs of care. The amounts PCMC receives from Medicare and Medicaid are not sufficient to cover the costs of care. . . . For 2002, PCMC calculated the difference to be $7,418,150 in the case of Medicare patients and $3,105,217 for Medicaid patients. . . .

During 2002, Provena Hospitals' "net patient service revenue" was $713,911,000. . . . Provena Hospitals' "expenses and losses" exceeded its "revenue and gains" during this period by $4,869,000. In other words, the corporation was in the red. The following year, this changed. The corporation's revenue and gains exceeded its expenses and losses by $10,548,000. . . . This surplus existed even after provision for uncollectible accounts receivable (i.e., bad debt) in the amount of $7,101,000. Virtually none of PCMC's income was derived from charitable contributions. The dollar amount of "unrestricted donations" received by PCMC for the year ending December 31, 2002, was a mere $6,938. . . . In years when PCMC realizes a net gain, the gain is "reinvested in order to sustain and further [the corporation's] charitable mission and ministry." . . .

In 2002, PCMC . . . advertised in newspapers, phone directories, event playbills, and Chamber of Commerce publications; on television and radio; and through public signage. It also advertised using "booths, tables, and/or tents at community health or nonprofit fundraising events; sponsorship of sports teams and other community events; and banner advertisements at sponsored community events." . . . None of its ads that year mentioned . . . a charity care policy in place at the hospital [which] . . . provided that the institution would "offer, to the extent that it is financially able, admission for care or treatment, and the use of the hospital facilities and services regardless of race, color, creed, sex, national origin, ancestry or ability to pay for these services." The charity policy was not self-executing. An application was required. Whether an application would be granted was determined by PCMC on a case-by-case basis using eligibility criteria based on federal poverty guidelines. A sliding scale was employed [based on income and assets]. . . .

[I]f a patient failed to obtain an advance determination of eligibility under the program, normal collection practices were followed. PCMC would look first to private insurance, if there was any, then pursue any possible sources of reimbursement from the government. Failing that, the hospital would seek payment from the patient directly. . . . Staffed by a small group of employees in Joliet, the Extended Business Office would typically make three or four phone calls and send three or four statements to patients owing outstanding balances. If a balance remained unpaid following such efforts, which typically did not extend beyond three months, Provena Hospitals would treat the account as "bad debt" and refer it to a collection agency. . . .

During 2002, the amount of aid provided by Provena Hospitals to PCMC patients under the facility's charity care program was modest. The hospital waived $1,758,940 in charges, representing an actual cost to it of only $831,724. This was equivalent to only 0.723% of PCMC's revenues for that year and was $268,276 less than the $1.1 million in tax benefits which Provena stood to receive if its claim for a property tax exemption were granted.[1] The number of patients benefitting from the charitable care program was similarly small. During 2002, only 302 of PCMC's 10,000 inpatient and 100,000 outpatient admissions were granted reductions in their bills under the charitable care program. That figure is equivalent to just 0.27% of the hospital's total annual patient census. . . .

Analysis

Under Illinois law, . . . tax exemption under federal law is not dispositive of whether real property is exempt from property tax under Illinois law. . . . [The state's constitution] provides that the General Assembly may, by law, exempt from taxation property . . . "used exclusively for agricultural and horticultural societies, and for school, religious, cemetery and charitable purposes." . . . In *Methodist Old Peoples Home v. Korzen*, 233 N.E.2d 537 (Ill. 1968), we identified the distinctive characteristics of a charitable institution as follows: . . . (2) it earns no profits or dividends but rather derives its funds mainly from private and public charity and holds them in trust for the purposes expressed in the charter; (3) it dispenses charity to all who need it and apply for it; . . . and (5) it does not appear to place any obstacles in the way of those who need and would avail themselves of the charitable benefits it dispenses. . . .

There is no blanket exemption under the law for hospitals or health-care providers. Whether a particular institution qualifies as a charitable institution and is exempt from property tax is a question which must be determined on a case-by-case basis. . . . Provena Hospitals plainly fails to meet the second criterion: its funds are not derived mainly from private and public charity and held in trust for the purposes expressed in the charter. They are generated, overwhelmingly, by providing medical services for a fee. . . . The only charitable donations documented in this case . . . were so small, a mere $6,938, that they barely warrant mention. Provena Hospitals likewise failed to show by clear and convincing evidence that it satisfied factors three or five. . . . When the law says that property must be "exclusively used" for charitable or beneficent purposes, it means that charitable or beneficent purposes are the primary ones for which the property is utilized. Secondary or incidental charitable benefits will not suffice, nor will it be enough that the institution professes a charitable purpose or aspires to using its property to confer charity on others. . . .

[M]ore than a century ago . . . we explained that "[t]he reason for exemptions in favor of charitable institutions is the benefit conferred upon the public by them, and a consequent relief, to some extent, of the burden upon the State to care for and advance the interests of its citizens." . . . Conditioning charitable status on whether an activity helps relieve the burdens on government is appropriate. After

1. The disparity between the amount of free or discounted care dispensed and the amount of property tax that would be saved through receipt of a charitable exemption is in no way unique to the case before us here. Excluding bad debt, "the amount of uncompensated care provided by as many as three-quarters of nonprofit hospitals is less than their tax benefits." J. Colombo, *Federal & State Tax Exemption Policy, Medical Debt & Healthcare for the Poor*, 51 St. Louis L.J. 433, 433 n.2 (2007).

all, each tax dollar lost to a charitable exemption is one less dollar affected governmental bodies will have to meet their obligations directly. If a charitable institution wishes to avail itself of funds which would otherwise flow into a public treasury, it is only fitting that the institution provide some compensatory benefit in exchange. While Illinois law has never required that there be a direct, dollar-for-dollar correlation between the value of the tax exemption and the value of the goods or services provided by the charity, it is a *sine qua non* of charitable status that those seeking a charitable exemption be able to demonstrate that their activities will help alleviate some financial burden incurred by the affected taxing bodies in performing their governmental functions.

. . . To be sure, Provena Hospitals did not condition the receipt of care on a patient's financial circumstances. Treatment was offered to all who requested it, and no one was turned away by PCMC based on their inability to demonstrate how the costs of their care would be covered. The record showed, however, that during the period in question here, Provena Hospitals did not advertise the availability of charitable care at PCMC. Patients were billed as a matter of course, and unpaid bills were automatically referred to collection agencies. . . . As a practical matter, there was little to distinguish the way in which Provena Hospitals dispensed its "charity" from the way in which a for-profit institution would write off bad debt. . . .

The minimal amount of charitable care dispensed by Provena Hospitals at the PCMC complex cannot be rationalized on the grounds that the area's residents did not require additional services. For one thing, the argument that there really was no demand for additional charitable care in Champaign County is one that Provena Hospitals cannot comfortably make. . . . [A]pproximately 13.4% of Champaign County's more than 185,000 residents have incomes below the federal poverty guidelines. That amounts to nearly 25,000 people. In addition, nearly 20,000 county residents are estimated to be without any health-care coverage. There is no reason to believe that these groups of indigent and/or uninsured citizens are any healthier than the population at large. To the contrary, experience teaches that such individuals are likely to have significant unmet health-care needs. . . .

Further undermining Provena Hospitals' claims of charity is that even where it did offer discounted charges, the charity was often illusory. As described earlier in this opinion, uninsured patients were charged PCMC's "established" rates, which were more than double the actual costs of care. When patients were granted discounts at the 25% and 50% levels, the hospital was therefore still able to generate a surplus. . . . Moreover, it appears that in every case when a "charitable" discount was granted or full payment for a bill was otherwise not received, the corporation expected the shortfall to be offset by surpluses generated by the higher amounts it was able to charge other users of its facilities and services. Such "cross-subsidies" are a pricing policy any fiscally sound business enterprise might employ. We cannot fault Provena Hospitals for following this strategy. . . . We note merely that such conduct is in no way indicative of any form of charitable purpose or use of the subject property. . . .

Provena Hospitals argues that the amount of free and discounted care it provides to self-pay patients at the PCMC complex is not an accurate reflection of the scope of its charitable use of the property. In its view, its treatment of Medicare and Medicaid patients should also be taken into account because the payments it receives for treating such patients [fell $10 million short of covering] the full costs of care. . . . Accepting Medicare and Medicaid patients is optional. While it is consistent with Provena Hospitals' mission, it also serves the organization's financial interests. In exchange for agreeing to accept less than its "established" rate, the corporation receives a reliable stream of revenue and is able to generate income from hospital resources that might otherwise be underutilized. . . . Mindful of such considerations, our appellate court has held that discounted care provided to Medicare and Medicaid patients is not considered charity for purposes of assessing eligibility for a property tax exemption. . . .

Provena Hospitals asserts that assessment of its charitable endeavors should also take into account subsidies it provides for ambulance service, its support of the crisis nursery, donations made to other not-for-profit entities, volunteer initiatives it undertakes, and support it provides for graduate medical education, behavioral health services, and emergency services training. This contention is problematic for several reasons. First, while all of these activities unquestionably benefit the community, community benefit is not the test. Under Illinois law, the issue is whether the property at issue is used exclusively for a charitable purpose. . . .

With respect to the ambulance subsidy, the costs for most patients who were transported by ambulance appear to have been covered by third-party insurers. The deficit claimed by Provena may therefore result primarily from the reduced rates insurers are allowed to pay, something which clearly would not qualify as charitable in nature. . . . We further note . . . that the ambulance service provided noncharitable benefits to the institution. It complemented PCMC's emergency room, which it was required by law to provide and which was operated by a for-profit corporation, and enhanced PCMC's ability to fill its beds and cover its fixed costs.

The volunteer classes and services cited by Provena Hospitals included such items as free health screenings, wellness classes, and classes on handling grief. Again, while beneficial to the community, they were not necessarily charitable. Private for-profit companies frequently offer comparable services as a benefit for employees and customers and a means for generating publicity and goodwill for the organization. . . . In a competitive health-care environment, [offering free services] may be an effective means for increasing awareness of the hospital, encouraging others outside the immediate community to use its services.

Provena Hospitals' reliance on expenses associated with the medical residency program is also problematic. . . . [I]n addition to generating direct payments from the University, Provena Hospitals' participation in the program unquestionably adds to PCMC's prestige and enables it to supplement its medical staff with well-trained, if inexperienced, physicians. While we cannot exclude the possibility that there is some charity in this relationship, it is difficult to know in which direction such charity flows, from Provena Hospitals to the University of Illinois or vice versa. . . .

We likewise find no error in the Department of Revenue's rejection of Provena Hospitals' request for a religious exemption. . . . [M]edical care, while potentially miraculous, is not intrinsically, necessarily, or even normally religious in nature. . . .

[Two other justices joined the majority opinion, and two dissented, for a 3-2 split.]

Justice Burke, dissenting in part.

I join that portion of the plurality opinion which holds that Provena Hospitals failed to demonstrate it was entitled to a religious exemption. . . . I do not join that portion of the plurality opinion which addresses the doctrine of charitable use. . . . By imposing a quantum of care requirement and monetary threshold, the plurality is injecting itself into matters best left to the legislature. The legislature did not set forth a monetary threshold for evaluating charitable use. We may not annex new provisions or add conditions to the language of a statute. . . . The Michigan Supreme Court in Wexford Medical Group v. City of Cadillac, 713 N.W.2d 734 (2006), aptly set out this principle:

> . . . To set such a threshold, significant questions would have to be grappled with. For instance, a court would have to determine how to account for the indigent who do not identify themselves as such but who nonetheless fail to pay. A court would have to determine whether facilities that provide vital health care should be treated more leniently than some other type of charity because of the nature of its work, or even if a health care provider in an undeserved area, such as petitioner, is more deserving of exemption than one serving an area of lesser need. A court would need to consider whether to premise the exemption on whether the institution had a surplus and whether providing below-cost care constitutes charity. Clearly, courts are unequipped to handle these and many other unanswered questions. Simply put, these are matters for the Legislature.

. . . Similarly, in Medical Center Hospital of Vermont, Inc. v. City of Burlington, 566 A.2d 1352 (1989), the Vermont Supreme Court, in rejecting the taxing authority's argument that the amount of free care dispensed must exceed revenues, concluded there was nothing in any Vermont case that required an institution to dispense *any* free care to qualify as charitable for purposes of the charitable property tax exemption. . . . The court declared: "In our opinion, pegging charitability to a stated amount of free care rendered would not be workable in determinating an organization's taxable status. Instead, uncertainty would reign. . . ." Rather, "[t]he better inquiry, it seems to us, is the one used by the trial court in this case: whether health care was made available by the plaintiff to all who needed it, regardless of their ability to pay." . . . "As plaintiff pointed out at trial, if the economy in the Burlington [VT] area were to fall off dramatically and unemployment to soar, fewer people would be covered by health care insurance through employers and, consequently, more free care would be rendered to those in need. Should the economy make a turnaround the following year, the amount of free care given might fall again should unemployment levels drop."

I find these authorities persuasive. . . .

Notes: The Basis for Health Care Tax Exemption

1. *The Benefits of Charitable Exemption.* "The voluntary [i.e., charitable nonprofit] hospital, like the government hospital, generally enjoys exemption from the federal income tax and from state and local property taxes. This has been true historically and it is true today. Any general repeal of the exemptions is most unlikely in the near future, despite the criticism of some respected authorities who see the exemptions as 'mindless subsidies' of the industry which could be carried out much more effectively in other ways. The complexities of current tax law are such, however, that even in a basically exempt industry the law impinges on many aspects of hospital operations and can be manipulated one way or another with resulting impact in

hospital developments. It thus constitutes a de facto type of public regulation." A. Somers, Hospital Regulation: The Dilemma of Public Policy 38 (1969).

The requirements for maintaining tax exemption have such a strong influence because the financial stakes are so high. Hospitals own considerable real property that is subject to local property tax, and they generate a very high volume of revenues potentially subject to sales tax. Even "nonprofit" hospitals such as Provena often earn many millions of dollars a year, which would be subject to state and federal corporate income tax. Equally important, tax-exempt hospitals are eligible to use tax-exempt bond financing, which significantly lowers their capital costs. Perhaps the most obvious benefit of tax exemption—eligibility to receive tax-deductible gifts—is the least important since hospitals no longer rely substantially on donations.

2. *Unrelated Business Income.* A related concern is whether various activities of hospitals generate "unrelated business income." This is income from activities that are not connected with the hospital's exempt functions. The consequence of earning such income is not nearly so severe as finding private inurement. Usually, this merely results in an "unrelated business income tax" (UBIT) imposed only on that designated portion of income. IRC §§511-513. However, if unrelated income constitutes a "substantial portion" of the hospital's total operations, it can threaten the entire exemption. See, e.g., GCM 39684 (Sept. 28, 1984) (hospital subsidiary that provided purchasing and data processing services to nonexempt hospitals lost exemption because of "substantial, nonexempt commercial purpose").

The major decision applying the unrelated business income tax to hospital operations (which coincidentally comes from the same city as *Provena*) is Carle Foundation v. United States, 611 F.2d 1192 (7th Cir. 1980). It sets forth the general rule that income from nonhospital patients is unrelated to the institution's exempt function. Thus, for instance, a nonprofit hospital's pharmacy sales to outpatients are taxable, even if sold to patients of physicians on the medical staff with offices in the hospital's own building, because these are not hospital patients. The service exempts pharmacy and laboratory sales to nonpatients only in "unique circumstances" where the hospital is the only available source for the service to nonhospital patients. Rev. Rul. 85-110. Why is it necessary to define the hospital's exempt function so narrowly? Why not conceive of the hospital's purpose as providing health care services generally to the community at large? This seems to be another example of the IRS's antagonism toward physicians benefiting from the exemption.

3. *Charity Care vs. Community Benefit.* What do you think about the *Provena* dissent's argument that, even if hospitals no longer provide significant charity care, it should be sufficient if they simply maintain an "open door" policy by which they accept anyone who seeks care, regardless of ability to pay? Consider the role physicians play in determining whether a patient is admitted to a hospital. Suppose a hospital does not require its physicians to accept charity cases.

The IRS further liberalized its free care policy in 1983, ruling that even free emergency services are unnecessary if an emergency room isn't needed in the community or if the hospital is a specialized one that offers limited treatment (e.g., eye hospitals or cancer hospitals). Rev. Rul. 83-187.

In a replay of the IRS's 1969 ruling, will states like Illinois change their position if national health care reform further reduces the need for charity care? In Dialysis Clinic, Inc. v. Levin, 938 N.E.2d 329 (Ohio 2010), the court held, over a dissent, that a dialysis clinic was not excused from having to show some level of charity care simply because almost all patients with kidney disease are covered by Medicare or Medicaid if they don't have private insurance.

The ACA requires tax-exempt hospitals to assess the health needs of their community, to report what community benefits they provide, and to have clear charity care policies that they publicize. It also prevents tax-exempt hospitals from charging low-income patients any more than the hospital receives from commercial insurers, and prohibits aggressive collection actions against patients who are eligible for the hospital's financial assistance policy. However, the ACA does not require hospitals to show any particular quantum of charity care or community benefit.

Prof. Jill Horwitz argues that hospitals need not provide more charity care than for-profits in order to justify tax exempt status. Instead, it suffices that they provide a broader range of services, including those that are not profitable. Jill R. Horwitz, Why We Need the Independent Sector: The Behavior, Law, and Ethics of Not-For-Profit Hospitals, 50 UCLA L. Rev. 1345 (2003). Professor Bloche argues that a charity care requirement is "deeply problematic" because it requires hospitals to fund the care for some patients by increasing charges to others. This "cost shifting" can be seen as an implicit form of "internal" taxation that is highly objectionable compared with a broad-based income tax: It is essentially a hidden tax on the sick that does a poor job of targeting resources to where they are most needed—preventive and primary care. M. Gregg Bloche, Health Policy Below the Waterline: Medical Care and the Charitable Exemption, 80 Minn. L. Rev. 299 (1995). True enough, tax exemption is not a good substitute for national health insurance, but do these imperfections justify excusing hospitals from any concrete obligation in exchange for the exemption? Other law professors argue for a looser test for exemption based on enhancing access to care in the community or promoting population health, or advancing religious missions, where this can be clearly documented. See note 8.

4. *Measuring Charity Care.* Following *Provena,* the Illinois revenue department denied exemption to several other hospitals, including Northwestern University's—causing a great stir from hospitals statewide, concerned that the new standards were too demanding or unclear. The state legislature responded in 2012 with a statute that requires hospitals to quantify that their charitable services equal or exceed what their state tax bill would have been but allows hospitals to count reimbursement shortfalls under Medicaid and from a range of essential services such as emergency rooms and burn units. A few other states have enacted similar laws requiring tax-exempt hospitals to document that the value of their charity care and other community benefits exceed either some set percentage of operations or exceed the value of their tax exemption, but federal bills that would do the same have not advanced in Congress. However, the ACA requires tax-exempt hospitals to at least study community needs and report on how the hospital is helping to meet them.

Where states impose a charity care standard, they must next decide how to measure the amount and value of unreimbursed services. Hospitals attempt to measure this value in terms of their listed charges rather than actual costs, but these list prices are rarely charged in full to insurance companies. Sometimes, hospitals even try to count as free care these voluntary "contractual adjustments" with paying customers. See St. Margaret Seneca Place v. Board of Property Assessment, 640 A.2d 380 (Pa. 1994) (accepting this argument with respect to Medicaid payments to nursing home, but only to extent that payments were less than average costs). Do you agree with the *Provena* majority that hospitals should not be allowed to count their uncollectable accounts since this is no different than for-profit hospitals that write off their bad debts? According to one estimate, the amount of uncompensated care that nonprofit hospitals provide above and beyond what similar for-profits provide amounts to only a small fraction of the value of the charitable tax exemption. Congressional Budget Office, Nonprofit Hospitals and the Provision of Community Benefits (Dec. 2006).

5. *The Nonprofit Ethos.* Hospitals argue that the "community benefit" justification for exemption captured in the 1969 revenue ruling is warranted because nonprofit hospitals are inherently superior to their for-profit counterparts. The debate between the two hospital sectors has raged for decades, ever since large corporate chains began to acquire significant numbers of for-profit hospitals in the late 1970s. The seminal article is A. Relman, The New Medical-Industrial Complex, 303 New Eng. J. Med. 963 (1980), but the core issues go back even further, as one court explained:

> Because the "care of the sick" has traditionally been an activity regarded as charitable in American law, . . . we deem it important to scrutinize the contemporary social and economic context of such care. We are convinced that traditional assumptions bear little relationship to the economics of the medical-industrial complex of the 1980s. Nonprofit hospitals were traditionally treated as tax-exempt charitable institutions because, until late in the nineteenth century, they were true charities providing custodial care for those who were both sick and poor. The hospitals' income was derived largely or entirely from voluntary charitable donations, not government subsidies, taxes, or patient fees.[7] The function and status of hospitals began to change in the late nineteenth century; the transformation was substantially completed by the 1920s. "From charities, dependent on voluntary gifts, [hospitals] developed into market institutions financed increasingly out of payments from patients." The transformation was multidimensional: Hospitals were redefined from social welfare to medical treatment institutions; their charitable foundation was replaced by a business basis; and their orientation shifted to "professionals, and their patients," away from "patrons and the poor." . . .
>
> Also of considerable significance . . . is the increasing irrelevance of the distinction between nonprofit and for-profit hospitals for purposes of discovering the element of charity in their operations. The literature indicates that two models, described below, appear to describe a large number of nonprofit hospitals as they function today. (1) The "physicians' cooperative" model describes nonprofit hospitals that operate primarily for the benefit of the participating physicians. Physicians, pursuant to this model, enjoy power and high income through their direct

7. Paul Starr, The Social Transformation of American Medicine 150 (1982). "Voluntary" hospitals, like public hospitals (which evolved from almshouses for the dependent poor), performed a "welfare" function rather than a medical or curing function: The poor were housed in large wards, largely cared for themselves, and often were not expected to recover. See id. at 145, 149, 160. Early voluntary hospitals had paternalistic, communal social structures in which patients entered at the sufferance of their benefactors, "had the moral status of children," and received more moralistic and religious help than medical treatment. Id. at 149, 158.

> or indirect control over the nonprofit hospitals to which they bring their patients. The nonprofit form is believed to facilitate the control by physicians better than the for-profit form. Pauly & Redisch, The Not-For-Profit Hospital as a Physicians' Co-operative, 63 Am. Econ. Rev. 87, 88-89 (1973). This model has also been called the "exploitation hypothesis" because the physician "income maximizing" system is hidden behind the nonprofit facade of the hospital. Clark, Does the Nonprofit Form Fit the Hospital Industry?, 93 Harv. L. Rev. 1416, 1436-1437 (1980). . . . (2) The "polycorporate enterprise" model describes the increasing number of nonprofit hospital chains. Here, power is largely in the hands of administrators, not physicians. Through the creation of holding companies, nonprofit hospitals have grown into large groups of medical enterprises, containing both for-profit and nonprofit corporate entities. Nonprofit corporations can own for-profit corporations without losing their federal nonprofit tax status as long as the profits of the for-profit corporations are used to further the nonprofit purposes of the parent organization. . . . The emergence of hospital organizations with both for-profit and nonprofit components has increasingly destroyed the charitable pretentions of nonprofit organizations.

Utah County v. Intermountain Health Care, Inc., 709 P.2d 265 (Utah 1985). Documenting the court's observations, health policy researchers have produced an extensive body of empirical findings that fail to reveal any major differences in the cost or quality of care delivered by nonprofits and for-profits. See, e.g., Jill Marsteller et al., Nonprofit Conversion: Theory, Evidence, and State Policy Options, 33 Health Serv. Res. 1495 (1998); David Cutler ed., The Changing Hospital Industry (2000). Others, however, point to notable instances where profit motivation has run amok, such as Columbia/HCA. The following exchange from a generation ago gives a glimpse of the still highly charged nature of this debate:

> Nonprofit hospitals . . . receive billions of dollars annually in subsidies from the rest of us taxpayers through various tax exemptions. Our research showed that nonprofit hospital chains did not provide benefits to society that justified this multibillion dollar gift. When compared with for-profits, the nonprofit hospital chains had the same prices and the same level of access for patients with no or low levels of health insurance. Moreover, they had higher costs, more employees, less efficient use of beds, and much older capital than for-profits. The net result was that the nonprofits performed less and cost much more—billions of dollars more!

Regina Herzlinger, An Author Replies, 65 Harv. Bus. Rev., Mar.-Apr. 1987, at 135, replying in support of Regina Herzlinger & William Krasker, Who Profits from Nonprofits?, 65 Harv. Bus. Rev., Jan.-Feb. 1987, at 93 (nonprofits "do more to maximize the welfare of the physicians who are their main consumers"). Uwe Reinhardt, a leading health economist, responded: "[T]his study is a truly shoddy statistical analysis. . . . The author's bias for privatization screams out from every page of the study. I'm concerned by the apparent attempt to propagate personal bias in the guise of science." N.Y. Times, Apr. 2, 1987, at 32, col. 3. A later round of this never-ending debate can be found in 25(4) Health Aff. W287 (June 2006).

Regardless of the evidence, nonprofit advocates claim that it is wrong to profit from people's medical misfortunes. Economists respond that the profit incentive is not inherently evil and may produce better service because it reacts more quickly and efficiently to consumer demands. But, absent any evidence that a systemic, material difference exists between the two hospital sectors, this debate turns to intangibles such as whether nonprofits promote a superior institutional ethos because they are devoted primarily to healing, not to generating profits. The danger of accepting this justification on faith is that even defenders of the exemption concede that "self-satisfaction and self-righteousness . . . is perhaps an occupational hazard" among nonprofit hospital administrators, who tend to "have an almost reflexive belief in the inherent superiority of voluntary health care." Id. at 4-5. Skeptics observe that hospital administrators respond more to where the money comes from than to abstract mission statements in corporate documents. At one time, nonprofits received substantial funding from donations, but now they rely almost entirely on public and private insurance, as well as borrowed capital. Because the sources of financing for both types of hospitals are nearly identical, many observers conclude that their administrative style and institutional ideology are virtually indistinguishable. Defenders of the community benefit standard respond by pointing to counterexamples such as Columbia/HCA. They also encourage nonprofit hospitals to document their community responsiveness and social accountability by cataloguing their various public-spirited programs and activities, such as health education, free screenings, and other good works. Federal law now follows the lead of several statutes in requiring tax-exempt hospitals to conduct these community benefit assessments and file periodic reports. What do you think about the *Provena* majority's perspective that these are merely marketing devices to create good will among potential customers?

6. *What if You're Not a Hospital?* Both the federal government and the states are more demanding of *non*hospital health care enterprises. Both refuse tax exemption to physician practices. See, e.g., Covenant Healthcare System, Inc. v. City of Wauwatosa, 800 N.W.2d 906 (Wis. 2011). And clinics and nursing homes are regularly denied exemption based on a low volume of free care. Similarly, the IRS refused to give charitable status to a nonprofit pharmacy, claiming that the sale of prescriptions is too "inherently commercial" to qualify under the "promotion of health" standard. Federal Pharmacy Service v. Commissioner, 625 F.2d 804 (8th Cir. 1980). Is there any reason to distinguish between the charitable status of inpatient versus outpatient health care services, hospital versus other institutional services, or surgery versus medication?

Both states and the federal government are also distinctly hostile toward extending the charitable exemption to physician groups. Under the modern rationale for hospital exemption, is there any justification for this distinction either? The IRS's position is that physicians would personally benefit too much if their professional corporations were exempt, in violation of the private inurement and private benefit prohibitions discussed in the following readings. Reluctantly, the IRS is willing, however, to exempt medical school faculty groups and very large and prestigious physician groups such as the Mayo Clinic that run a hospital, conduct medical research, and set physician salaries through a somewhat independent governance process. See D. Bromberg, The Tax-Exempt Clinic, 8 Exempt Org. Tax Rev. 557 (1993).

7. *HMO and ACO Exemption.* Equally controversial is whether HMOs or ACOs qualify for charitable tax exemption. The materials above cite state court opinions on either side of the HMO question. Federal tax policy is somewhat confusing. For ACOs, the IRS has ruled that those participating in Medicare's "shared savings

program" are eligible for exemption, but not if the ACO serves only commercial insurers, since doing only that lacks sufficient public benefit. See IRS Public Letter Ruling 201615022.

For HMOs to be tax exempt, the IRS requires them to offer open enrollment and community rating, discounted fees for low-income subscribers, and support for research and education. For a time, it was thought that these attributes were sufficient for all HMOs, based on a Tax Court decision, Sound Health Ass'n v. Commissioner, 71 T.C. 158 (1978), but a subsequent court decision drew a different line. In Geisinger Health Plan v. Commissioner, 985 F.2d 1210 (3d Cir. 1993), the court found that these factors were not sufficient for an HMO that it incorrectly classified as an IPA. (It was actually a group or network model, one that resembles a staff model except that it contracts with full-time physicians rather than employs them.) The court's major concern was that contracting for, rather than directly providing, medical services is not a charitable purpose, even though the contracting parties were part of a hospital system each of whose other components is tax exempt.[4] Does this make sense to you? It is an apparent attempt to draw some distinction between HMOs that are more like hospitals, and those that are more like ordinary insurance. Nonprofit health insurers like Blue Cross lost their exemption by virtue of a 1986 statutory enactment, §501(m). To preserve some meaningful distinction between Blue Cross and HMOs, the HMO exemption appears limited to staff model HMOs, which retain physicians full-time and own their own hospitals.

This position was affirmed by the Tenth Circuit in a case where the IRS revoked the exemption for an HMO owned by a tax-exempt hospital because, following *Geisinger*, the HMO did not operate its own medical facilities. The court ruled that "an organization cannot satisfy the community benefit requirement based solely on the fact that it offers health care services to all in the community in exchange for a fee. . . . Rather, the organization must provide some additional 'plus.' " First on the list of these "pluses" was "free or below-cost services," though the court acknowledged that "devoting surpluses to research, education and medical training" might also suffice. IHC Health Plans v. Commissioner of Internal Revenue, 325 F.3d 1188 (10th Cir. 2003).

Commenting on this decision, Prof. Colombo says: "What the heck is going on here? . . . The only answer I have been able to come up with is that sometime after issuing Rev. Rul. 69-545, folks at the Service realized that there were an awful lot of businesses that 'promote health' in this country by providing services or goods at a fee to anyone who can pay. . . . But instead of simply admitting that Rev. Rul. 69-545 was a well-meaning mistake and then revoking it (or limiting it to acute-care hospitals only), the Service embarked on what now is a 20-year struggle to find alternative means of limiting the scope of Rev. Rul. 69-545 while pretending that it still governs tax exemption for all health care providers. The Service's war on HMOs is one example of this struggle." John Colombo, The IHC Cases: A Catch-22 for Integral Part Doctrine, A Requiem for Rev. Rul. 69-545, 34 Exempt Org. Tax Rev. 401

4. The court also reasoned that extending free services and discounted membership to subscribers was not the same as serving the community at large, even though membership was open to the community at large.

(2001). See also John D. Colombo, The Failure of Community Benefit, 15 Health Matrix 29 (2005).

Are there any reasons that health policy and law might want to favor nonprofit HMOs or ACOs? Are the distinctions the IRS draws sensitive to these reasons? The loss of tax exemption is one reason given by many Blue Cross plans for converting to for-profit status in recent years.

To complicate matters even further (if that's possible), HMOs can still qualify for a lesser form of charitable exemption under §501(c)(4) for "social welfare" organizations. The major difference is that entities under this form of exemption are not eligible to receive tax-exempt donations or tax-exempt bond financing. However, nonprofit indemnity insurers like Blue Cross are not eligible for even this lesser status. Again, there is no easily discernible logic to this pattern. See generally Loren Rosenzweig, *Geisinger*, HMOs and Health Care Reform, 72 Taxes 20 (1994); Symposium, 9 Exempt Org. Tax Rev. 271 (1994).

8. *Further Readings.* For analysis and critique of the **federal position on hospital tax exemption**, see Mark Hall & John Colombo, The Charitable Status of Nonprofit Hospitals: Toward a Donative Theory of Tax Exemption, 66 Wash. L. Rev. 307 (1991); Jack E. Karns, Justifying the Nonprofit Hospital Tax Exemption in a Competitive Market Environment, 13 Widener L.J. 383 (2004); Comment, 20 Rev. Litig. 709 (2001); Symposium, 15 Health Matrix 5 (2005); Symposium, 25(4) Health Aff. w287 (Aug. 2006).

On **community benefits** (note 3), see John Colombo, The Role of Access in Charitable Tax Exemption, 82 Wash. U. L.Q. 343 (2004); Jessica Berg, Putting the Community Back into the "Community Benefit" Standard, 44 Ga. L. Rev. 375 (2010); Michael J. DeBoer, Religious Hospitals and the Federal Community Benefit Standard, 42 Seton Hall L. Rev. 1549 (2012); Mary Crossley, Health and Taxes: Hospitals, Community Health and the IRS, 16 Yale J. Health Pol'y L. 51 (2016); Dan Diamond, How Hospitals Got Richer off Obamacare, Politico, July 17, 2017.

On **charity care** (note 4), see Sayeh Nikpay & John Ayanian, Hospital Charity Care: Effects of New Community-Benefit Requirements, 373 New Eng. J. Med. 1687 (2015); Nancy M. Kane & William Wubbenhorst, Alternative Funding Policies for the Uninsured: Exploring the Value of Hospital Tax Exemption, 78 Milbank Q. 185 (2000); John Colombo, Federal and State Tax Exemption Policy, Medical Debt and Healthcare for the Poor, 51 St. Louis U. L.J. 433 (2007).

Regarding whether **nonprofits are superior** (note 5), see Horowitz, supra, 50 UCLA L. Rev. 1345 (2003); Daniel Fox, Policy Commercializing Nonprofits in Health: The History of a Paradox, 93 Milbank Q. 179 (2015); Kathleen Boozang & Tim Greaney, Mission, Margin and Trust in the Nonprofit Healthcare Enterprise, 5 Yale J. Health Pol'y L. & Ethics 1 (2005); Eleanor D. Kinney, For Profit Enterprise in Health care: Can it Contribute to Health Reform?, 36 Am. J.L. & Med. 405 (2010); George Nation, Non-Profit Charitable Tax-Exempt Hospitals: Wolves in Sheep's Clothing, 42 Rutgers L. Rev. 141 (2010); David Cutler ed., The Changing Hospital Industry (2000).

On **exemption for physicians** (note 6), see John Colombo, Are Associations of Doctors Tax Exempt? Analyzing Inconsistencies in the Tax Exemption of Health Care Providers, 9 Va. Tax Rev. 469 (1990); Kenneth Levine, Obtaining 501(c)(3) Status for Professional Medical Corporations, 2 DePaul J. Health Care L. 231 (1998).

The following books cover **health care tax exemption generally** under both federal and state law: John D. Colombo et al., Charity Care for Nonprofit Hospitals (2010); T. Hyatt & B. Hopkins, The Law of Tax-Exempt Healthcare Organizations (2d ed. 2004); Douglas Mancino, Taxation of Hospitals and Health Care Organizations (2d ed. 2005). Federal tax law is further discussed in the sources cited throughout these notes. A very good general treatise is F. Hill & D. Mancino, Taxation of Exempt Organizations (2002). The best practitioner journal is the Exempt Organization Tax Review. For a broad overview of multiple issues, see David Studdert et al., Regulatory and Judicial Oversight of Nonprofit Hospitals, 356 New Eng. J. Med. 625 (2007).

HARDING HOSPITAL, INC. v. UNITED STATES

505 F.2d 1068 (6th Cir. 1974)

PHILLIPS, Chief Judge.

The sole issue presented in this appeal is whether Harding Hospital, Inc. (the Hospital) qualified under 501(c)(3) of the Internal Revenue Code of 1954 as an organization exempt from federal income taxes. . . .

The Hospital, a nationally recognized psychiatric institution, treats mental and nervous diseases. It utilizes a method of treatment known as milieu therapy in which a patient's total environment is controlled on an around-the-clock basis and structured toward rehabilitation.

The Hospital was originally a corporation for profit. In December 1961, its articles of incorporation were amended to adopt its present name and to qualify under Ohio law as a corporation not for profit. . . . Before amending its articles of incorporation, the Hospital had a contract with a medical partnership composed of seven doctors. This medical partnership performed all the psychiatric treatment on 90 to 95 percent of the patients admitted to the Hospital. Immediately after the Hospital's change in status in 1962, the medical partnership was incorporated as the Harding-Evans Medical Associates, Inc. (the Associates).

Starting in 1962, and for the years in question, the Hospital entered into contracts with the Associates whereby the Associates provided medical supervision in the Hospital, teaching and supervision in the residency and other training programs, and medical service to the Hospital's indigent patients without a charge or at a reduced rate. For these services, the Hospital paid the Associates an annual amount of $25,000. This amount was raised to $35,000 as of July 1, 1968. Further, the agreement provided that the Associates were to pay the Hospital $1,000 per month as rental for facilities, equipment and business office services. This rental was increased to $35,000 per year as of January 1, 1965. It subsequently was lowered to $15,000 per year as of July 1, 1968, at the same time that the amount which the Hospital paid the Associates for medical supervision was increased from $25,000 to $35,000.

Since 1963, individuals not connected with the Associates have constituted a majority of the Board of Trustees of the Hospital. During the years in question, the Board consisted of nine members, only two of whom had any connection with the Associates of the Hospital prior to the 1961 reorganization.

The Harding-Evans Foundation (the Foundation) was set up in 1959 and is an entity separate from the Hospital and the Associates. The Foundation is a tax exempt organization, the principal activity of which is to provide a residency program in the field of psychiatry for the physicians. The Foundation collects charitable funds and expends them on the residency training program at the Hospital. . . .

Section 501(a) of the Code provides that the following organizations, which are listed in §501(c)(3), are exempt from federal income taxation:

> Corporations . . . organized and operated exclusively for religious, charitable, scientific, testing for public safety, literary, or educational purposes, or for the prevention of cruelty to children or animals, no part of the net earnings of which inures to the benefit of any private shareholder or individual, no substantial part of the activities of which is carrying on propaganda, or otherwise attempting, to influence legislation, and which does not participate in, or intervene in (including the publishing or distributing of statements), any political campaign on behalf of any candidate for public office.

In the context of the present case, this section essentially imposes three requirements for exemption: (1) the corporation must be organized and operated exclusively for charitable purposes; (2) no part of its net earnings may inure to the benefit of a private individual or shareholder; and (3) it cannot engage in certain lobbying and political activities. The government stipulated that the Hospital did not offend the third requirement for exemption. . . . [W]e proceed to determine if the district court was correct in holding that the Hospital "was operated almost exclusively for the benefit of the members of the . . . Associates and was not operated exclusively for charitable purposes." . . .

Based on the five factors set forth below, we hold that the Hospital was not entitled to tax exemption under §501(c)(3) during the years in question. We do not single out any one or combination of these factors as the consideration crucial to our holding. We conclude only that all these factors, as they occurred in the aggregate in this case, require denying the appellant Hospital the tax exemption for the years in question. . . .

(1) and (2) [The court observed that the hospital received virtually no charitable donations], and did not have a specific plan or policy for the treatment of charity patients during the years in question. . . . [P]ractically all patients presented themselves as paying patients and only when their funds were exhausted did the Hospital treat them on a charitable basis.

(3) Since the doctors who were members of the Associates treated between 90 and 95 percent of the patients admitted to the Hospital, they derived substantial benefit from the existence and operation of the Hospital. This was the primary source of the doctors' professional income. Although the Hospital did not pay over any of its net earnings to the Associates, except for the annual sum for supervision, this virtual monopoly by the Associates of the patients permitted benefits to inure to the Associates within the intendment of the statute. Sonora Community Hospital, supra, 46 T.C. at 526.

(4) Associates also benefitted from the agreement with the Hospital whereby the Associates paid $35,000 annually as rental for office space, equipment, and business office services. See the fourth requirement of Rev. Rul. 56-185. The $35,000 amount was reduced to $15,000 as of July 1, 1968. . . .

The Hospital introduced the testimony of an appraiser who indicated, in sum, that the $35,000 figure was a fair rental for the office space. That essentially meant that the Associates were not adequately compensating the Hospital for the use of the equipment and business office services (including secretarial assistance). Further, when the annual rental was reduced to $15,000, the Associates were not adequately compensating the Hospital for office space alone.

(5) The Associates also received a private benefit from the agreement whereby the Hospital paid an annual sum of either $25,000 or $35,000 to the Associates for hospital supervision. . . .

On the basis of these five factors, the judgment of the district court is affirmed.

HOSPITAL-PHYSICIAN JOINT VENTURES

General Counsel Memorandum [GCM] 39862 (Dec. 2, 1991)

Issue

Whether a hospital, tax exempt because it is described in §501(c)(3), jeopardizes its exempt status by forming a joint venture with members of its medical staff and selling to the joint venture the gross or net revenue stream derived from operation of an existing hospital department or service for a defined period of time. . . .

Facts

[The memorandum describes several hospital/physician joint ventures that all resemble the following example:] "Z-Hospital" proposed to establish a for-profit stock corporation for certain purposes that would be jointly owned in equal shares by the hospital and physicians on its medical staff. The new corporation would in turn establish and serve as the general partner in four limited partnerships (Z-LPs). The Z-LPs were to be formed to allow medical staff physician participation in the operation of four Z-Hospital outpatient departments. The four departments, Outpatient Surgery, Outpatient Diagnostic (CT Scan, Ultrasound, etc.), Ophthalmology, and Cardiac Nuclear Medicine, represented in the aggregate about 4 percent of Z-Hospital's gross revenues.

Z-Hospital stated that it would "in effect, lease the individual departments for a limited time period to the limited partnership[s]." Apparently, the Z-LPs would pay Z-Hospital an actuarially established price (discounted to present value) for the revenue stream of each of the subject departments. In addition, the Z-LPs would pay Z-Hospital a fee for managing the facilities and reimburse the hospital for all fixed and variable costs incurred in operating the departments. [In other words, the hospital would continue to own the equipment and deliver and bill for the services, but all the money would flow through the LPs. They would pay the hospital for its existing revenue stream and reimburse the hospital for actual expenses, but they would keep any remaining revenues.] Thus, according to the hospital, physician-investors would benefit only if utilization of the facilities increased because, in effect, they shared only in profits over and above the level the hospital already received.

Z-Hospital represented that it would retain, through its interest in the for-profit corporation, an interest in each Z-LP. Fifty percent of each Z-LP would be held by the corporation and 50 percent sold to medical staff physicians [for $5,000 each]. Z-Hospital also stated that it would retain actual control of the facilities through a management agreement, and that it alone would determine the rates charged patients for services in those facilities.

The stated reason for the proposed transactions was to maintain or increase utilization of Z-Hospital's various services, both inpatient and outpatient, so that it could provide the highest level of service at the lowest price to the public. Z-Hospital told the Service that, if it carried out the transactions, its utilization rate (then 65 percent) would be maintained or increased rather than experiencing a decline. At conference, Z-Hospital's chief financial officer predicted significant adverse effects if the hospital did nothing. The hospital was located in an overbedded service area and faced competition from two nearby hospitals, one for-profit, the other non-profit. It also faced potential competition from a private physician who was planning to develop free-standing outpatient facilities to be jointly owned with other doctors. Z-Hospital argued that failure to undertake the proposed transaction would raise a probability that it would be unable to continue providing the same high level of service to the community so, it reasoned, the transaction should be viewed as furthering its charitable purposes.

Z-Hospital maintained that the ventures would help it by creating incentives for medical staff physicians to increase inpatient admissions. The ventures would also create incentives for medical staff physicians to increase referrals to ancillary departments. These factors, combined with a feared loss of outpatient department business to competitors if the ventures were not undertaken, led the hospital to believe it would be better off by proceeding than by not doing so. . . .

Analysis

The joint venture arrangements described above are just one variety of an increasingly common type of competitive behavior engaged in by hospitals in response to significant changes in their operating environment. Many medical and surgical procedures once requiring inpatient care, still the exclusive province of hospitals, now are performed on an outpatient basis, where every private physician is a potential competitor. The marked shift in governmental policy from regulatory cost controls to competition has fundamentally changed the way all hospitals, for-profit and not, do business.

A driving force behind the new hospital operating environment was the federal Medicare Program's 1983 shift from cost-based reimbursement for covered inpatient hospital services to fixed, per-case, prospective payments. This change to a diagnosis-related prospective payment system (PPS) dramatically altered hospital financial incentives. . . . Hospitals realized that, in addition to attracting more patients, they needed to control utilization of ancillary hospital services, discharge Medicare beneficiaries as quickly as is medically appropriate, and operate more efficiently. . . . Once hospital and physician economic incentives diverged, hospitals began seeking ways to stimulate loyalty among members of their medical staffs and to encourage or reward physician behaviors deemed desirable. . . . Since most medical staff physicians are not hospital employees, and typically do not provide services to or receive direct compensation from the hospitals at which they practice, managers have had to look for innovative ways to influence their behavior. . . .

Whenever a charitable organization engages in unusual financial transactions with private parties, the arrangements must be evaluated in light of applicable tax law and other legal standards. . . . We believe the transactions described above cannot withstand such scrutiny. . . . [T]hese transactions must be viewed as jeopardizing a hospital's tax exempt status for three reasons: they allow inurement of part of a charitable organization's net earnings to the benefit of private individuals; they confer more than incidental benefits on private interests; and they may well violate federal law [prohibiting referral fees. Only the first] of these reasons is discussed below. . . .

[Section 501(c)(3)] describes as charitable only an organization "no part of the net earnings of which inures to the benefit of any private shareholder or individual." . . . Violations of this prohibition are commonly referred to as private inurement, or simply, inurement.

Protecting charitable organizations against private inurement serves important purposes. A charitable organization is viewed under the common law and the Internal Revenue Code as a trust whose assets must irrevocably be dedicated to achieving charitable purposes. The inurement prohibition serves to prevent anyone in a position to do so from siphoning off any of a charity's income or assets for personal use.

The proscription against inurement generally applies to a distinct class of private interests—typically persons who, because of their particular relationship with an organization, have an opportunity to control or influence its activities. . . . While most physicians on the medical staffs of the subject hospitals presumably are not employees and do not provide any compensable services directly to the hospitals, they do have a close professional working relationship with the hospitals.[8] . . . Individually, and as a group, they largely control the flow of patients to and from the hospital and patients' utilization of hospital services while there. . . .

Even though medical staff physicians are subject to the inurement proscription, that does not mean there can be no economic dealings between them and the hospitals. The inurement proscription does not prevent the payment of reasonable compensation for goods or services. It is aimed at preventing dividend-like distributions of charitable assets or expenditures to benefit a private interest. . . . Rev. Rul. 69-383, 1969-2 C.B. 113. In that ruling, the Service approved payment to a hospital-based radiologist of a percentage of the adjusted gross revenues from the radiology department in return for management and professional services. . . . Unlike the instant cases, the hospital in Rev. Rul. 69-383 was billing (presumably on a global charge basis) and collecting for the radiologist's professional services, as well as its own facility charge. Thus, the percentage compensation at issue represented an allocation of a portion of the global charge (referred to as the "professional

8. When considering hospital-physician relationships, the Service should be aware that many . . . "hospital based" physicians, notably radiologists, anesthesiologists, pathologists, medical residents, and some emergency room physicians typically are employees or contractors paid by the hospital. . . . Some states have laws . . . [that] restrict hospitals' ability to employ physicians to render professional services to patients. For federal employment tax purposes, however, physicians may be classified as hospital employees notwithstanding such laws.

component") to the physician to compensate him for his services. The hospital retained the remainder (the "technical" or "facility component") as compensation for use of its facilities and equipment. This type of arrangement was typical for pathology and radiology departments prior to the 1982 enactment of changes affecting Medicare reimbursement for hospital-based physicians. See Mancino, Nonexempt Uses of Tax-Exempt Hospital Bonds, 24 J. Health & Hospital Law 73, 79-80 (1991). Due to Medicare changes, the typical arrangement today provides for even hospital-based physicians to bill separately for their professional services, while the hospital bills separately for the technical component. Thus, while never revoked, Rev. Rul. 69-383 has little relevance to most hospital-physician relationships today, including the instant cases. In these cases, only hospital revenues derived from the technical or facility component are at issue.

Even while approving the specific arrangement in Rev. Rul. 69-383, the Service cautioned that the presence of a percentage compensation arrangement will destroy the organization's exemption where it transforms the principal activity of the organization into a joint venture between it and a group of physicians or is merely a device for distributing profits to persons in control. Also, it is equally clear that, if salaries or total compensation are not reasonable, they will result in inurement. . . . There is no de minimis exception to the inurement prohibition. . . . See also Lowry Hosp. Ass'n v. Commissioner, 66 T.C. 850 (1976) (use of hospital's funds to make substantial unsecured loans to nursing home owned by hospital's founding physician inured to his benefit). . . .

The proper starting point for our analysis of the net revenue stream arrangements is to ask what the hospital gets in return for the benefit conferred on the physician-investors. Put another way, we ask whether and how engaging in the transaction furthers the hospital's exempt purposes. Here, there appears to be little accomplished that directly furthers the hospitals' charitable purposes of promoting health. No expansion of health care resources results; no new provider is created. No improvement in treatment modalities or reduction in cost is foreseeable. We have to look very carefully for any reason why a hospital would want to engage in this sort of arrangement. . . .

Whether admitted or not, we believe the hospitals engaged in these ventures largely as a means to retain and reward members of their medical staffs; to attract their admissions and referrals; and to preempt the physicians from investing in or creating a competing provider. Even putting aside any legality issues [under Medicare fraud and abuse laws], . . . the structure of these transactions is problematic. Giving (or selling) medical staff physicians a proprietary interest in the net profits of a hospital under these circumstances creates a result that is indistinguishable from paying dividends on stock. . . . We do not mean to suggest that a §501(c)(3) hospital cannot have an appropriately structured incentive compensation plan for employees in which profits are a factor in the compensation formula. . . .

Another key principle in the law of tax exempt organizations is that an entity is not organized and operated exclusively for exempt purposes unless it serves a public rather than a private interest. Thus, in order to be exempt, an organization must establish that it is not organized or operated for the benefit of private interests such as designated individuals, the creator or his family, shareholders of the organization, or persons controlled, directly or indirectly, by such private interests. However, this private benefit prohibition applies to all kinds of persons and groups, not just to those "insiders" subject to the more strict inurement proscription. . . . Any private benefit arising from a particular activity must be "incidental" in both a qualitative and quantitative sense to the overall public benefit achieved by the activity if the organization is to remain exempt. . . . Such benefits might also be characterized as indirect or unintentional. . . .

In our view, some private benefit is present in all typical hospital-physician relationships. Physicians generally use hospital facilities at no cost to themselves to provide services to private patients for which they earn a fee. The private benefit accruing to the physicians generally can be considered incidental to the overwhelming public benefit resulting from having the combined resources of the hospital and its professional staff available to serve the public. . . . In contrast, the private benefits conferred on the physician-investors by the instant revenue stream joint ventures are direct and substantial, not incidental. . . .

Similar issues and arguments were considered in GCM 37789. There, a tax exempt hospital proposed to lease to certain members of its medical staff land adjacent to the hospital upon which the physicians would construct a medical office building. The agreement called for below market rent (99 years at one dollar per year), and the hospital also proposed to lend the physicians a portion of the construction costs on fair market terms. This Office determined that a more than incidental private benefit would flow to the physicians from the below market rental and that the hospital should lose its exemption if it entered into the transaction. . . .

Thus far, our discussion has focused principally on the sales of the revenue streams involved in the instant arrangements. We also need to address the joint venture aspect. This area of the law has undergone significant change over the last decade. In Plumstead Theatre Soc'y, Inc. v. Commissioner, 74 T.C. 1324 (1980), *aff'd*, 675 F.2d 244 (9th Cir. 1982), the Tax Court disagreed with the Service's earlier stand [that opposed] charitable organization participation as a general partner in a limited partnership. . . . The Service no longer contends that participation as a general partner in a partnership is per se inconsistent with exemption. . . . However, close scrutiny is necessary to ensure that the obligations of the exempt organization as general partner do not conflict with its ability to pursue exclusively charitable goals. Thus, in all partnership cases, the initial focus should be on whether the joint venture organization furthers a charitable purpose. . . . This requires a finding that the benefits received by the limited partners are incidental to the public purposes served by the partnership. Hospital participation in a joint venture is inconsistent with exemption, then, if it does not further a charitable purpose or if there is inadequate protection against financial loss by the hospital or improper financial gain by the physician-investors. See [GCM 39005 (Dec. 17, 1982)]; GCM 39444 (July 18, 1985); GCM 39546 (Aug. 14, 1986). . . .

GCM 39732 considered three cases in which hospitals or affiliated exempt organizations participated as general partners in joint ventures with medical staff physicians to establish (1) a free-standing physical therapy center, (2) a free-standing ambulatory surgery center, and (3) a magnetic resonance imaging facility. . . . [W]e concluded that participation in the partnerships (and activities) in question furthered their exempt purposes. In each case, a new health care provider or resource was made available to the community. Also, the joint venture entity itself actually became the property owner or service provider, subject to all the attendant risks, responsibilities, and potential rewards.

In the instant cases, we have moved from joint venture ownership of property and operation of an activity typically viewed as promoting the health of the community to a shell type of arrangement where the hospital continues to own and operate the facilities in question and the joint venture invests only in a profits interest. These arrangements, despite the joint venture cloak, are merely an arrangement between an exempt hospital and its medical staff physicians through which the hospital shares its net profits from designated activities with the physicians. The partnership's only true function is to purchase, receive, and distribute the net revenue stream from the activity. A hospital's participation in this type of partnership does not clearly further any exempt purpose.

In each of the cases at issue, the hospital has stated that its reasons for participating in the joint venture were to maintain or enhance utilization of its facilities. . . . In our view, there are a fixed number of individuals in a community legitimately needing hospital services at any one time. Paying doctors to steer patients to one particular hospital merely to improve its efficiency seems distant from a mission of providing needed care. We question whether the Service should ever recognize enhancing a hospital's market share vis-á-vis other providers, in and of itself, as furthering a charitable purpose. In many cases, doing so might hamper another charitable hospital's ability to promote the health of the same community. . . .

In addition, . . . the instant arrangements are distinguishable from the medical office building fact pattern in Rev. Rul. 69-464, 1969-2 C.B. 132. In that ruling, the Service recognized that leasing of office space adjacent to a hospital to members of the medical staff under the circumstances described furthers the hospital's exempt purposes by (1) increasing its efficiency, (2) encouraging fuller utilization of its facilities, and (3) improving the overall quality of its patient care. The hospital established that having members of the medical staff practicing next door would result in greater use being made of its diagnostic facilities, implying that attracting business may have been one reason for the arrangement. . . . Of course, the analysis would be completely different if, as in GCM 37789, the physicians paid below fair market rent. In the instant cases, the arrangements do not appear to result in improved patient convenience, greater accessibility of physicians, or any other direct benefit to the community. . . .

[In conclusion,] . . . participation in the subject net revenue stream purchase joint ventures is inconsistent with a hospital's continued exemption as a charitable organization. . . . Depending on the facts, revocation of the hospital's exemption might well be appropriate in such cases.

Notes: Private Inurement and Joint Ventures

1. *The Consequence of Private Inurement.* Finding private inurement can be fatal to tax exemption. Not only is the specific venture taxable, but the hospital's entire exemption can be revoked retroactive to the initiation of the venture. In the past, the "nuclear bomb" of complete revocation was the only enforcement measure the IRS could employ. The IRS is now authorized, however, to impose "intermediate sanctions" such as a fine proportionate to the size of the venture or the degree of inurement. As a consequence, IRS enforcement of compensation, joint ventures, and conflicts of interest has greatly intensified. It now issues a virtual code of conduct that nonprofit entities must comply with or pay a series of graduated penalties.

See IRC §4958; Hill & Kirschten, Federal and State Taxation of Exempt Organizations ¶2.03[3][f].

2. *Private Benefit.* Observe the differences noted in the General Counsel Memorandum (GCM) between the private inurement prohibition and the requirement that charities not operate for the private benefit of any individual. The private benefit proscription does not require monetary payment, it is not limited to "insiders," but it does have a de minimis exception. *Harding Hospital* gives one prime example of private benefit: a hospital that does not open its medical staff to all physicians in the community. The other examples—below-market office space rental, and excess compensation for administrative services—might be classified as either private inurement or private benefit.

3. *Physician Recruitment.* If it is impermissible for hospitals to secure the loyalty of their *existing* medical staff members, can they devise various incentives to attract *new* staff members? Generally, the answer to that is also no, unless the hospital is in an underserved area (such as an inner city or a remote rural setting) where it is difficult to recruit physicians. Then, if the hospital can show a need for the particular physician, the IRS has approved a list of limited recruitment incentives to assist with the transitional costs of moving and setting up a new practice. Examples include income guarantees, office support, subsidized malpractice insurance, and loan guarantees. Hermann Hospital Closing Agreement, *reprinted in* 3 BNA Health L. Rep. 1519 (1994); Rev. Rul. 97-21 (1997).

4. *Whole Hospital vs. Ancillary Joint Ventures.* The gist of the GCM appears to be that joint ventures that create new facilities may be permissible, but not those that merely reallocate revenue streams from existing operations. What if a hospital were to shift its entire operation over to a for-profit entity? At first glance, it would seem to be a foregone conclusion that this is impermissible. However, careful lawyering can do wonders in this arena. Using a vehicle known as a "whole hospital" joint venture, some for-profit hospital companies like Hospital Corporation of America (HCA, which was formerly Columbia) have been able to acquire management of nonprofit hospitals without sacrificing their tax exemption. The nonprofit entity contributes all its operating assets, including the hospital, to the joint venture, which it jointly owns, in exchange for a lump sum of money from the for-profit company. The joint venture then hires a management firm to run the hospital. In Rev. Rul. 98-15, the IRS ruled that the original nonprofit entity will retain its tax exemption if (1) it has majority control of the joint venture, (2) the agreement imposes specific operational requirements necessary to ensure that the hospital will continue meeting the community benefits test for charitable purpose, and (3) the management contract is with a firm that is unrelated to the for-profit party.

In St. David's Health Care System v. United States, 349 F.3d 232 (5th Cir. 2003), the court found that a fact issue existed over whether a nonprofit hospital had ceded operational management to HCA. The court rejected the trial court's summary judgment ruling that the particular agreement adequately protected the board's control over the hospital's charitable purpose, noting that the hospital had only a 50 percent share of the voting control over the joint venture and that the manager was paid a percentage of net revenues, which creates an incentive to maximize profits. On remand, however, the trial court found that the nonprofit hospital board did retain sufficient control because it had an "escape clause" that allowed it to back out if the management firm did not pursue charitable purposes adequately.

For commentary, see Gary J. Young, Federal Tax-Exemption Requirements for Joint Ventures Between Nonprofit Hospital Providers and For-Profit Entities, 13 Ann. Health L. 327 (2004).

Although this ruling is permissive with respect to whole hospital joint ventures, the ruling raised concerns among hospital lawyers that some or all of its requirements will affect other, more traditional, joint ventures such as constructing a medical office building, or opening a satellite clinic. See Gerald Griffith, Revenue Ruling 98-15: Dimming the Future of All Nonprofit Joint Ventures?, 31 J. Health & Hosp. L. 71 (1998). For instance, in Redlands Surgical Services v. Commissioner, 113 T.C. No. 3 (July 17, 1999), aff'd per curiam, 242 F.3d 904 (9th Cir. 2001), the Tax Court applied this ruling to deny exemption to a nonprofit entity formed by an exempt hospital to purchase an outpatient surgery center. The center was purchased through a joint venture between the exempt hospital and an unrelated for-profit company that owns surgical centers across the country. The Tax Court found the absence of a charitable purpose, and an unallowable level of private benefit, because the joint venture agreement gave complete operational control to the for-profit chain, and the surgery center provided no free care to indigents and had only a minuscule amount of Medicaid business. (The lengthy full opinion in this case is well worth reading for the detail it gives about the corporate and contractual documents and entities used to form joint ventures of this sort.)

In analyzing these situations, it is important to clarify what the main issue is. Usually, the issue is *not* whether the venture *itself* is exempt, since usually it clearly is not. Rather, it is whether the nonprofit's participation in a for-profit venture jeopardizes the nonprofit's exemption. *Redlands Surgical* is an unusual case that attempts to, but fails to, obtain exemption for the joint venture. No one suggested the joint venture might threaten the hospital parent's core exemption. As long as the joint venture is ancillary to a hospital's main activity, lawyers assume that the IRS will continue to allow an exempt hospital to put a portion of its assets at risk for legitimate purposes, even if the hospital does not retain full control of the venture's operations. See generally John D. Colombo, A Framework for Analyzing Exemption and UBIT Effects of Joint Ventures, 34 Exempt Org. Tax Rev. 187 (2001).

Notes: Hospital Reorganization and Integrated Delivery Systems

1. *Holding Companies.*

> For most of this century, the legal structure of the hospital was uncomplicated. Most hospitals were operated as single nonprofit organizations or, perhaps, as public corporations. As health care delivery has become more complex, however, so have the corporate structures of health care institutions. . . .
>
> The holding company structure is usually the result of a reorganization of a single hospital corporation into a group of affiliated corporations. The resulting corporations typically include a parent holding company, a hospital subsidiary and additional subsidiaries from which other components of the reorganized health care "system" are operated—components such as outpatient facilities, or real estate holdings. . . .
>
> Complex hospital corporate structures are a relatively recent phenomenon. Hospital reorganizations began in the 1970s and were widespread by the early 1980s.

The typical restructuring involved a freestanding hospital operated through a single, usually nonprofit, corporation. The reorganization resulted in the replacement of this simple corporate structure with a "parent holding company" controlling one or more operating subsidiaries, including a hospital subsidiary. As a result of this reorganization movement, few hospitals currently operate as stand-alone corporations without the benefit of a corporate parent, a so-called sister affiliate or a subsidiary.

The earliest hospital reorganizations were motivated primarily by Medicare reimbursement incentives. Prior to the adoption of the prospective payment system (PPS) . . . [r]eorganizing the hospital along the lines of the "parent holding company" model provided a number of different reimbursement advantages. . . . As part of a corporate reorganization, departments with low Medicare usage could be placed into separate corporations, leaving the bulk of hospital overhead costs to be allocated only among the Medicare-intensive departments that remained within the primary hospital corporation. Putting the low-usage activities in legally separate entities was thought to make it more difficult for the Medicare program to succeed in challenging overhead allocations. Separate incorporation of different components of hospital operations could also be used to avoid interest income offsets, to avoid provider cost limits, or, possibly, to obtain charge-based (as opposed to cost-based) reimbursement for certain services.[4]

Because most hospitals are no longer reimbursed on a cost basis, these reasons are now largely obsolete. Nevertheless, market incentives and regulatory rules still create significant additional reasons for hospitals to consider the holding company structure advantageous. . . . For example, in some states a hospital might be required to obtain a certificate of need to build a parking garage or a medical office building, whereas a separate corporation created for these specific purposes might be able to initiate the same project without CON review. . . . [Also], nonprofit health care systems may find it advantageous to put operations that generate unrelated business income into separate taxable subsidiaries in order to avoid jeopardizing tax-exempt status.[5] . . . [Finally], [s]eparating diverse functions into distinct entities can also create more precise accountability and awareness of corporate performance. Thus, the goal of hospital reorganization is often to use separate corporations to reflect separate lines of business. . . .

Reorganization may also create competitive advantages for the health care system by providing greater flexibility for participation in the creation and operation of health care networks and other innovative transactions. . . . [T]he recent

4. See generally David Frankford, The Complexity of Medicare's Hospital Reimbursement System: Paradoxes of Averaging, 78 Iowa L. Rev. 517 (1993).

5. . . . [However,] health care delivery systems may become so obsessed with diversification that corporations are created that have nothing to do with the initial and overall mission of the system. For example, Hamot Medical Center in Erie, Pennsylvania was publicly scrutinized when an affiliate was discovered to have purchased a marina for $375,000. In a fight to maintain its tax-exempt status, the hospital argued that the affiliate was furthering the hospital's purposes "by promoting urban redevelopment." A court reviewing the tax-exempt status of the Medical Center concluded that the hospital's primary business was no longer health promotion, but funding of affiliates that competed with local businessmen. School District of City of Erie v. Hamot Medical Center, 144 Pa. Commw. Ct. 668, 602 A.2d 407 (1992). . . .

> development of integrated delivery systems has made the creation of a parent corporation even more important than in the past.

Stephen Bernstein, Complex Corporate Structures, *in* Health Care Corporate Law: Facilities and Transactions (M. Hall & W. Brewbaker eds., 1996).

2. *Hospital Reorganization and Integration.* These reorganizations have led to a number of rulings concerning the extent to which hospital holding companies and other complex corporate structures comply with the requirements for charitable tax exemption. Under specialized doctrines known as the "integral part test" and the "shared service organization" rule, there are two basic issues: (1) which subsidiaries will lose exemption if their functions are examined separately from the hospital's; and (2) will the parent company qualify for exemption even though it is a "shell" corporation that offers no charitable service directly, and even though a number of its subsidiaries are run as for-profit ventures? The answer to the former is explored above in terms of each of a number of different health care ventures (HMO, nursing home, physician group practice, etc.). The answer to the latter is generally yes, following the "integral part" thinking described above. The leading ruling is *Northwestern Medical Corp.*, described in Tax Notes, Sept. 9, 1993, where the IRS approved the exemption of a "superparent" for a regional hospital network composed of several hospital systems, each with its own exempt parent. In Wilson Area School District v. Easton Hosp., 747 A.2d 877 (Pa. 2000), the court upheld the charitable status of a non-profit hospital that owned a number of for-profit subsidiaries because the subsidiaries helped to further the hospital's general health care purposes.

3. *Integrated Delivery Systems.* The most important application of these corporate restructuring rulings is to so-called vertically integrated networks or integrated delivery systems (IDSs), those that contain not only hospitals but also nursing homes, home health agencies, physician groups, and an HMO. The IRS's rulings at first followed a de facto rule that participating physicians may constitute no more than 20 percent of the governing board, based on obscure precedents dealing with tax-exempt bond financing. After sustained criticism, the IRS relaxed this limit to 49 percent as long as physician board members are insulated from decisions about physician compensation and other conflict of interest protections are in place. Lawyers await IRS guidance on similar issues relating to ACOs.

Is a limit on physician board membership consistent with the corporate practice of medicine doctrine? Is it consistent with realistic business planning? Hospital-based networks need to include physicians in order to offer the better management and coordination of care that health policy seeks, but hospitals find it difficult to form tight affiliations with physician groups without giving them substantial governance authority.

4. *Are Hospital-Run Systems Optimal?* Although the IRS may have relaxed somewhat its opposition to physician governance, it still appears essential that tax-exempt networks be hospital run. Otherwise, it would be difficult to invoke the generous "promotion of health" precedents that apply to hospitals and difficult to meet the free emergency service requirements. On the other hand, hospital control may not prove to be the optimal, or even a viable, organizational structure for emerging ACOs. The Friendly Hills system that received the first integrated system ruling in

the 1990s abandoned its exempt status less than two years later and split up into several for-profit components owned by the physicians, and many other provider-owned networks formed in the 1990s failed or were bought out by larger insurers. A prominent health management consultant gives several, highly opinionated reasons this may have occurred:

> [T]here are a lot of Walter Mitty-like fantasies of power being realized in the creation of integrated systems. Some executives believe that management is finally about to triumph over physicians. . . . My experience . . . taught me early on that physicians crave order but despise authority. . . . While many physicians fall prey to an illusion of omnicompetence and believe that their medical training endowed them with superior management judgment, most are incapable of submitting to the authority of anyone, even a fellow physician. . . . As a consequence, many lack the interpersonal skills or civility to function as part of a larger enterprise. When physicians are unhappy, they whine—deafeningly. They passively resist initiatives that they cannot overtly oppose, often doing so with dazzling flair and elegance. They will agree in public meetings and subvert privately. They wait for temporary weakness in administrative personnel and savage them. . . . In short, . . . a sizeable fraction of the current generation of private practitioners or medical school faculties are poor candidates for participating in any integrated health care enterprise. . . . One thing becomes clear.

Jeff Goldsmith, Hospital/Physician Relationships: A Constraint to Health Reform, 12(3) Health Aff. 161 (Aug. 1993). However, Goldsmith is equally dubious of hospital control:

> The hospital is not the appropriate nucleus of an integrated health care system. . . . Rather, the hospital is a high-maintenance core asset whose use must be rigorously limited by managed care incentives. Outside the integrated enterprise, the hospital is merely a vulnerable vendor of a surplus commodity. Owning a lot of hospital beds in the emerging managed care world will be as advantageous as owning a lot of rubles in post-Soviet Russia.

Problem: Choosing a Corporate Form

Florence Nightingale Hospital has decided to form an HMO in which it wants to give physicians a major stake, in order to foster allegiance and encourage cost-effective treatment. You are consulted as a legal and management expert to advise the hospital on the consequences of forming the HMO as a nonprofit vs. a for-profit entity. What are the relevant considerations with respect to tax exemption, the ability to raise capital, the role of physicians, and operational constraints?

3. The Corporate Practice of Medicine

This section explores an old body of law known as the corporate practice of medicine doctrine, which now may appear archaic, but which has profound influence on the entire structure of the health care delivery system.

BARTRON v. CODINGTON COUNTY

2 N.W.2d 337 (S.D. 1942)

SMITH, Judge.

. . . The central question of law to be determined is whether certain exhibited bargains between Codington County and the Bartron Clinic, a corporation for profit, pursuant to which such corporation furnished medical and surgical services, and medicines to the county indigent, are illegal and unenforceable.

The "Bartron Clinic" was incorporated in February of 1929, "to conduct and operate a general medical and surgical hospital and clinic and employ duly licensed physicians, surgeons, nurses, students, and other persons to carry on the business of said corporation." Its 750 shares of capital stock were originally issued and held by duly licensed physicians and surgeons, and by nurses and other employees of the corporation. . . . Except for some minor services of an intern, all of the professional services involved herein were performed by duly licensed physicians and surgeons employed at fixed salaries by the corporation, and all charges therefor accrued to and were made by the corporation. The corporation owned all equipment used by the doctors and maintained the supply of drugs furnished patients. The corporation did not hold a license to practice medicine and surgery, nor to operate a pharmacy.

On January 3, 1933, the county and the corporation executed and delivered two contracts in writing wherein the corporation agreed to furnish hospitalization, medical and surgical services and medicine to the county for its poor persons. . . .

The court [below] found that there was not in connection with the organization of the Bartron Clinic, or at any time thereafter, any purpose or intent whatsoever on the part of Dr. Bartron or anybody else connected with said corporation to place the actual control of the practice of medicine with any person other than duly licensed physicians; that there was not at any time throughout the existence of said corporation any control, or effort to exercise control, as to the actual practice of medicine on the part of anybody other than a licensed physician and no interference, or attempted interference, by anybody other than a licensed physician, with the actual practice of medicine; that the actual purpose and intent of Dr. Bartron in promoting the organization of said corporation was to establish what amounted to a system of profit sharing, whereby the prominent and leading employees of said hospital and clinic business would have some actual interest in the success thereof.

[This case] originated as a claim before the county commissioners in aggregate amount of $3,649.63 for medicine supplied the county indigent between January 1, 1938 and September 1, 1938. . . . [T]he court found that the professional services were actually rendered by duly licensed physicians, except for a small item for intern's services, and that the medicines were prescribed by such physicians in treatment of the county poor, and that all of this was done pursuant to directions and orders of the county commissioners.

The court concluded as a matter of law . . . that it is unlawful and contrary to public policy for a corporation to practice medicine or surgery and to operate a pharmacy or sell medicine without a license as required by the statutes of South Dakota. These conclusions are challenged here by appropriate assignments of error. . . .

When conduct opposed to the public interest is made the subject of a bargain the courts ordinarily refuse to accord a party thereto a remedy predicated thereon. . . . While decision has rarely turned on the naked issue of public policy, the expressions of the courts indicate a current of opinion, to which there are but few dissentients, that such practice contravenes the public interest and is contrary to public policy.

The leading case is that of In re Cooperative Law Co., 198 N.Y. 479, 92 N.E. 15. The court said:

> The practice of law is not a business open to all, but a personal right, limited to a few persons of good moral character, with special qualifications ascertained and certified after a long course of study, both general and professional, and a thorough examination by a state board appointed for the purpose. . . . The relation of attorney and client is that of master and servant in a limited and dignified sense, and it involves the highest trust and confidence. It cannot be delegated without consent, and it cannot exist between an attorney employed by a corporation to practice law for it, and a client of the corporation, for he would be subject to the directions of the corporation, and not to the directions of the client. There would be neither contract nor privity between him and the client, and he would not owe even the duty of counsel to the actual litigant. The corporation would control the litigation, the money earned would belong to the corporation, and the attorney would be responsible to the corporation only. His master would not be the client but the corporation, conducted it may be wholly by laymen, organized simply to make money and not to aid in the administration of justice which is the highest function of an attorney and counsellor at law. The corporation might not have a lawyer among its stockholders, directors, or officers. Its members might be without character, learning or standing. There would be . . . no stimulus to good conduct from the traditions of an ancient and honorable profession, and no guide except the sordid purpose to earn money for stockholders. The bar, which is an institution of the highest usefulness and standing, would be degraded if even its humblest member became subject to the orders of a money-making corporation engaged not in conducting litigation for itself, but in the business of conducting litigation for others. *The degradation of the bar is an injury to the state.* . . .

Debasement of the learned professions is in fact inimical to the public welfare. The public is the ultimate beneficiary of its professional social organisms, and of the private, as well as of the unselfish public, exercise of the skills and talents of its professional practitioners. Although the members of the legal profession in their individual capacities as officers of the courts of justice sustain a relationship to the public without parallel in the medical professions, in all other respects the services of the two professions are of equal importance to the public, and debasement of the one, in our opinion, would constitute no less a public evil than would the degradation of the other.

These professions, as they exist in our social structure, rest upon a foundation of sturdy, sterling human character which, in turn, has been and is being shaped and moulded by the impact of traditional ideals and points of view. The licensing statutes with their emphasis on character and professional conduct evidence a fixed public desire and will not only to foster, but to develop and reinforce, these basic attributes of its professional servants. . . . We are therefore persuaded that that which tends to debase the learned professions is at war with the public interest and is therefore contrary to public policy.

Does practice of the learned professions by a profit corporation functioning through duly licensed practitioners tend to debase the professions? We pause to emphasize the word *tend* because the learned trial court has found that the Bartron Clinic was innocent of any unethical intention or practice, and that its licensed officers and employees controlled its professional activities. Our present concern is with the tendency of the challenged conduct. Though the exhibited instance of that conduct has accomplished no evil, if its inherent tendency be at war with public interest, it is contrary to public policy.

Because of the rights with which the law invests a stockholder in a corporation for profit, recognition of such a means of conducting a professional business involves yielding the right of participation in control of its policies and in its earnings to lay persons. . . . The object of such a company would be to produce an earning on its fixed capital. Its trade commodity would be the professional services of its employees. Constant pressure would be exerted by the investor to promote such a volume of sales of that commodity as would produce an ever increasing return on his investment. To promote such sales it is to be presumed that the layman would apply the methods and practices in which he had been schooled in the market place. The end result seems inevitable to us, viz., undue emphasis on mere money making, and commercial exploitation of professional services. To universalize the use of this method of organizing the professions, or to permit such a use to become general, would ultimately wipe out or blight those characteristics which distinguish the business practices of the professions from those of the market place. Such an ethical, trustworthy and unselfish professionalism as the community needs and wants cannot survive in a purely commercial atmosphere. . . .

That such is the tendency of the profit corporation when used to conduct a professional practice is not a matter of mere fancy or conjecture. It is a matter of common knowledge that this form of organization has been tried in the field of dentistry and resulted in such unethical and commercial practices as induced the legislature of this and many other states to pass statutes expressly prohibiting its use.

Being convinced that the practice of the learned professions by a profit corporation tends to the commercialization and debasement of those professions, we are of the opinion that such a mode of conducting the practice is in contravention of the public interest and is against public policy. It follows that we are of the view that insofar as the bargains of the Bartron Clinic and Codington County dealt with medical and surgical services, they were illegal. [As a result, the court refused to order the county to pay for medical services it had received, but the court did allow the clinic to keep funds previously paid.]

■ RIGHT OF CORPORATION TO PRACTICE MEDICINE

Note, 48 Yale L.J. 346 (1938)

Efforts to obtain adequate medical care at reasonable cost have stimulated extensive experimentation with methods of medical organization. The result has been widespread development of such diversified types as private group clinics, employee health associations, county physician bureaus, health insurance plans, and medical cooperatives. Many of the sponsors of these systems have attempted to take advantage of the corporate form in order to achieve limited liability and continuity of existence. Groups of physicians have incorporated to operate their own clinic; laymen have formed corporations, hiring physicians to treat patients for profit; and aggregations of prospective patients have organized nonprofit cooperative corporations. Yet the legal existence of these corporate types has been jeopardized at one time or another by attempted application of the principle that corporations may not practice the learned professions. . . .

While numerous state statutes directly forbid the corporate practice of law, express prohibition of the corporate practice of medicine is rare. Instead, denial of the right of some corporations to practice medicine has been based upon those statutes in every state which outlaws performance of the healing art by unlicensed persons. The obvious inability of a corporate entity to meet the educational and character requirements prerequisite to a license is said to inhibit a corporation from practicing medicine. To bolster this interpretation of the statutes, courts have commonly resorted to arguments of public policy. Since the judiciary do not possess an intrinsic power to regulate the medical profession as they do the legal, the validity of this viewpoint is necessarily dependent upon the soundness of the courts' inference that state licensing statutes automatically forbid utilization of the corporate power.

Courts which profess to deny all corporations the right to have any connection with medical activities have apparently misconstrued the purpose of the state licensing statutes. These statutes are designed to preserve the public health by excluding from practice persons with inadequate ability, morality, and training. Since the diagnosis and treatment of disease are obviously purely personal functions, a corporation can perform them only through the medium of doctors. But the mere fact that a corporation employs physicians, or is operated by physicians, provides no valid basis for requiring the corporation itself to be licensed. As long as the doctors are properly licensed and their professional activities are not interfered with by unlicensed persons, the purpose of the statutes is fully effected, for no one without proper qualifications is then directly or indirectly administering to the public. This is true even though laymen may be entrusted with considerable control over administrative details. Only when lay officers or directors exercise substantial supervision over the professional activities of the physicians employed is there ground for arguing that the corporation is enabling unlicensed persons to practice medicine. Thus the real issue is not whether corporations generally are unlicensed to practice medicine, but whether in each individual case physicians are *actually* controlled in their purely professional functions by unlicensed persons in such a manner as to nullify the purpose of the licensing statutes. . . .

Even in states following [this doctrine], numerous corporations engage unchallenged in activities which have all the indicia of corporate practice of medicine as defined by the same courts. It is common knowledge that private hospitals, sanitariums, fraternal organizations, educational institutions, and industrial concerns all administer medical services to their constituents through staffs of physicians hired and paid on a full or part time basis. Similarly, salaried physicians undertake part time contract practice on behalf of various companies, particularly railroads, to treat passengers and employees. The explanation for such discrimination may be that the social utility of these types of corporate medical service has long been tacitly recognized; nevertheless, the fact remains that some corporate forms have been permitted in the face of the same state licensing statutes which are so rigorously invoked against others.

Since the legal construction of state licensing statutes is by no means inexorable, their varying application to certain corporate forms is probably attributable to the judges' evaluation of social policy arguments against corporate medical practice. Impairment of the intimate doctor-patient relationship and commercialization of the medical profession are the two general social policy objections most commonly cited by the courts. The first evil will result, it is feared, from possible restrictions upon the patient's freedom of choice of physician and from a division of the physician's loyalty between patient and corporate employer. If the old-fashioned family doctor is used as the norm, this objection might assume serious proportions. But when the challenged corporate forms are compared with the many types of corporate medical service already accepted, any distinguishing basis must be fanciful indeed. Furthermore, consistency would require that the same charge be levelled against noncorporate forms such as county, municipal, and private partnership clinics. And even if the choice of doctors should be unusually restricted within a particular corporate scheme, many patients might prefer that scheme to other types of private group medical services or to receiving inadequate or no medical treatment whatsoever. . . . Moreover, insulation of the doctor from administrative and economic cares and elimination of the patient's concern over cost may actually enhance the relationship between patient and physician.

More plausible is the second social objection to the corporate furnishing of medical service. It is feared that the profession may be commercially exploited by laymen who, not being amenable to ethical standards, are free to engage in high pressure solicitation of patients and sharp competitive advertising. But the fact that this fear may at times be well-grounded should not justify resort to the drastic measure of barring corporate medical service entirely. A more sensible solution is for the state to combine its recognized regulatory powers over corporations and professions in order to curb objectionable professional activity. And even without special regulation, the state can undoubtedly hold contract physicians to the same standard of ethics as private practitioners. Moreover, the opposition of the American Medical Association to this type of corporate medical practice assures a zealous and vigilant supervision by a body duty-bound to report to the state injurious professional activity.

. . . Some courts persist in trying to solve such cases by repeating generalizations which are meaningless in the abstract. A more realistic judicial approach would disregard the corporate form as such and inquire instead whether the actual setup is so provocative of abuses that the only solution is to deny the corporation existence altogether. However, the public interest in furthering experiments in medical care may suffer much by trusting to haphazard decisions by tribunals ill-fitted to investigate intricate specific cases. The surer method of achieving the benefits of corporate medical organization without possible attendant evils would be by enactment of legislation specifically authorizing the corporate form but carefully regulating its activities so as to insure the highest response to professional ethics by the corporation as an entity and by its physicians.

BERLIN v. SARAH BUSH LINCOLN HEALTH CENTER

688 N.E.2d 106 (Ill. 1997)

NICKLES, J.

. . . The [Sara Bush Lincoln] Health Center is a nonprofit corporation duly licensed under the Hospital Licensing Act to operate a hospital. In December 1992, Dr. Berlin and the Health Center entered into a written agreement whereby the Health Center employed Dr. Berlin to practice medicine for the hospital for five years. The agreement . . . contained a restrictive covenant which prohibited Dr. Berlin from competing with the hospital by providing health services within a 50-mile radius of the Health Center for two years after the end of the employment agreement. On February 4, 1994, Dr. Berlin informed the Health Center by letter that he was resigning effective February 7, 1994 and accepting employment with the Carle Clinic . . . located approximately one mile from the Health Center. Shortly thereafter, the Health Center sought a preliminary injunction to prohibit Dr. Berlin from practicing at the Carle Clinic. . . . The circuit court, finding the entire employment agreement unenforceable, granted Dr. Berlin's motion for summary judgment. . . . [T]he circuit court determined that the Health Center, by hiring Dr. Berlin to practice medicine as its employee, violated the prohibition against corporations practicing medicine.[3] . . .

. . . The corporate practice of medicine doctrine prohibits corporations from providing professional medical services. Although a few states have codified the doctrine, the prohibition is primarily inferred from state medical licensure acts, which regulate the profession of medicine and forbid its practice by unlicensed individuals. See A. Rosoff, The Business of Medicine: Problems with the Corporate Practice Doctrine, 17 Cumb. L. Rev. 485, 490 (1987). The rationale behind the doctrine is that a corporation cannot be licensed to practice medicine because only a human being can sustain the education, training, and character-screening which are prerequisites to receiving a professional license. Since a corporation cannot receive a medical license, it follows that a corporation cannot legally practice the profession. The rationale of the doctrine concludes that the employment of physicians by corporations is illegal because the acts of the physicians are attributable to the corporate employer, which cannot obtain a medical license. See M. Hall, Institutional Control of Physician Behavior: Legal Barriers to Health Care Cost Containment, 137 U. Pa. L. Rev. 431, 509-10 (1988). The prohibition on the corporate employment of physicians is invariably supported by several public policy arguments which espouse the dangers of lay control over professional judgment, the division of the physician's loyalty between his patient and his profitmaking employer, and the commercialization of the profession. See A. Willcox, Hospitals and the Corporate Practice of Medicine, 45 Cornell L.Q. 432, 442-43 (1960).

This court first [applied] the corporate practice doctrine [to strike down a restrictive covenant] in Dr. Allison, Dentist, Inc. v. Allison, 360 Ill. 638 (1935), [whose facts were essentially the same as here, except that Dr. Allison was a dentist

3. [This case challenges the legality of the employment relationship as a whole. The legality of restrictive covenants in particular has also been challenged. — EDS.]

working for a dental office, not a physician at a hospital] . . . Soon after the *Allison* decision, this court . . . addressed the corporate practice doctrine as it pertained to [physicians working in a clinic, in a ruling essentially the same as in Bartron v. Codington County, supra] People ex rel. Kerner v. United Medical Service, Inc., 362 Ill. 442 (1936). . . . Prior to the instant action, apparently no Illinois court has . . . specifically addressed the issue of whether licensed hospitals are prohibited from employing physicians. We therefore look to other jurisdictions with reference to the application of the corporate practice of medicine doctrine to hospitals.

. . . [N]umerous jurisdictions have recognized either judicial or statutory exceptions to the corporate practice of medicine doctrine which allow hospitals to employ physicians and other health care professionals. . . . First, some states . . . determined that a hospital corporation which employs a physician is not practicing medicine, but rather is merely making medical treatment available. See, e.g., State ex rel. Sager v. Lewin, 128 Mo. App. 149, 155, 106 S.W. 581, 583 (1907); State Electro-Medical Institute v. Platner, 74 Neb. 23, 29, 103 N.W. 1079, 1081 (1905). Under the second approach, the courts of some jurisdictions determined that the corporate practice doctrine is inapplicable to nonprofit hospitals and health associations. These courts reasoned that the public policy arguments supporting the corporate practice doctrine do not apply to physicians employed by charitable institutions. See, e.g., Group Health Ass'n v. Moor, 24 F. Supp. 445, 446 (D.D.C. 1938); People ex rel. State Board of Medical Examiners v. Pacific Health Corp., 12 Cal. 2d 156, 159-61, 82 P.2d 429, 431 (1938). In the third approach, the courts of several states have determined that the corporate practice doctrine is not applicable to hospitals [that] employ physicians because hospitals are authorized by other laws to provide medical treatment to patients. See, e.g., Rush v. City of St. Petersburg, 205 So. 2d 11 (Fla. App. 1967); St. Francis Regional Medical Center, Inc. v. Weiss, 254 Kan. 728, 869 P.2d 606 (1994).

We find the [third] rationale . . . persuasive. . . . The Medical Practice Act contains no express prohibition on the corporate employment of physicians.[1] Rather, the corporate practice of medicine doctrine was inferred from the general policies behind the Medical Practice Act. . . . The [hospital licensing] statutes clearly authorize, and at times mandate, licensed hospital corporations to provide medical services. . . .

In addition, we find the public policy concerns which support the corporate practice doctrine inapplicable to a licensed hospital in the modern health care industry. The concern for lay control over professional judgment is alleviated in a licensed hospital, where generally a separate professional medical staff is responsible for the quality of medical services rendered in the facility.[2] Furthermore, we believe that extensive changes in the health care industry since [1936], including

1. In contrast, the Dental Practice Act, applied by this court in *Allison*, expressly prohibited a corporation from furnishing dentists and owning and operating a dental office.

2. Moreover, in the instant case, the employment agreement expressly provided that the Health Center had no control or direction over Dr. Berlin's medical judgment and practice, other than that control exercised by the professional medical staff. Dr. Berlin has never contended that the Health Center's lay management attempted to control his practice of medicine.

the emergence of corporate health maintenance organizations, have greatly altered the concern over the commercialization of health care. In addition, such concerns are relieved when a licensed hospital is the physician's employer. Hospitals have an independent duty to provide for the patient's health and welfare. See Darling v. Charleston Community Mem. Hosp., 33 Ill. 2d 326 (1965) (recognizing hospital's duty to assume responsibility for the care of its patients).

We find particularly appropriate the statement of the Kansas Supreme Court that "[i]t would be incongruous to conclude that the legislature intended a hospital to accomplish what it is licensed to do without utilizing physicians as independent contractors or employees. . . . To conclude that a hospital must do so without employing physicians is not only illogical but ignores reality." *Weiss*, 869 P.2d at 618. Accordingly, we conclude that a duly-licensed hospital possesses legislative authority to practice medicine by means of its staff of licensed physicians and is excepted from the operation of the corporate practice of medicine doctrine. Consequently, the employment agreement between the Health Center and Dr. Berlin is not unenforceable merely because the Health Center is a corporate entity. . . .

Harrison, J. and Miller, J., dissenting:

. . . [N]one of the statutes invoked by my colleagues supports their position. The most that can be said of those statutes is that they authorize hospitals to operate facilities for the diagnosis and care of patients and to make emergency service available regardless of ability to pay. . . . None of those endeavors, however, requires that hospitals have the power to employ physicians directly or to charge patients for the physicians' services. All may be accomplished by granting staff privileges to duly licensed private physicians, and the Hospital Licensing Act presumes that hospitals will staff their facilities in precisely that way. . . . [T]he General Assembly has expressly authorized the employment of physicians by Health Maintenance Organizations (HMOs) under the Health Maintenance Organization Act. If the General Assembly had intended to grant the same authority to hospitals, I believe that it would have been similarly straightforward and unambiguous in doing so. In addition to creating special rules for HMOs, the General Assembly has also decided to allow physicians to employ various forms of business organizations in practicing their profession. Physicians may incorporate in accordance with the Professional Service Corporation Act, they may form corporations to provide medical services under the Medical Corporation Act, they have the right to practice in a professional association organized pursuant to the Professional Association Act, and they can organize and operate limited liability companies to practice medicine under the recently amended Limited Liability Company Act. Again, however, none of these provisions pertains to hospitals, and no inference can be drawn from any of them that the General Assembly intended to alter the prohibition against the corporate practice of medicine by hospitals. . . .

Notes: Corporate Practice of Medicine and Choice of Entity

1. *The Fundamental Structure of American Medical Institutions.* This body of law may appear obscure and antiquated, but it continues to have fundamental importance for the structure of institutional and economic relationships in American medicine. Observe, for instance, that the prohibition of institutions charging for

medical services explains why doctors are paid separately from hospitals and why there used to be a distinction between Blue Cross and Blue Shield and still is between Medicare Part A and Part B. This doctrine also explains why, only in North America, hospital medical staffs are independent and self-governing. Elsewhere in the world, hospital physicians are uniformly employed or compensated by the hospital.

Challenging this traditional order is hospitals' current interest in forming ACOs that better coordinate across different practice settings. This ACO movement is causing a significant increase in hospitals employing physicians who practice in the community. See R. Kocher & N. Sahni, Hospitals' Race to Employ Physicians: The Logic Behind a Money-Losing Proposition, 364 New Eng. J. Med. 1790 (2011). Will the corporate practice of medicine doctrine permit this? For a thorough discussion of various legal and practice issues, see Leigh Walton et al., Hospitals Employing Physicians, 22(2) The Health Lawyer 1 (Dec. 2009).

2. *Legal Landmines.* Following the 1930s and 1940s, the corporate practice of medicine doctrine entered a period of relative quiescence in the courts. It still continued to thrive, though, in state attorneys general opinions during the 1950s, in response to the growing technological sophistication of medical care and hospitals' resulting relationships with radiologists, pathologists, and other hospital-based specialists. Activity at even that level slackened noticeably over the ensuing decades, leading one to consider whether the doctrine hasn't been quietly defused. However, in Professor Rosoff's apt metaphor, corporate practice prohibitions survive as "legal landmines, remnants of an old and nearly forgotten war, half-buried on a field fast being built up with new forms of health care organizations. Occasionally, usually at the instigation of those who resist the change not taking place, one is detonated, with distressing results." A. Rosoff, The Business of Medicine: Problems with the Corporate Practice Doctrine, 17 Cumb. L. Rev. 485 (1987).

Instances of modern application in addition to those discussed in *Berlin* include Conrad v. Medical Board of California, 55 Cal. Rptr. 2d 801 (Ct. App. 1996) (hospital district may not employ physicians); and Isles Wellness, Inc. v. Progressive Northern Insurance Co., 703 N.W.2d 513 (Minn. 2005) (holding after extensive debate that the doctrine is still alive and it bars the employment of chiropractors by a clinic with lay owners). However, another decision in the latter case held that violation of the doctrine does not automatically render void any contracts entered into by the clinic. 725 N.W.2d 90 (Minn. 2006).

3. *Doctrinal Foundations.* The corporate practice doctrine is founded on two distinct bases: the Medical Practice Act and common-law public policy. The courts rarely draw this distinction, however. *Bartron* is one court that did. In another portion of the opinion, the court, influenced by the Yale Note, rejected the literal terms of the Medical Practice Act as a basis for a corporate practice challenge. In doing so, it stands almost alone.

4. *Statutory Arguments.* The *Allison* decision, discussed in *Berlin,* provides an example of the typical reasoning of the statutory basis for the corporate practice prohibition: "The qualifications [to practice a profession] include personal characteristics such as honesty, guided by an upright conscience and a sense of loyalty to clients or patients. . . . These requirements are spoken of generically as that good moral character which is a prerequisite to the licensing of any professional man. No corporation can qualify. It can have neither honesty nor conscience. . . ." 196 N.E.

799, 800 (1935). Does this line of reasoning differ in form or in substance from the following?

- The actions of drivers hired by a corporation are attributed to the corporation
- An eyesight examination is required for a driver's license
- Corporations cannot take an eye exam
- Therefore, a corporation that hires drivers is guilty of driving without a license

See Sloan v. Metropolitan Health Council, 516 N.E.2d 1104, 1107 (Ind. Ct. App. 1987) (rejecting the doctrine on this basis).

5. *Public Policy Arguments.* Addressing corporate practice from a common-law public policy perspective, how far should the courts go in striking down private contractual arrangements? Many of the original and leading cases address situations of apparent quackery in the peripheral medical professions (dentistry, optometry, etc.). See Laufer, Ethical and Legal Restrictions on Contract and Corporate Practice of Medicine, 6 Law & Contemp. Probs. 521, 526 (Autumn 1939). *Bartron,* however, applies a strict rule despite the completely upright behavior of the individual doctors. Are there any countervailing harms to banning corporate practice, or should the courts lean as far as possible in the direction of a pristine practice setting? In 1979, the Federal Trade Commission (FTC) permanently enjoined the AMA from enforcing *ethical* prohibitions against corporate practice because of the anticompetitive effects of the AMA controlling the economic and organizational aspects of medical practice. American Medical Ass'n, 94 F.T.C. 980, 1015 (1979), aff'd by equally divided court, 455 U.S. 676 (1982).

How great of a concern is the threat of divided loyalty, that is, the responsibility an employed physician owes to her employer as well as to her patient? Is the loyalty any greater than that owed by one physician *partner* to another? Than that owed by a physician to other patients? Is it not possible to serve two masters so long as they do not impose inconsistent duties?

And what of the commercialization concern, that is, that introduction of a profit motive will tend to debase the profession? Clearly a profit motive exists in medical practice regardless of the organizational form of practice. Doctors are the highest paid profession in the country. What additional concerns are introduced by *incorporating* a profitable practice? Consider whether there isn't a form of hypocrisy or self-interest in keeping only nonphysicians from sharing in medicine's rich rewards.

6. *Implicit Exceptions.* The holding in *Berlin* would appear to exempt from the corporate practice prohibition all hospitals, nursing homes, and licensed outpatient clinics, but only to the extent covered by their licenses. Could a hospital operate a chain of physician offices under this rationale? In a subsequent decision, the Illinois Supreme Court refused to apply *Berlin* to a nonprofit corporation that owned physician offices as a joint venture between a hospital and a physician group because the particular corporation used did not hold a hospital license. Carter-Shields v. Alton Health Institute, 777 N.E.2d 948 (Ill. 2002). The court also refused to find an exception based on the hospital's or the corporate entity's nonprofit status, holding that "nonprofit status is unrelated to . . . safeguarding the physician's professional judgment from lay interference or protecting the public's general health and welfare."

What other exceptions to the doctrine are mentioned in *Berlin*? See, e.g., Conrad v. Medical Board of California, 55 Cal. Rptr. 2d 901 (Ct. App. 1996) (hospital district may retain physicians only as independent contractors, not as employees). Not all courts agree with these exceptions, however.

7. *PCs and LLCs.* The dissent in *Berlin* observes that exceptions to the corporate practice prohibition are sometimes explicit in licensing statutes. The most prominent example is a professional corporation (PC). Practice groups organized like the one that was invalidated in *Bartron,* that are entirely owned by member physicians, are now permitted by PC laws widely adopted during the 1960s. A PC essentially allows physicians and other licensed professionals (lawyers included) to enjoy the liability protections of corporate organization while enjoying the tax benefits of practicing as a partnership. (Note, though, that tax reform legislation in the 1980s substantially restricted PC pension and retirement benefits, the major tax advantage.) See J. Philipps et al., Origins of Tax Law: The History of the Personal Service Corporation, 40 Wash. & Lee L. Rev. 433 (1983). Do these laws change the public policy recognized in *Bartron*? Cf. Sloan v. Metropolitan Health Council, 516 N.E.2d 1104, 1107 (Ind. Ct. App. 1987) (dictum) ("We believe that the Professional Corporation Act . . . totally abolished [the] public policy [prohibiting a corporation to practice medicine], if, indeed, it ever existed.").

Professional corporation statutes typically require owners to remain liable for each other's professional negligence, as in partnerships, and they restrict ownership to professionals who have similar categories of practice licensure (M.D.s, lawyers, dentists, etc.). This gives rise to disputes over whether physicians can employ or share ownership with other licensed medical professionals. See, e.g., Columbia Physical Therapy v. Benton Franklin Orthopedic Assoc., 228 P.2d 1260 (Wash. 2010) (holding that corporate practice doctrine does not bar physician group from employing physical therapists, but only because physical therapy is a subcomponent of medical practice).

An innovation to the PC format that has gained widespread popularity is known as a professional limited liability company (PLLC). State laws authorizing limited liability companies have proliferated in response to an IRS ruling that makes it easier to avoid corporate taxation. Classically, corporations, which are taxed as entities, were distinguished from partnerships in which there is no entity-level tax, only the ordinary income tax paid by individual members. This distinction was based on certain classic attributes of corporations, such as limited liability, centralized management, and freely transferrable investment interests, which the IRS ruled could not be fully replicated by contract without incurring corporate tax. See United States v. Kintner, 216 F.2d 418 (9th Cir. 1954). It is this ruling the IRS relaxed, opening the way to a whole new species of business organizations. The modern "check-the-box" regulations allow closely held entities to choose either partnership or corporate tax treatment, regardless of their form. 26 C.F.R. §301 (1997).

This flexible taxation approach is now available to closely held business entities, regardless of the kind of entity in question. For a time, however, it was available only by virtue of special state laws that created a new breed of business entity known as "limited liability companies" (LLCs). These are hybrids of partnerships and corporations in that they limit members' liability to the extent of their investment, like corporations, but they avoid an entity-level tax, like partnerships. LLCs also offer advantages over other hybrids such as limited partnerships and subchapter S corporations. Where authorized by statute, professional LLCs mimic PCs by making this new organizational form available to licensed professionals. However, these PLLC statutes usually contain some of the same provisions on governance authority and liability exposure that are in the PC statutes.

LLCs are widely used for physician practices, as well as for law firms. However, the restrictions hamper their use for larger, multi-specialty practice groups or for vertically integrated delivery systems. Therefore, more complex arrangements have emerged, such as a limited partnership composed of LLCs. See generally Ribstein & Keatinge on Limited Liability (2d ed. 2004); Symposium, 32 Wake Forest L. Rev. 1 (1997); Symposium, 40 Wake Forest L. Rev. 751 (2005).

8. *HMO Exemptions.* The corporate practice prohibition is recognized as one of the major historical stumbling blocks in early HMO development. Developments, The Role of Prepaid Group Practice in Relieving the Medical Care Crisis, 84 Harv. L. Rev. 887, 960-961 (1971). State HMO enabling statutes frequently provide protection from this doctrine, but it is nevertheless puzzling that the federal HMO Act initially did not include this body of state law in its preemption provision when enacted in 1973. However, 1988 amendments to the federal Act significantly broadened its preemptive provision to strike all state laws that "impose requirements that would inhibit" HMOs. 42 U.S.C. §300e-10(a)(1)(E). Does it make sense to limit this preemption to only federally qualified HMOs, to the exclusion of other innovative forms of health care financing and delivery?

9. *The Future.* The conflict between the corporate practice prohibition and the need for organizational experimentation, a dominant theme in the 1938 Yale Note, has an eerie resonance with present day circumstances. Do you agree with *Berlin* that the doctrine's public policy foundations no longer apply? Most commentators argue that the doctrine should yield to modern developments. See Nicole Huberfeld, Be Not Afraid of Change: Time to Eliminate the Corporate Practice of Medicine Doctrine, 14 Health Matrix 243 (2004); Adam Freiman, The Abandonment of the Antiquated Corporate Practice of Medicine Doctrine: Injecting a Dose of Efficiency into the Modern Health Care Environment, 47 Emory L.J. 697 (1998); M. Hall, Institutional Control of Physician Behavior: Legal Barriers to Health Care Cost Containment, 137 U. Pa. L. Rev. 431, 510 (1988); A. Rosoff, supra; Note, 7 Health Matrix 241 (1997); Note, 40 Vand. L. Rev. 445, supra. Others, however, argue that the doctrine should be revived in order to restrict the practice of medicine over the Internet—see, e.g., Brian Monnich, Bringing Order to Cybermedicine: Applying the Corporate Practice of Medicine Doctrine to Tame the Wild Wild Web, 42 B.C. L. Rev. 455 (2001)—or to protect physicians against excessive forms of managed care—see Andre Hampton, Resurrection of the Prohibition on the Corporate Practice of Medicine: Teaching Old Dogma New Tricks, 66 U. Cin. L. Rev. 489 (1998).

Problem: Hospital and Physician Contracting

Florence Nightingale Hospital (FNH) realizes that, in order to survive in the current marketplace, it must promote greater loyalty, corporate identification, and clinical integration with its physicians. It would also like to capture some of the money physicians are making from treating hospital patients. FNH could simply hire all or a portion of its medical staff, but it is concerned about the legality of doing this. Which of the following approaches would you suggest to minimize that concern, without sacrificing the business objectives?

1. Form a nonprofit subsidiary that hires as many physicians as it wants because it falls within an exception to the corporate practice prohibition. Then it can bill for all medical and hospital services, pay the physicians a salary, and keep the profits (or absorb the losses).
2. Encourage the physicians to form a for-profit entity of their own, and then contract with that entity. The billing and financial arrangements would be the same as just described (billing by hospital; contract with physicians for fixed rates that generate a profit).
3. Contract with each physician separately, but not to deliver medical services, only to manage their office practice, so that FNH would provide office space and clerical support, and would do the billing and collection for these physicians, but it would turn these revenues over to the physicians, less a 15 percent management fee.

C. MEDICAL STAFF STRUCTURE

This part of the chapter explores the structure of the relationship between physicians and health care facilities. It begins with the classic organization of the hospital medical staff, which is both central to and unique to the medical system in the United States. Later cases explore in more detail the fierce disputes that can arise over medical staff membership, and how these bodies of hospital law apply to membership in managed care networks.

■ DOCTORS, PATIENTS, AND HEALTH INSURANCE: THE ORGANIZATION AND FINANCING OF MEDICAL CARE
Herman Miles Somers & Anne Ramsay Somers
1961

[Read the excerpt at page 8.]

1. *Medical Staff Bylaws*

Physicians' rights and status with hospitals are defined by medical staff bylaws. Virtually unique from any other kind of organization, hospitals typically have two sets of bylaws, one for the medical staff and another for the hospital administration as a whole. The next two cases explore the relationship between these two governance structures, and whether it is possible to restructure the hospital medical staff.

■ ST. JOHN'S HOSPITAL MEDICAL STAFF v. ST. JOHN REGIONAL MEDICAL CENTER
245 N.W.2d 472 (S.D. 1976)

St. John's Hospital Medical Staff is an unincorporated association whose members . . . hold medical staff privileges at . . . the St. John Regional Medical Center

[in] Huron, South Dakota. . . . In October 1947, as construction of the [hospital] neared completion, the Sisters of the Franciscan Order proposed certain medical staff bylaws to regulate the affairs of the physicians wanting to use the hospital. . . . The interpretation and effect of these articles formulate the main issues of this action. The "Amendment Article" provides: "These by-laws may be amended after notice given at any regular meeting of the staff. Such [amendments] . . . shall require a two-thirds majority of those present for adoption. Amendments so made shall be effective when approved by the governing body." . . .

In 1972, the [hospital] wished to make certain changes in the bylaws.[2] The attempted changes were unacceptable to the medical staff and an impasse developed, . . . [so] the board of directors of the [hospital] unilaterally adopted new medical staff bylaws which were not approved by the medical staff. The [hospital] now insists that the medical staff is bound by the bylaws so adopted. . . . The [hospital] argues that . . . the power to amend the articles must be lodged in the directors in order to avoid . . . the possibility of independent hospital liability in some future case of malpractice. After a review of the record, we find these arguments to be without merit. . . .

As a general rule, the bylaws of a corporation . . . constitute a binding contract between the corporation and its shareholders. . . . In the present case, we hold that the 1947 medical staff bylaws do constitute a contract which is, by its express terms, subject to amendment when the amendment is agreed to by both the medical staff and the [hospital]. The principles which govern the construction of contracts also govern the construction and interpretation of corporate bylaws. . . . Therefore, both the medical staff and the [hospital] are bound by them until they are amended in accordance with the procedure set out [above]. . . .

South Dakota statutes recognize the power in a corporation to delegate a voice in the adoption of new bylaws to another entity. Such is the case here. The original articles of incorporation and [hospital] bylaws authorize the medical staff to promulgate medical staff bylaws. These medical staff bylaws call for a specific amendment procedure which must be followed. The [hospital] by ignoring th[is] procedure and by not including the medical staff in the attempted bylaws amendment has breached this contractual relationship with the medical staff.

MAHAN v. AVERA ST. LUKES

621 N.W.2d 150 (S.D. 2001)

Orthopedic Surgery Specialists (OSS) . . . commenced this action against Avera St. Lukes (ASL) alleging breach of contract. . . . ASL is part of a regional health care system sponsored by the Sisters of the Presentation of the Blessed Virgin Mary of Aberdeen, South Dakota. [It is the only facility in a 90-mile radius.] Since 1901, the Presentation Sisters have been fulfilling their mission statement

2. E.g., one change would allow the Chief Executive Officer of the [hospital] to temporarily suspend the clinical privileges of a staff physician upon a determination that the action must be taken immediately in the best interests of the patient care in the [hospital]. Another change would require [hospital] approval of all officers of the medical staff.

"to respond to God's calling for a healing ministry . . . by providing quality health services" to the Aberdeen community. . . .

In mid-1996, ASL's neurosurgeon left Aberdeen. . . . During the process [of recruiting his replacement], ASL learned that most neurosurgeon applicants would not be interested in coming to Aberdeen if there was already an orthopedic spine surgeon practicing in the area. This was due to the small size of the community and the probable need for the neurosurgeon to supplement his or her practice by performing back and spine surgeries. . . . ASL was successful in recruiting a neurosurgeon who arrived in December, 1996. Around this time, ASL learned that OSS, a group of Aberdeen orthopedic surgeons, had decided to build a day surgery center that would directly compete with ASL. During the first seven months that OSS' surgery center was open, ASL suffered a 1,000-hour loss of operating room usage.

In response, . . . [ASL's Board] closed ASL's medical staff with respect to physicians requesting privileges for [spine surgery] . . . [and] closed ASL's medical staff to applicants for orthopedic surgery privileges. . . . The effect of "closing" the staff was to preclude any new physicians from applying for privileges to use hospital facilities for the named procedures. The Board's decision did not affect those physicians that had already been granted hospital privileges, including the physician-members of OSS. . . .

In the summer of 1998, OSS recruited Dr. Mahan, a spine-fellowship trained orthopedic surgeon engaged in the practice of orthopedic surgery. . . . Mahan officially requested an application for staff privileges with ASL [but] these requests were denied due to the Board's decision. . . . Mahan and OSS commenced this action against ASL, challenging the Board's decision to close the staff. The circuit court determined that ASL had breached the Staff Bylaws by closing the staff . . . without first consulting the staff. . . . The circuit court reasoned that because [the Board had delegated power regarding medical staff issues], the Board no longer had the power to initiate actions that affected the privileges of the medical staff. . . .

It is well settled in South Dakota that "a hospital's bylaws constitute a binding contract between the hospital and the hospital staff members." St. John's, 245 N.W.2d at 474. . . . [However,] under South Dakota law, "[t]he affairs of a [nonprofit] corporation *shall* be managed by a board of directors." . . . Pursuant to its authority, the Board of ASL has delegated certain powers associated with the appointment and review of medical personnel to its medical staff. These designated powers are manifested in the Staff Bylaws. Plaintiffs now claim that the Staff Bylaws trump the decision-making ability of the Board as to all decisions relating in any way to, or incidentally affecting, medical personnel issues. We do not agree.

The circuit court failed to give sufficient weight to the fact that the Staff Bylaws are derived from the Corporate Bylaws. . . . Their legal relationship is similar to that between statutes and a constitution. They are not separate and equal sovereigns. . . . The Corporate Bylaws state that "[t]he business and the property of the Corporation shall be managed and controlled . . . by a Board of Trustees. . . ." In addition, the Corporate Bylaws provide that . . . "the Members of the Board of Trustees shall have and exercise the authority . . . to delegate to the Medical Staff the authority to *evaluate the professional competence* of staff Members and applicants for staff privileges and to hold the Medical Staff responsible for *making recommendations* to the Members of the Board of Trustees concerning initial staff appointments, reappointments and the assignment or curtailment of privileges, *all subject to the final approval of the Members of the Board of Trustees*" (emphasis added). . . .

Clearly, under these explicit powers, the Board has the authority to make business decisions without first consulting the medical staff. . . . Plaintiffs rely on the Staff Bylaws as their source of authority to assume the Board's power. Yet, even within the Staff Bylaws, there is no explicit provision granting the medical staff control over personnel issues. Instead, the circuit court found that the actions of the Board violated "the spirit of the bylaws taken as a whole." Such reliance on the "spirit of the [Staff] bylaws" turns the corporate structure of ASL upside down. . . . ASL cannot continue to offer unprofitable, yet essential services including the maternity ward, emergency room, pediatrics and critical care units, without the offsetting financial benefit of more profitable areas such as neurosurgery. The Board . . . surely has the power to attempt to insure ASL's economic survival. . . .

[T]he circuit court determined that this was not an administrative decision by the Board. Instead it held this was a decision regarding the "granting or withholding [of] staff privileges," and that the action fell "within the provisions of the medical staff bylaws." . . . According to the circuit court, in matters of personnel, the Board has only "secondary approval authority . . . ; no actions originate with the Board itself." The circuit court further concluded that the Board is only allowed to give its "seal of approval" at the final stages of staff actions. As support for this view, the circuit court cited the Staff Bylaws . . . as follows: "Initial appointments and reappointments to the Medical staff shall be made by the Governing Body. The Governing Body shall act on appointments, reappointment, or revocation of appointment only after there has been recommendation from the Medical Staff as provided in these Bylaws." The circuit court also cited a provision in the Credentialing Manual to support its claim that the Board has essentially only rubber stamp authority. That provision states that "[t]he Board shall either accept or reject the recommendation of the Credentials and Executive Committee. . . ." Finally, the circuit court found that the procedure for hearings and appellate review [by the Board] was further evidence that the Board was not allowed to originate any actions relating to the medical staff, it was only allowed to hear appeals.

These provisions have been misconstrued by the circuit court. . . . The purpose of this limited delegation of authority was to obtain input from the staff on areas of its expertise. Decisions relating to the competence, training, qualifications and ethics of a particular physician are matters for which the medical staff is uniquely qualified, while the Board admittedly has limited expertise in those areas. Under the Corporate Bylaws, it is *only* in those confined areas of expertise that the staff has any authority at all. . . . [T]he medical staff gives recommendations to the Board on issues relating to appointment and privileges. However, this case is not about appointments or the assignment or curtailment of privileges. It is about an administrative decision to close ASL's staff for certain procedures; therefore, the medical staff has no part in the decision and the Staff Bylaws do not apply. . . . The procedure for hearings and review only applies if a decision by the Board "will adversely affect [the practitioner's] appointment to or status as a member of the Medical Staff or his exercise of clinical privileges. . . ." The disputed action by the Board did not affect any physician's appointment or status as a member of the staff. . . .

Within its broad powers of management, some of the business decisions made by the Board will undoubtedly impinge upon matters that relate to or affect the medical staff of the hospital. This fact is unavoidable. However, merely because a decision of the Board affects the staff does not give the staff authority to overrule a valid business decision made by the Board. Allowing the staff this amount of administrative authority would effectively cripple the governing Board of ASL. . . .

In its decision, the circuit court attempted to distinguish between this present situation and the situation wherein a hospital enters into an exclusive contract. We find this attempt to be unpersuasive. An exclusive contract arises when the hospital contracts with an outside physician or group of physicians, whereby the hospital agrees that the physician or group of physicians shall be the only personnel allowed to use certain facilities in the hospital, such as radiology units or emergency room units. Such exclusive contracts are common practice for most hospitals today, and have been almost universally found valid and enforceable, even if not explicitly provided for in corporate bylaws. In the past, ASL has closed several areas of its facility to physicians not part of an exclusive contract. Such areas include anesthesiology, radiology, emergency room care, pathology, EKG interpretation, pulmonary function interpretation and cardiac cathe[te]rization. Plaintiffs do not allege that the prior exclusive contracts entered into by ASL are invalid. . . . Yet there is no logical reason why ASL could close certain areas of its facility to all but a few physicians (via an exclusive contract), yet not be allowed to close its facilities to any new orthopedic surgeons performing certain, named procedures. . . .

The circuit court also concluded that ASL must accept an application from any doctor wishing to have privileges at ASL . . . if the staff is satisfied [that the doctor is qualified] . . . Such a construction of the Staff Bylaws reaches a result that is contrary to the Corporate Bylaws and common sense. Are we to force ASL to grant privileges to every qualified physician that may stand at its doorstep and announce that he or she will henceforth be using the hospital's facilities, simply because the staff said they could? . . . The result reached by the circuit court . . . is impractical in a corporate business environment. Imagine the confusion and lack of clear lines of management authority that would ensue at the hospital if the Board had only the minimal amount of control over its medical staff that the circuit court would give it. . . .

Hospitals have legally defined responsibilities and duties. . . . [T]he negligent act of a doctor can impute liability to a hospital under a theory of *respondeat superior* . . . [Also], separate liability for negligence attaches to a hospital when it has breached its own standards, or those available in the same or similar community or hospitals generally, such as allowing a known incompetent doctor to remain on staff. . . . It would be completely illogical to first impose a duty of reasonable care upon a hospital, and then later strip the hospital of the ability and power to implement the policies and programs required to fulfill that duty. . . . Therefore, the circuit court's judgment is reversed.

Notes: Hospital and Medical Staff Bylaws; Exclusive Contracts; Economic Credentialing

1. *The "Two-Headed Monster."* Notice how the medical staff credentialing process was caricatured in *Mahan*. The court ridiculed the idea that the hospital has to "grant privileges to every qualified physician that may stand at its doorstep and

announce that he or she will henceforth be using the hospital's facilities, simply because the staff said they could? . . . [This] is impractical in a corporate business environment. Imagine the confusion and lack of clear lines of management authority that would ensue at the hospital if the Board had only th[is] minimal amount of control over its medical staff. . . ." "Allowing the staff this amount of administrative authority would effectively cripple the governing Board." Yet many hospital administrators would say that this is precisely how hospitals have traditionally functioned, because hospitals are essentially required to maintain "open" medical staffs, and hospital boards are expected to, and do, simply "rubber stamp" medical staff recommendations. In the view of one experienced lawyer:

> The internal organization of hospitals has remained essentially uniform and unchanged for the past seventy years.[1] Today, as in the past, the hospital is composed of three independent lines of authority: the medical staff, the management, and the board of directors.[2] . . . The self-governing medical staff is a feature of hospitals found only in the United States and Canada.[3] . . . The thesis of this article is that the self-governing medical staff model is an anachronistic mode of hospital organization that generally impedes the delivery of high-quality, cost-effective care. As other commentators have suggested, the law has imposed an organizational structure on hospitals that conflicts with the current regulatory agenda of promoting such care.[4] . . . Consequently, federal and state laws should be amended or repealed to allow hospitals to organize themselves according to their own managerial vision of hospital organization.

Thaddeus J. Nodzenski, A Critical Analysis of the Self-Governing Medical Staff, 43 Okla. L. Rev. 591, 592 (1990). The unique structure of American hospitals has been described as "attractive as a two-headed monster" and as "stable as a three-legged stool." See H. L. Smith, Two Lines of Authority Are One Too Many, 84 Modern Hosp., March 1955, at 59.

2. *Is the Paradigm Shifting?* Many commentators have noticed a possible paradigm shift in progress. They see in decisions like *Mahan* the potential demise of the independent medical staff, to be replaced by an ordinary employment contract model that gives the hospital much greater control over medical as well as managerial policy. See Nodzenski, supra; Lawrence Casalino et al., Hospital-Physician Relations: Two Tracks and the Decline of the Voluntary Medical Staff Model, 27(5) Health Aff. 1305 (Oct. 2008). This development is also mirrored in financing structures like HMOs and other integrated delivery systems that combine hospital and physician services under a single capitation payment. Others observe that the increased sense of urgency to improve the quality of care has led to renewed calls

1. Harris, Regulation and Internal Control in Hospitals, 55 Bull. N.Y. Acad. Med. 88, 90-92 (Jan. 1979).

2. See Hall, Institutional Control of Physician Behavior: Legal Barriers to Health Care Cost Containment, 137 Pa. L. Rev. 431, 505-506 (1988).

3. The Report of the Joint Task Force on Hospital-Medical Staff Relationships of the AMA and the AHA 10 (1985).

4. See generally Clark Havighurst, Doctors and Hospitals: An Antitrust Perspective on Traditional Relationships, 1984 Duke L.J. 1071, 1087-1092; Hall, supra n.2, at 528-532.

for hospital management to assert more authority over the medical staff. John D. Blum, Feng Shui and the Restructuring of the Hospital Corporation: A Call for Change in the Face of the Medical Error Epidemic, 14 Health Matrix 5 (2004); Symposium, 12 Ann. Health L. 179 (2003).

Observe, though, that Nodzenski, who applauds increased authority of medical institutions, works for the hospital industry. Are his views sound nevertheless? The subordination of physicians is vehemently opposed by organized medicine, for reasons articulated in the discussion of the corporate practice of medicine doctrine in section B.3. Consider what weapons physicians have in their legal arsenal to oppose fundamental structuring of the hospital medical staff. Realize that this organizational structure emerged as the result of accreditation standards set by the Joint Commission (JCAHA), which require separate medical staff bylaws that are under the control of member physicians. In 2010, after years of sometimes acrimonious deliberation, the Joint Commission revised its medical staff standards to reinforce the elements of self-governance. 23(2) The Health Lawyer 10 (Dec. 2010). This self-governing structure is also embedded in law to the extent that many hospital licensing statutes incorporate the Joint Commission standards by reference. Other legal sources explored throughout this chapter support this structure less visibly. Consider, for instance, the impact of the charitable tax exemption, or the corporate practice of medicine doctrine, on how doctors relate to hospitals. Note also that this dual line of authority is mirrored in the structure of insurance, which pays hospitals separately from physicians, and which results in Blue Cross vs. Blue Shield, and Medicare Part A vs. Part B.

3. *Hospitalists.* Assuming that the traditional medical staff structure remains intact at least on paper, how far can a hospital feasibly go in circumventing this structure? Could a hospital use exclusive contracts for the entire array of medical services? It is not possible to consider this question fully until other bodies of law are explored, such as tax exemption and referral fee prohibitions that are discussed in sections B.2 and E, and even then the answer is far from clear. The issue may be joined, however, by the growing use of physicians known as "hospitalists"—hospital-based primary care physicians who replace patients' regular physicians in managing care when the patients are hospitalized, as is the practice in European hospitals. Hospitals view this hospitalist system as an effective way to impose greater managerial discipline on patient care decisions, in order to improve scheduling, reduce costs, and increase quality. Primary care physicians like the convenience of being able to concentrate their attention on their office-based practice, especially under HMO payment structures that do not reward them, or may even penalize them, for hospital care. However, many physicians view this as an invasion of their established patient relationships, and specialists see this as a threat to their source of referrals and income. So far, hospitalist programs are voluntary, in the sense that primary care physicians can use them at their discretion, but hospitals in theory could start to insist on using their employed staff.

4. *Bylaws Are Binding.* Are *St. John's* and *Mahan* in conflict? If not, how are they reconciled? If so, which has the better argument? Can you possibly justify *Mahan*'s statement that "this case is not about appointments or the assignment or curtailment of [clinical] privileges. It is about an administrative decision. . . . The disputed action by the Board did not affect any physician's appointment or status as a member of the staff"? What if this action were taken right after the orthopedic physician

group had just hired a new physician who was in the process of applying for staff privileges? Is *Mahan* limited to a circumstance of dire economic or medical necessity? Does it turn on the wording of the particular bylaws used by that hospital?

Many other courts have agreed with *St. John's* that medical staff bylaws constitute a contract and cannot be amended or ignored unilaterally by the hospital board. For instance, this was the holding in a suit involving a different Avera hospital, Medical Staff of Avera Marshall Regional Medical Center v. Avera Marshall, 857 N.W.2d 695 (Minn. 2014). Yet, most courts also agree with *Mahan* that hospitals are free to enter unilaterally into exclusive contracts or stop admitting new members to a portion or all of the medical staff. E.g., Garibaldi v. Applebaum, 742 N.E.2d 279 (Ill. 2000) (awarding an exclusive contract is an administrative decision and so does not require a medical staff hearing for excluded physicians because the decision is not necessarily based on physician competence); Radiation Therapy Oncology, P.C. v. Providence Hospital, 906 So. 2d 904 (Ala. 2005) (hospital board may close cancer radiation staff as a "valid business decision," related in part to quality of care); City of Cookeville v. Humphrey, 126 S.W.3d 897 (Tenn. 2004) (bylaws require only "consultation" and not approval by medical staff prior to hospital adopting exclusive contract that closed the radiology staff). But see Kessel v. Monongalia County General Hospital Co., 600 S.E.2d 321 (W. Va. 2004) (exclusive contract by a public hospital for anesthesia services infringes on the physicians' right to practice and patients' rights to choose their own physicians (even anesthesiologists!)).

Courts reconcile these two lines of authority in two ways: (1) They distinguish, as *Mahan* did, between administrative decisions reserved to the hospital board versus medical decisions made by the medical staff. When the reasons for action are economic, they fall in the board's realm to act unilaterally. How well does this square with *St John's*? (2) Courts also distinguish between the possession of clinical privileges and the right to exercise those privileges, reasoning that medical staff bylaws protect only the former, not the latter. This distinction arises in exclusive contract cases, where the hospital picks a certain set of physicians to staff a portion of the hospital, such as the emergency room or the room where anesthesia is administered. The result is that not only new doctors but also existing doctors lose the ability to practice in those areas of the hospital. Courts uphold this nonetheless by reasoning that, technically, the non-contracting doctors still retain their status as members of the medical staff and are entitled to practice in other areas of the hospital. One court said that "such reasoning simply defies logic. Hospital privileges are not, in reality, some amorphous grant [of status]. . . . They are instead quite specific descriptions of very particular acts a doctor is permitted to do in that facility. Precluding a doctor from performing those acts is, as Plaintiffs here assert, very much a denial or termination of hospital privileges." Aluko v. Charlotte-Mecklenburg Hospital Authority, 959 F. Supp. 729 (W.D.N.C. 1997). However, this court also "recognize[d] the very real needs that hospitals . . . have to respond in a rapidly changing health care market with its unique blend of savage competition and heavy-handed governmental regulation." The court reconciled these competing considerations by reasoning that it is not the form of restriction that matters (denial of staff privileges vs. limiting use of the facilities); rather, it is the reason given for the restriction: quality of care vs. an economic reason. Where the physicians' "professional reputations are intact, . . . there is no foreclosure of opportunity to practice their profession nor bar to seeking privileges in other institutions." Is this reasoning convincing?

In today's marketplace, might not a reputation for being a high-cost or inefficient physician potentially be just as damaging as having a reputation for poor quality? For a thorough analysis of these and other cases, see Bryan A. Liang, An Overview and Analysis of Challenges to Medical Staff Exclusive Contracts, 18 J. Leg. Med. 1 (1997). See generally Annot., 74 A.L.R.3d 1268 (1974).

5. *Economic Credentialing.* The focus in these cases on hospitals' motivation for closing departments or using exclusive contracts points to a broader issue of immense importance to health care law and public policy—whether hospitals can explicitly consider economic factors in choosing physicians, in addition to, or instead of, quality-of-care factors. In the trade, this is known as "economic credentialing." The decisions discussed in the next section express the traditional attitude that only quality factors are relevant, but they arose before cost concerns became so paramount. Now that public policy embodies cost concerns as well, can they be included in the balance of considerations? Indeed, it appears from some cases that financially motivated exclusions are *easier* to justify than those motivated by quality concerns, because only the latter must be pursued through the medical staff hearing process and justified under the bylaws. If one is concerned about patient care, shouldn't this distinction cut in exactly the opposite direction?

This issue remains largely unsettled, however. In those jurisdictions that require economically based exclusions to be pursued through the bylaws process, two obstacles remain: (1) the need to amend traditional quality-based medical staff bylaws to make sure economic concerns are allowable criteria for reviewing physicians; (2) the legal uncertainty over whether economic concerns can *trump* quality concerns. Physicians who are excluded from contracts and medical staff membership because their treatment patterns are too expensive will likely complain that the hospital is sacrificing high quality for low costs. Hospitals have been able to avoid this charge by arguing that cost savings do not in fact compromise quality (e.g., swapping one good high-cost doctor for another good low-cost doctor), or by arguing that lower-cost treatment produces higher quality (e.g., reducing the risks of unnecessary surgery or medication). See, e.g., Knapp v. Palos Community Hospital, 465 N.E.2d 554 (Ill. App. Ct. 1984) (physician whose costs were 31 percent higher than others also had serious quality problems from overutilization of tests and medication).

Another form of economic credentialing is known as "conflict credentialing," in which hospitals refuse privileges to physicians who establish specialty facilities that compete with the hospital's services, under the theory that there is an economic conflict of interest between the two parties. In an important ruling, the Arkansas Supreme Court held that it violates public policy and constitutes an unfair trade practice for a general hospital to exclude from its staff any physician with an ownership interest in a competing specialty hospital. Baptist Health v. Murphy, 373 S.W.3d 269 (Ark. 2010).

6. *Further Readings.* For discussion of the nature, status, and powers of the **hospital medical staff** (note 1), see William Brewbaker, Antitrust Conspiracy Doctrine and the Hospital Enterprise, 74 B.U. L. Rev. 67 (1994); James F. Blumstein, Of Doctors and Hospitals: Setting the Analytical Framework for Managing and Regulating the Relationship, 4 Ind. Health L. Rev. 209 (2007); Lawton Burns et al., History of Physician-Hospital Collaboration, *in* Crosson & Tollen, page 342. Discussing the increasing **tensions between hospitals and their medical staffs**, see John D. Blum,

Beyond the Bylaws: Hospital-Physician Relationships, Economics, and Conflicting Agendas, 53 Buff. L. Rev. 459 (2005); Robert Berenson et al., Hospital-Physician Relations: Cooperation, Competition, or Separation?, 26(1) Health Aff. w31 (Jan. 2006); Symposium, 26(1) Health Aff. w31 (Dec. 2006).

For discussions of **hospitalists** (note 3), including ethical and public policy issues, see Hoangmai Pham, Hospitalists and Care Transitions, 27(5) Health Aff. 1315 (Oct. 2008); J. Coffman & T. G. Rundall, The Impact of Hospitalists on the Cost and Quality of Inpatient Care in the United States: A Research Synthesis, 62 Med. Care Res. Rev. 379 (2005); R. M. Wachter & L. Goldman, The Hospitalist Movement 5 Years Later, 287 JAMA 487 (2002); David Meltzer, Hospitalists and the Doctor-Patient Relationship, J. Leg. Stud. 589 (2001).

On **economic credentialing** (note 5), see Beverly Cohen, An Examination of the Right of Hospitals to Engage in Economic Credentialing, 77 Temp. L. Rev. 705 (2004); Elizabeth A. Weeks, The New Economic Credentialing: Protecting Hospitals from Competition by Medical Staff Members, 36 J. Health L. 247 (2003); Comment, 88 Marq. L. Rev. 413 (2004); Blum, supra, 53 Buff. L. Rev. 459 (2005).

Notes: Physician Employment; Labor Law

1. *Covenants Not to Compete.* As illustrated by Berlin v. Sarah Bush Lincoln Health Center, page 437, physician contracts, both with hospitals and with medical clinics and groups, also usually contain restrictive covenants that prevent them from practicing with competitors in the vicinity for a defined period of time. Physicians have been somewhat more successful in attacking these contract provisions. Covenants not to compete, in this and other employment contexts, are viewed with suspicion by the courts because they tend to contravene public policies in favor of free trade and the right to work. Nevertheless, these covenants are upheld if they are reasonable as to duration, geographic scope, and the range of activities covered, and if they are not otherwise contrary to the public interest.

The issue of greatest relevance in the medical context is whether it violates public policy to restrain the practice of a physician whose specialized services are much needed in the community. For example, in Dick v. Geist, 693 P.2d 1133 (Idaho Ct. App. 1985), the court refused to enforce a restrictive covenant that would have excluded the two doctors who rendered 90 percent of the neonatal care in the community. One court refused to enforce a restriction against a general practitioner who left an HMO and took 167 of his patients with him, even though there was no local shortage of physicians. The court was particularly disturbed by a penalty clause that assessed $700 for each patient the doctor took with him. The court reasoned that this "financial wedge . . . needlessly hindered the continuation of existing and successful doctor/patient relationships . . . vital to the provision of health care." Humana v. Jacobson, 614 So. 2d 520 (Fla. Dist. Ct. App. 1992). See also Murfreesboro Medical Clinic, P.A. v. David Udom, 166 S.W.3d 674 (Tenn. 2005) ("The right of a person to choose the physician that he or she believes is best able to provide treatment is so fundamental that we can not allow it to be denied because of an employer's restrictive covenant."). However, another line of cases has reasoned that hospitals have an interest in the protection of their own patient relationships, or that the public interest is equally well served if a doctor is allowed to treat different patients in another part of the state. Concord Orthopaedics v. Forbes, 702 A.2d

1273 (N.H. 1997); Sisters of Charity Health System v. Farrago, 21 A.3d 110 (Maine 2011).

2. *Labor Laws.* In addition to the *private* law rights of *individual* doctors, the law is also concerned with the *public* law rights of *groups* of health care employees. By convention, the former set of issues is labeled "employment law" and the latter "labor law." Other employment law issues relating to "at will" employment, wrongful discharge, and various employment discrimination laws are explored at pages 463 and 473. The remainder of these notes survey labor law.

The National Labor Relations Act (NLRA), 29 U.S.C. §§151 et seq., establishes a comprehensive regulatory scheme, administered by the National Labor Relations Board (NLRB), to protect employees' rights to form a union, to require their employer to bargain with the union in good faith and honor collective bargaining agreements, and to strike if they are dissatisfied with the terms or conditions of their employment. Employed physicians' efforts to unionize must clear a critical hurdle. The Supreme Court has interpreted the NLRA as excluding from its protections "managerial employees," those who assist management in setting and implementing policy. NLRB v. Bell Aerospace, 416 U.S. 267 (1974). In NLRB v. Yeshiva University, 444 U.S. 672 (1980), the Court determined in a 5-4 vote that this exclusion applies to professional employees—in that case, university professors—who serve on important committees and heavily influence hiring decisions. In Delphic dictum, however, the Court cautioned that not all employed professionals are ipso facto managers: "[E]mployees whose decisionmaking is limited to the routine discharge of professional duties in projects to which they have been assigned cannot be excluded from coverage. . . . Only if an employee's activities fall outside the scope of the duties routinely performed by similarly situated professionals will he be found aligned with management." 444 U.S. at 690.

The meaning of this distinction for employed doctors remains a matter of considerable dispute. In FHP and Union of American Physicians and Dentists, 274 N.L.R.B. 1141 (1985), the NLRB determined that all 70 doctors employed by an HMO were "managerial" and therefore not able to unionize because they served on numerous peer review and patient care committees that formulate and effectuate clinical policy. Even though these are the same committees typically found in a hospital, a prior decision ruled that the employed physicians at a teaching hospital (ironically, at Yeshiva University's medical school) were not managerial because clinical policy there was merely advisory, and department chairs exercised most of the managerial power. Montefiore Hospital, 261 NLRB 569 (1982). The NLRB subsequently applied the *Montefiore* precedent to HMOs, finding physicians are not managerial. E.g., New York University Medical Center, 324 NLRB 887 (1997).

3. *Physician Unions.* Although the disturbing specter of a physician strike is virtually unheard of, labor union activity in the health care sector has increased considerably. Most of this activity involves nonphysicians such as nurses and technicians, but even among physicians there has been interest in unionizing as a way to counteract loss of clinical and economic autonomy. In 1999, the AMA's House of Delegates took the unprecedented step of calling for the AMA to form a national bargaining unit under federal law to represent employed physicians and residents. The politically conservative leadership of the AMA has long opposed the formation of a union, but the AMA membership insisted on this move to give physicians a

stronger voice against HMOs and hospitals, and to preempt efforts by other labor organizations that are eager to take the lead in forming physician unions. It is important to realize, though, that the NLRA covers only employees. This limitation would seem to exclude independent physicians on hospital or HMO medical staffs from the NLRA's protections. 329 NLRB No. 55 (1999). Despite this limitation, physician unionizing is still of pressing importance due to the great increase in physician employment, especially by hospitals or health systems.

One advantage physicians seek by unionizing is protection from the antitrust laws, by virtue of the antitrust exemption for labor activities. 15 U.S.C. §17. (Otherwise, every employee strike over wages would constitute per se price fixing.) Subsequent sections of these materials describe the antitrust difficulties physicians face when they organize into groups to negotiate with insurance companies, HMOs and PPOs over reimbursement rates. See section D.2. As a result, some doctors have attempted to label their negotiating groups "unions." The flaw in this tactic is that doctors traditionally have not been employees of insurance plans; they are, at best, independent contractors. Therefore, their collective actions could result in huge damages or even criminal sentences. See AMA v. United States, 317 U.S. 519 (1943) (rejecting labor exemption claim made by physicians who boycotted an HMO). To avoid this, physicians have sought legislative authority to engage in collective bargaining with HMOs (but not strikes or boycotts), in order to offset HMO market power. The physicians' first victory was in Texas in 1999; but so far, similar legislative proposals have not been adopted at the national level. Although state law cannot give physician unions the same status they have under federal labor law, it might (or might not) achieve the same objective of conferring an exemption from antitrust laws using the "state-action immunity" doctrine.

4. *Nurse Managers.* The "managerial employee" exclusion from the NLRA's protections has surprisingly proven troublesome for nurses as well. Nurse employees in hospitals and nursing homes historically had no problem qualifying unless they held explicitly supervisory positions. In 1994, the Supreme Court ruled, however, that nurses employed in a nursing home exercised sufficient de facto supervision over nurses' aides to meet the managerial exclusion because they controlled work assignments. Health Care & Retirement Corp. of America v. NLRB, 511 U.S. 571 (1994). The NLRB, however, has resisted following this precedent, for instance, by finding that hospital "charge nurses" do not have managerial status. In NLRB v. Kentucky River Community Care, 532 U.S. 706 (2001), the Court reversed the NLRB again, holding that it read the Act too narrowly in ruling that supervising nurses at a mental health facility are not managers. Yet, the NLRB once again resisted, ruling that only full-time charge nurses qualify as managers, and not those who have these responsibilities only part time. Oakwood Healthcare Inc., 348 NLRB No. 37 (2006).

5. *Disruption of Patient Care; Definition of Bargaining Units.* Until 1974, nonprofit hospitals, which constitute the bulk of the industry, were not covered by the NLRA. In that year, however, Congress amended the Act with provisions directed specifically to the health care industry. 29 U.S.C. §§152, 158, 169, 183. In doing so, Congress expressed a concern that union activity not disrupt patient care. Specifically, both the Senate and the House stated that "due consideration should be given by the Board to preventing proliferation of bargaining units in the health care industry" because too many unions within a single institution would pose an excessive

risk of crippling, repetitive strikes. 1974 U.S. Code Cong. & Admin. News 3950. This "nonproliferation" directive has been a constant thorn in the side of the NLRB's numerous attempts to determine the appropriate scope of hospital bargaining units for nurses and other nonphysician employees. See, e.g., NLRB v. HMO International, 678 F.2d 806 (9th Cir. 1982) (improper to exclude vocational nurses from RN's union) (noting the "nearly perfect record of reversals of the NLRB by the court of appeals in review of health care bargaining units").

In response to a series of court reversals, the NLRB, which is notorious for deciding all policy issues in adjudication, took the extraordinary step of initiating a rulemaking proceeding to define the proper approach to health care unit determinations. Its final regulations allow up to eight, but only eight, separate bargaining units in any hospital, regardless of local circumstances: RNs, physicians, other professionals, technicians, clerical, maintenance, security guards, and others. 29 C.F.R. §103.30. These rules generated intense opposition from health care management, which perceives that carving units into this many divisions greatly increases the ease of unionizing. The rule was upheld by the Supreme Court, however. American Hospital Ass'n v. NLRB, 499 U.S. 606 (1991). In nonhospital health care facilities, the proper size of bargaining units remains unsettled. See, e.g., Specialty Healthcare and Rehabilitation Center, 357 NLRB 83 (2011) (allowing nursing assistants at a nursing home to organize separately from other service workers).

6. *Further Readings.* For general discussions of labor law issues in the health care industry, see Grace Budrys, When Doctors Join Unions (1997); William Brewbaker, Physician Unions and the Future of Competition in the Health Care Sector, 33 U.C. Davis L. Rev. 545 (2000); Note, 9 J. Health & Biomed. L. 117 (2013); Comment, 36 Hous. L. Rev. 951 (1999); Comment, 19 Cardozo L. Rev. 1125 (1997); Note, 34 Colum. J.L. & Soc. Probs. 1-48 (2000); Note, 42 Ariz. L. Rev. 803-833 (2000); Note, 52 Vand. L. Rev. 1051 (1999).

Problem: Economic Credentialing

You are the lawyer for Florence Nightingale Community Hospital. The administrator approaches you about how best to amend the bylaws so that the hospital can get rid of doctors who are costing the hospital too much money under Medicare and HMO insurance. The administrator is concerned about which removal actions can be defended in court and which bylaw amendments are politically feasible with physicians. Advise the administrator on each of these options:

- Amend the Hospital Bylaws to give the hospital board authority to remove doctors from the medical staff for any reason, regardless of the medical staff's own recommendations, as long as the medical staff is first consulted.
- Amend the Medical Staff Bylaws to declare that an additional criterion for medical staff membership is to practice an efficient style of medicine that avoids wasting medical resources or providing unnecessary care.
- Amend the Medical Staff Bylaws to declare that any physician who consistently loses money for the hospital will be removed from the medical staff.
- Forget about amending any bylaws. Instead, go after physicians who are economic losers based on their general medical competence and their unwillingness to be cooperative.

- Keep but supplant the entire medical staff structure by limiting who can practice in each department through one-year renewable contracts with the 200 best doctors out of the present 300.

2. *Medical Staff Disputes*

Access to a hospital is essential for most physicians to carry on a practice. Hospitals, on the other hand, are coming under increasing legal and economic pressure to monitor who joins the medical staff. From the intersection of these two competing interests springs a powerful flow of litigation, in the health care field, second only to malpractice. These materials explore which legal theories are available to physicians wanting to challenge their exclusion, and how much scrutiny courts impose on these decisions. We begin with common-law doctrine, first as applied to hospitals and then to HMOs. Following that is antitrust law. As you read the first two cases, try to identify what species of common law is being used to review staffing decisions by private hospitals, and attempt to articulate what hospitals have to show to justify their decisions.

GREISMAN v. NEWCOMB HOSPITAL
192 A.2d 817 (N.J. 1963)

JACOBS, Judge.

In 1958, the plaintiff graduated from the Philadelphia College of Osteopathy with the degree of doctor of osteopathy. [See nn.3 and 4 in Weiss v. York Hospital at page 485 for a definition of osteopathy.] He served an internship, took the full medical boards in New York, and was given an unqualified license to practice medicine and surgery in that state. Thereafter, he was admitted to practice in Michigan, Florida and New Jersey. His New Jersey admission by the State Board of Medical Examiners constituted an unrestricted license to practice medicine and surgery within the borders of our State. See Falcone v. Middlesex Co. Medical Soc., 34 N.J. 582, 170 A.2d 791 (1961). In July 1959, he began the general practice of medicine in the City of Vineland and, in November 1959, he opened an office in Newfield which is in the Vineland metropolitan area. Until January 1962 he also engaged in the practice of medicine from his home in Vineland. He is the only licensed physician in Newfield, is the plant physician for a Newfield company engaged in heavy industrial work and for an additional company engaged in the making of glassware, and is the school physician for Newfield's public school as well as for a Catholic school in the same community. He states that he is the only osteopathic physician fully licensed to practice general medicine and surgery in the metropolitan Vineland area which is said to have a population approximating 100,000; the defendants state that there is another osteopathic physician practicing in Vineland but the suggested variance is of no real significance here.

In 1961, the plaintiff sought to file an application for admission to the courtesy staff of the Newcomb Hospital which is located in Vineland about a mile from his home. The hospital was incorporated in 1921, is operated as a general hospital, and is the only hospital in the Vineland metropolitan area. Its certificate of incorporation sets forth the purposes for which it was formed including . . . the care of sick and injured persons residing in the vicinity of Vineland. . . . The hospital is a nonprofit corporation and its governing body is a Board of Trustees consisting of not less than 15 members. It solicits and receives funds annually in the form of charitable contributions and has received funds from the Ford Foundation. Several years ago, it constructed a new building, the cost being borne almost entirely by public subscription. It receives funds from the City of Vineland for the treatment of indigent patients from within the city, and funds from the County of Cumberland for the treatment of indigent patients from other areas in the county. It receives tax exemptions available to nonprofit corporations operated for charitable and like purposes. It is eligible for federal funds under the Hill-Burton Act.

Despite suitable requests, the Newcomb Hospital refused to permit the plaintiff to file any application for admission to its courtesy staff. In taking that course it did not question his personal or professional qualifications nor did it purport to exercise a discretion in the process of administrative screening and selection. It rested entirely on a provision in the hospital bylaws which sets forth that an applicant for membership on the courtesy staff must be a graduate of a medical school approved by the American Medical Association and must be a member of the County Medical Society. The American Medical Association has long rejected schools of osteopathy, though the original supporting reasons have been largely dissipated. See Report of the Committee for the Study of Relations Between Osteopathy and Medicine, 158 JAMA 736 (1955). Admittedly, the plaintiff is not a graduate of a medical school approved by the American Medical Association and, because of his schooling, his application to the County Medical Society was never acted upon. The school he graduated from is an accredited school of osteopathy, has been approved as in good standing by the New Jersey State Board of Medical Examiners, and has long given the full traditional medical course as well as osteopathic teaching. . . .

The Law Division found that the Newcomb Hospital did not confine itself to any specialized branch of medicine and had assumed the position and status of the only general hospital open to the public within the convenient accessibility of the inhabitants of the metropolitan area of Vineland, including Newfield; that the plaintiff had suffered economic and other harm because he was not permitted to admit his patients to the hospital or to serve them professionally once they were admitted, or to use the emergency room services of the hospital; that his patients suffered restriction in their choice of physicians or hospital facilities because of the plaintiff's inability to attend them professionally at the hospital, and that this was not minimized by the fact that the plaintiff was permitted to visit them at the hospital without, however, any opportunity to read their charts or prescribe for them. . . .

The defendants contend that the Newcomb Hospital is a private rather than a public hospital, that it may in its discretion exclude physicians from its medical staff, and that no legal ground exists for judicial interference with its refusal to consider the plaintiff's application for membership. . . . Broad judicial expressions may, of course, be found to the effect that hospitals such as Newcomb are private in nature and that their staff admission policies are entirely discretionary. They are private in the sense that they are nongovernmental but they are hardly private in other senses. Newcomb is a nonprofit organization dedicated by its certificate of incorporation to the vital public use of serving the sick and injured, its funds are in good measure received from public sources and through public solicitation, and its tax benefits are received because of its nonprofit and nonprivate aspects. It constitutes a virtual monopoly in the area in which it functions and it is in no position to claim immunity from public supervision and control because of its allegedly private nature. Indeed, in the development of the law, activities much less public than the hospital activities of Newcomb, have commonly been subjected to judicial (as well as legislative) supervision and control to the extent necessary to satisfy the felt needs of the times. See Munn v. Illinois, 94 U.S. 113 (1877); German Alliance Ins. Co. v. Lewis, 233 U.S. 389 (1914); Nebbia v. New York, 291 U.S. 502 (1934).

During the course of history, judges have often applied the common law so as to regulate private businesses and professions for the common good; perhaps the most notable illustration is the duty of serving all comers on reasonable terms which was imposed by the common law on innkeepers, carriers, farriers and the like. See Falcone v. Middlesex Co. Medical Soc., supra, 34 N.J., at p. 594; Messenger et al. v. Pennsylvania R.R. Co., 36 N.J.L. 407 (Sup. Ct. 1873). In the *Messenger* case Chief Justice Beasley, speaking for the former Supreme Court, noted that a railroad, though a private corporation, is engaged in a "public employment," that it "owes a duty to the community" and that under considerations of public policy it must be held under obligation to serve without discrimination. On appeal, Justice Bedle, speaking for the Court of Errors and Appeals, expressed the view that although railroad corporations are private, they hold their property "as a quasi-public trust," and that as trustees they must conduct their operations in such manner so as to insure to every member of the community the equal enjoyment of the means of transportation.

Implemented by specific legislation, the supervision of private businesses and professions for the public good has gone far beyond the early common law fields. In Munn v. Illinois, supra, a state's imposition of maximum charges for the storage of grain in warehouses was sustained in an opinion which stressed that the private property was devoted "to a public use" and was therefore subject to public regulation; in German Alliance Insurance Co. v. Lewis, supra, a state's fixing of fire insurance rates was upheld on the ground that the business of insurance was "so far affected with a public interest" as to justify its regulation; and in Nebbia v. New York, supra, a state's extensive regulation of its milk industry was upheld in an opinion by Justice Roberts which frankly recognized that there is no closed class or category of businesses affected with a public interest, that the phrase means no more than that an industry, for adequate reason, is subject to control for the public good, and that "upon proper occasion and by appropriate measures the state may regulate a business in any of its aspects." . . .

It is evident that . . . similar policy considerations apply with equal strength and call for a declaration that . . . Dr. Greisman is entitled to have his application evaluated on its own individual merits without regard to the bylaw requirement rejected by the Law Division. His personal and professional qualifications are not in dispute here; he lives in Vineland, has an office in Newfield in the Vineland metropolitan area, has an unrestricted license to practice medicine and surgery, and is engaged in the general practice of medicine. All he seeks, at this juncture, is simply permission to file his application for membership on the courtesy staff of the Newcomb Hospital and have it considered to the end that, if he is passed on favorably in accordance with the hospital's valid bylaws, he and his patients, as such, will have hospital facilities when needed.

The Newcomb Hospital is the only hospital in the Vineland metropolitan area and it is publicly dedicated, primarily to the care of the sick and injured of Vineland and its vicinity and, thereafter to the care of such other persons as may be accommodated. Doctors need hospital facilities and a physician practicing in the metropolitan Vineland area will understandably seek them at the Newcomb Hospital. Furthermore, every patient of his will want the Newcomb Hospital facilities to be readily available. It hardly suffices to say that the patient could enter the hospital under the care of a member of the existing staff, for his personal physician would have no opportunity of participating in his treatment; nor does it suffice to say that there are other hospitals outside the metropolitan Vineland area, for they may be too distant or unsuitable to his needs and desires. All this indicates very pointedly that, while the managing officials may have discretionary powers in the selection of the medical staff, those powers are deeply imbedded in public aspects, and are rightly viewed . . . as fiduciary powers to be exercised reasonably and for the public good.

It must be borne in mind that we are not asked to pass on a discretionary exercise of judgment but only on the validity of the bylaw requirement. Therefore, we need not concern ourselves with any of the larger issues relating to discretionary limits or the general lengths to which a hospital may go in conditioning staff admissions on the approval of outside bodies. Viewed realistically, our proper concern here is whether the hospital had the right to exclude consideration of the plaintiff, solely because he was a doctor of osteopathy and had not been admitted, because of his osteopathic schooling, to his County Medical Society. . . . In this day there should be no hesitancy in rejecting as arbitrary, the stand that a doctor of osteopathy, though fully licensed by state authority and reputably engaged in the general practice of medicine and as the local school and plant physician, is nonetheless automatically, and without individual evaluation, to be considered unfit for staff membership at the only available hospital in the rather populous metropolitan area where he resides and practices. The public interest and considerations of fairness and justness point unerringly away from the hospital's position and we agree fully with the Law Division's judgment rejecting it.

Hospital officials are properly vested with large measures of managing discretion and to the extent that they exert their efforts toward the elevation of hospital standards and higher medical care, they will receive broad judicial support. But they must never lose sight of the fact that the hospitals are operated not for private ends but for the benefit of the public, and that their existence is for the purpose of faithfully furnishing facilities to the members of the medical profession in aid of their service to the public. They must recognize that their powers, particularly those relating to the selection of staff members, are powers in trust which are always to be dealt with as such. While reasonable and constructive exercises of judgment should be honored, courts would indeed be remiss if they declined to intervene where, as here, the powers were invoked at the threshold to preclude an application for staff membership, not because of any lack of individual merit, but for a reason unrelated to sound hospital standards and not in furtherance of the common good.

Affirmed.

NANAVATI v. BURDETTE TOMLIN MEMORIAL HOSPITAL

526 A.2d 697 (N.J. 1987)

POLLOCK, J.

This appeal arises out of the revocation of the staff privileges of Suketu H. Nanavati (Dr. Nanavati) as a cardiologist at Burdette Tomlin Memorial Hospital (the hospital). . . .

The background of this case is a dispute between Dr. Nanavati and Dr. Robert Sorensen, who at the time was the chief of cardiology, chairman of the Department of Medicine, and a member of the Board of Governors at the hospital. The dispute originated over the allocation of the reading of electrocardiograms (ECGs or EKGs), which, at $5 per reading, produced an annual income of approximately $75,000. Burdette Tomlin is the only hospital in Cape May County, and when he was granted staff privileges, Dr. Nanavati was the only board-certified cardiologist in the county. Before the arrival of Dr. Nanavati in 1979, Dr. Sorensen, an internist, enjoyed a virtual monopoly on reading ECGs. Dr. Nanavati was allowed to read ECGs one day each week, but when he requested an additional day, Dr. Sorensen rejected his request. The rejection stimulated Dr. Nanavati into criticizing Dr. Sorensen, who retaliated. As the discord between the two doctors escalated, Dr. Nanavati allegedly committed a series of violations of the hospital's bylaws. On August 2, 1982, the medical staff executive committee "voted unanimously to act toward the revocation of Dr. Nanavati's medical staff privileges." That action marked the beginning of lengthy proceedings before the hospital authorities and before federal and state courts in this state.

Pursuant to the hospital bylaws, the chairman of the medical staff executive committee requested the hospital executive committee to take corrective action. The executive committee forwarded the request to the chief of the Department of Medicine, who appointed an ad hoc committee to investigate the matter. The charges against Dr. Nanavati were captioned as "Acts of Disruptive Behavior" and "Failure to Cooperate with Hospital Personnel Regarding the Use of Facilities Especially During the Summer Months and the Emergent Admissions Procedures."

Underlying these charges is the contention that Dr. Nanavati caused disruption in violation of a bylaw provision requiring a staff doctor to

> be of a temperament and disposition that will enable him to work in harmony with his colleagues on the Medical Staff; with the professional, technical, and other personnel in the hospital, and with the administration, accepting criticism without resentment and offering it in a spirit and manner that is constructive and devoid of offense and malice. . . .

The further allegation is that Dr. Nanavati violated a bylaw provision that a staff member "must enjoy the reputation of being an ethical and conscientious practitioner and must strictly abide by the Code of Ethics. . . ." At no time has the hospital questioned Dr. Nanavati's technical competence.

On August 23, 1982, the ad hoc committee "found against Dr. Nanavati on all charges and specifications" and recommended as the only appropriate punishment "his discharge from the Medical Staff of Burdette Tomlin Memorial Hospital, together with the permanent deprivation of Burdette Memorial Hospital privileges." The executive committee of the medical staff affirmed that finding, and Dr. Nanavati appealed to an ad hoc committee of the medical staff, which unanimously found against him and recommended that he be dismissed from the staff of the hospital. In November, the hospital administrator advised Dr. Nanavati of the revocation of his staff privileges.

Dr. Nanavati immediately filed an action in the Chancery Division, which found that the proceedings had not been conducted in accordance with the hospital's bylaws, enjoined the revocation of Dr. Nanavati's privileges, and remanded the matter for further proceedings to be conducted in accordance with the hospital's bylaws. The Board of Governors thereupon appointed a hearing committee, which recommended on April 15, 1983, "that the action of the medical staff in dismissing Dr. Nanavati be affirmed." Two weeks later, on April 29, the board affirmed the hearing committee's recommendation. . . .

[On appeal] the Chancery Division independently reviewed the record by a preponderance-of-the-evidence standard. The court determined that Dr. Nanavati's staff privileges should not be revoked on the ground of disharmony, absent a showing of actual interference with patient care, and concluded that the record did not support any such showing. Consequently, the court issued a permanent injunction against revocation of his privileges.

Although the Appellate Division affirmed the trial court's finding that the hospital proceedings were invalid, it disagreed with other portions of the trial court's opinion and held that the trial court, in reviewing the revocation of hospital staff privileges, should not have made independent findings of fact, but should have determined whether the hospital's decision was supported by sufficient credible evidence. In addition, the Appellate Division ruled that mere disharmony, although an insufficient ground by itself, is a relevant consideration in revocation proceedings. . . .

We granted Dr. Nanavati's petition for certification to determine the appropriate standard of review of the decision by a hospital to terminate a physician's staff privileges and to determine further whether actual interference with patient care is required in order to terminate those privileges. . . .

Twenty-five years ago we rejected the notion that decisions of private hospitals concerning staff privileges were beyond judicial review. Greisman v. Newcomb Hosp., 192 A.2d 817. By analogy to private businesses affected by the public interest, we ruled that courts should intervene when a hospital denied staff membership "for a reason unrelated to sound hospital standards and in furtherance of the common good." In reaching that conclusion, we also declared that "reasonable and constructive exercises of judgment should be honored. . . ." Thus, courts should sustain a hospital's standard for granting staff privileges if that standard is rationally related to the delivery of health care. A decision is so related if it advances the interests of the public, particularly patients; the hospital; or those who are essential to the hospital's operations, such as doctors and nurses.

Although not quite so deferential when reviewing individual decisions denying staff privileges, courts still apply a relaxed standard of review to those decisions. The test for judicial review of such a decision is whether it is supported by "sufficient reliable evidence, even though of a hearsay nature, to justify the result."

We have previously explained the difference between the two tests by analogy to judicial review of administrative actions. Setting a standard for admission to staff privileges is roughly analogous to the kind of policy decision reflected in administrative rulemaking. Carrying forward the analogy, a hospital's use of that standard to decide a particular case is like quasi-judicial agency action. . . .

Underlying the more relaxed standard is our growing awareness that courts should allow hospitals, as long as they proceed fairly, to run their own business. That sense is tempered by the recognition that doctors need staff privileges to serve their patients, and that the public interest requires that hospitals treat doctors fairly in making decisions about those privileges. . . .

In prior cases, we have considered the denial of privileges to new applicants. . . . Although we have not previously decided a case involving the *revocation* of privileges, . . . [n]onetheless, the standard of judicial review should remain the same. . . .

[I]f a hospital is to care for its patients, the staff, particularly doctors and nurses, must work together. As important as cooperation is to other corporations, it is even more critical in a modern hospital, where no single doctor cares for all the needs of any one patient. Hospital doctors depend on their colleagues, nurses, technicians, and other employees for total patient care. . . . Consequently, a hospital may adopt a bylaw providing that the inability of a doctor to work with nurses and other doctors is a ground for denying or terminating staff privileges. . . .

Doctors, like other people, have quirks, and some doctors are more disagreeable than others. The mere fact that a doctor is irascible, however, does not constitute good cause for termination of his or her hospital privileges. McElhinney v. William Booth Memorial Hosp., 544 S.W.2d 216, 218 (Ky. 1977). Nor should allegations of "disharmony" ever be used as a ruse to deny or terminate staff privileges because of a doctor's race, religion, color, or gender. Likewise, a doctor should not be cut off from staff membership merely because he or she has criticized hospital practices and other doctors. . . . A hospital need not wait for a disruptive doctor to harm a patient before terminating his or her privileges. Nonetheless, more should be required than general complaints of a physician's inability to cooperate with others. To constitute disruptive behavior meriting termination of staff privileges, hospital authorities should present concrete evidence of specific instances of misbehavior, such as unjustified altercations with other doctors or nurses, violations of hospital routines or rules, breaches of professional standards, or the commission of some other act that will adversely affect health care delivery. . . .

The judgment of the Appellate Division is affirmed as modified, and the cause is remanded to the hospital.

Notes: Judicial Review of Medical Staff Disputes

1. *Overview.* Why might a hospital want to exclude a doctor? More doctors, after all, mean more patients. If it is in a hospital's economic interest to exclude only bad doctors, why should we bother to scrutinize the hospital's decision at all?

In addressing these questions, the principal focus of these notes will be the common-law fairness theory announced in *Greisman.* The notes explore first whether any judicial review is available, and then the scope of review. As *Nanavati* indicates, it is helpful to divide the scope of judicial review into two components—procedural and substantive—and, further, to divide substantive review into (a) the rationale for the general membership criteria contained in the bylaws and (b) the evidence supporting the application of the bylaws to an individual physician. The primary focus of these notes is on the next-to-last issue: the substantive validity of general criteria.

2. *Other Legal Causes of Action.* There are many other causes of action potentially available to excluded physicians besides common-law fairness. Pursued below in section D.1 are challenges under the federal antitrust laws. State antitrust statutes and common-law unfair competition theories are another hook for the same hat. Under tort law, excluded physicians can allege defamation, e.g., Purgess v. Sharrock, 33 F.3d 134 (2d Cir. 1994) ($5.1 million damages), civil conspiracy, Nashville Memorial Hospital v. Brinkley, 534 S.W.2d 318 (Tenn. 1976), or tortious interference with contract, supra. The prior section also discusses the use of contract law to require hospitals to adhere to their bylaws when reviewing the credentials of existing medical staff members. Several states create statutory causes of action. See, e.g., N.Y. Pub. Health Law §2901-c(1) (McKinney); Egan v. St. Anthony's Medical Center, 244 S.W.3d 169 (Mo. 2008) (implied statutory action). Doctors excluded from public hospitals can bring constitutional claims. Caine v. Hardy, 905 F.2d 858 (5th Cir. 1990). Finally, claims can be brought under the civil rights statutes that protect against discrimination based on suspect classifications such as race or disability, even though physicians, technically speaking, are not employees of the hospital.

Observe that each of these alternative legal theories is limited by elements of the cause of action that do not restrain the common-law fairness theory. But, even under that theory, if bylaws constitute a contract, can they be used to require physicians to waive any right to sue over credentialing decisions? See Estate of Blume v. Marian Health Center, 516 F.3d 705 (8th Cir. 2008) (such a provision does not violate public policy, in the absence of any claim that civil rights were violated).

3. *Constitutional Issues.* Care must be taken to distinguish the *common-law* fairness theory articulated in *Greisman* from *constitutional* due process and equal protection. While the content of the doctrines may (or may not) be the same, their origins are distinctly different. Only public hospitals, that is, those *owned* by state or municipal authorities, are subject to the Constitution; it is well settled that the extensive involvement of private hospitals with public funding and regulation is not sufficient to constitute state action. Blum v. Yaretsky, 457 U.S. 991 (1982); Philips v. Pitt County Memorial Hospital, 572 F.3d 176 (4th Cir. 2009).

A constitutional theory that has not succeeded, even at public hospitals, is the *substantive* due process argument that "all licensed physicians have a constitutional right to practice their profession. It is not incumbent on the state to maintain a hospital for the private practice of medicine." Hayman v. City of Galveston, 273 U.S. 414, 417 (1926).

4. *Judicial Review, Pro and Con.* The *Greisman* public-facility theory has not won uniform acceptance. Consider the validity of the following objection to the quasi-public facility theory:

> It is far from clear today why hospitals are under any greater obligation than typical employers to account to the courts for the fairness with which they screen applicants for professional positions or why health care professionals deserve any special legal help in surmounting marketplace barriers to their pursuit of a livelihood. The due process requirements that common-law courts have required private hospitals

> to observe in allocating staff privileges are in fact anomalous and find weak support in the common-law ground in which they are rooted.

Clark Havighurst, Doctors and Hospitals: An Antitrust Perspective on Traditional Relationships, 1984 Duke L.J. 1071, 1099-1100.

The following are a sampling of cases pro and con: *Pro judicial review*—Silver v. Castle Memorial Hospital, 497 P.2d 564 (Haw. 1972); Barrows v. Northwestern Memorial Hospital, 525 N.E.2d 50 (Ill. 1988); Mahmoodian v. United Hospital Center, 404 S.E.2d 750 (W. Va. 1991). *Contra judicial review*—Pepple v. Parkview Memorial Hospital, 536 N.E.2d 274 (Ind. 1989); Lakeside Community Hospital v. Levenson, 710 P.2d 727, 728 (Nev. 1985); Medical Center Hospitals v. Terzis, 367 S.E.2d 728 (Va. 1988). Canada, which is virtually the only other country with a medical staff structure similar to ours, follows the New Jersey approach. The leading case is Abouna v. Foothills Provincial General Hospital, [1978] 2 W.W.R. 130. See generally Craig W. Dallon, Understanding Judicial Review of Hospitals' Physician Credentialing and Peer Review Decisions, 73 Temp. L. Rev. 597 (2000); K. Van Tassel, Does the Hospital Peer Review Hearing Process Negatively Impact Healthcare Quality, Cost and Access?, 40 Pepperdine L. Rev. 911 (2013); Nicholas Bagley, Medicine as a Public Calling, 114 Mich. L. Rev. 57, 88 (2015).

5. *Monopoly Status.* In examining how faithful this body of law is to the common carrier/innkeeper precedent on which it is based, consider whether excluded physicians should be able to demand judicial review of the fairness of a private hospital's decision even if they (and their patients) have the choice of several other hospitals in town, or should the public-facility theory apply only where hospitals exercise monopoly power in their local markets? *Barrows*, supra, 525 N.E.2d 50 (Ill. 1988) (the former); Kelly v. St. Vincent Hospital, 692 P.2d 1350 (N.M. Ct. App. 1984) (the latter). Given that the great majority of all municipalities in the United States with an acute care hospital have only one or two, usually with similar medical staff membership, is it appropriate to overlook this technicality in those locations where there is effective competition?

6. *Physician Access vs. Patient Access.* Note that the common-law public service duties of common carriers were owed to their *customers*, not to their employees. As *Greisman* recognizes, then, excluded doctors have cause to complain only by virtue of their control over patient admissions to hospitals. Consequently, should the public-facility doctrine apply to doctors such as anesthesiologists and consulting specialists who do not admit patients? No one appears to have considered this issue.

7. *Extensions of the Quasi-Public Theory.* It is fascinating to speculate what other applications might exist for a doctrine as novel as this. One case has extended the quasi-public facility theory to physician (as opposed to hospital) services, holding that a patient refused service by the only practice group in town after lodging a complaint against one of the doctors in the group may maintain an action alleging an arbitrary refusal to serve. Leach v. Drummond Medical Group, 192 Cal. Rptr. 650 (Ct. App. 1983). Consider, also, whether private hospitals owe common-law fairness duties to their *employed* physicians. Ezekial v. Winkley, 572 P.2d 32 (Cal. 1977) (yes for existing employees but not for applicants).

And what about possible hospital duties extending directly to *patients*? The quasi-public characterization has been used by a few courts to prevent hospitals from refusing patients for arbitrary or invidious reasons. But can a hospital set limits on which services or accommodations it offers? For instance, could this doctrine be used by a woman in labor to demand that her husband be allowed to attend the birth? Hulit v. St. Vincent's Hospital, 520 P.2d 99 (Mont. 1974) (holding no, but only after finding that the hospital rule was "reasonable" and "fair"). Finally, if ancient common-law precedents are to be given full force in this context, note that common carriers were subject to heightened liability for accidents and to judicial scrutiny for the reasonableness of their rates!

8. *Valid and Invalid Criteria.* Among the numerous possible criteria for medical staff membership, those that are usually upheld include possessing a license to practice medicine, having board certification, or having satisfactory references. Criteria that are usually struck down include being a member in the local medical society and having a recommendation from one or more current members of the medical staff. See American Health Lawyers Ass'n, Peer Review Guidebook (5th ed. 2016); Annot., 37 A.L.R.3d 645 (1971).

9. *Deference to Medical Judgment.* Is *Nanavati* consistent with the following frequently quoted standard of review?

> No court should substitute its evaluation of such matters for that of the Hospital Board. . . . Human lives are at stake, and the governing board must be given discretion in its selection so that it can have confidence in the competence and moral commitment to its staff. The evaluation of professional proficiency of doctors is best left to the specialized expertise of their peers, subject only to limited judicial surveillance. . . . In short, so long as staff selections are administered with fairness, geared by a rationale compatible with hospital responsibility, and unencumbered with irrelevant considerations, a court should not interfere.

Sosa v. Board of Managers, 437 F.2d 173 (5th Cir. 1971). See also Branch v. Hempstead County Memorial Hospital, 539 F. Supp. 908 (W.D. Ark. 1982) ("this court does not intend . . . to become a super hospital governing board"); Sadler v. Dimensions Healthcare Corp., 836 A.2d 655 (Md. 2003) (applying a corporate law "business judgment" rule).

10. *The Hard Cases.* In *Greisman,* the hospital did not attempt to defend its exclusion of osteopaths on the basis of a quality-of-care rationale. If it had, what justification would suffice? Is it necessary to establish *poor* quality of care, or only a relative *difference* in the quality of care? Which of the following exclusionary policies do you think are valid?

- A hospital limits staff membership to licensed physicians (M.D.s or D.O.s), which necessarily excludes other licensed health professionals such as clinical psychologists, podiatrists, nurse midwives, and chiropractors. Shaw v. Hospital Authority, 614 F.2d 946 (5th Cir. 1985) (constitutionally permissible to exclude podiatrists).
- A tertiary care hospital limits staff membership to specialists who are board eligible or board certified, which necessarily excludes general practitioners, including many osteopaths. Silverstein v. Gwinnett Hospital Authority, 861 F.2d 1560 (11th Cir. 1988) (valid); Armstrong v. Board of Directors, 553 S.W.2d 77 (Tenn. 1977) (invalid).

- A Christian Science hospital excludes physicians who do not practice according to its religious beliefs. Cf. Watkins v. Mercy Medical Center, 520 F.2d 894 (9th Cir. 1975) (Catholic hospital may refuse to have abortions performed on premises, but may not exclude abortionists from staff).
- A hospital excludes osteopaths because they are trained under a different medical philosophy. Hayman v. City of Galveston, 273 U.S. 414, 417 (1926) (sufficient to pass constitutional muster); Stern v. Tarrant County Hospital District, 778 F.2d 1052 (5th Cir. 1985) (en banc) (same); Petrocco v. Dover General Hospital, 642 A.2d 1016 (N.J. Super. 1994) (permissible under *Greisman* for hospital to exclude chiropractors where it gave the issue careful thought and rational justification).

It may assist you in answering these questions to employ an equal protection type of analysis by asking what level of scrutiny do physician exclusion decisions warrant—minimum "rational basis," strict "compelling interest," or intermediate "substantial basis" scrutiny? Do you see any indication that courts heighten their level of scrutiny in response to suspicions about the genuineness of the asserted reasons for physician exclusion? Professor Havighurst, above, argues that medical staff decisions should be presumed valid when they appear to be made independently by the hospital motivated by its own business concerns, but should be scrutinized when it appears that physicians controlled or influenced the decision for competitive or personal reasons. Does this appear consistent with what the courts are doing?

11. *Disruptive Physicians.* Courts no longer seem to deliberate as closely as the *Nanavati* case did before upholding hospital decisions to discipline disruptive physicians. It now appears that a documented series of unprofessional behavior will suffice, regardless of whether patient care is actually threatened. See, e.g., Sternberg v. Nanticoke Memorial Hospital, 15 A.3d 1225 (Del. 2011); Guier v. Teton County Hospital District, 248 P.3d 623 (Wyo. 2011). This low-tolerance position is supported by the Joint Commission, which in 2009 adopted a standard that requires hospitals to police disruptive behavior.

12. *Economic Credentialing.* The debate in physician exclusion cases usually turns on whether the decision was motivated by the public interest in quality of care or by the existing doctors' interest in limiting competition. But what about the *hospital's* interest? Is it ever allowed to exclude a physician to advance its private economic interest, so long as that interest does not conflict with the public interest? In one limited context, courts have allowed explicitly self-interested hospital motives. They have held that a hospital has a "right to take reasonable measures to protect itself" against exposure to joint and several liability with a doctor by requiring all medical staff members to carry a certain level of insurance. Holmes v. Hoemako Hospital, 573 P.2d 477 (Ariz. 1977). See Annot., 7 A.L.R.4th 1238 (1977).

With the mounting pressure for improved efficiency in medical treatment, it is widely predicted that this question will take on much broader significance. Hospitals are contemplating using economic criteria in the credentialing process to screen out wasteful doctors. The notes at page 450 explore whether a body of law premised on excluding physicians for poor quality will accommodate physician exclusion for *excessive* quality. Assuming this is generally permissible, what evidence will be necessary in the particular case that a physician's treatment patterns are excessively costly: that the doctor's patients are more expensive than average, the most expensive of all, much more expensive than anyone else's? Will courts entertain objections by the doctor that his patients are especially difficult cases and therefore costly because (a) he is such a terrific doctor he gets all the hard cases; (b) he's been in practice longer and so naturally his patients are older and therefore sicker on average; (c) random luck of the draw? See Sokol v. Akron General Medical Center, 173 F.3d 1026 (6th Cir. 1999) (split decision on whether objections like these undermine statistics showing that a surgeon's patients died more frequently than those of other surgeons).

13. *Procedural Protections.* Much of the case law on medical staff disputes concerns only whether the excluded doctor received procedural due process. See, e.g., Kiester v. Humana Hospital Alaska, 843 P.2d 1219 (Alaska 1992); Silver v. Castle Memorial Hospital, 497 P.2d 564 (Haw. 1972); American Health Lawyers Ass'n, Peer Review Guidebook (1995). Physician credentialing usually proceeds through several stages: investigation by a departmental or hospitalwide credentialing committee; vote by the medical staff as a whole and/or its executive committee; consideration of the medical staff recommendation by the hospital board; and an evidentiary review hearing if the board's decision is negative. Courts require that an excluded physician, whether an applicant or an existing staff member, be given notice of the charges, an opportunity to present evidence, and the right to confront and cross-examine opposing witnesses. The decisionmakers in this quasi-adjudicatory hearing may not be exposed to ex parte communication and must not have prejudged the merits. Much of this law is codified in the Health Care Quality Improvement Act of 1986, which imposes fair procedure requirements as a condition for conferring an immunity on those who participate in the hospital peer review process. The major respects in which this act differs from the case law are (1) it allows the challenged physician representation by counsel, and (2) it disqualifies from the hearing panel anyone who is in "direct economic competition" with the physician. 42 U.S.C. §11112(b). Observe, though, that this Act's procedural steps are not mandatory or exclusive; they only create a safe harbor that establishes one manner in which a hospital can qualify for immunity. Cf. Owens v. New Britain General Hospital, 643 A.2d 233 (Conn. 1994) (only substantial, not strict, compliance with bylaw procedures is required). Nevertheless, the procedures specified in the Act have quickly become the industry standard in practice.

What problems do these requirements present for a small rural hospital? See Applebaum v. Board of Directors, 163 Cal. Rptr. 831 (Ct. App. 1980) (procedures unfair where five physicians served on both the initial review committee and the hearing committee); A. Southwick, The Law of Hospital and Health Care Administration 618 (2d ed. 1988) ("In hospitals having a relatively small medical staff the risk of bias and partiality increases. A hearing panel composed of persons from outside the hospital may then be necessary.").

Notes: Civil Rights and Disability Discrimination Laws

1. *Civil Rights Violations.* Another basis for scrutinizing hospitals' and HMOs' rejection of physicians are federal and state antidiscrimination laws. For instance, a number of medical staff dispute cases have been litigated under Title VII of the Civil Rights Act of 1964, as discrimination based on race, gender, or national origin. In general, courts hold that medical staff membership is sufficiently analogous to

employment to fall within the ambit of this statute. See generally Michael R. Lowe, Stirring Muddled Waters: Are Physicians with Hospital Medical Staff Privileges Considered Employees Under Title VII or the ADA Act When Alleging an Employment Discrimination Claim?, 1 DePaul J. Health Care L. 19 (1996).

Also of interest under Title VII is the 1978 amendment that includes pregnancy as an aspect of prohibited gender considerations. If a woman's pregnancy poses safety risks to customers or other third parties, then employers may take pregnancy into account in workplace decisions. International Union, UAW v. Johnson Controls, Inc., 499 U.S. 187, 200-203 (1991). However, employers may not discriminate against female employees out of concern for fetal health. Thus, a company cannot deny jobs to fertile women on the ground that chemicals in the workplace are hazardous to fetal development. Id. at 204-207 (holding that a battery-making company could not refuse employment to fertile women despite the exposure to lead in the workplace).

2. *Disability Discrimination.* Disability discrimination is another source of concern for hospitals and HMOs, both in their employment relationships and in their contractual and membership relations with independent physicians. As with Title VII, several courts have subjected medical staff decisions to scrutiny under the Americans with Disabilities Act (ADA) even though they do not, strictly speaking, involve employment relationships. In Ambrosino v. Metropolitan Life Ins. Co., 899 F. Supp. 438 (N.D. Cal. 1995), the court found that a state equivalent of the ADA applied to a physician's membership in a PPO. *Ambrosino* also held that past drug dependency constitutes a disability, even though present drug use and addiction does not. But see Wojewski v. Rapid City Reg'l Hosp., 450 F.3d 338 (8th Cir. 2006) (Rehabilitation Act does not apply to medical staff dismissal since the physician was not employed by the hospital). Consider also whether physician membership decisions could be scrutinized under the public accommodations title of the ADA.

Several cases alleging discrimination on the basis of disability have arisen when HIV-infected health care workers have been dismissed or reassigned because of their HIV infection. Although such persons are considered disabled for purposes of the ADA, they often receive little protection under the statute. For example, in Doe v. University of Maryland Medical System Corp., 50 F.3d 1261 (4th Cir. 1995), the court upheld a medical center's decision to permanently suspend a neurosurgical resident from surgical practice and offer him an alternative residency in a nonsurgical field. See also Bradley v. University of Texas M.D. Anderson Cancer Ctr., 3 F.3d 922 (5th Cir. 1993) (upholding a hospital's reassignment of an HIV-infected surgical assistant to the purchasing department); Estate of Behringer v. Medical Center, 592 A.2d 1251 (N.J. Super. Law Div. 1991) (upholding a hospital's revocation of surgical privileges of an HIV-infected physician under state discrimination statute).

3. *Membership in Managed Care Networks*

HMOs have also been drawn into disputes arising from physician selection decisions. When they exclude physicians from their networks, the stakes from the physicians' point of view can be just as high, but the reasons may differ, as may the available legal theories for judicial review. Think carefully about whether HMO physicians should have the same legal theory of action as hospital physicians, and, if not, which exclusion decisions and reasons are valid or invalid as a result.

■ POTVIN v. METROPOLITAN LIFE INSURANCE CO.

997 P.2d 1153 (Cal. 2000)

KENNARD, Judge.

After removal from defendant insurance company's "preferred provider" lists, plaintiff physician brought this action. Citing the common law right to fair procedure, which forbids arbitrary expulsions from private organizations under certain circumstances, plaintiff alleged he should have been given reasonable notice and an opportunity to be heard before his removal.

We first applied the common law doctrine of fair procedure in the late 19th century. . . . Some 50 years later, relying on the general principles underlying this doctrine, we held that a union could not arbitrarily deny full membership privileges to African-American workers. Thereafter, in the 1960's and 1970's, we extended the doctrine in a trio of decisions . . . involv[ing] the exclusion of a dentist from professional organizations [and] a hospital's expulsion of a surgical resident. The general principles this court enunciated in the[se] decisions apply in this case as well.

On September 10, 1990, Metropolitan Life Insurance (MetLife) entered into an agreement with Dr. Louis E. Potvin, an obstetrician and gynecologist, to include him as one of 16,000 participants on two of its preferred provider lists. Potvin had practiced medicine for more than 35 years; he was a past president of the Orange County Medical Association; and he held full staff privileges at Mission Regional Hospital, where he had served as Chairman of the Obstetrics and Gynecology Department for nine years. . . . The agreement . . . provided for termination by either party "at any time, with or without cause, by giving thirty (30) days prior written notice to the other party."

On July 22, 1992, MetLife notified Potvin in writing that effective August 31, 1992, it was terminating his preferred provider status . . . without cause. MetLife then stated that even though it did not have to give a reason, Potvin's "delistment from the provider network was related to the fact that [he] did not meet [MetLife's] current selection and retention standard for malpractice history." At the time, MetLife would not include or retain on its preferred provider lists any physician who had more than two malpractice lawsuits, or who had paid an aggregate sum of $50,000 in judgment or settlement of such actions. Potvin's patients had sued him for malpractice on four separate occasions, all predating his 1990 agreement with MetLife. In three of these actions, the plaintiffs had abandoned their claims, while the fourth case had settled for $713,000.

After MetLife failed to respond to Potvin's request for a hearing, Potvin filed this lawsuit. . . . Potvin alleged that MetLife's termination of his preferred provider status devastated his practice, reducing it to "a small fraction" of his former patients. He asserted that he was required to reveal his termination to other insurers and managed care entities, which then removed him from their preferred provider lists, and that he suffered rejection by "physician groups . . . dependent upon credentialling by MetLife" and by current MetLife preferred provider physicians, who ceased referring patients to him. The trial court granted MetLife's motion for summary judgment. . . .

II

The purpose of the common law right to fair procedure is to protect, in certain situations, against arbitrary decisions by private organizations. As this court has held, this means that, when the right to fair procedure applies, the decisionmaking "must be both substantively rational and procedurally fair." . . . In James v. Marinship Corp. 25 Cal.2d 721, 155 P.2d 329 (1944), . . . we upheld an injunction restraining the labor union and the employer, a Marin County shipbuilder, from "discharging or causing the discharge of . . . Negro employees because they are not members of a labor union with which their employer has a closed shop agreement, but which will not grant Negroes full membership privileges." . . . We explained: "It was well established at common law that innkeepers and common carriers were under a duty to furnish accommodations to all persons, in absence of some reasonable ground. . . . Where, as here, a labor union has attained a monopoly of the labor supply through closed shop agreements, such a union, like a public service business, may not unreasonably discriminate against Negro workers for the sole reason [of their race]." . . . Thereafter, . . . we went on to say: "one may not be expelled from membership in a private association without charges, notice and hearing. This common law protection against arbitrary expulsion, judicially declared, is of broader application and has been extended not only to labor unions [citations] and professional and trade organizations [citations], but to mutual benefit societies [citations] and other fraternal and social groups [citations]. The underlying theme of these decisions, variously stated, is that membership in an association, with its associated privileges, once attained, is a valuable interest which cannot be arbitrarily withdrawn. Thus, they comport with the broader principle that one on whom an important benefit or privilege has already been conferred may enjoy legal protections not available to an initial applicant for the same benefit." Exekial v. Winkley, 752 P.2d 32 (Cal. 1977). . . .

Plaintiff here points out that when an insurance company with fiduciary obligations to its insureds maintains a list of preferred provider physicians to render medical services to the insureds, a significant public interest is affected. One practical effect of the health care revolution, which has made quality care more widely available and affordable through health maintenance organizations and other managed care entities, is that patients are less free to choose their own doctors for they must obtain medical services from providers approved by their health plan. . . .

Our conclusion that the relationship between insurers and their preferred provider physicians significantly affects the public interest does not necessarily mean that every insurer wishing to remove a doctor from one of its preferred provider lists must comply with the common law right to fair procedure. The obligation to do so arises only when the insurer possesses power so substantial that the removal significantly impairs the ability of an ordinary, competent physician to practice medicine or a medical specialty in a particular geographic area, thereby affecting an important, substantial economic interest. . . . Here, plaintiff's amici curiae, the American Medical Association and the California Medical Association, . . . predict that in the near future no more than a handful of health care entities will dominate the managed care industry. If participation in managed care arrangements is a practical necessity for physicians generally and if only a handful of health care entities have a virtual monopoly on managed care, removing individual physicians from preferred provider networks controlled by these entities could significantly impair those physicians' practice of medicine.

Here, Potvin alleged that among the adverse effects of removal from MetLife's preferred provider lists were rejection by "physician groups which were dependent upon credentialing by MetLife" and devastation of his practice, which was reduced to "a small fraction" of his former patients. Proof of these allegations might establish that, in terminating a physician's preferred provider status, MetLife wields power so substantial as to significantly impair an ordinary, competent physician's ability to practice medicine or a medical specialty in a particular geographic area, thereby affecting an important, substantial economic interest. . . . We therefore agree with Potvin that the "without cause" termination clause is unenforceable to the extent it purports to limit an otherwise existing right to fair procedure under the common law.

Brown, J., dissenting.

With its decision today, the majority, in effect, declares that it is the public policy of this state that physicians are entitled to a minimum income. . . . What is the majority's authority for declaring this public policy, for singling out physicians for such special treatment? . . . Historically, the common law duty to serve arose in response to the fact that in the 15th century those engaged in certain public callings, for example, innkeepers and carriers, exercised virtual monopolies. "When the weary traveller reaches the wayside inn in the gathering dusk, if the host turn him away what shall he do? Go on to the next inn? It is miles away, and the roads are infested with robbers. The traveller would be at the mercy of the innkeeper, who might practice upon him any extortion, for the guest would submit to anything almost, rather than be put out into the night." (Wyman, The Law of the Public Callings as a Solution to the Trust Problem (1904) 17 Harv. L.Rev. 156, 159.) . . . Under the standard announced by the majority today, an insurer need not exercise monopoly power before the burdens of the common law right of fair procedure are imposed on it. Rather, . . . it is sufficient if the insurer has any significant share of a regional market. . . .

History has confirmed this court's judgment that the racial discrimination practiced by the union in *Marinship* was "an act against which the law has definitely set its face." However, it trivializes *Marinship* to suggest that anything like the same degree of public policy consensus has developed with regard to the question at bar. According to Dr. Potvin, the average physician who practices his specialty, obstetrics/gynecology, has been sued for malpractice 2.3 times. Metropolitan Life Insurance Company (MetLife) wishes to restrict its preferred provider lists to physicians with a slightly better than average malpractice history, to those who have not been sued more than twice. Potvin, by contrast, has been sued 4 times—nearly twice the average. Now the majority's public policy antennae may be more sensitive than mine, but I suspect the jury is still out on the question of whether an insurer should be able to control its costs by restricting its preferred provider lists to physicians with slightly better than average malpractice histories. That, surely, is a business judgment, and if the insurer makes the wrong judgment by depriving itself of doctors that patients insist upon, then the market will punish the insurer and force it to retreat from the impracticable standard. . . .

[T]his court has made doctors a protected class. Until the economy turned around recently, one could hardly open a newspaper without reading of yet another company that had laid off thousands of its employees. However, no one suggested that textile workers or bank employees, for example, had a right to a hearing before losing their jobs. The layoffs certainly affected "important, substantial economic interest[s]" of theirs. Indeed, they may well have exhausted their savings and lost their homes. And yet textile workers and bank employees must fend for themselves, while doctors are treated by the majority as if they are entitled to a minimum income. . . .

The majority insists that, "[o]ur decision here does not apply to employer-employee contractual relations. Rather, it applies only to an insurer's decision to remove individual physicians from its preferred providers lists." However, employers will not be comforted, for why wouldn't the majority's opinion apply to employer-employee contractual relations? . . . For that matter, why wouldn't the majority's opinion apply to the admission to, as well as the removal of physicians from, an insurer's preferred provider lists? . . .

The out-of-state case upon which the majority relies [Harper v. Healthsource New Hampshire, 674 A.2d 962 (N.H. 1996)] . . . provides little support for the majority's refusal to enforce the "without cause" termination clause of Potvin's contract with MetLife. . . . [U]nder the *Harper* rule, a physician terminated pursuant to a "without cause" provision is entitled to review only if "the physician believes that the decision to terminate was, in truth, made in bad faith or based upon some factor that would render the decision contrary to public policy." Indeed, under the *Harper* rule, the "without cause" termination provision of MetLife's contract with Dr. Potvin should be enforced because there is no showing that MetLife's decision was "made in bad faith or based upon some other factor that would render the decision contrary to public policy." Certainly it is not contrary to public policy for a business enterprise to seek to minimize its costs. Any successful business must do so, and in this era of spiraling health care costs, health care providers have a special societal responsibility to do so. . . . Therefore, to be competitive, a medical insurer would be wise to restrict its preferred provider lists to physicians with better than average malpractice histories, and, by his own admission, Dr. Potvin's malpractice history was considerably worse than average.

In conclusion, the judgment of the trial court granting MetLife's motion for summary judgment should have been affirmed.

[The decision was 4-3.]

Notes: Managed Care Contracting; Employment at Will; Interference with Doctor/Patient Relationship

1. *Medical Staff Disputes Deja Vu?* Managed care contracts between physicians and HMOs or PPOs usually contain some of the same due process hearing protections as do medical staff bylaws. This is also increasingly being required by state insurance regulations and by industry accreditation standards adopted by the National Committee for Quality Assurance. Managed care physician networks,

therefore, have taken on many of the same structural attributes of hospital medical staffs. John Blum, The Evolution of Physician Credentialing into Managed Care Selective Contracting, 22 Am. J. L. & Med. 173 (1996). There are two key differences, however. First, insurers retain the option in managed care contracts to use either for-cause or no-cause termination, and only the former invokes due process protections. Second, these due process protections apply, for the most part, only to physicians once they join the network. HMOs and PPOs are still free to reject physician applicants at the outset without judicial review of their reasons or process. Observe, though, tort law and state insurance regulation require managed care networks to review physicians' credentials before enrolling them. See Chapter 3.B. If this initial credentialing is commonplace, can due process requirements be far behind?

Despite physicians' concerns over no-cause terminations, physicians themselves often insist on putting these provisions in their managed care contracts. Can you imagine why? Suppose you were a doctor about to be terminated for good cause. What would you prefer? Realize that HMOs with formal peer review processes who seek immunity under the Health Care Quality Improvement Act must report to the National Practitioner Data Bank any adverse actions "based on competence or professional conduct." Lawyers also insist on no-cause provisions in part to comply with the referral fee laws that, for complex reasons, make it difficult to enter into short-term renewable contracts with doctors (the fear being that contract renewal will be used as an inducement to refer more business). An indefinite contract with no-cause termination therefore may be the only feasible way to maintain flexibility for both parties.

2. *"Deselection."* The unfortunate term that has emerged for terminating physicians from managed care networks is "deselection." Did the California Supreme Court disagree with the *substantive* reason for deselecting Dr. Potvin, or only the lack of procedural protections? As the dissent notes, other courts have allowed physicians to object only when they allege that the reason for termination violates public policy, as would be the case with an allegation of racial discrimination. More common are allegations that insurers retaliate against physicians for challenging insurers' limitations on coverage:

> Several California doctors have told the [California Medical Association (CMA)] that when they protested denials of treatment or UR policy with IPAs, PPOs, large group practices or integrated delivery systems, the organizations retaliated by exercising their right to terminate the physician without cause. One doctor reported denial of a necessary MRI scan. Repeated appeals by the doctor eventually overturned the UR decision, but the physician was terminated from the plan two weeks later. Another physician reported challenging a managed care plan's program that required his ill patients to travel long distances for second opinions. After listening to his criticisms, the plan terminated the doctor's contract. . . .
>
> HMO interests paint a different scenario. They say physicians challenge UR denials as a defensive medicine tactic, motivated by self-interest, to the detriment of cost-containment strategies and quality assurance initiatives. . . . But physician advocates still see the issue as part of an ominous trend that could be replayed across the country. . . . CMA pressed for state legislation that . . . provides legal recourse for doctors who can prove that they were fired from a managed care organization because they challenged a denial of necessary treatment or otherwise advocated on

> behalf of their patients. . . . "The legislators agreed with us that it was imperative to preserve the physician's role as the patient's advocate," said CMA General Counsel.

Brian McCormick, What Price Patient Advocacy?, Am. Med. News, Mar. 28, 1994. The California statute, Cal. Bus. & Prof. Code §2056, has been adopted in a number of other states. Under the common-law fairness theory, is it permissible to terminate a physician for being excessively costly, or for simply not being among the lowest-cost providers?

> Anecdotal evidence of physician deselection has received considerable publicity over the past year or two. . . . Reports range from one insurer's decision to drop more than 100 physicians from its network to another . . . [that] dropped 600 specialists from its HMO network, including most of its African American physicians. . . . One plan's approach, which has received substantial publicity, may typify what others are doing. The Blue Cross Blue Shield plan based in Washington, D.C., uses a profiling system called Pro/File that compares resource consumption by each practice with that of other doctors in the same specialty and the same region. Pro/File considers a broad array of utilization measures (e.g., numbers of laboratory tests and office visits and what they call long-range utilization), but not patient outcomes. An adjustment for case mix is implemented by comparing groups of patients with similar diseases, ages, and treatments. Critics claim that small sample size is a significant problem and that Pro/File judges only resource consumption and not quality of care. . . .

Physician Payment Review Commission, Annual Report to Congress 226 (1995). Minority physicians have been especially hard hit by deselection in some instances, it appears, because HMOs perceived that their patients are less profitable or because HMOs didn't wish to market themselves in certain locations. See Note, The Impact of Managed Care on Doctors Who Serve Poor and Minority Patients, 108 Harv. L. Rev. 1625 (1995).

3. *Other States, Other Cases, and Other Theories.* Cases like *Potvin* are still few and far between. When they do arise, courts more commonly adopt the legal theory mentioned in the dissent, which allows physicians to challenge no-cause terminations only if they can show the true reason violates public policy. This is an extension of the "whistleblower" suits that arise under employment law, where courts have recognized a public policy exception to the "employment at will" doctrine.

Under either theory of action, should courts exert as much scrutiny as they do over hospital staffing decisions? Does the level of scrutiny depend on the theory of review? Is *Potvin* saying that HMOs are "quasi-public" facilities, relying on the same factors invoked in *Greisman*? If not, what level of scrutiny is justified by the public policy limitation proposed by the dissent? One way to think about this is to consider, under each of these theories, who bears the burden of proof to show exactly what? For instance, under the dissent's public policy theory, should HMOs be allowed to exclude osteopaths from their networks? Does the dissent's theory require the HMO to provide any due process procedures?

Is the dissent correct that the majority's theory might also apply to physicians who are refused initial admission into managed care networks? Under the majority's approach, are there any substantive grounds that would not require due process procedures? In another California case, the court held that it was illegal to summarily remove a physician from a network even though he had been disciplined by the state licensing board for prior substance abuse, improperly prescribing Demerol, and treating patients under the influence of drugs. The court reasoned that the insurer failed to show that the physician was presently impaired or a threat to patients. Ambrosino v. Metropolitan Life Insurance Co., 899 F. Supp. 438 (N.D. Cal. 1995).

For analysis of the full range of issues, see Linda C. Fentiman, Patient Advocacy and Termination from Managed Care Organizations, 82 Neb. L. Rev. 508 (2003); Mark A. Kadzielski, Provider Deselection and Decapitation in a Changing Healthcare Environment, 41 St. Louis U. L.J. 891 (1997); Brian A. Liang, Deselection under Harper v. Healthsource: A Blow for Maintaining Patient-Physician Relationships in the Era of Managed Care?, 72 Notre Dame L. Rev. 799 (1997); William M. Sage, Physicians as Advocates, 35 Hous. L. Rev. 1529 (1999); Bethany J. Spielman, Managed Care Regulation and the Physician-Advocate, 47 Drake L. Rev. 713 (1999); Note, 49 Rutgers L. Rev. 1397 (1997); Note, 48 Wm. & Mary L. Rev. 677 (2006).

4. *Interference with the Doctor/Patient Relationship.* In this body of law, to what extent should courts be concerned with patients' interests in addition to physicians'? If a patient's physician is excluded from the patient's HMO, what option does the patient have? Does the HMO have a "monopoly" over the patient's business? In one case, the court ruled that patients do not have a right to challenge the termination of their physician, because they can be treated by other physicians in the network. Maltz v. Aetna Health Plans of New York, 114 F.3d 9 (2d Cir. 1997). However, in Harper v. Healthsource New Hampshire, 674 A.2d 962 (N.H. 1996), the court noted that "the termination of [Dr. Harper's] relationship with [the HMO] affects more than just his own interest. Several relationships in our society stand on a different footing from the rest. The most visible are those between wife and husband, lawyer and client, pastor and penitent, and physician and patient. In these relationships, society values truthfulness in communication above other competing interests, such as evidence in the search for truth in legal actions. Evidentiary privileges protect communication within these relationships from being revealed in litigation because society has determined that the relationship 'ought to be sedulously fostered.' "

This viewpoint suggests another possible theory of action. Tort law recognizes an action for tortious interference with advantageous relationships. Doctors whose clinical privileges are limited by a hospital often argue that the hospital interfered with their economic relationships with patients. Viewed as a business tort, this often fails because hospitals are pursing their own appropriate business interests and therefore lack the requisite bad motive. If the restriction of privileges is seen as interfering with something more sacred, however, these claims may have a greater chance of success. In Baptist Health v. Murphy, 210 Ark. 358 (2010), the court found tortious interference where a general hospital excluded physicians who owned competing specialty hospitals, reasoning that this policy "affronts the sense of justice, decency, and reasonableness [and] impinges on fundamentally important public policies without adequate countervailing justification . . . because [it] would disrupt the patient-physician relationship, discouraged specialty hospitals, [and] suppressed competition. . . . Baptist wanted to force patients to choose between it and the [excluding] physician[s], . . . [whose] interest was in patient-physician relationships and the continuity of care. [This interest] outweighed Baptist's interest in protecting its economic viability because no evidence supported Baptist's purported need for the Policy." See generally Annot., 87 A.L.R.4th 845 (1991).

5. *Immunity Laws.* There has been little litigation yet over whether the federal Health Care Quality Improvement Act discussed below creates an immunity from damages for formal peer review decisions by HMOs. It appears that immunity does not apply to no-cause contract terminations or to decisions based on economic grounds, but does apply to formal peer review actions based on quality concerns. Cf. Alexander v. Memphis IPA, 870 S.W.2d 278 (Tenn. 1993) (state immunity statute applies to peer review by IPA). Also, there is an unresolved possibility that these suits are preempted by ERISA, the federal law discussed in Chapter 3.C that overrides certain state laws affecting employer-provided health insurance. Compare Zuniga v. Blue Cross and Blue Shield of Michigan, 52 F.3d 1395 (6th Cir. 1995) (ERISA preempts breach of contract and due process claims by physician removed from a PPO) with Napoletano v. CIGNA Healthcare of Connecticut, 680 A.2d 127 (Conn. 1996) (ERISA does not preempt a similar action).

6. *Wrongful Discharge.* The public policy limitation on at-will employment and for-cause termination applies to nonphysicians as well. For some reason, these wrongful discharge cases seem to crop up with some regularity in the hospital industry, in the form of "whistleblower" cases, where an employee is fired in retaliation for reporting, for example, workplace safety problems to the proper authorities. See, e.g., Margiotta v. Christian Hospital, 315 S.W.3d 342 (Mo. 2010) (terminated after reporting hospital safety violations); Van v. Portneuf Medical Center, 212 P.3d 982 (Idaho 2009) (terminated after reporting unsafe helicopter). Also, observe that public hospitals are subject to constitutional as well as contractual restrictions in their employment decisions. Waters v. Churchill, 511 U.S. 661 (1994).

7. *Conscientious Objection.* Consider whether public policy should limit the ability to discipline medical employees for exercising conscientious objection to assisting in particular medical procedures, such as abortions or termination of life support. Most states have "conscience clause" statutes that expressly prohibit discharge for refusal to perform abortions, and federal law enforces a similar prohibition against providers and institutions that receive certain forms of federal health care funding.

8. *Negotiating Managed Care Contracts.* Most physicians belong to several (sometimes many dozens) of overlapping managed care networks. Once these networks are formed, insurers then market them to employers and to other insurers, thereby binding physicians to payment and coverage terms that may vary from one purchaser to the next. In deciding whether to sign these contracts, physicians must grapple with many crucial issues in addition to no-cause termination clauses. Other issues include their basic service obligation and payment rights, whether they can limit the number of patients they accept, whether they must indemnify the HMO for liability arising from patient care, and how disputes are resolved. The following exercise provides an opportunity to sample some of these issues.

Exercise: Negotiating a Managed Care Contract*

Florence Nightingale Hospital (FNH) is described at page 456. One of its competitors established a successful IPA-model HMO two years ago. Fearing loss of patients, FNH is forming the Florence Nightingale Managed Care Network (the Network). The objective is to sign up a number of physicians, mainly in primary care but also in common specialties, and then to market this network to these two sources: (1) large employers who provide health insurance to their workers on a self-insured basis and (2) large regional or national insurance companies (such as Blue Cross) who then offer the Network to their customers.

The Network is approaching each physician group individually and asking them to sign up nonexclusively, leaving them free to sign up with other networks or HMOs. The contract excerpts below contain some common sticking points in these negotiations. Read each pairing of contract options and determine what is at stake. Then, assume the position of lawyer/negotiator for either (a) the Network or (b) a physician group who wants to sign up but is concerned about the details. Meet with a representative from the other side and see if you can hammer out a deal, either adopting one version or the other, or making any changes you want.

Compensation

A. In exchange for providing Covered Services,* Physician shall receive usual, customary, and reasonable rates that similarly situated physicians charge for like services, less a discount of 15 percent; provided, however, that Physician agrees that the Network shall receive his or her "most favored" discount, such that, if Physician gives a greater discount to another network, insurer, employer, or health plan, Physician shall extend the same discount to the Florence Nightingale Network.

B. In exchange for providing Covered Services,* Physician shall receive the same compensation the Network pays other similarly situated physicians for like services, which will be according to a proprietary fee schedule maintained by the Network and which the Network shall be free to modify from time to time as it deems fit, so long as it applies the fee schedule consistently to all physicians in the Network who are similarly situated.

Availability of Physician's Services

A. Physician agrees to provide or arrange all Covered Services** sought by Members in return for the compensation stated above. Physician shall provide such services on a twenty-four per day, seven day per week basis. During the term of this Agreement, Physician must have and maintain full and unrestricted medical staff privileges at a hospital which is under contract with Network.

*This exercise is adapted from one developed by Jan Yarborough, a North Carolina lawyer.

**"Covered Services" is defined as "those health care services which the Network may be obligated to provide any employer or individual under a health insurance or health benefits plan sold by or on behalf of the network."

B. Physician shall provide Covered Services* sought by Members in the same manner provided to persons who are not Members in return for the compensation stated above. During the term of this Agreement, Physician must have and maintain medical staff privileges at a hospital in the geographic area covered by the Network.

Indemnification

A. Physician agrees to indemnify and hold harmless the Network against any negligent act or claim made with respect to items or services provided by Physician under this Agreement. The Network agrees to indemnify and hold harmless Physician against any negligent act or claim made with respect to items or services provided under this Agreement to the extent that the Network is solely responsible for the negligent act or claim.
B. [No indemnification clause at all. Each party is left to bear its own liability.]

Term and Termination

A. This Agreement may not be terminated as to any Physician prior to its expiration unless said Physician loses his or her license to practice medicine. Provided, however, the Physician shall have the option to terminate this Agreement in the event of the failure of the MCO to make payments when due.
B. This Agreement may be terminated by either party at any time without cause by written notice given at least one-hundred-twenty (120) days in advance of the effective date of termination without the need for prior consent of, or notice to any Member, Participating Provider, or other third party.

D. ANTITRUST LAW

Note: Introduction to Antitrust Law

Until the 1980s, the health care industry was remarkably complacent about the antitrust laws. Physicians openly threatened boycotts to enforce their interests; hospitals had few qualms about dividing markets with each other; and the AMA ruled supreme over the economics and organization of medical practice. No one thought to challenge this conduct because it was considered that the learned professions did not engage in the type of trade that is subject to antitrust scrutiny, that health care is an inherently local enterprise not subject to federal jurisdiction, and that lofty considerations of ethical practice and quality of care removed health care decisionmaking from base concerns of economic efficiency.

However, Supreme Court decisions systematically upset each of these assumptions. In Goldfarb v. Virginia State Bar, 421 U.S. 773, 787 (1975), the Court held that there was no antitrust exemption for professionals: "The nature of an occupation, standing alone, does not provide sanctuary from the Sherman Act." In Hospital Building Company v. Trustees of Rex Hospital, 425 U.S. 738 (1976), the Court held that hospital activities can meet the interstate commerce prerequisite to antitrust jurisdiction. And in American Medical Ass'n v. FTC, 455 U.S. 676 (1982), the Supreme Court upheld without opinion an FTC injunction against the AMA using its code of professional ethics to ban physician advertising and certain physician contractual arrangements.

The result of suddenly exposing an entire industry that was once exempt from antitrust law has been an explosion of litigation and counseling. Health care antitrust cases pop up all over the health care landscape faster than dandelions after a spring rain. Law firms have created new health care practice groups and old antitrust litigators have found an area of revival in an otherwise sluggish specialty. Antitrust liability can be a frightening prospect to physicians, hospitals, and insurers. Violations can be privately enforced in civil damage actions brought by injured plaintiffs, defendants face the possibility of treble damages, and losing defendants must pay the plaintiff's attorney fees. To top it off, professional liability insurance rarely covers antitrust exposure. Enforcement authority is also lodged in the FTC, which is empowered to bring civil injunction actions, and in the Department of Justice (DOJ), which, in addition, may prosecute criminal violations (although this almost never happens in health care cases). Both agencies also issue advisory rulings and general interpretative guidelines.

Health care antitrust cases have emerged with such force and prominence that antitrust analysis can no longer be reserved to the litigation specialist. Health care lawyers must have a working understanding of this area of the law in order to advise their clients effectively on how to plan their activities in advance to minimize antitrust exposure. Yet it is not possible in the course of this survey text to cover the entirety of a field as complex as health care antitrust.[5] Materials in this chapter and elsewhere explore some basic principles governing the more prominent areas of litigation. This section examines group boycott law in the context of the exclusion of practitioners from hospital medical staffs and managed care networks. The next section contains a discussion of the price-fixing ramifications of structuring various collaborations and joint ventures, and the following section explores antitrust merger doctrine as applied to hospitals and physicians. The following is a summary of antitrust law as it relates primarily to the first category of disputes, but it also explains principles that apply generally to all types of antitrust theories.

Physicians frequently challenge medical staff membership and network formation decisions under federal antitrust laws, contending that exclusion from the hospital or from a managed care network constitutes a concerted refusal to deal, which is pejoratively known as a group boycott. The primary basis for these suits is §1 of the Sherman Act, 15 U.S.C. §1:

5. For more comprehensive overviews, see Carl Ameringer, The Health Care Revolution: From Monopoly to Market Power (2008); Clark Havighurst & Barak Richman, The Provider Monopoly Problem in Health Care, 89 Or. L. Rev. 847 (2011); Thomas L. Greaney, Competition Policy and Organizational Fragmentation in Health Care, 71 U. Pitt. L. Rev. 217 (2009); Deborah Haas-Wilson, Managed Care and Monopoly Power: The Antitrust Challenge (2003); Spencer Weber Waller, How Much of Health Care Antitrust Is Really Antitrust? 48 Loy. U. Chi. L. Rev. 643 (2017); Martin Gaynor, Farzad Mostashari & Paul B. Ginsburg, Making Health Care Markets Work: Competition Policy for Health Care (Brookings, Apr. 2017); National Academy of Social Insurance, Addressing Pricing Power in Health Care Markets (Apr. 2015); Thomas L. Greaney, Chicago's Procrustean Bed: Applying Antitrust Law in Health Care, 71 Antitrust L.J. 857 (2004); William M. Sage & Peter J. Hammer, A Copernican View of Health Care Antitrust, 65 Law & Contemp. Probs. 241 (Autumn 2002); Symposium, 7 Hous. J. Health L. & Pol'y 183 (2007); Symposium, 31 J. Health Pol. Pol'y L. 417 (2006).

> Every contract, combination . . . or conspiracy in restraint of trade or commerce among the several states, or with foreign nations, is declared to be illegal.

The three elements of a §1 action, evident from the face of the statute, are (1) concerted, as opposed to unilateral, action; (2) an unreasonable restraint of trade; and (3) interstate commerce. A general overview of these three elements may be helpful to the uninitiated reader prior to tackling the principal cases.

1. *Conspiracy.* No Sherman Act §1 violation exists if the challenged activity is unilateral in nature, that is, if it is the action of a single entity. The theory underlying §1 is that competitive harm exists only where two or more economic actors collude to subvert the forces of competition. When a single hospital or HMO excludes a physician, concerted action is not readily apparent, even though many individual doctors and administrators within the hospital or HMO participate in the exclusion decision. The Supreme Court has clearly held that "[t]he officers of a single firm are not separate economic actors pursuing separate economic interests, so agreements among them do not suddenly bring together economic power that was previously pursing divergent goals. Coordination within a firm is as likely to result from an effort to compete as from an effort to stifle competition." Copperweld Corp. v. Independence Tube Corp., 467 U.S. 752, 769 (1984). This reasoning is referred to as the "intra-enterprise conspiracy rule": No conspiracy ordinarily can exist within a single business enterprise.

There are exceptions to this intra-enterprise conspiracy rule, however. A combination or conspiracy may exist within a single enterprise if one or more of its members have different, outside economic interests that are separate from the firm's. In such a situation, it is no longer the case that the various corporate actors are pursuing a single economic purpose, and, therefore, the potential for harmful collusion exists even within a single firm. For instance, the Supreme Court held in American Needle Inc. v. National Football League, 130 S. Ct. 2201 (2010) that although the NFL is a single enterprise for many purposes, it is a collection of competing teams when it comes to licensing logos and therefore an exclusive license for marketing all teams' apparel is subject to §1 scrutiny.

In the health care context, suppose a malpractice insurance company owned and operated by obstetricians were to deny coverage to a doctor because he worked with midwives. There would be no conspiracy if the company simply thought the doctor posed an excessive insurance risk, but a conspiracy would exist if the corporate actors were motivated by an outside interest unrelated to the concerns of insurance, namely to suppress competition from midwives.[6] Likewise, the threshold issue in hospital or HMO exclusion cases is whether the economic interest that medical staff members have in competition with excluded practitioners (and with each other) results in the concerted behavior required to invoke Sherman Act §1. If not, a claim must be stated under Sherman Act §2 concerning monopolization. Its elements are more restrictive and are covered only briefly in these materials.

2. *Unreasonable Restraint of Trade.* If concerted action is present, then the core substantive question becomes whether the challenged conduct results in an

6. These facts are suggested by Nurse Midwifery Associates v. Hibbett, 918 F.2d 605 (6th Cir. 1990), which found allegations similar to these to be sufficient to go to trial.

unreasonable restraint of trade. This is a complex and difficult inquiry, one that is not capable of completely accurate summation. Nevertheless, some preliminary analysis is useful before encountering the case law. First, observe that the language of the Sherman Act provides no useful guidance; it prohibits "*every* contract . . . in restraint of trade," which, taken literally, is an impossibility since *every* contract in fact restrains trade at least to some small extent by precluding the contracting parties from dealing with someone else for the subject matter of the contract. To make sense of the statute, courts have found it necessary to add a judicial gloss so that it prohibits only *unreasonable* restraints of trade. This generates what is known as the "rule of reason" test of illegality: A restraint is illegal only if its anticompetitive harms outweigh its procompetitive benefits. Such a finding often requires a complex, lengthy, and expensive inquiry. To avoid engaging in this burdensome undertaking in every case, the courts have crafted what is known as the "per se rule" of illegality: Certain restraints are automatically illegal if it is clear from their general nature that they are anticompetitive in the vast majority of situations. The primary example of per se illegality is horizontal price fixing, that is, price fixing among competitors.

In general, the *horizontal/vertical distinction* is crucial to characterizing and analyzing particular arrangements subject to antitrust challenge. A vertical arrangement is aligned up and down the chain of distribution for the good or service in question. A horizontal arrangement is one that exists among competitors at one level of this chain. For manufactured goods, the vertical chain is usually manufacturer-wholesaler-retailer. For medical services, the vertical alignment, generally speaking, is insurer-hospital-doctor. Practices or restraints that are only in a vertical alignment are, for the most part, much less of a concern for antitrust law because they are usually imposed by a single actor and they do not obviously restrain competition in the various affected horizontal levels. For instance, a manufacturer who restricts its dealers to certain cities or states so they don't compete with each other over its products imposes a vertical market division that enhances its ability to compete with other manufacturers. Therefore, it is judged under the rule of reason, whereas the same arrangement agreed to among the dealers themselves and imposed on the manufacturer would be a per se illegal horizontal market division.

In the context of medical staff disputes, plaintiffs attempt to invoke the rule of per se illegality for medical staff or network exclusion decisions by characterizing these decisions as both a horizontal and a vertical *group boycott* among the hospital and members of the medical staff, all of whom agree not to deal with the plaintiff. Unfortunately for litigants and for students of health care antitrust, there is considerable confusion about the precise application and boundaries of the per se rule against group boycotts. Despite several Supreme Court precedents declaring boycotts per se illegal, "exactly what types of activity fall within the forbidden category is . . . far from certain." Northwest Wholesale Stationers Inc. v. Pacific Stationery and Printing Co., 472 U.S. 284, 294 (1985). In this case, the Court explained that "the mere allegation of a concerted refusal to deal does not suffice because not all concerted refusals to deal are predominantly anticompetitive." Therefore, "a plaintiff seeking application of the per se rule must present a threshold case that the challenged activity falls into a category likely to have predominantly anticompetitive effects." Id. at 297. This intermediate stance between per se illegality and rule of reason balancing is sometimes known as the "quick look" approach, in that it requires the court to make an initial assessment of a practice's likely competitive impact before deciding which way to characterize it.[7] How this general directive might apply to medical staff disputes is the second principal issue explored in the following section.

When restraints are judged under the rule of reason, two key issues emerge in medical cases. The first is what role *quality of patient care* plays in proper antitrust analysis. There are several possibilities explored below. Enhanced quality of care could be a relevant competitive benefit to be weighed in the balance of competitive effects pro and con. Quality of care could also be viewed as a noneconomic benefit that outweighs the competitive harms from the restraint. Or, medical markets might be thought to be so infused with noneconomic quality concerns that they deserve a sweeping exemption or extraordinarily lenient scrutiny under antitrust laws. You will see from the readings below that considerable confusion still reigns over these central questions.

A related point of confusion is whether the competitive impact of a restraint is to be judged more by the parties' *subjective motivation and purpose,* or instead by the likely *effects* of their actions. Black-letter law states that actual probable effects, not intent, should control the analysis, such that a good intent will not save a bad act nor will a bad intent impugn a harmless act. Nevertheless, courts still frequently place great weight on subjective intent, either in predicting the restraint's likely effects or in deciding how to characterize the nature of the restraint (e.g., as vertical vs. horizontal, or as price fixing vs. refusal to deal). Often, motive comes strongly into play in distinguishing "ancillary" from "naked" restraints. An ancillary restraint is one that occurs as a side effect of pursuing a primarily procompetitive purpose, whereas a naked restraint occurs where the core purpose of the activity is anticompetitive. For instance, a hospital or HMO that excludes chiropractors from the

7. In a major 5-4 decision, California Dental Ass'n v. FTC, 526 U.S. 756 (1999), excerpted at page 330, the Supreme Court created considerable confusion about the appropriate standard of review in health care antitrust cases and in Sherman Act §1 cases generally. The FTC and the Ninth Circuit had ruled that it was illegal for the California Dental Association to ban most forms of price and quality information in advertising by dentists. (For instance, dentists could not claim in general terms that they offer discounted prices or are especially good with children.) This ban was struck down using both the per se rule and a "quick look" version of the rule of reason, finding no plausible pro-competitive justifications asserted for conduct that otherwise appeared to be a restraint of trade. The Supreme Court reversed and remanded for further consideration, holding that neither the per se rule, the full-blown rule of reason, nor the particular version of the "quick look" standard of review used in this case were appropriate in this particular case. Instead, the Court wanted to see a "less quick look" than had been given, explaining that each case requires "an enquiry meet for the case, looking to a restraint's circumstances, details, and logic." The Court appears to be saying that the standard of review and the burden of proof in §1 cases do not fall into discrete categories but must be viewed as a continuum in which the standard and burden are adjusted to the particulars of each case, at least for categories of cases that have not yet received clear Supreme Court pronouncements. Needless to say, this makes it even more difficult to predict how particular arrangements and activities will be evaluated by the courts or the antitrust enforcement agencies in the future. See Marina Lao, The Rule of Reason and Horizontal Restraints Involving Professionals, 68 Antitrust L.J. 499 (2000).

medical staff might be viewed as engaging in either a naked or an ancillary restraint depending on how one conceives of its primary purpose: making it more difficult for alternative providers to compete with M.D.s, or protecting its own reputation by not associating with nonphysicians. Naked restraints are obviously much harder to defend.

Yet another generic analytical issue that is critical in health care antitrust is *market power.* A given arrangement creates greater or lesser anticompetitive concerns according to the power that the parties have to raise prices, restrict output, or lower quality. If they lack this power, competitive forces will discipline any adverse consequences because the offenders will lose business to other firms—either those presently in the market or those that might enter in order to exploit the competitive opportunity created by the restraint. Therefore, market power—measured in terms of market share and barriers to market entry—is critical to assessing the likely effects of a restraint of trade. Courts increasingly are ruling that, under the rule of reason, defendants need not offer any justification for their behavior whatsoever unless the plaintiff makes a threshold showing of market power.

The easiest way to gauge market power is to measure the actor's market share. Market power tends to increase the smaller or more compact the market is. Therefore, a given restraint is worse when the market within which it occurs is smaller because it has a larger proportionate impact. *Defining the relevant market* is therefore critical to deciding many antitrust cases. Markets are defined in two dimensions: the relevant product (or service) and the relevant geography. Medical markets tend to be small and highly concentrated because service delivery is inherently local and because hospitals are large dominant institutions. Thus, it is easy to imagine a market for hospital services with only a single hospital. Simply put, this is a monopoly and so, by definition, anything the hospital does has serious competitive consequences because it enjoys extreme market power. Therefore, defendants in many health care antitrust cases struggle to characterize the market in terms that enlarge its *geographic or product scope.* They also attempt to show that, despite large market share, their market power is diminished by unique attributes of medical markets.

3. *Interstate Commerce.* Because antitrust litigation is usually long, complex, expensive, high stakes, and of an uncertain outcome, defendants are eager to find defects in the plaintiff's case that avoid trial or even discovery. The elements of the action just summarized rarely result in dismissing a claim at the pleadings stage. Therefore, a more forceful defense is to claim absence of federal jurisdiction. In order for federal antitrust jurisdiction to attach, a restraint must have a substantial effect on interstate commerce. Initially, this requirement too was controversial in this body of law because health care delivery, like other types of personal service, appears inherently local in nature, in contrast with the manufacture and distribution of products. The Supreme Court resolved, however, that a competitive impact on even small local medical markets has interstate effects because reimbursement, equipment, and supplies frequently cross state lines, even if patients do not. Summit Health v. Pinhas, 500 U.S. 322 (1991). Also, even if federal jurisdiction were lacking, most states have antitrust statutes similar to the federal laws, and some state attorneys general are notably active in enforcing these laws.

Still, courts often have a strong instinct that a single doctor should not be able to make a federal case out of a staffing decision at a single hospital or HMO. This instinct can express itself in some of the standard defenses outlined above or in other, somewhat more obscure, defenses summarized in the notes following these cases.

1. *Medical Staff Boycotts*

WEISS v. YORK HOSPITAL
745 F.2d 786 (3d Cir. 1984)

BECKER, Circuit Judge.

This antitrust case arises from the refusal to grant hospital staff privileges to a physician. The plaintiff, Malcolm Weiss, is an osteopath[2] who was denied staff privileges at York (Pennsylvania) Hospital. Dr. Weiss brought this suit, both individually and as representative of the class of all osteopathic physicians in the York Medical Service Area (York MSA), against York Hospital (York), the York Medical and Dental Staff, and ten individual physicians who served on the York Medical Staff Executive Committee and the York Judicial Review Committee. York is controlled by, and, at the time Dr. Weiss applied for staff privileges, was exclusively staffed by doctors who graduated from allopathic medical schools.[3]

The gravamen of Weiss' lawsuit is that, although allopaths (hereinafter referred to as medical doctors or M.D.s) and osteopaths (D.O.s) are equally trained and qualified to practice medicine,[4] his application for staff privileges at York

2. Dorland's Illustrated Medical Dictionary defines Osteopathy as

> a system of therapy . . . based on the theory that the body is capable of making its own remedies against disease. . . . It utilizes generally accepted physical, medicinal and surgical methods of diagnosis while placing chief emphasis on the importance of normal body mechanics and manipulative methods of detecting and correcting faulty structure.

Osteopathic physicians signify their degree as D.O. [See Joel Howell, The Paradox of Osteopathy, 341 New Eng. J. Med. 1465 (1999).—EDS.]

3. Allopathy is defined as a system of remedial treatment in which it is sought to cure a disease by producing, through medicines, a condition incompatible with the disease. See Funk & Wagnalls New Standard Dictionary of the English Language (1942). Allopathy constitutes the common or "regular" system of medical practice. Allopathic doctors, signify their degree as M.D.

4. At trial Dr. Merle S. Bacastow, an M.D. and the Vice-President of Medical Affairs at York, testified that at least since the mid-1960s there has been no difference in terms of medical training and ability to provide medical care between graduates of osteopathic medical schools and graduates of allopathic medical schools. This observation is born out by the fact that osteopaths and allopaths are equally qualified for state licensure to practice medicine and surgery within the Commonwealth of Pennsylvania. . . . See also Blackstone, The A.M.A. and The Osteopaths: A Study of the Power of Organized Medicine, 22 Antitrust Bulletin 405, 408-414 (1977). Professor Blackstone concludes that in general D.O.s receive somewhat shorter, less expensive, and less specialized training than today's highly specialized M.D.s. He states that this difference may justify limitations on the privileges of osteopaths that are similar to limitations

hospital was turned down solely because of his status as an osteopath. . . . In Weiss' submission, this scheme to exclude D.O.s from York Hospital was motivated by a desire to restrict the ability of D.O.s to compete with M.D.s, thereby increasing the profits of the M.D.s. [The jury found that the medical staff, but not the hospital, violated §1 of the Sherman Act.] . . .

II. The Facts

A. Hospital Services in the York MSA

There are two providers of in-patient hospital services in the York MSA: York, which is run by M.D.s, and Memorial Hospital (Memorial), which is run by D.O.s. York is by far the larger of the two, with approximately 450 beds and 2,500 employees. Memorial has 160 beds. The testimony at trial established that York had a market share of 80 percent of the patient-days of hospitalization in the York MSA.

In addition to York's overall market dominance, testimony at trial established that certain complex, highly technical "tertiary care" services and facilities are, for a number of reasons, only available at York. Included among the services offered only at York are therapeutic radiology, open heart surgery, cardiac catheterization, renal dialysis, neo-natal intensive care, short-term acute psychiatric care, monitored stroke treatment, audiology, burn care, cardiopulmonary laboratory, cardiopulmonary rehabilitation, electroencephalography, genetic counseling, prosthetic service, speech therapy, computerized axial tomography (CAT scan), and infusion aspirator. . . .

[I]n early 1976, Weiss and another osteopath named Dr. Michael Zittle, both of whom were engaged in family practice in the York MSA, applied for staff privileges at York. Dr. Weiss informed representatives of the York medical staff that if York excluded him because of his osteopathic training he would institute legal action.

The York medical staff considered the applications and Weiss' threat of legal action, and in November of 1976 amended its bylaws to permit admission of osteopaths at York. Dr. Weiss contends that the amendment of the bylaws was purely cosmetic, and that since 1976 the York medical staff has engaged in a deliberate covert policy of discrimination against osteopaths. . . .

---

imposed upon general practice M.D.s and family practitioners, but that it would not seem to justify the total exclusion of osteopaths. See id. at 411; Kissam, Webber, Bigers, and Holzgraefe, Antitrust and Hospital Privileges: Testing the Conventional Wisdom, 70 Calif. L. Rev. 595, 641 n.218 (1982) [hereinafter cited as Antitrust and Hospital Privileges]; Dolan & Ralston, Hospital Admitting Privileges and the Sherman Act, 18 Houston L. Rev. 707, 728 (1981) ("Osteopaths undergo training regimens quite similar to that of M.D. practitioners, except that greater emphasis is placed on family practice and on some manipulative practices. Regardless of the situation 30 years ago, it is highly unlikely that any significant qualitative difference between the two groups exists today."). [See also Enders, Federal Antitrust Issues Involved in the Denial of Medical Staff Privileges, 17 Loy. U. Chi. L.J. 331 (1986).—Eds.]

D. DOCTOR WEISS' APPLICATION FOR STAFF PRIVILEGES

In 1976 Doctors Weiss and Zittle applied for staff privileges in York's Family Practice Department. In accordance with the procedures outlined above, the Family Practice Department Credentials Committee and the chairman of the Family Practice Department considered the applications. On January 17, 1977, the department recommended that they be accepted. The Medical Staff Credentials Committee then reviewed the applications and also recommended acceptance. The Medical Staff Executive Committee, however, did not approve either application. Instead, it took the unusual step of deciding to conduct a further investigation. The Committee made extensive oral and written inquiries concerning the professional competence and moral character of both Weiss and Zittle. No such survey had ever before been conducted by the hospital before. Ultimately the investigation turned up some questions about Dr. Weiss' personality. The investigation also raised some glimmer of a question about Dr. Weiss' medical competence, but the sole "evidence" that was adduced was hearsay, often second or third level hearsay. Nevertheless, the Medical Staff Executive Committee, apparently based on this "new evidence," decided not to recommend Weiss for staff privileges.

On June 30, 1977, the hospital Board of Directors considered the recommendations of the various committees which had considered Weiss' and Zittle's applications. The board voted to approve Zittle's application and deny Weiss' application. . . . The Credentials Committee's written report is revealing in both its assessment of the "evidence" against Weiss, and in its frank recognition of the "controversy" at York over the admission of D.O.s to staff privileges:

The Committee invited Dr. Weiss to discuss the reactivation of his application and to direct certain questions to him. He was told of the developments in the past and precisely how his application has been handled and of the problems that had arisen. He was specifically told that almost everybody with whom we spoke acknowledged him to be an intelligent, competent, conscientious physician whose care of his patients in the Hospital was quite competent. He was told that the Chairman of his Department suggested that he probably was the best general practitioner. However, almost everyone to whom we spoke acknowledged that he has had personality problems in the past which have caused him to have difficult interpersonal relations with other members of the staff. He was told that because of this personality problem, his application was rejected. It was further explained to him that because of the controversy that accompanied the application of osteopaths to the York Hospital, it was felt that acceptance of his application would jeopardize that endeavor. We explained to Dr. Weiss that his admission to the staff would be met in some instances with outright hostility and in others with indifference and it was a matter of real concern to the Committee how he would react to this sort of reception. . . .

IV. The Sherman Act Claims

We now turn to the substantive-law questions presented by this appeal. . . .

A. SECTION 1 OF THE SHERMAN ACT

In order to establish a violation of §1 of the Sherman Act, 15 U.S.C. §1 (1982), a plaintiff must establish three elements: (1) a contract, combination, or conspiracy;

(2) restraint of trade; and (3) an effect on interstate commerce. Each of these three elements has been the subject of extensive analysis by the courts, and we now turn to a discussion of that case law and its application to the facts of this case, taking the elements up in turn.

1. Proof of an Agreement: Is There a Sufficient Number of Conspirators?

In order to establish a violation of §1, a plaintiff must prove that two or more distinct entities agreed to take action against the plaintiff. Before the district court, Weiss contended that the hospital and its medical staff were legally distinct entities and therefore capable of conspiring in violation of §1. He also asserted that the doctors who joined together to form the medical staff were separate economic entities who competed against each other so that, as a matter of law, the medical staff was a "combination" of doctors within the meaning of §1. Finally, Weiss argued that even if the individual doctors who made up York's medical staff were deemed by the court to be the equivalent of "officers or employees" of the hospital and therefore ordinarily not capable of conspiring with the hospital, nevertheless the doctors were acting for their own benefit in discriminating against osteopaths, and therefore fell within an exception to the ordinary rule that "officers or employees of the same firm do not provide the plurality of actors imperative for a §1 conspiracy." Copperweld Corp. v. Independence Tube Corp., 467 U.S. 752 (1984).

The district court concluded, and instructed the jury, that the medical staff was an "unincorporated division" of the hospital, and as such the two were legally a "single entity" incapable of conspiring. . . . However, . . . the district court held the defendant medical staff liable to the plaintiff class under §1. On the question who conspired with the medical staff, the court stated only:

> The York Hospital Medical and Dental Staff conspired with another person or entity to deny or impede reasonable, fair, equal, and full access to staff privileges at York Hospital by osteopathic physicians other than Plaintiff Weiss.

We agree with the plaintiffs that, as a matter of law, the medical staff is a combination of individual doctors and therefore that any action taken by the medical staff satisfies the "contract, combination, or conspiracy" requirement of §1. . . .

Antitrust policy requires the courts to seek the economic substance of an arrangement, not merely its form. The "substance" of an arrangement often depends on the economic incentive of the parties. The York medical staff is a group of doctors, all of whom practice medicine in their individual capacities, and each of whom is an independent economic entity in competition with other doctors in the York medical community. Each staff member, therefore, has an economic interest separate from and in many cases in competition with the interests of other medical staff members. Under these circumstances, the medical staff cannot be considered a single economic entity for purposes of antitrust analysis. . . . In substance, the medical staff is a group of individual doctors in competition with each other and with other physicians in the York MSA, who have organized to regulate the provision of medical care at York hospital. Where such associations exist, their actions are subject to scrutiny under §1 of the Sherman Act in order to insure that their members do not abuse otherwise legitimate organizations to secure an unfair advantage over their competitors. . . .

Finally, we deal with the plaintiff's assertion that the district court erred in charging the jury that the hospital could not conspire with its medical staff. The district court found that the medical staff was an unincorporated division of the hospital, and as such the court determined that the two could not conspire. Although we do not necessarily agree with the district court's characterization of the medical staff as an unincorporated division of the hospital, we agree with its basic conclusion that, with respect to the issues in this case, the hospital could not, as a matter of law, conspire with the medical staff. The medical staff was empowered to make staff privilege decisions on behalf of the hospital. As such, with regard to these decisions, the medical staff operated as an officer of a corporation would in relation to the corporation. Although the members of the medical staff had independent economic interests in competition with each other, the staff as an entity had no interest in competition with the hospital. Accordingly, we conclude that the district court correctly charged the jury that there could not be a conspiracy between the hospital and the medical staff.

2. *Proof of Restraint of Trade*

a. Introduction

Read literally, §1 prohibits every agreement "in restraint of trade." In United States v. Joint Traffic Ass'n, 171 U.S. 505, 19 S. Ct. 25, 43 L. Ed. 259 (1898), the Supreme Court recognized that Congress could not have intended a literal interpretation of the word *every*, and since Standard Oil Co. of New Jersey v. United States, 221 U.S. 1, 31 S. Ct. 502, 55 L. Ed. 619 (1911), courts have analyzed most restraints under the so-called rule of reason. As its name suggests, the rule of reason requires the factfinder to decide whether, under all the circumstances of the case, the restrictive practice imposes an unreasonable restraint on competition.[52]

The courts have also, however, applied a rule of per se illegality to certain types of business practices. The development of per se rules has resulted from a recognition that the case-by-case approach inherent in the rule of reason has significant costs, and that certain types of business practices almost always have anticompetitive effects without offsetting pro-competitive effects. In applying the per

52. Justice Brandeis provided the classic statement of the rule of reason in Board of Trade of City of Chicago v. United States, 246 U.S. 231, 238, 38 S. Ct. 242, 244, 62 L. Ed. 683 (1918):

> The true test of legality is whether the restraint imposed is such as merely regulates and perhaps thereby promotes competition or whether it is such as may suppress or even destroy competition. To determine that question the court must ordinarily consider the facts peculiar to the business to which the restraint was imposed; its condition before and after the restraint and its effect; the nature of the restraint and its effect, actual or probable. The history of the restraint, the evil believed to exist, the reason for adopting the particular remedy, the purpose or end sought to be attained, are all relevant facts.

se rules, a court eschews the ordinary evaluation of the effect of the challenged practice, and concentrates instead on the question whether the practice falls within one of the categories of practices condemned by the per se rule. In this case, the plaintiffs argued that the actions of the defendants were the equivalent of a boycott, or as it is sometimes called, a concerted refusal to deal, and thus illegal per se. We now turn to that inquiry.

b. Is Defendants' Exclusionary Conduct the Equivalent of a Concerted Refusal to Deal ("Boycott")?

The jury found that the defendants had engaged in a policy of discrimination against Dr. Weiss and the other D.O.s in the York MSA by applying unfair, unequal, and unreasonable procedures in reviewing their applications. In addition, the district court concluded that this unfair, unreasonable, and unequal treatment "could reasonably be anticipated [by the defendants] to cause osteopathic physicians to refrain from applying for staff privileges at the York Hospital." The question before us is whether these actions should properly be characterized as a "group boycott" or "concerted refusal to deal," in which case they are illegal per se under §1. If the defendants' actions cannot be so characterized, the rule of reason analysis would apply and the outcome of the case could be different. We conclude that the defendants' actions, as found in the district court, are the equivalent of a concerted refusal to deal.

The classic example of a concerted refusal to deal is the situation in which businesses at one level of production or distribution, e.g., retailers, use the threat of a boycott to induce businesses at another level, e.g., manufacturers, not to deal with competitors of the retailers. As Professor Sullivan has observed, "The boycotting group members, in effect, say to their suppliers or to their customers, 'If you don't stop dealing with non-group members, we will stop dealing with you.' If continued trade with group members is more important to a supplier or customer than is trading with non-group members, this threat will be effective." L. Sullivan, Handbook of the Law of Antitrust §83, at 230 (1977).

In this case York is a provider of hospital services; for the purpose of our analysis, the equivalent of the manufacturer in the example of a classical boycott. Similarly, the M.D.s are the equivalent of the retailers in the example, in the sense that physicians require access to a hospital in order to effectively treat patients. The difficulty with this analogy, at first blush, is that there is no evidence that the M.D.s have used coercion for the purpose of inducing York to exclude their competitors, the D.O.s. . . . In this case, however, because of the M.D.s' control over York's admission decisions, no coercion is necessary. . . .

[At this point, the court's opinion becomes somewhat confused. The following explanation may help to clarify the issues: The paradigm boycott case involves a "secondary boycott" (i.e., a boycott aimed at one party in order to exclude or discipline a third party) because competitors usually lack any ready means to boycott the target firm directly. A classic secondary boycott would have occurred here if the medical staff had threatened to leave the hospital if Dr. Weiss were admitted. An ordinary medical staff exclusion case differs from this paradigm only because doctors don't need to use this indirect threat if they possess the ability to keep out the unwanted practitioner themselves, that is, to engage in primary rather than a secondary boycott. — Eds.]

We recognize that the facts of this case do not precisely fit into the mold of the classical refusal to deal. The refusal to deal is less than total insofar as York admitted Dr. Zittle and a number of other osteopaths. Arguably then, what is at issue is not a boycott but mere discrimination, which sounds less like a per se antitrust violation. However, given the evidence of the different standards applied to osteopaths and M.D.s and the second-class citizenship afforded D.O.s upon admission to staff privileges at York, and in view of the adverse impact of these factors upon D.O. applications for York staff privileges, we are satisfied that the restrictive policy is, in purpose and effect, sufficiently close to the traditional boycott, that the characterization is appropriate.

The Medical Staff is, however, entitled to exclude individual doctors, including osteopaths, on the basis of their lack of professional competence or unprofessional conduct. If York's policy toward D.O.'s could be viewed as a form of industry self-regulation of this type, the rule of reason, rather than a per se rule, would be applicable. See generally L. Sullivan, Handbook of the Law of Antitrust §§86-88 (1977). We recognize, therefore, that in many cases involving exclusion from staff privilege, courts will, more or less openly, have to utilize a rule of reason balancing approach. This case is different, however, because York has not contended that osteopaths as a group are less qualified than M.D.s. See supra n.4. In the absence of such a contention, or another legitimate explanation for the discrimination, we conclude that a per se rule should be applied, since the effect of the practice is identical to that of the traditional boycott, and plainly anticompetitive.

Congruent with the foregoing discussion, the Supreme Court has adopted an exception to application of the per se rule of illegality where the case involves a learned profession and where the restriction is justified on "public service or ethical norm" grounds. Thus, unlike most cases where characterization of some activity as a classical boycott ends the inquiry, here, because the medical profession is involved, the rule of reason analysis may still control, as a "built-in" exception. We now turn to a discussion of this potential "escape hatch" to see if it can extricate the defendants from the "cut" of the per se rule.

c. The "Learned Profession" Exception

In Goldfarb v. Virginia State Bar, 421 U.S. 773, 788 n.17, (1975), in which the Supreme Court made clear that the medical profession is not exempt from the antitrust laws, the Court stated that the "public service aspect, and other features of the professions, may require that a particular practice, which could properly be viewed as a violation of the Sherman Act in another context, be treated differently." In Arizona v. Maricopa County Medical Society, 457 U.S. 332, 348-349 (1982), the Court partially explained this exception by stating that conduct which is normally subject to per se condemnation under §1 will instead be subject to rule of reason analysis where the challenged conduct is "premised on public service or ethical norms." In *Maricopa,* because the defendants did not attempt to justify their price fixing arrangements on either of these grounds, but instead attempted to argue that the maximum price levels were pro-competitive, the Court held that the per se rule controlled and consequently found that the defendants' conduct violated §1.

In this case, the defendants have offered no "public service or ethical norm" rationale for their discriminatory treatment of D.O.s. Indeed, their defense at trial was that they did not discriminate against D.O.s. Since the jury believed otherwise, we conclude that the per se rule governs this case. . . .[61]

V. Conclusion

In summary, we reach the following conclusions. First, we find that the district court's decision that the medical staff violated Sherman Act §1 as to the plaintiff class is supported by sufficient evidence, and we therefore will affirm the district court on this point. . . . [W]e also agree that the issuance of an injunction by the district court in this case was proper.

■ HASSAN v. INDEPENDENT PRACTICE ASSOCIATES

698 F. Supp. 679 (E.D. Mich. 1988)

Newblatt, District Judge.

Before the court are defendants' Motion for Summary Judgment. . . . Plaintiffs Shawky Hassan and Fikria Hassan are allergists who practice through the Allergy

61. Several circuit court opinions have held the rule of reason analysis, not the per se rule of illegality, controls in boycott cases involving the learned professions. We believe these cases are readily distinguishable from the instant case. In Wilk v. American Medical Ass'n, 719 F.2d 207 (7th Cir. 1983), a case involving the refusal of M.D.s to deal with chiropractors, the Seventh Circuit stated: "[B]oycotts are illegal per se only if used to enforce agreements that are themselves illegal per se—for example price fixing agreements." Id. at 221 (quoting Marrese v. American Academy of Orthopaedic Surgeons, 706 F.2d 1488, 1495 (7th Cir. 1983)). Since the court could find no per se illegal purpose for the A.M.A.'s medical ethics principle 3, which in essence provided that M.D.'s should not associate with chiropractors, it concluded that the rule of reason analysis governed in that case. We believe that the Seventh Circuit was correct in utilizing a rule of reasons analysis in the *Wilk* case because the defendants were plainly asserting a "public service or ethical norm" justification for their concerted refusal to deal with chiropractors. In Virginia Academy of Clinical Psychologists v. Blue Shield of Va., 624 F.2d 476, 484-485 (4th Cir. 1980), the Fourth Circuit stated: "Because of the special considerations involved in the delivery of health services, we are not prepared to apply a per se rule of illegality to medical plans which refuse or condition payments to competing or potentially competing providers." . . . [A] "medical necessity" justification was apparently raised by the defendants, and in our view that would have been sufficient to bring the defendants within the purview of Maricopa's exception for conduct based on "public service or ethical norms." Finally, in Kreuzer v. American Academy of Periodontology, 735 F.2d 1479 (D.C. Cir. 1984), the D.C. Circuit Court held that the rule of reason analysis governed a §1 challenge to a rule promulgated by the American Academy of Periodontology (AAP) that limited membership in the AAP to licensed dentists who practice periodontics exclusively, and who do not practice other forms of dentistry. The court labeled the effect of the AAP's rule a "group boycott" but concluded that "[w]hen a conspiracy of this sort is alleged in the context of one of the learned professions, the nature and extent of its anticompetitive effect are often too uncertain to be amendable to per se treatment." . . . [See also Betkerur v. Aultman Hospital Ass'n, 78 F.3d 1079 (6th Cir. 1996) (no per se horizontal boycott existed where independent obstetricians agreed to designate one neonatologist for most of their referrals; the relationship between the two kinds of doctors was vertical, not horizontal, and no economic motives were apparent).—Eds.]

& Asthma Center, P.C., a professional corporation wholly owned by the Drs. Hassan. Defendant Independent Practice Associates, P.C., (IPA) is an organization of physicians and osteopaths who provide medical care to subscribers of Genesee Health Care, Inc., doing business as Health Plus of Michigan (Health Plus), a state licensed, federally qualified health maintenance organization (HMO). . . . Plaintiffs allege . . . that IPA's participation in plaintiffs' separation from IPA and the group's subsequent refusal to readmit the doctors, constitute an illegal group boycott. . . .

IPA is the corporation through which the group of doctors that treat patients who subscribe to Health Plus practice. It is owned by the physicians who comprise the group. Health Plus, the HMO insurance contractor here, was formed by the Genesee County Medical Society in 1979. Its Board of Directors is made up of subscribers, the public and physicians. Health Plus is funded by subscribers who pay a fixed premium per month. With this money, Health Plus pays service providers, such as IPA, on a computed basis and also a fixed amount per member per month. IPA members are paid primarily on a fee-for-services basis, which the IPA determines according to a set maximum fee schedule. . . .

Defendants concede that IPA exists only to serve Health Plus patients. . . . Health Plus has experienced substantial growth since 1979 and its patient market share is 20 percent of the population in the area of Genesee-Lapeer-Shiawassee counties. . . . There is no evidence that IPA physicians cannot also belong to other such organizations.

Defendants contend that they face a competitive market. For example, they contend that the largest portion of Health Plus's membership is represented by General Motors (GM) employees. In order to obtain the GM business, defendants must compete on an annual basis by obtaining both GM and UAW approval as an authorized insurer and then, further, convince the employees to choose the Health Plus program. Thus, GM, the union, and the workers must be satisfied as to both price charged and benefits offered. . . . This has resulted in actions [to cut costs such as] denying physicians' applications for membership and terminations or resignations of physicians. . . .

Plaintiffs joined IPA in 1979, and until October of 1981, they were the only allergy specialists to provide such service to Health Plus subscribers. In 1980, a review of billing records revealed a high incidence of lab tests performed by plaintiffs and prompted the IPA's Care, Quality and Cost Committee to request justification for those tests from plaintiff Shawky Hassan. Moreover, the Committee began setting guidelines for allergy testing which prohibited routine testing. Further, in October of 1981, an IPA survey of allergy testing procedures indicated that plaintiffs performed far more tests than two other specialists, and a review of patient charts failed to satisfy the IPA that the Hassans' level of testing was justified. . . .

Health Plus sent out a notice that subscribers could no longer see the Drs. Hassan. . . . In August of 1983, the Hassans applied to IPA on behalf of their newly established Urgent Care Family Clinic to provide emergency care to IPA members. . . . On January 6, 1984, all of plaintiffs' applications were denied without explanation. The Hassan Clinic lost money and, in 1985, it was closed. . . .

1. Was There a Conspiracy?

. . . [E]ach physician in IPA has a practice or other profession independent of IPA or Health Plus. The inferences from the undisputed facts lead the court to the conclusion that there is at least a question of fact as to whether there was a conspiracy to exclude plaintiffs from IPA. First, Health Plus was created by physicians, the Genesee County Medical Society, who are members of IPA. Moreover, although IPA members may not dominate the Health Plus Board of Directors, one third of its members belong to IPA. . . . [T]here is at least an inference which must be viewed in a light most favorable to plaintiffs, that IPA members have effective control. . . .

2. Is There a Per Se Violation?

Defendants next argue that Northwest Wholesale Stationers, Inc. v. Pacific Stationery Printing, Co., 472 U.S. 284 (1985) precludes treatment of this case under the per se illegal group boycott rule. . . . In *Northwest Wholesale Stationers,* . . . a cooperative buying agency expelled a member without procedural means for challenging the expulsion.[40] . . . The Court [refused to apply the per se categorization, explaining: "A plaintiff seeking application of the per se rule must present a threshold case that the challenged activity falls into a category likely to have predominantly anticompetitive effects. The mere allegation of a concerted refusal to deal does not suffice because not all concerted refusals to deal are predominantly anticompetitive."] . . . Thus, the court in *Northwest Wholesalers* required that, [before invoking the per se rule], those plaintiffs . . . make a threshold showing (1) whether that practice is [not] justified by plausible arguments that it is intended to enhance overall efficiency and make markets more competitive; and (2) a showing that defendant possesses—(a) market power, and (b) exclusive access to an element essential to effective competition. . . .

The court agrees with defendants that the acts of expulsion and the refusal to readmit plaintiffs are justified by enhancing efficiency and making the market more competitive. First, despite plaintiffs' counsel's contentions at the hearing, the record shows that plaintiffs do not dispute the fact that IPA adopted its allergy testing policy to prevent excessive use of costly tests and that plaintiffs disagreed with this policy. It is also undisputed that cost containment objectives are procompetitive. . . .

Although plaintiffs contend that defendants' decisions or policies as to allergy testing were incorrect, that is irrelevant. The issue is not whether the decisions were correct but "whether there are plausible arguments that they were intended to enhance overall efficiency and make markets more competitive." Northwest, 472 U.S. 284 at 294. . . . Finally, plaintiffs contend that the decision to deny membership to plaintiffs was made by primary care physicians who were interested in providing allergy care themselves. Not only is there no evidence of this, but allegations that defendants' motives were manifestly anticompetitive are more properly considered under a rule of reason analysis. . . .

[As for market power,] 20 percent market share is not sufficient market power in light of the competition from other providers in the relevant market. However,

40. Northwest was a purchasing cooperative of approximately 100 office supply retailers which acted as a primary wholesaler for the retailers. In 1978, members of Northwest voted to expel Pacific, offering no explanation at the time nor giving Pacific notice, a hearing, or any other opportunity to challenge the decision. Pacific contended that the expulsion was a group boycott and a per se violation of §1.

market share does not always indicate whether a firm really has market power. Therefore, other factors must also be examined and these support defendants' position.

First, there are no significant barriers to entry into this market—that is, the market for health care finance.[47] In Ball Memorial Hosp., Inc. v. Mutual Hosp. Ins., 784 F.2d 1325, 1335 (6th Cir. 1986), the Seventh Circuit stated that:

> The insurance industry is not like the steel industry, in which a firm must take years to build a costly plant before having anything to sell. The "productive asset" of the insurance business is money, which may be supplied on a moment's notice, plus the ability to spread risk, which many firms possess and which has no geographic boundary. In this case, defendants' expert has stated in his affidavit that any health care insurer in Michigan may serve patients in this market. Plaintiffs have not identified any barriers to entry and, in fact, Greater Flint HMO and PPO, Trust, have recently entered the market.

. . . Plaintiffs, however, argue that defendants have market power through the percentage of physicians (75 percent) in this market who are members of IPA. . . . The authority they cite does not apply because it is concerned with a different problem—that of deterring the establishment of new HMOs. Those concerns would only come into play if IPA was able to affiliate with physicians on an exclusive basis. There is simply nothing in the record to indicate that IPA physicians are not free to affiliate with other providers.[50] . . . Accordingly, plaintiffs are not entitled to a finding of per se illegality.

3. Rule of Reason

Defendants next contend that there is no unreasonable restraint of trade as no significant anticompetitive effect has resulted from the plaintiffs' expulsion or resignation, and subsequent rejection for readmittance, from IPA. The test under the rule of reason is whether competition in the overall market has been harmed, the antitrust laws not having been intended to protect merely individual competitors. . . .

In this case, the undisputed facts indicate that there has been no anticompetitive impact on the overall market. First, as indicated above, IPA does not have significant market power. . . . Even assuming that defendants did have the requisite market power, there is no evidence that the exclusion of plaintiffs had an impact on

47. Although plaintiffs contend that the relevant market is the "prepaid market share," which includes only HMOs, the relevant market "consists of the . . . services with which defendants' product competes." In this case, Health Plus must compete with the other sources of health care financing. . . .

50. If there was exclusive affiliation, there would be a barrier to entry. [It can be seen from this discussion that antitrust law favors physicians contracting with networks on a non-mutually exclusive basis or under contracts of very short duration. However, another body of law regulating "referral fees" is hostile to these types of contracts.—Eds.]

overall competition . . . because the substitution of one company for another "does not limit competition in any substantial sense." . . .

The plaintiffs' expulsion or departure from IPA was followed (or shortly preceded) by the admittance of two new allergists. . . . Moreover, there is no indication that plaintiffs left the market, so the end result is that the public has just as many allergists from which to choose. Even if the plaintiffs were to leave the tri-county market, there is no reason to believe that they would not be easily replaced so that the market would be served by enough allergists. . . . Finally, competition is not harmed because there are a sufficient number of allergists and primary care physicians who can provide allergy services in the tri-county area. . . .

Next, plaintiffs claim that defendants' motives in excluding plaintiffs from IPA were anticompetitive.[56] Plaintiffs present no evidence of an anticompetitive motive other than that several doctors, primary care physicians who were involved in the decision stood to benefit from plaintiffs' exclusion. Not only does this ignore the fact that several allergists were admitted shortly before and after plaintiffs' expulsion, but it also ignores the rule of reason's requirement of injury to overall competition, not just to individual competitors. Thus, plaintiffs have failed to satisfy the requirements under the rule of reason. . . .

Having disposed of all plaintiffs' claims, judgment in this case shall hereby be entered for defendants.

Notes: Medical Staff Boycotts; Exclusion from Managed Care Networks

1. *Medical Staff Conspiracies. Weiss* ruled that all physicians participating in a medical staff credentialing decision constitute a "walking conspiracy" as a matter of law. Granted that some physicians on the York Hospital medical staff have an independent interest in competition with Dr. Weiss, is this true of neurosurgeons, pathologists, or specialists who are not engaged in a general practice? Even for those doctors who potentially are in direct competition—in Dr. Weiss' case, say, general and family practitioners—should the court find a conspiracy as a matter of law? Individual doctors might in fact ignore their competitive interests in making a staffing decision. Following *Weiss,* several courts have held that no conspiracy exists unless special facts are shown. In one, the court held that pediatricians who voted to exclude nurse midwives were acting merely as agents of a single hospital because nurse midwives compete only with obstetricians, not pediatricians. As for the obstetricians, conspiracy would not be presumed; the midwives must show at least the possibility that they acted for other than legitimate reasons. Nurse Midwifery Ass'n v. Hibbett, 918 F.2d 605 (6th Cir. 1990).

In contrast with its holding as a matter of law that a conspiracy existed *within* the medical staff, *Weiss* held that the medical staff *as an entity* cannot, as a matter of law, conspire with the hospital because it is part of the hospital. But if members of the medical staff conspire with each other by virtue of their independent stake in the decision, why not with the hospital as well? Compare Bolt v. Halifax

56. Plaintiffs rely on FTC v. Indiana Federation of Dentists, 476 U.S. 447 (1986), for the proposition that "where clear anticompetitive motives are present and no clear competitive benefits exist, an extended market analysis is not required."

Hospital Medical Center, 891 F.2d 810 (11th Cir. 1990) ("we hold that a hospital and the members of its medical staff are all legally capable of conspiring with one another" because "a hospital and the members of its medical staff are legally separate entities").

Which of these approaches best captures the realities of the hospital/medical staff relationship, the typical reasons for peer review, and who controls the decisionmaking? For a detailed analysis of these issues, see William Brewbaker, Antitrust Conspiracy Doctrine and the Hospital Enterprise, 74 B.U. L. Rev. 67 (1994) ("given the typical economic and managerial independence of physicians from hospitals, . . . [concerted action exists unless] it can be demonstrated that the medical staff acted in a purely advisory role").

2. *Monopolies.* Where concerted action is not found and Sherman Act §1 is not implicated, an antitrust claim might still be stated under various §2 theories covering unilateral refusals to deal. Usually, unilateral refusals are beyond reproach, even if the hospital or HMO enjoys a monopoly, because the antitrust laws do not proscribe monopolies per se, nor do they proscribe the lawful exercise of monopoly power rightfully obtained. Antitrust law prohibits only obtaining monopoly power in certain unfair ways, or abusing that power in certain ways. Depending on the circumstances, a monopolist's unilateral refusal to deal might be considered abusive. However, understanding the qualifications embedded in the previous two sentences is largely beyond the scope of these materials. The one §2 theory of particular note for hospital exclusions is the "essential facilities doctrine." This is based on a smattering of cases holding that, where access to a particular facility is essential for others to compete, the facility must be offered to all competitors on fair and reasonable terms. This doctrine applies, however, only where the hospital in question enjoys a monopoly position in the market.

3. *Different Levels of Scrutiny.* In order for the *Weiss* court to impose a rule of per se illegality, it first characterized the medical staff's decision as a class-based exclusion of all osteopaths not premised on any quality-of-care justification. How strong is the evidence for this characterization? Consider that the medical staff did amend its bylaws to allow in osteopaths and it in fact extended privileges to Dr. Zittle, a D.O. who applied at the same time as Dr. Weiss. Consider also the stated justification relating to Dr. Weiss' personality.

Where the exclusion is not class-based but is directed unambiguously to the professional competence of a single practitioner, plaintiffs have rarely succeeded. *Weiss* is unique in applying a per se rule because the jury found that the hospital's justification for an individual exclusion was a pretext, and the hospital did not offer any justification for a class-based exclusion of all osteopaths (which it believed it had not engaged in but the jury found it had). When exclusions *are* premised on quality of care, the *Weiss* court concedes that the rule of reason applies. Although rule of reason cases are usually long and complex, in hospital disputes courts usually find ways to dismiss the case quickly, on the pleadings or on motion for summary judgment, without going to trial. As one court explained:

> The cases involving staffing at a single hospital are legion. Hundreds, perhaps thousands of pages in West publications are devoted to the issues those circumstances present. Those cases invariably analyze those circumstances under the rule of reason—there is nothing obviously anticompetitive about a hospital choosing

> one staffing pattern over another or in restricting the staffing to some rather than many, or all. A hospital has an unquestioned right to exercise some control over the identity and number to whom it accords staff privileges. Malpractice concerns, quality of care, market perceptions, cost, and administrative considerations may all impact those decisions. Those hundreds or thousands of pages almost always come to the same conclusion: the staffing decision at a single hospital was not a violation of §1 of the Sherman Act. [Citations to 28 cases omitted.]
>
> The reasons advanced for that conclusion are varied. Insufficient nexus to interstate commerce, lack of standing, lack of antitrust injury, failure to show a detrimental effect on competition, the inability of a hospital to conspire with its staff, and insufficient market power in the relevant market are among the reasons relied upon for denying section 1 relief. Sometimes the conclusion follows a motion to dismiss; more often the decision is one of summary judgment, but often it appears that the record relied upon is the absence of facts indicating special circumstances raising antitrust concerns. . . .
>
> Before we enlist this court in the micromanagement of the staffing arrangements at [this hospital] under the aegis of the antitrust laws, we need better reasons than the plaintiffs have given us. . . . "If the law were otherwise, many a physician's workplace grievance with a hospital would be elevated to the status of an antitrust action. To keep the antitrust laws from becoming so trivialized, the reasonableness of a restraint is evaluated based on its impact on competition as a whole within the relevant market." Oksanen v. Page Memorial Hospital, 945 F.2d 696, 708 (4th Cir. 1991).

BCB Anesthesia Care v. Passavant Memorial Area Hospital Ass'n, 36 F.3d 664 (7th Cir. 1994) (dismissing at the pleadings stage a complaint by three nurse anesthetists that the hospital conspired with a physician anesthetist to terminate their contract for anesthesiology services). This is consistent with a general trend in antitrust decisions toward making it easier for defendants to obtain summary judgment where the plaintiff's basic theory "simply makes no economic sense." Matsushita Electrical Industrial Co. v. Zenith Radio Corp., 475 U.S. 574 (1986).

A few courts since *Weiss* have found, however, that intensive review of hospitals' staffing decisions is justified under antitrust law. For example, one court reversed the grant of summary judgment to a hospital that excluded a doctor on quality grounds after he set up a competing clinic explaining:

> [Dr.] Miller contends that his hospital staff privileges were revoked and his applications for reinstatement denied because defendants wished to stifle his competition. He contends that . . . he was treated more severely than other physicians whose competence was in question but who presented no economic threat to the defendants. Defendants' argument that they revoked Miller's staff privileges because of his professional incompetence and unprofessional conduct is a defense they may present before the jury which, if convinced, will absolve them of any antitrust liability. It is inappropriate and unprecedented, however, to . . . defer to the manner in which defendants themselves, who are parties in interest, weighed the evidence and drew inferences.

Miller v. Indiana Hospital, 843 F.2d 139 (3d Cir. 1987). It appears from the remainder of the opinion that the court envisioned a de novo jury decision on the hospital's actual motives, not on the doctor's actual competence. Where the motives are more clearly appropriate, then courts are almost always deferential to the hospitals' assessment of competence. This pattern in the case law contrasts with frequent statements by the courts that legality is tested more by anticompetitive effects than by anticompetitive motives. On remand, the district court in *Miller* granted summary judgment to the hospital based on a lack of market impact, even though this was the only hospital in the county.

4. *Standing and Injury to Competition.* Courts at first expressed their hostility to hearing these antitrust disputes by finding no federal jurisdiction due to the lack of any impact on interstate commerce, but as summarized in the introduction, this route was closed off by the Supreme Court in 1991. Subsequently, courts have sometimes ruled based on lack of standing, holding that if there were any injury to competition, it would be suffered by patients or by hospitals, not by the excluded doctor. See Todorov v. DCH Healthcare Authority, 921 F.2d 1438 (10th Cir. 1991) (the reduced competition that theoretically might result from a hospital's exclusive contract for CT scans would injure only consumers, not the excluded neurologist; his only injury is the inability to share in the allegedly illegal profits); Balaklaw v. Lovell, 14 F.3d 793 (2d Cir. 1994) (physician who lost exclusive contract has no standing to complain that he was replaced; remedy sought would not increase consumer choice); cf. Brunswick Corp. v. Pueblo Bowl-O-Mat, 429 U.S. 477 (1977) (competitor lacks standing to challenge merger of bowling alleys). More commonly, however, courts simply rule as in *Hassan* that no injury to competition exists and therefore no violation occurs if the doctors who remain possess no significant market power. A single competitor's loss of patients to another doctor or hospital does not harm the patients, nor does it necessarily threaten to raise prices or worsen quality. In a phrase, antitrust law, in contrast with tort law, is concerned with harm to competition, not harm to competitors.

The instinct that single-physician staffing decisions should not create a federal antitrust case is also captured in the Health Care Quality Improvement Act, which immunizes peer review of individual physicians based on quality concerns. This qualified immunity extends, however, only to damages actions, not to injunctive relief, and it does not cover exclusions (1) of nonphysicians, (2) of groups of physicians, or (3) based on economic or administrative concerns.

5. *Using Outside Reviewers.* For hospitals concerned that the antitrust exposure for aggressive peer review is still too intense, Professors Blumstein and Sloan offer an inviting solution: "hospitals concerned about antitrust exposure could avoid liability by . . . using outside professional consultants for quality assurance. . . . [The] lack of [outside reviewers'] competitive status with staff physicians would remove such peer-review activities from coverage under §1 of the Sherman Act. No capacity to conspire would exist." James Blumstein & Frank Sloan, Antitrust and Hospital Peer Review, 51 Law & Contemp. Probs. 7, 39-53 (Spring 1988). See also Mathews v. Lancaster General Hospital, 87 F.3d 624 (3d Cir. 1996) (no conspiracy as a matter of law despite possible economic motivation where hospital board acted independently and obtained outside review by independent consultant). Why do you suppose outside review is not more common, considering that it appears to create a nearly iron-clad defense against §1 antitrust claims? See Brewbaker, supra ("JCAHO standards may fairly be read to prohibit a governing body's unilateral decision to retain an external peer reviewer.").

6. *Further Readings.* For additional academic commentary on these lines of cases, proposing various degrees of scrutiny, standards of legality, and burdens of proof, see n.4 in *Weiss*; Blumstein & Sloan supra (advocating that, for certain "cartel-behavior" decisions, courts should take "a precautionary prophylactic approach . . . requiring defendants to establish an overriding procompetitive justification . . . [that] is not just theoretical but factually demonstrable."); Clark Havighurst, Doctors and Hospitals: An Antitrust Perspective on Traditional Relationships, 1984 Duke L.J. 1071, 1133-1134, 1157 ("To ensure that hospitals have reasonable freedom of action, . . . summary judgment or a directed verdict would be appropriate if documentary evidence and affidavits showed that the hospital's action reflected its [own] corporate concerns. . . . Under this test, a court would not concern itself . . . with whether the ostensible motives for the actions taken were the real motives or whether the adverse effect of the hospital action on competition among practitioners was outweighed by its actual contribution to fulfilling the hospital's objectives."). For an empirical analysis of this body of case law, see Peter J. Hammer & William M. Sage, Antitrust, Health Care Quality, and the Courts, 102 Colum. L. Rev. 545 (2002). See generally 89 A.L.R. Fed. 419 (1988).

7. *Exclusion from Managed Care Networks.* The paradigm boycott case consists of a hospital excluding practitioners for ostensibly quality-of-care reasons, but *Hassan* illustrates that this body of law also applies to exclusion by insurers and managed care networks, and exclusions based on economic grounds. Antitrust law is more familiar with these conventional commercial contexts and so, although these developments are somewhat novel in the industry, the legal analysis is in some ways easier. For a decision similar to *Hassan*, see Capital Imaging Associates v. Mohawk Valley Medical Associates, 996 F.2d 537 (2d Cir. 1993) (holding that member physicians of an IPA are capable of conspiring among themselves in deciding to award an exclusive radiology contract, but dismissing antitrust claim because of the IPA's small market share and consequent absence of any likely impact on prices or quality).

Levine v. Central Florida Medical Affiliates, 72 F.3d 1538 (11th Cir. 1996), presents perhaps the most startling set of facts. There, a general internist was able to earn $724,000 a year despite his exclusion from one of the area's largest PPOs. He complained that, had the exclusion not occurred, he would have been able to "score a [financial] touchdown." The court obviously found that the PPO lacked market power. The case is interesting for the way it treats a leading Supreme Court decision of importance for defining markets. Eastman Kodak v. Image Technical Services, 504 U.S. 451 (1992), held that a separate market could exist for the parts required to repair a Kodak brand photocopy machine depending on whether Kodak parts are interchangeable with parts for other brands. If not interchangeable, once the Kodak machine is purchased the buyers are locked into that brand's repair parts. Similarly, Dr. Levine argued that the PPO has extreme power in a small market because subscribers to a managed care network are locked into an "aftermarket" of network providers. The court observed, however, that subscribers in a PPO can go outside the network, only at extra costs that providers such as Levine were free to make up through discounts, and that subscribers were generally able to change health insurance once a year. See generally James Ponsoldt & Lance McMillian, The Judicial Legitimization of Horizontal Price-Fixing Among Partially Integrated Health Care Providers: An Antitrust/Health Care Case Study, 50 Ala. L. Rev. 465

(1999). For additional discussion of market definition for managed care entities, see section D.3.

8. *Illegal "Tie-Ins."* The Supreme Court has, so far, spoken directly on physician exclusion issues in only one case, Jefferson Parish Hospital District v. Hyde, 466 U.S. 2 (1984), but it was decided on a more obscure antitrust theory relating to "tie-ins." In that case, a physician challenged an exclusive contract for anesthesiology services that kept him from practicing in the hospital. He argued that requiring surgery patients to use the services of only designated anesthesiologists constituted a per se illegal tie-in: Surgery patients were forced to use only designated anesthesiologists even if they might want someone else. Surprisingly, the Court seemed to agree that surgery and anesthesia are indeed separate services, but it rejected the tie-in claim nevertheless because the hospital lacked the requisite market power to force the packaged sale on the patient.

9. *Reimbursement Limits.* A related line of cases are those concerning health insurers' limitations on reimbursement for certain medical services. Chiropractors, for instance, would be severely affected if Blue Cross/Blue Shield refused to pay for their services. However, if Blue Cross/Blue Shield merely determines on its own the terms under which it is willing to do business and separately reaches an agreement with individual providers, there is no horizontal conspiracy—or is there? Law professor Sylvia Law, in her influential study Blue Cross: What Went Wrong? (2d ed. 1976), explains that providers historically have dominated the Blues and used them to enforce their economic interests. See Virginia Academy of Clinical Psychologists v. Blue Shield, 624 F.2d 476 (4th Cir. 1980) (§1 violation established by Blue Shield's refusal to reimburse psychiatrists directly); Hahn v. Oregon Physicians' Service, 868 F.2d 1022 (9th Cir. 1988) (physician-controlled HMO that excluded podiatrists can be challenged as group boycott). Where insurers are not controlled by physicians, however, most courts conclude that they are free to unilaterally pay or not pay for whatever medical services and in whatever amounts they want. E.g., American Chiropractic Ass'n v. Trigon Healthcare, Inc., 367 F.3d 212 (4th Cir. 2004) (no conspiracy in limiting payments to chiropractors).

Nevertheless, in a bold move the Affordable Care Act (§2706) prohibits any health plan from "discriminating" against any category of licensed health care provider. Thus, regardless of antitrust law, insurers no longer may flatly refuse to pay alternative providers. However, the statute does not require that health plans include alternative practitioners in their contracted networks (which means the law has meaning only for health plans that cover out-of-network care). Also, the government has interpreted this anti-discrimination requirement narrowly to allow health plans to pay alternative practitioners less, and to set "medical management" limits on the "frequency, method, treatment or setting" for their services. CMS, Affordable Care Act Implementation FAQs (Sept. 15, 2013).

CALIFORNIA DENTAL ASS'N v. FEDERAL TRADE COMMISSION

526 U.S. 756 (1999)

[Read the excerpt at page 330, and the footnote on page 483.]

THE ROLE OF QUALITY OF HEALTH CARE CONSIDERATIONS IN ANTITRUST ANALYSIS

Thomas E. Kauper

51 Law & Contemp. Probs. 273 (Spring 1988)

For decades, health care services markets have functioned, for better or worse, without the constraints imposed on markets by competitive market pressures. . . . Self-regulation has been the norm. Actors in these markets long assumed that the antitrust laws were of little or no relevance to their conduct. As a result, health care services markets have been characterized by a variety of structures and actions which in most other industries would raise serious antitrust questions. The introduction of antitrust policy into these markets has therefore resulted in direct challenges to a broad range of conduct within a short period of time. . . . In virtually every instance, the concern over quality of care is likely to be raised in justification for the conduct under antitrust attack.

A doctor is denied hospital staff privileges. Hospitals deny access to midwives or chiropractors, or enter into exclusive contracts with providers for the performance of specialized services. Groups of local hospitals, acting on their own or through regional planning groups, determine which hospitals will have emergency or burn treatment facilities. Doctors agree on, or communicate about, the amounts they will accept in reimbursement from insurers, or collaborate to resist other efforts by insurers to reduce costs. A hospital is denied accreditation by an accrediting group which relies in part on judgments by other hospitals. A physician is denied specialist certification by an organization made up of such specialists. A hospital (or group of hospitals) opposes the issuance of a certificate of need to a potential competitor. . . . Running through this broad range of cases is a single issue which is the central focus of this study. When, if ever, should an antitrust court weigh the impact of conduct on quality of care? . . .

II. Quality of Care: A Framework for Analysis

A quality-of-care "defense" can mean a number of quite different things. First, the [defendants] may seek recognition of a limited professional services exemption from the antitrust laws. Adverse competitive effects then would have no antitrust consequences. Second, the [defendants] may contend that even if the [action] in question has adverse price and output effects, those effects are offset in some way by the social and economic benefits of avoiding deaths and physical harm to [patients]. Such a justification proceeds on the premise that quality of care is a national goal to be achieved even at the cost of competition. . . . Third, the [defendants] may assert that . . . quality of care is a relevant competitive factor or that there are no adverse price and output effects because of the preservation of a high quality of care. . . . [This] is a quite different argument from either the first or second; it is consistent with the view that antitrust analysis is confined to an examination of price and output effects. Fourth, the [defendant] may contend that its [action] is saved by a good purpose. In cases where violation may depend on the presence of an anticompetitive intent, a good purpose may negate the presence of the bad. . . .

The quality-of-care "defense" is thus not a single contention, but a series of distinctly different arguments. . . . But courts confronted with quality-of-care claims have too often failed to understand these differences. The result has been analytical confusion, much of which can be attributed to the Supreme Court. . . .

This confusion began with the Supreme Court's decision in Goldfarb v. Virginia State Bar Association, 421 U.S. 773 (1975), which found that the use of recommended fee schedules by the Fairfax County (Virginia) Bar Association violated §1 of the Sherman Act. The Court rejected the contention that the "learned professions" were not engaged in "trade or commerce" and were not therefore covered by the Sherman Act, noting that "the public service aspect of professional practice [is not] controlling in determining whether §1 includes professions." While *Goldfarb* dealt specifically with lawyers, it opened the door for the application of the antitrust laws to a wide variety of restraints involving health care markets. But in a now well-known footnote [17], inserted perhaps out of an abundance of caution, the Court sowed the seeds for the confusion about the relevance of quality-of-care concerns. [F]ootnote [17] states:

> The fact that a restraint operates upon a profession as distinguished from a business is, of course, relevant in determining whether that particular restraint violates the Sherman Act. It would be unrealistic to view the practice of professions as interchangeable with other business activities, and automatically apply to the professions antitrust concepts which originated in other areas. The public service aspect, and other features of the professions, may require that a particular practice, which could properly be viewed as a violation of the Sherman Act in another context, be treated differently. . . .

So the antitrust laws apply to the professions, but not quite. . . . *Goldfarb* was followed by the decision in National Society of Professional Engineers v. United States, 435 U.S. 679 (1978). The canons of ethics of the Society prohibited competitive bidding. This, according to the government, was tantamount to price-fixing. In defense, the Society asserted that the prohibition was necessary because competitive bidding would result in "inferior work with consequent risk to public safety and health," a contention contrary to the repeated earlier assertions by the Court, noted above, that it is competition which assures quality. The Court's conclusion in *Professional Engineers* that the Society's ban on competitive bidding could not be justified on quality-of-service grounds is hardly surprising. . . . *Professional Engineers* makes clear that antitrust rules are directed solely to the *competitive* effects of the restraint. . . . But the Court went on:

> We adhere to the view expressed in *Goldfarb* that, by their nature, professional services may differ significantly from other business services, and, accordingly, the nature of the competition in such services may vary. Ethical norms may serve to regulate and promote this competition, and thus fall within the Rule of Reason.

While verbally adhering to the *Goldfarb* footnote, this reservation is more precise. Rather than public service, the touchstone is the nature of the competition. If professional services differ from others, the differences are in the markets themselves. Evaluation of competitive effects must take such differences into account. . . .

The Supreme Court's trilogy of health care antitrust cases following *Goldfarb*—Arizona v. Maricopa County Medical Society, 457 U.S. 332 (1981). Jefferson Parish Hospital District No. 2 v. Hyde, 466 U.S. 2 (1984), and FTC v. Indiana Federation of Dentists, 476 U.S. 447 (1986)—leaves little doubt about the general applicability of the antitrust laws to health care activities and considerable doubt about how they are to be applied. . . .

The final case in the trilogy is *Indiana Federation of Dentists*, where protection of the quality of dental care was the primary justification offered by defendants. At issue was a collective refusal by Indiana dentists, through the Indiana Federation, to supply X-rays along with claim forms to a number of dental care insurers. In order to contain dental care cost, insurers operated under policies limiting payments to the cost of the "least expensive yet adequate treatment," and often insisted that patient X-rays be submitted as part of the claims review process. . . . [T]he Federation attempted to justify its action on quality-of-care grounds, asserting that because X-rays alone do not furnish an adequate basis for evaluating dental problems, insurers who rely solely on X-rays would decline to pay for treatment which was in the best interest of the patient. . . . The Court declined to apply a per se rule, noting, inter alia, that "we have been slow to condemn rules adopted by professional associations as reasonable per se," but found that the [FTC's] findings of anticompetitive effects were sufficient. . . . The decision gives little comfort to those urging that antitrust analysis in health care markets should take into account a variety of non-economic factors.

Can the quality-of-care strands taken from *Goldfarb* through *Indiana Federation of Dentists* be woven into a coherent whole? The questions are being narrowed, and the nature of inquiry is now more sharply focused. A clear pattern is emerging. First, and most obvious, the Supreme Court has never found professional activity having adverse price and output effects justified by concerns over the quality of service provided. Second, justifications based on the view that competition will necessarily result in quality deterioration are unacceptable. . . . The Court's repeated assertions that professional conduct, and conduct in health care markets in particular, should be evaluated under standards that differ significantly from those more generally applied has created confusion. . . . These imprecise references to public service and ethical norms have allowed lower courts to treat quality-of-care issues in a variety of inconsistent ways, and in a manner reflecting biases more than consistent principles of antitrust analysis. . . .

Despite the confusion caused by the *Goldfarb* footnote and its progeny, the Court in its health care cases is generally moving in a direction in which quality of care is simply a factor in the analysis of adverse competitive effects. . . . Market structures and forces may be different in health care markets, and these differences may be relevant in evaluating the price and output effects of particular conduct, but the antitrust principles applied remain the same. . . .

Firms compete not only on price, but also on quality of product or service. Both are integral factors in the consumer's decision to buy. . . . The most obvious example is a hospital's denial of staff privileges to a physician who is simply incompetent, or has a public reputation of incompetence. The hospital will contend that the effect of its action is to prevent debasement of the quality of care its patients receive. It is not, however, acting out of some purely altruistic, public service concern. The presence of such a physician on the staff will damage the hospital's reputation, and thus its ability to compete. It may also injure the reputation of other members of the staff through association, although this effect is less obvious. If these effects are strong enough, the hospital may lose patients not only through consumer choice but because other physicians, fearful for their own reputations, leave the staff, taking their patients with them. . . .

A court called upon to decide such a case need not consider these effects unless the denial of staff privileges is likely to have adverse price and output effects in the market served by the denied physician. In most cases, such effects are likely only when . . . the number of competing physicians with such privileges is small. Under these circumstances, the denial of entry may protect a cartel among those already established. Few denials of staff privileges to individual physicians (or other providers) are likely to have such adverse price and output effects.[131] But where they do, the reputational effects of granting privileges become relevant and should be treated in the same manner as [cost] efficiencies. The likelihood of these effects must be evaluated on the record. The problems of defining quality should not be an obstacle here. The focus is more on reputation than quality as such. It is not necessary to define quality in some absolute sense. . . .

Courts and commentators on occasion have suggested that with some types of conduct, a predicate to antitrust liability is a determination that the conduct was accompanied by a purpose to injure competition. . . . [But] [p]urpose is relevant only as a guide to a judgment about effects, both adverse and beneficial. Where those who know a market act for the avowed purpose of restraining it, their intention is some evidence that adverse effects will occur. Similarly, an unambiguous intention to promote efficiency is probative in determining whether conduct does so. . . . The role of purpose is evidentiary. Standing alone, it can neither justify nor condemn. . . .

Purpose is often relied upon in evaluating agreements among competitors to which rules involving boycotts might be applied. The reason apparently lies in those rules themselves. Traditionally, boycotts have been described as per se violations, illegal without consideration of effects. Until very recently the definition of boycott, for the purpose of this rule has been far too broad. . . . Virtually any professional association rule which is enforced through a denial of benefits, such as staff privileges or accreditation, can be described as a boycott. Emphasis on purpose in health care cases of this type has added flexibility and mitigated the harshness of the per se rule. With the Supreme Court's reformulations of boycott doctrine in Northwest Wholesale Stationers, Inc. v. Pacific Stationery & Printing Co., 472 U.S. 284 (1985), and FTC v. Indiana Federation of Dentists, there is less need for such reliance on the parties' purposes. These decisions move in the direction of effects analysis.[156] . . .

131. Adverse effects are more likely where an entire class of competitors or potential competitors (e.g., podiatrists, nurse-midwives) are denied hospital access. . . .

156. In *Northwest Wholesale Stationers,* the Court held that the per se rule did not apply to expulsion from a purchasing cooperative made up of plaintiff's competitors absent a showing that the cooperative "possesses market power or unique access to a business element necessary for effective competition." 472 U.S. at 298. Without such a showing, a court could not: find that the expulsion was per se illegal. The Court also noted that in prior cases in which

III. Translating Theory Into Reality: A Case Study

This section examines two decisions, Wilk v. American Medical Association[200] and Koefoot v. American College of Surgeons, 652 F. Supp. 882 (N.D. Ill. 1987), in which the boundaries of a quality-of-care, or patient care, defense, if any, are explored in depth. In both cases, the defendants placed primary reliance on the legitimacy of their efforts to guard the public in general, and their own patients in particular, against what, in their perception, was a significant threat to the quality of care provided. No other decisions discuss the issue as carefully or exhaustively. . . .

A. Wilk

In *Wilk*, plaintiff chiropractors asserted that the American Medical Association and its members conspired among themselves and with other groups including the American Hospital Association, American College of Surgeons, American College of Physicians, American College of Radiology, American Academy of Orthopedic Surgeons, and the Joint Committee on Accreditation of Hospitals (JCAH) to conduct a nationwide boycott of chiropractic providers. While the facts are complex, the central feature of the alleged boycott was a 1966 AMA resolution stating: "It is the position of the medical profession that chiropractic is an unscientific cult whose practitioners lack the necessary training and background to diagnose and treat human disease." . . . The effect of the actions of the AMA and its co-conspirators was to discourage cooperation between chiropractors and physicians in the form of referrals, consultations, and the sharing of clinical and research results, and to deny chiropractors hospital facilities, including X-ray and laboratory facilities. . . .

Throughout the litigation, the defendants insisted that they had acted to protect the public health and safety from what they believed to be a form of quackery, a type of treatment without foundation in science. . . .

The court of appeals found the [trial court's] per se instructions erroneous. . . . Relying on *Goldfarb*'s reservations, the court noted that an ethical standard dealing with the role of scientific method presented sufficiently novel questions to avoid per se analysis. . . .

Had the appellate court stopped at this point, its analysis would have been fully consistent with conventional antitrust doctrine, . . . [b]ut the court then concluded that in accord with *Goldfarb*'s reservation it was free "to modify the rule of reason test in a case involving a certain kind of question of ethics for the medical profession." . . . In the court's words, "a value independent of the values attributed to unrestrained competition must enter the equation." If the defendants' dominant motive was a concern over scientific method in the care of patients, their conduct was reasonable even if competition was restricted. [The court constructed a four-part affirmative defense that tested the sincerity and objectivity of this motive and

---

it had applied a per se rule, the practices were not justified "by plausible arguments that were intended to enhance overall efficiency." . . . The boycott analysis in *Indiana Federation of Dentists* is similar, although qualified by the observation that "we have been slow to condemn rules of professional associations as unreasonable per se."

200. 719 F.2d 207 (1983). Following reversal by the court of appeals, the case was retried in a bench trial. Wilk v. American Medical Ass'n, 671 F. Supp. 1465 (N.D. Ill. 1987).

whether the defendants chose the least restrictive means of achieving their purpose. The trial court found in a bench trial that the least restrictive means test was not met because the defendants could have achieved their purpose through education. The court ordered sweeping injunctive relief requiring the trade associations to tell their members they are free to make individual decisions about whether to associate with chiropractors.] . . .

B. KOEFOOT[223]

Over half of all board certified surgeons in the country are members of the American College of Surgeons (ACS). . . . Board certification or status as an ACS fellow is required to hold staff privileges in hospitals accredited by JCAH. . . . The "itinerant surgery" rule of the ACS prohibits:

> [t]he performance of surgical operations (except on patients whose chances of recovery would be prejudiced by removal to another hospital) under circumstances in which the responsibility for diagnosis or care of the patient is delegated to another who is not fully qualified to undertake it.

The effect of the rule is that ACS surgeons may delegate responsibility for postoperative care only to other surgeons.

Dr. Koefoot is a general surgeon who performs surgery in three hospitals in Grand Island, Nebraska, and in several community hospitals some 20 minutes away. He gives postoperative care to his patients in Grand Island, but delegates responsibility for such care to nonsurgeon general practitioners in the community hospitals. After his expulsion from ACS for violating the itinerant surgery rule, he filed an antitrust suit against ACS, attacking the rule as a form of market allocation used by ACS members to block entry, as a boycott of non-surgeons, and as a tie-in between surgery and post-operative care. . . . ACS has defended the rule as a legitimate ethical canon adopted to enhance the quality of care provided surgical patients. . . .

[T]he trial court held that the itinerant surgery violation was not a per se violation and set an agenda for the trial under the rule of reason. A "facially legitimate ethical canon," defined as a rule of professional practice that establishes standards of care "without reference to the economic interests of professionals," is not per se illegal. . . .

The trial court then dealt with the relevance of evidence offered by ACS to establish (1) that their motive was to safeguard the quality of patient care, and (2) that the practice of itinerant surgery was in fact harmful. As to the first, the court found *Wilk*'s patient care motive doctrine inapplicable. . . . [T]he later Supreme Court decisions in *Jefferson Parish* and *Indiana Federation of Dentists* . . . suggest that . . . [m]otive evidence is relevant and admissible, but only for the limited purpose of evaluating effect. Evidence that itinerant surgery was in fact harmful is relevant only to establish ACS's intent. . . . Because harm evidence is of limited relevance, and is a type of evidence that is likely to be prejudicial, the court concluded that its quality and quantity must be severely limited. . . .

223. Koefoot v. American College of Surgeons, 610 F. Supp. 1298, 1301 (N.D. Ill. 1985).

Uncomfortable with the *Wilk* patient-care-motive justification, the court confined it to cases involving allegations of pure quackery. It is apparent that the court was determined not to make judgments about the medical consequences of itinerant surgery and feared that evidence about harm would distract the jury from its assignment to focus solely on competitive efforts. [After trial, the jury found that the rule had no anticompetitive effect.] . . .

C. [ANALYSIS]

. . . [The *Wilk* court was correct that] the AMA nonaffiliation rule and related actions cannot be . . . characterized as procompetitive . . . protection of reputation for quality. Physicians do have a legitimate competitive interest in reputation. And particular physicians could well decide that their competitive stance would be damaged by affiliation with chiropractors. But an *agreement* not to affiliate could be so justified only if a physician's ability to compete is impaired if *other* physicians affiliate with chiropractors. If such affiliation is harmful to reputation, however, affiliation by others would appear to enhance the competitive posture of those who reject it. . . .

[The *Wilk* court was wrong, however, to construct a special patient care affirmative defense.] Invariably, denial of access to these alternative providers is explained as a measure to protect the public from inferior care, [but this is] an explanation which in this broad sense is not cognizable in an antitrust case. . . . There is no single quality-of-care defense in health care antitrust cases. To the extent such a defense might be predicated on a balancing of social gains against adverse price and output effects, it is inconsistent with the focus on competitive effects which is central in antitrust analysis. Nor can such a defense be based on a dominant laudable purpose. Intent is relevant only as a predictor of effect. Where effect is established, intent is no longer of consequence.

Conduct that promotes efficiency, ameliorates the effects of market failures or imperfections, or increases quality rivalry among providers is, to this extent, procompetitive and may improve quality of care by enhancing the competitive process. Any further accommodation of quality-of-care concerns is a direct challenge to the central role of the market in the determination of quality, and therefore to the relevance of antitrust itself. It is for legislatures, not courts, to grant antitrust exemptions or otherwise displace the application of the antitrust laws.

Notes: Quality of Care as a Defense; Allied Health Professionals; Professional Society Rules

1. On balance, does antitrust law or the common law fairness doctrine do a better job of subjecting hospitals and HMOs to the proper level of scrutiny for their staffing decisions? Does your answer differ with respect to matters of procedure and matters of substance?

2. *Other Readings.* For additional discussions of the role that quality of care plays in health care antitrust analysis, see Peter J. Hammer & William M. Sage, Antitrust, Health Care Quality, and the Courts, 102 Colum. L. Rev. 545 (2002); William M. Sage & Peter J. Hammer, A Copernican View of Health Care Antitrust, 65 Law & Contemp. Probs. 241 (Autumn 2002).

3. If only competitive effects are relevant to antitrust analysis, why is a Catholic hospital allowed to exclude abortionists? (Possibly because of overriding First Amendment concerns. Or, because such a policy does not advance the economic interests of member physicians, it does not constitute a conspiracy.)

Should Congress's 1986 enactment of an *explicit* qualified immunity in the Health Care Quality Improvement Act, discussed below, resolve any further debate about whether the courts should find an *implied* patient care affirmative defense?

4. *Recognition for Allied Health Professionals.* Both the *Weiss* case above and the *Wilk* case discussed by Prof. Kauper manifest the traditional medical establishment's longstanding hostility to competing schools of practitioners that are founded on less scientific theories of medicine. Chiropractors and osteopaths are only two among the several allied health professions that are engaged in active struggles to achieve professional recognition and hospital access. Similar challenges have been mounted by podiatrists, clinical psychologists, nurse anesthetists, and midwives, usually without success. See, e.g., Minnesota Ass'n of Nurse Anesthetists, 208 F.3d 2000 (8th Cir. 2000) (rejecting a boycott challenge to several hospitals' decisions to contract only with physician groups for anesthesia services).

An important indirect effect of this antitrust pressure has been to force a revision of the JCAHO accreditation standards. Prior to 1984, JCAHO standards were read as prohibiting hospitals from extending staff privileges to practitioners other than doctors and dentists. However, in that year, the JCAHO adopted an amendment that allowed hospitals to "include other licensed individuals permitted by law and by the hospital to provide patient care services independently." For a survey of these developments, see C. Dodd, Exclusion of Nonphysician Health Care Providers from Integrated Delivery Systems, 64 U. Cin. L. Rev. 983 (1996).

In some states, allied health professionals have won their contest in the legislature by obtaining statutory enactments that require hospitals to grant them equal consideration in extending clinical privileges. Representative is D.C. Code Ann. §44-507, which requires individual, nondiscriminatory consideration of the credentials of podiatrists, psychologists, nurse anesthetists, nurse midwives, and nurse practitioners. See also Ohio Rev. Code Ann §3701.351(B).

5. *Codes of Professional Ethics. California Dental Ass'n* and the *Koefoot* and *Indiana Federation of Dentists* cases discussed by Prof. Kauper are examples of the several challenges to various ethical restrictions in medical professional codes. The most prominent of these is American Medical Ass'n v. FTC, 94 FTC 980, 1015 (1979), enforced 638 F.2d 443 (2d Cir. 1980), aff'd mem. by an equally divided Court, 455 U.S. 676 (1982), which invalidated ethical prohibitions against advertising and certain physician contractual arrangements. For additional commentary, see the articles cited in note 2 above, and Clark Havighurst & Nancy King, Private Credentialing of Health Care Personnel: An Antitrust Perspective, 9 Am. J.L. & Med. 131, 263 (1983).

Problem: Medical Staff Boycotts of Allied Health Professionals

Centerville Psychiatric (CP) is a for-profit psychiatric hospital in a large town with two other free-standing psychiatric hospitals and with four general hospitals that have smaller psychiatric units. CP attempts to distinguish itself from its competitors by claiming to offer better doctors and more state-of-the-art structured treatment programs that combine intensive counseling and drug therapy for acute episodes of serious mental illness (so-called nervous breakdowns). This treatment approach contrasts with that in general hospitals, which is unstructured, much shorter in duration, and often administered by nonspecialists, and contrasts with other specialized psychiatric hospitals that offer long-term custodial treatment for more chronic conditions.

Consistent with its long-standing bylaws, CP's medical staff presently consists of only board-certified psychiatrists, which are specially trained M.D.s. Alfred Zock, Ph.D. is a psychologist of good reputation with an active counseling and therapy practice in Centerville. He has decided to break the mold by applying for medical staff privileges at CP. The major practical difference between psychiatrists and psychologists is that only the former can prescribe drugs; psychologists are limited by state licensing laws to "couch therapy." In the past, psychologists have been allowed to see CP patients who were under their care before coming to CP, but only if a staff psychiatrist approved and supervised the psychologist. Dr. Zock would like to admit his own patients directly and treat them at CP without supervision or prior approval. He has admitting privileges at one of the general hospitals in town, but he finds their facilities unsatisfactory.

The existing psychiatrists oppose Dr. Zock's admission because they like things the way they are, for both clinical and financial reasons. The hospital administration is also not in favor, partly because it does not want to antagonize its medical staff in a competitive hospital market where they can take their patients elsewhere, and partly because reimbursement rates under managed care insurance are usually higher for drug therapy than for counseling. On the other hand, it is clear many patients would prefer their own psychologist to be their primary physician.

As lawyer for CP, advise it on the safest way to exclude Dr. Zock. Consider whether to use primarily quality or economic criteria, whether to act under the existing bylaws, or to change them and then consider Dr. Zock individually. Consider what procedures to follow in making these decisions.

After reading about all these lawsuits arising from medical staff disputes, both under the common law fairness doctrine and under antitrust law, it may surprise you to learn that a federal statute confers broad immunity on participants in hospital and HMO credentialing or peer review processes. As you read the following case, note the various qualifications and limitations imposed on this immunity by considering to what extent it would apply to each of the medical staff dispute cases you read in the previous three sections of this chapter.

■ BRYAN v. JAMES E. HOLMES REGIONAL MEDICAL CENTER

33 F.3d 1318 (11th Cir. 1994)

Tjoflat, Chief Judge:

In this case, a Florida hospital, after completing a lengthy internal disciplinary process, terminated the clinical staff privileges of a staff physician. The physician sued the hospital, alleging various state and federal causes of action and seeking money damages. After an eleven-day trial, a federal jury concluded that the hospital had revoked the physician's staff privileges in violation of its bylaws and awarded the physician nearly $4.2 million in damages for breach of contract. The hospital appeals that judgment . . . contend[ing it] was immune from liability in money damages under the Health Care Quality Improvement Act of 1986 ("HCQIA"), (1988 & Supp. IV 1992), and under Florida law, Fla. Stat. Ann. Sec. 395.0193(5) (West 1993). . . .

Congress enacted the Health Care Quality Improvement Act to encourage peer review activities, "to improve the quality of medical care by encouraging physicians to identify and discipline other physicians who are incompetent or who engage in unprofessional behavior." H.R. Rep. No. 903, 99th Cong., 2d Sess. . . . In furtherance of this goal, HCQIA grants limited immunity, in suits brought by disciplined physicians, from liability for money damages to those who participate in professional peer review activities. See also H.R.Rep. No. 903, at 3, reprinted in 1986 U.S.C.C.A.N. at 6385 (noting that "[e]ven though defendants may often win these lawsuits, that may not be sufficient to guarantee enthusiastic, or even minimally adequate, peer review" because "[d]octors who are sufficiently fearful of the threat of litigation will simply not do meaningful peer review"). . . .

HCQIA provides that, if a "professional review action" (as defined in the statute) meets certain due process and fairness requirements, then those participating in such a review process shall not be liable under any state or federal law for damages for the results. 42 U.S.C. Sec. 11111(a)(1). . . . (In another set of provisions, HCQIA requires health care entities to report certain specific disciplinary actions taken against a staff physician (or the acceptance of a resignation or suspension in return for not conducting investigations or disciplinary proceedings) to a national clearinghouse established to collect and disseminate information on health care providers. Then, prior to admitting a physician to its staff, a hospital must obtain that physician's records from the clearinghouse. These reporting requirements were designed to "restrict the ability of incompetent physicians to move from State to State without disclosure or discovery of the physician's previous damaging or incompetent performance.". . .)

The statute attempts to balance the chilling effect of litigation on peer review with concerns for protecting physicians improperly subjected to disciplinary action; accordingly, Congress granted immunity from monetary damages to participants in properly conducted peer review proceedings while preserving causes of action for injunctive or declaratory relief for aggrieved physicians. Section 11111(a)(1) expressly excludes from its coverage [civil rights] suits brought under 42 U.S.C. §1983 or Title VII of the Civil Rights Act of 1964, but it clearly does apply to antitrust claims. . . . Because the statutory scheme is somewhat convoluted, we discuss the immunity provisions in detail. . . .

The standards that professional review actions must satisfy to entitle the participants to such protection are enumerated in §11112(a) as follows:

> For purposes of the protection set forth in section 11111(a) of this title, a professional review action must be taken—(1) in the reasonable belief that the action was in the furtherance of quality health care, (2) after a reasonable effort to obtain the facts of the matter, (3) after adequate notice and hearing procedures are afforded to the physician involved or after such other procedures as are fair to the physician under the circumstances, and (4) in the reasonable belief that the action was warranted by the facts known . . . .

Importantly, HCQIA also creates a rebuttable presumption of immunity: "A professional review action shall be presumed to have met the preceding standards . . . unless the presumption is rebutted by a preponderance of the evidence."

Section 11112(b) of HCQIA then enumerates the minimum, or "safe harbor" procedures that will, in every case, satisfy the adequate notice and hearing requirement of §11112(a)(3). . . . We discuss this checklist in more detail infra. . . . Congress was careful to explain, however, that "[a] professional review body's failure to meet the conditions described in this subsection shall not, in itself, constitute failure to meet the standards of subsection (a)(3) of this section." The legislative history of section 11112(a) indicates that the statute's reasonableness requirements were intended to create an objective standard of performance, rather than a subjective good faith standard. . . .

A review of the facts of this case reveal that HCQIA's limitations on monetary liability dictate the outcome of this appeal. . . . [Dr. Bryan] is generally acknowledged to be an excellent surgeon, often undertaking long, detailed vascular procedures that other physicians in the field avoid. Bryan also has a reputation for being a volcanic-tempered perfectionist, a difficult man with whom to work, and a person who regularly viewed it as his obligation to criticize staff members at Holmes [Hospital] for perceived incompetence or inefficiency. Hospital employees, however, often viewed Bryan's "constructive criticism" as verbal—or even physical—abuse. Because the Holmes board of directors found Bryan's behavior inappropriate and unprofessional, it terminated his medical staff privileges in November 1990. The means by which Holmes accomplished this termination is the subject of the dispute in this case. . . .

[P]rior to his termination, Bryan was the subject of more than fifty written incident reports involving unprofessional or disruptive behavior, usually complaints regarding Bryan's abusive treatment of nurses, technicians, and even fellow physicians. Some insight into the origins of this behavior came from Bryan himself during his testimony at trial. Shortly after completing his residency, Bryan obtained staff privileges at a Veterans Administration hospital in Miami. There, he explained, he soon learned that the hospital could not fire incompetent nurses and other technicians easily; the most effective way to avoid working with nurses he viewed as incompetent or inefficient, he discovered, was to insult them until they refused to participate in operations involving his patients. . . .

At first, the Hospital and the medical staff attempted to deal with Bryan's behavior informally. . . . The incidents continued unabated, however, over the next three years, and Hospital officials gradually began to take a more active approach in dealing with the problem. . . . On October 19, 1989 . . . the board advised Bryan by letter that his abusive behavior could no longer be tolerated and that any further incidents of unprofessional behavior would result in the permanent revocation of his staff privileges. . . .

Despite the board's warning, Bryan was involved in four additional incidents in the first five months of 1990; these four incidents led directly to the termination of Bryan's medical staff privileges. . . . After considering these latest incidents in light of Bryan's history of disruptive behavior and the hospital's varied attempts to correct such behavior . . . the executive committee recommended that Bryan's staff privileges be permanently revoked.

Once again, Bryan requested that a peer review hearing panel be appointed. Chaired by Dr. Joseph Chanda, the panel consisted of seven physicians, none of whom were vascular surgeons. . . . Bryan challenged the initial composition of the panel, alleging bias on the part of Dr. William Broussard, who advised Bryan to seek counseling for his interpersonal problems in 1982. Bryan also contended that the panel should be composed solely of surgeons. In response to Bryan's objections, [Dr.] Mills selected a new panel member to replace Broussard but did not remove the non-surgeons who had previously been named. . . .

The Chanda panel held four sessions of hearings; Bryan was represented by counsel at the proceedings, and he had both the opportunity to cross-examine the witnesses offered by the medical staff and to present witnesses and documentary evidence on his own behalf. A court reporter recorded the testimony at all of the hearing sessions. Two panel members were absent from at least part of the hearings, but Chanda testified at trial that the panel as a whole reviewed the testimony orally at the end of each session and during deliberations and that summarized what had transpired for the absent members. . . .

[T]he panel recommended that Bryan's clinical privileges be suspended for two years. After considering the Chanda panel's report, the executive committee stood by its recommendation that Bryan's staff privileges be revoked. Bryan appealed the executive committee's recommendation to the board of the directors; pursuant to the bylaws, the board appointed a board review panel, which also recommended revocation of Bryan's clinical privileges. The full board then considered the three recommendations . . . [and] unanimously voted to terminate Bryan's clinical privileges at Holmes. . . .

Bryan filed a complaint on behalf of himself and his professional association against the Hospital, the individual members of its board of directors, members of the medical staff executive committee, and two nurses. The complaint included federal and state antitrust claims as well as state law claims for defamation, negligent supervision of the peer review process (against only the individual members of the board of directors), and breach of contract for failing to follow the medical staff bylaws during the disciplinary process (against the Hospital). The complaint also included the following various ancillary claims: (1) constitutional and civil rights claims under 42 U.S.C. §1983 (1988); (2) federal contractual claims arising out of the Hospital's participation in the Medicare program; and (3) claims of "interference with prospective economic advantage" and intentional infliction of emotional distress. . . . The central allegation in the complaint was that the defendants, "individually and in concert, acted in bad faith and with intentional fraud, resulting in the destruction of Dr. Bryan's medical practice."

At trial, as before the Chanda panel, Bryan presented testimony from various expert witnesses explaining that Bryan's actions were proper and did not adversely affect patient care; nothing in the record, they testified, would justify the revocation of Bryan's clinical privileges. . . . Bryan also presented the testimony of witnesses who found fault with the Hospital's peer review procedures, particularly that a transcript of the Chanda panel hearings was not prepared for the Board's use and that the Chanda hearing officer had become too inquisitorial in his questioning. . . . At the close of Bryan's case, the district court . . . concluded . . . that the evidence supported Bryan's claims for breach of contract against the Hospital, and denied the Hospital's motion for a directed verdict because material issues of fact remained concerning the federal and state peer review immunity statutes. The court also found that the evidence supported Bryan's antitrust claims against the Hospital and accordingly submitted those claims to the jury. . . .

Congress clearly intended HCQIA to permit defendants in suits arising out of peer review disciplinary decisions to file motions to resolve the issues concerning immunity from monetary liability as early as possible in the litigation process. . . . Several courts have resolved the issue of HCQIA immunity from damages liability on summary judgment. See, e.g., Austin v. McNamara, 979 F.2d 728, 734-735 (9th Cir. 1991). . . . [I]f the standards of Rule 56 cannot be satisfied . . . the defense of qualified immunity should be decided by the court and should not be submitted for decision by the jury. . . .

If there are disputed subsidiary issues of fact concerning HCQIA immunity, such as whether the disciplined physician was given adequate notice of the charges and the appropriate opportunity to be heard, the court may ask the jury to resolve the subsidiary factual questions by responding to special interrogatories. Under no circumstances should the ultimate question of whether the defendant is immune from monetary liability under HCQIA be submitted to the jury. . . .

As the Ninth Circuit has explained, the rebuttable presumption of HCQIA . . . creates an unusual summary judgment standard that can best be expressed as follows: "Might a reasonable jury, viewing the facts in the best light for [the plaintiff], conclude that he has shown, by a preponderance of the evidence, that the defendants' actions are outside the scope of Sec. 11112(a)?" *Austin*, 979 F.2d at 734. If not, the court should grant the defendant's motion. In a sense, the presumption language in HCQIA means that the plaintiff bears the burden of proving that the peer review process was not reasonable. . . .

We must examine the record in this case to determine whether Bryan satisfied his burden of producing evidence that would allow a reasonable jury to conclude that the Hospital's peer review disciplinary process failed to meet the standards of HCQIA. . . .

The term "professional review action" is defined [as]:

> [A]n action or recommendation of a professional review body which is taken or made in the conduct of professional review activity, which is based on the competence or professional conduct of an individual physician (which conduct affects or could affect adversely the health or welfare of a patient or patients), and which affects (or may affect) adversely the clinical privileges . . . of the physician.

42 U.S.C. §11151(9). While its meaning is generally apparent, the statute does provide the following definition of "professional review activity":

> [A]n activity of a health care entity with respect to an individual physician—(A) to determine whether the physician may have clinical privileges with respect to, or membership in, the entity, (B) to determine the scope or conditions of such privileges or membership, or (C) to change or modify such privileges or membership.

42 U.S.C. §11151(10). . . .

A "professional review body" is defined as "a health care entity and the governing body or any committee of a health care entity which conducts professional review activity, and includes any committee of the medical staff of such an entity when assisting the governing body in a professional review activity." Furthermore, the term "health care entity" includes "a hospital that is licensed to provide health care services by the State in which it is located," [as well as "a health maintenance organization, [a] group medical practice, . . . or a professional society (or committee thereof) of physicians or other licensed health care practitioners that follows a formal peer review process for the purpose of furthering quality health care (as determined under regulations of the Secretary)"]. The Holmes decisionmakers in Bryan's case fall within those categories. . . .

As stated above, a professional review action must satisfy the four standards of §11112(a) in order to qualify for the immunity protections of §11111(a). . . . First, a review of the record makes clear that the decision to terminate Bryan's clinical privileges at Holmes was taken "in the reasonable belief that the action was in the furtherance of quality health care.". . . At trial, Bryan asserted that the members of the board of directors and the executive committee were primarily motivated by personal animosity and not by concern for patient care. He introduced no evidence, however, that such hostility determined the outcome of the peer review process. Moreover, Bryan's "assertions of hostility do not support his position [that the Hospital is not entitled to the HCQIA's protections] because they are irrelevant to the reasonableness standards of Sec. 11112(a). The test is an objective one, so bad faith is immaterial. The real issue is the sufficiency of the basis for the [Hospital's] actions." *Austin*, 979 F.2d at 734. . . .

Second, a review of the record reveals that the Holmes board of directors took its action "after a reasonable effort to obtain the facts of the matter." . . .

Third, Bryan's staff privileges were revoked only "after adequate notice and hearing procedures [were] afforded to the physician involved or after such other procedures as [were] fair to the physician under the circumstances." As noted above, §11112(b) sets forth the "safe harbor" conditions that a health care entity must meet regarding adequate notice and hearing. . . . As the summary of the facts of the case . . . reflects, each of these procedural requirements of §11112(b) was satisfied. Documents introduced at trial indicate that the Hospital complied with the notice requirements and that the hearings were held in a timely fashion and in accordance with the Hospital's bylaws. Bryan was afforded full rights of representation, cross-examination, and confrontation.

Bryan's principal argument is that the board of directors did not have a transcript of the Chanda panel hearings when it rendered its decision. Yet HCQIA, like the Holmes bylaws, requires only that the Hospital ensure that a record of the proceedings be made; Bryan had the responsibility to request a complete transcript if he thought the board should have one, and he did not.

It should be noted that §11112(b) specifically provides that the failure of a review body to meet the enumerated conditions does not, per se, constitute a failure to meet the standards of §11112(a)(3). Indeed, "[i]f other procedures are followed, but are not precisely of the character spelled out in [section 11112(b)], the test of 'adequacy' may still be met under other prevailing law." H.R. Rep. No. 903, at 10. Moreover, Bryan made no contemporaneous objections to the manner in which the hearing procedures were conducted; §11112(b) explicitly provides that compliance with its terms is not required if the physician voluntarily waives them. On the record of this case, we conclude that no reasonable jury could conclude that the Hospital had not afforded Bryan the adequate procedures.

Finally, there is no question that the board decided to terminate Bryan "in the reasonable belief that the action was warranted by the facts known." . . . Bryan concedes that the incidents that led to his termination actually occurred; his only argument is that they did not justify the severe sanction he received. HCQIA clearly grants broad discretion to hospital boards with regard to staff privileges decisions. Accordingly, as in all procedural due process cases, the role of federal courts "on review of such actions is not to substitute our judgment for that of the hospital's governing board or to reweigh the evidence regarding the renewal or termination of medical staff privileges." Shahawy v. Harrison, 875 F.2d 1529, 1533 (11th Cir.1989). . . . "[T]he intent of [the HCQIA] was not to disturb, but to reinforce, the preexisting reluctance of courts to substitute their judgment on the merits for that of health care professionals and of the governing bodies of hospitals in an area within their expertise." Mahmoodian v. United Hosp. Ctr., Inc., 185 W.Va. 59, 404 S.E.2d 750, 756 (1991).

Given that all of the §11112(a) standards were satisfied, we conclude that the Hospital was entitled to the immunity from damages liability granted by HCQIA in §11111(a). . . Bryan has not appealed the district court's refusal to grant injunctive relief. . . .

Notes: Peer Review and State Action Immunity

1. *Limitations of the Federal Statute.* Precisely which peer review actions does the federal immunity cover? A helpful guide is to check (carefully) how many of the preceding cases in this chapter it would preclude. Realize, for instance, that by virtue of the definition of professional review action, "actions against a class of physicians do not fall within the purview of this legislation." House Report No. 99-903, p. 21. Observe also that the statute applies only to actions against physicians, not against other licensed medical professionals. Finally, observe that the statute applies only to peer review actions based on quality or competence factors, not to those based on economic or administrative concerns. And, it is unclear exactly to what extent the statute applies to non-hospital "health care entities." (It applies to HMOs and other entities that conduct a "formal peer review process for the purpose of furthering quality health care," but it is a matter of interpretation whether this includes PPOs, IPAs, ACOs, etc.

How effective do you think the federal immunity is in encouraging vigorous peer review for those entities and decisions that it does cover, considering the showing that must be made to enjoy the immunity? Do the qualifications for immunity differ materially from the scrutiny imposed by common law judicial review? Are the immunity standards more exacting than common law? It appears that the statute's main effect is to shift the burden of proof and remove from the jury the merits of whether the hospital's decision was substantively and procedurally fair, allowing these issues to be decided at the summary judgment stage under a highly deferential standard of review. The Act also contains a fee-shifting provision that allows the court to order the plaintiff to pay the defendants' costs of litigation. See Smith v. Ricks, 31 F.3d 1478 (9th Cir. 1994) (upholding award of over $300,000 in fees and costs).

Does summary judgment appear appropriate where there is a genuine issue of whether an ulterior, anticompetitive motive affected the decision? Should that kind of question be submitted to the jury? What if a hospital does not follow the elaborate hearing procedures or the careful insulation from conflict of interest that occurred here? See Brader v. Allegheny Gen. Hosp., 64 F.3d 869 (3d Cir. 1995) (reversing dismissal of complaint on immunity grounds because full judicial review is especially important "now that the provision of health services is becoming increasingly concentrated and the opportunities for physicians more limited"); Islami v. Covenant Med. Ctr., 822 F. Supp. 1361 (N.D. Iowa 1992) (because the doctor's economic competitors were not excluded from the review process, "the jury [must] answer the question of whether the procedures . . . were fair given the entire factual circumstances; . . . the decision on immunity is hopelessly intertwined with a decision on the merits of the contract claim"); Brown v. Presbyterian Healthcare Servs., 101 F.3d 1324 (10th Cir. 1996) (jury was entitled to find lack of fair hearing where the hospital's inquiry focused too narrowly on only two patient records); Clark v. Columbia/HCA, 25 P.3d 315 (Nev. 2001) (reversing grant of summary judgment and finding no immunity as a matter of law because of evidence hospital was retaliating against physician for "whistleblowing"). But see Brader v. Allegheny Gen. Hosp., 167 F.3d 832 (3d Cir. 1999) (awarding summary judgment on immunity claim despite minor flaws in the peer review proceedings and allegations of bad faith motivations); Parsons v. Sanchez, 46 F.3d 1143 (9th Cir. 1995) (allegations of personal bias and animosity do not rebut presumption of immunity); Alexander v. Memphis Individual Practice Ass'n, 870 S.W.2d 278 (Tenn. 1994) (same, under state immunity statute, for physician excluded from IPA); Cooper v. Delaware Valley Med. Ctr., 654 A.2d 547 (Pa. 1995) (vague allegations of malice not sufficient to avoid summary judgment under state immunity statute); Cardwell v. Rockford Mem. Hosp. Ass'n, 555 N.E.2d 6 (Ill. 1990) (finding absolute immunity under state statute protecting hospital even if conduct was "willful and wanton"); Singh v. Blue Cross and Blue Shield, 182 F. Supp. 2d 164 (D. Mass. 2001) (awarding summary judgment to an HMO even though the evidence showed mixed economic and quality reasons for excluding physician). See generally Charity Scott, Medical Peer Review, Antitrust, and the Effect of Statutory Reform, 50 Md. L. Rev. 316 (1991) ("the Act appears to immunize only conduct that would not be actionable under the antitrust laws in the first place. . . . Remarkably, of the few . . . cases that courts have said were proper for jury resolution, only a handful could even in theory have qualified for immunity."); William Curran, Medical Peer Review of Physician Competence and Performance: Legal Immunity and the Antitrust Laws, 316 New Eng. J. Med. 597, 598 (1987) ("the shield for physicians now contains a plethora of gaping holes through which many a guided missile can reach its human target"); Clark Havighurst, Professional Peer Review and the Antitrust Laws, 36 Case West. L. Rev. 1117, 1161 (1986) ("the new act does more to complicate than to simplify litigation"); Symposium, 33 J. Leg. Med. 1 (2012).

2. *State Confidentiality Statutes.* In addition to the federal immunity statute, virtually every state has a confidentiality statute that makes the proceedings of peer review committees inadmissible in certain legal actions. These peer review confidentiality statutes apply primarily to malpractice actions claiming negligence on the part of the reviewed physician and to malpractice actions against the hospital claiming negligent peer review. These statutes usually do not, however, apply to the

physician's own action against the hospital, since the parties themselves usually want to introduce the records in order to litigate the propriety of what occurred in the proceedings. Possibly, a court might recognize an evidentiary privilege nevertheless to exclude such evidence in order to protect quality improvement activities. A federal court refused this invitation, however, in a case where the physician alleged racial discrimination motives, finding that the public policy in favor of ferreting out discrimination outweighs the competing policies in favor of hospitals protecting peer review committee deliberations. Virmani v. Novant Health Inc., 259 F.3d 284 (N.C. 2001). For critical commentary, see 80 N.C. L. Rev. 1860 (2002).

Several states have also passed immunity statutes similar to the federal HCQIA. An empirical study concluded that these state confidentiality and immunity statutes have no effect on the number of adverse peer review actions taken by hospitals. Susan O. Scheutzow, State Medical Peer Review: High Cost but No Benefit—Is It Time for a Change?, 25 Am. J.L. & Med. 7 (1999).

3. *State Action Immunity.* Another potential defense in medical staff disputes, one that is applicable only under the federal antitrust laws, is known as "state action immunity." In Parker v. Brown, 317 U.S. 341 (1943), the Supreme Court held that the antitrust laws do not apply to activity engaged in or required by the states. For instance, it would be spurious to charge a state regulatory agency with an antitrust violation for denying a certificate of need to a new hospital.

The state action defense potentially exists with respect to physician discipline even at *private* hospitals if state law mandates and "actively supervises" the private peer review process. This contention was the subject of Patrick v. Burget, 486 U.S. 94 (1988), which involved a doctor who was forced to resign from the staff of the only hospital in town in retaliation for refusing to join the group practice that composed a majority of the medical staff. The Ninth Circuit relied on the *Parker v. Brown* state action exemption in overturning a damage award of more than $2 million that had sent shock waves through the medical establishment. (It was this verdict that prompted Congress to enact the HCQIA immunity.) However, the Supreme Court reversed and reinstated the verdict, holding that private hospital credentialing decisions in Oregon are not sufficiently supervised by the state to bring them within the protection of this defense. The Court observed that Oregon so far has not recognized a common law right to judicial review of the substance of private hospitals' credentialing decisions.

Although *Patrick* was initially read as closing the door to state action exemption in medical staff disputes, it left open the slight possibility that this defense might be available in another state whose common law differs. However, it does not appear that even a *Greisman* common law theory of judicial review would meet the Court's objection that "[the courts do no] more than to make sure that some sort of reasonable procedure was afforded and that there was evidence from which it could be found that plaintiff's conduct posed a threat to patient care." And, the Supreme Court held that the mere fact that a hospital is owned by a public entity does not make it immune from antitrust merger scrutiny, since the state did not clearly articulate an anticompetitive purpose in creating the public hospital authority. FTC v. Phoebe Putney Health System, Inc., 568 U.S. 216 (2013).

Another area of dispute is whether state boards of medical examiners are immune from federal antitrust law when they impose restrictive conditions on physicians or their potential competitors. In an important decision, the Supreme Court ruled that the dental licensing board in North Carolina was not immune as a state actor in ruling that teeth whitening cannot be done by non-dentists, because the state had not articulated a clear policy against non-dental teeth whitening, and it did not actively supervise the licensing board's decisions. North Carolina State Board of Dental Examiners vs. FTC, 135 S. Ct. 1101 (2015). It remains to be seen how expansive this precedent might be (e.g., does it mean the licensing boards can be sued simply for disciplining a particular doctor), and what constitutes "active supervision" over licensing boards. Consider, also, the significance for the state bar. For discussion, see Note, 129 Harv. L. Rev. 371 (2015); Comment, 66 Emory L.J. 443 (2017); Comment, 63 UCLA L. Rev. 1110 (2016); Comment, 84 U. Chi. L. Rev. 1473 (2017).

4. *Immunity via State Certification.* State action immunity from antitrust suits has been reinvigorated in a number of states that have created procedures intended specifically to meet the "active supervision" requirement missing in private peer review. These states have implemented a state governmental review process leading to a "certificate of public advantage" (or COPA) in which private parties submit certain risky ventures that they want blessed with antitrust immunity. This state review process is designed to meet the active supervision requirements set forth in FTC v. Ticor Title Ins. Co., 504 U.S. 621 (1992). For the most part, however, these COPA statutes do not apply to peer review decisions. Instead, they are directed to joint ventures and mergers, in which hospitals and other providers seek to cooperate in order to achieve efficiencies and avoid costly duplication of facilities. See Randall R. Bovbjerg & Robert A. Berenson. Certificates of Public Advantage: Can They Address Provider Market Power? (Urban Institute, 2015).

2. *Price-Fixing Law*

ARIZONA v. MARICOPA COUNTY MEDICAL SOCIETY
457 U.S. 332 (1982)

Justice STEVENS delivered the opinion of the Court.

The question presented is whether §1 of the Sherman Act, 26 Stat. 209, as amended, 15 U.S.C. §1, has been violated by agreements among competing physicians setting, by majority vote, the maximum fees that they may claim in full payment for health services provided to policyholders of specified insurance plans. The United States Court of Appeals for the Ninth Circuit held that the question could not be answered without evaluating the actual purpose and effect of the agreements at a full trial. Because the undisputed facts disclose a violation of the statute, we granted certiorari and now reverse.

I

In October 1978, the state of Arizona filed a civil complaint against two county medical societies and two "foundations for medical care" that the medical societies had organized. The complaint alleged that the defendants were engaged in illegal price-fixing conspiracies. . . .

The Maricopa Foundation for Medical Care is a nonprofit Arizona corporation composed of licensed doctors of medicine, osteopathy, and podiatry engaged in private practice. Approximately 1,750 doctors, representing about 70 percent of the practitioners in Maricopa County, are members. The Maricopa Foundation was organized in 1969 for the purpose of promoting fee-for-service medicine and to provide the community with a competitive alternative to existing health insurance plans. The foundation performs three primary activities. It establishes the schedule of maximum fees that participating doctors agree to accept as payment in full for services performed for patients insured under plans approved by the foundation. It reviews the medical necessity and appropriateness of treatment provided by its members to such insured persons. It is authorized to draw checks on insurance company accounts to pay doctors for services performed for covered patients. In performing these functions, the foundation is considered an "insurance administrator" by the Director of the Arizona Department of Insurance. Its participating doctors, however, have no financial interest in the operation of the foundation.

The Pima Foundation for Medical Care, which includes about 400 member doctors, performs similar functions. For the purposes of this litigation, the parties seem to regard the activities of the two foundations as essentially the same. No challenge is made to their peer review or claim administration functions. Nor do the foundations allege that these two activities make it necessary for them to engage in the practice of establishing maximum-fee schedules. . . .

The fee schedules limit the amount that the member doctors may recover for services performed for patients insured under plans approved by the foundations. To obtain this approval the insurers—including self-insured employers as well as insurance companies—agree to pay the doctors' charges up to the scheduled amounts, and in exchange the doctors agree to accept those amounts as payment in full for their services. The doctors are free to charge higher fees to uninsured patients, and they also may charge any patient less than the scheduled maxima. A patient who is insured by a foundation-endorsed plan is guaranteed complete coverage for the full amount of his medical bills only if he is treated by a foundation member. He is free to go to a nonmember physician and is still covered for charges that do not exceed the maximum-fee schedule, but he must pay any excess that the nonmember physician may charge.

The impact of the foundation fee schedules on medical fees and on insurance premiums is a matter of dispute. The state of Arizona contends that the periodic upward revisions of the maximum-fee schedules have the effect of stabilizing and enhancing the level of actual charges by physicians, and that the increasing level of their fees in turn increases insurance premiums. The foundations, on the other hand, argue that the schedules impose a meaningful limit on physicians' charges, and that the advance agreement by the doctors to accept the maxima enables the insurance carriers to limit and to calculate more efficiently the risks they underwrite and therefore serves as an effective cost-containment mechanism that has saved patients and insurers millions of dollars. Although the Attorneys General of 40 different states, as well as the Solicitor General of the United States and certain organizations representing consumers of medical services, have filed amicus curiae briefs supporting the state of Arizona's position on the merits, we must assume that the respondents' view of the genuine issues of fact is correct.

This assumption presents, but does not answer, the question whether the Sherman Act prohibits the competing doctors from adopting, revising, and agreeing to use a maximum-fee schedule in implementation of the insurance plans.

III

The respondents recognize that our decisions establish that price-fixing agreements are unlawful on their face. But they argue that the per se rule does not govern this case because the agreements at issue are horizontal and fix maximum prices, are among members of a profession, are in an industry with which the judiciary has little antitrust experience, and are alleged to have procompetitive justifications. Before we examine each of these arguments, we pause to consider the history and the meaning of the per se rule against price-fixing agreements.

Section 1 of the Sherman Act of 1890 literally prohibits *every* agreement "in restraint of trade." In United States v. Joint Traffic Assn., 171 U.S. 505 (1898), we recognized that Congress could not have intended a literal interpretation of the word *every*; since Standard Oil Co. of New Jersey v. United States, 221 U.S. 1 (1911), we have analyzed most restraints under the so-called rule of reason. As its name suggests, the rule of reason requires the factfinder to decide whether under all the circumstances of the case the restrictive practice imposes an unreasonable restraint on competition.

The elaborate inquiry into the reasonableness of a challenged business practice entails significant costs. Litigation of the effect or purpose of a practice often is extensive and complex. Judges often lack the expert understanding of industrial market structures and behavior to determine with any confidence a practice's effect on competition. And the result of the process in any given case may provide little certainty or guidance about the legality of a practice in another context.

The costs of judging business practices under the rule of reason, however, have been reduced by the recognition of per se rules. Once experience with a particular kind of restraint enables the Court to predict with confidence that the rule of reason will condemn it, it has applied a conclusive presumption that the restraint is unreasonable. As in every rule of general application, the match between the presumed and the actual is imperfect. For the sake of business certainty and litigation efficiency, we have tolerated the invalidation of some agreements that a fullblown inquiry might have proved to be reasonable. . . .

[P]rice-fixing agreements are unlawful per se under the Sherman Act and . . . "no showing of so-called competitive abuses or evils which those agreements were designed to eliminate or alleviate may be interposed as a defense." United States v. Socony-Vacuum Oil Co., 310 U.S. 150, 218 (1940). In that case, a glut in the spot market for gasoline had prompted the major oil refiners to engage in a concerted effort to purchase and store surplus gasoline in order to maintain stable prices. Absent the agreement, the companies argued, competition was cutthroat and self-defeating. The argument did not carry the day:

> Any combination which tampers with price structures is engaged in an unlawful activity. . . . The Act places all such schemes beyond the pale and protects that vital part of our economy against any degree of interference. . . . Nor has the Act created or authorized the creation of any special exception in favor of the oil industry. Whatever may be its peculiar problems and characteristics, the Sherman Act, so far as price-fixing agreements are concerned, establishes one uniform rule applicable to all industries alike. . . . Under the Sherman Act a combination formed for the purpose and with the effect of raising, depressing, fixing, pegging, or stabilizing the price of a commodity in interstate or foreign commerce is illegal per se.

Over the objection that maximum-price-fixing agreements were not the "economic equivalent" of minimum-price-fixing agreements, [we held in] Albrecht v. Herald Co., 390 U.S. 145 (1968):

> Maximum and minimum price fixing may have different consequences in many situations. But schemes to fix maximum prices, by substituting the perhaps erroneous judgment of a seller for the forces of the competitive market, may severely intrude upon the ability of buyers to compete and survive in that market. Competition, even in a single product, is not cast in a single mold. Maximum prices may be fixed too low for the dealer to furnish services essential to the value which goods have for the consumer or to furnish services and conveniences which consumers desire and for which they are willing to pay. Maximum price fixing may channel distribution through a few large or specifically advantaged dealers who otherwise would be subject to significant nonprice competition. Moreover, if the actual price charged under a maximum price scheme is nearly always the fixed maximum price, which is increasingly likely as the maximum price approaches the actual cost of the dealer, the scheme tends to acquire all the attributes of an arrangement fixing minimum prices.

We have not wavered in our enforcement of the per se rule against price fixing. Indeed, in our most recent price-fixing case we summarily reversed the decision of another Ninth Circuit panel that a horizontal agreement among competitors to fix credit terms does not necessarily contravene the antitrust laws. Catalano, Inc. v. Target Sales, Inc., 446 U.S. 643 (1980). . . . The per se rule "is grounded on faith in price competition as a market force [and not] on a policy of low selling prices at the price of eliminating competition." Rahl, Price Competition and the Price Fixing Rule—Preface and Perspective, 57 Nw. U. L. Rev. 137, 142 (1962). In this case the rule is violated by a price restraint that tends to provide the same economic rewards to all practitioners regardless of their skill, their experience, their training, or their willingness to employ innovative and difficult procedures in individual cases. Such a restraint also may discourage entry into the market and may deter experimentation and new developments by individual entrepreneurs. It may be a masquerade for an agreement to fix uniform prices, or it may in the future take on that character.

Nor does the fact that doctors—rather than nonprofessionals—are the parties to the price-fixing agreements support the respondents' position. In Goldfarb v. Virginia State Bar, 421 U.S. 773, 788, n.17 (1975), we stated that the "public service aspect, and other features of the professions, may require that a particular practice, which could properly be viewed as a violation of the Sherman Act in another context, be treated differently." See National Society of Professional Engineers v. United States, 435 U.S. 679, 696 (1978). The price-fixing agreements in this case, however, are not premised on public service or ethical norms. The respondents do not argue, as did the defendants in *Goldfarb* and *Professional Engineers,* that the quality of the professional service that their members provide is enhanced by the price restraint. The respondents' claim for relief from the per se rule is simply that the doctors' agreement not to charge certain insureds more than a fixed price facilitates the successful marketing of an attractive insurance plan. But the claim that the price restraint will make it easier for customers to pay does not distinguish the medical profession from any other provider of goods or services. . . .

The respondents' principal argument is that the per se rule is inapplicable because their agreements are alleged to have procompetitive justifications. The argument indicates a misunderstanding of the per se concept. The anticompetitive potential inherent in all price-fixing agreements justifies their facial invalidation even if procompetitive justifications are offered for some. Those claims of enhanced competition are so unlikely to prove significant in any particular case that we adhere to the rule of law that is justified in its general application. Even when the respondents are given every benefit of the doubt, the limited record in this case is not inconsistent with the presumption that the respondents' agreements will not significantly enhance competition. . . .

It is true that a binding assurance of complete insurance coverage—as well as most of the respondents' potential for lower insurance premiums—can be obtained only if the insurer and the doctor agree in advance on the maximum fee that the doctor will accept as full payment for a particular service. Even if a fee schedule is therefore desirable, it is not necessary that the doctors do the price fixing.[26] The record indicates that the Arizona Comprehensive Medical/Dental Program for Foster Children is administered by the Maricopa Foundation pursuant to a contract under which the maximum-fee schedule is prescribed by a state agency rather than by the doctors. This program and the Blue Shield plan challenged in Group Life & Health Insurance Co. v. Royal Drug Co., 440 U.S. 205 (1979), indicate that insurers are capable not only of fixing maximum reimbursable prices but also of obtaining binding agreements with providers guaranteeing the insured full reimbursement of a participating provider's fee. In light of these examples, it is not surprising that nothing in the record even arguably supports the conclusion that this type of insurance program could not function if the fee schedules were set in a different way.

The most that can be said for having doctors fix the maximum prices is that doctors may be able to do it more efficiently than insurers. The validity of that assumption is far from obvious, but in any event there is no reason to believe that any savings that might accrue from this arrangement would be sufficiently great to affect the competitiveness of these kinds of insurance plans. It is entirely possible that the potential or actual power of the foundations to dictate the terms of such insurance plans may more than offset the theoretical efficiencies upon which the respondents' defense ultimately rests. . . .

IV

Having declined the respondents' invitation to cut back on the per se rule against price fixing, we are left with the respondents' argument that their fee schedules involve price fixing in only a literal sense. For this argument, the respondents rely upon Broadcast Music, Inc. v. Columbia Broadcasting System, Inc., 441 U.S. 1 (1979).

26. . . . [T]his case [does not] present the question whether an insurer may, consistent with the Sherman Act, fix the fee schedule and enter into bilateral contracts with individual doctors. . . . In an amicus curiae brief, the United States expressed its opinion that such an arrangement would be legal unless the plaintiffs could establish that a conspiracy among providers was at work. . . .

In *Broadcast Music,* we were confronted with an antitrust challenge to the marketing of the right to use copyrighted compositions derived from the entire membership of the American Society of Composers, Authors and Publishers (ASCAP). The so-called blanket license was entirely different from the product that any one composer was able to sell by himself. Although there was little competition among individual composers for their separate compositions, the blanket-license arrangement did not place any restraint on the right of any individual copyright owner to sell his own compositions separately to any buyer at any price. But a "necessary consequence" of the creation of the blanket license was that its price had to be established. We held that the delegation by the composers to ASCAP of the power to fix the price for the blanket license was not a species of the price-fixing agreements categorically forbidden by the Sherman Act. The record disclosed price fixing only in a "literal sense."

This case is fundamentally different. Each of the foundations is composed of individual practitioners who compete with one another for patients. Neither the foundations nor the doctors sell insurance, and they derive no profits from the sale of health insurance policies. The members of the foundations sell medical services. Their combination in the form of the foundation does not permit them to sell any different product. Their combination has merely permitted them to sell their services to certain customers at fixed prices and arguably to affect the prevailing market price of medical care.

The foundations are not analogous to partnerships or other joint arrangements in which persons who would otherwise be competitors pool their capital and share the risks of loss as well as the opportunities for profit. In such joint ventures, the partnership is regarded as a single firm competing with other sellers in the market. The agreement under attack is an agreement among hundreds of competing doctors concerning the price at which each will offer his own services to a substantial number of consumers. It is true that some are surgeons, some anesthesiologists, and some psychiatrists, but the doctors do not sell a package of three kinds of services. If a clinic offered complete medical coverage for a flat fee, the cooperating doctors would have the type of partnership arrangement in which a price-fixing agreement among the doctors would be perfectly proper. But the fee agreements disclosed by the record in this case are among independent competing entrepreneurs. They fit squarely into the horizontal price-fixing mold.

The judgment of the court of appeals is reversed.

Justices Blackmun and O'Connor took no part in this case [due to conflicts of interest].

Justice Powell, with whom The Chief Justice and Justice Rehnquist join, dissenting.

The medical care plan condemned by the Court today is a comparatively new method of providing insured medical services at predetermined maximum costs. It involves no coercion. Medical insurance companies, physicians, and patients alike are free to participate or not as they choose. On its face, the plan seems to be in the public interest. . . .

It is settled law that once an arrangement has been labeled as "price fixing" it is to be condemned per se. But it is equally well settled that this characterization is not to be applied as a talisman to every arrangement that involves a literal fixing of prices. Many lawful contracts, mergers, and partnerships fix prices. But our cases require a more discerning approach. . . . In Broadcast Music, Inc. v. Columbia Broadcasting System, Inc., supra, there was minimum price fixing in the most "literal sense." We nevertheless agreed, unanimously, that an arrangement by which copyright clearinghouses sold performance rights to their entire libraries on a blanket rather than individual basis did not warrant condemnation on a per se basis. Individual licensing would have allowed competition between copyright owners. But we reasoned that licensing on a blanket basis yielded substantial efficiencies that otherwise could not be realized. Indeed, the blanket license was itself "to some extent, a different product."

In sum, the fact that a foundation-sponsored health insurance plan literally involves the setting of ceiling prices among competing physicians does not, of itself, justify condemning the plan as per se illegal. Only if it is clear from the record that the agreement among physicians is "so plainly anticompetitive that no elaborate study of [its effects] is needed to establish [its] illegality" may a court properly make a per se judgment. National Society of Professional Engineers v. United States, supra, at 692. . . .

In a complex economy, complex economic arrangements are commonplace. It is unwise for the Court, in a case as novel and important as this one, to make a final judgment in the absence of a complete record and where mandatory inferences create critical issues of fact.

Notes: Price-Fixing Antitrust Liability; Managed Care Networks; Joint Ventures

1. *Foundation Plans.* Medical society "foundation plans," such as those considered in *Maricopa County,* arose in the 1970s as a way for the medical profession to resist the introduction of alternative financing and delivery systems such as HMOs. These arrangements illustrate the AMA's continuing "strategy of preemption and cooptation [through] professionally sponsored reforms." Clark Havighurst, Professional Restraints on Innovation in Health Care Financing, 1978 Duke L.J. 303. It is therefore not surprising that the Court found these plans to have anticompetitive potential, especially where they include most of the doctors in town. This ruling is borne out by subsequent developments in Phoenix, where the number of PPOs and HMOs increased from 1 to 18 within three years of the *Maricopa County* decision.

2. *Managed Care Provider Networks. Maricopa County*'s importance for health care markets extends far beyond the particular "foundation plans" the Court ruled on. Observe that these largely defunct foundations plans were structurally identical to present-day PPOs, which are now the dominant form of health insurance. PPOs give subscribers a discount if they seek care from doctors and hospitals within the preferred network, rather than allowing the completely free choice of providers, or forcing patients to use *only* contracted providers. Providers agree to accept discounted payments in exchange for the prospect of a higher volume of business, and they agree to abide by certain utilization review protocols. More recently, we have also seen the formation of ACOs (accountable care organizations), in which

providers affiliate not only to provide more competitive pricing, but also to coordinate care and contract for more value-based payment methods than traditional fee-for-service. Does *Maricopa County* remain convincing in the present-day climate where ACOs, PPOs, and other types of provider networks are seen as *pro*competitive innovations? Note that, due to recusals, the majority opinion has the support of only four justices.

One potential way to distinguish the *Maricopa County* arrangement from current market arrangements is whether the impetus for the formation of a provider network comes from purchasers rather than from providers. In a purchaser-based network, an employer or insurance company approaches doctors and hospitals individually and negotiates with each separately. But sometimes, providers take the initiative by jointly agreeing to offer their services as a package to employers or insurers. In the past, they have done so mainly on a discounted fee-for-service basis, through what are known as Independent Practice Associations (IPAs). These provider-initiated networks raise the distinct aura of per se illegal price fixing, yet it may be necessary for groups of providers to cooperate in order for potentially procompetitive activity to flourish, especially if providers are to be organized in a manner (such as ACOs) that permits different forms of payment such as capitation or outcomes-based payment incentives.

Thus, the primary legal concern for managed care provider networks is whether this can be done in a way that avoids price-fixing antitrust liability.

3. *Antitrust Enforcement Guidelines.* Both the DOJ and the FTC have enforcement authority over the antitrust laws. These agencies, in exercising their prosecutorial discretion, have taken a substantially more encouraging position against provider networks. In a joint set of "Statements of Antitrust Enforcement Policy in Health Care," called the "DOJ/FTC Antitrust Guidelines," the two agencies establish the following safety zones for physician (not hospital) networks:

> By developing and implementing mechanisms that encourage physicians to collaborate in practicing efficiently as part of the network, many physician network joint ventures promise significant procompetitive benefits for consumers of health care services. . . . To qualify for [an] antitrust safety zone, the physicians participating in a physician network joint venture must share substantial financial risk. . . . Risk sharing provides incentive for the physicians to cooperate in controlling costs and improving quality by managing the provision of services by network physicians. The following are examples of situations in which participants in a physician network joint venture can share substantial financial risk:
>
> (1) agreement by the venture to provide services to a health plan at a "capitated" rate; or . . .
> (2) use by the venture of significant financial incentives for its physician participants, as a group, to achieve specified cost-containment goals . . . [such as] withholding from all physician participants a substantial amount of the compensation due to them, with distribution of that amount to the physician participants based on group performance in meeting the cost-containment goals. . . .
>
> Physician network joint ventures that fall outside the antitrust safety zone . . . do not necessarily raise substantial antitrust concerns. . . . [They] will be analyzed under

the rule of reason, and will not be viewed as per se illegal, if the physicians' integration through the network is likely to produce significant efficiencies that benefit consumers, and any price agreements are reasonably necessary to realize those efficiencies. . . .

Physician network joint ventures that do not involve the sharing of substantial financial risk may also involve sufficient [clinical] integration to demonstrate that the venture is likely to produce sufficient efficiencies. Such [clinical] integration can be evidenced by the network implementing an active and ongoing program to evaluate and modify practice patterns . . . and to create a high degree of interdependence and cooperation among the physicians to control costs and ensure quality. . . .

In contrast to integrated physician network joint ventures, such as these, . . . there have been arrangements among physicians that have taken the form of networks, but which in purpose or effect were little more than efforts by their participants to prevent or impede competitive forces from operating in the market. . . . Determining that an arrangement is merely a vehicle to fix prices or engage in naked anticompetitive conduct is a factual inquiry that must be done on a case-by-case basis to determine the arrangement's true nature and likely competitive effects. . . . In assessing the competitive environment, the Agencies would consider such market factors as the number, types, and size of managed care plans operating in the area [and] the extent of physician participation in those plans. If in the relevant market there are many other networks or many physicians who would be available to form competing networks or to contract directly with health plans, it is unlikely that the joint venture would raise significant competitive concerns. . . . The Agencies will consider a broad range of possible cost savings, including improved cost controls, case management and quality assurance, economies of scale, and reduced administrative or transaction costs. . . .

Some networks that are not substantially integrated use a variety of "messenger model" arrangements to facilitate contracting between providers and payers and avoid price-fixing agreements among competing network providers. Arrangements that are designed simply to minimize the costs associated with the contracting process, and that do not result in collective determination by the competing network providers on prices or price-related terms, are not per se illegal price fixing. . . . For example, network providers may use an agent or third party to convey to purchasers information obtained individually from the providers about the prices or price-related terms that the providers are willing to accept. In some cases, the agent may convey to the providers all contract offers made by purchasers, and each provider then makes an independent, unilateral decision to accept or reject the contract offers. In others, the agent may have received from individual providers some authority to accept contract offers on their behalf. . . . The Agencies will examine whether the agent facilitates collective decision-making by network providers, rather than independent, unilateral, decisions.[65] . . .

65. Use of an intermediary or "independent" third party to convey collectively determined price offers to purchasers or to negotiate agreements with purchasers, or giving to individual providers an opportunity to "opt" into, or out of, such agreements does not negate the existence of an agreement.

Are the DOJ/FTC Antitrust Guidelines consistent with *Maricopa County*? See generally Scott Danzis, Revising the Revised Guidelines: Incentives, Clinically Integrated Physician Networks, and the Antitrust Laws, 87 Va. L. Rev. 531 (2001).

Observe that these safe harbors do not apply to "multi-provider" networks; that is, those that contain hospitals. Why might the antitrust risks be greater or different when hospitals are present?

4. *Joint Venture Techniques.* The *Maricopa County* decision and the enforcement guidelines suggest three possible avenues for organizing a provider network to avoid a per se price-fixing charge:

a. *Financial or clinical integration.* No horizontal price fixing exists if doctors integrate into a single economic entity that bears substantial financial risk. This can occur through true corporate integration in which doctors invest capital and form a joint business enterprise. Or, it can occur through contractual joint venture arrangements. In the latter case, the focus is on the degree of financial risk sharing or clinical integration. The DOJ/FTC Guidelines give examples, but provide no quantification. A portion of *Hassan v. Independent Practice Associates* held that a "risk withhold" payment system that placed 12 to 25 percent of the physicians' payments at risk succeeded in classifying an IPA physician network as a "legitimate joint venture" under *Maricopa County*, thus escaping per se condemnation. This escape hatch raises a number of additional questions.

First, is it necessary for all doctors to share substantial risk for all of their services, or only for some or most? Payment schemes for specialists often differ substantially from those for primary care physicians. In two simultaneous consent orders (St. Joseph's and Danbury), the DOJ indicated that it is sufficient if the controlling physicians bear substantial risk; physicians who are paid by the network only as subcontractors may be reimbursed on a fee-for-service basis. 60 Fed. Reg. 51,809, 52,015 (1995).

Second, are there other ways to establish integration besides financial risk sharing? After vehement argument from the AMA and others, the DOJ and FTC revised their initial guidelines to allow a showing of *clinical* integration to suffice, as quoted above. Observe how clinical integration is defined. Illustrations include utilization review, quality assurance, practice guidelines, and physician credentialing. Are these enough to demonstrate that physicians in different offices are practicing as a coordinated clinical enterprise, or are they merely "window dressing" as found in *Maricopa County*? In the first ruling to find clinical integration, the FTC ruled in February 2002 (letter regarding MedSouth, Inc.) that it would not constitute a per se violation for more than half the doctors in one part of Denver to jointly negotiate with insurers, as long as they did so on a nonexclusive basis (i.e., each doctor could opt out and negotiate independently). The FTC found clinical integration to exist because the doctors proposed to share medical information, develop practice guidelines, monitor performance, and reduce utilization. The FTC also "concluded that the joint contracting appears to be sufficiently related to, and reasonably necessary for, the achievement of the potential benefits [of clinical integration] to be regarded as ancillary to the operation of the venture." Does that sound plausible to you? Especially noteworthy is the FTC's 2009 approval of the TriState Health Partners joint venture between the only hospital in Hagerstown, Maryland and most of the area's 300 physicians, finding enough indicia of increased clinical interaction among participating providers. For commentary, see Taylor Burke

& Sara Rosenbaum, Accountable Care Organizations: Implications for Antitrust Policy (Robert Wood Johnson Foundation, 2010), *reprinted in* 19 BNA Health L. Rep. 358 (2010); Thomas B. Leary, The Antitrust Implications of "Clinical Integration:" An Analysis of FTC Staff's Advisory Opinion to MedSouth, 47 St. Louis U. L. Rev. 223 (2003); Comment, 14 Ann. Health L. 125 (2005).

The third problem is that full-scale integration may not be the most attractive option for physicians, either from a business or from a legal antitrust perspective. From a business perspective, when provider groups assume substantial financial risk for medical treatment, they may as a result fall within the jurisdiction of state health insurance regulations that require them to maintain large capital reserves to protect consumers against their insolvency. See Chapter 3.B. From a legal perspective, consider what new antitrust problems would exist if 70 percent of the doctors in Phoenix had formed a joint venture. See the discussion of merger law that follows. On the other hand, what antitrust issues would exist if PPO physicians selectively limited membership to a smaller number of competitors? See the discussion of boycott law in section D.1; Reazin v. Blue Cross & Blue Shield of Kansas, 899 F.2d 951 (10th Cir. 1990) ($7.8 million verdict sustained in favor of hospital excluded by a PPO).

b. *Creation of a new product.* A second way to avoid per se price fixing, based on the reasoning of the *Broadcast Music* (*BMI*) case discussed in *Maricopa County,* is for physicians to attempt to form a new product. In *BMI,* the Court used the new product characterization to justify its holding that a "blanket license" for a library of music compositions did not constitute price fixing even though numerous music composers collectively agreed to market their compositions through a joint agency rather than dealing individually with each radio station and nightclub singer. See also NCAA v. Board of Regents, 468 U.S. 85 (1984) ("horizontal restraints on competition are essential if [an organized college football league] is to be available at all"). Why did the Court reject the Foundation plans' argument that the bulk sale of physician services to insurance companies and large employers, coupled with claims processing, quality assurance, and utilization review, constitutes a new health care product? What did the Court indicate would suffice to meet the new product test?

The DOJ/FTC Antitrust Guidelines do not speak in terms of a "new product," but instead analyze the *BMI* issue in terms of procompetitive efficiencies. The guidelines leave open the possibility that a network lacking financial integration may still be able to avoid per se condemnation if, after what some commentators call a "quick look" review, it appears not to be a "naked" restraint but instead is a "legitimate" joint venture. In such a case, the agencies will then weigh the procompetitive benefits against the anticompetitive harms. The agencies remain skeptical, however, that a network will actually survive this scrutiny if it in fact lacks financial and clinical integration. Therefore, it still appears necessary to show that a network does something more than merely facilitate marketing of physician services.

c. *The "messenger" model.* The easiest way to avoid per se condemnation is to show that no horizontal price agreement exists at all. This is so if physicians individually respond to unilateral price offers from potential buyers. See n.26 in the opinion. The "messenger model" is an attempt to capitalize on this notion by using the physician network as merely a means to communicate and coordinate individual offers, counteroffers, and acceptances. The difficulty is that such coordinated price negotiations could easily be viewed as constituting an implicit horizontal agreement among the doctors, especially where most of them end up agreeing to the same prices. Consider, for instance, whether doctors could legally agree in advance to be bound by the best price a joint negotiator is capable of obtaining from each purchaser? The DOJ and FTC have taken a strict stance against versions of the messenger model that resemble this "black box" variation. In various rulings, they have looked with disfavor on price negotiations initiated by quotes from the providers rather than bids from the purchasers, and they have ruled against an arrangement where physicians are bound in advance to negotiators' best prices unless they opt out. North Texas Specialty Physicians v. FTC, 528 F.3d 346 (5th Cir. 2008). This still leaves intact the possibility of an "opt-in" messenger arrangement, and at least one court has ruled that even an "opt-out" arrangement is legal where a nonphysician risk-bearing entity (e.g., an HMO) takes the initiative in formulating the fee schedule. Levine v. Central Florida Medical Affiliates, 72 F.3d 1538 (11th Cir. 1996).

5. *Safe Harbors for ACOs.* The FTC's rulings on "clinical integration" lay the groundwork for the government's emerging position on the new ACOs that are expected to take shape, to participate in Medicare's new "shared savings" program. Some commentators fear that when independent hospitals and doctors form ACOs, this will lead to greater market power, thereby driving up health care costs and insurance premiums. See, e.g., T. Greaney, The Affordable Care Act and Competition Policy: Antidote or Placebo? 89 Or. L. Rev. 811 (2011). Others complain that antitrust law is a major barrier to providers forming more effective coordination and integration of care.

Attempting to walk this fence, the DOJ and FTC issued a special set of antitrust guidelines for ACOs, building on their more general guidelines above. 76 Fed. Reg. 67026 (2011). In brief:

1. Qualifying ACOs are automatically regarded as clinically integrated, and thus subject to only rule of reason scrutiny;
2. A safe harbor applies to ACOs whose providers constitute less than 30 percent of the local market in each category or service, or, in rural areas, no more than one hospital or one physician per specialty;[8]
3. ACOs that fall outside the safe harbor are warned to avoid certain activities that raise competitive concerns, or to seek specific agency approval for such arrangements, but agency review is not mandatory. These activities of concern include interfering with insurers' cost-savings efforts, or requiring participating providers to deal with the ACO exclusively.

See Deborah Feinstein et al., ACOs and Antitrust Enforcement: Promoting Competition and Innovation, 40 J. Health Pol. Pol'y & L. 873 (2015); T. Greaney, Regulators as Market-Makers: ACOs and Competition Policy, 46 Ariz. L.J. 1 (2014).

6. *Virtual Merger: Beware.* Antitrust enforcers have also turned their attention to the price-fixing implications of what are known as "virtual mergers" or "joint

8. In addition, to receive safe harbor protection: ACOs may not contract exclusively with just one insurer; and participation by hospitals and rural physicians must be nonexclusive, meaning they are free to join other ACOs. Also, the guidelines provide detailed instructions for computing market boundaries and shares.

operating agreements." In these arrangements, two or more entities attempt to accomplish the substance of a merger without actual common corporate ownership, through detailed agreements that provide for joint or coordinated operations and management. Sometimes, this is done to avoid various corporate law restrictions that prevent complete merger, for instance, between religious and nonreligious hospitals, but sometimes this is done because the boards of the different entities simply can't agree on a full merger but still want to attempt joint operations. In such cases, the parties run the risk of per se illegal price fixing if the contractual arrangements do not create sufficient financial or corporate integration. For instance, in Medical Center at Elizabeth Place v. Atrium Health System, 817 F.3d 934 (6th Cir. 2016), the court surprised health lawyers by ruling (in a 2-1 decision) that a carefully constructed joint operating agreement did not create a single entity for antitrust purposes, thus exposing the participating hospitals to potentially per se liability in their managed care contracting. The court emphasized that, despite consolidating many of their operations, the participating hospitals did not give up their separate "corporate consciousness" but remained competitive rivals in important respects, analogizing to the NFL, which, the Supreme Court held is engaged in concerted action when it coordinates licensing for the teams' logo'ed sportswear. American Needle v. National Football League, 560 U.S. 183 (2010).

OCEAN STATE PHYSICIANS HEALTH PLAN, INC. v. BLUE CROSS & BLUE SHIELD OF RHODE ISLAND

883 F.2d 1101 (1st Cir. 1989)

LEVIN H. CAMPBELL, Chief Judge.

. . . Defendant Blue Cross, a nonprofit corporation established in 1939, has long been the largest health insurer in Rhode Island. It purchases health services from physicians, hospitals, and other health care providers on behalf of its subscribers. . . . Plaintiff Ocean State is a for-profit health maintenance organization (HMO) that began operations in 1984. Like Blue Cross, Ocean State contracts with physicians to provide medical care to its subscribers, and then pays its contracted physicians on a fee-for-service basis. . . . Eighty percent of the shares of the Ocean State corporation are owned by its participating physicians. A physician may participate in more than one health insurance program. . . .

Apparently because Ocean State provided more coverage and charged lower premiums, many subscribers switched from Blue Cross to Ocean State. By the spring of 1986, Blue Cross had lost approximately 30,000 of its 543,015 enrollees, while Ocean State's enrollment had exceeded all expectations, growing to 70,000. . . . [T]o meet the challenge presented by Ocean State, Blue Cross instituted a three-pronged attack:

First, Blue Cross launched its own HMO "look-alike," dubbed HealthMate, which it marketed to employers who were offering the Ocean State plan to their employees. Like Ocean State, HealthMate provided 15 percent more coverage than the standard Blue Cross plan, including such added benefits as office visits, prescription drugs, and "good health" benefits. . . .

Second, Blue Cross instituted an "adverse selection" policy of pricing. "Adverse selection" refers to the tendency for younger and healthier people to opt for HMOs such as Ocean State when they are made available, leaving older and sicker people (on the average) in the standard Blue Cross pool. Because of such adverse selection, Blue Cross expected the health care costs for standard Blue Cross to be higher in those employer groups that offered an HMO option than in those employer groups that did not. . . . Blue Cross instituted a pricing plan that took account of this projected difference in health expenses. Under this policy, employers were offered three different rates for traditional Blue Cross coverage. The rate was lowest for an employer who offered only traditional Blue Cross, intermediate for an employer who also offered a competing HMO (usually Ocean State) and HealthMate, and highest for an employer who also offered a competing HMO but declined to offer HealthMate.

Third, Blue Cross initiated a policy, which it called "Prudent Buyer," of not paying a physician more for any service or procedure than that physician was accepting from any other health care cost provider (such as Ocean State). Blue Cross established this policy after it became apparent that Ocean State's contracting physicians were accepting about 20 percent less for their services from Ocean State than they were receiving from Blue Cross. . . . After the implementation of Prudent Buyer, about 350 of Ocean State's 1,200 physicians resigned, in many cases apparently in order to avoid a reduction in their Blue Cross fees. . . .

Ocean State alleged that Blue Cross's conduct violated, inter alia, §2 of the Sherman Act, which makes it unlawful to "monopolize . . . any part of the trade or commerce among the several States." Ocean State charged that Blue Cross launched HealthMate not because it was a viable long-term product, but in order to put Ocean State out of business. Through the adverse selection policy, Ocean State claimed, Blue Cross was able to raise its rates for standard Blue Cross for employer groups offering HealthMate—which, in turn, influenced employers not to make HealthMate available. Finally, Ocean State claimed that Blue Cross instituted the Prudent Buyer policy not in order to save money, but rather to induce physicians to resign from Ocean State. . . .

After a lengthy trial, the jury found Blue Cross "guilty" on the §2 claim, but it awarded no damages on this claim. . . . [T]he district court granted Blue Cross's motion for judgment notwithstanding the verdict. . . .

B. The Effect of the McCarran-Ferguson Act

The McCarran-Ferguson Act ("the Act"), 15 U.S.C. §§1012(b), 1013(b), exempts from the antitrust laws all conduct that is (1) part of the "business of insurance"; (2) "regulated by state law"; and (3) not in the form of "boycott, coercion, or intimidation." Blue Cross argued to the district court that both the introduction of HealthMate and the use of the adverse selection rate factors—but not the Prudent Buyer policy—were exempted from antitrust scrutiny by the Act. . . .

The Supreme Court has identified "three criteria relevant in determining whether a particular practice is part of the 'business of insurance' exempted from the antitrust laws": first, whether a particular practice has the effect of transferring or spreading a policyholder's risk; second, whether the practice is an integral part of the policy relationship between the insurer and the insured; and third, whether the practice is limited to entities within the insurance industry. Union Labor Life Insurance Co. v. Pireno, 458 U.S. 119 (1982). See also Group Life & Health Insurance Co. v. Royal Drug Co., 440 U.S. 205 (1979). . . .

Both HealthMate and the adverse selection policy qualify as the "business of insurance" under these criteria. HealthMate is an insurance policy which operates by spreading policyholders' risk; adverse selection is a pricing policy that inherently involves risk-spreading. Both HealthMate and adverse selection directly involve the relationship between the insurer (Blue Cross) and the insured (its policyholders). Such policies are, more or less by definition, limited to entities in the "insurance industry" as broadly construed. Accord Health Care Equalization Committee v. Iowa Medical Society, 851 F.2d 1020, 1029 (8th Cir. 1988).

Ocean State . . . bases [its] argument [against immunity] on a misreading of *Royal Drug*. In that case, the Supreme Court characterized Blue Shield's contacts with its health care providers as "merely arrangements for the purchase of goods and services by Blue Shield." But the Court took care to distinguish Blue Shield's provider contracts from its subscriber contracts. . . . This distinction was emphasized in Justice Brennan's dissenting opinion: "Neither the Court . . . nor the parties challenge the fact that the . . . policy offered by Blue Shield to its policyholders—as distinguished from the contract between Blue Shield and the [providers]—is the 'business of insurance.' " . . . [Based on this distinction], we conclude that the challenged actions of Blue Cross with respect to HealthMate and adverse selection are exempt from antitrust scrutiny under the McCarran-Ferguson Act.

C. The Prudent Buyer Policy

The Prudent Buyer policy involves Blue Cross's relationships not with its subscribers but with its provider physicians. Blue Cross makes no claim that this policy is protected by the McCarran-Ferguson exemption. We agree with the district court, however, that the Prudent Buyer policy . . . as a matter of law, [is] not violative of §2 of the Sherman Act.

Section 2 of the Sherman Act makes it unlawful to "monopolize . . . any part of the trade or commerce among the several states." 15 U.S.C. §2. The offense of monopolization has two elements: (1) the possession of monopoly power in the relevant market and (2) the willful acquisition or maintenance of that power as distinguished from growth or development as a consequence of a superior product, business acumen, or historic accident. United States v. Grinnell Corp., 384 U.S. 563 (1966). On this appeal, Blue Cross does not dispute its monopoly power in the market for health care insurance in Rhode Island. Ocean State, for its part, concedes that Blue Cross acquired its historical advantages legitimately. The issue in dispute is whether Blue Cross maintained its monopoly position through improper means.

Section 2 does not prohibit vigorous competition on the part of a monopoly. To the contrary, the primary purpose of the antitrust laws is to encourage competition. What §2 does prohibit is "exclusionary" conduct by a monopoly, often defined as "behavior that not only (1) tends to impair the opportunities of rivals, but also (2) either does not further competition on the merits or does so in an unnecessarily restrictive way." 3 P. Areeda & D. Turner, Antitrust Law ¶626b at 78. . . .

In the case at hand, the record amply supports Blue Cross's view that Prudent Buyer was a bona fide policy to ensure that Blue Cross would not pay more than any competitor paid for the same services. . . . Blue Cross estimated that it saved $1,900,000 through this policy. We agree with the district court that such a policy of insisting on a supplier's lowest price—assuming that the price is not "predatory" or below the supplier's incremental cost—tends to further competition on the merits and, as a matter of law, is not exclusionary. It is hard to disagree with the district court's view: "As a naked proposition, it would seem silly to argue that a policy to pay the same amount for the same service is anticompetitive, even on the part of one who has market power. This, it would seem, is what competition should be all about."

This conclusion is also compelled by this court's holding in Kartell v. Blue Shield of Massachusetts, 749 F.2d 922 (1st Cir. 1984), that a health insurer's unilateral decisions about the prices it will pay providers do not violate the Sherman Act—unless the prices are "predatory" or below incremental cost—even if the insurer is assumed to have monopoly power in the relevant market. *Kartell* concerned Blue Shield of Massachusetts's ban on balance billing, a price policy according to which Blue Shield paid participating physicians only if they agreed not to make any additional charges to the subscriber. We held that, for antitrust purposes, a health insurer like Blue Shield must be viewed "as itself the purchaser of the doctors' purchases." As such, the insurer—like any buyer of goods or services—is lawfully entitled to bargain with its providers for the best price it can get. "[E]ven if the buyer has monopoly power, an antitrust court . . . will not interfere with a buyer's (nonpredatory) determination of price." . . .

Ocean State argues that *Kartell* is a "vertical" case (involving the effects of Blue Shield's policy on its provider physicians), while the present case is "horizontal" (involving the effects of Blue Cross's policy on its competitor, Ocean State). But the distinction is of no consequence. In both cases the challenged activity is the price that the buyer offers to the seller. . . . Even a monopoly can engage in a competitive course of conduct, so long as it does so for valid business reasons (such as the desire to get the lowest possible price), rather than in order to smother competition. . . .

[E]ven if we assume for argument's sake that Blue Cross selectively applied Prudent Buyer [only to Ocean State physicians], its conduct remains legitimate. It was primarily Ocean State physicians who were selling their services at a lower price to another provider (Ocean State) than to Blue Cross. Indeed, it was Ocean State's lower pricing policy—in particular, its 1986 decision not to return its participating physicians' withholds for 1985—that gave rise to Prudent Buyer. Therefore, it seems only logical—and not illegitimate—for Blue Cross to have focused its efforts in applying Prudent Buyer on Ocean State physicians. . . .

Finally, Ocean State points to evidence in the record that Blue Cross officials hoped that Prudent Buyer—together with HealthMate and adverse selection—would have the effect of destroying or weakening Ocean State. For example, there was testimony that Blue Cross's president had expressed—in none-too-polite terms—a desire to emasculate Ocean State. Another Blue Cross executive wrote in a handwritten note that "not one guy in the state isn't going to know the implication of signing with Ocean State." . . . The jury may reasonably have concluded, on the basis of this and other evidence, that Blue Cross's leadership desired to put Ocean State out of business. But the desire to crush a competitor, standing alone, is insufficient to make out a violation of the antitrust laws. . . . As long as Blue Cross's course of conduct was itself legitimate, the fact that some of its executives hoped to see Ocean State disappear is irrelevant. Under these circumstances Blue Cross is no more guilty of an antitrust violation than a boxer who delivers a perfectly legal punch—hoping that it will kill his opponent—is guilty of attempted murder. . . .

Notes: Vertical Restraints by Insurers

1. *Horizontal Conspiracy vs. Vertical Pricing.* The *Kartell* decision discussed in *Ocean State* was written by Justice Breyer when he sat on the First Circuit. Prior to that, he was an antitrust professor at Harvard. Justice Breyer offered the following important distinction elsewhere in his opinion:

> There is no suggestion that Blue Shield's fee schedule reflects, for example, an effort by, say, one group of doctors to stop other doctors from competing with them. Cf. Virginia Academy of Clinical Psychologists v. Blue Shield of Virginia, 624 F.2d 476 (4th Cir. 1980) (Blue Shield found to be a combination, not of policyholders, but of physicians [with respect to decision not to cover services of psychologists]). . . . *Maricopa* [therefore] is simply not on point. . . . [It] involved a horizontal agreement among competing doctors about what to charge.

Considering the origins of Blue Cross/Blue Shield, however, a few older decisions have agreed with *Virginia Academy* by finding that Blue Cross in particular constitutes a "walking horizontal conspiracy" among its controlling doctors. Glen Eden Hospital v. Blue Cross & Blue Shield of Michigan, 740 F.2d 423 (6th Cir. 1984) (possible conspiracy). Also, it is always possible to find that, in a particular case, an insurer and providers have conspired even apart from the insurer's internal structure. E.g., West Penn Allegheny Health System, v. UPMC, 627 F.3d 85 (3d Cir. 2010) (reinstating claim that Blue Cross and the area's dominant hospital conspired against smaller hospital); Reazin v. Blue Cross & Blue Shield of Kansas, 899 F.2d 951 (10th Cir. 1990) ($7.8 million verdict sustained in favor of hospital excluded by a PPO). And, apart from antitrust law, the new ACA prohibits any health plan (including self-insured employers) from "discriminating" against any category of licensed health care provider. What exactly this regulatory law means for insurers' many pricing decisions remains to be seen, but, in today's health care market structure, most courts agree with *Kartell* that insurers' vertical pricing decisions are beyond *antitrust* reproach. E.g., SmileCare Dental Group v. Delta Dental Plan, 88 F.3d 780 (9th Cir. 1996) (insurer can prevent dentists from waiving co-payments).

The focus of these notes is on areas of special importance to health care where insurers' cost-containment initiatives might pose antitrust violations in a *vertical* dimension. Challenges might arise either under a §1 rule of reason analysis, or under the §2 monopolization theory outlined in *Ocean State*, depending on whether the action is wholly unilateral or involves a vertical agreement. Other types of vertical restraints and §2 theories relevant to health care markets—more to hospitals than to insurers—are discussed in the notes at pages 497 and 501 in terms of "unilateral refusals to deal," the "essential facilities" doctrine, and illegal "tie-ins." For general commentary see Peter J. Hammer & William M. Sage, Monopsony as an Agency and Regulatory Problem in Health Care, 71 Antitrust L.J. 949 (2004).

2. *Most Favored Nation Clauses.* The "prudent buyer" policy at issue in *Ocean State* is more commonly known as a "most favored nation clause." Many antitrust experts consider this aspect of the decision to be wrong, or at least overstated. See Arnold Celnicker, A Competitive Analysis of Most Favored Nations Clauses in Contracts Between Health Care Providers and Insurers, 69 N.C. L. Rev. 863 (1991). To understand why, consider the following scenario: A dominant insurer with market

power attempts to ward off a new insurer by insisting that the dominant's participating physicians and hospitals contract exclusively with it, that is, they lose all of their existing business if they take any of the new business. This would clearly constitute a potential antitrust violation if there were no legitimate business reason for demanding exclusivity (such as that exclusive arrangements foster better-quality service or lower prices). See Aspen Skiing Co. v. Aspen Highlands Skiing Corp., 472 U.S. 585 (1985) (sustaining jury finding that monopolist illegally excluded competitor by refusing to give the competitor's customers the same all-inclusive lift ticket discount package it gave its own customers). The main difference between this extreme scenario and *Ocean State* is that the most favored nation provision made it very expensive, but not impossible, to do business with the new insurer: Physicians who accepted the insurer's terms in effect had to discount all their business by 20 percent.

Most favored nation provisions obviously make it more difficult for a new insurer to stimulate downward pressure on prices for physicians' services and, ultimately, for its own insurance product. Thus, these vertical restraints potentially have horizontal effects. Accordingly, the DOJ and FTC take a dim view of these agreements. See Beth Ann Wright, How MFN Clauses Used in the Health Care Industry Unreasonably Restrain Trade Under the Sherman Act, 18 J.L. & Health 29 (2003); Cascade Health Solutions v. PeaceHealth, 515 F.3d 883 (9th Cir. 2007) (ordering new trial because of jury instructions in a $16.2 million antitrust verdict against a hospital's use of a most favored nation's provision with a health care facility plan). Is it possible to justify *Ocean State* nevertheless based on its unique facts, in which, with respect to HMO insurance in particular, Blue Cross was doing badly in the market and its only response was to meet Ocean State's price where they competed head to head? Doesn't this justification turn on an assessment of Blue Cross' motive and purpose, and are these not quintessential factual issues for the jury to resolve?

3. *Exclusive Contracts.* For reasons explained in the preceding note, the DOJ and FTC also take a dim view of exclusivity agreements in managed care agreements and joint ventures, preferring that providers remain free to participate nonexclusively in several networks or arrangements. This can be seen in their health care antitrust enforcement guidelines. Under the general guideline:

> The Agencies will not challenge, absent extraordinary circumstances, an *exclusive* physician network joint venture comprising *20 percent or less* of the physicians in each physician specialty with active hospital staff privileges who practice in the relevant geographic market. . . . The Agencies will not challenge, absent extraordinary circumstances, a *nonexclusive* physician network joint venture comprising *30 percent or less* of the physicians in each physician specialty with active hospital staff privileges who practice in the relevant geographic market. In relevant markets with less than four [or five] physicians in a particular specialty, a . . . physician network joint venture otherwise qualifying for the antitrust safety zone may include one physician from that specialty [on a nonexclusive basis]. . . . The Agencies will determine whether a physician network joint venture is exclusive or nonexclusive by its physician participants' activities and not simply by the terms of the contractual relationship . . . [using] the following indicia of nonexclusivity, among others: . . . (2) that physicians in the network actually . . . contract with other networks or managed care plans. . . .

Statements of Antitrust Enforcement Policy in Health Care, 5 BNA Health L. Rep. 1295 (emphasis added). This viewpoint is echoed in the more recent guidelines for ACOs. See also *Hassan*, excerpted at page 492. Others argue, however, that exclusive arrangements can be procompetitive when used to form tighter clinical and financial bonds among providers that make different networks more distinctive. According to several leading scholars, preserving freedom to choose too often has been used by providers to resist market power from insurers, by keeping them from engaging in competitive bidding. Charles Weller, "Free Choice" as a Restraint of Trade in American Health Care Delivery and Insurance, 69 Iowa L. Rev. 1351 (1984).

4. *Monopolization.* When vertical restraints are challenged under §2, it is necessary to establish the existence (or at least the "dangerous probability") of monopoly power. (Sometimes, the technical term *monopsony* is used to describe a *buyer* as opposed to *seller* monopoly.) Blue Cross has a very large market share in many states, especially in the Northeast. See, e.g., *Reazin*, supra (60 percent market share sufficient to support finding of monopolization); *Kartell*, supra (75 percent market share presumed to be a monopoly for sake of argument). Other courts, however, have found no monopoly power despite large market share because competing insurers elsewhere in the state or the nation face few inherent barriers to entering the same market or expanding their existing market share. The leading discussion is Ball Memorial Hospital v. Mutual Hospital Insurance Co., 784 F.2d 1325 (7th Cir. 1986) (no market power despite 50 to 80 percent market share). Is this a realistic assessment given the start-up capital costs of (1) complying with state insurance regulations concerning solvency and (2) assembling a managed care network of providers? The issue of market share and market power in managed care settings is considered further in the following section.

3. Antitrust Merger Law

FTC v. TENET HEALTH CARE CORP.

186 F.3d 1045 (8th Cir. 1999)

BEAM, Circuit Judge.

Tenet Healthcare and Poplar Bluff Physicians Group, Inc., doing business as Doctors' Regional Medical Center (collectively, Tenet) appeal the district court's order enjoining the merger of two hospitals in Poplar Bluff, Missouri. . . . The district court found a substantial likelihood that the merger would substantially lessen competition between acute care hospitals in Poplar Bluff, Missouri, in violation of section 7 of the Clayton Act, 15 U.S.C. §15. We reverse.

Poplar Bluff is a city of 17,000 people in southeastern Missouri. It is located in Butler County, which has a population of 40,000. It is the largest city in several counties and has numerous major employers and manufacturing operations. Sikeston, Missouri, and Cape Girardeau, Missouri, both towns with populations of over 40,000 are forty and sixty miles away from Poplar Bluff. The population in the area surrounding Poplar Bluff is concentrated in Scott and Stoddard Counties, which lie between Poplar Bluff and Cape Girardeau. Poplar Bluff is within a few hours' drive of several large metropolitan centers including St. Louis, Missouri, Memphis, Tennessee, and Jonesboro, Arkansas.

Tenet Healthcare Corporation presently owns Lucy Lee Hospital in Poplar Bluff. Lucy Lee is a general acute care hospital that provides primary and secondary care services.[1] Lucy Lee has 201 licensed beds, 185 of which are staffed. It operates ten outpatient clinics in the surrounding counties. Its average daily census was 75 in 1994, 76 in 1995 and 104 in 1996. Doctors' Regional Medical Center in Poplar Bluff is presently owned by a group of physicians. It is also a general acute care hospital providing primary and secondary care services. It has 230 licensed beds, of which 187 are staffed. Its average census in 1994 was 106, in 1995 was 99, in 1996 was 95 and in 1997 was 77. It also operates several rural health clinics in the area. Though profitable, both hospitals are underutilized and have had problems attracting specialists to the area.

Tenet recently entered into an agreement to purchase Doctors' Regional for over forty million dollars. Tenet plans to operate Doctors' Regional as a long-term care facility and to consolidate inpatient services at Lucy Lee. It plans to employ more specialists at the merged facility and to offer higher quality care in a comprehensive, integrated delivery system that would include some tertiary care.[2] Pursuant to the Hart-Scott-Rodino Act, 15 U.S.C. §18a, the hospitals filed a premerger certification with the FTC. Shortly thereafter, the FTC filed a complaint alleging that the hospitals' merger would lessen competition for primary and secondary inpatient hospitalization services in the area. . . .

The evidence adduced at the hearing shows that Lucy Lee and Doctors' Regional are the only two hospitals in Poplar Bluff, other than a Veteran's Hospital. . . . There are several [larger, regional] hospitals in the surrounding area [that] offer the same or a greater range of services. . . . In addition, there are smaller rural hospitals located in nearby towns, . . . [which] have fewer than fifty beds and provide only primary care.

Lucy Lee's and Doctors' Regional's patient bases are composed primarily of patients who are covered by Medicare and Medicaid and thus remain largely insensitive to price differentials. Most of the remaining patient admissions at Lucy Lee and Doctors' Regional are covered by health insurance, under a plan administered by a managed care organization.[5] These organizations include health maintenance

1. Primary care involves relatively simple medical or surgical procedures. Secondary care is somewhat more complex, including procedures such as hernia repair or patient services related to a heart attack.

2. A comprehensive, integrated healthcare delivery system is one that provides service along the spectrum of healthcare: inpatient clinics, home health, hospitalization, inpatient and outpatient surgery, and short- and long-term convalescent or rehabilitation care. Tertiary care is sophisticated, complex, or high-tech care that includes, for example, open heart surgery, oncology surgery, neurosurgery, high-risk obstetrics, neonatal intensive care, and trauma services. Quaternary care is even more sophisticated and includes organ transplants.

5. Another form of healthcare coverage is traditional indemnity insurance. Traditional indemnity insurers cover a percentage of an insured's healthcare costs, with the remainder covered by the insured. Indemnity insurance is not implicated in this case, because it has become virtually nonexistent in the Poplar Bluff area. Historically, indemnity insurers have not attempted to gain discounts from providers.

organizations (HMOs)[6] and preferred provider organizations (PPOs).[7] Hospitals are willing to discount their stated rates to managed care payers in order to entice the managed care entity to send its enrollees to that hospital. Managed care organizations have had a presence in Poplar Bluff for approximately fifteen years. Most employers in the Poplar Bluff area either subscribe to or administer a PPO. Both Lucy Lee and Doctors' Regional have entered into discount agreements with numerous managed care entities and employers.

The hospitals in Cape Girardeau, on the other hand, refused to negotiate with managed care plans until recently, when, at the insistence of area employers, Southeast Missouri Hospital entered into a discount arrangement with HealthLink, a managed care organization. Healthcare prices in Cape Girardeau have historically been significantly higher than prices in Poplar Bluff. However, there is also a perception of higher quality service at Cape Girardeau hospitals. Since the entry of managed care in the Cape Girardeau market, there has been some reduction in prices. . . . Cape Girardeau hospitals now [advertise] in Poplar Bluff.

Market participants, specifically, employers, health plans and network providers testified that they had negotiated substantial discounts and favorable per diem rates with either or both Lucy Lee and Doctors' Regional as a result of "playing the two hospitals off each other." These managed care organizations and employers testified that if the merged entity were to raise its prices by ten percent, the health plans would have no choice but to simply pay the increased price. They testified that they perceive it is essential for the plans to include a Poplar Bluff hospital in their benefit packages because their enrollees would not travel to other towns for primary and secondary inpatient treatment. They stated that their employees and subscribers find it convenient to use a Poplar Bluff hospital; are loyal to their physicians in Poplar Bluff and would not be amenable to a health benefit plan that did not include a Poplar Bluff hospital.

The evidence shows that patient choice of hospitals is determined by many variables, including patient/physician loyalty, perceptions of quality, geographic proximity and, most importantly or determinatively, access to hospitals through an insurance plan. Managed care organizations have been able to influence or change patient behavior with financial incentives in other healthcare markets. This practice is known as "steering." Representatives of Poplar Bluff managed care entities testified, however, that they did not believe such efforts would be successful in the Poplar Bluff market, . . . in spite of the fact that such tactics had been successful in other markets. . . .

Lucy Lee and Doctors' Regional obtain ninety percent of their patients from zip codes within a fifty-mile radius of Poplar Bluff. In eleven of the top twelve zip

6. An HMO generally charges a set fee which covers all of an enrollee's healthcare needs, including hospitalizations. HMO enrollees are required to obtain care only from those physicians and hospitals who provide a discounted rate to the HMO. HMOs often have their own clinics and enrollees are obligated to go to those clinics for care. In addition, HMOs often consult with hospitals to ensure that costs of hospitalization remain as low as possible.

7. In a PPO, the PPO negotiates discounted rates with certain physicians or hospitals and then provides financial incentives, such as low deductibles or low co-payments, to its enrollees to use those providers.

codes, however, significant patient admissions—ranging from 22% to 70%—were to hospitals other than those in Poplar Bluff. There is no dispute that Poplar Bluff residents travel to St. Louis, Memphis, and Jonesboro for tertiary care. . . . [T]he FTC presented the testimony . . . based on an analysis of DRG data[9] that patients seeking care outside Poplar Bluff were seeking a more sophisticated level of service than that available in Poplar Bluff. . . . The evidence also shows, however, that significant numbers of patients in the Poplar Bluff service area travel to other towns for primary and secondary treatment that is also available in Poplar Bluff.

The evidence shows that the healthcare industry is rapidly changing. The emergence and growth of managed care—a system in which a third-party monitors healthcare resources and expenditures—has had a large impact on healthcare. This monitoring has caused a corresponding decline in the number and length of inpatient admissions. Many procedures that formerly required a hospital stay are now performed on an outpatient basis. Another trend has been growth of outreach efforts such as rural clinics to extend the service area of a hospital. Patient loyalty to a certain doctor has diminished as patients' out-of-pocket expenditures have increased. . . .

Discussion

The determination of a relevant market is a necessary predicate to the finding of an antitrust violation. . . . A relevant market consists of two components: a product market and a geographic market. *See* Department of Justice, Federal Trade Commission, Antitrust Division, 1992 Horizontal Merger Guidelines, 57 Fed.Reg. 41552. The parties agree that the relevant product market at issue in this case is the delivery of primary and secondary inpatient hospital care services. They disagree, however, on the relevant geographic market.

A geographic market is the area in which consumers can practically turn for alternative sources of the product and in which the antitrust defendants face competition. . . . A properly defined geographic market includes potential suppliers who can readily offer consumers a suitable alternative to the defendant's services. Determination of the relevant geographic market is highly fact sensitive. . . . A monopolization claim often succeeds or fails strictly on the definition of the product or geographic market. . . .

The FTC proposes a relevant geographic market that essentially matches its service area: a fifty-mile radius from downtown Poplar Bluff. It is from this service area that the two hospitals obtain ninety percent of their patients. A service area, however, is not necessarily a merging firm's geographic market for purposes of antitrust analysis. The FTC's proposed geographic market includes four other hospitals:

9. A DRG is a numerical code that serves to classify patients into one of 503 clinically cohesive groups that demonstrate similar consumption of hospital resources and length of stay patterns. These classifications are used by the federal government in administering Medicare and Medicaid programs and by insurers to evaluate reimbursement, utilization of resources, treatment protocols, related conditions, and demographic distribution. Examples of DRGs would be "extracranial vascular procedures," "chronic obstructive pulmonary disease," and "specific cerebral vascular disorders."

a Tenet-owned regional hospital in Kennett, Missouri, and three rural hospitals. The FTC contends that its evidence shows that the merged entity will have a post-merger market share of eighty-four percent of this geographic market.[10] Tenet, on the other hand, proposes a relevant geographic market that encompasses a sixty-five mile radius from downtown Poplar Bluff in addition to Barnes Hospital in St. Louis. The proposed area includes [20] hospitals. . . .

Because we conclude that the FTC produced insufficient evidence of a well-defined relevant geographic market, we find that it did not show that the merged entity will possess such market power. . . . The evidence in this case falls short of establishing a relevant geographic market that excludes the Sikeston or Cape Girardeau areas. The evidence shows that hospitals in either or both of these towns, as well as rural hospitals throughout the area, are practical alternatives for many Poplar Bluff consumers. In adopting the FTC's position, the district court improperly discounted the fact that over twenty-two percent of people in the most important zip codes already use hospitals outside the FTC's proposed market for treatment that is offered at Poplar Bluff hospitals. . . . If patients use hospitals outside the service area, those hospitals can act as a check on the exercise of market power by the hospitals within the service area. The FTC's contention that the merged hospitals would have eighty-four percent of the market for inpatient primary and secondary services within a contrived market area that stops just short of including a regional hospital (Missouri Delta in Sikeston) that is closer to many patients than the Poplar Bluff hospitals, strikes us as absurd. The proximity of many patients to hospitals in other towns, coupled with the compelling and essentially unrefuted evidence that the switch to another provider by a small percentage of patients would constrain a price increase, shows that the FTC's proposed market is too narrow. . . .

The district court rejected the Cape Girardeau hospitals as practicable alternatives because they were more costly. In so doing, it underestimated the impact of nonprice competitive factors, such as quality. The evidence shows that one reason for the significant amount of migration from the Poplar Bluff hospitals to either Sikeston, Cape Girardeau, or St. Louis is the actual or perceived difference in quality of care. . . . As the district court noted, healthcare decisions are based on factors other than price. It is for that reason that, although they are less expensive, HMOs are not always an employer's or individual's choice in healthcare services. *See* Blue Cross and Blue Shield United of Wisconsin v. Marshfield Clinic, 65 F.3d 1406, 1412, 1410 (7th Cir. 1995) (Posner, J.) (noting "[g]enerally you must pay more for higher quality" and "the HMO's incentive is to keep you healthy if it can but if you get very sick, and are unlikely to recover to a healthy state involving few medical expenses, to let you die as quickly and cheaply as possible.") . . .

We further find that although Tenet's efficiencies defense may have been properly rejected by the district court, the district court should nonetheless have considered evidence of enhanced efficiency in the context of the competitive effects of the merger. The evidence shows that a hospital that is larger and more efficient than Lucy Lee or Doctors' Regional will provide better medical care than either

10. An inference of monopoly power can be drawn from an 84% market share. . . . Market shares of less than 60% are generally not sufficient to create an inference of monopoly power.

of those hospitals could separately. The merged entity will be able to attract more highly qualified physicians and specialists and to offer integrated delivery and some tertiary care. . . . [Therefore,] the merged entity may well enhance competition in the greater Southeast Missouri area. . . .

The district court also relied on the seemingly outdated assumption of doctor-patient loyalty that is not supported by the record. The evidence shows, and the district court acknowledged, that the issue of access to a provider through an insurance plan is determinative of patient choice. Essentially, the evidence shows that patients will choose whatever doctors or hospitals are covered by their health plan. Undeniably, although many patients might prefer to be loyal to their doctors, it is, unfortunately, a luxury they can no longer afford. . . . As much as many patients long for the days of old-fashioned and local, if expensive and inefficient, healthcare, recent trends in healthcare management have made the old healthcare model obsolete.

The reality of the situation in our changing healthcare environment may be that Poplar Bluff cannot support two high-quality hospitals. Third-party payers have reaped the benefit of a price war in a small corner of the market for healthcare services in Southeastern Missouri, at the arguable cost of quality to their subscribers. . . . We are mindful that competition is the driving force behind our free enterprise system and that, unless barriers have been erected to constrain the normal operation of the market, a court ought to exercise extreme caution because judicial intervention in a competitive situation can itself upset the balance of market forces, bringing about the very ills the antitrust laws were meant to prevent. This appears to have even more force in an industry, such as healthcare, experiencing significant and profound changes.

■ SAINT ALPHONSUS MEDICAL CENTER v. ST. LUKE'S HEALTH SYSTEM

778 F.3d 775 (9th Cir. 2015)

HURWITZ, Circuit Judge:

This case arises out of the 2012 merger of two health care providers in Nampa, Idaho; [Saltzer Medical Group and St. Luke's Health System]. . . . Although the district court believed that the merger was intended to improve patient outcomes and might well do so, the judge nonetheless found that the merger violated § 7 [of the Clayton Act] and ordered divestiture.

As the district court recognized, the job before us is not to determine the optimal future shape of the country's health care system, but instead to determine whether this particular merger violates the Clayton Act. In light of the careful factual findings by the able district judge, we affirm the judgment below.

I. BACKGROUND

Nampa, the second-largest city in Idaho, is some twenty miles west of Boise and has a population of approximately 85,000. Before the merger at issue, St. Luke's Health Systems, an Idaho-based, not-for-profit health care system, operated an emergency clinic in the city. Saltzer Medical Group, the largest independent multi-specialty physician group in Idaho, had thirty-four physicians practicing at its offices in Nampa. The only hospital in Nampa was operated by Saint Alphonsus Health System. . . . The largest adult primary care physician ("PCP") provider in the Nampa market was Saltzer, which had sixteen PCPs. St. Luke's had eight PCPs and Saint Alphonsus nine. Several other PCPs had solo or small practices.

Saltzer had long had the goal of moving toward integrated patient care and risk-based reimbursement. After unsuccessfully attempting several informal affiliations, . . . Saltzer sought a formal partnership with a large health care system. In 2012, St. Luke's acquired Saltzer's assets and entered into a five-year professional service agreement ("PSA") with the Saltzer physicians. Saltzer received a $9 million payment for goodwill. The initial PSA contained hortatory language about the parties' desire to move away from fee-for-service reimbursement, but included no provisions for implementing that goal. . . .

C. PROCEDURAL HISTORY

. . . [St. Alphonsus sued in 2012, alleging] anticompetitive effects in the relevant markets for "primary care physician services," "general acute-care inpatient services," "general pediatric physician services," and "outpatient surgery services." . . . In March 2013, the FTC and the State of Idaho filed a complaint in the district court seeking to enjoin the merger pursuant to the Federal Trade Commission Act, the Clayton Act, and Idaho law.[1] This complaint alleged anticompetitive effects only in the adult PCP market. The district court consolidated this case with the one filed by [St. Alphonsus], and after a nineteen-day bench trial, found the merger prohibited . . . because of its anticompetitive effects on the Nampa adult PCP market.

The district court expressly noted the troubled state of the U.S. health care system, found that St. Luke's and Saltzer genuinely intended to move toward a better health care system, and expressed its belief that the merger would "improve patient outcomes" if left intact. Nonetheless, the court found that the "huge market share" of the post-merger entity "creates a substantial risk of anticompetitive price increases" in the Nampa adult PCP market. Rejecting an argument by St. Luke's that anticipated post-merger efficiencies excused the potential anticompetitive price effects, the district court ordered divestiture. This appeal followed. . . .

III. THE CLAYTON ACT § 7 ANALYSIS

The great Yankee catcher Yogi Berra is reputed (likely apocryphally) to have said that it's "tough to make predictions, especially about the future." Yet that is precisely what this case requires. Because § 7 of the Clayton Act bars mergers whose effect "may be substantially to lessen competition, or to tend to create a monopoly," judicial analysis necessarily focuses on "probabilities, not certainties." This "requires not merely an appraisal of the immediate impact of the merger upon competition, but a prediction of its impact upon competitive conditions in the future . . .

1. The Idaho Competition Act is "construed in harmony" with federal antitrust law, Idaho Code §§ 48-102(3), -106, and the district court held that the antitrust analysis is the same for each. The parties do not contend otherwise.

B. THE RELEVANT MARKET

. . . . Although the parties agree that the relevant product market in this case is adult PCPs, St. Luke's vigorously disputes the district court's determination that Nampa is the relevant geographic market. We find no clear error in that factual finding. . . . A common method to determine the relevant geographic market, and the one used by the district court, is to find whether a hypothetical monopolist could impose a "small but significant nontransitory increase in price" ("SSNIP") in the proposed market [without driving away much business]. . . .

Market definition thus perforce focuses on the anticipated behavior of buyers and sellers. In the health care industry, insurance companies effectively act both as buyers and sellers. Noting that "the vast majority of health care consumers are not direct purchasers of health care—the consumers purchase health insurance and the insurance companies negotiate directly with the providers," the district court correctly focused on the "likely response of insurers to a hypothetical demand by all the PCPs in a particular market for a [SSNIP]."[2]

The district court found that a hypothetical Nampa PCP monopolist could profitably impose a SSNIP on insurers. Citing testimony that Nampa residents "strongly prefer access to local PCPs," the court found that "commercial health plans need to include Nampa PCPs in their networks to offer a competitive product." "Given this dynamic—that health plans must offer Nampa Adult PCP services to Nampa residents to effectively compete—Nampa PCPs could band together and successfully demand a [SSNIP] (or reimbursement increase) from health plans."

St. Luke's argues that the district court erred by considering only the current behavior of Nampa consumers, not their likely response to a SSNIP. St. Luke's is of course correct that geographic market definition involves prospective analysis—it predicts consumer response to a hypothetical price increase. But that is precisely what the district court did. The court not only examined present Nampa consumer behavior, but also concluded that it would not change in the event of a SSNIP.

This determination was supported by the record. Evidence was presented that insurers generally need local PCPs to market a health care plan, and that this is true in particular in the Nampa market. For example, Blue Cross of Idaho has PCPs in every zip code in which it has customers, and the executive director of the Idaho Physicians Network testified that it could not market a health care network in Nampa that did not include Nampa PCPs. Evidence also indicated that consumers would not change their behavior in the event of a SSNIP. Experts testified that because health care consumers only pay a small percentage of health care costs out of pocket, the impact of a SSNIP likely would not register. Similarly, there was testimony that consumers choose physicians on factors other than price. The court

2. This "two-stage model" of health care competition is "the accepted model." John J. Miles, 1 Health Care & Antitrust L. § 1:5 (2014). In the first stage, providers compete for inclusion in insurance plans. See Gregory Vistnes, Hospitals, Mergers, and Two-Stage Competition, 67 Antitrust L.J. 671 (2000). In the second stage, providers seek to attract patients enrolled in the plans. Because patients are "largely insensitive" to price, the second stage "takes place primarily over non-price dimensions." Thus, antitrust analysis focuses on the first stage.

was unconvinced by evidence that insurers could defend against a SSNIP by steering consumers to non-Nampa PCPs. . . .

C. THE PLAINTIFFS' CASE

Once the relevant geographic market is determined, a prima facie case is established if the plaintiff proves that the merger will probably lead to anticompetitive effects in that market. The district court held that the plaintiffs established a prima facie case because of the post-merger entity's: (1) market share; (2) ability to negotiate higher PCP reimbursement rates with insurers; and (3) ability to "charge more [ancillary] services at the higher hospital billing rates." The court also found that "entry into the market has been very difficult and would not be timely to counteract the anticompetitive effects of the Acquisition." St. Luke's does not challenge the barriers-to-entry finding; we review the others in turn for clear error. . . .

The district court calculated the post-merger Herfindahl-Hirschman Index (HHI0 [a measure of market concentration] in the Nampa PCP market as 6,219, and the increase as 1,607. St. Luke's does not challenge these findings. As the district court correctly noted, these HHI numbers "are well above the thresholds for a presumptively anticompetitive merger (more than double and seven times their respective thresholds, respectively)." The district court also found that St. Luke's would likely use its post-merger power to negotiate higher reimbursement rates from insurers for PCP services. . . .

Because St. Luke's and Saltzer had been each other's closest substitutes in Nampa, the district court found the acquisition limited the ability of insurers to negotiate with the merged entity. Pre-acquisition internal correspondence indicated that the merged companies would use this increased bargaining power to raise prices. . . .

3. Ancillary Services

The district court's finding that St. Luke's would raise prices in the hospital-based ancillary services market[3] is more problematic. The court found that St. Luke's would "exercise its enhanced bargaining leverage from the acquisition to charge more services at the higher hospital-based billing rates." Because insurers and providers typically negotiate for all services as part of the same contract, the district court found that St. Luke's increased leverage with respect to PCP services would allow it to demand higher fees for ancillary services.

The problem with this conclusion is that the district court made no findings about St. Luke's' market power in the ancillary services market. Absent such a finding, it is difficult to conclude that the merged entity could easily demand anticompetitive prices for such services. Perhaps the court was suggesting that St. Luke's would engage in tying, "a device used by a seller with market power in one product market to extend its market power to a distinct product market." Although

3. Ancillary services, such as x-rays and diagnostic testing, are sometimes performed by doctors in conjunction with PCP examinations. Before the merger, Saltzer provided many ancillary services at its physicians' offices. Insurance companies and Medicare often offer higher reimbursements for ancillary services performed at a hospital-based outpatient facility.

various antitrust statutes address tying, Clayton Act § 7 does not expressly prohibit the practice. . . .

D. [THE POST-MERGER EFFICIENCIES DEFENSE]

Because the plaintiffs established a prima facie case, the burden shifted to St. Luke's to "cast doubt on the accuracy of the Government's evidence as predictive of future anticompetitive effects." The rebuttal evidence focused on the alleged pro-competitive effects of the merger, particularly the contention that the merger would allow St. Luke's to move toward integrated care and risk-based reimbursement.[4]

The Supreme Court has never expressly approved an efficiencies defense to a § 7 claim [and has several times ruled or reasoned in ways that appear inconsistent with this defense]. . . .Notwithstanding the Supreme Court's statements, four of our sister circuits (the Sixth, D.C., Eighth, and Eleventh) have suggested that proof of post-merger efficiencies could rebut a Clayton Act § 7 prima facie case. The FTC has also cautiously recognized the defense, noting that although competition ordinarily spurs firms to achieve efficiencies internally, "a primary benefit of mergers to the economy is their potential to generate significant efficiencies and thus enhance the merged firm's ability and incentive to compete, which may result in lower prices, improved quality, enhanced service, or new products." Merger Guidelines § 10. However, none of the reported appellate decisions have actually held that a § 7 defendant has rebutted a prima facie case with an efficiencies defense; thus, even in those circuits that recognize it, the parameters of the defense remain imprecise. . . .

We remain skeptical about the efficiencies defense in general and about its scope in particular. It is difficult enough in § 7 cases to predict whether a merger will have future anticompetitive effects without also adding to the judicial balance a prediction of future efficiencies. . . . Nonetheless, we assume, as did the district court, that because § 7 of the Clayton Act only prohibits those mergers whose effect "may be substantially to lessen competition," a defendant can rebut a prima facie case with evidence that the proposed merger will create a more efficient combined entity and thus increase competition. For example, if two small firms were unable to match the prices of a larger competitor, but could do so after a merger because of decreased production costs, a court recognizing the efficiencies defense might reasonably conclude that the transaction likely would not lessen competition. . . . The [Clayton] Act focuses on "competition," so any defense must demonstrate that the

4. The district court found that a core reason for high health care costs is the prevalent fee-for-service reimbursement model, based on the apparently uncontested opinions of expert witnesses. Experts have recommended moving toward integrated care and risk-based reimbursement. "In an integrated delivery system, [PCPs] and specialty physicians work as a team, with PCPs managing patient care and specialty physicians consulting and providing care as needed." Risk-based reimbursement (also known as capitation) means that "providers receive reimbursement from insurers in the form of a set amount for each patient rather than a payment for each service rendered. The set amount is based on the average expected health care utilization for the patients given such factors as their age and medical history." "Capitation motivates providers to consider the costs of treatment as they will share in the savings if they can keep actual costs below the set amount they receive."

prima facie case "portray[s] inaccurately the merger's probable effects on competition." In other words, a successful efficiencies defense requires proof that a merger is not, despite the existence of a prima facie case, anticompetitive. . . .

St. Luke's argues that the merger would benefit patients by creating a team of employed physicians with access to Epic, the electronic medical records system used by St. Luke's. The district court found that, even if true, these predicted efficiencies were insufficient to carry St. Luke's' burden of rebutting the prima facie case. We agree.

It is not enough to show that the merger would allow St. Luke's to better serve patients. The Clayton Act focuses on competition, and the claimed efficiencies therefore must show that the prediction of anticompetitive effects from the prima facie case is inaccurate. Although the district court believed that the merger would eventually "improve the delivery of health care" in the Nampa market, the judge did not find that the merger would increase competition or decrease prices. Quite to the contrary, the court, even while noting the likely beneficial effect of the merger on patient care, held that reimbursement rates for PCP services likely would increase. Nor did the court find that the merger would likely lead to integrated health care or a new reimbursement system; the judge merely noted the desire of St. Luke's to move in that direction.

. . . [Moreover], [t]he court found "no empirical evidence to support the theory that St. Luke's needs a core group of employed primary care physicians beyond the number it had before the Acquisition to successfully make the transition to integrated care," and that "a committed team can be assembled without employing physicians." The court also found that the shared electronic record was not a merger-specific benefit because data analytics tools are available to independent physicians. . . .

But even if we assume that the claimed efficiencies were merger-specific, the defense would nonetheless fail. At most, the district court concluded that St. Luke's might provide better service to patients after the merger. That is a laudable goal, but the Clayton Act does not excuse mergers that lessen competition or create monopolies simply because the merged entity can improve its operations. . . .

St. Luke's nonetheless argues that the district court erred in ordering divestiture because (1) divestiture will not actually restore competition; (2) divestiture eliminates the transaction's procompetitive benefits; and (3) a proposed conduct remedy was preferable. We find no abuse of discretion in the district court's choice of remedy. . . .

Notes: Hospital, Physician, and Insurer Mergers

1. *You Can't Win Them All. Tenet* is emblematic of the remarkable string of losses in hospital merger cases the federal government suffered prior to this decade. Prof. Greaney gives this explanation:

> Segments of the judiciary are openly hostile toward applying traditional competition concepts to the health care sector . . . [and so] have dealt a number of important setbacks to government agencies and private plaintiffs litigating antitrust matters. A close examination of these cases reveals an admixture of factors ranging from plain judicial error, to subtle changes in legal doctrine, to a shifting jurisprudence that is

> increasingly deferential to professionalism in health market interactions. An undercurrent has been that a backlash against managed care has contributed to decisions that shield providers from the antitrust laws.
>
> The unfavorable reception to antitrust cases in court appears to have had a corresponding chilling effect upon federal enforcement efforts. . . . Cases involving serious misconduct have resulted in mild civil sanctions rather than criminal prosecutions, and the overall level of investigatory and advisory activity appears to have declined. . . .
>
> The most pronounced change in the law has been in merger enforcement. . . . Since 1995 federal and state enforcers have lost all seven cases litigated in federal court. . . . [T]he government's failures in court have undoubtedly encouraged consolidation across the health care industry. Because they may supply precedent on issues such as market definition, the hospital merger decisions are likely to have a profound impact in other areas of antitrust concern such as physician consolidation, network formation, and restraints of trade. Experienced attorneys giving advice to physicians and hospitals see a judicial imprimatur for consolidation. As one practitioner put it, the cases "make almost any merger worth trying."

Thomas L. Greaney, Whither Antitrust? The Uncertain Future of Competition Law in Health Care, 21(2) Health Aff. 185 (Mar. 2002).

St. Luke's reflects the government's more recent track record. For another decision applying a similar analysis, see FTC v. Penn State Hershey, Medical Center, 838 F.3d 327 (3d Cir. 2016) (enjoining the merger of the two largest hospitals in the Harrisburg, Pennsylvania area).

2. *Undoing Mistakes.* The FTC, not wanting to let the courts have the last word, has adopted a policy of challenging mergers several years after they are consummated if evidence shows that actual effects have been adverse for competition. In the first such case, the FTC ordered partial divestiture in a merger that was approved four years earlier of the only two hospitals in Evanston, Illinois (which borders Chicago), based on evidence that the merger allowed the hospital to increase its payment rates under managed care contracts. However, the FTC declined to order a corporate breakup. Instead, it ruled only that the two facilities must conduct certain of their operations separately, such as negotiating for managed care contracts. In re Evanston Northwestern Healthcare Corporation, No. 9315 (FTC, Aug. 2, 2007). More generally, note 10 cites the increasing evidence that both horizontal and vertical mergers among providers tend to drive prices up, and that claimed efficiencies are rarely achieved.

3. *Joint Ventures and Other Transactions.* Merger analysis and related monopolization charges are not restricted to outright acquisitions. They are also relevant to a variety of contractual networks and joint venture arrangements. Consider, for instance, a sole community hospital's forming of a joint venture with its medical staff to enter into managed care contracts with insurers and employers, or a joint venture between the only two hospitals in town to purchase and share the town's only MRI scanner. One issue, discussed in the previous section, is whether or not a joint venture has sufficient integration to avoid scrutiny under Sherman Act §1; if not, the joint venture might constitute a "walking conspiracy," incurring *per se* liability. But, if the venture is viewed as a single enterprise, the participants still need to consider whether its creation violates merger law.

For this second purpose, the DOJ/FTC Antitrust Enforcement Guidelines, quoted at page 526, create safe harbors of either 20 or 30 percent market share for physician networks depending on whether the physician affiliations are exclusive or nonexclusive. The product market is defined in terms of the number of physicians practicing in the specialty. The guidelines also observe that joint ventures between competitors to purchase expensive high-tech equipment have never been challenged by the agencies and are not likely to be if efficiency justifications can be given for cost-sharing. However, in one notable decision, the Eleventh Circuit held that a dominant hospital monopolized the market for "durable medical equipment" (wheelchairs, oxygen equipment, and other items used in patients' homes) by entering into a joint venture with one equipment supplier and then having the hospitals' nurses steer its patients to that supplier when they left the hospital. Key Enterprises v. Venice Hospital, 919 F.2d 1550 (11th Cir. 1990).

4. *Geographic Markets.* In contrast with *Tenet*'s treatment of the geographic market definition, Judge Posner had the following to say about a proposed merger of two of the three hospitals in Rockford, Illinois:

> It is always possible to take pot shots at a market definition (we have just taken one), and the defendants do so with vigor and panache. Their own proposal, however, is ridiculous—a ten-county area in which it is assumed (without any evidence and contrary to common sense) that Rockford residents, or third-party payors, will be searching out small, obscure hospitals in remote rural areas if the prices charged by the hospitals in Rockford rise above competitive levels. . . . For highly exotic or highly elective hospital treatment, patients will sometimes travel long distances, of course. But for the most part hospital services are local. People want to be hospitalized near their families and homes, in hospitals in which their own—local—doctors have hospital privileges.

United States v. Rockford Memorial Corp., 898 F.2d 1278 (7th Cir. 1990). See also William G. Kopit, Price Competition in Hospital Markets: The Significance of Managed Care, 35 J. Health L. 291, 319 (2002) ("The assertions [in *Tenet*] in support of the defendant's market definition are completely without factual support").

5. *Product Market Definition.* The second aspect of market determination is defining the relevant product. Note that the *St. Luke's* court distinguished between the market for primary care and the market for "ancillary" services. Similarly, the DOJ/FTC Guidelines treat each practice specialty as a distinct market, and the ACO Guidelines instruct how specialties are to be defined.

For hospitals, although *Tenet* did not contest the issue, how was the product market defined in that case and how might it have differed? Compare *Rockford Memorial*, supra:

> If you need a kidney transplant, or a mastectomy, or if you have a stroke or a heart attack or a gunshot wound, you will go (or be taken) to an acute-care hospital for inpatient treatment. The fact that for other services you have a choice between inpatient care at such a hospital and outpatient care elsewhere places no check on the prices of the services we have listed. . . . If you need your hip replaced, you can't decide to have chemotherapy instead because it's available on an outpatient basis at a lower price. . . . Hospitals can and do distinguish between the patient who wants a coronary bypass and the patient who wants a wart removed from his foot; these services are not in the same product market merely because they have a common provider.

6. *Insurance Markets.* Consider how the market definition issues might differ when antitrust cases involve insurers rather than providers. Because insurers can

sell nationally, it is possible to argue for a national market, but the need to meet regulatory requirements in each state tends to restrict insurance markets to no greater than a state and the surrounding region. Should insurance markets be even smaller, however, due to the fact that, to be competitive, insurers need to contract with local providers?

Regarding product markets, should "Medicare Advantage" insurance be considered a separate market from commercial insurance? And, for commercial insurance, are there separate markets for employers versus individuals, or for employers that do and do not self-insure (and thus contract for administrative services and network access). According to some courts, market share is defined not only by *existing* competitors but also by *potential* competitors. See, e.g., Little Rock Cardiology Clinic v. Baptist Health, 591 F.3d 591 (8th Cir. 2009) (refusing to limit market definition to patients covered only by private insurance, reasoning that patients can also opt to pay for cardiology services out of pocket); City of New York v. Group Health Inc., 649 F.3d 151 (2d Cir. 2011) (refusing to limit market to the insurers currently offered to New York City employees).

Some insight into government policy on these questions is provided by the Justice Department's decisions in 2016 to block two separate mergers among four of the five largest insurers in the country: Aetna with Humana, and Cigna with Anthem (the largest Blue Cross conglomerate). The DOJ distinguished among all of the different product markets just noted, and considered geographic markets to be as small as a single county for some products (although national for very large employers, and metropolitan areas for most commercial insurance). It remains to be seen whether these positions will be upheld in court or altered by the Trump administration.

7. *Antitrust Two-Step.* As both of these cases indicate, it is necessary to analyze hospital and physician mergers in the context of not only their own markets, but also the insurance markets that determine how they are paid. The *St. Luke's* decision refers to this as the "two-stage model." Notice, for instance, the *Tenet* court's description of hospitals in neighboring Cape Girardeau for refusing to contract with managed care plans, at least for a time. This happens regularly around the country, even in metropolitan areas. Hospitals or physician groups that control a significant share of the market have learned that when push comes to shove, insurers will often back down and give in to demands for higher rates. Insurers often feel they can't afford to have major gaps in their networks because larger employers look for insurers that cover most doctors and hospitals in the area.

Coupled with providers' market power is a regulatory requirement in most states that managed care plans maintain adequate hospital and physician networks (both primary care and specialists) in each county where they do business. At an extreme, having a major gap in the network may mean giving up a license to sell the product in certain counties. More commonly, however, regulators allow managed care plans to continue doing business but require them to pay non-network providers their full, non-discounted rates if the local network does not have adequate capacity for the number of people enrolled locally. Therefore, regulators constrain the ability of HMOs to send people long distances for care.

Based on these considerations, some economists believe that market concentration among insurers has the pro-competitive benefit of forcing dominant hospitals and provider groups to be more willing to negotiate. Other economists, however, disagree, as did the DOJ in its 2016 decision (just noted) to block mergers among some large national insurers—in part because larger insurers that obtain price concessions do not necessarily pass those savings on to consumers. See Leemore S. Dafny, Evaluating the Impact of Health Insurance Industry Consolidation (Commonwealth Fund, Nov. 2015); Richard Scheffler & Daniel Arnold, Insurer Market Power Lowers Prices in Numerous Concentrated Provider Markets, 36 Health Aff. 1539 (2017); Kate Ho & Robin S. Lee, Insurer Competition in Health Care Markets, 85 Econometrica 379 (2017).

8. *Natural Monopolies.* Observe that market share statistics are not the sole consideration. A hospital merger even in a highly concentrated market is unlikely to lessen competition and, indeed, might help competition if one or both of the hospitals would not survive financially without the merger, or if a merged hospital would offer better service at lower cost. These arguments are known as the "failing firm" defense and the "efficiencies" defense. Although *Tenet* did not find that these arguments were sustained as affirmative defenses, the court did note that "the reality of the situation . . . may be that Poplar Bluff cannot support two high-quality hospitals." This suggests the presence of "natural monopoly" conditions. In line with this thinking, the DOJ/FTC Antitrust Enforcement Guidelines establish a safe harbor for mergers between two hospitals, no matter how small the market, where one has fewer than 100 beds and 40 patients a day.

9. *Are Nonprofits Different?* For a time, it was disputed whether the FTC has jurisdiction over nonprofit entities, due to the wording of the FTC's governing statute. Although the Supreme Court rejected this argument as an absolute defense in *California Dental Ass'n*, above, the substance of the argument sometimes surfaces when nonprofit hospitals argue they are not likely to abuse market power since they are not driven by a profit motive. On this score, one district relied heavily on the difference in nonprofit governance in approving the merger of the two dominant hospitals in a medium-sized town (Grand Rapids). The court observed that having community and business leaders on the nonprofit hospital board dampens the incentive to raise prices, and it pointed to research that markets dominated by nonprofit hospitals have lower prices. The court concluded:

> In the real world, hospitals are in the business of saving lives, and managed care organizations are in the business of saving dollars. Managed care organizations' interest in maintaining a competitive edge cannot be allowed to trump either hospitals' conscientious endeavors to continue to provide comprehensive, high quality health care . . . or the consumer public's right to receive the same. Permitting defendant hospitals to achieve the efficiencies of scale that would clearly result from the proposed merger would enable the . . . combined entity to continue the quest for establishment of world-class health facilities in West Michigan, a course the Court finds clearly and unequivocally would ultimately be in the best interests of the consumer public as a whole.

FTC v. Butterworth Health Corp., 946 F. Supp. 1285 (W.D. Mich. 1996), aff'd, 121 F.3d 708 (6th Cir. 1997). However, in the *Rockford* case discussed above, the court reasoned to the contrary:

> [T]he defendants contend that they have no incentive to act anti-competitively because . . . monopoly profits garnered by a not-for-profit company cannot be distributed to anyone, let alone corporate decisionmakers. Instead, any excess of

> revenues over expense must be farmed back into the firm's operation. . . . The court rejects the defendants' narrow view as to the motivation behind anti-competitive action. . . . The not-for-profit decisionmaker may desire more money for a new piece of equipment or to hire a new specialist or for a better office, salary or title, or just to keep the firm afloat in particularly lean or dangerous times. . . . Simply put, decisionmakers need not be solely interested in the attainment of profit to act anti-competitively."

717 F. Supp. 1284.

10. *Further Readings.* On the government's **track record in court** (note 1), see Barak D. Richman, Antitrust and Nonprofit Hospital Mergers: A Return to Basics, 156 U. Pa. L. Rev. 121 (2007); Thomas L. Greaney, Thirty Years of Solicitude: Antitrust Law and Physician Cartels, 7 Hous. J. Health L. & Pol'y (2007); Jennifer R. Conners, A Critical Misdiagnosis: How Courts Underestimate the Anticompetitive Implications of Hospital Mergers, 91 Cal. L. Rev. 543 (2003); Casenote, 130 Harv. L. Rev. 1736 (2017).

For analysis of the **legal issues in the *St. Luke's* case**, see T. Greaney & D. Ross, Navigating Through the Fog of Vertical Merger Law, 91 Wash. L. Rev. 191 (2016); Roger Blair et al., Hospital Mergers and Economic Efficiency, 91 Wash. L. Rev. 1 (2016).

Addressing how **states could take a more prominent enforcement or oversight role**, see Erin Fuse Brown & Jaime King, The Double-Edged Sword of Health Care Integration: Consolidation and Cost Control, 92 Ind. L.J. 55 (2016).

On the **empirical effects of hospital and physician mergers** (note 2), see Erin Fuse Brown, Jaime King & David Cutler, Hospitals, Market Share, and Consolidation, 310 JAMA 1964 (2013); Jeff Goldsmith et al., Integrated Delivery Networks: In Search of Benefits and Market Effects (NASI, Feb. 2015); David Dranove & Andrew Sfekas, The Revolution in Health Care Antitrust: New Methods and Provocative Implications, 87 Milbank Q. 607 (2009); Kristin Madison, Hospital Mergers in an Era of Quality Improvement, 7 Hous. J. Health L. & Pol'y 265 (2007); Note, 90 B.U. L. Rev. 431 (2010); Symposium, 36 Health Aff. 1527 (2017).

On antitrust analysis for **nonprofit hospitals** (note 8), see Barak D. Richman, The Corrosive Combination of Nonprofit Monopolies and U.S.-Style Health Insurance: Implications for Antitrust and Merger Policy, 69 Law & Contemp. Probs. 139 (Autumn 2006); Clark Havighurst & Barak Richman, The Provider Monopoly Problem in Health Care, 89 Or. L. Rev. 847 (2011).

Problem: Rural Hospital Merger*

Rural County has a population of 15,000, a small primary care hospital, and ten physicians, including seven general and family practitioners, an obstetrician, a pediatrician, and a general surgeon. All the physicians are solo practitioners. The nearest urban area is about 60 miles away in Big City, which has a population of 300,000, and three major hospitals to which patients from Rural County are referred

*This problem is excerpted directly from the DOJ/FTC antitrust guidelines.

or transferred for higher levels of hospital care. However, Big City is too far away for most residents of Rural County to use for services available in Rural County.

Insurance Company, which operates throughout the state, is attempting to offer "managed care" programs in all areas of the state, and has asked the local physicians in Rural County to form an IPA to provide services under the program to covered persons living in the county. No other managed care plan has attempted to enter the county previously.

Initially, two of the general practitioners and two of the specialists express interest in forming a network, but Insurance Company says that it intends to market its plan to the larger local employers, who need broader geographic and specialty coverage for their employees. Consequently, Insurance Company needs more of the local general practitioners and the one remaining specialist in the IPA in order to provide adequate geographic, specialty, and backup coverage to subscribers in Rural County. Eventually, four of the seven general practitioners and the one remaining specialist join the IPA and agree to provide services to Insurance Company's subscribers under contracts providing for capitation. While the physicians' participation in the IPA is structured to be nonexclusive, no other managed care plan has yet entered the local market or approached any of the physicians about joining a different provider panel. In discussing the formation of the IPA with the Insurance Company, a number of the physicians have made clear their intention to continue to practice outside the IPA and have indicated they would be interested in contracting individually with other managed care plans when those plans expand into Rural County. Insurance Company requests your legal advice about whether this network formation is likely to be challenged by the federal government.

E. REFERRAL FEE LAWS

Many of the transactions and relationships surveyed in this chapter are affected by an entirely different set of laws that happen to be motivated by the same concerns about excess commercialization and distorting incentives: the collection of federal and state laws that prohibit or regulate referral fees. By referral fees, we mean explicit or implicit incentives to generate or refer medical business. These referral fee laws are unfortunately but unavoidably complex, and they have effects that permeate the medical enterprise. They are taken very seriously by lawyers, doctors, and institutions because their violation can result in denial of payment, inability to enforce contracts, or even criminal penalties. As you become acquainted with this highly specialized body of law, try first to focus on the gist of what it prohibits and why, and then begin to consider its less obvious applications and implications.

UNITED STATES v. GREBER
760 F.2d 68 (3d Cir. 1985)

WEIS, Circuit Judge.

In this appeal, defendant argues that payments made to a physician for professional services in connection with tests performed by a laboratory cannot be the basis of Medicare fraud. We do not agree and hold that if one purpose of the payment was to induce future referrals, the Medicare statute has been violated. . . .

Defendant is an osteopathic physician who is board certified in cardiology. In addition to hospital staff and teaching positions, he was the president of Cardio-Med, Inc., an organization which he formed. The company provides physicians with diagnostic services, one of which uses a Holter-monitor. This device, worn for approximately 24 hours, records the patient's cardiac activity on a tape. A computer operated by a cardiac technician scans the tape, and the data is later correlated with an activity diary the patient maintains while wearing the monitor.

Cardio-Med billed Medicare for the monitor service and, when payment was received, forwarded a portion to the referring physician. The government charged that the referral fee was 40 percent of the Medicare payment, not to exceed $65 per patient.

Based on Cardio-Med's billing practices, counts 18-23 of the indictment charged defendant with having tendered remuneration or kickbacks to the referring physicians in violation of [the Medicare fraud statute]. . . . The proof as to the Medicare fraud counts was that defendant had paid a Dr. Avallone and other physicians "interpretation fees" for the doctors' initial consultation services, as well as for explaining the test results to the patients. There was evidence that physicians received "interpretation fees" even though defendant had actually evaluated the monitoring data. Moreover, the fixed percentage paid to the referring physician was more than Medicare allowed for such services.

The government also introduced testimony defendant had given in an earlier civil proceeding. In that case, he had testified that ". . . if the doctor didn't get his consulting fee, he wouldn't be using our service. So the doctor got a consulting fee." . . .

I. Medicare Fraud

The Medicare fraud statute was amended [in] 1977. Congress, concerned with the growing problem of fraud and abuse in the system, wished to strengthen the penalties to enhance the deterrent effect of the statute. To achieve this purpose, the crime was upgraded from a misdemeanor to a felony. . . . A particular concern was the practice of giving "kickbacks" to encourage the referral of work. Testimony before the congressional committee was that "physicians often determine which laboratories would do the test work for their medicaid patients by the amount of the kickbacks and rebates offered by the laboratory. . . . Kickbacks take a number of forms including cash, long-term credit arrangements, gifts, supplies and equipment, and the furnishing of business machines."

To remedy the deficiencies in the statute and achieve more certainty, the present version of 42 U.S.C. §[1320a-7b(b), Social Security Act §1128B(b)(2)] was enacted. It provides:

> [W]hoever knowingly and willfully offers or pays any remuneration (including any kickback, bribe or rebate) directly or indirectly, overtly or covertly in cash or in kind to induce such person—. . . to purchase, lease, order, or arrange for or recommend purchasing . . . or ordering any . . . service or item for which payment may be made . . . under [Medicare or Medicaid] shall be guilty of a felony.

The district judge instructed the jury that the government was required to prove that Cardio-Med paid to Dr. Avallone some part of the amount received from Medicare; that defendant caused Cardio-Med to make the payment; and did so knowingly and willfully as well as with the intent to induce Dr. Avallone to use Cardio-Med's services for patients covered by Medicare. The judge further charged that even if the physician interpreting the test did so as a consultant to Cardio-Med, that fact was immaterial if a purpose of the fee was to induce the ordering of services from Cardio-Med.

Defendant contends that the charge was erroneous. He insists that absent a showing that the only purpose behind the fee was to improperly induce future services, compensating a physician for services actually rendered could not be a violation of the statute. The government argues that Congress intended to combat financial incentives to physicians for ordering particular services patients did not require.

The language and purpose of the statute support the government's view. Even if the physician performs some service for the money received, the potential for unnecessary drain on the Medicare system remains. The statute is aimed at the inducement factor.

The text refers to "any remuneration." That includes not only sums for which no actual service was performed but also those amounts for which some professional time was expended. "Remunerates" is defined as "to pay an equivalent for service." Webster Third New International Dictionary (1966). By including such items as kickbacks and bribes, the statute expands "remuneration" to cover situations where no service is performed. That a particular payment was a remuneration (which implies that a service was rendered) rather than a kickback, does not foreclose the possibility that a violation nevertheless could exist. . . .

We conclude that the more expansive reading is consistent with the impetus for the 1977 amendments and therefore hold that the district court correctly instructed the jury. If the payments were intended to induce the physician to use Cardio-Med's services, the statute was violated, even if the payments were also intended to compensate for professional services.

■ LIMITATION ON CERTAIN PHYSICIAN REFERRALS

*42 U.S.C. §1395nn**

(a) Prohibition of certain referrals.

(1) In general. Except as provided in subsection (b) of this section, if a physician (or an immediate family member of such physician) has a financial relationship with an entity specified in paragraph (2), then the physician may not make a referral to the entity for the furnishing of designated health services [under Medicare or Medicaid and the entity may not seek payment for such services]. . . .

(2) Financial relationship specified. A financial relationship of a physician (or an immediate family member of such physician) with an entity specified in this paragraph is—

*This statute is known as the Stark Law, after its sponsor, Rep. Pete Stark. It was enacted in 1993.

(A) except as provided in subsections (c) and (d) of this section, an ownership or investment interest in the entity [through equity or debt], or

(B) except as provided in subsection (e) of this section, a compensation arrangement between the physician (or an immediate family member of such physician) and the entity. . . .

(b) General exceptions to both ownership and compensation arrangement prohibitions. Subsection (a)(1) of this section shall not apply in the following cases:

(1) Physicians' services. In the case of physicians' services provided personally by (or under the personal supervision of) another physician in the same group practice as the referring physician.

(2) In-office ancillary services. In the case of services . . . that are [billed by and] furnished personally by the referring physician, personally by a physician who is a member of the same group practice as the referring physician, or personally by individuals who are directly supervised by the physician or by another physician in the group practice. . . .

(c) General exception related only to ownership or investment prohibition for ownership in publicly traded securities and mutual funds. Ownership of the following shall not be considered to be an ownership or investment interest described in subsection (a)(2)(A) of this section: Ownership of investment securities which may be purchased on terms generally available to the public and which are [publicly traded on the stock exchanges] or [are] in a corporation that [has] . . . stockholder equity exceeding $75,000,000. . . .

(d) Additional exceptions related only to ownership or investment prohibition. The following, if not otherwise excepted under subsection (b) of this section, shall not be considered to be an ownership or investment interest described in subsection (a)(2)(A) of this section: . . .

(2) Rural provider. . . . [I]f substantially all of the designated health services furnished by such entity are furnished to individuals residing in [a] rural area.

(3) Hospital ownership. In the case of designated health services provided by a hospital if the referring physician is authorized to perform services at the hospital, and the ownership or investment interest is in the hospital itself (and not merely in a subdivision of the hospital). [The ACA placed a moratorium on this "whole-hospital" exception—denying it to any new hospitals or hospital expansions starting in 2012, but grandfathering existing arrangements.—EDS.]

(e) Exceptions relating to other compensation arrangements. The following shall not be considered to be a compensation arrangement described in subsection (a)(2)(B) of this section:

(1) Rental of office space; rental of equipment. Payments made by a lessee to a lessor for the use of premises [or equipment] if—

(i) the lease is set out in writing, signed by the parties, and specifies the premises covered by the lease,

(ii) the space [or equipment] rented or leased does not exceed that which is reasonable and necessary for the legitimate business purposes of the lease or rental and is used exclusively by the lessee when being used by the lessee, . . .

(iii) the lease provides for a term of rental or lease for at least one year,

(iv) the rental charges over the term of the lease are set in advance, are consistent with fair market value, and are not determined in a manner that takes into account the volume or value of any referrals or other business generated between the parties,

(v) the lease would be commercially reasonable even if no referrals were made between the parties, and

(vi) the lease meets such other requirements as the Secretary may impose by regulation as needed to protect against program or patient abuse.

(2) Bona fide employment relationships. Any amount paid by an employer to a physician (or an immediate family member of such physician) who has a bona fide employment relationship with the employer for the provision of services if—

(A) the employment is for identifiable services,

(B) the amount of the remuneration under the employment is consistent with the fair market value of the services and is not determined in a manner that takes into account (directly or indirectly) the volume or value of any referrals by the referring physician, [and]

(C) the remuneration is provided pursuant to an agreement which would be commercially reasonable even if no referrals were made to the employer. . . .

(3) Personal service arrangements. [This subsection covers independent contractors, and requires terms that reflect fair market and are unrelated to the volume of services, similar to the two exceptions above for leases and employment. The contract must cover at least 1 year, and must provide for fixed compensation set in advance.] . . .

(5) Physician recruitment. In the case of remuneration which is provided by a hospital to a physician to induce the physician to relocate to the geographic area served by the hospital in order to be a member of the medical staff of the hospital, if the physician is not required to refer patients to the hospital, and the amount of the remuneration under the arrangement is not determined in a manner that takes into account (directly or indirectly) the volume or value of any referrals by the referring physician. . . .

(g) Sanctions. [Medicare and Medicaid services delivered in arrangements that violate this section will not be paid for. Also, a knowing violation can result in the imposition of civil monetary penalties or exclusion from the Medicare and Medicaid programs.]

(h) Definitions and special rules. For purposes of this section: . . .

(1) The term "compensation arrangement" means any arrangement involving any remuneration between a physician . . . and an entity. . . . The term "remuneration" includes any remuneration, directly or indirectly, overtly or covertly, in cash or in kind. . . .

(3) The term "fair market value" means the value in arms length transactions . . . and, in the case of a lease of space, not adjusted to reflect the additional value the prospective lessee or lessor would attribute to the proximity or convenience to the lessor where the lessor is a potential source of patient referrals to the lessee. . . .

(5) . . . [T]he request by a physician for the item or service, . . . [or] the establishment of a plan of care by a physician which includes the provision of the designated health service, . . . constitutes a "referral" by the "referring physician." [The definition then clarifies that no referral occurs when certain specialists such as radiologists or pathologists order their own services or services rendered under their supervision.]

(6) Designated health services. The term "designated health services" means any of the following items or services: clinical laboratory services, physical therapy services, occupational therapy services, radiology services, . . . durable medical equipment and supplies, . . . home health services, . . . outpatient prescription drugs, and inpatient and outpatient hospital services. [Note that this list does not include basic physician services but only specified "ancillary" services

that physicians might provide or arrange for. The inclusion of hospital services covers only the facility's services (nursing care, testing, use of operating room, etc.) and not physicians' personal professional time.]

■ U.S. ex rel. DRAKEFORD v. TUOMEY HEALTHCARE SYSTEM

792 F.3d 364, 382. (4th Cir. 2015)

DIAZ, Circuit Judge:

In a *qui tam* action in which the government intervened, a jury determined that Tuomey Healthcare . . . knowingly submitted 21,730 false claims to Medicare for reimbursement. The district court then entered final judgment for the government and awarded damages and civil penalties totaling $237,454,195. . . . [W]e affirm the district court's judgment.

I. A

Tuomey [pronounced "TOO-mee"] is a nonprofit hospital located in Sumter, South Carolina, a small, largely rural community that is a federally-designated, medically-underserved area. At the time of the events leading up to this lawsuit, most of the physicians that practiced at Tuomey were not directly employed by the hospital, but instead were members of independent specialty practices.

Beginning around 2000, doctors who previously performed outpatient surgery at Tuomey began doing so in their own offices or at off-site surgery centers. The loss of this revenue stream was a source of grave concern for Tuomey because it collected substantial facility fees from patients who underwent surgery at the hospital's outpatient center. ... To stem this loss, Tuomey sought to negotiate part-time employment contracts with a number of local physicians.

In drafting the contracts, Tuomey was well aware of the constraints imposed by the Stark Law. While we discuss the provisions of that law in greater detail below, in broad terms, [it] prohibits physicians from making referrals to entities where "[t]he referring physician . . . receives aggregate compensation . . . that varies with, or takes into account, the volume or value of referrals or other business generated by the referring physician for the entity furnishing" the designated health services. 42 C.F.R. § 411.354. Pursuant to the Stark Law, [a] hospital may not submit for payment a Medicare claim for services rendered pursuant to a prohibited referral.

Beginning in 2003, Tuomey sought the advice of its longtime counsel, Nexsen Pruet, [which conferred with a physician compensation expert, a former Inspector General for the US Department of Health and Human Services, and another prominent healthcare law firm. Under the contracts Nexsen Pruet drafted, each physician's base salary] . . . was adjusted from year to year based on the amount the physician collected from all services rendered the previous year. The bulk of the physicians' compensation was earned in the form of a productivity bonus, which paid the physicians 80 percent of the amount of their collections for that year. The physicians were also eligible for an incentive bonus of up to seven percent of their earned productivity bonus. In addition, Tuomey [paid for medical malpractice insurance, employment taxes, and billing and collections costs].

The contracts had ten-year terms, during which physicians could maintain their private practices, but were required to perform outpatient surgical procedures exclusively at the hospital. Physicians could not own any interest in a facility located in Sumter that provided ambulatory surgery services . . . .

Tuomey ultimately entered into part-time employment contracts with nineteen physicians. Tuomey, however, was unable to reach an agreement with Dr. Michael Drakeford, an orthopedic surgeon. Drakeford believed that the proposed contracts violated the Stark Law because the physicians were being paid in excess of their collections . . . and thus the government would view it as an unlawful payment for the doctor's facility-fee-generating referrals.

To address Drakeford's concerns, Tuomey suggested a joint venture as an alternative business arrangement, whereby "doctors would become investors . . . in . . . a management company that would provide day-to-day management of the outpatient surgery center," and both Tuomey and its co-investors would "receive payments based on that management [structure]." Drakeford, however, declined that option.

Unable to break the stalemate in their negotiations, in May 2005, Tuomey and Drakeford sought the advice of Kevin McAnaney, an attorney . . . [who had formerly served in the Office of Counsel to the DHHS Inspector General]. In that position, McAnaney wrote a "substantial portion" of the regulations implementing the Stark Law. McAnaney advised the parties that the proposed employment contracts raised significant "red flags" under the Stark Law. . . . McAnaney also warned Tuomey that the contracts presented "an easy case to prosecute" for the government.

Drakeford ultimately declined to enter into a contract with Tuomey. He later sued the hospital under the *qui tam* provisions[5] of the [federal False Claims Act (FCA)], alleging that because the part-time employment contracts violated the Stark Law, Tuomey had knowingly submitted false claims for payment to Medicare. As was its right, the government intervened in the action . . . .

[An initial trial found that the hospital had violated the Stark Law, but not the False Claims Act, presumably because its violation of Stark was not "knowing or reckless," but the Fourth Circuit reversed and remanded for a new trial, based in part on the initial judge excluding testimony about Kevin McAnaney's view of the contracts' legality. In the second trial, the] jury found that Tuomey violated both the Stark Law and the FCA. It further found that Tuomey had submitted 21,730 false claims to Medicare with a total value of $39,313,065. The district court trebled the actual damages and assessed an additional civil penalty, both actions required by the FCA. From the resulting judgment of $237,454,195, Tuomey appeals.

II. B

. . . The Stark Law is intended to prevent overutilization of services by physicians who [stand] to profit from referring patients to facilities or entities in which they [have] a financial interest. The statute prohibits a physician from making a referral to an entity, such as a hospital, with which he or she has a financial relationship, for

5. [This "whistleblower" law, 31 U.S.C. §3729, allows private parties to sue on behalf of the government to recoup money paid under any claim that was knowingly false or fraudulent. Successful qui tam "relators" (as they are called) can earn a bounty of 15-30 percent of the recovered amounts.]

the furnishing of designated health services. If the physician makes such a referral, the hospital may not submit a bill for reimbursement to Medicare. Similarly, the government may not make any payment for a designated health service provided in violation of the Stark Law. . . .

Inpatient and outpatient hospital services are considered designated health services under the law. A referral includes "the request by a physician for the item or service." A referral does not include "any designated health service personally performed or provided by the referring physician." However, there is a referral when the hospital bills a "facility fee" (also known as a "facility component" or "technical component") "in connection with the personally performed service."

A financial relationship constitutes a prohibited "indirect compensation arrangement," if . . . "[t]he referring physician . . . receives aggregate compensation . . . that varies with, or takes into account, the volume or value of referrals or other business generated by the referring physician for the entity furnishing" the designated health services . . . . The statute, however, does not bar indirect compensation arrangements where: (1) the referring physician is compensated at fair market value for "services and items actually provided"; (2) the compensation arrangement is "not determined in any manner that takes into account the volume or value of referrals"; [and] (3) the compensation arrangement is "commercially reasonable" . . . .

. . . A reasonable jury could find that Tuomey violated the Stark Law when it paid aggregate compensation to physicians that varied with or took into account the volume or value of actual or anticipated referrals to Tuomey. . . . There are two different components of the physicians' compensation that we believe so varied. First, each year, the physicians were paid a base salary that was adjusted upward or downward depending on their collections from the prior year. In addition, the physicians received the bulk of their compensation in the form of a productivity bonus, pegged at eighty percent of the amount of their collections. . . . In sum, the more procedures the physicians performed at the hospital, the more facility fees Tuomey collected, and the more compensation the physicians received in the form of increased base salaries and productivity bonuses. . . .

Tuomey next argues that . . . it did not knowingly violate the FCA. Specifically, Tuomey claims that because it reasonably relied on the advice of counsel, no reasonable jury could find that Tuomey possessed the requisite intent to violate the FCA. Because the record here is replete with evidence indicating that Tuomey shopped for legal opinions approving of the employment contracts, while ignoring negative assessments, we disagree. . . .

McAnaney's testimony, summarized above, is alone sufficient to sweep aside Tuomey's claim of error. . . . According to McAnaney, compensation arrangements under which the contracting physicians are paid in excess of their collections were "basically a red flag to the government." He noted that similar cases had previously been prosecuted, although all of them were ultimately settled. McAnaney also pointed out that the ten-year term of the contracts, combined with the thirty-mile, two-year noncompete provision, would reinforce the government's view that Tuomey was "paying [the physicians] above fair market value for referrals." . . .

Nonetheless, a defendant may avoid liability under the FCA if it can show that it acted in good faith on the advice of counsel. . . . Tuomey contends that it provided full and accurate information regarding the proposed employment contracts to [their law firm] Hewson, who in turn advised Tuomey that the contracts did not run afoul of the Stark Law. But as the government aptly notes, "[i]n determining whether Tuomey reasonably relied on the advice of its counsel, the jury was entitled to consider all the advice given to it by any source."

. . . Tuomey defends its dismissal of McAnaney's warnings by claiming that his opinion was tainted by undue influence exerted by Drakeford and his counsel. But there was evidence before the jury suggesting that Tuomey also tried to procure a favorable opinion from McAnaney. . . . Thus, a reasonable jury could conclude that Tuomey ignored McAnaney because it simply did not like what he had to say. . . .

IV

Finally, Tuomey makes several challenges to the $237,454,195 judgment entered against it. . . . A defendant found liable under the FCA must pay the government "a civil penalty of" not less than $5,500 and not more than $11,000 "plus 3 times the amount of damages which the Government sustains because of that person." In this case, the jury found that Tuomey had submitted 21,730 false claims, for which it awarded actual damages of $39,313,065, which the district court trebled. The district court then added a civil penalty of $119,515,000 to that sum, which it calculated by multiplying the number of false claims by the $5,500 statutory minimum penalty. . . .

According to Tuomey, the civil penalty assessed was improperly inflated because the jury was permitted to take into account both inpatient and outpatient procedures performed by the contracting physicians. . . . Tuomey is incorrect.

It is true that the contracts solely addressed compensation for outpatient procedures. . . . [However, if] a physician has a financial relationship with a hospital, then the Stark Law prohibits the physician from making any referral to that hospital for the furnishing of designated health services. . . . Inpatient hospital services are designated health services. And a referral includes "the request or establishment of a plan of care by a physician which includes the provision of the designated health service." Plainly, then, inpatient services constitute a prohibited referral for the furnishing of designated health services, and the district court properly instructed the jury to factor them into the damages calculation.

Tuomey also asserts that the jury's damage award is flawed because the government . . . did not identify the "referring physician," and thus failed to prove that the alleged false claims came about through a prohibited referral. . . . . [However,] several courts have accepted that the "'attending/operating' physician identified in [Medicare claims form] qualifies as a referring physician," ... [and that] the fact that one of the physicians with whom the hospital has a financial relationship is identified as an "operating" or "attending" physician is sufficient evidence that the physician was also the "referring physician" absent evidence to the contrary. . . .

Tuomey next argues that the district court erroneously assessed the penalty based on [each of] the 21,730 [claims] forms Tuomey submitted to Medicare for reimbursement. . . . Instead, Tuomey asserts that the number of false claims should be limited to four [based on the number of times the hospital submitted annual reconciliations for aggregate Medicare payments]. Tuomey provides no Stark Law case to support its argument. Rather, each time Tuomey submitted to Medicare a [claims] form asking for reimbursement for a prohibited referral, it was knowingly asking the government to pay an amount that, by law, it could not pay. Consequently, we find the district court did not err in finding that each [claims] form constituted a separate claim.

Tuomey also . . . argues that the true measure [of actual damages] is not the sum total of all claims the government paid (as the court instructed the jury), but rather the difference (if any) between the true value of the services provided by Tuomey and what the government actually paid. According to Tuomey, since "there was no evidence that the Government did not get what it paid for[,] . . . there were no actual damages under the FCA." Here again, Tuomey's view of the law is incorrect.

The Stark Law prohibits the government from paying any amount of money for claims submitted in violation of the law. . . . The Stark Law expresses Congress's judgment that all services provided in violation of that law are medically unnecessary. By reimbursing Tuomey for services that it was legally prohibited from paying, the government has suffered injury equivalent to the full amount of the payments. . . .

C

Finally, Tuomey argues that the district court's award of $237,454,195, consisting of damages and a civil penalty, is unconstitutional under the Excessive Fines Clause of the Eighth Amendment and the Due Process Clause of the Fifth Amendment. While the award is substantial, we cannot say that it is unconstitutional. . . .

[T]he Supreme Court has directed courts to evaluate the degree of reprehensibility of the defendant's conduct by considering whether [among other factors not present here] ". . . the conduct involved repeated actions or was an isolated incident; and the harm was the result of intentional malice, trickery, or deceit, [rather than] mere accident." Clearly, Tuomey's conduct "involved repeated actions" as it submitted 21,730 false claims. Thus, while the penalty is certainly severe, it is meant to reflect the sheer breadth of the fraud Tuomey perpetrated upon the federal government. . . .

Next, we consider the disparity between actual harm and the punitive damages award. . . . Here, we can properly regard the entire civil penalty, $119,515,000, as punitive. On the other hand, the actual damages of $39,313,065 are entirely compensatory. As discussed above, the additional sum of $78,626,130 resulting from the trebling of actual damages is a hybrid of compensatory and punitive damages. . . . Assuming further that Drakeford receives the minimum amount allotted by the statute–that is fifteen percent of the total recovery–the relator would be entitled to $11,793,920 of the trebled award, leaving $66,832,210 to be allocated to punitive damages. By this calculation, the portion of damages that is compensatory is $51,106,985 and the $186,347,210 balance is punitive. . . .

[The Supreme Court] has suggested that "an award of more than four times the amount of compensatory damages might be close to the line of constitutional impropriety." Here, the ratio of punitive damages to compensatory damages is approximately 3.6-to-1 . . . . We therefore conclude that the damages award is constitutional under the Fifth and Eighth Amendments.

Finally, we do not discount the concerns raised by our concurring colleague regarding the result in this case. But having no found no cause to upset the jury's verdict in this case and no constitutional error, it is for Congress to consider whether changes to the Stark Law's reach are in order.

WYNN, Circuit Judge, concurring:

. . . I agree with the majority that the jury's determination that Tuomey violated both the Stark Law and the False Claims Act must stand. Our standard of review at this juncture is a highly deferential one. . . . Nevertheless, I am troubled by the picture this case paints: An impenetrably complex set of laws and regulations that will result in a likely death sentence for a community hospital in an already medically underserved area. . . .

"The Stark Law is a strict liability statute so it is immaterial whether one intended to violate the law; an inadvertent violation can trigger liability." Paula Tironi, The "Stark" Reality: Is the Federal Physician Self-Referral Law Bad for the Health Care Industry?, 19 Annals Health L. 235, 237-238 (2010). Individuals and entities that violate the Stark Law can be subject to severe monetary penalties and exclusion from federal health care programs. These "steep civil sanctions and program exclusions may be ruinous. Health care providers are open to extensive liability, their financial security resting uneasily upon a combination of their attorneys' wits [and] prosecutorial discretion." Jo-Ellyn Sakowitz Klein, The Stark Laws: Conquering Physician Conflicts of Interest?, 87 Geo. L.J. 499, 503-504 (1998).

Despite attempts to establish "bright line" rules so that physicians and healthcare entities could "ensure compliance and minimize . . . costs," 66 Fed. Reg. 860 (2001), the Stark Law has proved challenging to understand and comply with. Indeed, "[t]he Stark law is infamous among health care lawyers and their clients for being complicated, confusing, and counterintuitive; for producing results that defy common sense, and sometimes elevating form over substance. . . . Charles B. Oppenheim, The Stark Law: Comprehensive Analysis (AHLA 5th ed. 2014). . . .

Against this problematic backdrop, the availability of an advice of counsel defense should perhaps be especially robust in Stark Law cases prosecuted under the False Claims Act. . . . In the context of the Stark Law, it is easy to see how even diligent counsel could wind up giving clients incorrect advice. Between the law's being amended to have a broader scope but then narrowed with various exceptions, along with the promulgation and amendment of copious associated rules and regulations, "the Stark Law bec[ame] a classic example of a moving target. For lawyers, who must depend on the predictability of the law when they give counsel to their clients, such unpredictability [i]s an unusually heavy burden." Steven D. Wales, The Stark Law: Boon or Boondoggle? An Analysis of the Prohibition on Physician Self-Referrals, 27 Law & Psychol. Rev. 1, 21.

In this case, there can be no doubt that Tuomey sought and followed the advice of its long-time counsel, Nexsen Pruet. . . . Nevertheless, as the majority opinion notes, "a reasonable jury could have concluded that Tuomey was . . . no longer acting in good faith reliance on the advice of its counsel when it refused to give full consideration to McAnaney's negative assessment of the" contracts. . . .

This case is troubling. It seems as if, even for well-intentioned health care providers, the Stark Law has become a booby trap rigged with strict liability and potentially ruinous exposure—especially when coupled with the False Claims Act. Yet . . . the jury did not act irrationally when it determined that Tuomey violated both the Stark Law and the False Claims Act. Accordingly, I must concur in the outcome reached by the majority.

[Note: To avoid bankruptcy, Tuomey hospital was subsequently purchased by a larger hospital chain, and the sales proceeds were used to settle with the government for $72.4 million. The government also assessed a $1 million fine against the hospital's former CEO.]

■ A PUBLIC POLICY DISCUSSION: TAKING THE MEASURE OF THE STARK LAW

American Health Lawyers Association Public Interest Committee
*(2009)**

The Stark Law starts with an extremely broad prohibition. All physician referrals to an entity are prohibited unless the physician's financial relationships with that entity fit within one or more exceptions. Given the equally broad definition of financial relationships, the Stark Law has virtually ubiquitous application in the healthcare delivery system. The practical implications of the Law are greatly magnified by the fact that where the entity has a non-excepted financial relationship with a physician, the entity is prohibited from billing for any designated health services referred to it by that physician. In addition, the Stark Law is a strict liability statute in that the referral prohibition and the prohibition on billing are not dependent on the parties' intent. . . .

The strict liability provisions of the Stark Law combined with its breadth have yielded both positive and negative results. . . . [The Law] is credited with eliminating physician ownership of freestanding diagnostic centers and blamed for encouraging physicians to provide an ever growing range of services through their group practices. The Law has made it more difficult for physicians to have an ownership interest in a provider of designated health services but prompted an expansion of leasing and management services arrangements. . . .

The proscriptive structure of the Stark Law requires the creation of an exception for each and every permissible financial relationship. Given the dynamics of the healthcare industry, the Law is destined to impede changes that involve relationships that do not fit within existing exceptions. This, in turn, creates pressure for an ever-increasing number of exceptions, enhancing the complexity of the law and undermining the industry's ability to understand and comply with its provisions. The mechanical application of the Stark Law can also result in overpayment liabilities that are highly disproportionate to the conduct giving rise to the offense.

On the other hand, the Stark Law's broad prohibition and lack of an intent element make it easier for CMS and government enforcement agencies to use. . . . The sharp rise in the number of Stark-based False Claims Act cases is a testament to the utility of the statute. . . .

 In its role as a public resource on health law, the AHLA from time to time convenes panels of experts representing diverse viewpoints to explore issues of significance to the health law and health policy communities. The views expressed in this paper are a summary of the positions expressed by such experts and should not be construed as an endorsement of any position by the AHLA or its members.

The Dangers of Disproportionality: The risk that a Stark violation might result in a level of exposure that could effectively bankrupt a hospital is a scenario that haunts administrators. For example:

> [A]ssume that in 2001, a hospital enters into a medical director agreement with its most productive cardiac surgeon. The terms of the agreement are commercially reasonable and the compensation is set at fair market value. In 2002, the medical director agreement expires but the hospital mistakenly assumes that the agreement automatically renewed and continues to pay the surgeon. The surgeon also thinks the written agreement is still in place and continues to provide the services and submits weekly timesheets documenting the hours devoted to his medical director duties. In 2009, the hospital discovers that the medical director agreement expired in 2002. Under the Stark Law, the hospital has had a non-excepted financial relationship with the cardiac surgeon for the past seven years and all reimbursement that the hospital received during that period for services provided to Medicare [or Medicaid] patients pursuant to referrals from that cardiac surgeon are subject to recoupment by the government.

The repayment liability in this instance could be millions of dollars. If the hospital made the same type of faulty assumption with respect to five agreements, the potential exposure grows accordingly. If this Stark violation is used as the basis for a False Claims Act case, civil penalties and treble damages could also be recovered.[6] In short, the hospital's total exposure flowing from an expired medical director agreement could well be ruinous. . . .

While the potential exposure for a Stark violation is enormous, historically the likelihood of enforcement has been low. CMS has not been actively seeking recoupment based on violations of the Stark Law. Enforcement of Stark through the False Claims Act is random and often not the sole or even primary focus of the government's case. The risk of a hospital facing disproportional penalties for an innocent Stark violation, however, is exacerbated to the extent that prosecutorial discretion has been effectively abdicated to whistleblowers under the *qui tam* provisions of the FCA. Given all these factors, the industry has viewed Stark enforcement as akin to lightning striking—unpredictable but deadly. . . . [M]ost hospitals, even when faced with a claim with little merit, will settle rather than roll the dice in a government enforcement action. . . .

[*Dealing with Technical Violations.*] As noted above, there is general consensus that the Stark Law is exceedingly complex and highly technical. . . . Some participants noted that the complexity of the Stark Law arises in part from its history of "reactive" rulemaking. According to this perspective, the cycle has been that (1) the agency promulgates an exception or a rule, (2) following implementation, someone identifies a potentially abusive practice in the industry; and (3) the agency reacts, not by taking a different tact, but by either amending the existing rule or creating "an exception to the exception" to address the perceived concern. Although this

6. [In part, this is because the Fraud Enforcement and Recovery Act of 2009 defines "false claim" to include the knowing retention of overpayments that were thought to be proper at the time the claim was made, but which are later discovered to be improper.—Eds.]

cycle may seem logical, it has resulted in a maze of regulatory definitions, special rules, and exceptions. . . .

Several participants in the Convener Session noted that when confronted with evidence of a Stark violation, providers' [options are to]: . . .

- Do nothing.
- Fix the problem and don't look back.
- Fix the problem and return the entire "overpayment."
- Identify a government agency, make a disclosure and attempt to negotiate a compromise.

All options pose substantial risks. . . . Disclosure to [CMS,] the Department of Justice or local US Attorney's Office could be viewed as an admission of wrongdoing and neither [CMS,] the DOJ nor the US Attorneys are known for their willingness to compromise claims for less than the face amount of the repayment obligation. . . .

Given the backdrop of potentially ruinous liability under the FCA, . . . the industry has been casting about for a practical means of addressing Stark violations once they are identified. . . . [S]everal participants suggested that CMS establish a Stark self-disclosure protocol to give the industry a practical means of addressing Stark violations once they are identified.

Notes: Referral Fees

1. *Sources of Law.* There are four sources of referral fee prohibitions, two federal and two state.[9] The most threatening are the two federal statutes discussed in the principal readings (the Stark law, and the Medicare/Medicaid fraud and abuse statute, which is also called the "anti-kickback statute"). Many states also criminalize referral fees or prohibit physician referral arrangements. In California, for instance, "the . . . receipt or acceptance, by any [physician] of any rebate, refund, commission . . . or other consideration, whether in the form of money or otherwise, as compensation or inducement for referring patients . . . to any person . . . is unlawful . . . and is punishable [as a felony]." Cal. Bus. & Prof. Code §650. Finally, state medical practice acts frequently enumerate fee splitting as one of the grounds for revocation or suspension of a physician's license to practice. A typical statute allows disciplinary action by the board of medical examiners for "division of fees . . . received for professional services with any person for bringing or referring a patient." See generally Note, 43 Brandeis L.J. 465 (2005).

Litigation under the state laws is becoming more common, as a basis for challenging the legality of various business arrangements, some of which are very common. See, e.g.:

- Medical school's 10 percent "dean's tax" on its clinical departments' revenue constitutes illegal "fee splitting" with respect to part-adjunct, part-time faculty.

9. In addition, in contrast with prohibitions of referral incentives is the related prohibition of "gainsharing" incentives to reduce Medicare or Medicaid services, which is quoted and discussed in Chapter 3.E.3.

Odrich v. Trustees of Columbia University, 764 N.Y.S.2d 448 (N.Y. App. Div. 2003).

- Courts differ on whether ordinary office management contracts are illegal in which physicians pay a percentage of revenues or profits for running their business operations. Compare, e.g., Necula v. Glass, 647 N.Y.S.2d 501 (1996) (illegal) *with* Epic Medical Management v. Paquette, 244 Cal. App. 4th 504 (2015) (legal).
- Physicians who resell prescription drugs at a markup do not violate the state's anti-kickback statute. Wright v. Jeckle, 144 P.3d 301 (2006).

Also, consider whether "Groupons" for doctors might be illegal fee-splitting. Michael Bolongna, Online Coupons from Doctors: Fee-Splitting?, 20 BNA Health L. Rep. 1513 (2011) (discussing legality of Groupons for doctors).

Representative Stark introduced his law after increased attention to the abuses that result when physicians own or invest in the medical facilities where they practice or to which physicians refer business. This ownership interest in the facility means they profit not only from their own service fees but also from the earnings of the facility. This extra incentive to in essence refer business to themselves causes increased utilization of the facilities. Several studies have shown, for instance, that physicians who own or invest in clinical laboratories or expensive diagnostic equipment such as MRI scanners order from 40 to 100 percent more tests of this nature than do other doctors with similar patients.

Although the aim of the Stark self-referral statute is essentially the same as the anti-kickback statute, its structure is fundamentally different. First, it is primarily civil, not criminal; the main effect is to disallow payment for medical services in arrangements that violate the statute. Second, it does not have the same large gray areas of legal uncertainty; under Stark, you are either on base or you are out, whereas anti-kickback liability depends on a more subjective intent to induce referrals.

2. *Seeking Safety Under the Anti-Kickback Statute.* Greber v. United States rules that any intent to induce referrals poisons the arrangement, even if payments are in exchange for physicians' services. However, close attention to the facts suggest that the decision may not be this ominous. Do you see any indications that the "interpretation services" were a bogus front to disguise what was in reality a true kickback scheme? Nevertheless, several other Circuits have adopted the same broad interpretation of the federal statute, dashing the hopes of those who initially read that decision as limited. United States v. Borrasi, 639 F.3d 774 (7th Cir. 2011). Only the First Circuit has made a conviction at least marginally more difficult by requiring a showing that there be a "primary" rather than merely an "incidental" purpose to induce referrals.

Under the broader interpretation of the anti-kickback statute, wouldn't it potentially be a felony punishable by five years' imprisonment for a rural hospital to recruit a badly needed specialist to the community, for a doctor to discount his services by waiving insurance deductibles and coinsurance, or for a health care institution to pay its doctors a bonus as a reward for efficient practice? As startling as this may seem, a case can be made that each of these activities falls within the literal terms of the statute and entails at least some intent to induce referrals. Enticing a physician to join the medical staff necessarily involves implicit or explicit incentives to refer the physician's patients to that hospital. Price discounts can be characterized as payments to refer one's patients to one's self for treatment. And efficiency bonuses can induce doctors to admit patients to a particular hospital or encourage them to direct patients to a particular insurance plan. Beverly Cohen, An Examination of the Right of Hospitals to Engage in Economic Credentialing, 77 Temp. L. Rev. 705 (2004).

To reduce legal uncertainty, the Department of Health and Human Services (DHHS) has issued a series of "safe harbor" regulations specifying payment practices that are deemed legal under the anti-kickback statute despite their potential referral incentive. 42 C.F.R. §1001.952. These safe harbors track fairly closely the particular financial relationships that the Stark Law allows as exceptions to its general prohibition. Among the more important ones are those covering physician recruitment, space rental, management contracts, price discounts, certain joint ventures, and physician investments in certain health care entities. In addition, private parties may seek a ruling from DHHS about whether it will challenge particular transactions under the anti-kickback statute (but not under Stark).

The difficulty with these safe harbors and Stark exceptions is that they identify only a limited list of uncontroversial and conventional transactions, and thus they provide little guidance for novel, unanticipated business arrangements that fall outside their scope. Many of the private rulings have also been extremely cautious. For instance, in one ruling (subsequently reversed by regulation), DHHS stated that hospitals may not restock ambulance supplies for free since this might act as an inducement to bring patients to one emergency room rather than another, and in another ruling, it said that an ambulance company may not give nursing homes a discount on some of their patients for fear this might induce nursing homes to refer other, non-discounted patients to the ambulance company. Also, the DHHS ruled that it is potentially illegal for a hospice to offer free services to terminally ill patients who do not have insurance coverage. Some rulings have been more permissive. One approved a joint venture arrangement in which physicians own or invest in an outpatient surgery clinic. Nevertheless, this ruling was limited to surgery because the facility fee is only a small fraction of the procedure fee that surgeons earn regardless of their investment in the facility; therefore, having a stake in the facility fee creates very little added incentive to perform more surgeries.

3. *What's a Lawyer to Do?* Safe harbor regulations and private rulings on particular transactions help to reduce uncertainty over what is and is not a "kickback," but to a great extent, the health care industry must simply rely on the government's good sense to exercise discretion in choosing to challenge only truly abusive arrangements. Is it comforting that federal prosecutors simply overlook the fact that so many accepted and socially beneficial relationships in the health care industry potentially violate a felony statute? Professor Blumstein provides a colorful metaphor for this legal state of affairs:

> [T]he modern American healthcare industry is akin to a speakeasy—conduct that is illegal is rampant and countenanced by law enforcement officials because the law is so out of sync with the conventional norms and realities of the marketplace. . . . This poses a formidable civil liberties concern as prosecutors exercise enormous prosecutorial discretion, which is subject to abuse.

The Fraud and Abuse Statute in an Evolving Healthcare Marketplace: Life in the Health Care Speakeasy, 22 Am. J.L. & Med. 205 (1996).

Also, consider the dilemma that lawyers face in giving advice under these ambiguous laws. In Kansas the U.S. Attorney prosecuted two lawyers who drafted agreements under which a hospital paid physicians to manage nursing home patients, an arrangement that was found to be a criminal violation of the anti-kickback statute. United States v. Lahue, 261 F.3d 993 (9th Cir. 2001). The prosecutor presented evidence that some of the physicians overbilled Medicare and solicited kickbacks for recruiting patients. However, in dismissing the case against the lawyers, the trial judge ruled (March 9, 1999) that they tried in good faith to structure an arrangement that they thought complied with the law, and they should not be faulted for technical failures or other people's hidden motivations, considering the complexity, ambiguity, and evolving nature of this law. See Stuart M. Gerson & Jennifer E. Gladieux, Advice of Counsel: Eroding Confidentiality in Federal Health Care Law, 51 Ala. L. Rev. 163 (1999).

In the *Tuomey* case, however, which was decided on the more strictly worded Stark Law, former members of the hospital's board of trustees sued their lawyers for malpractice in giving the flawed advice that led to the disastrous legal outcome.

4. *Whistleblowing and Fessing Up.* In *Tuomey*, note the motivation of the physician who initially brought the situation to light. This illustrates that every disappointed business partner, disgruntled employee, patient, or lawyer is a potential bounty hunter under the referral fee statutes. Also, note the handsome "bounty" reward that went to Dr. Drakeford. Plaintiffs' lawyers who pursue such cases naturally would receive a substantial share of such awards.

Congress finally heard the cries for help from the health care industry and its lawyers. The ACA required that CMS adopt a "self-disclosure protocol" that allows CMS to reduce refunds when providers voluntarily reveal previously unknown technical Stark violations. According to one analysis, the approach CMS took "is so punitive and difficult to navigate that very few health-care providers have made disclosures, despite specific legal requirements to do so." Jean Veilleux, Catching Flies with Vinegar: A Critique of the Centers for Medicare and Medicaid Self-Disclosure Program, 22 Health Matrix 169 (2012).

5. *Separating the Wheat from the Chaff.* Is it possible in a health care system as complex as ours to intelligently regulate which potentially distorting incentives are allowable and which are not? See David Frankford, Creating and Dividing the Fruits of Collective Economic Activity: Referrals Among Health Care Providers, 89 Colum. L. Rev. 1861, 1937 (1989) ("Laws like [this] are absolutely incapable of logically defining, much less policing against, inflated prices. [T]hey fail even to create a language for comprehensible debate. They simply obfuscate the issues."). Is any kind of physician payment incentive completely beyond reproach? Even straight salary has the perverse effect of inducing physicians to spend less time with patients or to make excessive referrals to other doctors. Consider the following from the prestigious Institute of Medicine's influential report For-Profit Enterprise in Health Care 153 (B. Gray ed., 1986):

> All compensation systems—from fee-for-service to capitation or salary—present some undesirable incentives for providing too many services, or too few. No system will work without some degree of integrity, decency, and ethical commitment on the

> part of professionals. Inevitably, we must presume some underlying professionalism that will constrain the operation of unadulterated self-interest.

Realizing this, could it be dangerous to single out individual incentives from the overall mix of counteracting incentives and regulate each one (or only some of them) in isolation? Even unadulterated referral fees might be beneficial if they are used to counteract the incentive that general practitioners have to not refer patients to specialists when needed. Mark Pauly, The Ethics and Economics of Kickbacks and Fee Splitting, 10 Bell J. Econ. 344 (1974) ("it is possible for fee splitting to offer incentives which actually improve patient welfare"). Dr. Arnold S. Relman, former editor of the New England Journal of Medicine, would respond:

> The situation is different when physicians seek income beyond fee for service and make business arrangements with other providers of services to their patients. Such arrangements introduce a new and unnecessary conflict, which strains the physician's fiduciary commitment to the patient. Unlike the conflicts of interest in the fee-for-service system, these new arrangements are usually not fully disclosed to the patient, and therefore are more difficult to control.

Dealing with Conflicts of Interest, 313 New Eng. J. Med. 749, 750 (1985). Do the rule of necessity and the absence of disclosure justify felony imprisonment?

Regardless, these laws are not written to prohibit only unnecessary and undisclosed incentives. Another way, then, to draw sensible distinctions is to determine whether a transaction implicates these laws' core purposes. Mark A. Hall, Making Sense of Referral Fee Statutes, 13 J. Health Pol. Pol'y & L. 623 (1988). Referral fee statutes are intended to prevent three abuses: ordering unnecessary services, increasing charges for needed services, and influencing with financial considerations the decision of where best to refer a patient. To illustrate with the most common target of referral fee criticism, a clinical laboratory kickback to doctors who order tests might induce doctors to order unnecessary tests, increase a lab's billings for tests that are necessary, or persuade doctors to send tests to an inferior lab.

One might reason, then, that a less blatant practice does not violate referral fee statutes if the practice does not conflict with any of the three mentioned purposes, even though the practice might fall within the literal language of these sweeping prohibitions. For example, one might think that the waiver of insurance deductibles and co-payments should not be prosecuted because this practice does not result in any increased costs to the government; indeed, it reduces costs for beneficiaries.

This purpose-based analysis provides only limited guidance, however. Any incentive that has a referral aspect in a literal sense will always conflict with at least one of the stated purposes—namely, the potential to influence *where* a patient is referred. Moreover, incentives usually have some impact on whether a service should be ordered at all. For instance, on the question of waiving co-payments and deductibles, DHHS issued a safe harbor regulation that allows such price discounts by hospitals and HMOs, but not by doctors. It reasoned that deductibles and co-payments are meant to deter ordering unnecessary care, and only hospital care is sufficiently urgent that reducing patient cost-sharing is not likely to increase program costs.

An alternative definitional model is to determine whether or not referral fees are earned through arm's-length non-referral services paid at fair market value. A classic situation is the rental of hospital space and equipment to in-house pharmacies and radiologists in exchange for a percentage of their gross receipts. Since hospital pharmacies and radiologists obtain their patients from the hospital, these rental payments have the clear potential to induce referrals. Courts and regulators analyzing this situation have distinguished between earned and unearned referral fees: Fees incidentally related to a referral are valid if they do not exceed the fair market value of legitimate non-referral services bargained for at arm's length. Hall, Making Sense of Referral Fee Statutes, supra. This conceptual guide is prominent in a wide variety of anti-kickback safe harbor regulations and Stark Law exceptions.

The utility of the fair market guide is weakened, however, by the fact that referral-neutral reference points to judge market value are often lacking in the medical marketplace, since the market value of a service or relationship often stems precisely from the business it generates. Consider, for instance, a hospital that seeks to recruit badly needed new physicians. Although this may be good for the community, it is also good for the hospital's business. Any "market value" for new physicians surely must reflect, in part, the increased admissions that hospitals expect.

Therefore, safe harbor rules and exceptions often stress a more subjective assessment of whether the fees in question are intended to generate referrals. But, because purity of intent is difficult to prove, the safest route, also reflected in the rules, is often to structure payments so that their amount does not depend on the number and value of referrals made. But, sometimes, this simply is not possible. For instance, when hospitals or HMOs consider purchasing physician office practices, in order to employ the physicians, the true market value of the practice obviously depends in part on components such as good will, customer lists, patient records, and employee contracts that relate directly to how much existing patients are likely to continue seeing the physician. This calls into question the legality of any amount paid in excess of simply the hard assets of the office practice.

6. *Impact on Organizational Form.* Professor Frankford, above, argues that the referral fee prohibition distorts health care institutional arrangements by concentrating more power within medical institutions. This is because "referrals" do not occur within institutions, only between them, and the safe harbors are more protective of larger than smaller institutions. In short, there is less legal exposure if health care institutions grow to absorb more physicians and sources of payment. 89 Colum. L. Rev. 1861. In this regard, referral fee laws might be seen as an unnatural stimulus for fully integrated rather than more loosely formed delivery systems.

Professor Blumstein, above, observes that these laws also threaten various contractual arrangements that are transitional states between no integration and full integration. Casting into doubt the financial relationships that exist in partially or "virtually" integrated models (such as hospital/physician joint ventures and physician office management contracts) makes the movement toward full integration more difficult.

Observe, also, that the referral law's bias toward complete integration is at odds with the corporate practice of medicine doctrine, which prohibits physician employment, and it is in tension with tax exemption law that imposes greater scrutiny when doctors are "insiders." Also, the safe harbors protect physician ownership in for-profit entities, but have no equivalent protection for physicians who are insiders in nonprofits, which discourages adoption of the nonprofit form.

Critics have also observed that referral fee prohibitions make little sense in the context of bundled or capitated payment systems because these laws were meant to address the abuses of fee-for-service reimbursement, and incentives within managed care systems are likely to reduce costs in the long run by encouraging more efficient practice patterns. Recognizing this, a 1999 safe harbor protects providers who practice under capitation and other "at risk" incentives that discourage overutilization. Similarly, a 2011 ruling protects provider payments within ACOs that participate in the Medicare shared savings program. And, a 2015 law protects the sharing of payments among providers under Medicare's new approach that bundles payment based on certain episodes of illness (see Chapter 3.E.4).

7. *Further Readings.* For description and analysis of the **safe harbors and the exceptions** to the self-referral statute, as well as the effect these statutes have on contemporary business arrangements, see Rebecca Olavarria, MACRA and Stark: Strange Bedfellows at the Heart of Health Care Reform, 62 Wayne L. Rev. 131 (2017); Nancy L. Zisk, Investing in Health Care, 36 Seattle U. L. Rev. 189 (2012); Alice G. Gosfield, Medicare and Medicaid Fraud and Abuse (2015); Patrick Sutton, The Stark Law in Retrospect, 20 Ann. Health L. 15 (2011); Jean M. Mitchell, The Prevalence of Physician Self-Referral Arrangements After Stark II, 26(3) Health Aff. W415 (Apr. 2007); James Belanger & Scott Bennett, The Continued Expansion of the False Claims Act, 4 J. Health & Life Sci. L. 26 (2010); Robert Lower & Robert Stone, Off with Their Heads! Summary Execution for Technical Stark Violations—And a Proposal to Commute the Sentence, 3 Health & Life Sci. L. 112 (2010); Leigh Walton et al., Hospital Syndications: Opportunities and Options, or Poised for Extinction?, 21(4) The Health Lawyer 1 (Apr. 2009); Paul DeMuro, Eye of the Storm: The Government's Focus on Hospital-Physician Arrangements, 21(5) The Health Lawyer 30 (June 2009).

For a sampling of the burgeoning literature on ***qui tam* health care actions**, see Dayna Matthew, *Qui Tam* Litigation Under the False Claims Act, 69 Wash. & Lee L. Rev. 365 (2012); Beverly Cohen, KABOOM! The Explosion of *Qui Tam* False Claims Under the Health Reform Law, 116 Penn. St. L. Rev. 77 (2011); A. Kesselheim & D. Studdert, Whistleblower-Initiated Enforcement Actions Against Health Care Fraud and Abuse in the U.S., 149 Ann. Intern. Med. 342 (2008). See section A.2 for additional discussion of the **False Claims Act**.

8. *A Look Back.* Look back over this chapter as well as Chapter 3 to observe the many ways in which federal and state regulation of health care fail to achieve a coordinated and purposeful public policy. One searching for imperfections might justifiably assert that health care corporate and regulatory law suffers from each of the following pathologies:

- ERISA unthinkingly creates a regulatory vacuum that is only erratically filled by state or federal insurance regulation.
- State corporate practice of medicine law is anachronistic and unpredictable.
- Insurance regulation fails to achieve a level playing field between traditional and innovative forms of health care delivery, and confuses consumer protection with provider protection.

- Tax exemption law discourages the formation of nonprofit HMOs and is too lenient on hospitals.
- Fraud and abuse law deters legitimate ventures and fails to see that incentives in a fee-for-service era are fundamentally different than those in an era of bundled payment and pay-for-performance.
- The details of each of these particular bodies of law point in inconsistent directions on fundamental questions such as how tightly integrated financing and delivery systems should be and the proper role of physicians in their ownership and management.

In your view, are these hypothetical criticisms valid?

Problem: Medicare/Medicaid Fraud and Abuse

You are outside counsel to the Florence Nightingale Healthcare Corporation, which among its other operations owns a durable medical equipment (DME) subsidiary, which sells equipment for home use such as crutches, wheel chairs, and oxygen concentrators. You learn that the subsidiary has had certain business practices about which you have some question under the Medicare and Medicaid Anti-Fraud and Abuse provisions:

- Salesmen regularly offer home health agency employees a "premium" whenever their clients order DME from the subsidiary.
- The subsidiary offers "rebates" to patients who use its equipment.
- The subsidiary pays hospital and home health agency personnel for assisting its patients in learning how to use its products.
- Some arterial blood gas test results may have been "massaged a bit" by the DME in order to facilitate Medicare payment for oxygen concentrators.

What advice would you give?

Problem: Reverse Referral Fees

You are outside counsel to the Florence Nightingale Healthcare Corporation (FNHC), which is concerned that expenses in some of its ancillary departments are causing it to lose money under Medicare and HMO insurance. It would like to start charging its hospital-based physicians for some of the costs of running their departments. Its current relationship with these physicians is one in which they have exclusive contracts to work in these departments, but no money changes hands between them. The hospital handles all billing, staffing, and overhead, but it bills separately for facility charges vs. professional fees, and the physicians keep all the professional fees the hospital collects on their behalf. This is the standard practice in the industry. FNHC has the following suggestions for changing this arrangement:

- Have the radiology group pay for services, supplies, personnel, utilities, maintenance, and billing services furnished by the hospital. In a nonhospital, office-based setting, this package would normally cost about $100,000 to $150,000 per year. The hospital will charge the radiology group only $25,000 at first, but increase the charges to $100,000 over four years. Payments are due only if the hospitals' gross revenue derived from radiology services exceeds $1,000,000 in the previous year.

- The hospital's clinical laboratory, under the direction of the pathology group, would pay the hospital a 20 percent fee for "specimen collection and handling services" when a physician on the FNHC medical staff orders a test from the clinical lab.

What advice would you give?

Comprehensive Review Problem: Forming an Integrated Delivery System

Review the introductory discussion at page 340 and the description of Florence Nightingale Hospital at page 346. Now, consider the following methods the hospital might pursue for closer affiliation with physicians, in order to begin to form an integrated delivery system or an accountable care organization. Suppose this affiliation was undertaken either to market a comprehensive managed care insurance plan and participate in the Medicare shared savings program, or, less ambitiously, to establish an outpatient clinic. How would each of three possible integration/affiliation models fare under each of several business and legal factors that have been reviewed in this chapter? Fill in the following chart by indicating whether each business or legal factor would view each arrangement favorably (+), negatively (–), or in neutral/mixed way (/).

	Physician Autonomy	*Clinical and Financial Integration*	*Corporate Practice of Medicine*	*Antitrust*	*Referral Fee Law*	*Tax Exempt*
Corporate Ownership The hospital's corporate parent buys out physician practices and employs the physicians.						
Physician-Hospital Organization (PHO) Hospital and several physician groups form joint-venture partnership, contribute equal capital, and split the proceeds.						
Management Services Organization (MSO) Hospital contracts with independent physicians to provide office management services and to act as negotiating agent with insurers/ employers.						

Glossary of Organizational Terms and Acronyms

In previous generations, it was necessary to learn a specialized vocabulary to study law and medicine. This is still true, but in the past that vocabulary was purely medical. Today, it includes many obscure organizational terms as well. This is a selected glossary of organizational terms and acronyms, adapted from Prospective Payment Assessment Commission, 1996 Report to Congress.

ACA	Affordable Care Act of 2010
ACO	Accountable Care Organization
AFDC	Aid to Families with Dependent Children
AHA	American Hospital Association
AHRQ	Agency for Health Care Research and Quality
AMA	American Medical Association
CDHC	Consumer-Directed (or Driven) Health Care
CMS	Center for Medicare and Medicaid Services
COBRA	Consolidated Omnibus Budget Reconciliation Act of 1985
CON	Certificate of Need
DHHS	*See* HHS
DRG	Diagnosis-Related Group
ERISA	Employee Retirement Income Security Act of 1974
ESRD	End-Stage Renal Disease
FDA	Food and Drug Administration
HCFA	Health Care Financing Administration, now CMS
HHS	Health and Human Services, Department of
HIPAA	Health Insurance Portability and Accountability Act

HIV	Human Immunodeficiency Virus
HMO	Health Maintenance Organization
HRA or HSA	Healthcare Reimbursement or Health Savings Account (*see also* MSA)
IDS	Integrated Delivery System
IPA	Independent Practice Association
JCAHO	Joint Commission on Accreditation of Healthcare Organizations
MSA	Medical Savings Account
MSO	Management Services Organization
NCQA	National Committee for Quality Assurance
OBRA	Omnibus Budget Reconciliation Act
PHO	Physician-Hospital Organization
POS	Point of Service
PPACA	Patient Protection and Affordable Care Act
PPO	Preferred Provider Organization
PPS	Prospective Payment System
RBRVS	Resource-Based Relative Value Scale
SNF	Skilled Nursing Facility
SSI	Supplemental Security Income
TEFRA	Tax Equity and Fiscal Responsibility Act of 1982
UR/UM	Utilization Review, or Utilization Management

Accountable Care Organization (ACO)—An organization or network of physicians and/or hospitals that is able to receive payment from public or private insurers on a bundled basis that holds the provider group collectively responsible for the cost and quality of patients' care.

Adverse Selection—A term of art in insurance economics that describes the tendency of people who expect to have greater need for insurance to have more interest in purchasing insurance.

Community Rating—A method of determining an insurance premium structure that reflects expected utilization by the population as a whole, rather than by specific groups.

Consumer-Driven Health Care—An alternative to managed care, which seeks to activate patients to be cost-conscious consumers at the point of treatment, by requiring them to pay more out of pocket, and by providing better information about treatment options and costs.

Cost Shifting—Increasing revenues from some payers to offset uncompensated care losses and lower net payments from other payers.

Diagnosis-Related Groups (DRGs)—A system for determining case mix, used for payment under Medicare's PPS and by some other payers. The DRG system classifies patients into groups based on the principal diagnosis, type of surgical procedure, presence or absence of significant comorbidities or complications, and other relevant criteria. DRGs are intended to categorize patients into groups that are clinically meaningful and homogeneous with respect to resource use. Medicare's PPS currently uses 490 mutually exclusive DRGs, each of which is assigned a relative weight that compares its cost lines to the average for all DRGs.

Fee-for-Service—A method of reimbursing health care providers in which payment is made for each unit of service rendered.

Fiscal Intermediary—An insurer or other private company that the government contracts with to administer Medicare or Medicaid payments to providers.

Gainsharing—An awkward term referring to hospital arrangements that reward physicians for their participation in initiatives or programs that save costs or improve quality.

Health Maintenance Organization (HMO)—A managed care plan that integrates financing and delivery of a comprehensive set of health care services to an enrolled population. HMOs may contract with, directly employ, or own participating health care providers. Enrollees are usually required to choose from among these providers and in return have limited co-payments. Providers may be paid through capitation, salary, per diem, or prenegotiated fee-for-service rates.

Health Savings Account (HSA)—A tax-sheltered account, similar to an IRA, and also known as a Healthcare Reimbursement Account (HRA) or Medical Savings Account (MSA), that is used to pay for medical expenses. It is coupled with high-deductible or "catastrophic" insurance, such that the HSA can pay for most ordinary expenses and insurance is used only for very expensive treatment.

Integrated Delivery System (IDS)—Any number of different arrangements among doctors, hospitals, other medical facilities, and insurers in which a full range of medical services is offered to employers, subscribers, or insurers. Includes conventional arrangements such as HMOs, as well as more innovative arrangements known as PHOs, PSNs, or MSOs, which are discussed in Chapter 10.

Managed Care—Any system of health service payment or delivery arrangements in which the health plan or provider attempts to control or coordinate health service use to contain health expenditures, improve quality, or both. Arrangements often involve a defined delivery system of providers having some form of contractual relationship with the plan.

Moral Hazard—A term from insurance economics describing the fact that insurance makes people less concerned about the costs of their behavior for costs that are covered by insurance.

Peer Review Organization (PRO)—An organization that contracts with HCFA to investigate the quality of health care furnished to Medicare beneficiaries and to educate beneficiaries and providers. PROs also conduct limited review of medical records and claims to evaluate the appropriateness of care provided.

Physician-Hospital Organization (PHO)—A joint venture or affiliation among one or more hospitals and physicians or physician groups. The venture might encompass the full range of medical services, or only one or a few services.

Point-of-Service (POS)—A health plan allowing the enrollee to choose to receive a service from a participating or a nonparticipating provider, with different benefit levels associated with one or the other types of providers.

Preferred Provider Organization (PPO)—A health plan with a network of providers whose services are available to enrollees at lower cost than the services of non-network providers. PPO enrollees may self-refer to any network provider at any time.

Prospective Payment—A method of paying health care providers in which rates are established in advance. Providers are paid these rates regardless of the costs they actually incur.

Prospective Payment System (PPS)—Medicare's acute care hospital payment method for inpatient care. Prospective per case payment rates are set at a level intended to cover operating costs for treating a typical inpatient in a given diagnosis-related group. Payments for each hospital are adjusted for differences in area wages, teaching activity, care to the poor, and other factors.

Relative Value Scale—An index that assigns weights to each medical service; the weights represent the relative amount to be paid for each service. The relative value scale used in the development of the Medicare Physician Fee Schedule consists of three cost components, physician work, practice expense, and malpractice expense.

Risk Adjustment—A method to assess the relative severity or likelihood of medical conditions for different groups of patients, in order to adjust comparative measures of quality or cost. Risk adjustment is used, for instance, to increase or reduce payments to health plans to compensate for health care expenditures that are expected to be higher or lower than average. Risk adjustment is also used to determine whether differences in medical outcomes are due to patients' underlying conditions or instead to how providers treat them.

Uncompensated Care—Care rendered by hospitals or other providers without payment from the patient or a government-sponsored or private insurance program. It includes both charity care, which is provided without the expectation of payment, and bad debts, for which the provider has made an unsuccessful effort to collect payment due from the patient.

Utilization Review (UR)—A review of services delivered by a health care provider to evaluate the appropriateness, necessity, and quality of the prescribed services. The review can be performed on a prospective, concurrent, or retrospective basis.

Table of Cases

Primary cases are indicated by italics.

Index